D1570879

DATE			
AUG	1992		

IN PURSUIT OF SATAN

IN PURSUIT OF SATAN

THE POLICE AND THE OCCULT

ROBERT D. HICKS

PROMETHEUS BOOKS
Buffalo, New York

In Pursuit of Satan: The Police and the Occult. Copyright © 1991 by Robert D. Hicks. All rights reserved. No part of this book may be reproduced in any manner whatsoever without written permission, except in the case of brief quotations embodied in critical articles and reviews. Inquiries should be addressed to Prometheus Books, 700 East Amherst Street, Buffalo, New York 14215, 716-837-2475.

95 94 93 92 91   5 4 3 2

Library of Congress Cataloging-in-Publication Data

Hicks, Robert D., 1952-
    In pursuit of Satan : the police and the occult / Robert D. Hicks.
        p.   cm.
    Includes bibliographical references.
    Includes index.
    ISBN 0-87975-604-7
    1. Crime—United States. 2. Law enforcement—United States. 3. Cults—United States. 4. Satanism—United States. 5. Occultism—United States. I. Title.
HV6791.H515   1990
364.1'88—dc20   90-43473
                                                                                CIP

Printed in the United States of America on acid-free paper.

To Reginald Scot,
author of *The Discoverie of Witchcraft* (1584)

CONTENTS

PREFACE

I did not enjoy writing this book. The word *Satanism* evokes in some people everything from disdain for superstition to tremors of fear. Similarly, for those like me, who have decided to enter a public forum to advance arguments about what Satanism (whatever it is) has to do with crime, the road is paved with invective, calumny, and rumor, but also with insight, temperance, and skeptical thinking. Skeptical thinking to some connotes peremptory doubt, an inclination to dismiss out of hand. But skeptical thinking is not that: rather, to be a responsible skeptic is to follow a habit of scientific thinking. A skeptic wants to examine what evidence supports claims, wants to see unusual phenomena replicated and verified, and above all, where the behavior of people is concerned, holds to few immutable truths. Deduction and induction, a sifting and weighing of facts, a formulation of hypotheses, a search for evidence that both supports *and refutes* the hypotheses, all form the habit of skeptical thinking.

This book skeptically examines the myriad claims that bear on the law-enforcement preoccupation with Satanism, satanic crime, and occult and cult crime. But Satanism at present is a divisive word: professionals in law enforcement, social work, psychiatry, psychology, and education usually align themselves and others into two categories: believers and nonbelievers. And thus again we have the skeptic—according to the believer —as one who dismisses satanic claims out of hand. Supervisory Special Agent Kenneth V. Lanning of the FBI has implored professionals on both sides to find a middle ground. Few have heeded the message; conferences present as speakers either believers or nonbelievers. Ideally, we need a good interdisciplinary mix of points of view. Satanism seminars should not be proselytizing experiences; they should encourage debate and restraint.

Some people in law enforcement, social work, and allied professions believe that a clandestine network of Satanists exists who kidnap, abuse, and murder. These same people are educated, have had years of professional experience, enjoy deserved reputations for excellence in their work, yet still claim proof of a satanic network. I invite such people—my intended audience—to consider and debate my arguments. Whatever stand one takes about the pervasiveness and influence of Satanism and the occult in society, much less their importance, I ask only *restraint*. Police officers must consider the fears engendered in their communities by their speculation and third-hand information. The creation of community fears will only stigmatize the innocent and promote suspicion among neighbors. I ask professionals to consider carefully the consequences of transforming fears of Satanists into public policy. To browbeat small children into believing that Satanists abused them at a day-care center, to detain a Wiccan at a police station for questioning about his or her beliefs, or to create files on suspected Satanists can have disastrous consequences.

But not all professionals find the public anxiety over matters satanic a topic for analysis. Some have found new careers in appearing on television talk-shows, lecturing to parents about what threatens their children, and casually dropping to journalists contrived figures for the numbers of human sacrifices performed in the United States. Some, unfortunately, come from the ranks of law enforcement, proffering apocalyptic or millenarian visions of the satanic cancer in society. Such people, in essence, offer a religious or moral message on behalf of a government agency. Government leaders should champion a legal stance, certainly no mean feat in a multicultural society. But police officers can claim no mandate from the Constitution, their state laws, nor their sworn oath according to the Police Code of Ethics to offer pronouncements on what music people listen to, what books they read, or what thoughts they think.

Few members of the law-enforcement community have taken the time to combat publicly the overstatements, generalizations, clearly false and absurd "facts," and excursions into illogic relating to the impact of Satanism and the occult on crime. Those who do are soon confronted with an organized crusade to protect teens and small children from the alleged satanic threat. To fight this perceived menace, people have banded together to influence the legislative process in Virginia, Idaho, Texas, Illinois, and other states to enact laws or modify criminal codes. Skeptics have not responded in kind. Nevertheless, a former police officer (now a "cult expert") has circulated the story that I give lecture tours paired with a Scientologist (I don't); two self-professed cult survivors have contacted a Virginia newspaper to discredit my skeptical views by claiming that I am a leading Satanist who sexually abuses them regularly (I have not even met either woman); a radio evangelist has claimed that I am a "witch"; and a Lyndon LaRouche periodical dismisses me as an apologist for Satan as well as claiming that I am a field marshal in Satan's army.

A word on apologists. Carl Raschke's recent book, *Painted Black* (Harper & Row, 1990), an exemplar of all that I argue against in this book), dismisses folks like Kenneth Lanning as cult apologists. Presumably I fall into the same category. But I apologize for no one and nothing: if some people profess spiritual beliefs in Satan, they must fend for themselves, as all of us must defend our own views. I simply contend that debates about such beliefs should be deferred to social critics and scholars, not to the police.

Raschke, a University of Denver academic, inveighs against "apologists"—his term—for certain arguments they make, including the assertion that "Satanism is an established religion with canons and rituals as well as an elitist philosophy that cannot appeal to everyone"; that no "epidemic of satanic crime" exists; that "all the fuss about satanist corruption and criminality adds up to nothing more than a hysterical tremor, or a conscious plot, on the part of Christians. . . ." (pp. 131-132). He goes on to enumerate apologists' "strategies of persuasion familiar to students of propaganda," such as pseudo-distinctions and genetic fallacies. However, I don't recognize his model of apologetic thinking in the likes of Kenneth Lanning, one of those Raschke attacks. Raschke has not responded to argument; he simply indulges in name-calling as a way to support his assertions.

Raschke's arguments against skepticism are akin to those used by child-welfare and social workers who bridle against any criticism of the methods used to investigate multiple-victim child-abuse cases in day-care centers. Well-meaning people in child-concerned professions quickly and loudly attack those who criticize such methods by responding that "apologists" (1) deny the existence and prevalence of child abuse in the United States and therefore perpetuate the problem; or (2) have through their criticism betrayed the children and the now-adult victims of child abuse. Both of these arguments are intended to end debate and deflect criticism. "Your criticism of day-care investigations harms the children," some argue. Skepticism about such investigative methods should sharpen and refine them; skepticism does *not* deny the existence of child abuse or the need to combat it.

I do not purport to be a cult expert. On the contrary, my relevant experience as a law-enforcement officer (Tucson Police Department, Arizona; later a civilian manager for the Pima County Sheriff's Department, Arizona), trainer, planner, researcher, and analyst (law-enforcement specialist for the Virginia Department of Criminal Justice Services, and earlier a cryptologic officer, U.S. Navy), plus my educational background in anthropology (B.A., M.A., University of Arizona) have all formed my observations and judgments. I *do* know something about empiricism, inductive and deductive reasoning, and research, which also ground my role as a critic of law-enforcement trends. So I have no alarmist picture to paint of a threatened America; rather, I criticize law enforcers for suspending the critical judgment they otherwise display in conducting criminal investigations and maintaining public order at a point when they are confronted with Satanism, cults, pagans, witches, and the like.

For anyone who reads this book and concludes that I side with child molesters, that I am a cult member, that I can't free myself from my own prejudices against Christians, take note: (1) I acknowledge the widespread problem of child abuse, whether characterized by neglect, inattention, or outright violence. I support vigorous prosecution of those who violate criminal laws in harming children—or anyone else, for that matter. (2) I do not believe that any Christian conspiracy exists to perpetrate a satanic hysteria upon the populace. (3) I acknowledge that some people will commit crimes—sometimes very violent, vicious crimes—in fealty to Satan. I further acknowledge that some people will employ the imagery or trappings of the occult, of Satan, or of some other mystical source in committing crimes. Some people will act also in concert with others to commit crimes, perhaps meeting legal definitions of a criminal enterprise, syndicate, or conspiracy. (4) I acknowledge that some people find that certain books, images, and music exercise a powerful hold on the imagination, inspiring or stimulating certain actions.

Raschke also takes a tsk-tsk attitude toward sociologists and anthropologists who, when conducting ethnographic work, frequently "go native" and become too tolerant of the people they study. Such tolerance, to Raschke, gets in the way of reasoned judgment. To Raschke, if someone's satanic views mean a belief in the correctness of harming others, then the views ought to be condemned out of hand. An anthropologist or sociologist may indeed make such judgments about beliefs or practices of the culture under study; but for purposes of an ethnography, judgment is not the point. Raschke doesn't understand what he criticizes: participant observation of another culture seeks to understand and describe, not to offer thumbs up or down. The ethnographic information contained herein is meant to explicate beliefs; the explication is intended to reduce mindless fears of other people's differences.

Again, the main objective of this book is to encourage restraint, introspection, critical analysis, and perspicacity. Some cult survivors *may* be telling accurate accounts of human sacrifice; satanic cults *may* be running day-care centers; and playing Dungeons & Dragons *may* lead some children to acquire the Black Arts. If such phenomena exist, then they must be proved. As this book demonstrates, I have found no proof that pernicious satanic phenomena exist on a scale worthy of new criminal laws and specialized police task-forces.

That said, I have many to thank for helping me research and write this book. Several people who are themselves writing about facets of the Satanism phenomenon offered immeasurable help in discussing their ideas, allowing me to use their own research materials, and generously passing on key papers, monographs, news articles, and notes: journalist Debbie Nathan, sociologist Jeffrey S. Victor, anthropologist Phillips Stevens, Jr., sociologist David G. Bromley, psychologist Frank J. MacHovec, and folklorist and author of popular books on urban legends Jan Harold Brunvand. For information on role-playing games, I thank Michael Stackpole, Loren Wiseman, William Flatt, and Paul Cardwell, Jr. Several others who contributed important research material include Barry Karr, executive director, Committee for the Scientific Investigation of Claims of the Paranormal; Kendrick Frazier, editor of the *Skeptical Inquirer*; psychologist Richard Noll; Shawn Carson, who coauthored *Satanism in America*; Supervisory Special Agent Kenneth V. Lanning, FBI; anthropologist Sherrill Mulhern; sociologist Marcello Truzzi; Connie J. Kirkland; Sonji Pearson; Patrick Harris, Virginia Department of Criminal Justice Services; Zeena LaVey; Gayle Olson-Raymer, who wrote *Occult Crime: A Law Enforcement Primer* for the California Office of Criminal Justice Planning; Lieutenant Mike Jones, Division of Capitol Police (Virginia); Investigator E. Mahaffey, Hall County Sheriff's Department (Georgia); Valerie Voight; Paul Sulin; Lee Darrow; Morton Stavis, Esq.; Rex Springston, journalist, *Richmond News Leader*; and Alexander R. Jones, Church of Scientology. I thank the staff of the Virginia State Library, and Michelle Willingham in particular, for helping to ferret out obscure sources and handle many interlibrary-loan requests. To Kathleen R. D. Sands, my thanks for reviewing the draft and compiling the index. To Doris Doyle, Prometheus Books, my gratitude for careful editing. I reserve profound gratitude for Steve Squire, librarian, Virginia Department of Criminal Justice Services, who has tirelessly contributed in every way toward this book; in fact, he may have expended more energy on it than I have. Although I take responsibility for any and all errors, Steve deserves much credit for all arguments within this book that appear sharp, critically sound, and cogent. Finally, I thank Donald K. Shipley, without whose help this book could not have been written.

The Spring and Summer 1990 issues of the *Skeptical Inquirer* contain my two-part article, "In Pursuit of Satan," which this book absorbs. Readers interested in the arguments I advance and in works by the sociologists and anthropologists cited, should study the forthcoming book, *The Satanism Scare*, edited by sociologists Jim Richardson and Joel Best, to be published in 1991 by Aldine.

Finally, the views expressed herein are my own and do not necessarily reflect views or policies of the Virginia Department of Criminal Justice Services.

December 1990

Chapter 1
TALK OF THE DEVIL

Talk of the devil and he'll appear.

Erasmus (1500)

Introduction

In Lancashire, England, in 1632, a boy left his job tending cattle to gather plums. To justify to his parents his absence from work, the young cowherd explained that he had seen two stray greyhounds running toward him. He thought he might use them as hunting dogs. When he went after the dogs, however, a hare crossed the dog's path, and he noticed that they did not even try to pursue it. Angry at their laziness, the cowherd began to beat the dogs. Presently, the animals were transformed into new beings: one a small boy, the other a woman whom the cowherd knew. The woman offered to pay him not to mention the incident, but he refused: "Thou art a witch," he said. The woman then withdrew a string from her purse, which instantly became a bridle, and when she affixed it to the head of the small boy accompanying her he turned into a white horse. The young cowherd and the woman then flew off on the back of the horse and alighted near a house, which they entered. Joining a company of people there (with odd horses of various colors), they partook of a feast.

When pressed, the cowherd later named eighteen neighbors who he claimed were present at the feast. Although he was familiar with the details of a similar Lancashire story about events that had taken place twenty years earlier and had resulted in a furious witch-hunt, authorities took his comparatively innocuous story about the dogs as *casus belli* for a fresh outbreak of witch hatred. The cowherd's claim led to many arrests, and he himself toured as a witch-finder.[1] The case remained a *cause célèbre* for decades and became the basis of Thomas Shadwell's 1682 play *The Lancashire Witches*.

The Lancashire story, like many others in Europe over the past few centuries, exhibits important characteristics: the boy told an alarming narrative of the supernatural; he implicated neighbors; authorities sought arrests based on the child's uncorroborated statements; the presence of evil in the boy's story (witches working magic) sparked community rancor aimed at people for whom no defense appeared credible. Historian Wallace Notestein observed of Tudor and Jacobean witchcraft cases: "[They] would lead one to suppose that in England no rules of evidence were yet in existence. The testimony of children ranging . . . from six to nine was eagerly received."[2]

In 1985 in Bakersfield, California, a jury sentenced a young woman who worked in a fast-food restaurant to 405 years in prison for molesting children. The trial, which included other women defendants, examined allegations by children that several adults met "regularly to sodomize and molest their own sons, daughters, nephews or nieces, often after forcing drugs or alcohol on them. Children said they saw cameras apparently filming the sexual acts."[3] Children claimed that the adults had formed a satanic cult and had killed and mutilated babies. After much questioning, the children identified a widening circle of adult participants, including even an attorney, a deputy sheriff, and a social worker investigating the case. An attorney who represented one of the defendants

> said the Salem trials began in 1692 with two children who, after repeated questioning, identified many local people as witches. "The Salem witchcraft fever did not break until the children made absolutely unbelievable accusations, pointing their damning fingers at the governor's wife," [the attorney] said. "They also accused those most eager in the prosecution of witches. Once disbelieved in a few particulars, they lost the power to condemn [those] they undoubtedly never sought."[4]

In my role as a law-enforcement specialist with the Virginia Department of Criminal Justice Services, beginning in 1986 I took a professional interest in what had become a trendy topic on the police seminar circuit: cult crime. At first alarmed by what I learned at the seminars, I became progressively more skeptical, then even more alarmed by the cult experts' anti-intellectual and anti-rationalist stance. The law-enforcement model of cult crime appeared to me shoddy, ill-considered, and rife with errors of logic (including faulty causal relationships, false analogies, lack of documentation, and unsupported generalizations) and ignorance of anthropological, psychological, and historical contexts. Above all, I fault cult experts for their ignorance of a historical context: in this book I draw an analogy between seventeenth-century English and American witchcraft cases and contemporary hysteria over today's equivalent of witches—cultists—to make the point that none of the cult investigators' claims represents new phenomena. Modern cult-crime claims traverse a familiar historical landscape replete with public venom against nonconformists, creation of scapegoats for real or imagined social ills, the political exploitation of rumor and innuendo as a basis for public policy, and a willingness to sacrifice civil liberties because of the argued necessity to protect our children from an imminent threat.

"Children Do Not Lie"

In the Bakersfield case, ostensibly investigated by the Kern County Sheriff's Department, deputies—in pursuit of criminal charges but largely untrained and unsupervised in conducting child-abuse cases—deferred the responsibility of questioning children to a zealous social worker. Consequently, the investigation went to court based on children's statements in paraphrased form that were glossed over by unwarranted conclusions containing inaccuracies and "without supporting facts."[5] The children themselves, removed from their homes during the investigation, had many opportunities to talk with one another, obtain new information, and adjust their stories to correspond with what investigators pressed them to say in repeated interviews. Owing mainly to the dominant participation by the social worker for the local Child Protective Services (CPS), the deputies relied on and deferred to CPS staff,

> who perform functions quite different from police officers in a child-abuse investigation . . . [and who focused] the interviews primarily on protecting the child at the expense of investigating and determining the facts in the case.[6]

Further,

> The prevailing attitude of the interviewers was that "children do not lie." As a result, interviewers tended to take children's statements at face value and failed to do necessary corroborative investigative work. This attitude seriously impaired the entire interview process and, indeed, the investigation itself.[7]

But despite the flawed investigation, several women were given the longest sentences meted out in California legal history.[8] Unlike seventeenth-century English and American witchcraft trials, the criminal-justice systems of the American states have thus far not condemned anyone to death for putative cult crimes; yet law enforcers have made arrests, separated children from their accused parents, confiscated books and magazines about the occult in violation of the First Amendment, and conducted searches of property owned by non-Christian ethnic minorities in violation of the Fourth Amendment, all in the pursuit of Satan. However, *like* seventeenth-century witchcraft cases, investigations have relentlessly pursued an ideology that dictates a specific criminal mold with identifiable satanic attributes. This ideology bears analogy to pseudoscientific claims, which by their nature are unprovable.

Pseudoscience and the Occult

To assert that a criminal satanic conspiracy exists might constitute a working hypothesis with testable assumptions. If, for example, I posit that a satanic cult murders young, transient, unemployed men as a form of propitiation to the Devil, then one might expect occasionally to stumble on physical evidence, such as bodies (or body parts); to obtain interviews with witnesses to abductions; or to garner information from informants whose scruples about murdering have caused them to break ranks with their satanic fellows. But, in fact, no such evidence turns up, no witnesses come forth, and no information is volunteered—nothing. Instead of abandoning the hypothesis, the investigating officer rationalizes the lack of evidence as proof of the cult's success: the murderous cult members remain covert, entrenched in otherwise responsible, common occupations; they dispose of *all* evidence at the site of their ritual murders; they *never* break ranks for any reason. Their success is measured by their invisibility and by their adroit management of crime scenes in never leaving traces of their activity. The cult's success, then, must be taken as self-evident; we no longer need proof. We know that cultists are sacrificing people to Satan because we know that they do it. And if the conspiracy claim still faces doubt, one throws the onus of proof onto the skeptic: "Well, prove that it *isn't* so!"

Further, this ideology guides police officers inevitably to find what they seek. Where one finds cops who specialize in investigating cults, one finds cults. In the seventeenth century, when a witch-finder came to town, someone—perhaps an impoverished, cranky old woman—was hanged shortly thereafter. Psychologist Terence Hines has observed that the "most common characteristic of a pseudoscience is the nonfalsifiable or irrefutable hypothesis. This is a hypothesis against which there can be no evidence—that is, no evidence can show the hypothesis to be wrong."[9] But irrefutable hypotheses can be verified. "So, irrefutable hypotheses are only that—irrefutable. They could be verified, if the evidence to support the hypothesis existed. Of course the promoters of irrefutable hypotheses have been forced to fall back on them precisely because no evidence exists to support them. Thus, an irrefutable hypothesis is a sure-fire sign of a pseudoscience."[10] The pseudoscience of the satanic-cult proponents is a farrago of social-science methods and theories, many of which are long obsolete. Its advocates are infused with an ignorance of history and cultural development and are fueled by xenophobia and parochial thinking.

Finding Witches

Throughout this century we have witnessed purges, pogroms, even *autos da fé* to rid societies of alleged subversives and quiet public fears. Since the Senator Joe McCarthy epoch, journalists have dubbed the search for scapegoats "witch hunts." The term derives from the now-popular conception of the 1692 Salem, Massachusetts, witchcraft cases dramatized by Arthur Miller in *The Crucible,* a play that appeared during the McCarthy inquisition. It held up a mirror in which the political actors of the day recognized everyone's face but their own. The term *witch hunt* may appear trite, then, in connection with the current satanic scare. But concerning the Bakersfield child-abuse case and similar others, most notably cases in Jordan, Minnesota, and at the McMartin Preschool in California (discussed in Chapter 5), historical parallels between the seventeenth century and the 1980s should make us uncomfortable. Philip Jenkins and Daniel Katkin, both Pennsylvania State University professors of the administration of justice, warn that these recent cases "indicate that children are indeed capable of both lies and fantasies about sexual abuse, and that entirely fictitious testimony can be drawn forth by careless or malicious prosecutors and therapists."[11]

Katkin and Jenkins further note the similarity of contemporary day-care-center abuse cases and the Salem trials "even to the precise form of illicit gatherings alleged to have taken place. Such parallels [can] be explained in terms of the ideological assumptions guiding investigators and prosecutors in two eras."[12] Aware that the comparison with Salem might seem ingenuous, Katkin and Jenkins admit that the "comparison may seem eccentric; yet another account of the Puritan experience in Massachusetts may seem gratuitous; but the parallels . . . are clear and disturbing."[13] Arthur Miller's play dramatizes the trials in a way that communicates how people's fears can transform the innocuous into proofs of devilry and how fears can mold the emotional responses of citizens into hysteria. In *The Crucible,* which largely follows the facts, the inquisition against several Salem adults appears jeopardized when one of the possessed girls, Mary Warren, confesses that her fits were pretense and alludes to the influence of Abigail Williams. But Abigail immediately feigns a fit, utters a chilling cry, and screams at a phantom hovering near the ceiling of the courtroom, a ruse that convinces the officiating deputy governor Danforth of the girls' possession, and the witchcraft executions continue.[14] In the Bakersfield case, during the court proceedings the judge asked a six-year-old witness to identify a defendant, one who had once disciplined her. " 'Don't let him get me! Don't let him kill me!' she screamed hysterically, whereupon she ran into the arms of Judge Friedman, who said after the trial he felt 'she was definitely traumatized, as were the other children.' "[15] The two cases are seemingly very different, but one can usefully compare the response of judicial authorities to apparently hysterical behavior in children.

But the law-enforcement interest in satanic cults has not been limited to a few well-publicized day-care-center cases of child abuse. Law enforcers have pursued an ideology that they, in turn, pass off to the public under the rubric of crime prevention and to other officers as investigative intelligence. Law-enforcement officials throughout the United States flock to training seminars about satanic cults and crime. In Virginia alone, I estimate that in 1988 cult officers (that is, those who teach or specialize in satanic or occult crime) and their allies gave at least fifty seminars to the public—usually in churches and schools—as well as exclusive courses to law-enforcement officers who earn in-service credit from them to retain their certification to continue working in their profession. The seminars, orchestrated by a loose network of investigators, former police officers (now cult consultants), therapists, and clergy, offer a world-view that interprets both the familiar and explainable and the unfamiliar and poorly understood in terms of increasing participation by Americans in satanic worship. The seminars claim further that Satanism has spawned gruesome crimes and aberrant behavior that *might* presage violent crime. In particular, law-enforcement officials have developed a model of "The Problem," a scheme widely disseminated through training seminars as well as through networks of investigators, newsletters, and public presentations.

Who gives these seminars and what topics do they address? A small sampling of seminar brochures hints at the universe of social problems blended into a distilled, simple model of criminality. Officers attend the "Sects, Cults and Deviant Movements" seminar (designated as "intermediate," for "investigators with experience in this field"), a four-day course presented by the Institute of Police Technology and Management at the University of North Florida. They learn such esoterica as "analysis of modern medieval vs. countercultural satanism"; "dynamics of paganism"; "in-depth study of Afro-Cuban-American Santeria, Palo Mayombe and brujeria"; "ritual sites, symbols, languages and scripts"; "multigenerational ritualistic abuse"; and "multiple-personality disorder and disassociative states." The Fifteenth Annual Florida Attorney General's Crime Prevention Conference, held in Sarasota in October 1989, listed a plenary session titled "Responding to Occult Religious Activities." The University of Delaware runs a three-day course, "Occult and Cult Crime Investigation," given by Thomas Wedge, a "nationally recognized authority on the investigation of traditional and nontraditional occult and cult related crimes." Wedge, a former probation officer who now makes his living on the cult circuit, leads officers to "discover what these groups believe, their methods of recruitment, the types of rituals they perform and their influence on criminal behavior."

An influential speaker, Patricia A. Pulling, who founded Bothered About Dungeons and Dragons (BADD), offers a one-day workshop, "Teen

Satanism and the Occult," to mental-health professionals in Staunton and Waynesboro, Virginia. In a brochure festooned with no fewer than twenty-two inverted pentagrams, Pulling describes her credentials as a "private investigator" whose "list of degrees, honors and awards is innumerable [*sic*]," who "has been a guest on several hundred shows from coast to coast," including *60 Minutes* and CBN's *700 Club*. For mental-health professionals in Hampton, Virginia, Pulling taught "The Hidden Danger: Adolescent Involvement in Satanism and the Occult," and discussed the "use of culture in Satanism and the occult," " 'Black Metal' and other occult music," "fantasy role-playing games," and "teen devil worship." She warns that "the practices of witchcraft and satanism among adolescents are on the rise in this country." Concerning the role-playing games, she states, "Adolescents involved with one role-playing game, Dungeons and Dragons, have been linked to at least 125 documented suicides and murders in the last ten years."

Even the prestigious National Crime Prevention Institute of the University of Louisville offers "Occult Crimes: Prevention, Reduction and Detection." The program contains the standard litany: involvement in Satanism through role-playing games and "heavy metal" music, examination of Palo Mayombe and Santeria and their links with drug trafficking, and what to look for at crime scenes. And if seminars don't fill the hunger for information, one may purchase "occult investigative aid" software (along with "profiling rape suspects" and "profiling sexually motivated homicides") for a minimum of $995 from the International Protection of Assets Consultants, Inc., of Salt Lake City, Utah. Finally, for those seeking a bizarre time, longtime Satan-impugner Mike Warnke will give a public talk in one's own town: Warnke bills himself as "Former Satanist High Priest, Now America's Number 1 Christian Comedian." But is the concern of these cult seminars justified?

Civil Blasphemy

I argue that the current preoccupation of law enforcers with Satanism and cults involves nothing new: the seventeenth-century analogy given earlier suggests a firm historical and cultural context for satanic claims. Further, I suggest that the news media have largely defined the law-enforcement model of cult activity, since the evidence officers cite for cult mayhem is generally nothing more than newspaper stories. Frequently, a close reading of the same stories reveals that the vast majority of nasty incidents cannot be attributed to cults, but the police often infer causality anyway. I suggest that the actual police problem with cults, as determined by their threat to public order, is very small, has nonsupernatural explanations, and requires no new law-enforcement resources, no new laws, and no new definitions of crime and criminality.

In a recent university commencement address, humanities professor Arthur Schlesinger, Jr., observed that "little is more surprising these days than the revival of blasphemy as a crime."[16] In describing recent governmental mortification over the "desecration" of flag-burning, he notes:

> We are witnessing the rise of what Charles Fried, Ronald Reagan's Solicitor General, calls the "doctrine of civil blasphemy." Whether religious or secular in guise, all forms of blasphemy have in common that there are things so sacred that they must be protected by the arm of the state from irreverence and challenge—that absolutes of truth and virtue exist and that those who scoff are to be punished.[17]

I suggest that civil blasphemy has indeed evolved as a crime, though it is not codified as such, because it subsumes conservative Christian views. For example, cult-crime officers now elevate minor misdemeanors—annoying and offensive ones, to be sure, but still misdemeanors—to felonious proportions when Christian values are assailed. Destruction of a cemetery cross, vandalizing a grave, spray-painting "666" on a church door receive considerable investigative time because the perpetrators—to investigators, obviously cult members—have deliberately and maliciously sought to harm Christian values by demeaning Christian property in symbolic fashion.

Entering blasphemy on the list of criminal motives is part of the government-sponsored investment of law-enforcement resources in hate and bias crime. A bias crime might be a church vandalism, but what distinguishes a garden-variety destruction of property from a church vandalism is the psychological hurt done not to just one property owner but to an entire community. The government interest in bias crime, while only recently introduced into local law-enforcement policy, does not elevate Christian sentiments only; it cuts across ethnic and religious boundaries and includes phenomena from cross-burnings to synagogue vandalism. (The government interest in bias crime as it corresponds to cult crime is discussed in Chapter 7.)

Nevertheless, the promotion of bias crime plays into the government's use of criminal myths. For example, the government has transmogrified the drug dealer into a demon whose color is black or brown, whose expression is cinematically Mephisthophelean, who dresses like a fashionable pimp, and whose business acumen and ruthlessness represent a mix of J. R. Ewing from *Dallas* and Lee Iacocca. This drug dealer of mythic proportions directs drug-related crimes. He oversees trafficking, debauches our children, and procures arsenals from arms manufacturers. In short, he is omnipotent; his omnipotence derives from his omniscience; and his omniscience is sustained by the vast sums paid to informants, many of whom occupy responsible, influential positions. Federal government myth-making has drawn this picture of the drug dealer in order to appropriate money to serve no clear strategy but to attack the scapegoats of well-to-do white society: such scapegoats are always found in barrios and ghettos.

While the federal goverment has not constructed a satanic myth, local governments, through their police, have: I argue that criminal myths have their uses in designating scapegoats. The satanic cults *are* scapegoats for a variety of social ills, and I view such scapegoating as a product of xenophobia stroked by a millenarian fear. The cult-cop world-view entertains, although unwittingly, a racism that is supported by a fundamentalist Christian vision that seems apocalyptic in respect to a coming millennium. At the threshold of the new millennium, Satan bars our passage. But we must ask: Do law enforcers truly believe in an anthropomorphic, supernatural Satan who walks among us, tempting people to, and guiding, criminal activities?

Satan Walks Among Us

Arthur Lyons, a writer who has closely observed and reported on Satan, quoted a 1982 Gallup poll that found that 34 percent of adult Americans considered the Devil a "personal being who directs evil forces and influences people to do wrong," while another 36 percent perceived the Devil as "an impersonal force that influences people to do wrong."[18] Lyons, in his recent book, *Satan Wants You* (an update of his 1970 book on the same subject), finds Americans' belief in the Devil increasing. In a survey of high-school biology teachers, 44 percent responded affirmatively to the statement, "Satan is an actual personality working in the world today."[19] Yet another study of the belief of North Americans found that between 1964 and 1973 certainty that the Devil exists rose, yet certainty that God exists *declined.*[20]

Many other studies have reflected Americans' growing beliefs in various occult ideas;[21] in particular, a National Science Foundation survey of scientific literacy, a subject not unrelated to views of the Devil, found, not surprisingly, that "only about 1 in 18 [adults] knows enough about the vocabulary and methodology of science to function effectively as a citizen and consumer." The survey's finding reflects the influence of pseudoscientific and occult beliefs on people's inability to think scientifically.[22] Some police officers, who in general are politically and religiously conservative,[23] have recently shown susceptibility to pseudoscientific beliefs as manifested by their uncritical embracing of the satanic-cult explanation of crime. Paradoxically, the same police officers have welcomed new scientific investigative tools, particularly the advancements in forensic techniques, such as criminal identification through DNA analysis and fingerprint-matching through the Automatic Fingerprint Identification System.

At a distance of three and a half centuries from the last major outbreak of witchcraft trials, we may shake our heads in disbelief at the seventeenth-century Englishman's respect for logic, proof, and legal inquiry. Certainly, we think, witches cannot invite such responses—public shaming, excommunication, hanging, and burning—in the contemporary United States. Witches belong to 1960s communes and New Age feminists, some say, but pose no threat to society at large. Even if some Americans do take fright at neighbors who meet in covens, surely our legal authorities would never react to stories of lawbreaking that implicate the Black Arts except in a manner strictly confined by the Bill of Rights and our criminal codes.

A Satanic Sampler

Unfortunately, a survey of news stories reporting the activities of cults, Satanists, and pagans reveals no such assurances about our legal system. By our so-called sophisticated standards, the "proper" handling of witchcraft cases in Tudor or Stuart England was only superficially concerned with a review of the facts and reflected a belief pattern characteristic of a remote time, a more *primitive* time. Despite the changing definition of what constitutes judicial proof since the seventeenth century, however, the same belief system has now pervaded American policing. But *we* know better than those Englishmen of the 1600s because *we* are modern, sophisticated folks. Or are we? I offer a sampling of recent journalistic attention paid to satanic cults:

—In 1988, police arrested four teenagers for vandalizing a cemetery; allegedly they were trying to remove body parts from a grave for satanic rituals.[24] The judge denied bond because she felt that, once freed, the boys would run amok during the upcoming Walpurgisnacht (April 30), a satanic holiday. In the opinion of the judge, the boys couldn't control their own behavior because they were in thrall to Satan.

—In Mississippi, police arrested two brothers for trying to kill a judge through a hoodoo spell. (Hoodoo, a variant of voodoo, survives in the American South primarily among impoverished blacks.) The brothers had arranged with a Jamaican "voodoo priest" to cast a death spell, using a photograph of the judge and a lock of his hair. Although the brothers got caught by ingenuously asking the judge's wife for the hair and the photograph, the police nevertheless charged them with conspiracy to commit murder based on the hex alone.[25]

—In Virginia, an article described cult paraphernalia left at a popular riverside park, but a park official wasn't worried: the paraphernalia could not be the work of dangerous Satanists because "real satanists don't leave any traces," he observed.[26]

—Chicago police investigator Jerry Simandl says of cult crime, "I think it's going to be a growing problem as we go into the nineties." He further notes that, although no national statistics have been compiled on the problem, there is a network of Satanists who perform child molestation and murder as a form of worship. A deputy sheriff warns that Satanists sacrifice as many as fifty thousand people a year, "mainly transients, runaways, and babies conceived solely for the purpose of human sacrifice."[27]

—An article surveying the law-enforcement interest in cults recounted the first of several preschool and day-care-center cases in which uncorroborated children's testimony caused indictments of many adults for sexual abuse. The children said that adults dressed in robes performed ceremonies involving not only rape but murder, cannibalism, and mutilation.[28]

—Detective Don Rimer of the Virginia Beach, Virginia, Police Department lectures church groups on satanic cults, despite his own department's disavowal of any satanic problem in the area. Rimer, "a Christian and father of two," not only warns parents about the satanic influence of rock music, but "he also observed that Papa Smurf, a seemingly innocuous cartoon character, has appeared in several television episodes wearing a pentagram, symbolic of satanic worship." Such occurrences, Rimer said, are "small victories for cults."[29]

—Patricia A. Pulling, who in addition to running BADD also runs a "detective agency," estimates that 8 percent of the population of Richmond, Virginia, "is involved in one degree or another in a multi-tiered secret Satanic society that ranges from teen-age dabbling with a few incantations to the fully committed at the upper levels who command lower levels to do their bidding."[30] She further observes, "We've found that the people in Satanism can be found on all levels of society. . . . Across the country, doctors, lawyers, clergymen, even police are involved in this."

—Glendale, Arizona, police went to the Good Shepherd School for Girls and found "upside-downed [sic] crucifixes and swastikas spray-painted on the walls, candle wax dripped in patterns on the floor and other evidence associated with devil worship."[31] The police cautioned that vandalism was not the problem, but rather "the possibility that practitioners may commit ritualistic crimes associated with devil worship, including animal mutilation and homicide."

—Teenager Thomas Sullivan listened to heavy-metal rock music, played Dungeons & Dragons, and toyed with satanic symbols, a recent and abrupt conversion from life as a high-school athlete, overachiever, excellent student, and churchgoer. But after he murdered his mother and then committed suicide, Sullivan's neighbors imagined the presence of evil spirits. "The mayor and local clergy in this [New Jersey] town gave voice to what others feared: The boy was possessed by the devil."[32]

—More than 250 police investigators convened in Killeen, Texas, for a seminar on satanic cults. "It's a crazy situation—local cops trying to understand a national problem like this," said Sandi Gallant, a San Francisco Police Department investigator who became one of the first cult cops. "There are horrendous, ritual crimes being committed. Until this conference, most of the police here never heard about this stuff," she said.[33] Speakers at the conference maintained that police at crime scenes ignore or overlook cult-crime clues because, until attending the seminar, they hadn't yet learned to interpret them properly.

—A Cincinnati photographer traveled through rural Kentucky taking photographs under a grant from the Kentucky Arts Council. By coincidence, "rumors that devil worshipers were searching for blond, blue-eyed victims for sacrifices reached the town from surrounding counties about the same time." The photographer, however, had taken photographs of children, prompting the rumor "that a woman was taking pictures of blonde-haired, blue-eyed girls, potential victims for devil worshipers." After receiving threats, and after the local high-school principal chased her from school yelling, "Get out, get out," the photographer fled.[34]

—Cultists supposedly rampaged through Raleigh County, West Virginia, threatened to damage a church, "sacrificed dogs," and disturbed graves. According to a local Baptist minister, "There have been a lot of rumors, and there have been some things that happened, like one girl [whom cultists] tried to pull out of a window in her bedroom and an older woman who was taken out of her house." A local sheriff's spokesman observed, "Any time a sign is knocked down or a dog gets run over, people try to connect it with Satan worship. . . . We really didn't connect [the events] with cult worship, but we are convinced that there are things happening and young people are being threatened to join the satanic worship group."[35]

—Dick Burke, a member of the Fellowship of Christian Police Officers, lectures school administrators and teachers about teen Satanism. He makes the case that the presence of Satanism inevitably means criminal behavior. "Burke also explained that every single juvenile that he had interviewed and who has told him that they were into the occult or a satanist has had a criminal record. [Burke] explained this by saying that occult and satanic activity is oppositional to the Judeo-Christian standards under which our laws are designed."[36]

—Convicted murderer Henry Lee Lucas maintains that he killed because of the dictates of a cult known as "The Hands of Death." Lucas, who claims to have killed about 360 people during eight years, said that "the cult killed by contract and performed ritual cremations and crucifixions of animals and humans to promote 'a reincarnation of the devil.' " Lucas's born-again Christianity has prompted his explanation of his former misdeeds.[37]

—Pasadena, Texas, school officials moved to create a new student dress code that would ban the peace symbol of the 1960s, the inverted Y inside a circle. "School administrators learned the symbol's devilish significance at a seminar on cults conducted last spring at the University of Houston."[38] The symbol, apparently, includes a very un-Christian upside-down cross.

—Thomas Wedge, the former probation officer who makes his living giving cult seminars, poses for a photograph: he stands grim-facedly eyeing the cameraman, wearing a dark suit, holding a skull, and surrounded by burning candles and an arrangement of books with such titles as *The Satanic Bible, The Necronomicon,* and *Sex Magick.* He warns, "For those of us who work in law enforcement, we're encountering something entirely different than anything we've ever come across—something we've never had to deal with before." He further observes, "There are no absolutes in Satanism—and that's the danger. They can do anything they want to do, and nothing at all is forbidden."[39]

—In a rare editorial comment by a police executive in a national magazine, Chief Donald W. Story of the Matteson, Illinois, Police Department echoes Wedge in citing the newness of the satanic phenomenon. He warns, "Satanism intentionally twists, perverts, or reverses everything that is considered good in order to mock the traditional Judeo-Christian religions. The belief system, as practiced by many, is commonly characterized as 'What's good is bad, and what's bad is good.' This type of moral system is 180 degrees opposite to that of civilized people." Story argues the need for officers to be vigilant about Satanism for their own safety's sake. People who become involved in Satanism undergo personality changes that "with certain triggering mechanisms" cause people to become "extremely violent." Finally, he says, "Our society deserves to be protected from this menace."[40]

—The same law-enforcement message shows up in religious periodicals. Erling Jorstad, a history professor at St. Olaf College in Northfield, Minnesota, notes "a gruesome fact: Satanism in its many forms is growing in popularity." Jorstad, citing law enforcers, says that "1.4 million teens and adults are involved in satanic worship in one way or another." Also citing the "growing number of occult bookstores" that promulgate such dangerous literature as *The Satanic Bible* by Anton LaVey, he notes that "Devil Worship is a totally self-centered, self-gratifying perversion of religion."[41] Jorstad liberally cites law enforcers as the source of his information.

—Perhaps Satanism will prove a mitigating circumstance in criminal trials. A Virginia pastor accused of sex crimes involving a girl blamed his difficulties on the Devil. "Satan really started trying to ruin his life, [the pastor] said, after he told . . . authorities that a woman he had been counseling had witnessed the sacrifice and cannibalization of a child. . . . Investigators found no evidence to support the story." Facing counts of forcible sodomy and rape, the pastor philosophized, "I've never had to rape a woman in my life. . . . I've had quite a few try to rape me."[42]

These incidents reveal the scope of belief in the Devil's involvement with crime and the resulting bedevilment of the police. Above all else, law enforcers cite such episodes of malevolence as new phenomena. What police officers don't *know* and only *suspect* has superseded the facts and circumstances of probable cause, the legal elements of arrest, in cases with the barest scent of satanic presence.

A Caveat About This Study

One cannot easily analyze the law-enforcement concern with satanic cults for two reasons. First, the sources of information are irregular and are sometimes obscure or not verifiable (e.g., there is no public access to ongoing criminal investigations). Relevant court cases appear here and there citing Satanism in anecdotal fashion: that Satanism has not figured significantly in case verdicts is evidenced by the lack of a "Satanism" subject heading in indices of legal cases. Also, no one comprehensive index exists of all court cases in the country: in the LEXIS system, for example, only state appellate, higher court, and federal-court decisions figure into the compilation.

Second, the eclectic nature of the law-enforcement model of cult crime makes focused criticism difficult. The information law enforcers use to document cult activities derives largely from newspaper articles. Reporters often cater to the lurid and the macabre, frequently implying cause-effect relationships or hinting at dark deeds.

For example, articles on teen suicides sometimes note that the victim was known to listen to heavy-metal rock-music or to play Dungeons & Dragons. Some law-enforcement officials and concerned parents perceive a cause-effect relationship: Dungeons & Dragons introduces young lives to the occult and may prompt suicides. Patricia A. Pulling, founder of the Virginia-based BADD, whom I noted earlier, infers such a relationship when she claims that many teen suicides are linked to the game; she bases her conclusion only on newspaper articles (including some from the *Weekly World News*) as authoritative sources. Law-enforcement literature makes the same mistakes. For example, *Law Enforcement News,* a publication of the John Jay College of Criminal Justice in New York City, began an article on cult crime with: "A 14-year-old Jefferson Township, N.J., boy kills his mother with a Boy Scout knife, sets the family home on fire, and commits suicide in a neighbor's back yard by slashing his wrists and throat. Investigators find books on the occult and Satan worship in the boy's room."[43] But did the boy have a collection of spiders? A stack of pornographic literature under his bed? A girlfriend who just jilted him? Newspaper accounts never mention other possible explanations since only those touched by a nameless, faceless evil will explain why good boys go bad. Of course some news articles show critical inquiry, but they are few in number and do not support cult-cops' views.

Articles by gullible journalists who merely recount what cult-cops tell them are passed around the cult seminars as proof of cops' assertions about cults. As such, the articles constitute a sort of reflexive bias. The journalist interviews the cult investigator; the investigator offers guesses and suppositions about the nature and scope of the problem; the journalist publishes the officer's views; the officer then uses the article as a seminar handout to prove that the satanic-cult menace exists.

Typical cult-crime seminars across the country maintain the same threat, cite the same news articles, pass out photocopied material of signs and symbols without documentation, and portray their generalizations, suppositions, hints, and allusions as fact. Most cult officers giving seminars have had little or no experience in what they teach except for having attended other cult-crime seminars. For example, the Virginia State Police has developed a slide show for presentation to citizens' groups and law enforcers and has assigned an investigator from each field station to double as cult investigator and slide-program presenter. Nevertheless, when I spoke opposite a State Police investigator who presented the slide show, accompanied by a hyperbolic talk, he admitted that he works as an accountant for the State Police and has never investigated a putative cult crime. Although I was paired with the investigator so that "pro and con" views of the cult problem would be presented, days before the presentation both the investigator and his supervisor argued with me that there was no need for the "con" view, or my skeptical view, since the slide presentation consisted of established and recognized facts, such as the link between Dungeons & Dragons and teen suicides. The investigator argued that giving a skeptical view would simply damage the work the State Police was trying to do, and besides, State Police policy precluded its officers from participating in debates on the matter.

This book represents a critical examination of the dogma of the cult seminars. Taking nothing for granted, I questioned source material, tracked down documentation, and queried the primary sources whenever possible. Aside from attending some of the seminars and collecting documentary material, I had to limit myself to telephone calls and correspondence with other researchers and investigators: I had neither the money nor the time to investigate firsthand some of the more celebrated cult-case allegations. I can only hope that the critical questions I raise about the cult-seminar dogma will challenge others to do the same. What *precisely* have the self-appointed cult experts investigated in the way of crimes connected to cults, and what cults? How do the presenters define their terms, if they do at all? When they do cite sources, it is important to consult them. I found that the sources, upon careful study, rarely confirmed the generalizations of cult cops. Further, the same news articles cult investigators cite frequently give a larger dimension or a wider interpretation to phenomena than what the investigators claim. Often the news reports even *contradict* satanic assertions. When one sifts through the claims to separate cause from effect, the question arises: Are generalizations about cult activity supported by the evidence?

This book, then, tries to face the cult cops on their own ground. I want to force them to become more specific, more critical and empirical, and to generalize less. I argue my skepticism on the basis of cult investigators' own documents, assertions, and cited supporting research. To pursue this end, I also cite news articles, and many of them illustrate that some members of the news media have presented a picture of Satanism much different from the dogmatic viewpoint taught at cult seminars. I do so also to show that the *same sources* as those cited by cult cops tell or suggest stories different from those inferred by the investigators.

Chapter 2 presents an outline of the model of cult crimes presented at the seminars. Chapter 3 discusses definitions and distinctions, particularly those that cult cops don't but should make. Chapters 4 and 5 analyze the most salient evidence of satanic conspiracy posited by cult cops, the cult survivors' claims, and the child-abuse cases involving day-care centers, respectively. In Chapter 6, I discuss the claims concerning teenagers, focusing on the alleged links between fantasy role-playing and suicide and murder. Finally, in Chapter 7, I offer an interpretation of the hysteria surrounding Satanism in terms of folklore research, and do so within a historical context. In the same chapter, I present the civil-liberties issues regarding this satanic hysteria. In conclusion, I return to my comparison of cult seminars and cult cops with witch-finding, and offer some recommendations to concerned citizens and to the police.

A Note on Terminology

Cult cops parley significant terms interchangeably and synonymously. The words *cult, occult, ritualistic,* and *satanic* are used simply to connote a sense of evil, despite firm distinctions in the social-science literature. Chapter 3 is devoted to the problem of definition, yet throughout this book I use the terms in a loose sense. A new California guide to occult crime for police officers offers the following definitions:

> Occult activity involves the use or knowledge of actions and/or rituals connected to supernatural beliefs and/or supernatural powers.

Satanic activity involves a belief that Satan will bring personal power over oneself, others and the external environment and, in turn, such power will permit the believer to live by whatever moral and ethical codes one wishes to adopt.

Ritualistic activity involves repeated physical, sexual, psychological, and or spiritual acts.[44]

The definitions of "occult" and "ritualistic" activity could even apply to Christian behavior. Nevertheless, except for Chapter 3, I use the terms largely as cult cops use them: to designate a faceless, evil, criminal conspiracy. I use the term *occult* largely to denote spiritual interests apart from Christianity or any other organized religious belief with a historical dimension—interests that may include everything from what we now call New Age to parlor tricks like Ouija boards and tarot cards.

Chapter 2
BELIEVING IN HELL

Believing in Hell must distort every judgment on this life.

Cyril Connolly (1945)

Logic, n. The art of thinking and reasoning in strict accordance with the limitations and incapacities of the human misunderstanding.

Ambrose Bierce, *The Devil's Dictionary*

A cult seminar given under the aegis of the senior judge of the Superior Court of Lake County, Indiana, Juvenile Division, promises to give instruction "on the identification of four levels of ritualistic criminal activity: primary level (international network), secondary level (organized groups), third level (self-styled), and fourth level (dabbler)" (seminar handout, May 13, 1988).

Detective Gary Sworin, of Luzerne County, Pennsylvania, similarly observes that "Satanic cults come in different stages . . . and we're going from one extreme to the other—[one] is the self-styled or what we call the dabbler. . . . Then going to the other extreme, we have the hard core people . . . involved in the Satanic cult activity . . . where people are killed, offered up as sacrifices. . . ." (Transcript of satanic-cult seminar, Oct. 4, 1988, Freeland, Pa.).

Detective Bill Lightfoot, of the Richmond, Virginia, Bureau of Police also teaches the four-level model. His description of the continuum includes such phenomena as "backmasking," i.e., incorporating disguised satanic messages in rock-music albums; these secret messages supposedly stimulate kids to do ill when the music plays at 180 hertz. According to Lightfoot, "level one," or traditional Satanists, are people born into Satanism, most of whom occupy the "worker" level; an elite few achieve high rank as cult leaders who manipulate members at will (Cult-crime seminar, Petersburg, Va., Sept. 13, 1988).

In a handout at a seminar conducted in Richmond, Virginia, by Patricia Pulling's BADD organization, Wisconsin probation officer Steve Daniels writes: "Among the professionals who study, research and investigate satanic activity, there is generally a consensus that there are between three and five levels of satanic activity, ranging from the teenage dabblers to the extremely sophisticated, highly technological, international satanic commission" (Advanced ritualistic-crime seminar, Sept. 23–24, 1988).

The Massachusetts State Police advise their officers: "Like all religions, Satanism has a body of followers. People are drawn to this belief by the desire to acquire power and control. A believer in Satan is predisposed to doing evil, i.e., enticed by his/her own lusts; a good person cannot be overcome and forced to do evil."[1]

The Massachusetts State Police has streamlined this model into three types of Satanists, leaving out public groups, such as the Church of Satan. But the Massachusetts document offers some gems of criminal intelligence:

> The most startling element of the world of the occult, particularly Satanism, is the practice of animal and human sacrifice. The theory is that a living creature is a storehouse of energy. When killed, the victim's energy force is liberated and produces an extremely high psychological charge to those who commit and witness its death.
>
> The ideal victim is healthy and virgin to insure minimal dissipation of its force. A male child of high intelligence possesses the greatest force and therefore offers the highest spiritual attainment to would-be sacrificers.[2]

I offer these examples to demonstrate the similar messages conveyed through law-enforcement training. Their universal sameness reflects the lack of critical discussion and the concomitant refinement of theory that should take place. One of the earliest cult seminars I found, sponsored in 1984 by the San Diego County Sheriff's Department,[3] parleys the same message as those held in 1989: no significant refinement of the satanic paradigm has occurred. In fact, many of the same handouts on investigative tips continue to circulate five years later. The sameness of the message becomes dogma, which in turn assumes folkloric value as rumors, urban legends, or subversion myths. The four-tiered model evolved without professional debate; it coalesced almost seven years ago, introduced by so-called cult experts, including investigator Sandi Gallant of the San Francisco Police Department, evangelist Mike Warnke, Patricia Pulling (BADD), psychiatrist Lawrence Pazder, and television producer Ken Wooten. Significantly, most of the satanic-cult-conspiracy proponents were not even police professionals.

Now cult cops appear everywhere: officers attend a few cult seminars, return to their departments, and organize portfolios of Satanalia so that they themselves can give seminars to teachers, parents, and enforcers; they join informal networks of other cult cops, then parade their own consciousness-raising seminars by inventing a *mise-en-scène* replete with Black Mass artifacts, books adorned with garish pentagrams, and resurrected photographs of Anton LaVey's 1966-67 Church of Satan featuring nude women as altars. News reporters follow the seminars, giving them wide coverage and quoting alarmed citizens, their consciousness appropriately raised in response to the cult cops' glib and slick ideology. Indeed, the seminar presentations resemble late-night television appearances by hucksters sharing secrets on how to make millions in real estate. Vague on causal relationships and ambiguous on the investigative value of seminars, cult cops leap logical problems in favor of *tableaux vivants* featuring priests and cult survivors with lurid tales backed by slides of graffiti, dead animals, and occult bookstores. Further, officers attending the seminars earn in-service credit and thus advance their careers.

Characteristically, law-enforcement cult seminars parley their model of satanic cults largely without any substantiation or documentation beyond news clippings, television reports (from *20/20, Oprah Winfrey, Geraldo, Sally Jessy Raphael,* or local coverage), plus inside tips from "ongoing investigations," usually nothing more than sporadic surveillance of modern witchcraft practitioners or secondhand conversations with investigators from other jurisdictions. A few cult cops, such as investigator Jerry Simandl of the Chicago Police, have worked directly with so-called cult survivors (while they undergo therapy for multiple-personality disorder) or with day-care-center abuse cases, but they number relatively few. Simandl has maintained that no cult experts exist. The only experts, he says, are the investigators working directly with victims.[4] But the four-tiered model convinces because it takes phenomena familiar to the officer and imbues them with new meanings: officers learn a new lexicon to describe old phenomena and therefore see the cult problem as a new threat to public order.

Definitions

Characteristically, cult-crime officers—the self-proclaimed experts who teach the seminars—do not define the object of their concern. They use the terms *cult, occult, ritualistic,* and *satanic* interchangeably but with the connotation of disruption, coercion, mind control by a charismatic leader, and, of course, criminality. As FBI's Kenneth Lanning has observed about cult seminars, cult cops link multifarious phenomena—day-care-center child abuse, human sacrifice, cemetery and church vandalism, modern satanic or witchcraft practices, teen suicide, heavy-metal music, and fantasy role-playing games—to the four-tiered model, fusing the levels into a continuum.[5]

Cult cops extend the terms mentioned above to religious practices dubbed "nontraditional," e.g., voodoo, Santeria, Native American practices, and African-derived religions. Definitions of these religious beliefs are discussed in Chapter 3. The "nontraditional" label masks an implicit bias that Christianity is *the* traditional belief, the norm. The same law enforcers who employ the term *nontraditional* don't even see the irony of introducing their seminars with the caveat that officers must respect First Amendment rights and not interfere with noncriminal religious practices. Lanning notes: "Many law enforcement officers begin their presentations by stating that they are not addressing or judging anyone's religious beliefs, and then proceed to do exactly that."[6]

The "nontraditional" label permeates the cult seminars and the hand-outs. In an undated handout with no source cited (distributed at a seminar given in Dunkirk, N.Y., by Detective Paul Hart of the Jefferson Township, New Jersey, Police Department, April 11, 1989), one reads:

> Many non-traditional satanic cults are using drugs, child abuse, human sacrifice and forms of mind control to keep their members from defecting. Many of their criminal acts center around the personality of the coven leader. Determine what form of his/her teachings the group is following. Study their symbols, dates activities are performed, instruments used in the ceremonies, etc. Note the holidays honored by the cult; particularly—birthdates of leaders, the solstices of June 22nd, December 22nd, April 30, etc. [Of course, one is limited only to two solstices per year, on or about June 22nd and December 22nd, give or take a few days.] In missing children cases, determine whether dates of disappearance are kept confidential as any public awareness will drive the cult into even greater secrecy.

This paragraph washes much occult laundry, superstition, and generalization, entertaining elements like witchcraft (mention of covens) and the solstices (evoking Celtic mythology), and foments, in systematic fashion, the sub-version myth (see Chapter 7). The description of "nontraditional satanic cults" and their activities constitutes only one of the tips given in the handout. But one sees the cavalier use of *nontraditional.* Normally, the label attaches to non-Christian beliefs in cult seminars, thus damning everyone from the hardcore criminal Satanists to a *botanica* who provides medicinal herbs in a Cuban community, hardly a criminal matter.

The failure to separate a religious belief from a religion's adherent who commits a crime is evident in a handout prepared by Kurt Jackson when he was an officer with the Beaumont, California, Police Department: "Crimes that have been committed by some strange religious Cults, Sects, or Individuals, are particularly difficult to investigate much less try to understand them."

Cult expert Dale Griffis of Tiffin, Ohio (a retired police captain from Tiffin's police department), has even developed an "Investigation Manual for Non-Traditional Groups." As a "case management file," the manual looks like any comprehensive investigative file, listing physical characteristics of a suspect, as well as his or her clothing, family, associates, vehicles owned, and financial and educational background, but also asks for the "last church attended" and "religious training." Consistent with the cult-seminar model, the manual also asks that an investigator note a suspect's (or victim's) past psychological problems, whether he or she is gifted or possesses a learning disability, his or her food preferences, favorite idol or role model, recent personality changes, musical tastes, and sexual activity.

Moving on to the group's activities, the manual asks investigators to describe security devices in use at meetings, whether lookouts were used, and what passwords were mentioned. Members and associates of the group must be listed next, along with their roles in the group ("passive" or "violent"). One then has the opportunity to categorize the group, e.g., witchcraft, "voodoo-island," Satanist, survivalist, "identity" (includes the Ku Klux Klan and other white-supremacist groups), terrorist, "psychological/self-help (self-awareness)," political, New Age, destructive religious cults, money-making groups ("pyramidal sales using mental manipulation"), and "cults of no name." No group with an explicit Christian label appears.

Similarly, one can check off a list of locations for meetings or rituals that includes abandoned churches, crematories, mortuaries, private/public schools, preschools, riverbeds, underground, statues or monuments, and even the zoo. The section on deities and rituals provides a challenge to any investigator's imagination. After the listing "deities or demons," one must check yes or no to whether the leader is godlike. Next, one lists the method for calling Satan and whether a subject is dedicated to Satan, a horned god or goddess. But the "ritual events" section of the manual reads like an inventory of demonic devices from the fifteenth-century witch-finding guide, the *Malleus Maleficarum*. Aside from the mundane entries, such as dancing, drums, and chanting, one indicates whether the following activities occurred before, during, or after the ceremony: bloodletting, blood writing, drinking of urine (either "plain" or "mixed with blood"); flesh eating (again, a choice: "fowl," "animal," "human"); sex acts (interesting parallelism: types to choose from include "animals," "corpse," "children," "homosexual," "lesbian," followed by a shortened list of choices for "sex orgies").

The forced-choice list of "ritual events" includes sadomasochistic acts, mutilations, kidnapping, martial arts, and pornography. The last category offers subcategories to check: adult sex film; child film; or "snuff porn" films (pornographic films that allegedly include actual killings). The list even includes "fantasy games," clearly directed at Dungeons & Dragons, asking the investigator to indicate whether the suspect was a player or game leader, how often he or she played the game, and the time spent. Next comes a flow chart of responses to a cult's "mental manipulation," asking the investigator to select the character attributes in a suspect or victim. The list, which Griffis borrows from his doctoral dissertation (which will be discussed below), includes, for example, under "disfunctional [*sic*] brain response," confusion, emotional depression, and change in speech pattern, and under "recruitment" one finds the categories of "ego destruction" and "id destruction." Under the former, the attributes are guilt, fear, and the threat of Satan; under the latter, isolation, personal confrontation, and restricted sex drive. Although Griffis uses the chart in his dissertation, he has borrowed the concepts from Robert J. Lifton's *Thought Reform and the Psychology of Totalism* (W. W. Norton, New York, 1961), a study of the "brainwashing" (to use the popular but not clinically accurate term) of prisoners of war in Korea.

Other ritual artifacts listed in check-off fashion include candles (by color and shape), "cauldrons" (where one lists the contents); chalices; incense burners; "runes/Grimoires/Book of Shadows"; and "Key of Solomon." Aside from the checklists, however, the manual contains few questions that would afford a knowledgeable investigator greater insight into behavior. Griffis does ask whether the interrogated person knows the meaning of symbols; whether the victim or suspect appears "to be afraid of any super type power," if the interviewee loses attention when questioned; and whether the interviewee becomes nervous at the mention of certain figures.

Griffis concludes the manual by listing some investigative hints, such as stressing the necessity for a thorough crime-scene search and carefully measuring everything at a crime scene and diagramming the site. Some forensic pointers occur here, such as examining a corpse for "ligature or restraint marks," the presence of which could betoken an autoerotic death, a homicide, or less likely, a cult killing. Some of the hints offer puzzling notions, such as: "Do not break up activity if circle of power is closed"; (concerning animal remains) "type of animal: does it have cloven hoofs?"; "Persons involved in occult activity generally keep a log of events"; "Look for drawings—gives idea of quest for power."

The last notion, which appears in the manual alongside other recommendations of what to look for in writings, involves a satanic Rorschach test to assess a person's predelictions. Iconographical or literary interpretations, of course, are pseudoscientific at best; but when performed by nonclinical police officers, they become a game anyone can play. Some of the ritual artifacts and processes listed in the manual appear in contexts suggesting that the officer should not only respect cult-related paraphernalia and ceremonies because the cult members believe them to carry supernatural force, but officers should pay heed because supernatural demons actually lurk and skulk among us these days. The Griffis guide is so attuned to the Christian notion of satanic worship that its investigative usefulness is diluted. If the object of the guide is to help an officer formulate a criminal motive to explain behavior, the lengthy guide becomes redundant and cumbersome. One suspects that Griffis listed many possible ritual activities and artifacts so that an officer can hunt for the particular cluster of attributes that signify an "Aha!" touchstone that would explain a crime in satanic terms. The Griffis guide, then, serves officers who try to fit crimes into satanic models: it provides enough categories to match many behaviors to cult attributes. Further, the Griffis guide has had wide national circulation among police departments.

Fundamentalist Bias

Some conservative fundamentalist Christian views drive the cult-crime model, insofar as cult officers frequently communicate fundamentalist concepts at seminars. Cult officers employ fundamentalist rhetoric, distribute literature that emanates from fundamentalist authorities, and sometimes offer bibliographies giving many fundamentalist publications. Further, cult cops sometimes team up with clergy to give Satanism seminars. The most notable circular among cult-crime investigators, the *File 18 Newsletter,* published by the Idaho-based Cult Crime Impact Network, Inc., follows a Christian world-view in which officers who claim to separate their religious views from their professional duties nevertheless maintain that salvation through Jesus Christ is the only sure antidote to satanic involvement, whether criminal or noncriminal, and point out that no police officer can honorably and properly do his or her duty without reference to Christian standards.[7]

Other cult-crime seminar speakers make a living at it: Thomas Wedge maintains a Baptist line of thinking at his seminars by beginning with his own brand of "Theology 101."[8]

Further, cult officers distribute handouts at seminars showing symbols to identify at crime scenes, accompanied by their meanings. The handouts typically cite no sources but many derive from Christian material. For example, the peace symbol of the 1960s is now dubbed the "Cross of Nero." Someone decided that the upside-down "cross" on the symbol somehow mocks Christianity.[9] In fact, the symbol originated in the 1950s, combining semaphore representations for the letters "n" and "d" for "nuclear disarmament."[10]

Fundamentalist Christianity motivates many proponents of cult-crime conspiracy theories in other ways. Arguing against their theories is, to them, attacking their world-views. To some officers, arguing against the cult-crime model denies the existence of Satan as a lurking, palpable entity who appears to tempt and torture us. Satan becomes the ultimate crime leader: the drug lord, the Mafia don, the gang boss. Chicago police investigator Jerry Simandl has demonstrated the cult officer's world-view in his work. He doesn't just investigate crimes; he also interprets cult behavior, particularly that which threatens Christians. He supposedly can tell whether a church vandalism was committed mindlessly by kids or purposefully by a cult group: "For example, an organ might be vandalized by having its keys broken. That means the vandals were seeking to deny a congregation the ability to 'communicate with God' through music."[11] Simandl draws amazing inferences about a crime that experiences the lowest clearance rate because police find no suspects and no evidence beyond the destroyed property. To paraphrase Mark Twain's remark about science, with church and cemetery vandalism one gets wholesale returns of conjecture on a trifling investment of fact. Church vandalism so shocks Christian sensibilities that a cult officer— armed with his new world-view that cults cause crime—can only interpret the crime as satanic.

Evil is, indeed, the operative word. Law enforcers who meld cult-crime theories with their professional world-views have transformed their legal duties into a moral confrontation between good and evil. Larry Jones, an Idaho police officer who coedits the *File 18 Newsletter,* projects a fundamentalist bias. Jones believes a satanic network exists in all strata of society, a network that maintains extreme secrecy to shroud its program of murder.

Defensive about the lack of physical evidence of cult mayhem, Jones states:

> Those who deny, explain away, or cover up the obvious undeniably growing mountain of evidence often demand statistical evidence or positive linkages between operational suspect groups. At best, this demand for positive proof of a "horizontal conspiracy" is naive. . . . Consider the possibility that the reason supposedly unrelated groups in different localities over various time periods acting-out in a similar manner, is that consistent directives are received independently from higher levels of authority. Instead of being directly linked to each other, these groups may be linked vertically to a common source of direction and control. . . . Those who accept this theory as a reasonable possibility need to rethink the meaning, scope, and effects of the term conspiracy![12]

In other words, if the evidence doesn't seem to fit a particular conspiracy theory, just create a bigger conspiracy theory. Jones and other cult officers impose their model on a pastiche of claims, exaggerations, and suppositions. *File 18 Newsletter* recounts newspaper factoids from around the country and assumes the truth of journalists' musings about satanic connections and crime.

The Christian-biased view leads cult officers to deny facts that contradict their theories. For example, one of the recent murders dubbed satanic by cult officers was that of Stephen Newberry, a teenager from Springfield, Missouri, whose friends bashed him to death with a baseball bat. Even though Larry Jones quotes local investigators, a prosecutor, a psychologist, and an academic cult expert, all of whom claimed that *no* satanic sacrifice occurred but instead blamed drug abuse, Jones nevertheless offers the opinion that the experts

> do not give credit to the strong influence of the tenets of the satanic belief system over its initiates. In some cases the subjects become involved with satanism . . . prior to the onset of family problems. . . . The only true and lasting solution to "devil worship" or satanic involvement is a personal encounter with true Christianity.[13]

Jones's earlier guess that a "vertical conspiracy" might exist—a higher leader directing groups to do murderous business within an authoritarian cult led by a charismatic leader—is a phantasm of the cult officer's mind: the police have not unequivocally identified any such satanic groups.

I noted earlier that in not defining terms, cult cops use the label "nontraditional" belief to encompass anything not Christian, particularly Satanism, but also ethnic religious practices such as voodoo, Santeria, and Native American beliefs. Cult cops don't see the irony of making implicit judgments about others' religious beliefs while at the same time introducing their seminars with the caveat that officers must respect First Amendment rights and not interfere with noncriminal religious practices. *File 18 Newsletter* ingenuously advises readers not to interfere with constitutionally protected civil liberties, yet nonetheless judges "nontraditional" groups or cults according to its own standards.

In a discourse on Wicca, a neopagan form of witchcraft, Larry Jones posits, for example, that *any* belief system must set absolute standards of conduct. Relative ones won't do because they "open the door to excesses."[14] He can find fault with Wicca only by abstracting the standard that measures somehow the legitimacy of belief systems. While concluding that Wicca is benign and its practitioners claim no connection with Satanism, Jones nevertheless describes much of Wicca as derived from "Luciferian" Aleister Crowley, to whom he attributes ties to Satanist and black-magic organizations, a connection that might surprise many Wiccans. So nontraditional beliefs just can't win. If beliefs that don't pose absolute standards of conduct can harbor dangerous deadbeats, then Buddhists must be next in line for final judgment in the pages of the *File 18 Newsletter*.

Arthur Lyons reports that in 1986 subscribers to the *File 18 Newsletter* received an accompanying publication, a reprinted article, "America's Best Kept Secret," from *Passport,* a Christian magazine. The article was "rife with unsubstantiated allegations, inaccurate statements, and biblical references," stating that the "best-kept secret" is the satanic conspiracy comprised of white, middle-class Americans.[15] In fact, the article referred to the "WICCA Letters," a spurious document (reminiscent of the anti-Semitic *Protocols of the Elders of Zion*) that purports to document an international witches' plan for world subversion. Lyons noted that even a San Bernardino County, California, deputy sheriff investigating a ritualistic child-abuse case mentioned the "WICCA Letters" to corroborate his belief that a satanic conspiracy caused the abuse.[16] A recent investigative report suggests a source for the "WICCA Letters":

> The source . . . seems to be one Dave Gaerin, a deputy sheriff in the juvenile division of the San Diego County [Sheriff's] Department. Several years ago, Gaerin initially reported on his "discovery" of these letters in an issue of *Exodus*, published by a fundamentalist ministry in San Antonio, Texas, and described his "decoding" (translating?) of the transcripts. Likewise, Larry Jones notes that Gaerin "originally developed the information" . . . . To the best of our knowledge, no one has ever seen the original documents.
>
> [*File 18 Newsletter*] also includes commentary by Rev. Peter Michas, an "expert" on Satanism, who opines that the letters point toward the accomplishment of WICCA's goals, "culminating in the physical reign of Satan on earth on June 21, 1999. . . ."[17]

Jones's persistence in projecting his bias on evidence continues. Although Lyons mentioned the *Passport* mailing as having occurred in 1986, *File 18 Newsletter* continues to recommend "America's Best Kept Secret."[18] But Jones has found ways to fight skepticism. In defense of the lack of evidence for a satanic conspiracy, he tosses the question back: "To people who say, prove to me these secret cults exist, I say, prove they don't."[19] To this inanity, the reply comes easily: Police officers have no legal obligation to prove that the satanic mastercult doesn't exist. Officers operate under a well-founded reasonable suspicion to look into wrongdoing, or the possibility of wrongdoing, and they make arrests based on probable cause. Both *reasonable suspicion* and *probable cause* have fairly precise definitions supported by reams of case law. Jones's argument is hardly unique: "I can't prove that UFOs exist, perhaps, but just prove to me that they don't!" The reasoning is the same.

The Cult-Crime Model

Cult seminars begin with a capsule history of satanic cults. Such history lessons bend toward Christian views of church history gleaned from lightweight fundamentalist sources, in many cases, or from popular works on the occult. Investigator Lightfoot of the Richmond, Virginia, Bureau of Police (who at one time investigated Satanism full-time and lectured nationwide to erstwhile cult-busters) teaches that Satanism began in the eighth century and arose from paganism, reaching sophistication in the twelfth century through development of the Black Mass by the Cathari. Modern Satanism culminates in the mid-twentieth century, for example, with Adolf Hitler's SS troops. Hitler receives special attention with lurid anecdotes about his daily consumption of belladonna, digitalis, and excrement to serve his hellish ideology (Ritual-crime in-service seminar, Peters-burg, Va., Sept. 13, 1988). Finally, we have twentieth-century Aleister Crowley, dubbed the pernicious father of it all, and Anton LaVey's Church of Satan and Michael Aquino's Temple of Set, the two most commonly cited examples of public Satanists today. And all this from a police investigator with no credentials in the history of religion.

Even Lyons's casual history of Satanism differs considerably from that posed by Lightfoot and other cult cops. Lyons, a writer and researcher, notes the earliest appearance of a recognizable Satan in sixth-century B.C. Persia.[20] He points to the larger context of Manichean sects of the Middle Ages, which included not only the Cathari but also the Albigenses and Waldenses. In short, cult cops don't even have to look much beyond lay writers like Lyons for a more accurate history of Satan, but in cult seminars, oversimplified history is the rule. Cult officers tie the history lesson to their construction of a present-day reality: Dale Griffis says, "We are seeing in the streets the sign of Armageddon" (Advanced ritualistic-crime seminar, Richmond, Va., Sept. 22, 1988). Professional cult expert Thomas Wedge simplifies matters even more to conform to his thumbnail Christian version of history. In his "Theology 101," he states, "Satan wanted to become God; he wanted other angelic beings to worship him." When God cast Satan out of heaven, "one-third of the angels chose to follow him." Within this Miltonian scenario, then, modern Satanists try to convince the other angels to do their bidding.[21]

The current milieu of criminal cultists, claim cult cops, encompasses not only Satanists but also witches. Lightfoot posits three types of witches—black, white, and gray, those practicing evil magic, good magic, and both, respectively. As an indirect acknowledgment that magic has some inherent supernatural power, Lightfoot warns that white witches might even volunteer to help law-enforcement agencies, but officers should beware: "In reality, they're doing magic for good purposes. Nothing stops them from practicing black magic" (Ritual-crime in-service seminar, Petersburg, Va., Sept. 13, 1988). Witches, say Lightfoot, learn their craft formally through institutions. Witches apparently must formally study their craft because of the multifarious deities who must be invoked for magical purposes. Lightfoot asserts that witches pray to 300 deities and that, of course, they pray *for* something. Satanists, who by implication occupy a distant branch of the same pagan family tree, don't pray to their deities; they *demand,* because theirs is a "self-indulgent religion" based on two themes: "All humans are inherently evil," and "Life is a struggle for survival of the fittest." Witches' matter-of-fact social Darwin-ism certainly places them at odds with conservative Christianity, as sources such as the *Passport* special issue (1987) vehemently attest.[22]

As a further example of cult cops' confusion of labels and identities, Griffis describes witchcraft as a *new* phenomenon and contrasts it to cults with a long history, such as Santeria (a conflation of Santa Maria, the mother of Christ), an Afro-Cuban religion that, because of Cuban immigration over the past twenty years, has sought a niche in United States society. Griffis, who is sometimes unable to separate a particular belief from the criminals who profess it, says of Santeria and like religions, "These groups are mean." In particular, he notes, Santeria "has proven a good religion to the drug pusher" (Advanced ritualistic-crime seminar, Richmond, Va., Sept. 22, 1988). Griffis goes on to identify modern witchcraft groups as evincing the New Age philosophy of "If it feels good, do it"; to Griffis, New Agers are "professedly" at odds with Satanists. In fact, he suggests that law enforcers should not accept a group's identity merely on its say-so: some cultists belong to "bifurcated groups" that ostensibly practice white witchcraft but instead practice Satanism.

To cult cops, the two most salient characteristics of cults and those that also pose the greatest threat to plain, simple, decent folks are the do-your-own-thing ethos coupled with the quest for power. Detective Gary Sworin of Luzerne County, Pennsylvania, muddies the subject thus:

> We have to look an awful lot deeper because of the fact that any cult, whether it be passive cult [sic] . . . or destructive cults which are the Satanic cults, they're all there for one purpose, and the one purpose is power. They want control. They want the power. They want to be the only person or the centralized person to handle this, to control that power. . . . [It is] behind everything that they do and usually the motive is their own gain. . . . And if it means the destruction of people who are involved, the destruction of their followers, they're going to do that because they don't care what's going to happen to you as a follower or what you're involved in. Their ultimate goal . . . [is] power. (Satanic-cult seminar, Freeland, Pa., Oct. 4, 1988)

Cult cops, then, ascribe to cults the a priori attributes of power-seeking through magic, encouraged by an unrestrained, if-it-feels-good-do-it philosophy. The First Amendment caveat that cult cops introduce, then, becomes impossible to follow. Such attributes, even without further evidence of wrongdoing, necessitate police action of some kind: interviews, surveillance, or other forms of information-collecting.

Dabblers in Satanism

Dabblers, the outer or fourth level, are said to be mostly children, teens, or very young adults who, in unsophisticated fashion, play with occult bits and pieces. At this level, according to cult officers, Dungeons & Dragons (D&D) and like games attract kids to the occult, as does heavy-metal rock music with satanic lyrics. Some investigators here introduce the implantation (backmasking) of satanic messages into heavy-metal rock music. Chapter 6 discusses in greater detail the two most significant occult lures of teens— fantasy games and rock music.

Again, cult cops speak effusively about the many dangers to teens in Western civilization, implying causal relationships. Patricia Pulling, for example, dangles impressive statistics before her police-seminar audiences: In 1988, she said, 66 percent of high school seniors admitted to regular use of alcoholic beverages, and she noted that teen suicides have tripled in the past three decades (Cult seminar, Arlington, Va., Sept. 13, 1988). Pulling offers a typical profile of the occult-endangered teen: white, male, generally middle- or upper-class, "actively recruited" between the ages of 11 and 17. (Pulling's own son, "Bink," who committed suicide, fits this description.) While faceless adult Satanists are said to recruit teens through free drug-and-sex parties, apparently teens who are rebellious, exhibit curiosity, come from a sexually abusive background (sometimes), or who lack self-esteem, may stumble into trouble on their own. As for the satanic recruiters, they find susceptible teens through fantasy games, boys' clubs— even the Boy Scouts—heavy-metal concerts, and at the homes of acquaintances. At the recruiting parties—no friendly neighborhood gatherings, these—the Satanists supposedly offer kids free beer and drugs, and eventually free sex as well. According to this scenario, adult Satanists then photograph the drunken, stoned kids in compromising situations and use the photographs as blackmail when they order the kids to break into churches or to otherwise become criminals in service to the Evil One.

Pulling and other cult cops identify the criminal problems most likely to involve occult-blinded kids. First, officers must remain alert for school difficulties, most commonly violence. Second, status offenses, particularly running away, may mean that the child has been spending time with occult groups rather than studying. Most prominently, such teens indulge in grave-robbing to obtain bones for satanic rituals and in defacing Christian monuments, even extending to vandalism and burglaries of churches to desecrate such property or to steal religious artifacts for use in ceremonies. At seminars, cult cops show many slides of defaced or broken tombstones and melted wax in opened mausoleums. Bill Lightfoot also advises on the meanings of particular colors of wax.

But the real *bête noir* of youth is the fantasy role-playing game, usually Dungeons & Dragons. Even cult cops admit that the "basic" levels of the game involve mythological themes, normally innocuous; but to quote Patricia Pulling, more than 50 percent of the advanced material that some witches and satanists still practice is "real occult." Cult cops ascribe to the game the same dictum that applies to Satanism generally, that the game's purpose is to obtain power and wealth and to stay alive during the process. Since the game minimizes the finality of death, kids may feel encouraged to experiment, first with killing animals, later with killing people or committing suicide. Pulling attributes about 100 murders and suicides to D&D (Cult seminar, Arlington, Va., Sept. 13, 1988), a figure within the range of 95 to 150 cited in most seminars. Investigator Lightfoot asks, "Every kid that plays D&D will not get into Satanism, but how many kids do we lose before we have a problem?" (Cult-crime seminar, Petersburg, Va., Sept. 13, 1988).

According to Dale Griffis, through playing the game, "some kids cross over an imaginary line and start connecting their D&D world with the real world" (Advanced ritualistic-crime seminar, Richmond, Va., Sept. 22, 1988). To Griffis, the kids who seek solace in Satanism (sometimes through D&D) from loneliness exist "on the precipice of a whirlpool" and will evolve toward self-mutilation or worse.

Detective Paul Hart, of the Jefferson Township, New Jersey, Police Department, stated in a cult seminar that, while he knew of no adult criminal satanic cults, "that is not to say that they are not out there" (Cult-crime seminar, Dunkirk, N.Y., April 11, 1989). As an object study, Hart cites the case of Tommy Sullivan, who killed his mother and committed suicide. Showing a note purporting to be Tommy's pact with the devil, Hart nevertheless says, "As best we could determine, Tommy had no adult contact" (that is, with adult Satanists). Six weeks before Tommy's suicide (which occurred just following the 1987 Christmas vacation), he had written a school paper about Satanism. As the *coup de grâce,* Hart paraded Tommy's pictures of heavy-metal rock musicians and horror films. Hart implied a connection between all of these factors and the crime, but did not consider the alternative hypothesis for the suicide-murder as "severe low esteem." When sociologist Jeffrey Victor interviewed Hart, he questioned the connection with Satanism. Hart replied that Tommy did not want to attend a Catholic school, that his domineering mother led him to perceive that he had very little control over his own life, and that his family fostered "perfectionist" expectations. When Victor asked what was cause and what was effect, Hart replied that "Satanism is probably always a symptom of much deeper psychological problems [in kids]."

In short, Sullivan's crimes could not be attributed to the manipulation of Satan, yet Hart—and other cult cops—dangle such near-misses to seminar audiences and imply causal connections. Undoubtedly, sooner or later a teen will kill someone and announce that the Devil made him do it, but documented incidents appear hard to come by. At a cult-crime seminar (Richmond, Va., Sept. 22, 1988), Pulling offered "documentation" of the Sullivan-Satan connection in a handout, a photocopied article from the *Philadelphia Inquirer.*[23] The article's author, completely taken in by satanic claims, stated, "After an eighth-grader's fascination with Satanism culminated . . . in his mother's murder and his own suicide, it wasn't difficult for residents to imagine the presence of evil spirits in these hills. The mayor and local clergy in this Morris County town gave voice to what others feared: The boy was possessed by the devil." Sullivan had been, until three months before his death, a model kid: an "overachiever" in school and in sports, one who worked to earn money and attended church weekly. Yet the cult experts who solemnly extrapolated moral lessons from the boy's death, Pulling, Sandi Gallant, Larry Zilliox, Jr. (former director of the National Cult Awareness Network of New York and New Jersey), and the Reverend James J. LeBar, a longtime cult advisor to the Catholic church, quickly voiced their I-told-you-so's.

Sullivan had been a D&D player; he loved heavy-metal rock music. LeBar, particularly, relies on innuendo and implied causality: "In every instance of this kind of [satanic] activity, the perpetrator was an avid fan of heavy metal. One becomes suspicious, although I wouldn't say that it alone is a causative factor. But look at the power of advertising to change people from [drinking] Coke to Pepsi and back to Coke again in the flick of a television commercial."[24] LeBar, then, manages to inject into the suburban horror of Sullivan's murder-suicide the largely disproved realm of subliminal effects of commercial advertising, even hinting at a satanic connection. Fundamentalists, and most cult cops, continue to cite subliminal messages in everything from innocuous television sitcoms to rock music, finding entire blasphemograms authored in furtherance of Satan's subversion of our civilization.

To create distance from Tommy Sullivan's final acts and his model teenhood, the cult experts—Pulling, LeBar, Gallant, et al.—posit that fine, upstanding, responsible, and smart white boys like Sullivan present "a profile of a teenager most likely to succumb to the attraction of devil worship and the occult."[25] The Reverend Richard Rento, another local priest, confronted the question, "Can what happened to Tommy happen to us?" Rento quoted a student: "Nothing happened to Tommy. Tommy happened to it." In other words, one must look to an extrasomatic explanation for sordid behavior: Tommy could not have been capable of such viciousness without the cumulative influence of D&D, heavy-metal rock music, and the like. Such explanations hark back centuries, perhaps millennia. Of course Rento and LeBar can claim familiarity with the *Malleus Maleficarum* and exorcism rites, and the existence of a corporeal Satan serves Catholic theology. But even if one accepts the satanic causality, what difference would it make? If Satan led Tommy Sullivan to murder his mother and then take his own life, does knowledge of this impetus mitigate or aggravate the horror? If one, however, accepts the satanic explanation, particularly if the explanation agrees with a Christian world-view, then one must search for Satan's influence elsewhere; and as the FBI's Kenneth Lanning has pointed out, the pursuit of Satan may blind law enforcers to other legitimate police questions:

> A teenager's excessive involvement in satanism and the occult is usually a symptom of a problem and not the cause of a problem. Blaming satanism for a teenager's vandalism, theft, suicide, or even act of murder is like blaming a criminal's offenses on his tattoos: both are signs of the same rebelliousness and lack of self-esteem that contribute to the commission of crimes.[26]

The dabbler's signature is satanic graffiti: cult cops build files of photographs of signs and symbols that appear on or in derelict buildings, bridges, and elsewhere. Cult cops rarely consider the possibility that such graffiti represent mindless vandalism. Special Agent John Polak of the Virginia State Police, in a slide program produced by his department, shows a view of a bridge covered in spray-painted graffiti (Cult-crime lecture, Chesapeake, Va., June 23, 1989). Although most of the bridge's graffiti do not relate to anything satanic or occultic, Polak points out one spray-painted feature that he insists is satanic. To emphasize the importance of the eyesore, Polak states that two years earlier an unsolved homicide occurred near the bridge. He offers no further details; instead he invites the audience to draw a causal inference from the homicide and the defacing mark. Other cult cops describe graffiti's configuration of symbols, the colors used, the orientation to cardinal directions, and the like, to infer a precise meaning.

Cult cops teach other law enforcers to watch for satanic graffiti in their neighborhoods. Of course local newspapers cover the cult-seminar circuit, so when officers in rural Kansas learn what to look for, a journalist advertises that information to the community. One suspects that the appearance of satanic graffiti following barnstorming seminars may derive more from local kids finding new expressions of teenage *angst* than from Satanists leaving their mark.

Sheriff's deputies in Camden, New Jersey, finding markings and graffiti consisting of "obscure symbols, what appeared to be runic writings," coupled with the usual cemetery vandalism, packed themselves off to a cult seminar, one of the largest regional ones hosted periodically by the University of Delaware.[27] Consequently, the New Jersey State Police assigned two officers to investigate cult crimes. One of the Camden County deputies has begun to read the standard satanic works and has sought to interpret local vandalisms and animal deaths as satanic. His undersheriff, not without a modicum of humor about the whole business, said of his deputy, "I started to check every now and then to see if he was hanging upside down in his closet."[28]

Other police chiefs remain skeptical, even after attending training by Chicago's cult cop, Jerry Simandl. After investigating much graffiti, Clinton, Illinois, Police Department Chief Michael Norrington discovered that the satanic symbols "had been incorrectly drawn by junior-high-school children. 'The cases we've had have not been serious activity. It has been pranksters. In other words, maybe they've picked up on something they've heard,' " the chief said.[29] Simandl nevertheless warns that "parents who find signs their child might be involved in devil worship should contact police so an evaluation can be completed by experts."[30] What experts? Simandl and other satanic-conspiracy ideologues, apparently, will dispassionately analyze a child's behavior upon request. One of the more disturbing aspects of Patricia Pulling's book, *The Devil's Web,* involves her clinical assessment of children brought to her by exasperated mothers. Pulling has even entered schools to conduct interviews to gather the "proof" she seeks of satanic or occult influence.[31]

Who, then, are dabblers and what problem do they present to law enforcement? Shorn of conspiratorial dimensions, dabblers are teens who behave like teens. Smart, inquisitive teens don't have to look to Satanism for compulsive behavior: the cult cops have stopped short of explicitly proclaiming causal connections but like to proffer bright kids as satanic fodder. Cult cops prefer to serve up a potpourri of incidents, usually taken from newspapers, incidents that include as an aside a dead boy's interest in the occult, in D&D, or in heavy-metal rock music. The same pastiche of news clippings, of course, serves conservative Christian interests in banning or at least restricting the availability of such music and games. Pulling cites schools she has convinced to ban D&D playing or game paraphernalia from school property.[32] Some kids *may* commit crimes and proclaim that Satan made them do it, but such crimes have always been rare. Law enforcers have customarily investigated them as they would any other felony, with thoroughness and detailed documentation for prosecution. No evidence, save the undocumented anecdotes in Pulling's own book, exist to support her assertions that satanic cults hold sex-and-drug parties for our smart, unblemished youth. In this, Pulling generalizes from just one or only a few incidents.

For example, Pulling distributes at her seminars a clipping from the Pottsville, Pa., *Republican.* Local Coaldale police arrested a sex-and-drug "cult" consisting of six people who combined occult trappings with drug-taking, drinking, and sex with children. But the chief said of the case, "It's not a satanic cult. It's more witchcraft and definitely sex-oriented."[33] The incident offered no indications of involvement by any but the six adults, nor had the "cult" operated for much more than a few months, nor were many teens involved as victims. Such stories citing clandestine Satanists or other cultists *do* appear, however, in many documented and studied urban legends. (See Chapter 7.)

Self-styled Satanists

The third level of satanic involvement includes self-styled Satanists, like the mass murderers John Wayne Gacy and Henry Lee Lucas (both cited at cult seminars). These men, also social isolates, invented ideologies to affirm their behavior. Some cult officers even maintain that such criminals do their evil deeds as a form of satanic sacrifice to give them power, but other law enforcers, such as Griffis, believe that self-styled Satanists borrow from the occult because satanic ideology permits or encourages their crimes. This idea is the plausible component of the model: sociopaths or psychopaths, already distanced from common standards of behavior, may choose a perceived ideology that comports with their behavior.

An example cited by Pulling is that of Robert A. Berdella, whose victim's decomposing head was found in Berdella's backyard.[34] Subsequent investigation revealed other human artifacts of other murders. But what made this case something beyond garden-variety homicide? Berdella's slayings were related, apparently to torture and sadistic homosexual sex. The police evidently discovered on Berdella's premises about 240 photographs of men being tortured. But the article itself alludes neither to Satanism nor to cults of any kind.

The involvement of satanic imagery or paraphernalia follows no set pattern with psychopathic or sociopathic criminals; the imagery could have judicial value to form motive, or, more likely, to help a defense attorney characterize a defendant's state of mind during the commission of a crime. After all, American jurisprudence looks to the criminal state of mind, or *mens rea*, to establish whether the accused committed a crime willfully, maliciously, knowingly, or perhaps didn't understand his own behavior or the consequences of his behavior. A defense attorney would find satanic excuses, then, within his client's interests.

Sometimes the claims of self-styled Satanists may backfire. In the trial of Thomas Lee Bonney for the murder of his teenaged daughter, jurors viewed a videotape of Bonney under hypnosis, during which he assumed the identity of Satan. The Satan persona evidently constituted a separate personality, an *alter*. In the tape, the Satan persona describes the murder (although Bonney later stated that the man in the videotape must have been someone else).[35] A subsequent news article revealed that the prosecutor dubbed Bonney a fake, his multiple-personality disorder also a fake, and even the psychologist who certified the disorder admitted that "he did not take extensive precautions to guard against suggesting [the personalities'] possible existence to Bonney."[36]

Cult involvement as claimed by imprisoned murderers has thus far yielded no evidence of widespread conspiracies. Henry Lee Lucas, a self-confessed mass killer, has told of his putative cult involvement, an association cited as true by Pulling and other cult cops, despite the lack of evidence. Lucas even claims that his "devil's organization" required homicide as an initiation rite. Lucas further states that he murdered 360 people within eight years,[37] a figure he apparently feels comfortable admitting publicly in view of his recent conversion to Christianity. As Lucas put it, "the cult killed by contract and performed ritual cremations and crucifixions of animals and humans to promote a 'reincarnation of the devil.' "[38] While describing his cult involvement, Lucas nevertheless cites his own lifelong hatred of women, fostered in no small part by his own mother's prostitution. That, plus the social isolation imposed on him by those who ostracized him, led to his becoming "what everybody wanted [him] to become." In a notable moment of retrospection, Lucas laments the women hitchhikers he picked up: "But they'd start in about sex and money and such, and that's something I don't go for. That's why so many of them ended up dead. They just didn't want to be treated as human beings." Despite Lucas's obvious attempts to stoke public interest in his case by invoking a mysterious cult that guided his murders, Pulling cites him as, in his own way, a victim of a megacult: in her book, one sees a photograph of a contrite Lucas standing next to a sympathetic Pulling, the accompanying text offering testimony to the probable truth of Lucas's cult claims because Pulling *feels* that he is telling the truth.

Cult cops and the various other cult aficionados have no difficulty finding lurid and macabre examples of murders committed by self-described satanic killers. Such killers, however, have not to date revealed unequivocal evidence of their cult associations in a causative sense. Cult cops have also not considered the circumstances and timing of confessed satanic cult explanations: those who confess such connections or motivation are in prison, and therefore have already been convicted, some of them awaiting execution. Why would they not take the opportunity to dissemble when television reporters thrust microphones in their dreary faces? Nevertheless, some convicted killers, such as Richard Ramirez, the "Night Stalker," flamboyantly hails Satan in the courtroom, and flashes his pentagram-painted hand to the jury. Yet the investigation of his crimes—and the basis of his conviction—rests upon a time-honored, standard technique: empiricism supported by diligent investigation.

Organized Satanists

The second level of satanic involvement includes public groups, such as the Church of Satan and the Temple of Set. Cult officers ambiguously define the threat presented by this level since organized groups formally prohibit acts of violence. But cult seminars imply a fortiori that such groups promote self-indulgence to the point of attracting psychopaths and criminals. The *likelihood* of public satanic organizations attracting bad people, then, justifies law-enforcement surveillance.

At this point in the cult cops' exposition of their model, they peg two twentieth-century personalities who have molded the contemporary philosophy of their respective movements: Aleister Crowley and Anton LaVey. Crowley, frequently described in cult seminars as an "influential Satanist," indulged in pagan shenanigans during the early twentieth century. He became involved with (although many cult officers mistakenly say that he founded) the Order of the Golden Dawn and the Ordo Templi Orientis, "the largest practicing Satanic cult operating today," according to Lightfoot (Cult-crime seminar, Petersburg, Va., Sept. 13, 1988). Further, say the police, the main belief fostered by groups deriving from Crowley's legacy involves sexual perversion.

LaVey, on the other hand, a former police photographer and circus performer, founded the Church of Satan in San Francisco in 1966 at the zenith of Haight-Ashbury hippiedom. Police officers teach that LaVey's two books, *The Satanic Bible* and *The Satanic Rituals Book,* can be dangerous, and they observe incredulously that both can be found in shopping-mall bookstores. In particular, law enforcers cite LaVey's nine dicta of the Church of Satan, which include:

1. Satan represents indulgence, instead of abstinence!
2. Satan represents vital existence, instead of spiritual pipe dreams!
3. Satan represents undefiled wisdom, instead of hypocritical self-deceit!
4. Satan represents kindness to those who deserve it, instead of love wasted on ingrates!
5. Satan represents vengeance, instead of turning the other cheek!
6. Satan represents responsibility to the responsible, instead of concern for psychic vampires!
7. Satan represents man as just another animal, sometimes better, more often worse, than those that walk on all fours, who because of his divine spiritual and intellectual development has become the most vicious animal of all!
8. Satan represents all of the so-called sins, as they lead to physical or mental gratification!
9. Satan has been the best friend the church has ever had, as he has kept it in business all these years![39]

Cult officers maintain that LaVey's dicta foster in his followers the attitude, "If it feels good, do it," thus justifying criminal acts. Scholar of religion Gordon Melton has referred to *The Satanic Bible* as "assertiveness training with a twist,"[40] and in a way LaVey reads like a New Age tract on the power of one's inner resources, a notion therefore heretical to some conservative Christians. For example, LaVey has written: "The Satanist, realizing that anything he gets is of his own doing, takes command of the situation instead of praying to God for it to happen. Positive thinking and positive *action* add up to results."[41]

More important, *The Satanic Bible* repeatedly warns the reader away from violence. The book encourages any form of sexual expression "so long as it hurts no one else."[42] *The Satanic Bible* explains:

> Therefore, Satanism *does not* advocate rape, child molesting, sexual defilement of animals, or any other form of sexual activity which entails the participation of those who are unwilling or whose innocence or naivete would allow them to be intimidated or misguided into doing something against their wishes.[43]

Further, under no circumstances would Satanists harm animals or babies.[44]

With these proscriptions, LaVey then introduces magic as the means to egocentric ends. A very important insight into understanding magic concerns its efficacy: "*It matters not whether anyone attaches any significance to your working [magic], so long as the results of the working are in accordance with your will*" (emphasis in original).[45]

Aleister Crowley, described as "the most renowned magical practitioner and theoretician of the twentieth century,"[46] added a more wicked dimension to the philosophy of "if it feels good, do it," for in his *Book of the Law* (written before World War I) he stated, "Do what thou wilt shall be the whole of the law."[47] The statement quoted by law-enforcement officers out of context implies to them license for murder. In context, however, one reads a metaphorical jaunt through the ancient Egyptian pantheon full of erotic and occasionally Masonic allusions. One might infer from the context that the law officers' quotation, too, is figurative speech.

The *Book of the Law,* as dictated by a shadowy "prophet" to Crowley, contains a damning quotation: "Love is the law, love under will. There is no law beyond Do what thou wilt." But the text even explains the credo by pointing out that people move through their lives according to their destinies, that people act according to experience, impulse, and the "law of growth." In short, people are controlled by destiny: they cannot act apart from it. "Do what thou wilt" means "Do what accords with your destiny." A recent biography of Crowley points out that he did not intend the phrase to mean, "Do what you like," but rather, as he later wrote, "Find the way of life that is compatible with your innermost desires and live it to the full."[48] The same biographer adds that an exegesis of the work may be impossible because Crowley himself claimed that he didn't understand all of it.

Elsewhere in the *Book of the Law,* one finds metaphorical language as well, which undoubtedly has dissuaded many cult cops from reading through the object of their scorn. For example, cult seminars overlook the good parts:

> Hold! Hold! Bear up thy rapture; fall not in swoon of the excellent kisses!

> Harder! Hold up thyself! Lift thine head! breathe not so deep—die!

> Ah! Ah! What do I feel? Is the word exhausted?[49]

Instead, cult seminars sometimes suggest that Crowley believed in human sacrifice, despite the lack of evidence for the claim (although rumors to that effect circulated). In particular, cult cops read literally such passages as:

> For perfume mix meal and honey and thick leavings of red wine: then oil of Abramlin and olive oil, and afterward soften and smooth down with rich red blood. . . . The best blood is of the moon, monthly: then the fresh blood of a child, or dropping from the host of heaven. . . .[50]

Nevertheless, say law enforcers, deviant people use Crowley's prescription to justify sex crimes, child molesting, and murder. To add to the mystery, Lightfoot held up a copy of Crowley's book at a seminar, stating that one can only obtain it from a certain Pennsylvania occult bookstore or from the Ordo Templi Orientis, and that he himself could not disclose how he obtained his copy (Cult-crime seminar, Petersburg, Va., Sept. 13, 1988). Taking his statement as a challenge, I examined his copy, noting the title page carried an ISBN number and the reprinting publisher's name, Samuel Weiser, Inc. With help from directory assistance, I called the publisher's customer-relations representative. I discovered that the company, which publishes many New Age books, still prints Crowley in paperback, so I placed an order for the *Book of the Law*. I alarmed the representative by explaining what the officer had said about the impossibility of obtaining a copy, to which the surprised woman said, "But we'll sell it to anyone who asks!" I received my copy within ten days.

LaVey, on the other hand, operates without a deity. To the Church of Satan, the Evil One is no deity but rather a symbolic adversary. The Church of Satan, then, pulls a clever trick:

> "What are the Seven Deadly Sins?" LaVey is fond of asking. "Gluttony, avarice, lust, sloth—they are urges every man feels at least once a day. How could you set yourself up as the most powerful institution on earth? You first find out what every man feels at least once a day, establish that as a sin, and set yourself up as the only institution capable of pardoning that sin.[51]

Since people's guilt, apprehension, and anxiety about such urges feel worse to them than experiencing the urges themselves, the Church of Satan offers people a release: indulge yourselves, says this Church, as long as you abide by the law and harm no one. Lyons reports examples of Church of Satan psychodramas that engineer people's confrontations with their own fears, such as a woman afraid of her domineering husband who role-plays him to help reduce his menacing effect on her. Further, the rituals of the Church of Satan frequently invoke fictional deities. "In joining the Church of Satan, these people not only managed to inject a little mystery and exoticism into their otherwise banal lives, they achieved a mastery of their own fates by the practice of ritual magic."[52] Lyons's point was confirmed by the participant-observation experiment of anthropologist Edward Moody, who found the Church of Satan therapeutic.[53]

If LaVey's ideology is contrived of fiction, symbolism, and a deliberate antidote to establishment Christianity, and Crowley's writings on magick (his spelling) offer up *sui generis* metaphysical gropings with plenty of Egyptian name-dropping (what we now call New Age), why the law-enforcement interest? Cult cops focus on these two because they have published, because their philosophies are within easy reach. No other "satanic" ideologies exist that have so openly and publicly philosophized. They make easy targets. One of the first articles on this subject in a law-enforcement journal even pointed out that LaVey uses a symbolic Satan and noted in context that LaVey's church condemns sex crimes, including bestiality, but nevertheless stated, "It seems contradictory for a group to encourage all forms of sexual expression, and at the same time place parameters on that activity."[54] Again, in the fashion of *File 18 Newsletter,* law enforcers can't resist criticizing non-Christian beliefs.

Cult cops grasp firmly the only tangible evil they can find for public vilification at cult-crime seminars: published, easily available books. Other dangerous satanic books cited by cult cops include *The Necronomicon,* an anthology of scholarly writings (laced with fabrications) on Near Eastern religion and myth, with introductory material designed to add hocus pocus. For example, *The Necronomicon* names no author or editor, but the publisher states that the original manuscript is a secret, claiming that the book "concerns deep, primeval forces that seem to *pre-exist* the normal archetypal images of the tarot trumps and the Golden Dawn archetypal figures."[55] With that, the book includes tables of ritual symbols from sources such as H. P. Lovecraft and archaeological finds from ancient Sumer. The bibliography contains, *inter alia,* Otto Neugebauer's landmark study, *The Exact Sciences in Antiquity,* and every anthropology student's favorite, Sir James Frazer's *The Golden Bough.* The latter book appeared on a display table at a Lightfoot seminar. Lightfoot, dubbing it a link to the occult and therefore dangerous, recommended that officers confiscate it when necessary (Cult-crime seminar, Petersburg, Va., Sept. 13, 1988). But according to a game designer, *The Necronomicon* actually came about as an "in" joke among horror- and fantasy-fiction writers within Lovecraft's circle as "a book of forbidden knowledge. . . . Reading even a small portion of the book would be enough to drive anyone mad. The words, in theory, writhed across pages made of human flesh."[56]

In short, the purported guides to the occult—whether LaVey, Crowley, or *The Necronomicon*—hold no particular force or power other than what readers, and especially cult cops, impart to them. The books either derive from scholarly sources or represent modern invention. While some police officers dub the books evil, others claim the books are dangerous because weak-minded persons may pluck criminal ideas from them, the same objection cult cops bring to bear against organized Satanists—those with noncriminal public stature. But although law-enforcement authorities may fear the books' generation of threatening ideas, cult cops have no business citing their presumed malevolent influence: our constitutional form of government, theoretically at least, precludes officials warning us away from any literature, no matter how unpopular or objectionable the content. But cult officers indeed have appointed themselves conservators of our libraries. In fact, Dale Griffis has recommended that officers contact public libraries for names of patrons who have borrowed books on the occult.[57]

Cult cops have cited, then, numerous books à la LaVey and Crowley as bona fide compendia of occult knowledge rising from the dim horizon of some *arcanum arcanorum* of medieval alchemists and witches. Cult cops' willingness to imbue many books with the supernatural complements the sèance atmosphere they create at cult seminars by constructing elaborate facsimiles of supposed satanic altars—thus creating the very thing they seek to prevent. The reaction of cult cops and their allies to the popular and academic literature on the occult is simply silly. One law-enforcement guide, an otherwise valuable exposé of con games and swindles, addresses Satanism as perhaps the biggest con of all and advises officers:

> . . . Continue your education in this area by reading as widely as possible on the subject. But note: intense study of resource books and materials by occult sources or practitioners is hazardous. Preferred is studying overviews and synopses by credible authors who have studied the occult traditions. The unknown realm of the occult beckons with many lures. Study and/or experimentation are to be avoided. There are safer ways to test for poisonous chemicals than by tasting them.[58]

The same authors—police officers—simply turn the podium over to Larry Jones of *File 18 Newsletter*. They quote Jones:

> When confronted with those criminals who are led or controlled by supernatural, evil beings, philosophies or motivations, traditional police tools are not effective. If a cop is in a head-to-head confrontation with the prince of darkness or his troops, then that cop had better have the 'defeater of Satan' on his side as well as every bit of spiritual armor and assistance available . . . Mike Warnke (of Warnke Ministries . . .) told me that, in his opinion, the Christian police officers were the best prepared to be on the cutting edge in the fight against satanic crimes.[59]

Detective Gary Sworin, of Luzerne County, Pennsylvania, similarly reports that body-snatching demons arise from the printed page:

. . . Since 1984 we've been doing a lot of investigating and probably a lot of—an awful lot of reading, and I've found myself sitting at home, reading some of the things—reading through *The Satanic Bible,* reading through some of the literature that's passed out by these organizations and by these groups. Sometimes I could sit there for hours because all of a sudden I just get wrapped up and drawn right into it.

My wife will come in and she starts yelling right away. "What's going on? Are you starting to change your reading? . . . Something's happening to you!" And then I sit back and I think, oh-oh, what did I do, like there's something wrong. But she's right sometimes because of the fact that I'm getting so wrapped up in it. Is it curiosity? Yes. . . . And if I can be curious, you can be darned sure that a youngster can be curious after reading something like that that says it's really out of this world, the greatest thing going. Gosh, my curiosity is up. I got to really see what happens here. (Satanic-crime seminar, Freeland, Pa., Oct. 4, 1988).

Sworin teamed up with the Reverend Maurice Raymond of St. Anthony's Roman Catholic Church in Freeland, Pennsylvania, who had his own remarks about the supernatural danger posed by *The Satanic Bible.* He recounted an anecdote about his "biggest problem":

A young man came to my door. It was a Wednesday evening because we were getting ready for prayer meeting, and he rang the doorbell. I opened the door and he pushed right through me. He almost walked through me, literally. And he's pacing up and down in the office and he's holding his head, and he's—I said, "What's the matter with you?" And he said, "I saw the devil." And he slammed down the Satan bible on my desk, which I'm very afraid of; I won't touch it. (Satanic-crime seminar, Freeland, Pa., Oct. 4, 1988)

Public, second-level Satanists have become straw men for cult cops. They profess an ideology, one quite open and widely disseminated, that bears no criminal message save the blasphemy perceived by Christian groups for whom police officers become mouthpieces. The police alliance with Christian Satan-hunters represents an ethical failing: law enforcers through satanic-cult seminars enforce a by-no-means universal Christian ideology.

Traditional Satanists

The primary level of Satanists is said to include members of families who have practiced their beliefs secretly for generations, those who abuse children in day-care centers, murder, kidnap, and rape. Such Satanists, according to the cult "experts," comprise an international underground, tightly organized and covert, responsible for upwards of 50,000 human sacrifices a year (many of which involve babies bred specially for murder). These traditional, dangerous Satanists supposedly exist in a realm beyond publicly accessible, organized groups. Overall, though, traditional Satanists belong not to different denominations of the same thing but rather to an international megacult tightly organized in a clandestine hierarchy.

Whole families are said to participate, raising children to a lifetime of human and animal sacrifices, kidnapping, ongoing mental and physical abuse, and child pornography, to name the primary activities. Griffis tags the Ordo Templo Orientis as such a group and believes that their mind-control methods of enforcing slavish participation in cult ceremonies include the use of symbols to trigger criminal responses in members: for example, a black rose or a greeting card with a frog on it, both cuing devices like the famous card deck in the film *The Manchurian Candidate* (Advanced ritualistic-crime seminar, Richmond, Va., Sept. 22, 1988).

Primary-level Satanists' belief in magic propels them to sacrifice people: through killing, they release some primal energy force that enriches the participants, say the cult officers. The abuse of children itself is a form of worship. While for most ritual purposes the children of traditional Satanists will suffice, sometimes Satanists must look elsewhere for sacrificial fodder: usually at day-care centers. Investigator Bill Lightfoot related that a particular day-care center abused kids as a matter of course. Once the parents had dropped off their children for the day, the day-care staff allegedly bussed the children to an airfield, loaded them onto an airplane, and then flew them to a ceremonial site. Day-care staff—while robed—then forced children to lie in open coffins that were then lowered into the earth. Onlookers threw dirt on the children, who cried for help. The high priest then retrieved and sexually assaulted the children. Supposedly, the point of the ritual was to reduce the children's self-esteem. After the rituals, day-care staff returned children (by airplane) to the center, where the unsuspecting parents picked them up at the end of the day, none the wiser (Cult-crime seminar, Petersburg, Va., Sept. 13, 1988). Such stories are hardly atypical: cult cops, from Jerry Simandl of Chicago to those reported in the pages of *File 18 Newsletter,* uncritically repeat as true such claims of abuse.

Lightfoot's story expresses a paradigm of day-care-center Satanism that has appeared in widely publicized cases throughout the country, leading to mass indictments, ruined reputations, and a handful of convictions—none of them related to the occult, despite the wide-ranging allegations of cult activity.[60] Because of the complexity of the day-care-center cases, they will be discussed in detail in Chapter 5.

But to Griffis, "occult cults" (his name for traditional Satanists) go one further: they engage in ritual murder to bind members to the cults. Charles Manson is believed to belong to this variety: his imprisonment apparently has not reduced his involvement. According to Jerry Simandl, drug use also permeates all levels of satanic involvement. To cult officers, society has much to fear from primary-level Satanists. Thomas Wedge says, "It doesn't matter what you and I believe. It's what *they* believe that makes them dangerous. . . . For the first time, we in law enforcement are dealing with something we can't shout at."[61] To Virginia Beach police investigator Don Rimer, the secret primary-level Satanists present an insidious threat. "They will go to any lengths to satisfy their needs."[62] Griffis adds, "The most dangerous groups are the ones we know nothing about. . . . They are the real underground."[63]

Law enforcers' dogged belief in a faceless satanic conspiracy, despite the lack of evidence, relies on *nonevidence:* to them, what one doesn't find proves the strength of the conspiracy. Since traditional Satanists measure their success by leaving no evidence, the more successful they become at kidnapping, child abuse, and murder, the fewer clues they leave behind. Richmond, Virginia, Bureau of Police Lieutenant Lawrence Haake once admitted that he had no evidence of satanic human sacrifices, but added, "No evidence can be evidence."[64] Patricia Pulling tries to link unsolved homicides to human sacrifices: "They certainly have found a number of unsolved murders with no motive, haven't they?"[65] Another self-appointed expert, Sergeant Alan Alves of the Freetown, Massachusetts, Police Department, asserts: "The organized satanists leave absolutely no evidence. They're killing. That's what they believe in. They have to make sacrifices. They're killing babies."[66] Of course Alves himself admits that he has never made a satanic-crime arrest nor uncovered evidence of human sacrifice. But the lack of evidence does not inhibit detailed claims about Satanists' ceremonial doings. Deputy sheriff Larry Dunn from Washington State, backed by cult survivor Jacquie Balodis, claims that "devil worshipers sacrifice 50,000 humans a year, mainly transients, runaways, and babies conceived solely for the purpose of sacrifice."[67] But how would Satanists dispose of the evidence of such slaughter? One cult survivor who claims to have witnessed human and animal sacrifice says: "They'd burn everything up at the end. What they didn't burn, they would bury. They would have to have it done before the sun came up."[68] Another survivor related that body parts were also eaten.

The *belief* in the transcendent traditional Satanists has become the test of faith for cult cops. San Francisco police officer Sandi Gallant: "With organized groups, it's very deliberate that we're not finding any evidence of criminal activity. They're much too careful and hide their tracks very well."[69] To pursue such a belief has one apparent value: one can assert anything about traditional Satanists without having to demonstrate how one arrived at such assertions. In Chapter 1, I noted that the defining characteristic of a pseudoscientific assertion is its irrefutability. Therefore, when cult cops assert as true a complex model of traditional satanic behavior, they rely on a certain argument in the face of skepticism: "Prove to me that they *don't* exist."

The same belief forces cult cops to further assert that traditional investigative techniques don't work in such cases. Of course they won't work: "traditional" investigative techniques require an empirical approach to solving a crime—constructing demonstrable hypotheses governing how crimes were committed (based on physical evidence). If such techniques don't work with traditional Satanists, we are left with the evidence available to the seventeenth-century witch-finder: spectral evidence. Spectral evidence includes visions of demonic doings, visions shared only by those afflicted by the demons, not by the investigators who can only observe the fury of the afflicted persons. The shocking nature of young women's paroxysms before the Salem courts convinced the inquisitors of the truth of the women's indictments of others as witches. Similarly, the coaxed statements of very young children that satanic activities occurred in day-care centers, uncorroborated by physical evidence, has led to record-setting prison sentences for day-care staff-members with no criminal backgrounds whatever.

Cult cops, then, play a dangerous game indeed when passing on to others in cult seminars their detailed nightmares about the undetected and undetectable. The game becomes Kafkaesque when cult cops offer as investigative guides the popular cinema: Lightfoot has described the film *Rosemary's Baby* as an accurate depiction of Satanism of the clandestine sort, and *The Believers,* of Santeria-inspired crime (Ritual-crime in-service seminar, Petersburg, Va., Sept. 13, 1988).

One doesn't have to look far to measure the effects of cult-crime seminars to see how attendees interpret Satanism for new audiences. For example, in an article on satanic cults in *Family Violence Bulletin,* published by the University of Texas at Tyler, Paula Lundberg-Love writes of a seminar she attended titled "Ritualistic Child Abuse and Adolescent Indoctrination." Quoting the seminar instructor, president of the Cult Awareness Council in Houston, Lundberg-Love writes that "some satanic cults are created for the expressed purposes of child prostitution or the production of child pornography" and that " 'religion' has proved to be a good 'front' for organized child prostitution and pornography rings." To reinforce the notion that we can't do much about this, she points out that "in many states, ritualistic behavior [whatever that is] is not against the law."[70]

In recounting the amazing and startling facts she learned, Lundberg-Love offers the following detailed insight about how Satanists undertake their mayhem:

> There are also individuals within the cult to whom particular tasks are assigned. Transporters are the people who take babies and ship them out-of-state. Spotters have the task of looking for recruits or objects. Breeders are, as their name implies, used for the purposes of breeding. The production of "snuff" films

(films in which an individual is actually killed) is associated with these persons. [The seminar instructor] suggested that juveniles may be being used to transport these films across the border.[71]

Without even its collective tongue pressed against its cheek, the Houston Cult Awareness Council has performed shrewd investigative work in uncovering the clandestine mechanics of a satanic international conspiracy so slick and sophisticated that its members remain faceless, having never been identified, and its murderous activities remain covert because the Satanists leave no traces of their nefarious undertakings. Yet this model of the cult's activities is quite specific and detailed and based entirely on spectral evidence: the stories, unconfirmed and uncorroborated, of cult survivors' tales (see Chapter 4). Of course we have no evidence of satanic child prostitution, no evidence that women breed babies for sacrifice, and no satanic snuff film has ever turned up. But to many people, Lundberg-Love's article carries credibility: she is the associate director of the Family Violence Research and Treatment Program at the University of Texas, Tyler. And her story derives from cult cops and their allies.

Interestingly, the first case of a criminal investigation involving snuff films has occurred: In August 1989, numerous FBI agents, working with San Jose, California, Police Department officers, arrested two Virginia men for the criminal conspiracy of devising a scheme "to either purchase or abduct a minor boy" and then, after "holding the boy in captivity for up to two weeks, while videotaping acts of sexual molestation," to murder him and dispose of the body by washing it in acid "to remove incriminating forensic evidence." The U.S. attorney handling the case said "that as far as he knows, the existence of snuff films has been talked about in law-enforcement circles for years, but has not been substantiated," least of all where Satanists are concerned.[72]

Cult officers say that the ranks of secret Satanists boast the intelligentsia of our society, hence the moneyed power behind the rituals. Pulling maintains that satanic ranks burgeon with "doctors, lawyers, clergymen, even police."[73] She believes that "adherents of this violent religion" number about 300,000 nationally. Apparently, the secret Satanists are not new: only through cult seminars do police learn how to recognize their existence (and learn to use spectral evidence). And in particular, traditional Satanists sacrifice almost 50,000 people annually, a figure contradicted by the national homicide figures published annually by the FBI, which show a total of about half this figure for each of the past few years.[74]

Despite this large-scale conspiracy, police still have uncovered no convincing evidence of primary-level Satanists' murderous activities. The only consistent stories we have of them comes from two sources: the day-care-center abuse cases, discussed in Chapter 5, and those of cult survivors, discussed in Chapter 4.

The Continuum

In discussing the myriad attributes that attach to each level of satanic involvement, the FBI's Lanning observed:

> The implication often is that all are part of a continuum of behavior, a single problem or some common conspiracy. The information presented is a mixture of fact, theory, opinion, fantasy, and paranoia, and because some of it can be proven or corroborated (desecration of cemeteries, vandalism, etc.), the implication is that it is all true and documented. The distinctions among the different areas are blurred even if occasionally a presenter tries to make them.[75]

Indeed, cult cops themselves find the four-tiered model comfortable for categorization of the entire domain of both observed and imagined behavior of Satanists and satanically influenced people. But they ambiguously describe the links between the levels. Unaccustomed to sociological models, the cult cops find it easy to interpolate a progressive scheme in the four-tiered approach. Back to Detective Sworin:

> Participation . . . could mean starting out with just listening to some heavy metal rock music, starting to read Satanic bibles, starting to be involved in a ritual, Satanic ritual, and then gradually lead to bigger and so-called, in their perspective, better things. You generally will be involved in what they call a black mass. You'll then be taken in and initiated as one of their members and one of the cult people. . . .
>
> Very definitely that's what we're talking about here because of the fact you're starting out—or they're starting out with something that's very, very minimum, very small, which is dabbling, putting markings up and drawings up. And then all of a sudden it starts to progress, and all the contributing factors that we listed all come together and finally something happens where we go from what we know, what we should do, to the other extreme of what they want us to know and they want us to do. And at that point we're lost. And that really is the sad part. (Satanic-cult seminar, Freeland, Pa., Oct. 4, 1988)

But just as the satanic model of criminal behavior has no observable basis—the suggestions of Sworin and others deriving mainly from cult survivors—the notion of a continuum of behavior rests upon no empirical foundation. I suggest that some cult cops infer a continuum from the model because it presents a tidy ribbon with which to wrap a neat package. Yet, to accept the four-level model as a continuum, one would have to accept a progression through four rather distinct clusters of personality traits, with very different behaviors. The dabblers, theoretically, can be anyone, but those most susceptible to the dabbling influence include underachieving Caucasian teenage boys, often loners, but smart; organized, public Satanists include adults of all persuasions, backgrounds, and incomes. Self-styled Satanists also may be loners, but they display psychopathological behavior that by definition exists virtually within an isolated social context. Finally, the traditional, clandestine Satanists exhibit absolute social conformity: such conformity takes the shape of social responsibility, since these dastardly folks occupy prominent and visible public roles, such as ministers, judges, teachers, lawyers, and police officers.

In short, each tier of the model presupposes a very distinct personality type and corresponding social role, and some of the personality types are entirely inconsistent with the social roles predicted by the model. For example, the model would have us believe that dabblers are social isolates, and that their isolation may lead them to turn to Satanism for power over others who show more social success. Yet if satanically afflicted teens drift upward in the so-called continuum to become public Satanists, they now exhibit a strong group affiliation. Moving right along, our erstwhile dabblers might find organized, public Satanism too benign for their carnivorous tastes, so they become self-styled Satanists. Dale Griffis has described self-styled Satanists as having "a connection with serial killers" (Advanced ritualistic-crime seminar, Richmond, Va., Sept. 22, 1988). Yet serial killers, typified by the lone psychopath who, for psychosexual reasons, commits *ritualistic* murders, don't show any consistent group affiliation of any kind. Serial killers, as rare as they are, drift from job to job and cannot maintain any ongoing emotional ties, whether to friends or lovers or a group. But if self-styled Satanists enter the worldwide conspiratorial circle of the primary level, magically, it seems, they can now maintain an absolute group dedication and loyalty, follow absolute orders with absolute secrecy and yet to all appearances command respectable, authoritative roles in society—and this, for psychopaths who by definition cannot hold jobs of any kind for very long, much less jobs of prominence and stature. But as anthropologist Sherrill Mulhern has noted, cults of the public kind generally shun personality types that might become serial killers; cults oust them (Fifth International Conference on Multiple Personality/Dissociative States, Chicago, Ill., Oct. 8, 1988). Yet we are supposed to believe that somehow the extremist, traditional Satanists have no trouble socializing with serial killers.

The *continuum* that some cult cops infer from the model, then, requires one to accept large doses of contradiction and inconsistency. To quote Mulhern:

Naturally, the basic premise [of the continuum idea] is false. By definition, a continuum is something in which no part can be distinguished from neighboring parts except by arbitrary division. The first thing remarkable about the alleged satanic levels is that each level is a self-contained whole, defined by specific, real or imagined, exclusive parameters. The continuum is not in observable behavior, it exists only in [cult cops'] . . . minds! The fact that [some cult cops and therapists] both come up with the same "continuum levels" without talking to each other is offered as proof for [the model's] validity. (My reaction is "So what!" It is again the same type of validation which is constantly being offered for the violent ramblings of the adult [cult] survivors.) It goes without saying, this false conceptual framework is being spread throughout the therapeutic community.[76]

But to cult cops, the continuum's appeal has not diminished and evolves toward public alarm-raising. Officer Terry Wheeler of the Glendale, Arizona, Police Department lectured to school officials that painted satanic graffiti does not present a danger of vandalism but, instead, "the possibility that practitioners [satanic dabblers, that is] may commit ritualistic crimes associated with devil worship, including animal mutilation and homicide."[77]

Signs and Symbols

Cult seminars offer attendees handouts of symbols to recognize and investigative steps to take. Cult cops tout the symbols and associated paraphernalia—beads, books, candles, among other things—as possibly dangerous. Officers may not recognize the significance of artifacts and symbols, and an "officer who violates them by touching them could be killed by cult members seeking revenge," say cult cops.[78] The handouts I have examined, which came from cult seminars in Virginia, Arizona, Texas, Kansas, Illinois, Pennsylvania, California, South Carolina, and Massachusetts, are the same. They offer the same investigative hints and illustrate the same symbols with the same assigned meanings. In Chapter 7, I argue that through the cult seminars, and particularly through the attendant handouts, cult cops invent urban legends, rumors, and subversion myths. In fact, the same handouts rarely note the sources of the material. When handouts cite sources, most often they list conservative Christian ones, such as the WATCH Network based in El Paso, Texas, and the Mike Warnke Ministries, or organizations representing other interests with unsubstantiated claims, such as BADD.

The investigative tips derive from the stories of cult survivors blended with fanciful speculation derived from reading popular works on witchcraft and Satanism. Occasionally, the tips come from actual criminal cases.

The following handout, with no source cited, represents a typical list of investigative touchstones. The list reads like a mystery writer's *aide memoire:*

Crime Scene Investigations

1. Mockery of Christian symbols (inverted cross, vandalized Christian artifacts).
2. Time of occurrence may be between 0100-0300 hours.
3. Use of silver implements.
4. Discovery of candles or candle drippings (candles may be in the shape of genitals, or colored black or white).
5. Unusual drawings or symbols on walls or floors: baphomet [defined in another handout as an "idol worshiped by those attending black mass," while another merely pictures it as an inverted five-pointed star], hexagram, pentagram or horn of death, etc.).
6. Use of parchment (for making contracts [with the devil]).
7. Non-discernable alphabet. . . .
8. Animal mutilations, including removal of specific body parts such as: anus, heart, tongue, ears, front teeth and front legs and genitals.
9. Use of animal parts and bones to form signs and symbols on ground.
10. Absence of blood on ground or in animal.
11. Use of stone or metal altar containing the following artifacts: black candles, silver chalice, white handled knife, salt, knotted colored cords (each color represents rank of members).
12. Effigies like clay figures, voodoo dolls stuck with pins or otherwise mutilated.
13. Bowls of powder or colored salt, drugs and herbs.
14. Skulls with or without candles.
15. Bones used or taken from graves such as: femur, fibia [*sic*], index finger, skull, and other large bones of the body.
16. Robes, especially black, white and scarlet.
17. Jewelry such as amulets.
18. Colored plastic drop cloths may have been used to protect walls and floors from evidence such as blood or feces, then used to remove evidence from crime scene and dispose of it.
19. Rooms draped in black or red (look for holes in walls, floors and ceilings left by nails).
20. Books on satanism, such as "Magick" or "Book of Shadows," videotapes, record albums and cassettes.
21. Bells or gongs.

Such general investigative hints appear in combination with two other lists: "occult-related homicide clues" and "items to be listed on a search warrant." The former list, which according to Detective Kurt Jackson of the Beaumont, California, Police Department, came from the San Diego Sheriff's Office and the San Francisco Police Department, offers the following:

1. Where the body is located: Most cult meetings or rituals are held in deserted isolated areas. Wooded areas away from people, desert areas, graveyards, abandoned buildings, churches and/or residences.
2. Position of the body: Note direction of body, whether the body is formed in the shape of a circle (facing inwards or outwards), it may be nailed to a cross or formed in the shape of one, it may be hanging from something like a tree either by its feet, hands or neck. If rigor mortis is present the body may still show signs of having been tied down (bondage).
3. Missing body parts or organs: In occultic blood rituals many times parts of the human body and/or organs are removed. They may have been eaten (cannibalism) or kept for use in another way. Usually the parts most often used are the head, heart, hands, genitalia and the eyes, ears, nose, tongue or lips. Sometimes the cadaver will have appeared to have been boiled and the body fat within the cadaver will be missing. This will be determined at the autopsy.
4. Body dressed or undressed. . . .
5. Stab wounds or cuts: Particularly important, the size and location of stab wounds or cuts, if done in patterns or symbols, if done to allow blood letting or draining. Incisions to the sex organs, mutilation. Note the number of cuts and/or bruises if in numbered patterns (i.e., in 3's, 6's, 7's or 13's). The location of human teeth marks or cannibalism.
6. Ink marks or tattoos: . . . Again look for patterns and/or symbols. It may even be a message written in an unknown alphabet or code.
7. Painted with a substance or paint. . . .
8. Branded with a branding iron or any burns. . . .
9. Jewelry on or near the cadaver. . . .
10. Jewelry that is missing. . . .
11. Any cords or colored ropes on or near the body: Check for implements of bondage. . . .
12. Any implements near the body. [A list of "ritual items" follows which includes candles, cords, containers of salt, an "alter" [sic], an athame or ritual knife, a chalice, a circle drawn on the ground, human or animal body parts, parchments, "a cauldren" [sic], "voodoo" dolls, and a book of shadows or a grimoire (book of spells).]
13. Oils or incense on the body . . . .
14. Wax dripping from candles on or about the body. . . .
15. Human and/or animal feces found on or consumed by the victim. . . .
16. Signs of hands and feet having been tied or shackled, rope burns, etc., . . .
17. Stomach contents of urine, feces, semen, blood, drugs, wine or portions, etc., not common to the human body. . . .
18. Lungs with ingested matter (smoke, liquid, blood). . . .
19. The absence of blood in the cadaver or on the ground: For most religious cults blood is extremely important to them, they believe the life force or spirit is contained in the blood. The lack of blood present within the body is a good indicator of occultic involvment. These groups will drain the body and either drink or bathe in the blood. Most of the time they won't waste any of it.
20. Semen near or inside the cadaver: . . . Sex with a dead body (necrophelia [sic]) is a common initiation for new members to a group.
21. The presence of occult ritual paraphernalia or Christian artifacts. . . .
22. Mini storage lockers: . . . Many times the groups will store their ritual

paraphernalia and supplies there.
23. Biblical verses and graffiti written in blood. . . .
24. Nondiscernible alphabets, witches [*sic*] alphabet, cabalistic writings, etc.: Many of these cults or groups will write or send messages in code or use strange or old alphabets like the Runic or Theban alphabet, including ancient Hebrew or Greek.
25. Animals [*sic*] body parts. . . .
26. Drawings or photographs of victims: Many groups . . . will want to keep a record of their ceremonies and also for use in blackmailing others into silence.
27. Dates of rituals, calenders [*sic*], etc.: . . . Some satanic or black witchcraft cults are religiously required to perform certain rituals on [certain] dates.
28. Computer ties in the home: If you suspect cult involvement and that the victim had computer ties in his home, we know many cults and groups are highly organized and use computers to amass information, send messages between members and to break into other computer systems for personal gain, thefts, secrets, etc.
29. Photography of mock weddings, child pornography or sexual activities fixated on anal abuse: Some groups will keep a photographic record of their activities or use such photos or films for blackmail purposes. Some cults take pleasure in desecrating known religious and/or social functions.
30. Marks of the beast—the alphabetical letter numbers for heaven and hell, 666, occult symbolism, etc. . . .

As with the former list, at least a third of the homicide clues constitute a lesson in very basic crime-scene investigation: all but the most doltish police officers will carefully document the position and posture of a victim, the presence of wounds, what type, the presence or absence of various bodily or other fluids, whether a victim was dressed or undressed, and so on. Assuming an investigating officer encountered the candles, painted occult symbols on walls, again, only inept officers would fail to note such characteristics in a report or crime-scene diagram, much less photograph them. Such bizarre attributes, of course, might be meaningful in discovering the identity of an unknown murderer. Yet some of the clues have never been borne out: for example, cult survivors maintain that photographers work at cult rites; hence item number 29. Yet no such photographs have ever turned up; this is similar to the absence of evidence about snuff-film claims.

Law enforcers have in some cases tried hard to lay Satanism before the judge. In the trial of Scott Waterhouse in Maine for the murder of a young girl, prosecutors introduced Waterhouse's Satanism: Waterhouse admitted to satanic beliefs that involved sexual and violent rituals. Although convicted, the defense appealed by arguing that the defendant's satanic beliefs lacked probative value and might prejudice a jury. The conclusion of the Maine Supreme Court, however, is not surprising:

> We conclude that the evidence of satanism and the defendant's belief therein is relevant for the permissible purposes of proving the identity of the perpetrator as well as his intent. . . . It was for the jury to decide whether such motivations were actually at work in this case, but the evidence of satanic beliefs is certainly probative of motive and, therefore, of the identity of the perpetrator. . . . On the issue of intent, which the State has an affirmative burden to prove, the consistency between the circumstances of the crime and satanism's emphasis on sex, destruction and denigration of weakness, makes it more likely that if defendant killed the victim, he did so intentionally rather than by accident, i.e., through recklessness or criminal negligence. Thus, the evidence of satanism is probative on the issue of intent.[79]

As far as an officer is concerned, he or she must undertake a complete, comprehensive investigation of the crime. If the officer discovers evidence of satanic beliefs *that figure significantly in the commission of a crime,* the officer arrests, and the court may convict. What the court has affirmed in the Waterhouse case presents nothing new: if a personal belief can help the police *identify* a criminal and establish the criminal's *mens rea,* or state of mind, then the belief enters the investigative case file. *The police invocation of Satanism in this criminal case came about as a consequence of standard investigative practice.* Officers investigating this case (of a "self-styled Satanist," to use the cult-seminar term) did not need a list of occult arcana to arrest the criminal.

Cult seminars feature as one of the bona fide satanic murder cases that of *California v. Clifford St. Joseph.* This 1985 murder involved a victim who was found with a pentagram carved in his chest, slashed wrists, ankles, back, and buttocks, a mutilated testicle, wax dripped into the right eye, and very little blood present. The case went without leads until a man arrested for drunkenness told police that he was trying to rescue a friend who, he claimed, was "drugged against his will, forced to submit to sexual acts, and would soon be the victim of a Satanic cult murder." Subsequent investigation revealed a few men who indulged in sadistic homosexual sex, and police arrested one of them, St. Joseph, for murder, sodomy, and false imprisonment. A jury convicted St. Joseph in 1988.

The St. Joseph case appears in many cult seminars as proof of the widespread tenacity of Satanism in prompting the commission of crimes. Sandi Gallant believes this case to constitute one of the three bona fide satanic murders.[80] Others, such as Ken Lanning, discount this as a "satanic murder,"[81] focusing instead on the sadomasochistic sex. Nevertheless, the successful police investigation of the case hinged on several characteristics:

1. "Good, careful crime scene investigation that stresses how to take a circumstantial case and back it up with physical evidence . . . This was really a case of circumstantial evidence built upon physical evidence."
2. "Know how to back up very bizarre, shocking stories of marginal witnesses

with physical evidence that can back up their stories." All of the witnesses were marginal—two were male prostitutes and the third was a lifelong criminal.

3. "Careful documentation of every circumstance at both crime scenes." The officers who responded to the call at the residence [that produced the informant] carefully documented everything they witnessed and everything that the arrestees said. . . .

4. "Knowledge of and how to utilize the best available laboratory technology relative to evidence collection. [In this case, physical evidence consisted of an analysis of bloodstains and fibers.]

5. "Vertical prosecution. These cases are just too complicated without bringing the D.A. in from the very first day. The legal ramifications are daily battles and the police need to have the legal system readily available."[82]

In this case, the police confronted bizarre behavior, behavior that officers undoubtedly found repulsive. Nevertheless, this case represents a textbook example of informed insight, thorough documentation, inductive and deductive reasoning. In short, despite the case's complexity (particularly the reliance on physical evidence and the concomitant laboratory analysis), officers followed the dictates of their professional experience and did not blind themselves to investigating crime by pursuing allegations of Satanism. No one questions the existence of sordid criminality, however it is associated with sadistic heterosexuality or homosexuality, and perhaps even with self-professed satanic beliefs. The presence or absence of satanic beliefs has nothing to do with the prevalence of murder and sex crimes. To investigate the St. Joseph case, officers did not need cult-seminar handouts accompanied by an inventory of occult symbols, runic alphabets, or a reading knowledge of ancient Hebrew.

Undaunted, cult cops disseminate pages upon pages of symbols that one might encounter on a heavy-metal album cover, at an altar, or painted on the underside of a bridge. Such symbols include: an upside-down cross, the Star of David, an Egyptian *ankh,* a swastika, images of goats' heads, plus various configurations of moons, stars, crescents, circles, and arrows. The peace symbol of the 1960s appears in a tainted fashion: one learns that it represents the "Cross of Nero" and that its appearance as a broken, upside-down cross (as perceived by some Christian literature and cult cops) denotes a degradation of Christianity. An Episcopalian cleric, the Reverend Michael Rokos of Maryland, former president of the Cult Awareness Network, even claims that this symbol derives from a pagan, pre-Christian past, and cites *Gods and Beasts,* by Dusty Sklar, as a source of documentation;[83] yet a check with that source revealed nothing. Cult cops and their allies prefer to ignore the symbol's recent provenance: as I noted earlier, the symbol derives from civil protest against atomic weapons. Thus far I have been unable to find the symbol at all in any context before the 1950s.

Cult cops distribute lexicons of occult arcana to accompany their drawings of symbols and signs. In one of the most slickly packaged versions of the cult cops' model, "Introduction to Satanism," a syllabus prepared by instructor Paul Banner of the South Carolina Criminal Justice Academy in Columbia, student-officers quickly become conversant with titillating new words: e.g., *belomanay* ("Technique of inscribing the name of the enemy on an arrow and shaking up the arrows in a quiver. The arrow was directed at the enemy whose name was inscribed thereon."); *apotropaion* ("a charm that protects someone against evil spirits or the Evil Eye"); *catoptromancy* ("divination by means of mirrors"); and *tephramancy* ("divination by looking for messages in ashes, often burned tree bark"). Banner's compilation also has charming nineteenth-century line-drawings of various devils, such as Astaroth and Orbas (with a man's limbs, a horse's head and rear legs). Such illustrations, of course, present no useful law-enforcement insight or any investigative aid: Banner obviously included them in his notebook of occult symbols and among his photocopies of newspaper clippings and investigative clues (the same lists that I presented above) to communicate the *frisson* of dabbling in the netherworld. Banner, like other cult cops, seeks to guide law enforcers' fears, ignorance, and lurking suspicion that such symbols just *might* have supernatural power after all. Police officers have never collected such material at routine training seminars: generally, the purpose of professional seminars is to convey necessary but comparatively mundane details about how to complete case reports, how to handle physical evidence, how best to offer testimony in traffic cases, and how to defuse a family fight. Only in cult seminars do they enter the chamber of the medieval alchemist, meet new bad guys like the modern Merlin, Aleister Crowley, absorb some loose ends of the history and sociology of magic and pagan worship, manipulate new symbols that terrify some people, play amateur cryptoanalyst with alphabets and codes.

Cult seminars cite two examples as proof that widespread satanic cults not only exist but carry out a program of murder, kidnapping, and animal mutilation to propitiate the Evil One: the Son of Sam killings and the murders recently discovered in Matamoros, Mexico.

Son of Sam

Freelance writer Maury Terry, in his 1987 book, *The Ultimate Evil: An Investigation into America's Most Dangerous Satanic Cult*,[84] argues not only that David Berkowitz did not act alone in committing the New York Son of Sam killings but that Berkowitz et al. acted in consonance with a satanic mandate. Terry, in fact, lectures frequently to cult seminars, particularly to warn that a Charles Manson II is afoot, a killer with a fruitful future if left unchecked. Terry also wrote the preface to Pulling's book, *The Devil's Web.*

For example, Terry encounters reports of animal sacrifices, particularly of German shepherds in the Yonkers area, and notes that 85 dead shepherds and Doberman pinschers appeared in Walden, New York, over a year's period, 1976 to 1977. Although the dogs had not been killed by any consistent technique, Terry says, that "officials believed a cult was behind the killings."[85] Terry goes on to offer the reasons that Satanists sacrifice animals: "As abhorrent as these practices sound, they aren't the product of the mind of a demented Hollywood scriptwriter: they are real, and are being performed today." And who is his law-enforcement source on this? Dale Griffis, whom he quotes: "But the activities are so bizarre, so apart from the norm, that many—police and public alike—will contrive any explanation at all to rationalize away crimes that are obviously cult-connected. There is a massive education program to conduct."[86]

Once tipped off to Satanism, Terry read a smattering of books and then imposed a loose model of sacrificial activity on the evidence and his own surmises to construct a theory. For example, he reexamined the Son of Sam letters, written to the police before Berkowitz was arrested, and found linguistic or numerological coincidences:

> . . . The Sam letters were sprinkled with occult references. . . . They included "wemon," as in demon; "brat," as in imp or small devil; "outsider," the title of an occult book; "Beelzebub," the demon known as Lord of the Flies; "the hunt," a reference to the goddess Diana, queen of the Black Sabbath and leader of the Wild Hunt; and "I'll be back, I'll be back," words identical to those spoken by Satan in the book, *Black Easter.*[87]

One Sam letter contained the phrase "I am the 'monster'-'Beelzebub'—the 'Chubby Behemouth' [*sic*],"[88] which Terry explores further (again, in a post facto attempt to fit facts to theory), linking Behemoth to its occult representation as an elephant (but, of course, Behemoth has been portrayed as a variety of large monsters), and the Latin word for elephant, *elephas,* happens to be in the name of the Elephas Disco in Queens, where one Sam killing occurred. But, to Terry, "the most important satanic clue was contained in the letter's first sentence: "Hello from the gutters of N.Y.C., which are filled with dog manure, vomit, stale wine, urine, and blood."[89] To Terry, such elements constitute the raw ingredients for a Black Mass: even the word *stale* refers not to wine but to animal urine, meaning that cultists drank urine instead of wine. Such connections led Terry to consider whether the Sam killings occurred on satanic holidays: while anyone can play interpetive games with anonymous letters to the police (in which misspellings and grammatical mistakes are given ritual significance), the calendar is unequivocal—either murders occurred on certain days or they did not. Terry could not come up with a connection here, but rationalized it anyway: "The attacks hadn't occurred exactly on the holidays, but we reasoned that the shootings were public displays, and the cult may have done other things privately on the days themselves."[90]

While Terry's book offers convincing evidence that the Son of Sam killings involved a second killer, evidence that prompted authorities to reopen the case, his evidence for a satanic conspiracy doesn't work. Post facto assumptions and assertions about interpretations of the Sam letters, or the presence of occultic graffiti near sites of murders or animal mutilations, proves no case at all. Terry credits as significant that Berkowitz once knew so-and-so who happened to attend a party given by someone, who committed murder with Charles Manson. Such tenuous connections are not the stuff of which solid investigations are built. He also places much stock in the hints and insinuations that Berkowitz has offered during jail interviews to conclude that a one-time Charles Manson–affiliated cult, "The Process," hovers over the Sam murders and others, notably the California murder of Arlis Perry in a chapel, with further connections to the Ordo Templi Orientis. Interestingly, Terry's evidence for the second Sam murderer derives from evidence with direct application to the case: eyewitness accounts, including reconstructed images of suspects' faces, plus an intensive examination of crime scenes to deduce how the murderer came and went, to calculate crucial timings, and so on.

Yet when constructing the satanic theory, Terry relies on different standards of evidence: he places unequal weight on circumstances and facts that he labors to apply to his conspiratorial model. For instance, Terry cites an incident in which a police officer apparently stumbled into a pagan or satanic ceremony involving a handful of people. (Terry cannot distinguish the ceremony as pagan, satanic, or anything else, but assumes its satanic nature because one member wore a red cape and held two German shepherds on chains.) He notes disdainfully that local law enforcers had no evidence to link the ceremony to Son of Sam cult meetings that took place nearby—that is, meetings with Berkowitz and his cronies. Terry notes, " 'They have no evidence to say it *wasn't* connected, either.' "[91]

As I mentioned, a considerable component of Terry's theory derives from hints and suggestions that Berkowitz himself offered. Arthur Lyons, in discussing Terry's book, notes that Berkowitz later recanted some of his statements as " 'baloney,' made up to bolster an insanity plea."[92] Lyons also says that he finds Terry's linguistic evidence unconvincing, citing, for example, Terry's mention that the Sam letters spelled *colour* in the British style, thus linking the author to "The Process," which, in turn, borrowed from Englishman Aleister Crowley. As for the Process/OTO connection, "Although there is ample evidence that Manson had been influenced by

The Process, there is no evidence whatsoever that The Process and the O.T.O. had overlapping membership or ideas, or that Manson ever had any contact with the O.T.O." Terry's loose assertions about the O.T.O. have gotten him into scalding water. The O.T.O. brought suit against Terry for defamation, and Terry appealed the court's finding for the plaintiff all the way to the New York Supreme Court. "The case was subsequently settled out of court, with a cash settlement paid to the O.T.O. as well as an agreement to strike all references to that organization from all future editions of the work."[93]

Matamoros

The Matamoros murders discovered in April 1989 in Mexico, just across the border from Brownsville, Texas, have provided many cult cops with a lucky boost in seminar audiences. Until Matamoros, the cult seminars had few macabre examples to offer of the pernicious influence of cults: the Jonestown, Guyana, mass suicide of almost one thousand people presented the most notorious symbol of cults' "mind-control methods." Even a superficial review of the facts of Matamoros, however, raises questions about the incident's utility as an exemplar of what happens when people enter a satanic cult. Even as this book goes to press, several pulp paperbacks have appeared on supermarket shelves purporting to carry the true, inside look at the Matamoros killings. These books, written by journalists who have managed to obtain jailhouse interviews with key dramatis personae, offer no more than the same photographs that appeared accompanying the wire releases and a reiteration of newspaper claims embellished by quotations from the interviews. We may never know all of the relevant facts about Matamoros, however, because the so-called cult leader, Adolfo de Jesus Constanzo had himself killed; and because the methods of Mexican justice, which included a public parade of the arrestees before television cameras, differ significantly from those used in the United States.

In particular, the identification of evidence connected to the murders, and the confiscation of artifacts at the site (such as the purported ritual instruments), did not follow recognizable American judicial safeguards. The so-called "cauldrons" found at the ranch near Matamoros, supposedly filled with offal mixed with human remains, numbered about three, yet the Mexican authorities allowed at least one to remain at the site for weeks, keeping it stoked with unidentifiable organic matter. In fact, visitors tramped through the site almost immediately upon discovery of the murders, with many artifacts of evidentiary value remaining on the premises for some time and being handled by many people. The gathering of police, journalists, and the curious certainly tainted the integrity of the crime scene, which was not consistently protected during the investigation, and is thus analogous to an archaeologist trying to survey a site disrupted by grave robbers. Nonetheless, what I present here is a recitation of the evolution of Matamoros events through news reporting, since the reporting itself, particularly in the early stages, fostered the connection of murders with satanic ritual, giving cult seminars the documentation sought to prove a demonic impetus. Following the reconstruction of events, I identify the major themes that cult cops and their allies—Patricia Pulling, in particular—have tried to cull from the murders to justify their world-view that admits to clandestine, murderous conspiracies.

Almost from the moment the Matamoros killings were disclosed to the public, authorities had discovered most of the key details of what happened and who did it, although the immediate and overpowering presence of news reporters and their cameramen greatly influenced—and perhaps also inhibited—construction of sound hypotheses by investigators. From the first, Texas newspapers referred to the Matamoros gang as "satanic drug smugglers" who had "sacrificed" several people, including the twelve bodies discovered thus far, at least three of which were those of U.S. citizens.[94] Much of the publicity surrounded the killing of University of Texas student Mark Kilroy, whose body had already been disinterred at the Santa Elena ranch near Matamoros. Even as newspapers around the world directed attention to Matamoros, some officials said that the "rites" associated with the "sacrifices" "were designed to bring demonic protection to the smugglers' contraband activities."[95] U.S. Customs official Oran Neck, however, noted "overtones" of religious rituals from Cuba and Haiti, particularly Santeria. But Lieutenant George Gavito of the Cameron County Sheriff's Department maintained that "the killings were part of satanic rituals in which the suspects prayed to the devil" to avoid arrest, a mistake that has fueled journalists' insistence on applying the "satanic" label to the killings. Despite the label, Texas newspapers, in any event, had already identified the so-called cult leader, Constanzo, and clarified that, despite initial claims, no evidence of cannibalism was present at the site. Significantly, though, Texas newspapers reported one salient detail missing from many national publications: the prevalence of violence in the northern Mexican drug trade. Matamoros may have contributed the human-sacrifice claim and the association of Afro-Cuban rites, but the murders were hardly unique: earlier, nine corpses turned up on a ranch near Agua Prieta, Sonora, just outside the Arizona town of Douglas. The nine "had been tortured, mutilated and bound," according to Mexican police.[96] But the North American public heard no more about the Agua Prieta murders.

On the same day, April 12, 1989, the *El Paso Times* also reported that "satanic rituals" had been intended to protect drug smugglers, but added that the victims had been "sacrificed *and* cannibalized" (my emphasis).[97] Oran Neck referred to the "kettles full of human parts, blood, skulls of animals that had been burnt" and the newspaper mentioned what was soon to occupy a focus in subsequent reporting, discovery of a "caldron" that contained "brains and hearts" of victims, which the murderers then ate, according to Cameron County Sheriff Alex Perez. The *El Paso Times* noted that Kilroy had been selected at random as an Anglo male sacrifice, whose body was discovered without a brain. Also the same day, Associated Press releases outside of Texas gave fewer details, certainly fewer quotations, but occasionally introduced new "facts": in particular, that the "satanic" sacrifices had been going on for nine months and that the victims had all been males.[98] Still other newspapers, reporting from wire dispatches, the same day diluted the story to all but what the press deemed to represent the salient points: that people were chosen randomly for sacrifice and that the sacrifices served "a satanic cult of drug smugglers."[99]

By the next day, Mexican authorities had paraded four suspects, all in their early twenties, before a news conference: Elio Hernandez Rivera, who said of the victims, "We killed them for protection";[100] Sergio Martinez; David Serna Valdez; and Serafin Hernandez Garcia. For the first time we learned of an at-large accomplice of Constanzo's: Sara Villareal Aldrette, whose "blood-spattered house" in Matamoros, police maintained, might have been the scene of "ritual murders of children" (a standard satanic-cult practice), suggested by photographs and clothing of children found in the house. But by April 13, authorities, if they had only casually mentioned "satanic" the day before, did so no longer; quoted officials "described the murders as a twisted blend of sacrificial and black-magic practices from Haiti, Cuba and Jamaica," Constanzo having promised that his rituals would protect the traffickers from harm.[101] And also on April 13 officials had disclaimed any cannibalism but noted that body parts had been used in rituals. *New York Times* reporter Peter Applebome examined the Santa Elena ranch site, describing the scene as a "still life" and observed that the site had been left unguarded, with reporters and others sifting through the various artifacts, including "a large cauldron" by the front door "in which a horseshoe, turtle, goat's feet and other animal remains floated in a dank soup with large sticks protruding from it," adding that "human blood and body parts were mixed in and boiled as part of the ritual killing" (quoting the ubiquitous "officials").[102] For the next several days, reporters supplied various descriptions of the contents of this and other "cauldrons," though no news accounts noted that any forensic examination of their contents took place, either by Mexican or U.S. authorities.

But the Texas coverage of events, by April 13, described the Constanzo gang as a "drug-smuggling voodoo cult," and the mysterious Aldrete (revised from the first-reported "Aldrette") now received the press's epithet of "the witch of the operation," a label that persisted in perpetuating the satanic image.[103] Nevertheless, the centerpiece photograph of the *El Paso Herald-Post* article showed Texas Attorney General Jim Mattox at the Santa Elena ranch, in which Mattox "shows members of the news media caldrons used in satanic rituals." Although at first the arrestees accused the at-large Constanzo of murdering the victims himself, we now learned that Hernandez Rivera had been "authorized" to make human sacrifices, and this against an emerging picture of the drug smuggling: Constanzo and the others had funneled about 1,000 pounds of marijuana into the U.S. monthly. But despite the loose usage of "satanic" by the press, some authorities for the first time invoked Santerian religious practices, and the Associated Press quoted anthropologist Mercedes Sandoval that "there is no evidence, however, that Santeria has ever sanctioned human sacrifice," a point little noticed by the press thereafter. The press continued to project the murders as somehow a natural consequence of Santerian belief, not until much later pointing out that Constanzo employed diverse bits and pieces of religious practices in rituals serving criminal purposes. Nevertheless, the *El Paso Times* on April 13 referred to the Constanzo gang as a "voodoo cult" but noted the authorities' growing conviction that most of the murders were not arbitrary human sacrifices but rather represented revenge for drug deals that went sour.[104]

For the next several days, authorities at the Santa Elena ranch continued their excavation of shallow graves, watched by scores of reporters and the growing crowd of Mexicans who came to the site to seek missing relatives and friends among the unearthed corpses. Some bodies had been identified: Kilroy and "a Mexican policeman, a federal police volunteer, a 16-year-old youth."[105] But the intensive search was on for Constanzo and Aldrete, whom Mattox also now described as "the witch of the operation."[106] Mattox also continued to emphasize that most of the victims fell prey to random human sacrifice, though officials had by now said "that two of the killings were reprisal murders of associates of the drug traffickers."[107]

Mexican reporting, on the other hand, offered up details not circulated in U.S. accounts, while still catering to the lurid. *Diario de Juarez* referred to the dead as victims "de los narcotraficantes diabolicos" and identified the cauldrons as *ngangas,* a term carrying meaning in several Afro-Caribbean religions.[108] The same article referred to the authorities' having confiscated many weapons, from automatic rifles to machetes, and expensive cars with high-tech communications equipment. Because of obvious interest among the Mexican public, the local newspaper reported attempts to identify the bodies, adding that the Mexican police related that the arrestees told them that the corpses were all drug traffickers, whom they killed "en altares de sacrificio en ceremonias satanicas" with one motive: vengeance.[109]

While the search went on for both Constanzo and his "witch" (also called "a voodoo priestess") and more bodies turned up, officials could now speculate on the religious trappings. Most authorities told the press that the drug gang followed no particular cult or religious belief, although the notorious Tom Wedge, described in an article in the *Austin American Statesman* as "a Columbus, Ohio, author who has written a book on cults and gives seminars to law enforcement organizations," pronounced the rites "Abakua," an association disputed by every other expert interviewed.[110] David Brown, "an expert in Afro-Cuban religions at the Smithsonian Institution," offered the consensus of those with direct knowledge of Afro-Caribbean rites that "the killings probably were the work of someone who had distorted religious beliefs."[111] Brown added, "The idea of using a religion for one's purposes does not link the religion to that person's purposes."[112] The same article now used *nganga* instead of *cauldron,* and for the first time mentioned Palo Mayombe as the religion whose rites Constanzo adapted.

The nature of the Matamoros-based drug smuggling came to receive more attention: the *New York Times* reported that the volume of marijuana distributed by the Constanzo group approached *2,000* pounds per *week.*[113] Further details emerged about Aldrete: she had been an honor student at Texas Southmost College, a "friendly, hard-working" physical-education major whose association with the drug smugglers astounded and even frightened friends and teachers. The Aldrete paradox, coupled with rumors circulating in the Rio Grande Valley that children had been kidnapped by the Constanzo gang, had led parents to keep their children from school. "The ultimate mystery, however, still remains the behavior of the cult members, most of them from relatively well-to-do middle-class Mexican families."[114] By April 15, the press were quoting authorities as certain in their attribution of Constanzo's rites to Palo Mayombe; and one of the arrestees, Elio Hernandez Rivera, told how he was ritually scarified by Constanzo to make him officially a priest with the authority to sacrifice humans.[115] Also, through Hernandez Rivera, we heard the first disclosure that the film *The Believers* (which portrayed Santerian practices by rich urban North Americans, involving human sacrifices with lurid and supernatural special effects) was shown to gang members repeatedly to reinforce their desire to kill and, importantly, that Constanzo began to work Santerian rituals with gang members 14 months earlier, switching to Palo Mayombe rituals only nine months before.[116]

By April 16, officials revealed how the Matamoros murders came to light. Hernandez Rivera had tried to drive his truck through a drug checkpoint at the Mexican border, believing himself invisible.[117] The regional police, headed by Mexican federal police commander Juan Benitez Ayala, tracked Rivera to the Santa Elena Ranch. Expecting to find drugs at the ranch, the police moved in, and on a hunch one investigator showed a photograph of Mark Kilroy to the ranch's caretaker, who recognized Kilroy and led police to the discovery of more than a dozen graves. Again, reporters inevitably felt compelled to describe the *nganga* ritual artifacts at the site, in particular the "copper caldron" in the shed where murders occurred, a pot containing "something that looked like brains."[118] By now, Lieutenant Gavito of the Cameron County Sheriff's Department disclaimed any satanic connection for the Constanzo activities, but instead invoked Santeria and Palo Mayombe.

Also by April 16, one of the arrestees, Serafin Hernandez Garcia (a United States citizen), led investigators to a second ranch also owned by the Hernandez family, Rancho Los Leones, to search for more corpses.[119] Arrestees now began to describe Aldrete as the gang's "godmother," one who recruited gang members and helped lure victims to their deaths. Officials now disclosed that several bodies had been found mutilated and eviscerated of brains, eyes, ears, hearts, and genitals; some of the victims had even been tortured and mutilated while yet alive.

By April 17, corpses began to show up at Rancho Los Leones.[120] Unlike the mutilated bodies at Rancho Santa Elena, 20 miles away, the three bodies at Los Leones had not been mutilated; instead they had been killed by machete blows. The motive of the killings: a "drug deal gone sour." In fact, the same day the *New York Times* carried a Matamoros update that emphasized the context of border drug violence, describing the Constanzo murders as "only the latest incident in what has become a steady drumbeat of violence, most of it drug-related."[121] Border Patrol official Norbert Gomez described the growing "pre-demand violence" near the border; rather than committing a robbery by pointing a gun and demanding money from a victim, he observed that now assailants will shoot victims first and then rummage through their pockets for money. Officials attributed the savage methods to "the increasing competition among rival [drug] dealers."[122] The *New York Times,* almost alone of the major newspapers covering Matamoros, had looked beyond Matamoros to the wider violence-ridden drug trafficking in the region, thereby offering a valuable and insightful dimension to border goings-on within which Matamoros constitutes a bizarre but not unique episode. But authorities began to discuss Santeria and Palo Mayombe as associated in undefined ways with other drug smuggling.

By April 17, additional bodies turned up, at least one at a new location, the Ejido [collective farm] Santa Librada, two miles from Rancho Santa Elena.[123] Constanzo's Mexico City home had been located and searched, although he remained at large, but police nevertheless began to examine the possibility that Constanzo had murdered there as well. U.S. officials arrested Serafin Hernandez Rivera on April 17 in Houston for marijuana smuggling, noting that the Hernandez family had been involved in marijuana smuggling from Matamoros for at least a dozen years.[124] In fact, Serafin's father, Brigidio Hernandez, owned the Santa Elena ranch. Elio, Serafin's brother, had been arrested earlier. The men had another brother, Saul, who himself had been killed by drug dealers.

During the weeks preceding the discovery of Constanzo, many of his associates and various involvements came to light. The Mexican press noted that the Constanzo connections extended to several different Mexican cities and even included "un comandante de la Direccion Federal de Seguridad" (a commander with the Mexican Federal Directorate of Security).[125] By April 19, fifteen corpses had been exhumed, mostly "those of drug traffickers and not random victims of an occult-influenced drug ring's human sacrifices," according to the local commander of the Federal Judicial Police, Ayala.[126] The next day, even the FBI came forward to announce drug trafficking links between the Matamoros gang and the Houston area, noting that Constanzo had made major purchases there.[127] But, meanwhile, in Brownsville, Texas, rumors of child kidnapping surfaced again: "Reports that cult leaders had threatened to kidnap children for sacrifice if fellow cult members were not freed sent the parents to schools to pick up their children."[128]

Constanzo, whom his arrested associates dubbed *el padrino* (the godfather), apparently maintained several residences in Mexico City (with "occult altars"), did not take drugs himself (and even killed a gang member who did), and cut a flamboyant figure within the gay community.[129] He also mingled with the upper-class social circuit in Mexico City, particularly with those who also practiced Santeria in some form, even assisting his acquaintances with various rituals.[130]

Meanwhile, back in northern Mexico, Mexican authorities razed the hut at Rancho Santa Elena, where the murders had occurred. Anthropologist Rafael Martinez, a specialist in Palo Mayombe, considered Constanzo a "psychopath" whose murders "have shocked practitioners of a religion that uses human bones to gain magical power." He referred to Constanzo as having "practiced a twisted form of Palo Mayombe."[131] Martinez tried to distance the practice of Palo Mayombe (discussed further in the next chapter) from Constanzo's use of ritual in drug trafficking. Days later, authorities explained the destruction of the shack at the ranch as a form of "exorcism": apparently a *santero* had performed a rite to purify the site.[132,133] The Matamoros priest explained that church attendance was up; parents had either restricted their children from attending school or at least escorted them to and from school; at Texas Southmost College in Brownsville, an "overflow" crowd attended a seminar on Satanism and the occult.

Finally, on May 6, the police caught up with Constanzo. Once the police had found him, Constanzo ordered his associate, Alvaro de Leon Valdez, to kill him and his lover, and the now-infamous Aldrete surrendered. Mexican police paraded all of the arrestees before cameras and newspeople, the quondam *narcosatanicos* looking sheepish behind a table covered with garish "satanic cult items."[134] To further the view of authorities that Constanzo and his associates simply adapted a capilotade of rites and rituals to drug smuggling, Aldrete explained that Constanzo had "invited her to join 'Christian Santeria' and asked her to use voodoo to help people with problems."[135] The *New York Times* report of the same news conference referred to the artifacts on display as "voodoo paraphernalia" and further dubbed the Matamoros gang a "voodoo cult," quoting Aldrete as suggesting that "the ritual killings were part of another voodoo-like faith that she called Palo Mayombre [*sic*]."[136] The choice of Mark Kilroy, the arrestees revealed, came from Constanzo himself, who had "ordered them to grab a white person to sacrifice."[137] But Constanzo remained a mystery: he had even killed and dismembered a man who had "refused to vacate an apartment Constanzo had been renting," a killing authorities had to point out was not a human sacrifice.[138]

A post mortem on Constanzo revealed that authorities knew little about him; he had grown up in Miami in an environment of Santeria, certainly (Palo Mayombe came later), but "he is remembered as someone who swiftly developed a reputation as a sorcerer skilled at ridding the body of evil."[139] Anthropologist Martinez said that Constanzo "really knew his Palo Mayombe," citing the confiscated diary in which Constanzo made jottings in Spanish and Bantu.[140] In 1984, Constanzo moved from Miami to Mexico City, where he made money in drug trafficking. As for his influence on others, journalists compared him to Charles Manson and Jim Jones. Aldrete maintained that Constanzo led his followers "through the sheer force of his personality," saying, "If he tells you to do something right now, if he orders you, you will do it. I don't even know why, but you will do it"[141]

Constanzo attached himself to an ongoing drug trade run by the Hernandez family in Matamoros, entering with a reputation as a "drug dealer with a propensity for cheating and killing," according to Lieutenant Gavito. Further, Constanzo arrived with connections and influence; on the mystical side, he had performed *limpias,* or cleansing rites, for well-to-do Mexicans, cultivating clients who included the Mexican head of Interpol.[142] Anthropologist Martinez explains that many Mexican drug traffickers have relied on Palo Mayombe for spiritual protection, a connection pushed by cult seminars, which frequently fail to note the widespread benign and legal practice of the religion. Other evidence of Constanzo's wealth and influence began to surface: the Mexican press listed his residences and automobiles as an indication of his connections,[143] Mexican authorities arrested Salvador Vidal Garcia, a federal narcotics officer, who said that Constanzo was his godfather.[144] Later, U.S. authorities found commercial (and not ritual) links between the Matamoros drug traffickers and a Chicago crime syndicate that may have purchased drugs from them.[145]

Yet another post mortem, while catering to the odd sensationalist and with unfounded assertions here and there, delivered some insights into the Matamoros business. Writing for the *Texas Monthly,* Gary Cartwright conveyed the atmosphere within which the murders came to public attention, particularly noting how North American news media representatives converged on Rancho Santa Elena, followed by representatives from tabloid television programs, such as *Geraldo* and *Oprah,* trying to scoop the skullduggery. Investigators Gavito and Neck on the U.S. side of things emphasized that "drugs caused this to happen."[146] Gavito further explained how Mexican police methods differ from ours: coupled with the public parade of suspects and artifacts, Mexican police obtained confessions quickly from arrestees by shaking bottles of mineral water and squirting their contents up the noses of recalcitrants.

The pressure of publicity and the ease of obtaining worldwide press exposure unquestionably influenced the pronouncements of some politicians, police, and the arrestees. Spurred by the death of Mark Kilroy, news accounts stressed the apparent random sacrifice of the student over the larger context of border drug violence and drew erroneous connections between Mexican drug-running and religious ritualism; and in almost racist fashion, the media overlooked the impact of drug trafficking on Mexican families. Those hundreds of impoverished, voiceless Mexicans who descended upon Rancho Santa Elena to watch the exhumation of bodies in hopes of finding answers to their own anguish had no role in the U.S. media happening. Mexican authorities seemed to court U.S. camera teams: Cartwright also notes that Comandante Ayala "made no attempt to seal off the crime scene. During almost any hour of the day journalists could be found stomping about the ranch . . . looking for something—anything—that no one else had found."[147] Meanwhile, at least one arrestee, Sergio Martinez, was forced to dig up corpses at gunpoint. Even at the shack where the butchery occurred, beside the door, "apparently arranged by the federales so that the media could not miss their significance" stood the *ngangas,* the "caldrons."[148]

Matamoros should evoke questions about drug trafficking. The Constanzo business may not reflect credit on Mexican authorities, but, of course, the trafficking would not exist without complicity on the U.S. side of the border by other drug dealers and consumers. Nevertheless, cult seminars, without further analysis, offer up the Matamoros morality play as evidence of the pernicious effects of the mind-control methods of cults, or Satanism's pervasive influence in our society, of proof that satanic conspiracies can exist. While we may never know all the pertinent details of how the Matamoros killings happened, particularly the process by which a group of middle-class young people briefly combined to torture and murder, cult cops have exploited the incident to alarm police and public audiences. Specifically, we must ask: How have cult cops exploited Matamoros and why do Constanzo's escapades capture their interest?

I assert that Matamoros has appealed to cult-cops for three reasons. First, the nine-month spree of murder included the abduction of innocents, a theme which figures significantly in some cult-seminar claims and also in rumors, urban legends, and subversion myths. North American news media pictured Mark Kilroy as such an innocent: a clean-cut, sturdy American college kid out on a lark had vanished from Matamoros, abducted by strangers bent on human sacrifice. The idea of such a purposeful abduction, if advanced before the facts of Matamoros came to light, would have been dismissed as improbable. The Reverend Michael Rokos, former president of the National Cult Awareness Network, maintains, though, that Kilroy had been lured into Constanzo's clutches by tempting offers of drugs and sex ("Kids, Drugs, Cults: Treating Cult Survivors" seminar, Oct. 19, 1989, Richmond, Va.). Whether or not Kilroy had been distracted by such an offer, his abduction represents a nightmare come true for many Americans. To intensify the nightmare, Kilroy was abducted in Mexico: here, the innocent is truly helpless in lacking a language skill, friends, protectors. Anyone who has sojourned in a foreign culture occasionally entertains fears of helplessness: not being able to reach a hospital; running out of money; falling prey to a crime. Kilroy's abduction and death reifies such fears. And further, cult cops can point to Kilroy as a bona fide abduction for human sacrifice. If this happened to him, then what about the many runaway children or missing adults?

Of course, extrapolating from Kilroy's example is not logical. In a sense, the abduction and vilification of innocents occurs quite frequently in the United States in other contexts: physical and sexual abuse, rape, and murder. But the psychopathology of the Matamoros killers, while deserving of intense study, perhaps should be understood on its own terms. Glib and superficial comparisons to the Reverend Jim Jones or to Charles Manson don't produce insights; they only heighten fears without offering instruction on how to reduce or eliminate the minatory presence of murderous behavior. The Matamoros gang embarked on a program of murder for a very short time; they concealed very little evidence of their crimes. In fact, when the police traced one of the Hernandez brothers, who ran a border checkpoint, to Rancho Santa Elena, it was only on a hunch that an officer showed the ranch caretaker a photograph of Kilroy. The caretaker recognized the photograph, and the story of the abduction emerged promptly, followed briskly by the discovery of bodies. Using Kilroy's death as proof of the purported modus operandi of a satanic network, cult cops posit that murderous cults envelop their activities in secrecy, acknowledging that such cults have never been infiltrated, nor their members arrested. But the Matamoros murders could not be sustained as proof of a satanic cult for long; too many people were involved, only a casual attempt was made to dispose of evidence, and the gang members seemed to disclose their crimes quite readily.

Few Americans understand the religious attributes of Santeria or Palo Mayombe, preferring to reduce their understanding to the following equation: Palo Mayombe derived from African rites. Such rites involved animal and human sacrifice. Palo Mayombe, therefore, by using human and animal remains in ceremonies, sanctions and encourages human sacrifice. In a racist vein, some Americans would observe that we ought to expect such behavior from foreigners, particularly Mexicans. But Charles Manson has proved that we don't need foreigners to commit multiple murders. While not taking up the question of what motivated Charles Manson's followers, the Matamoros gang did not need Palo Mayombe to murder. The members were drug smugglers with commercial ties extending from Mexico City to Chicago. Their business exhibits a low tolerance for error and competition: murder is a way of life. The abduction and murder of Kilroy may indeed symbolize the destruction of the innocent, but all the evidence advanced about Matamoros to date suggests that the Matamoros gang succumbed to a pathology of murder that collapsed when the gang went beyond being faceless Mexican drug dealers and traffickers and abducted a middle-class U.S. citizen, mobilizing his friends and the authorities to search for him.

Second, cult cops cite Matamoros as indirect proof of the international satanic conspiracy, because the case proves that people like us, fairly well educated with middle-class upbringings, can form secret loyalties that involve murder. The press took Sara Aldrete as an example: friendly, bright college student by day, "high priestess" or "witch" by night, terms that Aldrete shunned when arrested. By the time of her arrest, of course, the news accounts had thus painted her role, so any denials on her part could not alter the image. To the press, Aldrete confirmed the cult-seminar model of such people looking and sounding like anyone else, and perhaps occupying responsible jobs. One cannot defeat a conspiracy theory that posits that cultists are indistinguishable from the rest of us, thus rendering anyone and everyone as suspect. In a sense, though, cult cops are right: criminals cannot be identified by hair color or cranial capacity (although some police training has in fact revived such century-old ideas) or the cut of their clothes; criminals can look like anyone. The logical consequence of this realization ought to be that innocence is presumed until the officer has probable cause to arrest. Cult cops, though, reason that we must look for bizarre or at least unconventional habits or mores as indications of more insidious behavior. Such persons, then, should be investigated and placed under surveillance. But cult cop logic would not have worked in Aldrete's case: she evinced nothing out of the ordinary in her role as college student. To use Aldrete as exemplar of the secret, murderous cultist ultimately serves no law-enforcement purpose: law enforcers should simply leave people alone unless a well-founded reasonable suspicion exists of criminal behavior.

Aldrete's participation in murder has not been made clear anyway; some authorities alleged that she lured victims to her death, yet Aldrete publicly announced that she was not a direct party to murder, having not witnessed any, although she certainly aided and abetted drug trafficking and did not leave the group or approach authorities when she learned that Constanzo and the others had murdered. We may never know precisely the extent of her involvement in the killings, but the image of her as a conjuring, beguiling (the Mexican press made much of her good looks) witch remains, thanks to the news media's insistence that the Matamoros events fit a Halloween mold.

Third, cult cops have taken Matamoros as *satanic* because the newspapers have used the term. If newspapers use it, and Texas Attorney General Mattox uses it as an opportunity to advise Texans against the Satanist forces who left behind the Matamoros bodies on their march to world subversion,[149] then why should cult cops not reap the same rewards of frightened audiences? The North American news media irresponsibly transmuted religious rituals and beliefs practiced by many quite innocuously and legitimately into hellishness. Once the newspapers latched onto "satanic" as the explanatory adjective, they refused to relinquish their claim on the word. Even after authorities investigating Matamoros disclaimed cannibalism and explained that Constanzo practiced a mishmash of rites borrowing from Palo Mayombe, among other beliefs, the "satanic" label has persisted.

Journalists wax prelatic when discussing "objectivity" in news reporting, as if such a singular point of view exists and can be acquired. Yet reporters habitually tag any reported person or event with descriptors: a man who takes a gun and shoots people in a crowded post office appears in print as a "former Vietnam veteran," despite the twenty years separating the Vietnam experience from the reported killing. The same man also could be described as "church elder" or "model airplane hobbyist." But the newspapers, in their search for clear motivations, imagine that the man must have suffered post traumatic stress disorder owing to his Vietnam experience, since other news stories and the entertainment media nowadays emote with Vietnam recollections. Such descriptors, of course, shape people's thinking: readers will not recall events or persons without the associated descriptors. Thus, Matamoros, in news reporting, must appear accompanied by "satanic" or "voodoo" or "Black Magic," or, for those newspapers that can correctly spell the names, Palo Mayombe or Santeria. My brief chronology of reporting on Matamoros shows the newspapers' inability to get it right. While reporters learned to quote knowledgeable investigators who described Constanzo's use of religious ritual as a blend of varied practices and beliefs, the same newspapers continued to use "satanic" in photo captions. And the cult cops quote the press as their source of information, and they borrow the press adjective *satanic* to advance Matamoros as a satanic sacrifice.

Cult Cops

Cult cops come in many molds, though mostly of the self-appointed variety. Investigator Gary Lupton of the Prince William County, Virginia, Police, typifies the dabbler variety. Lupton, "who's become the county's resident expert on the Devil," holds the local school administrators "rapt" while journalists, including two from the *Washington Post,* scribble down his every prophetic utterance. He asserts to the school, "A couple of hundred students are involved in Satanism."[150] A juvenile-crime investigator, Lupton says he spends most of his time holding seminars and attending workshops. Spouting a familiar litany, Lupton became converted to the cult-cop world-view by "attend[ing] four seminars, two given by law-enforcement organizations and two by . . . B.A.D.D." Some cult cops, like Dale Griffis, train other cult cops; others, like Lupton, carry the alarmist word to a worried professional audience of teachers, school administrators, therapists, counselors, and church officials; and, of course, he teaches his own department.

A few cult cops give seminars for a living. Thomas Wedge panders a glib and polished presentation to the public, professional audiences, and the police. A former Logan County, Ohio, probation officer, Wedge conflates his Baptist convictions with his reconstituted history of the Devil, giving his audiences "Theology 101."[151] His massive presence onstage is complemented by his own altar; for the *Salt Lake City Tribune,* he poses grim-facedly holding a skull, his double-chin illuminated by candles, *The Necronomicon* in the foreground.[152] "He has been a cult cop for fourteen years, and he travels around the country dispensing what he calls the 'simple facts' of satanism . . . for $350 per student."[153] He continues: "These satanists aren't foolin' around, now that's a simple fact." He is fond of saying, "Remember, as weird as this all sounds to many of you, we're talking about what they believe, not what you believe."[154] His formula is simple: "Traditional Christian religions are based on fear and abstinence, while satanism is a religion based on self-worship . . . since carnal and selfish feelings are natural, the satanist believes they should be indulged freely."[155] This formula, coupled with the ghoulish imagery Wedge projects, creates the very entity he claims to be combatting: I have already shown that the no-holds-barred, *sui generis* Satanism preached by self-styled cult experts like Wedge has become the *idée fixe* of the cult-seminar circuit.

Not all law enforcers who speak at seminars are as critically mindless as Wedge. Detective Patrick Metoyer of the Los Angeles Police Department, for example, does not readily leap to speculation involving breeders of babies for sacrifices. Says Metoyer to journalist Larry Kahaner:

> There are things that occur that have a basis in Satanism, but there is no way that we can collectively put them into a container and say, Okay, we've had this number of Satanic crimes. We can't do that. . . . There's no way you can justify monitoring a criminal commnity when you can't show quantitatively that the crime exists. Crimes that appear to have some religious motivation or some deviant activity do not get the kind of reporting or recognition they deserve.
>
> If you're asking whether we need that type of category, however, my answer is no. We can do our jobs, get our convictions without it. In fact, I tell anyone who asks me, don't get into the Satanic stuff with your case. Why? It will give your man an opportunity to plead diminished capacity. Juries have trouble believing this bizarre material. Don't make life difficult for yourself.
>
> If we had a purely Satanic crime in Los Angeles proper, one where the alleged murderer said, "Yeah, I killed him because it was the only ritual I knew that I could perform effectively," if we had one like that, I would say, yes, we had one. We have not.[156]

Unlike many other cult cops, San Francisco's Sandi Gallant has redefined her position according to new ideas and new research, yet her earlier claims, promulgated throughout the law-enforcement community by handouts listing clues, signs, and symbols, continue to influence many through the cult-seminar *samizdat*. Gallant, nevertheless, whom journalist Debbie Nathan has described as "a born-again Christian and former maven in the San Francisco 'red squad' intelligence office that used to spy on the Bay Area left,"[157] still has not distanced herself from conspiracy claims.

Dale Griffis, Cult Cop Extraordinaire

While cult cops like Gallant and Wedge influence large numbers of other law enforcers, mental-health professionals, and school officials, and appear in public, usually provoking fireworks on television programs like *20/20, Oprah,* and *Geraldo,* many law enforcers look to Dale Griffis for a definitive academic interpretation of cultic goings-on because he titles himself *Dr.* Griffis. A retired police captain from Tiffin, Ohio, Griffis obtained a doctorate from Columbia Pacific University in San Rafael, California. Since his doctorate was bestowed in law-enforcement administration and his dissertation was devoted to the cult problem, a discussion of his background and thinking might prove insightful about the cult-cop world-view.

Griffis retired from the Tiffin Police Department under a small shadow. The then-mayor of Tiffin (while Griffis was a captain) complained about

Tiffin's grandstanding about Satanism, and his police chief, David A. Martien, had "repeatedly warned [Griffis] about his large phone bill, run up talking about cults with other police agencies."[158] At the same time, several officers sued Tiffin to undo Griffis's appointment to deputy chief without a competitive exam (a suit that failed), and the Seneca County, Ohio, prosecutor investigated Griffis for "alleged misuse . . . of thousands of dollars in funds supposedly destined for Tiffin's Furtherance of Justice Fund. Foundation money solicited by Griffis ended up financing computer equipment and other materials for his outside work."[159] Even Jeff Rossi, coordinator of training at the Ohio Police Officers Training Academy said that Griffis might be forbidden to teach because of complaints that he spent his time telling about cult-busting rather than lecturing on the more mundane topic of handling investigations. At the time (1985), Griffis told a journalist, "I can't wait until I retire. Then I can do this [cults] full-time."[160] The journalist, who interviewed Griffis at his home, noted that Griffis's doctorate is his "badge of honor," that Griffis's "various pamphlets and mailings inevitably contain several references to his academic accomplishment."

But in 1985, Griffis was only getting his cult-busting feet wet. For example,

> [Griffis] triggered the excavation of five hundred square feet of parkland because a piece of red thread was spotted dangling from a pine. Red thread [Griffis explained] signified a satanic ritual site. On June 23rd [1985] Sheriff James Telb [Lucas County] authorized a dig in search of "fifty to seventy-five" ritually murdered bodies.[161]

Nothing turned up, of course. But now Griffis indulges his satanic interests full-time and graces the seminar circuit.

Griffis was tagged as a cult expert before his retirement. An early article about his work stated that even by 1984 Griffis had "lectured to police departments around the country on satanic worship, mind-control cults and destructive religious groups."[162] Griffis finds satanic worship on the increase, of course, but warns journalists that his primary obligation is to his brothers and sisters in blue: "You've got to remember there're a lot of sheriffs and a lot of police chiefs under a hell of a lot of pressure when I get there. . . . I'm there to help my brother police officers. I report to them, not to the public."[163] Nevertheless, Griffis's satanic model, whether in 1984 or in 1989, proclaims the same underground activity: "Satanists . . . tend to be well-educated, with comfortable middle-class or higher incomes. Their recruits often are children in their early teens, lured by sex, drugs and alcohol."[164] Even so, his study of Satanism penetrated beyond the handful of books that most cult cops read: he knows the background of *The Necronomicon,* for instance, but says of it and *The Satanic Bible,*

"Some people just can't handle it. It is hazardous to their psychological health."[165]

His doctoral work deserves scrutiny because his dissertation imparts the ideology that has influenced many and has shaped much of the cult-seminar dogma. According to brochures produced by his alma mater, Columbia Pacific University, the institution "recognizes life, work, and independent learning experiences in granting credit toward fully approved Bachelor's, Master's, and Doctoral degrees. . . . Most will earn their degrees within a year, through the completion of a Bachelor's Independent Study Project, Master's Thesis, or Doctoral Dissertation, along with a faculty-guided program of self-assessment and directed readings." Among "important facts and figures," one discovers an enrollment of 5,000 students at CPU, "making it the largest nonresident graduate university in the United States. There are over 400 part- and full-time members of the faculty." One doesn't even have to reside in the United States to earn a degree from CPU or complete the writing project in English. The campus exists in two components: a business office and a tiny campus nearby, which boasts "the library [not listed in the American Library Association Directory], administrative offices, and conference/residence facilities."

The institution, then, offers credit for life experiences, requires no academic work completed in residence, and offers no classroom courses. Nevertheless, CPU maintains that "some [employers] pay all or part of CPU's tuition fees for their employees or have accepted CPU degrees for employment placement or promotion." As examples, the brochure cites the U.S. Army, AT&T, Xerox Corporation, Rockwell International, and the U.S. Department of Education. Importantly, the brochure states that the California Department of Education's Superintendent of Public Instruction has bestowed on CPU "full institutional approval," meaning "that CPU's curriculum is consistent in quality with curricula offered by appropriate established accredited institutions."

But all is not rosy in San Rafael. In April 1989, a legislator introduced a bill, SB190, in the California legislature that "would make sweeping changes in the way California regulates private, unaccredited colleges, including the creation of a new state agency to take over the licensing responsibility now held by the state Department of Education."[166] The bill's author states that her proposal is "aimed at cracking down on what has become known as diploma mills, those accredited colleges and universities which can operate worldwide and too often award easy degrees."[167] Perhaps in response to the legislative interest, CPU has issued a "Questions and Answers" brochure, making plain its legal basis for granting degrees: CPU admits that it is not accredited and carries a license to grant degrees in California only.

In fact, CPU does not appear in standard listings of colleges and universities. However, the 1983 publication, *The Complete Guide to Nontra-*

ditional Education by William J. Halterman (published by Facts on File, New York), describes CPU and notes that "in some cases the degree requirements can be substantially satisfied by a project the student has already completed at the time of application and fully documents for the University records" (p. 34). Halterman warns, however, that although CPU offers "legal and legitimate degrees . . . they are not accredited. [The degrees] are quite good in the business world but are not always acceptable in academic environs." John Bear's 1982 book, *How to Get the Degree You Want* (Ten Speed Press), also contains an entry on CPU with a laudatory comment: "No other non-resident, Doctorate-granting institution has a staff with the credentials, reputation, and experience of Columbia Pacific. Many major universities, including Harvard, Yale, and Princeton have expressed a willingness to accept C.P.U. degrees" (p. 96). One wonders, though, precisely what Bear means by "expressed a willingness to accept." By 1988, John Bear, Ph.D. (from Michigan State University), in his updated *Bear's Guide to Earning Non-Traditional College Degrees* (also from Ten Speed Press), notes that "of 377 faculty described on a partial faculty list, 23% have their own Doctorate from Columbia Pacific, an unusually high percentage" (p. 101).

Griffis, when asked, freely offers the name of his doctoral institution. He does not misrepresent his credentials in any way. Nonetheless, to his audience, his being able to claim a "Ph.D." carries weight and authority, regardless of its nonacademic standing. When I contacted CPU to obtain a copy of his dissertation (since the standard dissertation-abstracts listings do not include CPU works), an administrator told me that CPU would only release a copy with the author's permission, a procedure quite unlike that of academic institutions. University Microfilms in Ann Arbor, Michigan, through which one can obtain copies of most dissertations from academic institutions, did not list Griffis's. Griffis himself loaned me a copy of his dissertation for study.

Griffis's undated dissertation, *Mind Control Groups and Their Effects on the Objectives of Law Enforcement,* apparently was not reviewed or approved by any committee of scholars. Rather, the only faculty member ackowledged is "mentor" Frank J. Bracelin, Ph.D., of Kirkland, Washington. According to academic counselor Dolores Brennan of CPU, Bracelin obtained his doctorate in health services and currently works as an investigator for the Washington State Board of Pharmacy. The dissertation runs 200 pages, contains a preface written by the Reverend John Charles Cooper, Ph.D., professor of religion at Susquehanna University, Pennsylvania, and one entire chapter, "Cults and the Law," was written not by Griffis but by a lawyer. A reading of the dissertation reveals poor scholarship. One does not find any critical sifting of academic or professional thinking about cults, what they are, how they view themselves, how they function, or how they sustain themselves. The dissertation does not even contain a comprehensive bibliography showing that its author has at least surveyed the literature of his field. Lacking focus and precision, the dissertation reflects sheer casuistry; Griffis tendentiously persists in linking—in a priori, indiscriminate fashion—cults, however defined, to the indoctrination model posited by psychiatrist Robert J. Lifton in his *Thought Reform and the Psychology of Totalism,* a study of Chinese methods of persuasion used on prisoners of war in Korea (which, ironically, Griffis doesn't cite in his bibliography), a book that has not only influenced Griffis but also has shaped the dogmatic arguments of other cult cops and such organizations as the National Cult Awareness Network.

One must first read through 43 pages of a speech emphasizing Griffis's law-enforcement experience and commitment to truth, justice, and the American way before arriving at the thesis. (Along the way to discovering the thesis, one must wade through a seven-page, single-spaced extended quotation from one source—*Deprogramming for Do-It-Yourselfers,* by R. K. Heller, to establish some basic pointers on hypnosis.) Finally, though, the thesis: "In fact, today, some Americans' lives are directed or, in some cases, controlled by other individuals who are skilled in the use of mind-control techniques. Orwell's '1984' is here, ten times worse than predicted, this phenomenon is often called MENTICIDE, a term coined by Dr. Joost Murlo" (pp. 43-44). Then Griffis offers another extended quotation—this one from Lifton's book—of the ingredients of mind control: milieu control, or control over the communication environment; mystical manipulation, a "planned spontaneity" to convince the subjects (victims?) that they represent the "chosen few"; a demand for purity, or the honing of thought to absolute polarities of good and evil, pure and impure; the cult of confession, or the inculcation of the compulsion or obsession to confess in order to purify the self; the teaching of the sacred science or ideology of those controlling the indoctrination; loading the language, or the use of brief, memorized seductive apothegms of philosophy that substitute for critical thinking; the doctrine taking precedence over the person, or the redefinition of identity to conform to doctrine; and, finally, dispensing with the right to existence, or the necessity to earn the right to exist by submission to a group's doctrine or ideology (pp. 44-47).

Griffis moves from Lifton to generalizations that presume that (1) cults, left undefined, have increased in membership and power in the United States; (2) cults practice Lifton's model for assuming mind control over adherents or members; (3) cults are dangerous. So who are these cults? Griffis states, "Today, it has been stated, over three thousand groups exist and can be identified" (p. 51). Of course Griffis offers no source for this quantity, but he nevertheless asserts a priori: "The interest, purpose, magnitude and ultimate goals differ from cult to cult: however all demand in common devotion, obedience, and, ultimately, submission" (p. 51). This perception continues to shape Griffis's public presentations: law enforcers have uncritically adopted it as an immutable truth about the way in which cults work, however undefined. This groundless assertion, for Griffis, leads to logical consequences: "Let it be noted that a common factor among recruits is that a high percentage suffer from sub-clinical depression" (p. 52), one of the first, but not the last, instances of Griffis invoking therapeutic language, here without any definition. Griffis offers anecdotal evidence to support his contentions, some of it even comical: "Recruiters [for cults] carry out their assignments with trained skills and precise detail. One only has to travel through O'Hare Airport to see this in operation" (p. 53).

His Figure 1, which follows page 53, offers in flowchart fashion Griffis's mind-control model. He uses the chart as a seminar handout, and indeed the handout has assumed a life of its own; cult seminars throughout the country use it to illustrate a variety of points. In the diagram, one learns that budding cult recruits are prey to "ego destruction" through "guilt, fear, threat of satan"; concomitant "id destruction" occurs through "isolation, personal confrontation, restricted sex drive." The next stage of indoctrination involves, similarly, two processes: "high excitement" (including "low food intake," "lack of sleep," and "love bombing") and "information distortion" (including "meditation," "guided fantasy," "subliminal oratory," and "misdirected thought input," the latter two terms not defined). Finally, the "snapped personality" is reached by two final processes, "acceptance without wisdom or judgment" (characterized by "no personal goals," "conformity," and "accepting leaders' thoughts," among others) and "dysfunctional brain response" (with attributes such as "confusion," "emotional depression," and "information process destroyed").

Griffis implies, though, that this thought-control process, a technique developed by Chinese communists, has been somehow adopted by feckless cult leaders. By imbuing the model with catastrophic implications, he fails to observe other environments—which we consider legitimate and even innocuous, or perhaps character-improving—in which the same methods obtain. For example, military indoctrination follows many of the same techniques: although people voluntarily enter the military these days, during basic training they enter milieu control, an acceptance of ritual and ritualized truths, made simple by rote and conformity in habit, speech, and appearance. Such techniques also exist in legitimate legal contexts, as sociologist David Bromley has demonstrated in his paper on the Tnevnoc cult (discussed in Chapter 3).[168]

To prove that his model works, Griffis undertakes a survey of cult survivors: "Unlike others who have researched this topic a forensic psychological aspect to cults was explored [sic]" (p. 59). Significantly, in his survey he assumes the truth of his thesis that cults indeed operate through mind-control methods described by Dr. Lifton, and he tests "several hypotheses," among them whether cult members "have tendencies toward depression" and, second, if persons "while under the influence of the cults . . . commit illegal acts" (p. 58). If the survey's bias of *assuming* the truth of what he wants to prove doesn't skew the results, his test subjects certainly might; Griffis finds his test subjects among ex-cult members now receiving counseling through Christian organizations. Griffis's survey, similar to his investigation manual discussed earlier, lists the attributes of his mind-control flowchart and asks the cult member to verify that he or she did indeed experience what he asks. For example:

> During Recruitment were you:
> _____ Love Bombed _____ On Diet
> _____ Given Little Sleep _____ Given Small Jobs
> _____ Watched at all times _____ Loud Music Played
> Other _____
> During lectures did your mind wander _____

In fact, Griffis's investigation manual employs some of the same questions, such as listing attributes of the group leader, and an inventory of group rites. With one exception, all of the survey questions assume the worst about a person's cult experience and certainly reflect the post-cult-experience indoctrination offered by Christian counselors. The one exception: "List some of the good qualities of the group." In answering this open-ended question, the ex-cult member must shift to a new mode of response. Until this question, the respondent must complete a forced-choice questionnaire. This one question requires the respondent to think abstractly before continuing to answer other forced-choice questions. In short, the respondent is likely to skip the question or supply a very terse answer. In fact, at this point, the respondent may be hard pressed to say anything good.

Following the question about good cult qualities, Griffis asks a few other short-answer questions: describe one's mental and physical condition while in the cult and since departing the cult; "A Law Enforcement Officer has primary goals in protection of life, limb, and property with secondary duties of enforcing the laws. What would you recommend to law officials in coping with cult and occult groups?" "How as a Police Officer can we help prevent people from being lost into cults?" Of course, in asking the last question, the respondents cannot respond as police officers since they are not officers, and both of these last two questions reveal Griffis's bias. Griffis applies a chi-square test to the responses on the 50 returned questionnaires, with a result that he "found to be statistically highly significant" (p. 68). Interestingly, while respondents predictably confirmed the Lifton model, they didn't do so exclusively: for example, 68 percent answered that they felt they could leave their group voluntarily. Thirty-six percent of the respondents reported that just before entering the cult they "felt everything hopeless" while 52 percent did not. Fourteen percent reported that after being out of the cult for three months they "felt everything hopeless," while 64 percent did not. The *decrease* in those feeling hopeless implied a therapeutic benefit to cult involvement. On many other similar questions, respondents reported an increase in depressive symptoms, but not consistently so, and generally not by a very significant increase. Since the respondent must identify his or her symptoms three months following cult involvement, one presumes that by this time the ex-cultists have undergone or still receive Christian therapy, which undoubtedly modifies one's self-perception and retrospective view of the cult experience, an influence Griffis doesn't discuss.

Griffis concludes that "42 percent [of respondents] displayed some signs of pre-clinical depression probably caused by the cult experience. Eight percent demonstrated actual depressed tendencies at entry and this figure rose to 100 percent at post experience interview. Almost all respondents described their mental health altered in some way during the time spent in a cult group" (p. 78). And what of criminal behavior? "Police agencies must concern themselves with [destructive cult] members, 46% of which will possibly kill an assigned target if requested according to questionnaire results" (p. 78).

Perhaps the most annoying facet of Griffis's dissertation is his predeliction for *ad misericordium* argument. To conclude his analysis of survey results, he includes the texts of impassioned letters by ex-cult members with the introduction, "Enforcement officials . . . in our democratic society should pay attention to the attached letters. The letters were unsolicited yet their messages are clear and appealing. . . ." (p. 80). He writes:

> Today peace officers are working the streets, basically using equipment, techniques and know how developed at times in-house. We have the same objectives to protect and serve as the old town marshals had yet new laws with staggering precedents shackle our efforts. . . . *What if:* Gurus, false prophets, criminal activists actually unleashed their controlled followers. we peace officers are their enemy—"SATAN'S SOLDIERS." . . . A handfull [*sic*] of officers know this inter-working of cult organizations, let alone the fact some deal in guns, fraud explosives [*sic*] and associate with foreign interests.
>
> Lectures, phone calls, visits and now this text have been done to inform my fellow officers. I am concerned over the apathy among our so-called professional leaders. . . . Our profession will be tried to the limits, let us hope we do not lose too many people before we see what man has made of man. . . .
>
> Let this document be a primer to the under standing [*sic*] of cult activities, mind control and a man's research for helping his personal peers. Let this only be the beginning! (pp. 186-187)

I am a veteran member of the "Thin Blue Line," that which lies between chaos and democracy. My studies and quest for knowledge are based on a [*sic*] honest desire to help my fellow police professionals. . . . Responsible citizens, no matter of their status in life, must take heed of the facts and ideas presented in the prior chapters. Stock also must be taken in the long term course which AMERICA is presently taking as our very laws are being used as a refuge for very questionable activities. (p. 94)

. . . Congressional investigations into the deaths of 913 people [Jonestown] and the murder of one of their own accomplished little because our legislators were unwilling to get entangled in a "religious issue." This liberal argument that the state or federal government should not intervene because of legal technicalities defining religion invites the argument that human lives may properly be sacrificed to support an abstract, artificial concept. . . .

We are now at a turning point in our history. . . . Already in the Middle East, religious zealots have become human bombs with sophisticated explosives killing over two hundred of our servicemen. What if such terrorist activity occurs in the U.S.? Will our society be able to sustain such an attack with our present liberal criminal justice system?

. . . Silence can no longer be tolerated especially in the areas of destructive cults. I am but one person limited by the sanctions placed on my profession. (p. 197)

As examples of destructive cults ("any group which uses psychological manipulation to impair, destroy, or make captive an individual's freedom of thought," p. 142), Griffis invokes mainly Christian groups (Children of God) or those with some allied spiritual sentiment (e.g., the Unification Church). He relies on the fairly abundant literature on such groups, notably from Christian sources. His treatment of the occult (which he separates into Satanism, white magic, and voodoo), offers virtually no evidence of criminal behavior, relying on his own dislike or even disgust for groups like the Church of Satan to convey his argument that such groups are a priori destructive. Griffis offers the usual cult-seminar comments about the Church of Satan, identifying it, in fact, as the most prominent satanic group with a growing membership, whose "followers are well educated and often professional people" (p. 87). As examples of the growing menace posed by occult groups, he offers the following (and notes that he cannot supply details of locations, dates, and so on, because "some of these cases are still open for investigation," p. 88):

1. Western metro city, two graveyards entered sixteen graves opened. Heads taken off corpse' [*sic*] and placed on stakes.
2. Five rabbits killed, heads placed on stakes all facing south.
3. Several cattle killed all sex parts removed with surgical precision.
4. A baby roasted in oven by mother, who stated the devil made her do it.

5. A homo-sexual [*sic*] was murdered, investigation showed he drank blood and was a devil worshipper.

6. Woman left dead along road. Corpse shows signs of cloved [*sic*] animal on top of her. Rape test shows possible pig semen.

7. Abandoned church entered, satanic symbols on walls with pentagram on floor. Several small animals found dead in area.

8. Occult book store opens in area of missing children.

9. Three states investigating similar group that during initiation sacrifices small children.

10. For sale in shopping mall satanic figurines. Two days later sheriff's offices received sightings of naked hooded people in farmers [*sic*] field . . . Solstice of September.

Of course Griffis can offer such examples with impunity since he can reserve identifying details because this list supposedly represents on-going investigations. On the other hand, one cannot help but question his sources. Items 1 and 7 represent verifiable incidents: documented cases exist of grave-yard vandalism, disinterment and mutilation of corpses. Item 2 may indeed have happened, but one can only surmise the connection with Satanism. Item 3 also represents a common occurrence and one usually caused by predators: the "surgical precision" claim is intended to arouse suspicion but in all likelihood a veterinarian has not confirmed an officer's explanation of the animal's death.

Items 4 and 9 smack of urban legends since both represent motifs that have enjoyed wide circulation in the United States and Europe. But Items 8 and 10 are ludicrous on their face, to use the judicial phrase. Aside from the fact that solstices do not occur in September, both items betray a mindset obviously incapable of judging causal relationships, an ability crucial in undertaking complex criminal investigations. And Griffis cites both as evidence of the pervasive influence of Satanism? His doing so falls within the cult-seminar mirage that Griffis himself has helped to foster: the willing suspension of empiricism nursed by the imagined minatory omnipresence of Satanism and other occult influences in the United States. Anyone who can cite Items 8 and 10 as evidence of the perverse influence of Satanism on Americans would also believe that the Iranian airliner shot down by the *U.S.S. Vincennes* in the Persian Gulf in 1988 was stocked with nude corpses in order to entrap us in an embarrassing international incident (a story that surfaced in many parts of the United States). Such are the causal relationships sought by interrogators in the seventeenth-century witch-finding cases, which will be discussed in the final chapter.

Griffis shears away qualifying statements in Lifton's study, marching onward with his mind-control model. But Lifton moves cautiously around the term *brainwashing,* noting its origin in the Chinese term *hsi nao,* meaning "wash brain" but converted by journalist Edward Hunter into "brainwashing."[169] But what of applying the term *brainwashing* to techniques of persuasion?

> Behind this web of semantic . . . confusion lies an image of "brainwashing" as an all-powerful, irresistable, unfathomable, and magical method of achieving total control over the human mind. It is of course none of these things, and this loose usage makes the word a rallying point for fear, resentment, urges toward submission . . . and for a wide gamut of emotional extremism.[170]

Lifton argues that *totalism*—his term—involves first a confession or a renunciation (a phrase apparently missing from most cult cops' descriptions of mind-control Satanists) followed by re-education in the Chinese communist mold. But Griffis and other cult cops ignore the significant cultural underpinnings of re-education. Lifton discusses at length the evolution of Chinese cultural values that make the model work. "[W]hat we see as a set of coercive maneuvers," he writes, "the Chinese Communists view as a morally uplifting, harmonizing, and scientifically therapeutic experience"[171] Granted, some cults may view their indoctrination methods the same way, but Griffis's failure to relate the Chinese prison-camp model to today's weekend cult-retreat damns his whole exercise. Can our well-fed, WASPish citizens experience full milieu control, as Lifton puts it, over prospective converts at a Moonie seminar the way brutalized prisoners of war in China experienced it? Further, and not to diminish the capacity of the manipulative process to impose new identities, can the thought-control model do good? Lifton found that the Chinese process could "produce a genuinely therapeutic effect. Western subjects consistently reported a sense of having been benefited and emotionally strengthened, of having become more sensitive to their own and others' inner feelings, and more flexible and confident in human relationships."[172] But regardless of whether the totalism experience produces ill or good, Lifton readily admits that the process didn't always succeed (some prisoners showed recalcitrance), and he points out that *no* milieu can ever achieve "complete totalism," just as "many relatively moderate environments show some signs of it."[173]

Griffis, in his treatment of occultism, tosses in for good measure Dungeons & Dragons and even involvement of the Society for Creative Anachronism (SCA), a largely national organization of people who foster an interest in medieval European culture by, in part, assuming fictional identities of lords, ladies, and other Chaucerian characters, and stage battles replete with lances, maces, armor, and chain mail. But Griffis nevertheless taints this innocuous group. His evidence: "A female former black arts follower turned S.C.A. member stalks the countryside singling out coven members. She does it as a game and carries her sword made from a leaf spring of a Ford pick-up truck" (p. 102). But Griffis cannot get the meaning of SCA correct: he believes the initials refer to the Society for the Consciousness of Acronyms (p. 102).

The ELF Incident

An incident occurred in Brown County, Indiana, a few years ago that not only illustrates the excessive police resources brought to bear over nothing but also communicates the strength of the cult-seminar world-view, in this case imparted by Dale Griffis. A neopagan group, the Elf Lore Family (ELF) had arranged an equinox ceremony (September 20-22, 1985), billed as a "Wild Magic Gathering," at a public park. The ELFers had arranged to meet at the last moment and to distribute flyers just before the event to forestall adverse community reaction. The ELF posters and handbills mentioned camping, feasts, dancing, "New Age workshops," "bardic tales and tunes," and other similar events. Many of the organizers described themselves as witches and even distributed "witchcraft fact sheets" to explain their beliefs, but they took no measures to educate the law-enforcement officers assigned to provide security for the event.[174]

To folklorist William Guinee, who studied the incident, it illustrated how "two opposing subcultures each with their worldview can produce separate legends from a single event. Separate rumors can arise from conflicts between antagonistic yet mutually supporting worldviews or systems of expectations."[175] By the ELF weekend gathering, a local church group had planned a strategy to proselytize the ELFers, and the local sheriff's department became involved through a deputy who had attended a cult seminar given by two Indiana state-police officers, both self-proclaimed experts, who had in turn received their information from Dale Griffis.

Guinee found "four major first-hand perspectives" concerning the incident from eyewitnesses: Deputy Sheriff Leon Walls from Brown County claims that he saw Devil worship at the gathering. He "saw people drinking blood, eating raw meat, dancing around the flames naked in a triple wedding ceremony, wearing devil-like costumes and having a ceremony with burning candles in the graveyard. He also heard rumors of the sacrifice of a goat."[176] By contrast, a conservation officer saw nothing of the kind, only people dancing and singing around a fire, and even stated to the press that he saw no evidence of Satanism. A local pastor, who arranged to have his congregation drive sorties through the gathering spot to toss around religious tracts ("Satan: The God of This World" and "The Burning Hell: Tortured Lost Souls Burning Forever"), saw *some* suspicious events: people dressed in black and red clothing, "a six-sided star in a circle, three scantily clad women, and something which might have been a candle on a tombstone."[177] But the pastor believed the group satanic because Christian witches cannot exist, contrary to some ELFers who considered themselves as such. An ELF elder denied the Satanism, reinterpreted the mystical symbols in terms of the group's ideology, and even claimed some police harassment.

The atmosphere of the gathering was confusing at best, with ELFers collecting the scattered religious tracts and burning them out of environmental concern (thus arousing greater fears in the pastor's congregation). The officers providing security maintained their distance, reluctant to communicate with the ELFers. But following the weekend, a local newspaper reported the gathering under the title, "Satanic Rites Held at Yellowwood Forest," referring to animal sacrifice, the drinking of blood in rituals, nude dancing, dancing by people in "devil-like costumes," and the eating of raw flesh. The reporter used only one source for the article: Deputy Sheriff Leon Walls. Guinee questioned why Walls made the statements he did to the press, noting that the local newspaper's "opinions have helped to inform the views of many others." Guinee observed, "The influence of second-hand opinions proved especially strong among the law enforcement element."[178]

Guinee traced Walls's satanic attributes to descriptions of Satanism provided at local training seminars, either conducted by Dale Griffis, communicated through his handouts (including the flowchart from Griffis's dissertation), or through the two Indiana state troopers. Griffis himself confirmed to Guinee that the attributes identified by Walls were the same one would expect to find among Satanists. That Griffis teaches these attributes "creates a suspicion that Walls may have been influenced by the idea that these features are representative of Satanism."[179]

Griffis took the time to convey to Guinee his mind-control model. Guinee responded to Griffis's flowchart that "what is being presented is largely a picture of non-mainstream religious groups in general."[180] Griffis's model contains 27 steps to cult mind-control, and he claims that the application of any 17 within 24 hours "will disorient a person." Guinee observed, "The first sixteen steps are fairly common religious practices or phenomena that are difficult to evaluate empirically. The last ten steps seem to be results rather than causes. Perhaps this fear that seventeen of the steps might be taken contributed to the concern over the E.L.F.'s weekend long celebration."[181]

One of the cult cops, Sergeant Richardson of the Indiana State Police, gave Guinee an explanation of the cult threat. His view deserves quoting at length because it depicts the half-formed ideas imparted by cult seminars—short on facts but long on innuendo, unsubstantiated causal relationships, generalizations, and a suspicion of intelligent people:

> You see these people are not illiterate. Usually it's quite the reverse. Usually they're extremely intelligent. You can look through the history of cults, and you'll find that by and large people involved in cults are extremely

intelligent. . . . Some very well respected people were involved in what we might call "cults." . . . There's been some very influential people in our past that have believed in some of these things. So they're very intelligent. So if you take that, with the high degree of intelligence we have out here at [the local university], it would certainly be a breeding ground. . . . If your mind is really active you'll explore whether it's possible that there's UFO's and what we believe in UFO's. You might take apart things and see how they relate to other areas. And these people, that's what they do, that's what they're paid for. . . .

[The interviewer asks Richardson if he perceives "any kind of inherent danger in these cults." The officer replies, "Sure," and then proceeds to explain the danger.] Well, you can take, where do you want to start? The popular game 'Dungeons & Dragons.' Something I know not that much about. I've never seen a 'Dungeons & Dragons' book, but I understand, a figure was given to me that there's been ninety-three deaths attributed to "Dungeons & Dragons." Sure, if you believe, if you believe in something . . . and you believe in this, so totally, that I say to you, I say—the Dungeon Master or player—"I've hexed you. I've got a curse on you, I've done this to you." And you're out, you're lost. And if you believe that I can do that and that I can curse you, then what do you have to live for? . . . A case is on record, two boys came back, wrote a note said "lost the game"—shot themselves.[182]

Richardson carefully observed that the ELF gathering was not satanic, remarking that his own post facto examination of the gathering place revealed evidence of "white witchcraft" only, but warned nonetheless that the gathering was not entirely innocuous, some "whackos" having attended and that "white witchcraft can lead to dark magic."[183]

Guinee comments on the prevalence of the view among law enforcers that "a very real and growing danger of mind control cults threatens America. These cults, they maintain, take numerous forms and often hide behind first amendment rights. Consequently the police are virtually stymied and impotent in the face of this threat."[184]

But the ELF incident influenced many beyond the participants in the gathering, both police and neopagans. The local newspaper, the *Brown County Democrat,* represented the event as satanic, based on Deputy Walls's comments, and Guinee noted that the local reporter "displayed little ethical concern over the actual course of events. Rather she seemed far more interested in an impressive headline. . . . She neither checked the accuracy of the report nor did she take the time to gather background information."[185] Since newspaper articles have formed the corpus of "evidence" at the cult seminars, the ELF incident, as documented by the local newspaper, now enters the files of cult cops as evidence of the threat of Satanism, and the article is exchanged and passed on throughout the country.

The remainder of this book will concern analyses of facets of the cult-cop model. In this chapter I have tried to illustrate the cult-cop world-view, how that view is communicated to wide audiences, begging the question of why professional law enforcers suspend their disbelief when the "Satan!" tilt light flashes. Significantly, the cult-cop model of Satanism in the United States has resolved into a tight, parsimonious construct, despite its many internal inconsistencies. Of course the success of the model lies in the manner of presentation. Cult cops must pitch the model with large doses of innuendo, implication, and wild extrapolation from a few facts, relying on selling the big picture rather than the details. The rest of this book examines the details.

Chapter 3
THE OTHER SIDE OF THE CASE

It must be remembered that we have only heard one side of the case. God has written all the books.

Samuel Butler, 1912

The previous chapter outlined the law-enforcement model of satanic cults and crime. Cult cops claim an increase in such crime with a concomitant increase in cults. In particular, they stress the inhuman philosophies and depredations of the many cults "out there." While the main object of concern has been satanic cults, cult seminars, by not defining terms, have been careless with exiguous facts and indulged in boundless (and groundless) speculation about cults generally. I now propose to sort out some definitions, which will prove no mean feat.

Scholars have defined cults in a variety of ways. Anthropologists, for example, generally define cults as adaptive or functional mechanisms. They describe cults in terms of what they do for their members. The American Indian phenomenon of the Ghost Dance ritual, for example, has been labeled "cultic." The Ghost Dance, a pan-Indian phenomenon of the late nineteenth century, was a ritual designed to invoke the coming of a messiah who would restore Indian lands and cultures to their pristine condition, excluding the marauding white civilization. The ritual clearly served the function of *revitalizing* Indian spiritualism when North American civilization had reduced Indian populations to living on reservations where they eked out a meager living.

I would like my readers to develop a sense of what a cult is and what it is not. In particular, I would like them to do this with difficulty. First, cults should *not* be easy to define. We should not find it easy to appoint whole classes of people, or merely people with common interests, to cults. The term *cult* frequently proves to be a pejorative label, one wielded to identify people unlike us; it is used by most as a word with no redeeming sociological value. Second, coupled with an unease in using the word *cult,* I examine here groups frequently tainted by name-calling at cult seminars, particularly neopagans and ethnic minorities who practice Afro-Cuban or native Hispanic religious beliefs. As I have previously argued, cult seminars have been notoriously lacking in the voice of the "nontraditional belief" and, for that matter, of secular professional behavioral science. Law enforcers appoint themselves experts in interpreting signs and symbols of religious beliefs whose adherents they've never met. Since no cult-crime seminar is complete without its excursion into Santeria, cult cops often grandstand about people who have never lived in or near their communities, in rural Virginia or Pennsylvania, for example. Cult cops prefer to identify cults' putative proselytizing through mind-control, their fraudulent recruitment of members, and their attraction to sociopaths as key criteria for classification, comparison, and evaluation.

Numbers

Before taking up the matter of what can be classified as a cult, satanic or otherwise, I will first dispense with the easier issue: How many cults exist? The fact is that no one knows. J. Gordon Melton, who created the Institute for the Study of American Religion, based in Santa Barbara, California, undertook the only survey to date of *all* religious groups that have surfaced publicly in the United States.[1] But as Melton found, some groups whose memberhips adopt self-identifying labels may not even claim a formal membership roll, much less articulate a commonly held credo. And even when trying to survey cults labeled as such, the groups may resist the categorization. Nevertheless, Melton probably comes closer to an accurate estimate of the number of cults than any cult cop's baseless generalization. "Using the broad definition of the social scientists, one can find some 500-600 cults or alternative religions in the United States. Of these, over 100 are primarily ethnic bodies confined to first- and second-generation immigrant communities," and total cult membership may reach 150,000 to 200,000.[2]

Against Melton's well-founded estimate of 150,000 to 200,000 cult members in the United States, cult cops and their allies have come up with tantalizing figures:

—Occult groups (undefined) are "usually organized into 'covens' consisting of 9 or 13 members." With 10,000 covens in the United States in 1946, growing to 135,000 in 1985, the total national membership may run to 500,000.[3]

—Cult members may number up to ten million.[4]

—About 3000 cults exist in the United States.[5] Griffis also says that only 500 of the total figure for cults deal with "the occult."[6]

—Cult membership in the United States may run about three million.[7]

So against Melton's estimate, cult cops have one in every 25 Americans a member of some type of cult. Interestingly, cult cops orient their seminars to satanic cults, yet when they offer any numbers at all, since they lack any statistics on satanic-cult membership, they simply introduce raw estimates of the *total* number of cult members, thus using the number alone to imply a threat. As an example of the cavalier use of statistics about cults, in an article about a cult survivor, Patricia Pulling offered a "conservative" estimate of 8 percent of Richmond, Virginia's population as "involved in Satanic worship at some level."[8] When reporter Rex Springston pointed out that 8 percent translates into 56,000 people, Pulling qualified the figure by saying that "she meant 8 percent of the area was involved in the occult, in which she included people dabbling in witchcraft and such New Age activities as channeling."[9] Pulling explained that she arrived at eight percent by "estimating 4 percent of the area's teenagers, and 4 percent of the adults, were involved. She added the figures."[10] When Springston countered that in mathematics "the sum amounts to only 4 percent of the total population, she said it didn't matter because 8 percent was probably 'conservative' anyway."[11]

Of course, cult cops maintain that the numbers have been increasing, a contention that Melton has rebutted. For example, Melton "has investigated hundreds of reports of alleged satanic activity and found only 20 to have any merit. The relatively small number of persons involved in some sort of organized Satan-worship has remained constant in recent years."[12] To those who claim that satanic cults have increased in recent years, Melton has observed that "[t]he real increase . . . has come in the number of Christian and citizens' groups claiming the Satanists are on the rise."[13] Melton even goes further to assert that purported satanic crimes have not increased in recent years, either: "Over the last 20 years the reported number of graffiti, church break-ins, teen-age informal covens and adult Satanist groups has remained constant."[14] But since we cannot get very far with prognostications about numbers, perhaps the most useful focus would be to define cults and cult involvement.

Defining Cults

Allan Eister has described the problems one faces in defining cults: Most definitions lack "solid empirical grounding," he writes.[15] Eister points out that cults may organize around charismatic leaders or they may not; they may arise in times of cultural stress or crisis or they may not. For that matter, cults don't necessarily advance religion. "Cults could indeed be 'secular' or could, without violation of the logical principles involved in defining the type, combine elements which could be defined as either."[16] After cataloging the attributes commonly cited for cults, Eister says that the " 'orientations' proffered by cults should be diverse and unconventional and they may be syncretistic, eclectic and perhaps esoteric and arcane as well."[17] In short, the binding or compelling interest that draws people to a cult could be anything.

J. Gordon Melton has written two works that show up in reference sections of most libraries: *The Encyclopedia of American Religions,* a two-volume survey that constitutes a who's who in religion, and *The Encyclopedic Handbook of Cults in America,* the more recent of the two, essentially an expanded treatment of the cults named in the former work, accompanied by an analysis of what cults are and how they work. In *The Encyclopedia of American Religions,* Gordon confronts the problem of definition, of what constitutes not only a cult, but also a church, a denomination, or a sect. Melton's classification criteria do not prove easy to define, as Melton himself admits, but he examines a group's size, whether a group is organized around a recognizable church, whether the church sought the loyalty of its members, and whether members shared a common "thought world" (not necessarily identical views), common heritage, or lifestyle.[18]

In his *Encyclopedic Handbook,* Melton deals with the definition of cults head-on: "The term 'cult' is a pejorative label used to describe certain religious groups outside of the mainstream of Western religion."[19] Surveying the literature, Melton finds that definitions of cults fall within three basic perspectives. The first view places cults within a larger scheme of religious groups, whether sects, churches, or cults. Social scientists here take the view that "cults represent a force of religious innovation within a culture."[20] The second domain of definition derives from the writings of Christian polemicists who argue the perversity of cults. The third view, largely a secular one, comes from those who seek to identify destructive cults—for example, parents whose children have been part of such groups.[21] The definition of cult, then, has depended on the object group taken as an exemplar of the definition. Melton takes up argument repeatedly against the more extreme Christian writers who take pains to name cults followed by *j'accuse* finger-pointing. In their attacks against new religious groups, "the secular anti-cultists gradually discarded any overtly religious language as a means of designating cults in order to appeal to government authorities and avoid any seeming attack upon religious liberties."[22] In short, the process of defining cults has often been inseparable from an attack on them. What makes Melton's works singular is that he tries to construct, in Linnaean fashion, a nonjudgmental model of religious groups, a model resembling a giant family tree.

Gordon returns repeatedly to the judgments passed on cults by Christian writers. In particular, he discusses the "destructive cult" category posited by many, a term, as we have seen, that has entered the fray within cult seminars. Through attacks on a few cults, " 'cults' have come to be seen as groups that share a variety of generally destructive characteristics" including the requirement that members swear absolute, total obedience to a messianic leader; the employment of deceptive recruiting tactics; psychological manipulation (mind control) to eradicate rational thought and induce guilt, forcing the members to rely on the group to solve personal problems; having as their only purpose the material well-being of their members and following an "ends justify means" philosophy; and having violent propensities.[23] Some of the same anticultists have announced that 3,000 to 5,000 destructive cults exist in the United States, a figure identical to that asserted by Dale Griffis, but "no evidence of the existence of such a large number of religious groups, either cultic or otherwise, has been produced."[24]

Clearly, cult cops have borrowed quite uncritically from Christian polemicists to construct a view of cults' destructive nature without first defining the term *cult*. Perhaps more important, the satanic-cult paradigm—replete with breeders of sacrificial babies, drug and sex parties, and so on—derives exclusively from the writings of Christian anticultists. Ironically, Anton LaVey has been right: Satan indeed may have been keeping in business some of the Christian ideologues who *invented* the satanic tradition in the first place. As Melton puts it, "The Satanic tradition has been carried almost totally by the imaginative literature of non-Satanists, primarily conservative Christians, who describe the practices in vivid detail in the process of denouncing them."[25]

Melton takes up the topic of cult violence, and in recounting the few incidents of it, observes that, for scholarly study, definitions of "cult-related violence" must be broadened and rethought. Citing the only scholarly work devoted to the topic, *Violence and Religious Commitment,* edited by Ken Levi (Pennsylvania University Press, 1982), Melton defines cult-related violence as "violent behavior which leads to bodily harm or death (homicide or suicide) of individuals or the significant destruction of property due to actions initiated within a nonconventional religion against either members or the general public and also actions by the public against nonconventional religions' members and property."[26] Melton cautions, though, that in examining cult-related violence, one must sort out the innuendo and unconfirmed reports, a very difficult activity in a time of public hostility on matters cultic. "Cult critics, when discussing the issue of violence, continually yield to the very attractive temptation to lump all cults together and brand all with the guilt of any one. Such guilt-by-association, which unfortunately has been integral to the media treatment of cult issues, is no less deplorable than the racism and anti-semitism from which it has been copied."[27]

In Chapter 2, I referred to Dale Griffis's survey of cult refugees (or self-proclaimed survivors), people all under Christian counseling. In Chapter 4 I will again take up the matter of cult survivors, some of whom have written public apostasies that rail against the inhumanity of their particular cults. But Melton advises, "Hostile reports of the defectors from unconventional religions must be double checked against independent sources, and unverified claims either rejected or, at best, put aside for possible future verification."[28] Above all, the reported incidents of cult violence do not support the "*false conclusion* suggested by many cult critics that *cult life is inherently dangerous and threatening*" (Melton's emphasis).[29] When one finds cult-related violence, particularly directed at children, the perpetrators are not followers of satanic churches; instead, "ritualistic" child abuse has arisen in large part inside conservative, evangelical Christian groups which take literally a biblical injunction about chastising children (Hebrews 12:6).[30] (This also was noted by Kenneth Lanning, in an advanced ritualistic-crime seminar, September 22, 1988, Richmond, Va.). Melton cites examples of such sects: the Gideons in Florida; River of Life Tabernacle in Montana; Stonegate Christian Community, West Virginia.

Psychiatry and psychology, also concerned with what defines the cult experience, have tried to separate "destructive cults" from the nondestructive variety. Psychologist Frank MacHovec defines a cult as

> a group of persons who share in a special interest differing from the established majority or current religious, social, or cultural values, who meet regularly to continue and extend their purpose or mission independent of previous relationships with family, friends, religion, school or career, with beliefs, practices and rituals which reinforce cult values and norms.[31]

This definition presumes that a cult interest must be nonconformist or unconventional, but many cults like those inventoried by Melton show quite conventional Christian beliefs, although with some aberration: either an unusual emphasis on doctrine or the adoption of an uncommon ritual. The notion of nonconformism appears also in the latter part of the definition, which suggests that the binding interest within the cult must exist independently of a person's familial and social milieu; yet as Melton has also shown, it ain't necessarily so. Groups of persons brought together by a special interest could involve friends or family, for example. By contrast, MacHovec defines a *destructive* cult as

> a rigidly structured absolutist group usually under an authoritarian, charismatic leader which isolates itself from established societal traditions, values, and norms, recruits members deceptively without informed consent, and retains them by continually reinforced direct and indirect manipulative techniques which cause personality and behavior change, deny freedom of choice, and interrupt and obstruct optimal personality development.[32]

Even this definition carries dilemmas. Absolutist groups that perform all of these characteristics but which we consider firmly *within* "established societal traditions," such as recognized or "legitimate" religious orders and the military, fall within the definition. Attempts to define "destructive" cults by their recruitment strategies and techniques that bring about behavioral change can end up as statements of bias against nonconformism; there is a danger in trying to establish some cults a priori as destructive by virtue of the psychology of the cult experience. As Melton pointed out, we need much more study of the cult phenomenon in order to devise definitions free from bias against nonconformism, definitions that embrace the varieties of religious experience. MacHovec's definition, though, doesn't limit itself to religious cults; and MacHovec, while wrestling with definitions, remains aware of the ease with which we set up biases against nonconformists: "In the context of world history, today's cult can become tomorrow's culture."[33]

Of course the whole subject of cults enters the psychiatric realm as aiders and abetters of mental disorders; after all, psychiatrists treat those who have left cults or, conversely, those who have left their families, friends, schools, and jobs to enter cults. More than a few psychiatrists believe that people must a priori require some therapy after emerging from a cult experience. To treat such people, however, psychiatrists must adopt working assumptions of what psychological response the cult experience requires; some psychiatrists, for example, assume the malevolence of the cult environment. Psychiatrist Marc Galanter has written that his profession can assess cult members only with great difficulty, because no method exists for understanding how they adapt to their religion while simultaneously departing from convention.[34]

In his most recent study, Galanter set out to convey a psychological understanding of the charismatic cult, which he defines as a group

> consist[ing] of a dozen or more members, even hundreds or thousands. It is characterized by the following psychological elements: members (1) have a shared belief system, (2) sustain a high level of social cohesiveness, (3) are strongly influenced by the group's behavioral norms, and (4) impute charismatic (or sometimes divine) power to the group or its leadership.[35]

Galanter's study applies systems theory to the examination of cults in "an evolutionary, sociobiological context."[36] He finds that charismatic cults offer one vital service to prospective members: the relief of psychological distress. In so doing, cults serve an evolutionary purpose:

> This "relief effect" serves to reinforce members' involvement in the group and also continually reinforces their acceptance of the group's beliefs by rewarding them for their conformity and acceptance. . . . Both anthropologic and ethologic evidence suggest that such affiliative behavior and biologically grounded drives improve the ability of a group to adapt and survive.[37]

In his study, Galanter finds a correlation between joining a group—a cult—the adoption of fidelity or loyalty to the group, and the easing of psychological distress.[38] He discusses recent studies of Christian fundamentalists that examine the relationship between faith and healing. Noting that the recent "upsurge in religious commitment" in the United States, "particularly in fundamentalist religion, has brought faith healing closer to the cultural mainstream," Galanter observed of recent research that fundamentalists "perceived their faith-healing experience as a definitive treatment *regardless* of the presence or absence of physical symptoms afterwards. . . . The primary function of faith healing was not necessarily to resolve symptoms, but to reinforce the group's religious perspective and thereby provide sick people with a means of avoiding harsh realities."[39] Whereas people who have been "healed" through faith must rely on large doses of denial to overcome their realization that, say, cancer symptoms are still present, Galanter found that "the ability to blind oneself to reality" through religious experience might alleviate psychological distress.

The study of psychological distress and affiliation with a religious group—a cult—evokes the study I cited in Chapter 2 by anthropologist Edward Moody, who explored the therapeutic value of rites in the Church of Satan.[40] The cult cops, however, have taken the Christian polemicist view of cults as perverse and heretical and therefore cannot admit to the psychological benefits of affiliation with nonconformist religious groups; they therefore, must doggedly pursue "mind control" models, making a priori assumptions that any cult affiliation will prove harmful. As I mentioned earlier, cult-cop Dale Griffis relies on the model of cults as a brainwashing phenomenon, based on research conducted by Robert J. Lifton.[41] But Griffis completely ignores the cross-cultural issue; he transfers a model of indoctrination practiced by Chinese communists to the modern social setting of middle-class America. The cultural background for the operation of Lifton's "totalism" and the circumstances of war at the very least raise important questions about the applicability of this model. While not commenting on Griffis's work, Galanter comments:

> Controlled communication in the small group also characterizes coercive persuasion, or brainwashing, where the individual is forced to adopt a group's views *against* his or her will. Robert Lifton has observed that brainwashing like that in Chinese Communist concentration camps required full control over the context of communication but in voluntary conversions contact must be maintained in a subtle (or deceptive) way, without forcing the individual to comply with the group's views.[42]

Galanter's point has been ignored by cult cops: in their militant insistence that cults psychologically kidnap recruits, cult cops fail to note that real cults (not the imagined satanic megacult) can never exercise *full* "milieu control" over prospective recruits—unless they begin running concentration camps in the United States. Rather, as Galanter suggests, persuasion can be accomplished in other ways, particularly when people enter cults voluntarily, as they do in the cases Griffis cites as applicable to Satanism. Cult cops cannot knowledgeably discuss recruitment into satanic cults, since there is no proof that *clandestine* satanic cults exist. Instead, cult cops have borrowed from documented groups such as the Unification Church to suggest that the Lifton model applies. But as Melton and others have pointed out, cults attract very few members who stay on: very, very few recruits last even two years, and most prospective members do not even return after an initial meeting, all of which portends little for "mind control" totalism.

Sociological views of cults, their recruiting techniques, and their ideologies have not presented a new international threat. In particular, sociologists Anson D. Shupe, Jr., and David G. Bromley, in outlining the recruitment and indoctrination practices of the Tnevnoc cult,[43] suggest strong biases in the way cult cops describe nonconformist religions, biases that predispose them to finding criminal behavior where none exists.

The Tnevnoc cult, which has implanted itself throughout the United States, is a "communal, sectarian group affiliated with a large and powerful international religious organization."[44] The cult aims to recruit young women, either teenagers or young adults, and does so openly at schools and colleges. Following indoctrination into the cult, young women eventually lose any power of will, succumbing entirely to the regimen of the cult. Cult members must abandon their former lives, even surrendering their outside friendships and personal possessions. Their activities, then, involve the cult exclusively. Members must arise at 4:30 in the morning, wear prayer beads attached to their wrists, engage in long, monotonous chants and prayers, and in one of the most bizarre activities, members consume food they are told represents the dead cult-founder's body. Women must even pledge in writing absolute obedience to the cult. To further distance itself from worldly affairs, the cult assigns new names to members and designates as their birthdays the dates of their entry into the cult. After hours of performing menial tasks, such as scrubbing floors, coupled with the incessant recitation of ritualistic prayers, members may occasionally transgress rules, for which they are punished harshly. For example, punishment might require women to go without food, having to beg on their knees for the crumbs from others' plates. But the most shocking ritual requires members to become brides to the dead cult-leader.

Cult cops use such language—focusing on the unfamiliar or the unconventional—to describe the rites and beliefs of those affiliated with "cults," a label that is used freely and without definition and is intended to evoke suspicion. But *Tnevnoc* is *Convent* spelled backward; the paragraph above describes the socialization of women into Christian convents. The description begs questions of fraudulent recruitment, dehumanization, possible criminality, mind-control manipulation, and Liftonesque milieu control. Bromley and Shupe observe how such language ignores the religious vision of "cult" members and their own self-discipline in achieving a goal of spiritual experience, activities requiring no governmental intervention.

> . . . The foregoing description of the Tnevnocs actually constitutes a caricature of the group insofar as it fails to convey the sense of majesty, purpose, personal fulfillment and belonging that Tnevnocs experienced individually and collectively. It also ignores the order, harmony, stability and integration of Tnevnoc communal organization. However, these same details also are missing from most contemporary accounts of new religious movements. It is precisely this lack of personal and organizational context and purpose which creates a sense that some of their practices are illegitimate and destructive.[45]

Bromley and Shupe observe that the view of unconventional, nonconformist religions as destructive has a historical dimension within the United States: "The stereotypes and litany of charges leveled against contemporary 'new religions' also are remarkably reminiscent of allegations against the earlier 'new religions': political subversion, unconditional loyalty of members to authoritarian leaders, brutalizing of members, sexual indiscretions, and possession of mysterious, extraordinary powers."[46]

In the Tnevnoc paper, Bromley and Shupe note that religious groups largely escape the stereotypes once they have achieved legitimacy. In fact, after surveying cult cops' claims about a number of small organizations with nonconformist beliefs, I concluded that only legitimacy distinguishes "religion" or "church" from beliefs denoted as "cult." In another work, Bromley and Shupe ask, however, "Is there a point at which individuals become so enmeshed in a religious group that they become incapable of autonomous action and outside intervention becomes needed?"[47] In this 1981 analysis of the cult controversy, Bromley and Shupe conclude that it is a hoax: "There is no mysterious brainwashing process used to trap and enslave millions of young Americans." And of the scare and hysteria: "It is not a deliberate fraud, but it is a deliberate attempt to horrify and anger us."[48] In short, the cult controversy, they suggest, must be understood as "a conflict of interest."[49] Similar to the points they raised in the Tnevnoc paper, Bromley and Shupe found that whenever a new religious group emerges, opposition appears immediately, characterized by atrocity stories, allegations of deception, coercive recruitment and retention of members, illegitimacy of beliefs, and so on, the very claims now made by cult cops about putative satanic groups.

And what of the claim that cults employ brainwashing techniques on their members?

> Attempts to shape attitudes are a part of every church, school system, military establishment, and government. Ultimately there is nothing wrong, in the moral sense, with the practice of shaping attitudes, even if it brings about radical change. The "wrongness" depends only on whether we approve of *who* is shaping the attitudes and for *what* purpose. This is the fundamental issue with which we as citizens must come to grips. . . . Mind control is more in the mind of the perceiver than some individual, identifiable practice.[50]

But again, *cult* still defies meaningful definition outside of the polemicists:

> . . . Cult is a fashionable buzz word thrown about haphazardly by the media, anticultists, establishment ministers who no longer worry about the label being applied to them, and even some social scientists who should know better. Although the term has a precise technical meaning, it has been run into the ground by persons who indiscriminately attach it to any group not conforming to a narrow range of so-called normal middle-class religions. Cults are thus touted as new, expanding at alarming rates, and potentially dangerous both to their members and to larger society.[51]

As for the "precise technical meaning," Bromley and Shupe observe: "Sociologically, a cult is the starting point of every religion."[52] Cults exhibit no bureaucracy or priesthood and normally consist of a charismatic leader and his or her followers. Cults *must* be nonconformist in trying to introduce a new religious tradition, so they emerge accompanied by some tension and conflict, which explains their quite natural need for self-protection.

I tend toward the view of cults as simply groups—normally oriented toward a religious principle, but not always—that have not yet achieved widespread legitimacy as perceived by the public at large. But we will now explore the salient cults usually described at cult seminars. We will do so largely with an *emic* perspective. Anthropologists bear in mind the *etic-emic* relationship when writing ethnographies. The terms derive from *phonetic* and *phonemic,* respectively, terms important to linguistic study.

When an anthropologist undertakes a phonetic analysis, he or she undertakes an inventory of a language's sounds according to a phonetic alphabet of symbols representing single, identifiable sounds.[53] A phonetic alphabet should prove useful for describing sounds in *any* language. However, the entire system of phonetics, as elaborate and developed as it is, remains a system created by linguists: it has no reality apart from linguistic analysis. The system derives from a multitude of considerations and designs of use to the linguist only: the speaker of a language, by contrast, would recognize no such system if asked to describe his or her own language.

The second component of linguistic analysis, after a scholar has transcribed a speaker's utterances by phonetic means, involves identifying the smallest *meaningful* sound units. The range of sounds available to any speaker is virtually infinite, yet any language contains a discrete set of sounds that speakers may use, and many that they *cannot* use because the culture does not recognize their use. So linguists move from a phon*etic* to a phon*emic* analysis to identify sounds significant to native speakers (as well as sounds not significant). In the end, the linguist will produce a phonemic alphabet of sounds *from the native speaker's perspective.*

An etic discussion of cults, then, places them within a scheme that has no reality to cult members. The criteria by which cult cops describe their prey conform to their own conservative Christian-based model of how cults function. Cult seminars would obtain a more insightful version of cults' raison d'être by having cult members describe their beliefs and values according to their own world-view. But cult seminars very rarely, if ever, seek such a perspective. However, law enforcers have learned through painful experience with racial tension to have members of ethnic minorities address police trainees on *their own* concerns about how police should treat them, so the emic notion is not entirely new to them.

For the remainder of this chapter, I will offer an emic glimpse into the beliefs of those groups most frequently discussed (and sometimes denigrated) at cult seminars. The descriptions of cults offered by Christian polemicists ignore this emic perspective. Christian polemicists may point to exposés from former cult members as emic, but they hardly qualify as such: cult apostates thrust forward by Christian groups have told tales of subversion and perversion taught them by Christian counselors as preparation for publicly announced conversions. Dale Griffis's investigative guide, which was described in Chapter 2, has been gauged to identify destructive behavior based on criteria that *always* flags the innocuous as criminal, or at least destructive.

Satanists

"Satanism as it now exists and has existed during the past two centuries has been a most unusual cult. It has produced almost no literature and individual groups have come and gone without connecting with previously existing Satanic groups or leaving behind any progeny."[54] In Chapter 2, I noted that Anton LaVey had founded the Church of Satan in 1966. Satanism, then, can refer either to the philosophy of the Church of Satan or to a separate, less well known organization, the Temple of Set, founded by Michael Aquino and Lilith Sinclair, two former members of the Church of Satan. Unlike the Church of Satan, the Temple of Set acknowledges a deity, in this case the Egyptian Set, who to members is a forerunner of the Christian Satan. The Temple of Set practices arcane ritual and, like the Church of Satan, doesn't recruit, but its members may number only hundreds, or perhaps little more than a thousand, while the Church of Satan has perhaps a few thousand. The Temple of Set doctrine has not been divulged to the public, except for some broad generalities, whereas, by contrast, LaVey's books, *The Satanic Bible, The Satanic Rituals* (1972), and *The Compleat Witch* (1970), have been widely publicized. LaVey's nine satanic dicta (cited in Chapter 2), more than anything else in *The Satanic Bible*, have received citations in everything from Christian publications to scholarly studies to cult-cop presentations. In all but scholarly publications, the nine dicta are taken as evidence of the perversity of the Church of Satan; yet as Melton points out, the church's philosophy actually is rather more tepid: "The Church of Satan promotes the development of strong individuals who seek the greatest gratification out of life and practice selfish virtues as long as they harm no other."[55]

Anthropologist Edward Moody spent several months as a participant-observer of the Church of Satan.[56] Not surprisingly, Moody cites "astounding" scientific ignorance of witchcraft (which he doesn't distinguish from Satanism), noting that most anthropologists explain witchcraft simply as an outlet for forbidden aggressions or as a label for punishable deviance.[57] Moody's experience led him to search for a common denominator among members: "All were deviant or abnormal in some aspect of their social behavior."[58] His choice of the word *abnormal,* though, doesn't imply criminal or perverse by any conventional standard; rather, it means "that they engaged in some behavior which was disturbing to other members . . . of their society. . . . The abnormal person, behaviorally, is deficient in either his ability to perceive or receive social stimuli, or in the skills necessary to make the appropriate response,"[59] according to Moody. He makes an insightful observation: "The deviant's behavior is not so much disturbed as disturbing, for the person who does not play according to the rules casts doubt on the validity of the game and causes anxiety in the minds of others who do play according to the rules."[60] So the members of the Church of Satan whom Moody observed exhibited "abnormality" in their difficulty in playing by social rules and in their lack of social skills.

When Moody looked beyond the maladroit social behavior for causes, he found them: members came from broken homes, alcoholic or abusive parents, or hostile siblings. As a result, he felt that prospective members came to the Church of Satan with a sense of social failure and inadequacy in order to seek the ability to achieve "the rewards, the monetary successes and sexual conquests" that define success in our culture.[61] "Having consciously or implicitly identified the source of his problems as the evaluative system, an essentially Judeo-Christian system of his culture, the pre-Satanist wishes to reduce the anxiety caused him by behavior at variance with his culture and his beliefs."[62] The budding Satanist's interest in his new affiliation, then, comes about quite predictably in order to reduce "cognitive dissonance," to resolve conflicts between what he perceives as impossible expectations of success thrust upon him and his low self-esteem.

For the novitiate, Church of Satan rituals teach that they are in fact evil, but "evil" undergoes redefinition: novitiates receive encouragement to speak of their evil thoughts and deeds, which are praised. "It is a tenet of the Satanic ideology that evil is relative to the time and place in which the deed is done . . . and only when one feels guilty about doing something is he really 'doing wrong' "63 The Church of Satan teaches, then, that man is an animal, and a naturally "self-aggrandizing and greedy" one at that. In a way, the novitiate undergoes a process not dissimilar to psychotherapy, which helps relieve guilt for "normal" behavior. But the Church of Satan progresses a step further by shearing away people's ingrained responses to Christian symbols, part of the "evaluative system" that judges human conduct in our culture. To remove symbolic meaning, or at least reduce its perceived import, the Church of Satan holds a Black Mass, a deliberate inversion of Christian symbols. Participants in the Black Mass who feel guilty about it receive ridicule. "Eventually the formerly anxiety-provoking stimuli bring disgust, anger, or laughter, but not fear."64

Once the Church of Satan has removed anxiety-producing stimuli, it has to make good its promise to teach magic. As an example of acquiring magic, Moody recounts the case of Billy G. Billy had been brought up in a fundamentalist Baptist atmosphere, quite sexually repressed. Later, he entered the Church of Satan with several problems: affliction by devils, or his fear of natural impulses; extreme anxiety when around women (having been taught that women pose dangers); a feeling of sexual ineptitude, which fed his sense of social impotence and anxiety. The casual talk about sex within the Church of Satan began to reduce his anxieties a bit, and since an attractive nude woman formed part of the "altar of flesh" in church rituals, Billy G. began to feel more comfortable with a woman's sexuality. Moody notes that this desensitization to the source of Billy's anxiety—women and sex—forms a commonly used therapeutic technique of taking "a previously anxiety-producing stimulus and condition[ing] a new response to it."65 The nude woman "on the altar makes no demand on him and does not move about; she just lies quietly. He sits in the darkness, his reactions masked, surrounded by friends—secure and safe from the negative consequences of his behavior. Eventually he relaxes."66

Eventually, Billy G.'s anxiety disappeared; he began talking with women in the group, showing more and more self-confidence in social settings. With his anxieties reduced, he then learned magic. Part of his magic training consisted of "how to flatter a girl [and] to how dress and groom oneself in order to be attractive to others. . . . Couching these rules in magical terminology merely underlines their importance and makes them more acceptable."67 Moving to more advanced levels of magic, Billy G. learned to practice Love Magic. First, he had to prepare an amulet, the ingredients proving difficult to obtain. Under admonitions from other members that the amulet will prove effective, Billy G. begins to feel confident, to feel better about the most troublesome part of his *rapprochement* with women: the possibility of sexual interaction. But the amulet is only a part of the process: he must learn the theory of Love Magic by transforming himself into a "love magnet."

Magic training continues: Billy learns that everyone gives off "vibrations" to others and the amulet's power must be directed to those emanations. In short, Billy learns to "emphasize and capitalize on some characteristic of [his] that is appealing to others. . . ." He develops a more realistic perception of himself and of his own capabilities, learning to magnify his strong points and de-emphasize his weaknesses."[68] Eventually, Billy G. takes women out on dates; makes friends with them; and has pleasant sexual experiences. "The benefits of Satanism . . . are obvious: he need be less anxious or fearful, he is more able socially, and he is actually more successful in many spheres of activity due to his enhanced ability to interact with others. He now has, after all, a better knowledge of the expectations of the rest of society, a better awareness of the rules of the cultural or social game."[69]

Moody offers insightful remarks about church participants' views on the efficacy of magic:

> If psychology explains personal interaction in terms of hypothesized "forces" at work, forces which are known and measured only through the perception of their effects, then how is that different, the Satanist asks, from magic? Satanists say, with some justification, "When magic becomes fact we refer to it as medicine or astronomy." . . The use of magical therapy helps to resocialize deviants and bring their behavior, for whatever reasons, closer to the cultural and social norms necessary to ensure the continued "smooth" running of the society. The Satanists are clearly better citizens after their magical therapy than before, if one is speaking in terms of social cohesion and equilibrium.[70]

Witches

If Satanists have had a difficult time in the face of public hysteria about abductions, sacrifices, and mutilated babies, self-professed witches, pagans, and Wiccans have fared no better. In response to an alarmist article in a local paper, J. Worthington Montgomery, representing the Mid-Atlantic Council of the Witches' League for Public Awareness, wrote:

Back to the article. [The author] wrote, "One popular 'proof' [of satanic activity]: bizarre confessions of people claiming past involvement in Witchcraft." Foremost, Witchcraft is in no way associated with satanism. To even infer so betrays ignorance of the facts. . . . Witchcraft pre-dates the Judeo-Christian worldview and has no "Satan," no "devil" and no "demons" in its belief structure. . . . Next, Witchcraft is a religion and is federally recognized as such. The words "Witchcraft" and "Witch" should always be capitalized. "Christian," "Methodist," "Catholic," "Jew" and "Protestant" are all capitalized; "Witch" should be capitalized as well.[71]

Nevertheless, the newspaper's editors responded that they would continue to use the lower case. The letter from Montgomery illustrates the annoyance felt by many witches at being lumped with baby-eating Satanists. Cult cops occasionally distinguish witches from Satanists, but nevertheless retain their suspicions. Cult-seminar slide-shows routinely depict, for "intelligence" value, local bookstores that retail in New Age, occult, or similar subjects, and even photographs of purported witches. The indefatigable Larry Jones of *File 18 Newsletter* mentions a seminar, exclusively for law enforcers, conducted by witches to explain the differences between witches and other groups, and while Jones acknowledges that a police-only seminar might prove useful, he nevertheless suspects that it could also be a move by witches to learn the identities of officers working the occult beat.[72]

Witches can provide plenty of anecdotes about police harassment.

[Bart] Myers, who attends occasional worship services at a Fredericksburg [Va.] coven, recalled being stopped by Stafford County deputies one night last spring as he was driving home from a meeting.

He was wearing a necklace with a doubled pentagram and the deputies asked if it was a sign of Satan. Then, he said, they asked to look in the trunk of his car. There they found his black witches [*sic*] robe and candles.

"They said, 'Were you participating in a Satanic ritual tonight?' They gave me a real hard time because I'm a Wiccan."[73]

Selena Fox, a well-known witch, who "runs the prime networking organization in the craft," according to Margot Adler (author of *Drawing Down the Moon*), took up residence with her coven in Brigham Township, Wisconsin, after her previous landlord cast her out for being a witch. When Fox and her husband applied for a zoning variance to allow improvements on their barn at their new residence, problems began: "A local fundamentalist church held a meeting and showed a movie about Satanism and the occult, with warnings about the evils of witchcraft."[74] Subsequently, local officials "grilled" Fox about her beliefs, but with help from the American Civil Liberties Union, after more than two years she obtained the zoning approval.

Why the fuss? Selena Fox draws an image of her congregation analogous to that of a patient parish priest: "A lot of Christians only go to church on Christmas and Easter," she says, "and a lot of pagans only come out on Halloween"[75]

Otter and Morning Glory Zell, who edit *Green Egg* magazine, describe the witches' ethos:

> The term "Neo-Paganism" is applied to the current revival of ancient Pagan religious values, including the sacredness of all Life and the worship of Nature. Modern Witchcraft has been a major component of the Neo-Pagan resurgence since England repealed its anti-Witchcraft laws in 1951.
>
> The many traditions of Neo-Pagan Witchcraft have few universal theological precepts, but one of them is certainly the veneration of the Moon Goddess, known most commonly by her Roman name, Diana. She is perceived as manifesting in triple form: as Maiden, Mother and Crone. These triple aspects are identified respectively with the waxing, full, and waning moons. Witches gather at *esbats* every full moon, to sing and dance in Her moonlight, share cakes and wine, and work magic to heal each other, their friends, and the Earth. . . .
>
> Many traditions of Neo-Pagan Witchcraft also honor the Consort of the Goddess in the form of the Horned God, who is seen as the Lord of Animals as well as seasonal ruler of the Underworld. The most familiar version of the Horned God is the Greek Pan. . . .[76]

Neopagans find their historical association with shamans, "or medicine men and women, of the tribal Celtic peoples of Europe."[77] Many argue their historical roots in pre-Christian paganism, which maintained beliefs and rites sub rosa during the ascendancy of Christianity. Since our modern Satan is a Christian construct, witches maintain that Old Nick resides entirely outside their belief system. In fact, witches continually labor to distance themselves from Satanists and Satanism.[78,79,80] Melton notes that witches perceive themselves as an alternative faith, commenting that, in his view, witchcraft constitutes a religion in that it offers a discrete world-view, circumscribes a relationship between humankind and a deity (although witches are polytheistic), and defines ethical codes.[81] Witches learn and refine their craft through maintenance of two essential books: a book of shadows, or grimoire, a diary of spells and magical procedures one has practiced; the other, a book of traditional rituals, usually copied by hand.

Most witches meet in covens; *esbats* are coven meetings to undertake coven business. Eight times a year celebratory events occur—the *sabbats,* or festivals: October 31, Halloween, the Celtic Samhain; February 2, Candelmas, or the Celtic Oimelc; April 30, or May Eve, the Celtic Beltane; August 1, or August Eve, the Celtic Lammas; and the lesser sabbats, the two solstices and the two equinoxes. During Wiccan ceremonies, covens gather around a circle; the circle offers protection and furthers concentration so that "magick" may be done. Ritual artifacts include an *athame,* or knife; a pentacle; a chalice; and a sword. Cult cops, frequently unable to understand the symbolic nature of the artifacts, see the athame as a lethal weapon *in potentia;* to witches, however, the athame only represents the male force in nature. Melton finds that witchcraft ceremonies evoke a poetic feeling in their mystical reverence of nature, ceremonies that, unsurprisingly, normally involve "psychic healing" and solving members' problems.[82]

The prime credo of witches is the Wiccan Rede: "An it harm none, do as you will" (similar to Crowley's in the *Book of the Law*). The Principles of Wiccan Belief, adopted in 1974 by the Council of American Witches, includes the following statements:

1. We practice rites to attune ourselves with the natural rhythm of life forces. . . .

2. . . . We seek to live in harmony with Nature, in ecological balance offering fulfillment to life and consciousness within an evolutionary concept.

3. We acknowledge a depth of power far greater than is apparent to the average person. Because it is far greater than ordinary, it is sometimes called "supernatural," but we see it as lying within that which is natually potential to all.

4. We conceive of the Creative Power in the Universe as manifesting through polarity—as masculine and feminine—and that this same Creative Power lives in all people. . . . We value sexuality as pleasure, as the symbol and embodiment of Life, and as one of the sources of energies used in magical practice and religious worship.

5. We recognize both outer worlds and inner, or psychological worlds . . . and we see in the interaction of these . . . dimensions the basis for paranormal phenomena and magical excercises. . . .

6. We do not recognize any authoritarian hierarchy, but do honor those who teach. . . .

7. We see religion, magick, and wisdom-in-living as being united. . . .

8. Calling oneself "Witch" does not make a Witch. . . . A Witch seeks to control the forces within him/herself that make life possible in order to live wisely and well, without harm to others, and in harmony with Nature.

9. We acknowledge that it is the affirmation and fulfillment of life . . . that gives meaning to the Universe we know. . . .

10. Our only animosity toward Christianity, or toward any other religion . . . is to the extent that its institutions have claimed to be 'the one true right and only way' and have sought to deny freedom to others and to suppress other ways of religious practices and belief.

11. As American Witches, we are not threatened by debates on the history of the Craft. . . .

12. We do not accept the concept of 'absolute evil,' nor do we worship any entity known as 'Satan' or 'the Devil' as defined by Christian Tradition. We do not seek power through the suffering of others, nor do we accept the concept that personal benefits can only be derived by denial to another.

13. We seek within Nature for that which is contributory to our health and well-being.[83]

The hallmark of modern witchcraft and neopaganism is eclecticism, a point overlooked by cult cops, who, if they differentiate among witches at all, simply divide them into practioners of white, black, and gray magic. Anthropologist T. M. Lurhmann, in her study of English witches, observed that "modern magic is a mixture of many different activities and ideas: paganism, astrology, mysticism, the range of alternative therapies, even Kabbalism—a Jewish mysticism grafted onto Christian magical practice in the Renaissance."[84] To Luhrmann, practitioners of modern witchcraft display two primary characteristics:

> First, they tolerate a surprising spiritual diversity. Central to the ethos is the notion that any path to a religion is a path to a spiritual reality, and whatever symbols and images one chooses are valid. Groups and their practices are creative, syncretic, and their rites often an amalgam of Egyptian headdress, Celtic innovation, and Greek imagery. The only dogma . . . is that there is no dogma. . . .
> Second, they practice what they call magic.[85]

At best, I can offer no firm definitions of what constitutes witches' beliefs, nor the beliefs of any other religion. In fact, thus far I have used the terms *witch* and *Wicca* interchangeably. The terms can be used safely as synonyms: practitioners of Wicca cite the term as deriving from the Anglo Saxon *wicce* which means "to turn, bend, or twist," or "a magickal shaper of reality," according to *Green Egg*.[86] Both witches and Wiccans form a subset of neopaganism. Melton distinguishes the neopagans from witches in terms of degree of emphasis: pagans may be slightly more oriented to nature than witches. Melton defines paganism as "a common reverence for the earth and nature as the prime focus of religious orientation."[87]

Sociologist Marcello Truzzi views modern witches as occultists, probably agreeing with Luhrmann's view that their philosophies show eclecticism. Truzzi finds that "occultism is broadly multidimensional and does not necessarily include magical elements nor need its concerns center about the supernatural."[88] Viewing witches in the broadest context, Truzzi finds that "the major concern of occultists is simply with the unknown, especially knowledge of that unknown to science."[89] Truzzi has developed a three-level model of occult groups, placing witches, and Satanists for that matter, in the third level: belief systems occupying this stratum offer metaphysical explanations for the place of human beings in the scheme of nature, using unfalsifiable (pseudoscientific) criteria to support their beliefs (rather like any other belief). Many witches, for example, cite their magick not as anti-scientific but as *extra*scientific, or at least not within the purview of empirical study. Mindful of emic-etic distinctions, Truzzi notes that modern witchcraft has acquired definition through external labeling, that is, through people designated witches by others. The external labeling, combined with modern witches' claims for a historical link with pre-Christian pagans, in Truzzi's view leads to "serious questions . . . about the theoretical value of the analytic construct *witchcraft* in light of its great cultural variations."[90] Truzzi, in fact, argues against the historical antecedents of modern witchcraft as is claimed in the writings of Gerald Gardner, widely credited for shaping the model of modern Wiccan belief. Both his 1954 book, *Witchcraft Today,* and Margaret Murray's 1921 study, *The Witch Cult in Western Europe,* offer the view that modern witchcraft is derivative of a pre-Christian model, but these views are commonly disparaged by modern historians.

In contravention of the police cult-model, which places abusive, charismatic leaders in charge of zombified people who are directed to commit crimes, Truzzi finds that covens are not headed by charismatic leaders; that most witches practice their craft alone; that organized witches number rather few, with an estimated 300 covens throughout the United States (in the early 1970s); that witches don't even recruit members.[91] In groping for a typology to distinguish Alexandrian witches from Gardnerian ones, Murrayite witches from drug-culture ones, Truzzi concludes: "We see that both analytically and empirically, witchcraft is a highly multidimensional form of occultism and generalization is most difficult." He cautions that "much more research is needed into the basic ethnography of these groups before fruitful generalizations can be stated."[92]

Luhrmann's study of British witches aims in large part to describe and explicate how "ordinary, well-educated, usually middle-class people" come to believe in magic, to accept the notion that under certain circumstances, with proper training, people can alter the physical landscape through magic.[93] Making observations similar to Truzzi's about witches' groups, she adds an observation about the people who become witches. As cult cops claim that witches and other nonconformist groups must be placed under surveillance because of the likelihood of their attracting sociopaths and criminals, Luhrmann points out that "magical practice does attract the mentally unstable, but the process of selection—the extensive social interaction, the lengthy correspondence course—means that relatively few of them are accepted."[94] (Unlike Truzzi's American findings, Luhrmann found British— that is, English—witches are quite sociable and given to forming groups of practitioners).

Cult cops imply that people on society's fringe may feel the greatest attraction to magic because it represents the shortest path to a selfish end: manipulating the universe to get what one wants. Since magic, which cult cops consider to be sophisticated self-deception, represents the means to material ends, then covens by definition must be shelters for deadbeats. But those who have undertaken ethnographic studies of witches find a much different story. Since Luhrmann examined how scientifically and rationally molded people can believe in magic (she doesn't employ the "k"), her conclusion soars beyond the parochial gropings of cult cops:

> So magical practice turns on the assumption that the ability to control the physical world arises through disciplined religious apprenticeship in which experiential, image-bound self-knowledge confers that power. This knowledge is not a body of objective facts but a process of understanding, a way of knowing. . . .
>
> Magic is an esoteric mystery rather than an instrumental science and symbolism is its religious heart.[95]

And even if criminal-minded people maintain the discipline to study the craft of magic and can pass muster at a coven esbat, what do weirdos learn through apprenticeship in magic?

> Esoteric knowledge makes the important uncertainties (like when one dies) inconsequential by mastering (or trying to master) our apparently irrational responses to them. As one [magic] manual says, "the objective of all these practices is to get YOU in total control of your SELF." And perhaps not surprisingly, the practices work. That is, they provide, to some extent, a greater sense of self-control and personal competence.[96]

Cult cops have displayed ambivalence about the practice of magic. On the one hand, they dismiss it as hocus-pocus, an attribute of immaturity, a harmless drudge not to be taken seriously. On the other hand, cult cops suspect that magic bears some inherent efficacy, just as reading occult books releases Pandoran demons. Investigator Bill Lightfoot tells officers that black witches (who practice magic for evil purposes) and white witches (who practice it for good) nevertheless practice the same magic, so beware when self professed white witches offer to help the police (Ritual crime in-service seminar, Petersburg, Va., September 13, 1988). But under the most rudimentary comparison between cult cops' claims about neopagans and witches' views of their own beliefs, the cult cop model can be dismissed as mere dross.

Margot Adler, journalist and self-proclaimed witch, wrote the first survey of the neopagans' view of themselves, their beliefs, and the practice of the craft in *Drawing Down the Moon*.[97] Where Luhrmann and Truzzi found difficulty in precisely fixing neopagan beliefs and values in an emic scheme, Adler makes the process of classification and description even more difficult: "The Pagan vision is one which says that neither doctrine nor dogma nor asceticism nor rule by masters is necessary for the visionary experience, and that ecstasy *and* freedom are both possible."[98] Not only are the charismatic, manipulative, mind-control leaders of neopagans extremely rare, if they exist at all, but their role has been rendered unnecessary anyway because magical beliefs are arrived at through personal experience and epiphany. And one cannot delimit neopaganism or witchcraft as religious beliefs: "This *religious* movement of people who often call themselves Pagans, Neo-Pagans, and Witches is only partly an 'occult' phenomenon. Often it is interwoven with the visionary and artistic tradition, the ecology movement, the feminist movement, and the libertarian tradition."[99]

Of course police officers themselves do not arise from any such tradition or movement; police officers generally espouse no such beliefs. The notion of magic lies outside officers' framework of beliefs, their understanding of causality; magic contradicts officers' scheme of how society operates, a scheme usually expressed in Darwinian terms saddled with pop-corporate-speak. For example, criminal conspiracies, particularly those involving drugs, are business deals that exploit the stupid, the powerless, and the ignorant, as police officers might put it. Deals are made, money exchanges hands, deadbeats get rich through sordid means roughly analogous to how legitimate big business operates: officers, like many citizens, suspect billionaires of having achieved wealth and position at others' expense. Such a world relegates myth to fairy tales, culture to women's clubs, and magic to nursery fantasies. Adler, in evoking the emics of neopaganism, says that most people define magic "*as superstition or belief in the supernatural* [her emphasis]. In contrast, most magicians, Witches, and other magical practitioners do not believe that magic has anything to do with the supernatural."[100]

Cult cops, through their seminars, cannot progress beyond inchoate ramblings about the paraphernalia and symbolism of neopagans, witches in particular, to construct definitions; definition-building implies a legerdemain of thought that must be learned. Social-science disciplines, of course, strive to teach how to compare, to differentiate, to classify, to subject hypotheses to testing, and to produce paradigms that in turn fuel working hypotheses requiring further testing. Definitions of beliefs *only* serve epistemological purposes within the jargon peculiar to a given discipline. Universally understood or accepted definitions of religious beliefs simply don't exist. Since cult cops receive no training and have no experience in the construction of theoretical models, they ignore definitions altogether and parley what is visible: symbols and paraphernalia. "Most popular talk about Witchcraft is about trappings," observes Adler.[101] She continues: "This misleads and mystifies. Our society teaches us to regard objects as the essentials. Thus we are apt to focus on ritual daggers and spells and strange herbs and all the paraphernalia of modern Wicca, thinking that these *are* the Craft." What cult cops cannot comprehend is that witchcraft, according to its modern practitioners, is a way of knowing, a way of perceiving one's relationship with a natural world, transforming it from a ball of polluted dirt to an equal partner in life's experiences. Redefining one's relationship with the planet takes on mythological proportions, and as Joseph Campbell has taken many volumes to convince us, myth is metaphor. Adler writes:

> What little we know of the Mysteries seems to indicate that [neopagan rites] emphasized . . . *experience* as opposed to *dogma,* and *metaphor* and *myth* as opposed to *doctrine.* Both the Mysteries and the Craft emphasize initiatory *processes* that lead to a widening of perception. Neither emphasizes theology, belief, or the written word. In both, participants expect to lead normal lives *in* the world, as well as attain spiritual enrichment.[102]

Anthropologist Max Warwick has enlarged the grouping of phenomena under the label "witchcraft." He finds that witchcraft, as most of us refer to the term, has links to changes in European life and culture during the various witch panics, coupled with millenarian movements.[103] Through anthropological language, he seeks the larger social dimension of the role played by witches. Historically, the accusation of being a witch "graphically summon[ed] up all forms of deviance," the very accusation itself "throw[ing] into sharper relief the positive moral precepts of the society to which the accused person belongs."[104] He sums up the various sociological lines of thinking about witches, the panics and accusations, either as an index of social tension; as concerned with cognition or the analysis of witchcraft belief systems as logical constructs (in emic terms); or witchcraft as the Freudian projection of fears and horrors onto accepted collective fantasies. Two much-cited classical anthropological works on witches, E. E. Evans-Pritchard's *Witchcraft, Oracles and Magic Among the Azande* and Clyde Kluckhohn's *Navaho Witchcraft,*[105, 106] don't question the existence or legitimacy of witches: witches do exist in non-European cultures. More important, witches do not exist in a social vacuum but serve social purposes, even as scapegoats, the traditional role they have occupied in European history, although not necessarily in other cultures. For that matter, the term *witches* in Evans-Pritchard's and Kluckhohn's works bears little comparison with the European variety (which is used as a convenient English-language referent).

Cult cops have not differentiated neopagans and Wiccans from those occupying the status of "witches" in other cultures, a distinction important for law enforcers in a country that prides itself on cultural pluralism. Immigrants, particularly from non-Christian cultures, have brought with them a panoply of beliefs that includes agents of the supernatural, witches, and sorcerers. In Kluckhohn's study of the Navahos, witchcraft, which occupies a particulary minatory role, "is obviously a means of attaining wealth, gaining women, disposing of women, and 'being mean.' In short, witchcraft is a potential avenue to supernatural power."[107] Rather than representing witches as the forbidden, the perverse, the heretical, Navahos perceive them as occupying a social niche. Kluckhohn discusses the *adaptive functions* of witchcraft (and, hence, its social necessity) as "providing a socially recognized channel for the expression . . . of the culturally disallowed."[108] In particular, the

> principal manifest "function" is that witchcraft lore affirms solidarity by dramatically defining what is bad: namely, all secret and malevolent activities against the health, property and lives of fellow tribesmen. This sanction is reinforced by attributing to witches all the stigmata of evil: incest, nakedness and other kinds of forbidden knowledge and act.[109]

As Kluckhohn points out, though, we shouldn't mislead ourselves into perceiving Navaho witchcraft as analogous with our European concept; Navahos don't even have a word that translates as "witch." And while they reify witches as something worth fearing, that very fear produces social control by deterring misbehavior that might otherwise occur. Clearly, though, the language of ethnographic inquiry about witches does not even begin to overlap with the language of cult seminars. Yet the language of anthropology betokens a depth of cross-cultural insight certainly missing from the seminars. That missing insight produces racist generalizations, as we shall see with Afro-Cuban and Native American beliefs. And although we have an abundant scholarly literature about non-European witches in their native context, we know comparatively little about ethnic minorities in the urban United States and the manifestation of their beliefs here. Anthropologist Phillips Stevens, Jr., has written, "for recent migrants and others who are not well integrated into urban social networks, witchcraft beliefs can have unfortunate implications."[110] And despite such beliefs surfacing into public view, they "receive little sympathetic attention by academic, clinical, judicial, theological, or popular agencies."[111] In fact, Stevens points out that such beliefs should not be relegated to the occult bin, as some fringe preoccupation with the unprovable and unknowable, but rather represent social problems. The stress of urban life guarantees that immigrants' beliefs must reckon sooner or later with judicial, economic, and educational institutions. In fact, the law-enforcement interest in Afro-Cuban beliefs may indirectly reflect their relatively recent emergence in United States society.

Non-Christian Beliefs

To suggest that ethnic-minority immigrants may be committing human sacrifice in the United States, Patricia Pulling distributed at one of her seminars a newspaper article about Liberian human sacrifice.[112] A mortician in Harper City, Liberia, had arranged for the killing of two boys as part of *juju* magic to ensure his winning a mayoral election. Those convicted of the murder and its associated criminal conspiracy included a Methodist preacher, a former judge, and a former prosecutor. Most of the Liberians quoted shamefully admitted the endurance of *juju* as the nation, a Christian one, tries to modernize itself. The judge who condemned the guilty to death called the boys' murder "wicked, barbaric and satanic."[113] The prosecutor in the case added: "As long as Satan is on Earth, I don't care what education you have, these practices will continue. It is impossible to eradicate such practices in the absence of the second coming of Jesus Christ."[114] Of course reading between the lines of indignant Western-minded Christian officials, one detects a deep cultural conflict which Pulling would dismiss as irrelevant, asserting that human sacrifices also happen in the United States; yet the article does not assert a satanic or cult motivation for the killings.

Anthropologist Jane Martin, quoted in Harden's article, said of a farmer's murder of his own son, "There is an extremely elaborate cosmological system in that area. It is very hard for outsiders to understand. . . . It is a part of the world where it is hard to separate mythology from reality."[115] Along with anthropologist Jeannette Carter, Martin pointed out that the death of any young person is never considered accidental in Maryland County, the region of Liberia where the murders had taken place. Such deaths are attributed to the envy or hatred of others. Both anthropologists were unsure why Harper City should witness human deaths in furtherance of *juju* despite the large number of Africans who follow the belief but do *not* get involved in murder. They speculated that an answer might reside in the cultural conflict between indigenous Africans in Liberia and the descendants of resettled freed American slaves. Martin thinks that rivalries between the two groups translate into competition for power, the *juju* becoming a significant ingredient in obtaining power. Along the same line, anthropologist Geoffrey Parrinder has found that ritual killing in Africa serves mainly political ends.[116]

Months later another "ritual murder" occurred in Liberia, that of a police officer. This time, the culprits included the country's defense minister whose first-degree-murder charge included the accusation of indulging in "ritual intended to promote his own selfish and greedy desire."[117] In this case, the *juju* explicitly served political ends: the defense minister intended the dead policeman's body parts to form part of "harsh medicine" to achieve the overthrow of Liberia's president, Samuel K. Doe. Although the Liberian cases have gone to trial and resulted in convictions of well-known citizens, many *juju* human-sacrifice stories remain unconfirmed and anecdotal.

Nevertheless, as the Liberian examples show, human sacrifice occurs, albeit rarely. But the importance of it comes from its consideration within a cultural and political context. That sacrifices of people have occurred in Liberia, and that *juju*-susceptible people from Africa have emigrated to the United States does *not* imply that similar murders occur here with frequency, if at all. For Pulling to even cite Liberian "ritual" murders as evidence of satanic influence on American kids is dishonest at best and betrays her lack of any critical analysis of purported evidence. After all, *juju* practitioners don't ackowledge Satan, don't design and market Dungeons & Dragons, and don't hold sex-and-drug parties for teens. So what does citing *juju* deaths prove for American law enforcement?

The citation of Liberian deaths described as "ritualistic" betrays the racism of associating murderous acts with various beliefs (as we have examined with the Matamoros killings in Chapter 2). The semantic trigger for implying the causal link between a non-Christian belief and a criminal practice is the word *ritualistic*. Newspapers use the word to precede *murder* or *crime* to imply that some hollow-eyed criminal, with a mind numb with religious fanaticism, committed the heinous act, driven to it by the compulsion of his belief. The FBI's Kenneth Lanning rails against the cavalier use of *ritualistic* because people forget that ritual governs our lives in benign fashion:

> During law enforcement training conferences on [ritualistic crime], ritualistic almost always comes to mean satanic or at least spiritual. Ritual can refer to a prescribed religious ceremony, but in its broader meaning refers to any customarily repeated act or series of acts. The need to repeat these acts can be cultural, sexual, or psychological as well as spiritual.[118]

Yet the word *ritualistic* inevitably appears in the context of describing ethnic religious practices foreign to mainstream Christianity. And the American press has been too willing to link "ritualistic" activities in furtherance of religious beliefs to crime. The Matamoros murders spurred several graduate students and faculty at Cornell University to write to the *New York Times:*

> Most newscasters have linked [the murders] to the Afro-Caribbean religions of Voudoun, Santeria and Palo Mayombe, analyzing the murderers' "cult" or so-called ritual practices as hypothetical human sacrifice. We, as anthropologists, . . . urge the news media and the public to bring extreme caution to analyses of religious motives for criminal activity. . . .
>
> Human sacrifice has no place in Voudoun, Santeria and Palo Mayombe. So far as we know, no specialists in Afro-Caribbean cultures or religions have been consulted in reaching the hypothesis that the murders are tied . . . to Afro-Caribbean religious beliefs and practices. . . .
>
> Whatever the religious practices of the murderers might be, their crimes are no more attributable to any particular religious system than are those of criminals whose religious affiliations are more familiar to the American mainstream.[119]

Hints of non-Christian rites easily fuse with the satanic in news articles, displaying a chronic inattention to definitions and distinctions. An odd finding in a largely lower-class black section of Richmond, Virginia, indicated the possible appearance of voodoo or hoodoo: a dental student chanced upon a burned box that apparently contained a jar with hundreds of human teeth (identified as such by the student), two tins of cheap jewelry, all atop a cardboard box, which the journalist described as "a makeshift altar," the artifacts constituting "the scene of a ritual."[120] The police duly investigated the scene, likewise pronouncing it ritualistic. But the journalist's conclusion implies a connection between the apparently innocuous find (which anthropologist Rafael Martinez in Miami speculated was hoodoo, the fact of its being burned reflecting a practitioner's abandonment of magic) and Satanism or witchcraft:

> Police sources say they are unaware of any practicing voodoo cults in the area, but that there is a coven operating within three blocks of the site.[121]

"Police sources" neglected to point out the connection between the "coven" and the "altar."

I have earlier suggested that Americans' intolerance of racial or ethnic pluralism might be increasing, as evidenced by the alacrity with which unconventional beliefs are tagged as "cultic" or "satanic," implying criminal and inhuman propensities. White Christian citizens seem to be faced with unfamiliar cultural goings-on, particularly in communities with growing populations of immigrants. Even the federal government every so many years takes a shot at the unconventional. For example, the government has waged an on-again, off-again battle with the Native American Church (NAC) because it uses peyote buttons, hallucinogens derived from the mescal cactus, as "sacraments."[122] In 1984, the police arrested Jack Warner, a resident of a reservation in North Dakota, for distributing peyote. In fact, the peyote, valued at $1,000, had been obtained from a licensed dealer by an NAC representative. Further, Warner had been arrested not for selling it but for *giving* it to an acquaintance for use in a healing ceremony. After the arrest, the federal attorney in the case announced that Warner and his wife had been "drug pushing" and that the investigation involved the seizure of peyote "with a street value of over $50,000."[123]

Peyote use in NAC ceremonies diffused from northern Mexico in the nineteenth century and eventually was absorbed into Native American rites. From its first appearance, the government has opposed its use as inimical to the "civilizing process." When peyote use came under the aegis of religious practice through an organized church, practitioners obtained First Amendment protection. So why were the Warners arrested? Jack Warner was white, his wife Hispanic. The government contended that only NAC members who are Native Americans may enjoy the protected use of peyote, whereas other races, even if they are NAC converts (as were the Warners), are liable to prosecution. The government contended, among other things, that "the Warners' religious use of peyote [was likened] to child sacrifices committed in the name of God."[124] As for the argument that non-Native Americans may not legally participate in NAC ceremonies, one defense lawyer noted that the "government's position was akin to arguing [that] one must be Hasidic to be a member of the Jewish faith, or Greek to be a member of the Greek Orthodox Church."[125] In the trial, the jury unanimously found the Warners innocent and even offered comments to the court "to let the government know we thought they had no business prosecuting these people for their religious beliefs," according to the foreman.

The government chose the peyote issue to promote a crackdown on drug trafficking. The government creates criminal demons—such as drug traffickers whose crimes metamorphose into holocausts—to gain political advantage and social control. Governments manipulate public sentiment by creating enemies or adversaries: in Chapter 1, I referred to the federal purges of communists in the late 1940s and early 1950s; in Chapter 7 I describe more current government myth-making about criminality and suggest that the satanic scare may rise to the level of federal interest. Such interest raises the danger of persecution of nonconformists and ethnic religious beliefs not recognized as "legitimate" by practitioners of institutionalized beliefs.

Some beliefs strikingly different from Christian ones have maintained themselves in secret in conservative white communities, whereas in other parts of the United States practitioners of such beliefs (those who dispense advice, counseling, or medicine) have negotiated at least mutual tolerance with established therapies and medical practices of white Americans. For example, Hispanic communities in the United States host native curers, or *curanderos,* largely known for offering folk remedies to community members afflicted with physiological or psychosomatic ailments. In Mora, New Mexico, for example, Gabriela Pino, a *curandera,* runs her own office, "decorated with scores of pictures of Jesus Christ and the Virgin Mary," in a community where she delivered one-third of all babies.[126] But despite widespread community acceptance and a congenial working relationship with some local "established" physicians, the 83-year-old Pino still feels stung by the label "witch." "The word frightens me," she admitted.[127] Perhaps unlike many witches, Pino claims that she received her calling from God, a divine gift. But to cult cops, *curanderismo* may appear indistinguishable from *brujeria,* conventionally defined as witchcraft. Both the *curandero* and the *brujo* (or *curandera* and *bruja*) create discomfort for cult cops because they have no parallel in white society: after all, we insist that counselors, therapists, and physicians ply their skills after professional scrutiny through licensing, which follows a period of specialized training and apprenticeship. To cult cops, *curanderos* and *brujos* are charlatans who obtain money for services they can't perform. Certainly, folk healers receive no licensing, no governmental regulation, and some deceive or obtain money fraudulently. Yet most of them obtain credibility through lifelong association with neighbors and their communities. What cult cops must accept is a community's perception of the efficacy of *curanderismo,* and they must recognize the social standing of *curanderos* as people of great influence. Perhaps half of all Hispanics in the southwest United States have consulted *curanderos,* the motivation to do so perhaps borne of poverty in many cases. Fernando M. Trevino, a professor at the University of Texas Medical Branch at Galveston, observed that perhaps one-fourth of all Hispanics (of an estimated 20 million in the United States) lack health insurance, so some Hispanics may never see a licensed physician. "For some of these people, it's alternative health care or no care at all."[128]

In many Hispanic and Native American communities, people acknowledge a supernatural realm manipulated by witches or sorcerers. The role of the supernatural cannot be confined to a very limited slice of a person's life, self-identify, feeling of self-sufficiency, or dependency. For example, a man who seeks the advice of a *curandero* may complain of a stomach ailment while acknowledging that a woman who claims that he cheated her paid a witch to place a hex on him. The man with the stomach problem might believe that the hex will produce his own death by slow degeneration of his bodily functions. So the *curandero* must offer advice on many levels: he must consider perhaps an herbal remedy to immediately ameliorate the stomach problem; discuss the cheating incident and offer a negotiated remedy to the woman's anger; and devise a magical solution to the hex without evoking another feud with the witch. The medical problem—possibly a psychosomatic one—links with a criminal problem as well. Does the woman have a criminal design? After all, she wished the man dead and in effect conspired with the witch to employ the proper means to make the man suffer to death. If the woman and the man both believe in the power of the associated hex rituals, are the elements of a crime present? Law enforcers don't have to answer this question, for rarely do citizens in ethnic enclaves even call the police for help in such matters.

Yet cult cops have tried to isolate *curanderos* and *brujos* from their cultural context and advertise them as dangerous sorcerers to be ferreted out. But the only example of such malevolence they can cite has been Adolfo de Jesus Constanzo, a probable psychopath who employed the trappings of *brujeria* to satisfy his own murderous ends. But cult cops have focused on the wrong issue; for the criminal-justice system, all practitioners (probation workers, police, judges, prosecutors, public defenders) need to look for a common ground within which to match formal criminal law (with its reliance on *mens rea,* or criminal states of mind combined with proscribed acts) with informal but no less binding notions of criminal cause and effect held by Native Americans, Hispanics, and other immigrants.

Recent immigrants from the Caribbean and disaffected black Americans have shown strong interest in Yoruba and allied beliefs (e.g., voodoo). Such beliefs not only involve folk healers but also disclaim Christian ideology, relying on ecstatic spiritual experiences (through dance and entering trances) and the sacrifice of animals. Cult cops frequently assume a priori that animal sacrifices smack of the occult, and they quickly label as cults such beliefs as Santeria and voodoo. Indeed, immigrants who sacrifice goats and chickens have run afoul of animal shelters and citizens' groups dedicated to ending cruelty to animals, most notably in large cities like Miami. That compromises must now take place between immigrant practitioners and their white Christian neighbors, that Afro-Cuban beliefs are no longer practiced sub rosa in some cities simply adumbrates a law-enforcement problem to come. Law enforcers will have to recognize new patterns of victimization among non-English-speaking immigrants and adjust community-relations and crime-prevention programs accordingly. Officers must adapt some of their methods to new citizens' views of crime and criminality, an argument that has been made, in fact, by criminal-justice scholars and practitioners since the race riots of the late 1960s, which spawned "community team policing" in the 1970s and its progeny, "community-oriented policing" in the 1980s.

For example, Yoruba has gained a firm hold in largely black, low-income sections of Richmond, Virginia, a city known for its predominant white conservatism. And according to Cecelia McDaniel Brown, who has taught about Yoruba at the University of South Carolina–Spartanburg, Yoruba worshipers have been "increasing geometrically."[129] The number of adherents in the United States has grown from an estimated 80,000 to 100,000 a decade ago to between 500,000 and 2 million today.[130] In a pellucid exploration of Yoruba beliefs and practitioners for a newspaper known for ultraconservatism, journalist Rex Springston broke new ground in Richmond by focusing attention on Yoruba as legitimate in its own right. Not surprisingly, he noted that "Yoruba practices in the Richmond area may help to account for persistent rumors of Satanic cults operating here. Yoruba believers . . . have traditionally been branded as Satanists by many Christian outsiders. And people who come across butchered animals in cemeteries or trash bins are often quick to think they've found the devil's work."[131] In extending a discussion of animal sacrifices to other African-derived beliefs, such as Santeria, Springston quoted a Santerian priest who responded sympathetically to police ignorance:

"It's a culture shock. . . . What happens is that the officer gets a call (of loud noise) and he knocks on the door and he knows nothing of the [Santeria] procedures, and he sees some guy dressed in white with a knife in his hand and blood on his pants. He's going to put everyone's hands up on the wall."[132]

In Chapter 1, I mentioned an incident in Tupelo, Mississippi, in which two men were jailed for conspiracy to murder a judge with a "death spell spun by a hoodoo priest in Jamaica using a faded photograph and a lock of His Honor's hair."[133] Criminal-justice officials have not made light of the case, oddly conferring magical potency on the Jamaican hoodoo priest's charm: "At first you want to laugh and make jokes, but then you think, well, the Devil does have many powers. . . . The judge's life might have been imperiled," said his secretary.[134] The local Baptist minister added: "There's a malevolent quality to this affair. Any cult that is organized for the purpose of doing evil I must regard as satanic."

University of Mississippi anthropologist William Ferris, commenting on the case, said he believes that the incidence of belief in hoodoo has increased over the past decade, particularly among the poor and illiterate. He even cited the case of a deputy sheriff on trial for several felonies, who, to intimidate jurors, had hoodoo powder strewn over the doorway to the court and successfully kept some jurors away. While the prosecutors in the case maintain that the efficacy of the hex is immaterial because only the criminal conspiracy is important, other Mississippians have been forced to confront the extent of their own beliefs not only in voodoo, hoodoo, and other variants, but about criminal causality.

Do hexes have a place in conventional American concepts of criminality? The Tupelo case presents possibilities that could easily arise with *curanderismo* or *brujeria*. Obviously, law enforcers trying to make sense of this might simply label the belief itself as criminal or at least potentially criminal. The problem of *potential* has proved significant in cult seminars. As I have noted with Wicca and Satanism, cult cops warn their fellow officers about beliefs because of the *potential* such beliefs hold of attracting criminals or people who *might* absorb criminal ideas by virtue of their spiritual beliefs.

Santeria and Palo Mayombe

Santeria and allied beliefs, such as Palo Mayombe, receive strong criminal identification at cult seminars and in the press, Matamoros notwithstanding. Law-enforcement authorities in Washington, D.C., and Miami "have linked Santeria worshipers to criminal activity, particularly drug trafficking. The criminals—many of them apparently Cuban convicts who came to the U.S. in the 1980 Mariel boat lift—pray for protection from the police and rival gangs."[135]

A California guide to occult crime for law enforcers offered the following:

> The occult groups law enforcers target as most prone to possible criminal involvement are Santeria, Palo Mayombe and Satanism. This does not mean these groups actually are involved in criminal activity, but rather that some evidence exists to link them to certain activities.[136]

Very simply, however, nothing in Santeria or Palo Mayombe instructs believers to commit crimes. What law enforcers have seen, on the other hand, includes increasingly successful international networks of drug trafficking, most based in Central or South America. Adherents of Santeria are not "most prone to possible criminal involvement"; on the contrary, many Central and South American drug traffickers bring their ethnicity to the crime. Some drug traffickers happen to practice Santeria, an elementary point that seems hopelessly elusive to cult cops. Should we say that in police-training seminars about organized crime, the Catholicism of *mafiosi* ought to be emphasized as a religion with criminal links?

The widespread interest in Santeria among Hispanics may indeed portend an upsurge in the number of adherents, just as some scholars have seen with Yoruba and an interest in *curanderismo*. Yet no statistics exist: the participation of United States citizens in African- or pre-Columbian-derived beliefs is largely undocumented. Yet some criminal contexts have surfaced in which Santeria appears as a sideshow:

—In Culiacan, Sinaloa, Mexico, reputedly one of the most active centers of illegal drug trade in that country, citizens have erected a shrine to Jesus Malverde, a man hanged as a bandit eighty years ago.[137] Malverde, apparently, has taken on mythical dimensions as a rural Robin Hood who dispensed the fruits of robbery to the peasantry. Mexicans leave money at the shrine in return for miracles; but as the drug trade has prospered, traffickers have begun to venerate Malverde as a saint. A local university literature professor observed, "But if you go to the shrine at night, you will see these guys in cowboy hats, full of jewelry, gold chains and fancy watches, pulling up in their big cars with the smoked glass windows."[138] While the shrine's caretaker maintains that "Malverde is not the patron saint of the narcos," he acknowledges that "Malverde protects all of humanity." But why Malverde? Apparently, in his renegade days during the last century, he gained a reputation for outwitting and eluding the police, a characteristic apparently admired by drug traffickers.

—The Colombian government confiscated an estate, called Castillo Marroquin, from a "mid-level" drug dealer named Camillo Zapata and transformed it into an army barracks.[139] The hillside mansion contained a chapel with stained-glass windows, a large carport with two Mercedes automobiles, a satellite dish, a sauna, an indoor swimming pool, topiary gardens, and a tennis court. But one room contained artifacts of Santeria: "Inside the Zapatas' shrine, bowls of fruit and eggs were arrayed as offerings before portraits of the saints."

—In the sideshow of sideshows, the U.S. military raid on Panama in December 1989, which netted President Antonio Noriega, yielded *el presidente's* "*brujeria* room" at his residence with a treasure in odd artifacts explicated for the American public by none other than the Army's "specialist on cults and deviant movements," Special Agent James L. Dibble.[140] If the Army can be believed, Noriega practiced everything from voodoo to Palo Mayombe, *brujeria,* and Santeria. Dibble's prize find was the "name of investigative journalist Seymour Hersh, who has written in the *New York Times* on Noriega's involvement in drug trafficking . . . written on a piece of paper inside a rotten tamale."[141] At last account, Dibble was hot on the trail of Rosileide dos Gracias Oliveira, a "Brazilian witch" who cohabited with Noriega, and who left behind her grimoire, a woman who may have helped Noriega with his "diabolical spells," according to Dibble.[142]

Several scholarly books outline the practices of Palo Mayombe and Santeria, most notably works by Migene Gonzalez-Wippler and Joseph Murphy.[143] But rather than discuss Santeria in detail, I shall limit my comments to the contribution of cross-cultural misunderstandings to cult-cop hysteria. The examples above show no links between Santeria and criminal behavior.

The cultural landscape often overlooked by North Americans, however, involves drug trafficking, seen not as an illegal enterprise by those who participate in it but more as a way of life open to the powerless. The cultural context of drug trafficking in countries much picked over by North American and European industrial interests is dismissed by those same interests. After all, some say, economic exploitation isn't responsible for drug dealing. But, in the face of political failure—the most persistent Latin American political issue has been land reform, or redistribution of land to *campesinos*—drug trafficking has proved one of the most lucrative stimuli to economic independence. Certainly, then, practitioners of Santeria, like many others, especially Roman Catholic *latinoamericanos,* have willingly pursued an escape from poverty through narcotics. Santeria has proved to be the "religion of choice" of drug dealers, claims Dale Griffis (Advanced ritualistic crime seminar, Richmond, Va., September 22, 1988). More accurately, though, drug trafficking has become the *profession* of choice by *some* practitioners of Santeria.

Cult cops encourage racism indirectly by singling out Santeria and Palo Mayombe as beliefs allied with criminality simply by isolating them from a mosaic of African-derived and indigenous pre-Christian beliefs. The Columbia University scholar George Eaton Simpson has examined not only Santeria but also about thirty related beliefs within Caribbean countries and South America and offers his own definition of *cult,* the term he extends to Santeria and like religions: a cult is "a religious protest against a system in which attention to the various individual functions of a religion has been . . . made ineffective by the extreme emphasis on social and ecclesiastical order."[144] With his view of Afro-Caribbean cults as politically derived, Simpson argues several psychological and social functions:

> Black religious cults and sects in the New World offer rewards of considerable value to their adherents, many of whom are dispossessed persons without rank or power in the societies in which they live.
>
> Religious ceremonies take believers away from the mundane affairs of life and are often exhilarating experiences. . . . A well-performed religious cult ceremony in the Caribbean or in South America provides dramatic entertainment for participants. Moreover, some believers gain "understanding" through being possessed by a deity, an ancestor, or some other spirit. . . .
>
> Taking part in the activities of a cult or sect provides emotional support for members who are forced to live in a world that they often peceive as hostile. At the same time, they compete for position within their religious group.[145]

In order to experience spirit possession or to enter a trance, characteristics not only of Santeria but also of most other Afro-Caribbean religions, one must be acculturated into the belief. "Possession behavior is culturally structured; the acts of possessed persons are so stylized that the initiated can identify the divinity possessing a devotee."[146] What Santeria and the other regional beliefs share is their syncretic nature: Nigerian Yoruba (mainly) plus Catholicism have spawned numerous deities and rites to promote health, to heal, to protect against unseen, imagined dangers, and to guide one in important, stressful decisions. Psychiatrist Mercedes Sandoval has argued that, for immigrants in the United States, Santeria has proved its anodyne qualities in reducing the stress of acculturation into this country. Such stress has been compounded by an "inability to speak English and the lack of understanding of the new power-hierarchy," not to mention the economic competition.[147]

Although cult cops prefer to reduce their claims to simple descriptions, Santeria and its related beliefs follow no firm dogma, as Simpson implied in his definition. (Afro-Caribbean cults arise partly in rebellion against the firmly delineated and impersonal cosmology of Roman Catholicism.) Investigator Bill Lightfoot of the Richmond, Virginia, Bureau of Police has compiled a guide titled "Occult Involvement by Non-Traditional Groups: Santeria and Brujeria Cults," which offers no useful description of Santeria save a very short paragraph describing the syncretism of African and Catholic beliefs, supplemented by pages of pictures of deities and their "meanings." The document implies that it can be used as a dictionary of Santerian beliefs so that officers can recognize the meanings of certain ceremonies. But Sandoval offers a different view:

> *Santeria,* characterized by its lack of homogenity, is not a religion tied to a narrow and strict orthodoxy or dogma. Each priest subjectively interprets the beliefs and frequently introduces variations in the rituals and mythology according to his own knowledge, convictions and the needs of his followers. Thus, *Santeria* is an abstraction of many different local cults which share one common denominator—the worship of the santo.[148]

The *santo,* or saint, is worshiped in the persona of *orisha* or *oricha,* the Yoruba deity. Practitioners may build personal shrines to the saints who favor them, offering even money or food. The *santero* is the priest, an important figure sought out for advice and guidance and for ritual treatment. Sandoval finds that Santeria in the United States has proved quite successful for a number of reasons. Santeria offers adherents "a closer contact with the supernatural through the always-present divination systems, and a relief from tensions through the role playing and the possession by the gods."[149] In particular, Santeria has provided psychiatric benefit:

> Field observations seem to show that Santeria had been very successful in treating psychosomatic disorders such as asthma, colitis, etc, which have experienced a sharp increase due to the tensions of the process of acculturation.[150]

Although Sandoval certainly makes no connection between Santeria and criminal behavior, she does provide some insights. Since the belief has no "ethical basis," adherents consider influencing the supernatural as their primary goal. Morality occupies a secondary consideration since

> the gods will be on your side, regardless of your moral standing, as long as you make offerings to them.
> *Santeria* is a task-oriented and present-oriented system, as task-oriented and as materialistic as American society seems to the Cuban exiles. *Santeria* also offers the believers a guilt releasing set of beliefs. . . . *Santeria* is a flexible religion, always open to and eager for new reinterpretation.[151]

And as Simpson notes, membership in *Santeria* or similar groups "compensates for lowly social positions in the larger society" of adherents.[152] The lack of a supreme Christian type of ethic doesn't damn Santeria but must be understood in a cultural and historical context of slavery and powerlessness as well as the remoteness of the deities proffered by white civilization. For U.S. immigrants, however, the practicing of Santeria has not been limited to lower classes: educated, middle-class Cuban expatriates practice it as an alternative to or in conjunction with their Catholic beliefs.

Medical examiner C. V. Wetli and anthropologist R. Martinez, both of Miami, have described the forensic aspects of Santeria, highlighting and explaining the ritual artifacts that law enforcers may be likely to encounter.[153]

They define the religion of Santeria as "a benevolent or neutral magic. The beliefs and traditions are variously interpreted by the believers, and there is no central dogma or bible. Nonetheless, certain tenets appear immutable. Among these are the syncretic depictions and the use of stones, herbs, and animal sacrifice for the rituals."[154]

Most of the forensic aspects of Santeria relate to Palo Mayombe, the Congo-derived "black magic sect of Santeria," which Wetli and Martinez describe:

> It is known as *palo mayombe* and its practitioners are called *paleros* or *mayomberos*. For personal gain or a fee, they will perform rituals to inflict mental or physical harm, or even death, on an individual. The practitioners are often locally reputed to be career criminals engaged in drug smuggling. A basic tool used by these paleros is the *nganga*—an iron cauldron filled with sacred dirt and containing human bones, blood, coins, and other items.[155]

The central question for law enforcers concerns the provenance of the human bones found in accidentally encountered *ngangas*. Of the cases cited in the article, Wetli and Martinez found that all came from either biological supply houses or, less frequently, from cemeteries. In fact, one practitioner produced for the police a receipt for a skull. Had people been killed for *nganga* bones? "Although no current instances of murder (to obtain bones or organs) have come to light, such an event may be a possibility. . . ."[156]

In another study, Wetli and Martinez focused on *brujeria,* which they broadly label "witchcraft or malevolent sorcery associated with Afro-Latin religious systems," singling out Palo Mayombe as the component of Santeria that maintains "malevolent sorcery and is invoked by criminal elements."[157] The authors are quick to note that the "black magic" nature of Palo Mayombe "should not be construed, however, to suggest that Santeria promotes malevolent or criminal activities, but that it may simply be used by such persons to promote their already established intentions."[158] The latter study offered a more detailed description and explication of police *nganga* finds, focusing once again on the use of human bones. And again, Wetli and Martinez found that the bones employed in rituals usually came either from biological supply houses, had been smuggled into the United States, or had been taken from cemeteries, but they cautioned: "Although grave robbings have been previously associated with this cult, they remain unusual events . . . in South Florida."[159]

> Despite the orientation of Palo Mayombe in malevolent sorcery, we have not encountered any deaths related to this cult in either a literal or preternatural sense. Outright homicide related to Palo Mayombe, however, was reported at the turn of the century [in a second-hand report in 1906].[160]

Despite a relationship between Palo Mayombe and Santeria, Wetli and Martinez also note that many *santeros* distance themselves from or resent an imputed affiliation. Nevertheless, both sects, if such a word can be applied, share common symbols and some ritualism. Adolfo de Jesus Constanzo may have applied elements of Palo Mayombe to his murderous drug business, but clearly the belief system allows for individualistic, personal interpretation and lacks a pronounced moral code, which thus allows its use for *any* purpose. At Matamoros, whatever Constanzo may have created in the way of rites or symbols doesn't apply to other practitioners of Palo Mayombe, nor do his actions portend similar excursions into homicide by other believers.

In summing up, obviously vast dissimilarities distinguish Santeria and neopaganism—Wicca in particular—from Satanism. I have tried to convey an emic notion of what each belief signifies to the believer: certainly the three beliefs operate in substantially different cultural contexts, ranging from therapeutic assertiveness for some white, educated, middle-class United States citizens, to an invocation of African-derived deities inherited by some Latinos from a past of slavery. Cult cops have isolated these beliefs from their cultural and historical contexts, implying as a common denominator a learned black art and dabbling in forbidden magic for selfish gain. The lure of the forbidden pathway to recruiting supernatural aid, we are to believe, attracts sociopaths and criminals. But in identifying the practice of black magic, cult cops nervously reify the magical realm of sorcery and spells as inherently dangerous stuff. Cult cops stop short of warning their fellows to remain on guard against demons called forth by others, but they seem to want to hedge their bets by assuming that *there's something out there anyway.*

By the eclecticism of their seminars, cult cops deliver racism through implication or sometimes do so explicitly. They find Satanism a priori dangerous because of its guiltless self-indulgence, presuming that criminality is sure to follow. Because many Cuban immigrants have joined the ranks of drug traffickers, as have immigrants from other Caribbean countries, the fact of their believing in Santeria and the fact of their asking *orichas* to protect their activities simply strikes cult cops as a perversion of Christianity. Cult cops rail at the self-interest: after all, *good* Christianity involves prayer for benevolent, magnanimous purposes, while Santeria involves shrines, Palo Mayombe involves macabre *ngangas,* and both involve primitive rites such as spirit possession. As George Eaton Simpson has described, Santeria nestles alongside almost thirty other beliefs involving similar ritualism, all derived from or influenced by African cultures. Yet cult cops single out Santeria, and to a lesser extent Palo Mayombe and voodoo, as the religion of criminals. Excursions into titillation—offering up examples of arcane rituals—serve no law-enforcement purpose.

If cult cops think that they are teaching something useful to their fellows, what is the result? Officers who attend the cult seminars walk away with a generalized suspicion that practitioners of Santeria, Wicca, or Satanism are up to no good, that all of these beliefs can be grouped under one label: satanic. Unlike officers in Los Angeles, Miami, and New York, those in Boise, Bismarck, or Kansas City will never find much use for their new training in Santeria, but they will learn to become suspicious when Latino immigrants come to town. And if they chance upon Wiccans casting a circle in a remote forest, the taxpayers will host surveillance, record-keeping on noncriminal activities by noncriminals, and perhaps even a frantic response by the regional police tactical team.

Chapter 4
CULT SURVIVORS AND THE "FEAR OF THINGS INVISIBLE"

And they that make little, or no enquiry into the naturall causes of things, yet from the fear that proceeds from ignorance it self. . . . are enclined to suppose . . . severall kinds of Powers Invisible; and to stand in awe of their own imaginations; and a time of distresse to invoke them; as also in the time of an expected good successe, to give them thanks; making the creatures of their own fancy, their Gods. . . . And this Feare of things invisible, is the naturall Seed of that, which every one in himself calleth Religion; and in them that worship or feare that Power otherwise than they do, Superstition.

Thomas Hobbes, Leviathan, 1651

In Chapter 2, I pointed out that cult cops offer two primary forms of evidence in the attempt to prove the existence of traditional Satanists— the clandestine international megacult allegedly responsible for human sacrifice on the scale of a holocaust: cult survivors' stories and child-abuse cases in day-care centers. Cult survivors, in fact, ascend quickly into celebritydom once they begin to "network" with other *survivors,* the term they apply to themselves. Tabloid television, through the national daytime video catharsis with Phil Donahue, Oprah Winfrey, and others emotes with survivor tales. And we receive regular titillation through nighttime televised happenings, such as Geraldo Rivera's lubricious twilight zone of alleged satanic-priests-turned-fundamentalist-Christians; cult cops solemnly pronouncing the unseen satanic murders going on in our neighborhoods; priests assuring us that the Devil does indeed lie in wait; and, of course, survivors. Discussions of child abuse in survivors' own purportedly multi-generational satanic families become daily episodes on television. Why do cult cops consider survivors important, and what have survivors contributed to the cult-crime picture?

Survivors, usually young women, once they have undergone perhaps years of therapy, sometimes announce themselves as people with a message. A woman under treatment by a Kansas City, Kansas, therapist has attested to having witnessed both animal and human sacrifices during the 1960s. But she "had been an amnesiac until about 18 months ago."[1] She participated in rituals at night, with participants burning or burying all traces of animals or humans before sunrise. One former cult survivor, Jacquie Balodis, also a talk-show regular, operates "Overcomers Victorious," a sort of witness-relocation program for cult survivors. Balodis claims to have counseled about 200 ex-cultists from the satanic underground network.[2] Like many cult cops, she posits 50,000 human sacrifices annually, unconcerned about the lack of evidence: "Bodies are never found because they are mutilated, eaten, burned or buried."[3]

"We did a lot of child sacrifice," says Balodis, explaining that her cult either kidnapped children for murder or bred them: "Her own first two children were among the victims."[4] She cautions that most therapists do not recognize the cult symptoms, that she herself underwent institution-alization three times before someone recognized her symptoms and culled the truth from her. Balodis, like most cult survivors, claims to suffer from multiple-personality disorder (MPD), a disorder officially on the books since 1980. In fact, she says she has experienced more than a hundred personalities since she left her cult in 1972.

But survivors aren't confined to the Midwest. In Richmond, Virginia, one July morning in the mid-1980s Cassandra Hoyer was alone at a friend's house and heard a knock at the door. When she answered it, two men, one with a gun, forced her to the bed and made her strip while the armed man put the gun to her head and pulled the trigger several times, revealing an empty chamber. Once she undressed, they painted her white on one side, black on the other. But Hoyer escaped, grabbing a shirt and her car keys on the way out. As she tried to start her car, a woman arose from the back seat, put a gun to Hoyer's head, and ordered her to drive to her therapist's office. When they arrived, the woman ordered Hoyer into the therapist's car, where she remained until the therapist "coaxed" her out of it, according to journalist Lisa Antonelli.[5]

Hoyer's problems didn't begin in Richmond. She spent her first 16 years in a Roman Catholic orphanage where she claims she unwillingly entered a satanic cult. The priests and nuns at the orphanage allegedly practiced Satanism, forcing the children to have sex with other kids and adults, and on holidays she was taken on trips to meet cult leaders around the country, as well as in Richmond. But Hoyer was no foot soldier in Satan's army: she had been selected to become a high priestess. At age nine, Hoyer claims, she and other child candidates for the title were strapped to and burned on crosses; only Hoyer survived. But years later, Hoyer went about her business, her cult past behind her, only to find that she had been brain-washed. Kathy Snowden, her therapist, says that cults program in members "unconscious responses which can later be reactivated by simple gestures, phrases and visual images."[6] Significantly, Snowden handled Hoyer the way other therapists have handled survivors: "Through networking with other medical professionals. . . . Snowden learned that the abuses and rituals which [Hoyer] endured were being reported by others."[7]

But in 1987, the cultists were on to Hoyer, trying to intimidate her back into the fold. They allegedly abducted her and took her to a place near Richmond for a ritual in which she watched a woman being burned to death and the body being eaten; then later she witnessed another sacrifice, which was followed by the cultists' raping her. Snowden and the police—that is, Lieutenant Lawrence Haake and Investigator Bill Lightfoot of the Richmond Bureau of Police—believe Hoyer's account although they cannot confirm it. The Medical College of Virginia records a doctor having removed from Hoyer's vagina a Chap Stick cap with a cigarette butt and a portion of a Q-tip. The meaning of this? Snowden learned from her network of therapists that the Chap Stick artifact "is a common ritual of reclamation."[8] Snowden's network has proved useful in many ways. Antonelli's article continues

> After listening to Snowden detail the chain of events [concerning the Chap Stick], one ritual survivor with whom Snowden conferred expressed surprise that [Hoyer] had not been through a 'marriage' to Satan, a ritual which victims commonly experience as part of the reclamation process. A week after that conversation, [Hoyer] was enroute to visit a friend . . . when her car was forced off the road. She was dragged out, staked to the ground and raped as an onlooker read from the Satanic bible. It was the identical ritual which Snowden's contact had described.[9]

Despite intense police interest in Hoyer's continuing problems, and despite their occasionally providing protection, no arrests have evolved out of these and other stories. Despite the uncritical treatment of her story by the Richmond press, despite the attestations of police that, indeed, satanic skulduggery exists and is out of control, and despite an apparently encouraging reception of the story by the Richmond public, many questions remain. In the article, both Hoyer and Snowden cite MPD as masking Hoyer's satanic history. As we shall see, even the psychiatric literature on the subject cautions that MPD sufferers, through therapy, become ruthlessly manipulative and even sadistic. (And in a seminar on her work, Snowden admitted that she had had no training in treating MPD victims [presentation at the Medical College of Virginia, Richmond, January 18, 1990].) Further, the various personalities the subjects manifest, which through therapy must be identified, explored, and "integrated" or "fused" into a smoothly running whole, do not necessarily relay accurate accounts of abuse. Rather, MPD sufferers' accounts can rarely be taken at face value and years of therapy may elapse before the sufferer even receives a diagnosis of MPD. Snowden feels that MPD has been severely underdiagnosed, as in the case of her patient, Cassandra Hoyer, who had been examined for many mental disorders.

But since some of these therapists have developed an extensive network across the country through which to share symptoms and treatment hints, is it possible that the therapists themselves participate in creating the cult stories? A skeptical question worth asking about the quotation above about the marriage ritual might be: Since Snowden elicited a new motif from Hoyer after learning from another survivor of the ritual only a week before, could Snowden not in some way have suggested the ritual to Hoyer? Or could the other cult survivor have communicated this information to Hoyer? As we shall see, therapists are not alone in forming networks: many cult survivors, like Jacquie Balodis, maintain an extensive network with other survivors, some even becoming freelance survivors available for conferences and training sessions.

But therapists who become *believers* step away from scientific procedures: the possibility of Hoyer fantasizing, or even injuring herself, does not enter the domain of diagnostic possibilities, even though MPD sufferers can exhibit many physiological symptoms attendant upon the presence of various personalities (change in linguistic patterns, for example, even speaking with a different voice tone and pitch; color blindness; a change in handedness, and so on). Further, since MPD sufferers show susceptibility to hypnosis and suggestion through therapy, might they not integrate fictional notions from therapists and other survivors into their personalities? A scientific inquiry into MPD would have to address such questions. But to therapists and cult cops two compelling circumstances lend veracity to survivors' stories: first, the emotional force with which survivors recall the trauma of cult involvement; second, the fact that survivors living far apart have told essentially the same stories.

San Francisco police officer Sandi Gallant speaks for many other cult cops: "It's the consistency in the stories that continues to make me take this whole thing seriously."[10] Chicago cult-cop Jerry Simandl says, "There isn't anyone who can lecture on this topic unless you're working with it" (Fifth International Conference on Multiple Personality/Dissociative States, Chicago, October 8, 1988). Simandl maintains that officers can receive a "true feeling," that is, a belief in the veracity of survivor stories.

Cult cops have in many cases allied themselves with cult survivors in training sessions and other public appearances, often on television. Simandl, for example, works occasionally with Bennett G. Braun, M.D., a psychiatrist who directs the Dissociative Disorders Program at the Rush-Presbyterian-St. Luke's Medical Center in Chicago. Braun happens to be one of the country's leading researchers on MPD as well as one of the major therapeutic sources who believes in the truth of cult survivors' claims. Simandl has interviewed many of Braun's patients and has constructed a model of satanic criminality identical to that outlined in Chapter 2, since he, too, takes cult survivors at their word. He argues repeatedly that one has to listen to survivors directly, to hear their stories expressed through the emotional vehemence of their abreaction (defined as an "emotional release after recalling a painful experience that has been repressed because it was consciously intolerable")[11] to understand why survivors must be taken at their word. In this opinion of veracity, he parrots therapists who have been overwhelmed by survivors' trauma, if not at least deeply impressed (Mini-workshop on the identification and treatment of victims of ritualistic cult abuse, Fifth International Conference on Multiple Personality/Dissociative States, October 8, 1988, Chicago).

Michelle Smith

The prototype cult-survivor was Michelle Smith who, with her psychiatrist husband, Lawrence Pazder, wrote *Michelle Remembers* (1980), a widely read and influential book.[12] In fact, both Smith and Pazder have become lecture-circuit regulars and frequent guests on television talk-shows. Presumably the couple now live off the proceeds. At publication, Smith received $342,000 in advances for a hard-cover and a paperback printing.[13] Nineteen eighty proved a singular year in one other important respect for survivor stories: the publication by the American Psychiatric Association of the third edition of the *Diagnostic and Statistical Manual of Mental Disorders (DSM-III)*, the professional handbook for diagnosing mental illnesses. For the first time in DSM-III, dissociative disorders (including MPD) emerged as a major category. Following both of these publications, cult-survivor stories proliferated, as did the survivors themselves; and growing numbers of therapists began to recognize and treat MPD.

Smith's story has become so influential in shaping the cult-survivor paradigm that it deserves detailed scrutiny. Smith had been undergoing treatment by Pazder for some time (he was not yet her husband) for a variety of problems before the satanic elements appeared. Smith described herself as a happy child, in the main, but with troublesome parents: a dipsomaniacal father and a passive and distant mother. She had had a Catholic upbringing in Canada. (At the time of her therapy, she lived in Victoria, British Columbia.) And one day, during therapy, Smith spontaneously regressed to a child persona through a self-induced trance and told her by now famous story. Before her confession (accompanied by screaming and yelling), she had alluded to a deep, dark secret; she complained repeatedly that she had a problem she couldn't discuss. Now it came out.

Rather than offer a chronology of Smith's alleged childhood experiences in a satanic cult, I will instead focus on the elements or motifs present in her tale. After all, what links cult survivors' stories are common motifs, not necessarily rituals experienced in identical ways in the same order by other people. Smith's book, then, relates the following:

—Participation in ceremonies replete with black candles, black drapes, goblets, dismembered bodies, sharing coffins with decomposing bodies, sexual abuse (including having "colored sticks" first dipped into a goblet and then inserted into her various orifices), having dismembered baby limbs rubbed on her, imprisonment in a snake-infested cage, confrontations with red spiders, watching other occult members rend kittens with their teeth, and having horns and a tail surgically attached to her body;

—Attendance at rituals in cemeteries, homes, mausoleums, and offices;

—Attendance at a ceremony where everyone dressed in white robes, where white cloth draped everything, including a corpse at the center of the ceremony, a pair of red shoes atop its chest, the same red shoes Smith had seen affixed to her "dazed" mother (who frequently appears at ceremonies, not as an active leader but as a stupefied, passive onlooker), and Smith herself being undressed and "probed";

—Rituals involving a man named Malachi and an "evil woman" who appeared frequently in Smith's stories, a woman who announced: "I am your special nurse" and forced Smith to defecate on a Bible and a crucifix. The nurse, in fact, drove a black car with a flamboyant hood ornament (a pouncing cat). Malachi cut a dead baby in half, rubbed it over Smith, and later placed her in a cage with snakes, the snakes apparently emanating from Smith's own body. In witnessing several cases of dismemberment, Smith once saw parts stitched to other parts, the Frankensteinian bodies, which were wired for electricity, squirming into life.

—A ceremony in which Smith was placed inside an effigy, a "statue," quite naked, from which she pushed baby parts out of its mouth. She did the same with snakes; she shoved them through the effigy's eyes which helped create a frenzy of dancing involving children. Smith somehow escaped from the effigy, only to be placed on a bed, straddled by a possessed woman who then vomited on her. Later, Smith spied her own mother, dressed in a white robe, her body stained red, holding a snake in her mouth. Upon hugging her mother, she then realized that she was hugging the evil woman.

How does Pazder analyze these stories? Although he stresses the need for skepticism, he remarks that Smith's story rings true because he had been to Africa where he "had encountered beliefs and practices that, had he not observed them directly, he would not have believed could exist within humanity—sacrifices, cannibalism, rituals of every sort. . . ."[14] Evocative of remarks made by other therapists about cult survivors' tales, Pazder concludes: "Michelle's reliving was relentlessly genuine. It maintained its remarkable intensity. It was too consistent to be false, had too much information, was too sophisticated from the psychological point of view to have been made up . . . It simply wasn't the kind of thing you fabricated if you were crazy or hysterical. It was being relived."[15]

The stories indeed conveyed much information, but could the information be verified? For example, the Satanists in Smith's circle supposedly cut off a finger in fealty to the Evil One, so presumably one might be able to spot them on the street. Further, in order to organize the events in which Smith participated, the Satanists must have shown skills of conference planning: obtaining snakes, making robes, arranging for members to give believable excuses to stay away from their jobs, ensuring no witnesses, arranging with cemeteries to exhume bodies, having effigies made, nabbing babies for sacrifice, efficiently cleaning up sacrificial messes, and so on. Yet no one could verify any of the details.

Since Smith relayed stories that supposedly represented a child's account of cult mysteries, Pazder pinned the recalled events to the years 1954 and 1955. He compared dates of Catholic movable feasts in 1954 and 1955 to the dates for the feasts in 1976 and 1977, the period within which Smith told satanic stories. His findings "showed there were startling correlations."[16] In particular, "Michelle's memories were corresponding almost to the day with events that had taken place exactly twenty-two years before. And in those years the Church's important dates (Ash Wednesday, Easter, Ascension, Pentecost, Corpus Christi, and the First Sunday of Advent) fell on the same days they did this year. The days and dates were the same. . . ."[17] Pazder admits that the correspondence might be a coincidence, and he planned to check further. While the Catholic Pazder seemed quite taken by the numerology, he mentions in *Michelle Remembers* here and there other clues to trauma—clues not pursued, at least not in the book. For example, Smith was married at the time of her therapy, a marriage with some problems; she had bouts of difficulty with alcohol; she had a painful childhood memory of an automobile accident in which smoke inhalation terrified her.

Smith's further adventures with Pazder involved priestly advice. On the feast of St. John the Baptist, a priest had arranged a fire near the church rectory. He prepared to burn a bench that had shown up in church, a bench with "precisely the symbols Michelle had described as being sewn on the cloaks" of participants in a satanic ceremony.[18] The priest had also prepared a prayer "meant to drive out anything evil in the fire." As the fire progressed, Pazder took photographs. When the good father sprinkled holy water on the fire, Pazder smelled, for an instant only, burning human flesh, a scent he learned to recognize in Africa. Days later, Smith was baptized, and the photographs were developed, and then the surprise: as he looked at the photographs of Smith and the priest, something else appeared. "But in the background—what was that? That figure beyond the fire . . . it seemed to be dressed in a long, flowing gown, and there was a glow around the head."[19] And who was the ghostly figure? The priest's mother said, "That's Mary with the child." The photograph appears in the book. I'm unable to find Mary or anyone else in it, but I invite readers to try their luck.

Smith then developed physiological symptoms to accompany her stories. She recounted a meeting with Satan himself (a drawing of him appears in the book), and as if reminding her of his evil nature, he wrapped his tail around her neck; and lo and behold, during her therapy the rash it had caused years before reappears on her neck.[20] Pazder photographed it, in fact, and the photograph appears in the book. Further, Pazder took Michelle to the local bishop to have the rash appraised. When the bishop saw it, he "then took a step backward. It was clear that it meant something to him."[21] Then the priest who had officiated at the fire examined it:

> "Hmmm." He looked closer. "The shape. I do sense something evil here," he said somberly.
> "It wasn't there—that mark—it wasn't there a week ago," Dr. Pazder told him.
> "It's where that thing's tail was wrapped around my neck."
> "It looks like the end of the tail," Dr. Pazder said, "the way you see the Devil in medieval pictures."
> "It is the classic image," Father replied. "These things become known."[22]

In fact, Smith even recounted in her book the speech given by Satan to his assembled. Among other things, the Devil says:

> Three times seven, seven times three,
> This is the time that belongs to me.
> From now until then the seasons turn again.
> I can do much to destroy and then
> Replace with words of hate and despair,
> Words as stupid as love and care.[23]

Even Pazder acknowledged that the words sounded "foolish," but his friend the priest pronounced an exegesis of them:

> But underneath, there is a lot there. Double and triple meanings. Satan will not humiliate himself to speak like ordinary people. He considers himself too brilliant for that. Remember, he is speaking to his high priests. There is important content there.[24]

The priest points out that Satan *wants* us to dismiss his words as puerile and meaningless.

Pazder's exploration of Smith's problems grew quickly beyond the therapist's couch to the rectory for a Catholic explication of what had happened to her. But in his search for material evidence of Smith's claims, Pazder's main exhibit was her rash; then numerological coincidences; next the priestly interpretation of events; and finally, linking Smith's ceremonies with the Church of Satan, the only extant example of anything approaching her stories. Pazder's link of Smith's cult to the "world-wide" Church of Satan raised some problems.[25] First, the Church of Satan was founded in 1966; it didn't exist in 1955. Second, the Church of Satan didn't much care for Pazder's association; when it sued him, he backed away from his conjecture.[26]

Pazder might have been correct when he said that whoever had abused Smith as a child had tried to make her feel guilt, and Smith herself said repeatedly during therapy, "I must be . . . a really rotten child."[27] But above all, Pazder *believes* her story:

> I happen to believe you . . . for many reasons . . . but mostly for what I feel *with* you. It feels real. You feel real. . . .
> You're describing it with what we call a visually eidetic memory. You seem to see things you are describing, in detail. I hear you describe what you see, and I don't hear it as a hallucination. It is too organized. Too long-term. It fits into the pattern of your life too well. You haven't been psychotic at any time. You aren't delusional—you don't believe in any of this happening in the here and now. . . . That's very different from a person who is delusional . . . .
> I don't think it really matters . . . whether people believe you . . . or not. I don't think that matters. *I think the way you are expressing the experience is very touching. It is authentic as an experience.* . . . [Emphasis added.][28]

Cult cops who take Smith's story as paradigmatic forget that Pazder's assessment is psychiatrist's talk, not a police officer's. *Feeling* the authenticity of Smith's story may aid a physician's clinical work, but police officers must operate on a well-founded, reasonable suspicion and make arrests based on probable cause.

Smith's account leaves out details about her family that might have significance. Again, Smith claims that her mother, who died in 1964, introduced her to the cult. Yet Smith's father has denied the incidents (he doesn't appear in the ceremonies). By all accounts, Smith loved her mother very much, as did her two sisters (not mentioned in the book), who attest that they never witnessed any satanic involvement. In fact, one sister was deeply distressed at Smith's representation of her mother. Not mentioned either was the Catholic Pazder's divorce or Smith's own divorce in order to marry Pazder, practices forbidden by the Catholic Church. Yet *Michelle Remembers* extols Catholic ceremonies and rituals as a way to combat the satanic terror.[29]

Further, Smith began her account by referring to a killing: At a satanic gathering, someone took a bottle and hit a "lump" under Smith's mother's skirt. The lump had been a woman, now dead, and the infamous Malachi put the dead woman *and* Smith in a car and pushed it down a mountain road. In the fiery crash, the dead woman was incinerated, but Michelle escaped, only to have to eat the woman's ashes. But one of Smith's relatives recounted that when Michelle was about five years old, while in a car with her family, she passed a traffic collision and saw a woman lying in the road. Michelle became hysterical.[30] Since *Michelle Remembers* offers readers details that conform with Pazder's assessment, one wonders what Freudian or Jungian interpretations could be brought to bear on Smith's pastiche of Catholic symbolism, lumps under her mother's skirts, toying with snakes, and the like. *Maclean's* magazine, which reported on Smith's claims, recommended Dustin Hoffman for the film role of Pazder.

In *Michelle Remembers,* Pazder did not diagnose Smith as having a dissociative disorder, MPD in particular, yet on the current lecture circuit, Smith presents herself as an MPD exemplar.

Multiple Personality Disorder

Since cult cops offer survivors as evidence of the satanic megacult, and since they have allied themselves with therapists who make the same claims, I must give an overview of current thinking about MPD and its bearing on tales of Satanism. Further, the alliance of police with therapists with Ph.D.s or M.D.s convinces many law-enforcement people that the megacult must exist. Conversely, therapists do the same: some psychiatrists have cited the cult-cop literature as external proof, or at least "confirmation," of survivors' claims.[31]

As I noted earlier, MPD did not occupy a prominent position within the classificatory scheme of medical disorders until the publication of *DSM-III* with its explication of dissociative disorders. The conceptualization of MPD was borne of work with "hysterical neurosis," hypnosis, and "the dynamic unconscious."[32] Now MPD constitutes one of four types of dissociative disorders as defined in the revised (1987) version of *DSM-III (DSM-IIIR):*

> The essential feature of these disorders is a disturbance or alteration in the normally integrative functions of identity, memory, or consciousness. The disturbance or alteration may be sudden or gradual, and transient or chronic.[33]

The disorder is grouped by one of the four types, depending on whether the person develops one or more additional personalities or whether "the customary feeling of one's own reality is lost and is replaced by a feeling of unreality,"[34] or if it affects the memory. MPD is an expression of the first type, where the dissociation results in new identities. The *DSM-IIIR* defines MPD as the existence within the person of two or more distinct personalities or personality states. Personality is here defined as a relatively enduring pattern of perceiving, relating to, and thinking about the environment and one's self that is exhibited in a wide range of important social and personal contexts. Personality states differ only in that the pattern is not exhibited in as wide a range of contexts. . . .

In children and adolescents, classic cases with two or more fully developed personalities are not as common as they are in adults. In adults, the number of personalities or personality states in any one case varies from two to over one hundred, with occasional cases of extreme complexity. Approximately half of reported cases have ten personalities or fewer, and half have over ten. . . .[35]

For MPD to be diagnosed, the subject must exhibit at least two *completely developed* personalities. "Personality states" can refer to "fragments," or relatively two-dimensional personalities that appear and reappear only within narrow contexts. To the characteristics given above, psychiatrist Bennett G. Braun adds that different personalities dominate the patient at any given time, and that "each individual personality is complex and integrated with its own unique behavior patterns and social relationships."[36]

Despite a decade-old working definition of MPD and dissociative disorders generally, the phenomenon has received little scientific scrutiny and uneven literature, and has been professionally discussed primarily in terms of clinical treatment or exchanging ideas on what works with patients. Further, some professional disagreement about causes and treatment "modalities" may even cause incorrect diagnoses of MPD, as psychiatrist Richard P. Kluft has written: "The issue is further complicated because different clinicians use different criteria or interpret criteria differently."[37]

But according to psychiatrist John C. Nemiah: "The natural history of the dissociative disorders has not received sufficient attention from clinical investigators, and the inadequacy of data precludes definitive statements either about their course or their prognosis."[38]

Psychiatrist Frank Putnam, a researcher at the National Institutes of Mental Health in Maryland, has stated that "our current knowledge about the treatment of MPD is derived exclusively from the work of clinicians, often in nonacademic settings, who have been sticking it out in the trenches with these complex and difficult patients."[39] He further advises that psychiatry still needs to sponsor "systematic studies" of MPD to provide a scientific basis and a standard of understanding and treatment.

Most current clinical trial designs require the randomized assignments of patients to different treatment groups for comparison of the efficacy of two or more modalities. In addition, single-blind and double-blind methodology is preferred to ensure objectivity in the collection of data.[40]

Parallel to Putnam's suggestion for scientific study, Kluft warns that whatever notions his colleagues adopt as firm truths about MPD, models do change: "One must hedge tentative interpretations of the data by acknowledging the possibility that some unanticipated confounding systematic artifact may yet be discovered that leads to a revision of our current understanding."[41]

Professional literature appeared with Braun's edited 1986 work, *Treatment of Multiple Personality Disorder,* and Kluft's *Childhood Antecedents to Multiple Personality* (1985), in addition to sporadic papers in medical or psychological journals. The apparent rise in MPD cases has caused the recent proliferation of professional literature: Braun cites 500 reported cases nationwide in 1979, 5000 in 1986.[42] Braun, in fact, had been the nexus (and remains so) of professional oral exchange of ideas and treatments since he initiated, in 1984, the annual International Conference on Multiple Personality/Dissociative States, sponsored by his own institution, Rush-Presbyterian-St. Luke's Medical Center. In the past few years, these conferences have examined the satanic-survivor claims in workshops.

For the purposes of this book, I here outline characteristics of, and issues concerning, the diagnosis and treatment of MPD that bear critically on cult-survivors' claims.

1. Therapists agree that MPD arises from psychological trauma. They also agree that child abuse, particularly the chronic variety—but if not child abuse, then at least *some kind* of childhood trauma—shows a very strong etiological link to MPD. Incest constitutes the most-often-reported type of sexual abuse, usually between a father or stepfather and a daughter or stepdaughter. Concomitantly, emotional abuse occurs involving some form of ridicule or degradation. Putnam stresses that our view of MPD, its symptoms, and its treatment rest upon a "strong consensus on diagnosis and treatment reached in the oral literature among clinicians" and that the MPD behaviors discussed in the literature constitute an agreed-upon "core set" that have been replicated clinically.[43] Dissociative disorders may begin and end abruptly, but "there may be a definite history of a specific, shocking emotional trauma or a situation charged with painful emotions and psychological conflict."[44] Nevertheless, according to Braun, "we still do not clearly understand what causes and maintains the symptoms of this disorder."[45] Braun also suggests that various stresses, perhaps not amounting to trauma, can induce MPD, "such as the death of a family member, frequent geographic relocation, and cultural dislocation."[46] Putnam adds that therapists should not become too cavalier about the association between MPD and child abuse:

> To date, it has not been proven that childhood trauma *causes* MPD. In most reports . . . there is no outside verification that any trauma occurred. An independent verification of alleged abuse, which often occurred, 10 or more

years prior to being reported in therapy, is almost impossible for the average therapist to obtain.[47]

Yet no therapist who works with MPD sufferers doubts the connection between child abuse and the presence of the disorder. Perhaps complicating matters, Putnam has written that clinicians, almost unanimously, view the dissociative process as occurring "along a continuum ranging from minor, 'everyday' examples (e.g., daydreaming) to psychiatric disorders" (including MPD).[48]

The multiple personalities, known as alters, in effect become a defense mechanism: alters represent an adaptive response, functionally distinct from the "main" personality through the barrier of amnesia.[49] The trauma, in fact, may arise from an emotional double-bind; for example, a parent may alternately beat and then hug the child. But not all people subject to severe or prolonged trauma react by developing MPD: "persons with an inborn biopsychological capacity to dissociate" develop it.[50] That the capacity for developing MPD seems innate constitutes a state-of the-art statement. MPD sufferers don't switch alters at random: "The 'spontaneous' transformation of the alert patient into a personality usually occurs when the patient encounters a stress with which he or she cannot cope."[51] So the prime mechanism through which MPD operates is spontaneous self-hypnosis, which also produces an insightful key to understanding what kind of personalities and how many will emerge, since their "essence is a hypnotic amnesia hiding experiences, emotions, and functions."[52]

The goal of therapy is to *integrate* the various personalities; and given the theory that MPD is "highly correlated" with childhood trauma, usually child abuse, therapists find that MPD sufferers are "highly responsive to psychotherapy" and that the integration of personalities is achievable.[53] But the therapy also presumes that child abuse, particularly child sexual abuse, shows a high incidence throughout the population at large. Some therapists believe that we should see in adult MPD patients the abused child who tries to tell his or her story but no one listens:

> If patients with multiple personalities can be understood as abused children in adult bodies (whose childhood traumata and responses to those traumatizations have been preserved through time by dissociation), their problems in being believed are likely to be similar to the problems encountered by children who attempt to tell their stories at an earlier point in their lives.[54]

As we shall see in Chapter 5, therapists' concerns that adult survivors were abused kids who couldn't communicate their abuse have important implications for the investigation of alleged "ritual abuse" of children in day-care centers. In the latter case, investigations and even arrests of day-care-center workers have been based on uncorroborated children's testimony,

testimony sometimes coaxed and shaped by therapists and police who assume that a child's denial that abuse has occurred is based on fear or a refusal to come to terms with "the bad thing that happened." This assumption has led to the axiom that children do not lie about abuse and its corollary that children's denial of abuse must be brooked. (In the MPD literature, the same idea occasionally crops up. Psychiatrists note that abused MPD patients might then deny that the abuse occurred, a denial that they say must be overcome.) The psychiatric literature on MPD reiterates, first of all, that not all therapists will even admit that the illness exists. And while Kluft explores the problems with *believing* MPD victims, he warns fellow professionals of the consequences to the MPD sufferer of the therapist's denial: "Part of choosing to believe abused children and adult patients with multiple personality disorder is choosing to confront our own complicity in the wishing away of these unbearable childhood experiences."[55, 56]

2. Working with MPD patients is time-consuming, demanding, and emotionally draining, not to say very complicated. To those who suggest that naive therapists unconsciously implant personalities in patients, psychiatrist Eugene Bliss points out, "In my experience many [patients] are hardheaded, stubborn, and unsuggestible."[57] Further, the "manifestations of dissociative disorders are varied, often complex, and frequently difficult to distinguish sharply one from another."[58] In fact, Braun finds that most patients undergo up to seven years of therapy before receiving a proper diagnosis of MPD.[59] The exhausting nature of MPD forces therapists to rely on a network of other therapists for support and to foster the networking of MPD sufferers for social support. "Because the MPD patient has so much information to integrate, his or her needs can seem overwhelming and exhausting to a single therapist. Social support systems are especially effective in this regard because they return the patient to the community and help prevent therapist burnout."[60] Braun recommends in-patient treatment of satanic-cult survivors because their stories of "ritualistic sex, human sacrifice, and cannibalism [are] so terrifying and overwhelming that [survivors require] the assistance of a trained staff available 24 hours a day to help these patients cope."[61]

3. Hypnosis plays an important role in invoking certain personalities. Some researchers have suggested that since "MPD was identified most often through hypnosis, the disorder could be an artifact of hypnotic suggestion."[62] The leading MPD therapists, however, discount the idea that hypnosis represents an iatrogrenic threat by creating personalities (iatrogenesis refers to the physician creating yet another disorder while trying to treat the original one). Bliss finds the iatrogenic argument "a red herring": "The key consideration is whether self-hypnotic processes are partially or mainly responsible for the psychopathology exhibited by the patient."[63] Putnam offers a subtly differing view: "The capacity to be hypnotized may be directly related to

...tilize a dissociative mechanism for coping with trauma."[64] ...also agree that MPD sufferers show "high hypnotizabil-...ticular, MPD patients show themselves quite adept at "spon-...pnosis," thus furnishing sufferers with an outlet to replicate ...ymptoms, personalities, and irrational behaviors."[67] In this regard, Buss finds some MPD sufferers to be "hypnotic virtuosos."[68] Psychiatrist George K. Ganaway has had to remind therapists that "they are treating patients who . . . are continually moving in and out of hypnotic trance states no matter what the therapists' intent may be regarding the use of hypnotic techniques."[69]

Perhaps hypnosis itself "can be appropriately characterized as a form of association," and hence a method to integrate personalities.[70] In an experiment with a hypnotically responsive subject, *not* an MPD patient, the subject, a woman, was induced to see ghosts, apparently responding to a suggestion made during hypnosis. And the woman became convinced about the reality of the hypnotically suggested ghost:

> . . . Although the woman subject was given only verbal information about what she would see, quite unconsciously she invented a pictorial image so convincing that the conscious part of her not only failed to recognize it as her own creation, but even when given a clear logical explanation she remained convinced that the ghost was real.[71]

So therapists' application of hypnosis must be done carefully. Memory recall, at best, is inaccurate. But during therapy, patients may come to believe their own inaccurate memories recalled in hypnosis. As Ganaway cautions, "virtually every study that has examined the subjects' confidence in the veracity of their memories has demonstrated that hypnosis increases confidence in the veracity of both correct and incorrect recalled material," and in some cases, patients may form "an entire belief system with its own set of supporting pseudomemories [that] can be cued by a simple suggestion from the interviewer, and, if not extinguished, could potentially become part of the subject's permanent sense of narrative truth."[72]

4. MPD sufferers can be ruthless and imaginative manipulators of their therapists. "The therapist must know that the patient will attempt to manipulate him or her throughout the course of diagnosis and treatment and must not take it personally."[73] Perhaps owing to the emotional double-bind associated with a childhood trauma, patients may inflict the same double-bind on the therapist. MPD sufferers, "like other victims of abuse, recreate situations for mastery."[74]

Putnam does not minimize the difficulties of working with MPD sufferers: "They produce complex transference and countertransference interactions and can wreak havoc on any research team or hospital ward that is not well informed and prepared."[75] Further, administering medicine to MPD patients creates other problems: they react with marked sensitivity to side effects and sometimes "exhibit marked placebo responses to any intervention."[76] Further, many MPD patients exhibit suicidal behavior, and an alter may punish another alter through self-mutilation.[77]

5. Perhaps intimidating to some therapists, an MPD sufferer's alters come complete with physiological idiosyncrasies. Braun calls these "somatic memories": "For example, the patient may remember being burned in the past and an actual blister may accompany this verbal report."[78] A recent article in the *New York Times,* reporting on the work of Braun and others, summarized the extent to which somatic memories might show up: "the abrupt appearance and disappearance of rashes, welts, scars and other tissue wounds; switches in handwriting and handedness; epilepsy, allergies and color blindness that strike only when a given personality is in control of the body."[79] The biological symptoms, some of which can be amazingly subtle (e.g., a child persona reacts in one way to a dose of medicine appropriate to a child, yet the same dose produces a different response in an adult alter, just as the small dose predictably would in an adult anyway), serve adaptive functions as well. According to psychiatrist Frank Putnam, "A given state of consciousness has its biological reality. . . . By keeping these states separate and distinct, the patients create biologically separate selves."[80]

6. Although therapists have found that MPD afflicts young and old, males and females, on the whole MPD seems more prevalent among women by a 9-to-1 ratio, generally afflicting those in their 20s to early 30s, and MPD may even exhibit a transgenerational nature within a family.[81, 82] Even children can display MPD. Family history, then, plays an important role in charting the development of MPD in a patient: "The interpersonal factors that continue to perpetuate the symptomatic manifestation of [MPD] are varied, but usually relate to the patient's family dynamics," and therefore treatment must consider not only the disorder per se but also "the unique dynamics and contributions of the individual, the family, and society."[83] Different researchers have come up with different sex ratios among MPD patients, but Putnam cautions that such ratios may display a bias because most patients seem to be women; he suggests that male MPD victims reside not in hospitals but in jails, noting the high percentage of incarcerated sex offenders.[84] Further, MPD sufferers experience "frequent" substance abuse.[85]

7. The diagnosis of MPD can be confused with other illnesses. For example, a person may exhibit a psychogenic fugue or psychogenic amnesia, both similar to MPD but distinct in that MPD involves repeated appearances of alters, whereas the fugue or amnesia involves a single episode.[86] Similarly, one could have schizophrenia or a "mood disorder with psychotic features," or perhaps not even a dissociative disorder at all. In fact, *DSM-IIIR* notes that MPD patients may even claim to be possessed by a spirit,

demon, or other entity, and possession experiences can belong to one of several kinds of disorders, not necessarily MPD. Psychiatrist Ganaway has discovered nonhuman alters in some subjects: "demons, angels, sages, lobsters, chickens, tigers, a gorilla, a unicorn, and 'God.' "[87] That alters can get mixed up with assaults by demons hints at a broader cross-cultural issue:

> [The multiple personality experience] is not interpreted in religious terms. The distinct personalities joined in the patient do not originate from outside the person, in another reality . . . but come about by forces or experiences internal to the individual. The entities in question are not spirits . . . they are "alters."[88]

Theoretically, depending on the religiocultural experience of the patient, exorcism could rid the body of demons and fuse personalities. In other religious rituals apart from mainstream Christianity, ecstatic and trance experiences constitute communion or joining with the deity, as in some Afro-Cuban beliefs. One wonders about the correspondence between such ecstatic experiences and the diagnosis of MPD and its treatment. And if the development of alters bears some analogy to spirit possession in people for whom trances are almost commonplace, we could emerge with yet some new model of MPD. Felicitas Goodman observes that "where the phenomenon of multiple personality differs from possession . . . is in ritual control."[89] "Nothing happens haphazardly in a ritual," so the closed environment within which spirits possess people (or within which they evince alters) results from control; control derives from learned behavior.

On the subject of perceiving demons, several psychiatrists have observed a relationship between patients' religious lives and the nature of their alters' personalities. Psychiatrist Philip M. Coons has noticed that an MPD sufferer usually has a parent or grandparent who practices fundamentalist Christianity, which in the patient is manifested by one alter strongly adhering to the belief, another alter not. Other therapists have found "a tendency for MPD patients to come from families with a strict, fundamentalist or authoritarian religion."[90] "Cognitive fallacies associated with literal religious interpretations" may help explain why fundamentalist Christianity plays some nebulous role in the expression of MPD.[91]

That no "definitive psychological or physiological test for MPD" exists confounds diagnosis.[92] Again, substance abuse complicates the picture. "Sedatives, hypnotics, and analgesics are the most commonly abused drugs, closely followed by stimulants and alcohol," but the drug abuse normally shows up in particular alters only.[93]

Survivors and MPD

Given the consensus on MPD among therapists, where do the survivors fit in? The same clinical sources cited above maintain virtual silence on the satanic-cult associations. Braun has suggested that this silence has not been by choice: he maintains that professional journals have shown reluctance to print clinical articles on the topic and that he himself has experienced difficulty trying to get his material published (personal communication, 1989). Braun's 1986 volume contains only one paragraph devoted to survivors, and that only to comment on the extreme examples of sadistic abuse cited by survivors and their need for around-the-clock hospital attention. Putnam, in his 1989 study, did not isolate survivors by virtue of their professed satanic backgrounds, but noted that "many multiples" told stories of elaborately cruel abuse:

> I am struck by the quality of extreme sadism that is frequently reported by most MPD victims. . . . Many multiples have told me of being sexually abused by groups of people, of being forced into prostitution by family members, or of being offered as a sexual enticement to their mothers' boyfriends. After one has worked with a number of MPD patients, it becomes obvious that severe, sustained, and repetitive child sexual abuse is a major element in the creation of MPD.[94]

Putnam, though, is careful to use the term *ritualized* in a broad context, noting that some patients appear to report abuse that involved some "cleansing" or "purifying" quality (as explained by the abuser to the child to justify an abusive act), none of which necessarily relates to satanic rites.

But while a professional literature on MPD did not begin to emerge until the early 1980s, clinical literature on satanic-cult survivors has been even slower in coming. Most of what exists is still oral history shared at the annual conferences on multiple personality/dissociative states hosted by Braun in Chicago. If any written material circulates as a consequence of the conferences, it usually takes the form of unpublished abstracts or short monographs. In some cases, nothing appears or circulates at all. The satanic-cult survivor workshops have sometimes occurred without audiotaping for public dissemination, and abstracts have not always been circulated. In short, in several cases no public traces of the workshops exist. The lack of publications following such workshops owes in part to therapists' fear. Many psychiatrists are concerned that by treating cult survivors, cult members may threaten the therapists themselves. Many therapists, in fact, have reported death threats. Kathy Snowden, the therapist in Cassandra Hoyer's case, and even Bennett G. Braun have reported such threats. In Braun's case, he will only treat patients who have left their cults; he views those who maintain their membership as too dangerous, believes his telephone has been bugged, and says that he still receives death threats (personal communication 1989).

Except for the work of a very few mental-health professionals, such as psychologist Richard Noll and psychiatrists George K. Ganaway and Frank W. Putnam, what little psychiatric writing has emerged on survivors and their therapy has uncritically embraced the literal truth of survivors' claims. And, although anthropologist Sherrill Mulhern has publicly questioned the views of Braun and other MPD researchers that, as evidenced by survivors' stories, murderous and abusive satanic cults exist, few within psychiatry have done so.

At the Fourth International Conference on Multiple Personality/Dissociative States in Chicago in 1987, social worker Maribeth Kaye and psychologist Lawrence R. Klein presented a paper to distinguish clinical indications of cult survivors from other garden-variety MPD symptoms. Their abstract states that "while the incidence of cult victimization among multiples is as yet undetermined, our limited survey data suggest it to be a significant phenomenon," and therefore therapists must be able to recognize "often subtle, embedded cues" that flag Satanism in order to "facilitate the abreactive work of their clients."[95] Of 42 patients under study in the Akron, Ohio, area, under the care of seven therapists, Kaye and Klein found that about half showed satanic experiences. Characteristic of other therapists who believe the cult stories, Kaye and Klein observe that the MPD sufferers "reveal experiencing remarkably similar ordeals" but they also maintain that while these patients independently and spontaneously admitted to satanic experiences (of the Michelle Smith variety), such information only appeared "in a veiled, obscure form," the full disclosure of details occurring only "in response to therapeutic probe."[96]

What distinguishes the MPD satanic-cult survivor from MPD non-satanic abuse survivors? Kaye and Klein believe that cult survivors have been "subjected to formal induction/brainwash procedures" and that therapy must resemble deprogramming. The "internalized messages" of ex-cultists are difficult to ferret out because they "have been purposefully and methodically implanted."[97] In fact, Braun follows a similar line of thinking by claiming that theoretically Satanists could *implant* alters in cult members (personal communication 1989). So what clinical indicators must therapists seek when dealing with suspected cult survivors? Kaye and Klein inventory them:[98]

1. The "seemingly endless array of symbols," particularly those mocking Christianity.

2. Ceremonial objects, such as those for the Black Mass, "the focal religious ceremony in the Satanic faith." Such objects include robes and candles of various colors, masks, and chalices.

3. Rituals, such as the Black Mass, with chants spoken in "Enochian,"

which "produce a hypnotic effect." Various rites apparently involve sexual and physical abuse, with "torture . . . inflicted as a purification rite." And, commonly, Satanists sacrifice humans, drink the blood and eat the corpses. Other popular rites include administering electric shocks, gang rapes, and mutilation of genitals. To maintain secrecy, cult leaders "further insure silence [by systematicaly implanting] trigger words or ideas . . . into the psyches of victims."

Despite the cluster of satanic attributes, Kaye and Klein recommend that therapists pursue treatment of survivors with the same methods and goals that they would apply to survivors of any other kind of trauma or abuse. To illustrate their points, Kaye and Klein cite the case of Kim, an alter of Selena, who tells a tale similar to Michelle Smith's but with violent embellishments. For example, not only did she undergo group rape, "but a knife would be inserted in her vagina and the blood smeared over her body."[99] In exploring one alter, who spoke with "an automaton-like personality," the therapists found that the persona was a product of torture: "Angel [the alter] related how holes were dug in the back of her head and in various other parts of her body. There the electrodes were implanted. Then the switch would be turned on/off."[100] Evidently, Kaye and Klein did not think to examine their patient for physical signs of such mutilation: if so, they didn't mention it.

Evocative of Lawrence Pazder's comments about feeling the authenticity of Michelle Smith's story, Kaye and Klein offer advice to therapists:

> In the face of the enormity of what we have learned, we have elected to focus upon our clients. To help them deal with their pain, see what they need to see, hear what they need to hear, feel what they need to feel, and learn what they need to learn. This is the scope of our present interventions.[101]

From the same conference on dissociative disorders, other therapists presented similar views. According to the abstracts of their talks:

—Kathy Lawson, presenting "Satanic Cult Worship and Multigenerational MPD," discussed the "satanic occult, symbols, cues, cult death contracts and the inter-marriages in the elite groups to form a high level of blood purity. This high level of blood purity allows entire communities to become 'locked in' to a higher system and create 'safe pockets' within states or regions."

—Julia Holland, in "Occult Ritualistic Behavior Modification: Dissociative Processes and Techniques," asserts that "new 'converts' are even sought in grammar schools," thus illustrating the enormity of the threat. She advises her fellow professionals of the therapeutic skills one must possess when deprogramming cult survivors: "Successful mental health care is often extremely dependent upon the therapists' specific knowledge of witchcraft, satanism, and the occult since so much is common ground, including frequently knowing/unknowing substance abuse as well as the . . . techniques of cult indoctrination and trance induction." Holland glibly and disingenuously observes that in hospitalized MPD patients the occult influence "can indeed be as terrorizing and mindbending as in the days of the Witches' Hammer, as evidenced by . . . increasingly common murders and suicides connected with satanism and the occult."

Of course, we have no evidence that such murders or suicides have become increasingly common, but as a dare to therapists to join her crusade, and as an excuse for her lack of a more precise definition of the cult-survivor phenomenon (and as a mitigating explanation for why her ideas have so many loose ends), Holland says, "These same groups ironically now claim and receive legal protection under the First Amendment as a 'religion.' " Of course the Church of Satan has received the legal tax status of a religious institution, to which Holland obliquely refers; but since the Church has nothing to do with her cult-survivor patients, her statement is dishonest. No group practicing murder or encouraging suicide receives any First Amendment protection. To make such a statement implies that the threat can never be mastered and can never be known thoroughly; to make such a statement keeps the myth viable.

A recent paper by psychiatrists Walter C. Young and Bennett G. Braun and psychologists Roberta G. Sachs and Ruth T. Watkins constitutes the closest thing to a scientific study of cult survivors that exists.[102] The study analyzes work with 37 patients who tell tales of satanic goings-on and begins by iterating commonly known ideas about the etiology of MPD. Since childhood trauma apparently brings about MPD, the authors advance the idea that satanic-cult experience could likewise induce dissociative disorders, and they match the patients' reports with those of children in day-care settings.[103] For their purposes, the authors define satanic cults as "intra-familial transgenerational groups that engage in explicit satanic worship which includes the following criminal practices: ritual torture, sacrificial murder, deviant sexual activity, and ceremonial cannibalism."[104] The definition is important since all of the patients in the study could identify *at least* one member of their own families as a Satanist. Further, therapists did not enlist law-enforcement help in investigating the stories.

Of 37 patients studied, 33 were women and 4 were men; all had been referred for evaluation *following* therapy for dissociative disorders. In fact, during their previous therapy, all patients had disclosed, in some fashion, stories about their own abuse at the hands of Satanists. Most of the patients, during the two-year evaluation conducted by Young et al., co-mingled in some ways, attending "some group activities and group psychotherapy together," although the authors felt that "there was minimal discussion" between them about their satanic experiences because the patients seemed secretive about their past.[105]

But the satanic stories did not come easily. While patients showed clear memories of some abuse at home, the "ritual abuse" (defined as specific satanic rituals) only "emerged gradually" over time, although occasionally "intrusive images of cult abuse arose unexpectedly while patients were in the process of working through memories of familial abuse. Reports occurred spontaneously as patients abreacted, dreamed, or experienced flashbacks of people wearing robes in rituals."[106] Hypnosis elicited details, although "in a piecemeal fashion." But constructing the satanic *tableau* was not left entirely to the evaluators: therapists also drew from patients' artwork, journals, and even their clinical records.

While the patients all reported abusive experiences, the details of their stories differed, as in "the color of robes worn by cult members, types of cult-related symbols and instruments, or details of rituals."[107] Of great interest to an analysis of these patients, yet not addressed in this paper, would be a discussion of the therapeutic methods used. The authors did not perform the initial diagnoses of the patients before the study began, so we are left to speculate about the means through which satanic elements surfaced during the years of therapy before the study. In an earlier version of their paper, Young et al. stated that the piecemeal utterances about satanic abuse appeared so disconnected and out of sequence, possibly due to the obvious pain of the patients, that the authors had to guide them through yes/no questioning, which prompted the patients to "verbalize their reports more directly." An additional methodological detail present in the earlier paper but absent in the current version was that the personae through which patients told satanic stories were those of children, usually "three years of age or earlier."[108]

But finally the therapy produced a list of elements constituting satanic ritual abuse, including:

1. Forced drug use;
2. Sexual abuse;
3. Witnessing, receiving physical abuse or torture;
4. Witnessing, participating in mutilation or killing of animals;
5. Witnessing, participating in mutilation or killing of people, particularly infants;
6. Receiving death threats;
7. "Marriage" to Satan;
8. Forced cannibalism;
9. Forced impregnation and sacrifice of own child.[109]

The clinical syndrome presented included "unusual fears, survivor guilt, indoctrinated beliefs, substance abuse, severe post-traumatic stress disorder [PTSD], bizarre self-abuse, sexualization of sadistic impulses, and dissociative states with satanic overtones."[110] Undoubtedly complicating the therapy, the PTSD symptoms loomed large, in that some patients evinced self-mutilation, heard voices, felt controlled by inner forces, or panicked, with "easy triggering by external stimuli."

Young et al. offer a clinical vignette of one patient, a 30-year-old woman whose psychiatric history included periodic hospitalization over a period of ten years, some involving self-laceration and suicide attempts. Her satanic-abuse stories emerged through a child alter; the abuse had continued into her sixteenth year. Her stories included not only those on the preceding list but also electrical shocks, serial rape, and even "a mock operation where she was told that a bomb was placed inside her body that would explode if she ever told secrets or did not obey the dictums of her cult."[111] In fact, during therapy the patient vacillated over whether she had been a victim or a murderer. Because patients implicated members of their own families, the study did not examine intrafamilial relationships, except those reported by the patients. The 30-year-old patient was afraid to receive any gifts or correspondence from family members, "as she felt they were meant to convey an order of silence."[112] The patient displayed particular anxiety "on both Christian and satanic holidays." One wonders how the therapists determined satanic holidays: since no fixed creed or dogma of Satanism exists, one may pick and choose what constitutes a satanic holiday.

So how do Young et al. size up their survivor patients? The authors raise questions of the reliability, verifiability, and credibility of the clinical details. The authors examine reliability in terms of whether the patients and the therapists who elicited their stories can be trusted. Verifiability translates into hard corroborative evidence. Both reflect credibility. Although Young et al. seem impressed that the patients reported similar stories while coming from diverse locations, the authors could "not rule out the possibility that these patients had read non-professional literature describing reports of satanic cult activity and ritual childhood abuse. They could have incorporated certain incidents from articles or books as 'pseudo-memories,'" or they have found "a powerful satanic metaphor for conveying and explaining other forms of severe abuse actually suffered."[113] On the other hand, the reported use of drugs during cult ceremonies might influence the reliability of recalled stories.

The authors also point out that if the patients were quite young at the time of abuse, then one would expect distortion in their stories by virtue of their inexperience and immaturity. "Reported experiences may be real, distorted, or fabricated, or they may represent the confusion of real, fantasied, or misperceived elements."[114] For example, one patient's dissociated personality cut inverted crosses on her body and marked the walls of her room with "cult symbols." While the primary personality remained unaware of what had happened, yet *another* alter appeared to assert that a cult member showed up in the patient's room, marked the wall, and then cut her. Yet the alter with the memory of the cult visitation remained convinced of the truth of her own account.[115] Finally, Young et al. note that while hypnosis does enhance recall or repressed memories in amnesiac patients, it may also result in the reporting of increased amounts of false information."[116]

Young et al. claim to have found some corroborative evidence of the patients' stories. One patient had a distorted nipple; another had scars on the back; one had a "satanic tatoo on his scalp."[117] Most impressive to the therapists, "when patient photographs of alleged cult members were shown to other patients from a similar geographic region," four patients identified the people in them by name and cult function. During the time of the study, the patients had no contact with one another. One patient's school records indicated a drop in school grades from ages 7 through 10, the same time that the patient supposedly endured the cult abuse.[118]

The authors find credibility of paramount importance. "The establishment of credibility is critical, not only for treatment purposes, but for ethical considerations as well. For instance, it would be important in instituting reporting procedures for law enforcement and child protection agencies."[119] Certainly, too, patients need confirmation of their victimization, in addition to assuaging their guilt, for as George Ganaway has noted, MPD patients display "an insatiable need to be believed."[120] In seeking external evidence, the authors refer to a paper by social worker Sally Hill and psychiatrist Jean Goodwin that attempts to survey pre-Inquisition historical sources describing satanic rituals, a paper that indeed identifies rituals similar to those described by the patients under study.[121] Young et al. assert that while the similarity between the historical sources and the patients' accounts doesn't necessarily prove anything, it *might* prove the cults' existence. Further, the authors seek analogies to their patients' experiences through literature on other cults of the non-Satanic variety, confirming that some cult members adapt by dissociation, that some cults indoctrinate people through fear, intimidation, and violence. Young et al. conclude by urging further attempts to independently verify patients' stories, and, citing the work of David Finkelhor and others who have examined day-care-center abuse cases (discussed in Chapter 5), posit a connection with "other current reports of children being ritually abused in daycare settings."[122]

Problems

The paper by Young et al. presents some scientific problems. First, the authors work with a biased sample of patients: their patients did not include those exposed to cults in childhood who did not develop dissociative disorders. Nor did the authors compare satanic stories with those told by other MPD patients, those who claimed abusive backgrounds but not of the satanic variety. Such an extended discussion of so-called satanic ritual abuse in a dissociative context is crucial to properly evaluating the patients' information. Most important would be scrutiny of the therapeutic process: How many therapists originally examined the 37 patients? What models or paradigms of MPD did they use? Were the other therapists social workers, psychiatrists, or psychologists? What standards of hypnotherapy did they observe? Regarding the "corroborative" nature of the anecdote about four patients independently identifying other cult members from photographs, we learn that the patients came from the same "geographical area." Could not cross-fertilization have occurred if the patients saw the same therapist, or several therapists who routinely met and discussed their MPD cases? For investigative purposes, Young et al. leave too many loose ends and fail to develop corroborative leads to help investigators or other therapists. Many explanations can be offered to account for mutilated nipples and scarified backs.

The inquiry by Hill and Goodwin identifies other therapists who dismiss MPD patients' stories as delusional as evidence of those therapists' inability to accept the possibility of sadistic child abuse. Hill and Goodwin stress the need for establishing the credibility of patients' claims as "a key issue in the treatment of patients who have experienced extreme childhood trauma."[123] Nevertheless, they seek to present "another data-based framework" to help therapists deal with stories of satanic mayhem. Their historical excursion into pre-Inquisitional sources produces some vindication of the satanic-cult rituals listed by Young and his colleagues in their attempt to find a scheme, a pattern, a model.

> Therapists, sometimes working in study or support groups, are collecting accounts from many different victims so that they can begin to recognize typical patterns. Victims too are meeting in groups or networking through newsletters to share their experiences. Written descriptions, by those victims who retain clear narrative memories, are being compiled for use in bibliotherapy. Law enforcement agencies are documenting material and eyewitness evidence in newly found cases which can be compared with accounts obtained clinically.[124]

Despite the networking, Hill and Goodwin may have overstated the usefulness of the information apparently being compiled by many therapists. Despite the assertion about the work of law-enforcement agencies, survivors' stories have not borne investigative fruit, at least not to confirm a satanic megacult. But the authors' historical sources confound the matter: they cite many secondary sources describing the early Gnostic sects, hardly satanic cults, and even invoke the work of Margaret Murray, long discredited by historians. Hill and Goodwin contrive a list of cult-worship elements that includes sacrifices of children or fetuses, chanting, drug-taking, ritual use of body fluids, cannibalism, animals, dismemberment of corpses, murder, to mention the salient ones. Certainly, Hill and Goodwin "do not suggest that concordance of a flashback image with historical accounts constitutes proof that the image derived from actual experience," but they suggest that clinicians consider, at least, the possibility.[125]

Psychologist Richard Noll has taken Hill and Goodwin to task for "citing historical materials in an undisciplined manner," perhaps "repeating the mistakes made by other such dilettantes in the past by doing so."[126] Noll points out that historians have not found evidence of millennia-old satanic cults practicing the Black Arts, but instead "it is the power of the *idea* of cannibalistic and orgiastic cults" that continues to enthrall us. Noll notes that among the "essential references" not cited by Hill and Goodwin is Norman Cohn's influential *Europe's Inner Demons: An Enquiry Inspired by the Great Witch-Hunt* (1975), a historical study of deviant European cults and religious movements. Cohn, for example, points out that the Romans harbored notions that the early Christians performed all of the macabre rituals that appear in the Hill/Goodwin compilation. Where cult-survivor patients are concerned, Noll suggests that, although some of their experiences are perhaps true, some may be "the screen memories of childhood abuse at the hands of adults (perhaps even parents) but which have taken on a mythic, almost archetypal form, in their representation of the essential evilness of the experience."[127] Like Young et al., Hill and Goodwin do not raise the issue of a connection between the use of imperfect therapeutic methods and the stories that emerge in sesssions with MPD patients. The paper by Young et al. and the shorter study by Kaye and Klein discuss clinical findings within the framework of therapeutic methods and psychiatric theory. Since the therapeutic goal of working with cult survivors is to integrate their multiple personalities, clinicians must identify and explore them, accept their presence, and negotiate with them on their own terms. The therapist must accept the reality of the experience as expressed by the primary personality or his or her alters. As Braun has pointed out, "I don't deny any reality." Braun emphasizes that therapists should not apply criminal criteria to handling MPD cases: " 'Reasonable doubt' criteria or anthropological criteria are not the criteria of a therapist" (Fifth International Conference on Multiple Personality/Dissociative States, Chicago, October 8, 1988). To accept expressions of trauma as detailed criminal acts or settings—that is, as eyewitness accounts—is not justified even according to the psychiatric literature, and certainly cannot be presumed according to the nature of MPD.

Braun may not deny any reality, but a cult survivor's reality or the realities of the MPD patient's many alters cannot be viewed as tape-recorded and accurate memories triggered by the therapist pressing the right button. "The questions of what really happened and when it happened are usually sources of painful confusion for MPD patients. Confusion of past and present; of real and unreal; and of dream, fantasy and memory may overwhelm them at times."[128] Therapists who take survivors' tales literally, even while acknowledging the suggestibility of memory and its biochemical erosion over time, seem to view memory as somehow somatically tape-recorded. But, because memory does not work that way, there are many obstacles to the acceptance of hypnotically refreshed statements of cult involvement.

Braun, at the Fifth International Conference on Multiple Personality/ Dissociative States, mixed psychiatric concerns with occasional acceptance of the literal truth of cult-survivors' claims. He maintained, "I am not judgmental for the past," perhaps a necessary precondition to accepting for therapeutic purposes a survivor's story. He emphasized, in fact, that one must accept at face value the claims of patients, taking care that the patient must first give information on Satanism. But as to precisely what kind of story a survivor is actually telling, Braun added that it's "hard to recreate something if you haven't had the experience"; the survivor's trauma "is an indication that something happened," but precisely what happened remains open to question. He even noted that a therapist must pace an interview with a survivor. If not, the patient might abreact to "a mountain of detail and information" and therefore reify shaky details through repeated questioning. Therapists can, he said, lead the patient and imprint satanic stories if one has not been careful and deliberate.

On the other hand, Braun said, "although I don't believe in Satan, I believe there is an evil" (also from the 1988 conference). At first, he maintained, he didn't believe the stories, but later they overwhelmed him and now he believes virtually everything he hears at least five times. He operates according to the "rule of five." If he hears the same stories by five people, perhaps some truth can be attached to them. In presenting a talk at the 1988 conference, when Braun listed attributes of survivors' stories (self-mutilation, influence of satanic calendar dates, numerology, symbols), he pointed out which were above or below the level of five, as if it were some measure of veracity rather than an arbitrary rule of thumb. He even cited his own epiphany about the use of cueing devices.

He recounted the story of a patient who received a card from her family, and who then tried to commit suicide. When the family later sent the same card to her, the patient tried suicide again. At this point, Braun's suspicion was drawn to the card. In fact, Braun found as highly significant the family's using the same apparently innocuous get-well card twice; so he began to examine it for clues and found a variety of numerological similarities and symbolism, all satanic, of course. The satanic 666 combination appeared everywhere: for example, the bucolic scene on the card showed birds in sixes, acorns in sixes, flowers and pickets in the fence in sixes, and a house surrounded by a fence with an open gate also carrying significance. The fence meant that the survivor couldn't escape the cult; the gate turned inward directed the message forcefully to the patient. The nearby tree signified hanging. The card's message—"Hope you make a recovery so fast it will seem the hospital visit was only a dream. Get well soon. We miss you and hurry home"—communicated a variety of messages to trigger, or cue, a response.

Since Braun assumed that the patient's view of her family as multi-generational Satan worshippers reflects truth, then the family's greeting cards represented sophisticated, subtle brainwashing devices evoking *The Manchurian Candidate*. This leads to Braun's "eight P's" of satanic involvement. To the four P's of drug abuse—pimps, physicians, prostitutes, and pushers—he adds politicians, police officers, pallbearers, and priests. Similar to his rule of five, he uses the eight P's as a checklist. When patients tell stories involving at least six of the eight P's, they begin to name public officials. Braun has recorded their names and placed them in several safe-deposit boxes—just in case.

I have suggested that in the MPD cases, therapists seem to view hypnosis as a playback button, yet abundant psychological literature militates against such a view of memory, particulary hypnotically refreshed memory. Further, the two studies of cult survivors I have discussed, by Young et al. and Kaye and Klein, both give detailed accounts of survivors' claims extracted through hypnosis. Also, both studies note that although patients who don't know one another told similar stories, the same patients could not at first deliver spontaneously "complete" satanic-abuse stories. Such stories had to be coaxed through therapy. Yet the authors of the two papers circumlocute when confronting the question of whether the therapeutic technique did help create and reify the stories. Perhaps most important, neither study represents a scientific double-blind test, which psychiatrist Frank Putnam suggested. The therapists conducting the studies were primed to absorb patients' satanic offerings. The patients studied were not new to therapy; in both studies, *other therapists* had first identified the patients as survivors and MPD sufferers and referred them to the researchers *because* the patients had either hinted, in disjointed fashion, at satanic deeds, or through therapy had developed accounts of satanic experiences.

I have chosen the word *motif* for a satanic abuse element, such as parents wearing robes of certain colors, or the killing of an infant, or sexual assault by members of a cult during a ceremony. I use the term *motif* in its folkloric sense, explored further in Chapter 7. Therapists cite the sameness of survivors' claims, particularly of those who come from diverse parts of the United States and could not have met one another. But survivors *do* influence other survivors. Tabloid television programs spread survivors' stories quite effectively. Besides, survivors construct networks to communicate with other survivors, a process encouraged by the therapists, who themselves communicate satanic imagery through their own networks. The folkloric *motif,* then, has significance here if one views the ongoing communication of satanic stories by survivors and therapists as being the equivalent of oral transmission of rumors, urban legend, and subversion myths. Psychiatrists who cite the sameness of stories have, in actuality, cited the sameness of *some* motifs. Survivors' stories are not comparable when *details* are matched. Survivors, in fact, do not tell the same stories; their stories merely exhibit the same dozen or so primary motifs.

For example, one primary motif concerns the wearing of robes for satanic ceremonies. If one believes the literal truth of a survivor's claims, one stops there: the other details do not take on importance. But to a folklorist, the other details are important, and to an anthropologist, even more so. What color robes were worn? Precisely what do the robes look like (length; type of fastenings; hooded or nonhooded, and so on)? Any difference between robes worn by men or women? At what point in the ceremony did participants don robes? Remove them? Were the robes decorated by any symbols? What kind of symbols? Did participants wear robes of specific colors and symbols depending on the longevity of their membership in the cult, of their status, of their sex, or of their specific functions at rituals? Or did robe colors and symbolism reflect mastery of the ritual trade? That is, did journeymen Satanists wear one color, apprentice Satanists another? What rules govern the storage and safekeeping of robes, or their cleaning? Any rules governing who makes the robes and how? Of what material? On the level of such details, the stories don't compare; but therapists, unlike police investigators or anthropologists writing an ethnography, don't seek the answers to such questions. Only the very broad motifs merit their attention.

Even the broad motifs require an improved synthesis if we are to accept the stories as factual. If satanic rituals are practiced within single families for generations, one would expect to find the careful preservation of ritual artifacts and techniques. The performance of a ritual requires the repeated performance, with little variation, of a set of activities within a given order. Do infant sacrifices require the attendance of a master Satanist, an itinerant analog to a circuit judge, someone to ensure the purity of the ceremony, the strict adherence to dogma? Can certain rites be performed only by certain people? Do infant sacrifices follow sexual abuse of children in a group setting? Or precede it? The ritual interment of children in coffins: What occasions demand this rite? What determines whether children are temporarily interred with snakes, decomposing bodies, or spiders? What role does magic or trickery play in ceremonies? Anthropologists undertaking fieldwork ask such questions of informants and understand that religious ritual in a society occupies an important role that pervades all other realms of social involvement.

But cult survivors don't make good ethnographic informants; their tales of lifelong involvement with satanic rituals simply don't blend plausibly with other facets of their lives. The rituals, in survivors' tales, deal only with the sexually sadistic. But in any ethnography, anthropologists discover how rituals shape the world-view, affect language, govern the socialization of the young into the values of their parents, and give people a sense of personal and communal identity. Yet the cult survivors, while claiming (through therapy) to have been part of a satanic subculture, can come up with none of this information to create a whole picture. The satanic underground could not exist without the willing involvement of some participants; coercion in sacrificing humans *must* coexist with nurturing behavior in other contexts to help convince the cult member of the correctness or rightness of his behavior *and* thinking. The satanic subculture would have to display the cruelty of a sacrificial ceremony paired with satanic-cult potluck *sabbat* dinners, with grandmothers exchanging recipes. Yet survivors' stories don't provide such information, despite the specificity of details of murder and abuse that emerge through therapy. The cult survivors' picture of satanic cults would have us believe that members come from esteemed professions, people whose public behavior appears model in every respect, yet covertly such people commit almost unimaginable brutality and cruelty, and do so willingly in fealty to Satan. This model has been perpetuated and elaborated by conservative Christians who can explain the inconsistencies in human behavior as attributable to Satan's power. Nevertheless, for therapists and investigators, the ethnographic imbalance should render the stories suspect.

Anthropologist Sherrill Mulhern, affiliated with the Laboratory of Rumors, Myths about the Future, and Cults, at the University of Paris, has studied cults and cult behavior for almost two decades, in large part training students to enter cults for study and then exit with both field observations and psyches intact. Her study population of more than 100 includes hypnotherapists, law-enforcement officials lecturing on the subject (as experts), psychiatrists and psychologists who are actively treating alleged cult survivors, adult survivors, and parents of alleged child victims (who are very active in Believe the Children), as well as teachers, teenagers, pastors, priests, and lawyers.[129, 130] Mulhern's study population continues to grow, and her research methods include participant observation, interviews, analysis of public presentations, written materials, and literature on child abuse. At this writing, Mulhern's research has not yet been published.

Mulhern's findings, presented in Chicago in 1988, indicate that "the network that links [the police cult experts, the therapists, the survivors, the concerned parents' organizations, the clergy] together is sufficient to completely explain the creation, elaboration, and spread of the satanic-cult rumor. I believe that they are the phenomenon."[131] Mulhern's research has been conducted under delicate circumstances: confidentiality of patients must be maintained; some Christian therapists have used their personal religious convictions to interpret what they've heard in therapy; some therapists "converted" to the satanic-cult ideology; and standard therapeutic procedures do not permit a therapist "to 'objectively' validate the traumatic scenario that patients produce" in a therapeutic session.[132] (On therapists' "conversion" to the satanic ideology, Mulhern observes that, in this context, "belief represents a resolution to the stressful cognitive dissonance which divides the therapist between his 'rational' version of probable reality and the emotional persuasiveness of the details of his patient's disclosures."[133]) Psychologically distressed people come to recognize themselves as "adult survivors" through therapy.

In effect, Mulhern's study reveals that many psychiatrists and psychotherapists have allowed themselves to be drawn into an impasse with highly hypnotizable patients. This has happened in spite of their earlier training in hypnosis. Mulhern found an extensive network of story-sharing among the professionals and alleged victims she studied, contradicting the claims of therapists who become convinced of the truth of survivors' stories because they emanate from people from different parts of the country who haven't met. For example:

> There is a series of interviews where a specific detail was transmitted from one adult survivor from California, during a "validation" group therapy session in Kansas City and where the detail was subsequently incorporated into the stories of local adult survivors. However, even when one goes through the laborious process of tracing down the origin of a specific detail, and thoroughly describing just how it has been transmitted from one group to another, committed believers in the cult rumor will counterattack with ten new extraordinary details which they claim "victims," who have never met each other, are all disclosing at the same time and which, they allege, prove the existence of the super cult![134]

Mulhern notes that many "believing" or "Christian" therapists who refuse to talk about their therapeutic methods cite medical codes of confidentiality, "which often translates into 'I only talk to those who share my beliefs.' " Mulhern's 1988 study examined whether any evidence exists to suggest the existence of a cult responsible for the "objectively real" memories of organized, ongoing, sadistic, sexual tortures that began in early childhood and were "recovered" in therapeutic sessions. Her answer was no. At that time, Mulhern asked two questions of the executive committee of the International Society for the Study of MPD: Had she reviewed all available and relevant data? Did any acceptable method exist whereby information obtained from people in altered states of consciousness could be validated as "objectively real," as opposed to "subjectively real," without seeking corroboration from extra therapeutic sources? In response to the first question, Mulhern had supplied her own sources, to wit, an analysis of hypnosis; an analysis of descriptions of actual non-Satanic cults "where violent . . . or deviant sexual practices had become normative and where there was documentary evidence of sacrificial murder/suicide"; an analysis of documented cases of child abduction; and an analysis of interviews with therapists treating alleged survivors, and their patients. The executive committee agreed that Mulhern had checked all relevant sources. Mulhern had shown that therapists' beliefs in the satanic ideology derived from four factors: violence of the abreaction; copious detail; the existence of "body memories of the abuse"; and the observation that victims who had not met had said the same things.[135] Mulhern also showed that the last "proof" could be accounted for by the networking process.

Concerning the second question, all but one member of the committee agreed that therapists could not validate as "objectively real" patients' memories based on the therapeutic context.

Mulhern has particularly warned of what she perceives as the "unholy alliance" of police and " 'converted' therapists." In this regard, I cite Bennett Braun and Jerry Simandl, the Chicago officer, as examples. Simandl and others like him, writes Mulhern, "constantly use the stories of [MPD patients] as if they were hard factual descriptions of a real existing organization."[136]

Some of Mulhern's assertions will be accepted with difficulty by therapists who foment satanic stories and by therapists who fail to recognize themselves as exemplars of Mulhern's study population (or who, in fact, were part of the study population). Therapists forget that both hypnotic age-regression and auto-hypnotic "switching" to child alters or personae are active processes occurring in the present, not an instant replay of the cerebral tape-recorder awaiting the push of the playback button. "The personalities of multiples are mental constructs. . . . When personalities are elicited" in therapy, "there is the mental 'interaction' among personalities . . . in the patient's mind, there is the taking possession of the body by the 'presenting' personality, and finally there is . . . the 'interacting out' of the presenting personality with the therapist." Such personae "are all imaginary personalities that the patient is seeing and hearing in [his or her head]" and "acting out."[137] Further, Mulhern has publicly debated Simandl, who has already convinced many people of the satanic conspiracy. To Mulhern, when "cult experts"

cite the "fact" that everyone is saying the same thing as proof of the cult's existence (everyone being the children of the various day-care cases and the adult survivors) I have continually responded that my research shows that alleged victims do not start out saying the same things, they learn to say the same things because their fragmented recollections and confabulations are being heard in the same way.[138]

Readers should recall the two studies cited earlier, those of Young et al. and Kaye and Klein. In both, the study populations consisted of patients who had already undergone therapy, received the MPD diagnosis, and who may have demonstrated hints, in very disjointed, nonsystematic form, of satanic elements. Through therapy, and in fact sometimes through yes-no questioning, the developed stories emerged. Simandl has stated many times that the most important clue to an MPD patient's veracity is the conviction (coupled with emotional intensity) with which they relate their stories. To Mulhern, that survivors tell their stories convincingly

> . . . is the problem. These patients are all highly hypnotizable people whose conscious sense of self is allegedly shattered across a variety of "personalities." You must recall that multiple personality disorder . . . is considered to be the result of a creative use of the imagination by a child who has the ability to dissociate and who is locked into a hopeless traumatic environment. By creating imaginary other personalities the child psychologically escapes from the abuse that he is physically forced to endure.
>
> In a very real sense, if this diagnosis is etiologically correct, these people become pathological liars in their own defense. And they are very good at what they do. . . . These patients are amazingly seductive and often ruthlessly manipulative. They are also constantly moving through dissociated states of consciousness which are in effect, rarefied trance states.[139]

Mulhern also discusses the difficulties in working with patients in an age-regressed hypnotic trance, because

> allegedly forgotten historical memory is constantly blended with confabulation and fantasy. It is impossible for either the therapist or the patient to isolate historical truth from confabulation without appealing to corroborating evidence obtained outside of the trance state. . . .
>
> This being said, it should be noted that there is one consistently observable effect of age regressed memory retrieval. The reliving of the past in a trance state allows the patient to emotionally invest the reconstituted past. Once the holes in memory have been filled in with whatever is available and emotionally experienced through abreaction . . . the teller of the story always becomes much more convincing, both to himself and to others. The hypnotically enhanced memory is immensely more credible due to the vivid details which have been "rediscovered!"[140]

Interestingly, Mulhern's observations about the limits of hypnosis, and about the pitfalls of literal acceptance of survivors' claims, all appear in literature by "believer" therapists. The difference, though, is that such therapists discount the pitfalls and embrace the stories' uncorroborated veracity because the detail that emerges in the therapeutically enhanced survivor stories and the emotional intensity with which satanic stories are told combine to override methodological caveats.

But not all psychiatrists investigating MPD uncritically accept survivors' tales as factual. Psychiatrist Frank Putnam feels that survivors' stories "have been spread by therapists who attend seminars on how to detect ritual abuse, as well as by" the published accounts, such as *Michelle Remembers*. "There is an enormous rumor mill out there. Patients pick up on stories, and therapists trade stories. . . . As far as I can tell, there has never been a case where the authorities have ever proven or verified any of the stories that these people have reported."[141] Gordon Melton adds, "You have to remember that Satanism has emerged as a reflecting board on which people have projected a wide variety of fantasies."[142] Melton thinks that "some incest victims weave satanic fantasies around their trauma because it is easier for them to accept abuse by a black-robed Satanist rather than a father who belonged to the Rotary."

Cultists on Parade

Despite the complexity of MPD, despite the therapeutic dangers cited in the psychiatric literature (of mishandling patients' abreaction; of suggesting satanic stories through hypnosis; of taking at face value the story of a hypnotically regressed adult talking in a child persona), nothing has hindered survivors from taking their tales to the masses. Apparently, the survivors who have paraded their claims on national television (and in the accompanying printed tabloids) now have integrated personalities in order to have the primary personality retell the hypnotically produced tales of the alters. Remember that before integration of personalities, the primary one would display no memory of the identities or experiences of the alter. And upon integration of personalities, survivors are now equipped to tell tall tales, and they do so repeatedly to many audiences. So when MPD patients appear on television, sometimes accompanied by their therapists (who occasionally abreact themselves when survivors tell their tales), they usually appear rational, poised, and self-confident, and can matter-of-factly assert that their babies were sacrificed and mutilated.

I suggest that both the therapeutic literature as well as Mulhern's research indicate profound reasons for doubting the veracity of survivors' satanic stories; yet no one doubts that survivors have in fact experienced trauma, possibly child abuse. That survivors implicate their own families as Satanists who enculturated them into a life of sadism and murder might be telling: every credible study of child abuse defines the most common abuser as a family member, usually a father or stepfather. In very pathological cases the entire family can be involved in ongoing sexual and physical abuse. I assert, though, that MPD sufferers are sick people in need of treatment. Survivors who market themselves as seminar speakers and therapists who parade them before awed audiences have produced a carnival side-show, a Bedlam of freaks for public amusement. Further, survivors can vex the attempts of law enforcers to conduct a legitimate investigation into their claims.

For example, Marti Johnston, a survivor paraded before seminars by the Cult Awareness Council of Pasadena, Texas, said that "she was the victim of ritualistic child abuse for 10 years and belonged to a satanic coven by age 20. She eventually rose within the satanic hierarchy to become a high priestess in two covens."[143] She told the standard tales: that ritual abuse was common, particularly to children, that Satanists' own children were abused at ceremonies, and that sometimes children were abducted from day-care centers for that purpose. To an audience of parents and teens, Johnson said:

> "I witnessed the sacrifice of an 8-year-old girl who was taken from the Harris County area." She described the crime in detail, saying the girl was drugged and then, with her eyes open in horror, killed slowly as other children watched."[144]

Naturally, the police wanted to talk to her about the murder. But then Johnston disappeared, refusing to talk further. The regional district attorney said, "We have no homicide to link [her story] to. Why she would make those claims and then be hesitant to talk with authorities is reason to question her motives."[145] So the police have been communicating sporadically with Johnston through an intermediary, Dorothy Seabolt of the Cult Awareness Council. Seabolt maintains that Johnston now fears for her own safety, especially because she also told audiences that about 100 covens existed within a 300-mile radius of Tomball, Texas, population 6,225. At her seminars, Johnston expressed her fears, saying that she stays on the move to escape "terminators" sent out by the cult to silence her. Speaking on Johnston's behalf, Seabolt guessed that the 8-year-old was taken out of Texas, sacrificed, then cremated, thus explaining the lack of evidence (although police can't even verify that an 8-year-old has been missing). Seabolt believes Johnston: "She's telling the truth because there're certain things only a former satanist would know about. True survivors know exactly how an altar is laid out, they know about rituals and the positions of officers in the organization."[146]

Joan Christianson, a cult survivor, a former prostitute and drug addict, and a born-again Christian even titles her letterhead "Survivor" and makes frequent appearances before seminars and on television to relay her sordid story, which contains the familiar motifs: childhood torture and rape; necrophilia; impregnation at a young age by cultists who made her bear babies for sacrifice (sometimes she says four, sometimes five), afterwards eating parts of their little hearts.[147] "She also passes out material explaining that Satanists are planning to defeat Jesus Christ at His Second Coming, which is supposed to happen any day now." The wealth of detail she provides to audiences astounds and amazes.

A New Mexico district attorney, Susan Martinez, paraded Christianson, having met her at a child-protection conference where "Christianson showed up along with parents of children in California's notorious McMartin pre-school abuse case,"[148] which will be discussed in Chapter 5. How does Martinez react to Christianson? While calling her "brave," she nevertheless says that Christianson's stories of satanic abuse may be

> "absurd, but so are a whole hell of a lot of other things that happen. And witchcraft has been with us for hundreds of years. Look at Salem!" She believes that child protection workers need to adopt such thinking in order to root out perfectly normal-looking people who secretly practice demonic tortures on kids."[149]

Christianson has been able to give us the benefit of her experience because her alters have been integrated through "spiritual therapy," thanks to the efforts of her "Baptist therapist." But despite her hobnobbing with the McMartin parents and giving the odd advice to investigators, Christianson's background becomes curiouser and curiouser:

> Christianson claims she has no birth certificate, and won't say where she is from or where she lives. She says she knows where a child's body is buried but can't find anyone to dig it up. She says she has pornographic photos of a McMartin student, but she won't produce them.[150]

At a cult seminar in El Paso on August 30 and 31, 1988, Christianson spoke on "Ritualistic Abuse of Children and Cult Survival" on behalf of a group of mental-health professionals and law-enforcement agencies. She began by telling her own story of involvement in Satanism, giving as side-effects not only MPD but also drug and alcohol abuse, prostitution, and the production of pornography. She went on to tell of other harmful satanic influences, such as heavy-metal rock music and entertainment violence through films and television. Concluding more or less with a Christian message, she advised mental-health practitioners on what signs betray sex-ual or "ritual" abuse in patients. To heighten the suspense, Christianson told of police officers who tried to infiltrate her cult: one ended up joining, the other was murdered. It is important to note that Christianson mentioned that she and other survivors have formed Speaking for Ourselves to promote their stories. In fact, Christianson claims that "in the seven years that I have been doing this I have gotten 10,760 phone calls,"[151] certainly attesting to a vigorous network of survivors.

Christianson may indeed have been an MPD patient, but what qualifies her to advise on therapeutic techniques or to lecture on the epidemiology of child abuse? Her résumé provides the answer. It states: "Her credentials are based on her life experience and her work with government and private agencies on this subject." But what does her résumé provide in the way of consulting "with government and private agencies"? Her background consists *only* of television and radio appearances dating to 1982. She lists associations with various police officers: Detective Kurt Jackson of the Beaumont, California, Police Department; Detective Ralph Bennet, Los Angeles Police Department; and one of the most often cited researchers promoting the satanic-abuse stories in day-care centers, psychologist Catherine Gould of Los Angeles. (Gould appears as a guest star in a San Francisco Police Department training film on ritual crime.)

To those who maintain that survivors have told the same tales throughout the country independently of one another, Christianson's résumé testifies to an expanding network of therapists and survivors. Not only does she cite an organization of survivors, but she has pandered her tales to therapists and survivors throughout California, listing more than twenty regional conferences of law enforcers and therapists. Her stature within the survivor community even caused the neopagans who produced a reference guide on cult crime to include her testimonial:

> And finally, I would like to state for the record, any record, that I am proud to know the people of the Pagan community that I met and I will stand up in front of *any group* of people and proudly proclaim that I do know Pagans and I like Pagans and most of all, I trust them. I am honored that I can and do refer Survivors and people who want to understand Pagans to these wonderful people.[152]

Undoubtedly neopagans everywhere will derive strength and reassurance from Christianson's paean. But one needs to hear a survivor in action to sense why therapists and many ordinary citizens find the survivors' stories so mesmerizing. Consider the following extract from a *Geraldo* television program, hosted by Geraldo Rivera, "Satanic Breeders: Babies for Sacrifice," aired on October 24, 1988. Rivera first establishes for his audience that his interviewees had all bred babies for sacrifice, including Gloria, who "was born specifically to be a breeder in her cult and had her first baby for them when she was just 12 years old," and discovers that another of his guests, Cheryl, had also given birth at the same age. Cheryl said that her parents had arranged for her impregnation.

Geraldo: You say your parents?

Cheryl: Yes. They were involved in a very large network of Satanists. And there was a doctor that ended up buying my children as they were born.

And my daughter, when she was born, she was sacrificed. They put her on the table and they drove an upside-down cross in her chest and took her out and buried her and carried me on a stretcher to watch.

[Rivera then probes further for details.]

Geraldo: Where were the babies sacrificed?

Cheryl: The babies were sacrificed in the L.A. area and it was in a mansion. Very high class people, in fact, very rich people.

In response to the detail of the account and Cheryl's apparent self-assurance, Rivera expresses doubts. His incredulity is matched by Cheryl's certainty. Once Rivera's doubt has been dispensed with, the last skeptical defense meekly in retreat, television audiences prepare to transcend their doubts and *believe*. An expression of doubt counts as a necessary step toward scaling the heights of belief; the expression of doubt counts as a test of proof.

Geraldo: The allegation, the story you tell—I like to think we're reasonable people here, Cheryl, but the charge is so inflammatory [against her parents], the charge is so repulsive, that it violates not only our basic standards of decency but also sorely tries our belief. Twelve years old—how certain are you that the events that you recount really happened?

Cheryl: I'm a hundred percent certain. I remember very well. I had blocked it through a process called multiple personalities and today I remember it as Cheryl. I remember the experience and I'm very repulsed by the whole thing. And I also remember my mother as, when I was between the ages of two and four, having a baby in a ritual and then sacrificing the baby, and in it there was a Catholic priest.

Geraldo: Go back to Wendy.

Cheryl: Okay.

Geraldo: Describe this room. Describe what you saw as a 12-year-old. Describe where you stood.

Here, of course, Rivera simply pushes the "play" button on Cheryl's cerebral tape-recorder for a memory playback. To the audience, this constitutes convincing stuff: the audience remains quite silent as Cheryl's eidetic memory, in a 12-year-old persona, regurgitates details.

Cheryl: That's pretty heavy. I was in a—it was like a surgery room. They had a mansion. They had a—what they called a surgical room and she was born and they induced labor. They took my babies early. There was another table, as she was born, and my son was put into a little basket and he was okay. I was on a table right here, there was another table here, and they took and they turned my head to watch. And they took and drove an upside-cross made out of wood into her chest.

Geraldo: Who did that? Who drove that? Who murdered that?

Cheryl: There was an argument between my father and the doctor about money and when the murder came up, it was—it was—I'm drawing a blank right now. I can't tell you right now.

Since Cheryl has faltered, Rivera needs to bolster her veracity, so he turns to cult-survivor Jacquie Balodis:

Geraldo: Do you believe her, Jacquie?

Jacquie: Yes. . . .

Later, another breeder, Gloria, manages to beat Cheryl's story by asserting that in her cult breeders gave birth at ages *nine* and *ten.* But the interview was not without a mildly comic dimension:

Gloria: Well, I come from Colorado, and we came out to California and that's where my family had used me. They were in the cult, I wasn't. And they impregnated me when I was nine and made me abort the baby, and they used the feces in their rituals. And they impregnated me again when I was ten and used the feces in the same type of ritual—

Geraldo: You're saying *feces.* You meant *fetus?*

The claims of Christianson and other survivors are received uncritically as factual accounts. But as I have argued, the psychiatric literature describing the treatment of MPD, the nature of MPD patients, and their possible histories of intrafamilial child-abuse all militate against quick acceptance of such tales at face value. If therapists who parade survivors before conferences simply reify for them the fantasies told by alters during hypnotically induced trances, then they have indeed created public exhibitions of sick people for our vicarious *frisson* of sexual terror. The proliferation of satanic imagery in cinema, television, and popular literature, and its skulking presence in our fears probably combine with the trauma experienced by children who develop dissociative disorders. Even if some MPD patients who have never met offer the same motifs, can we really separate their stories from the bombardment of *Geraldo* and his television cohorts, *Friday the Thirteenth* horrors at the movie theater, or our everyday fears of strangers? This last point will be discussed in Chapter 7: the confrontation with our fears as expressed through rumor panics, urban legends, and subversion myths.

I suggest that *Michelle Remembers* constitutes such legend. FBI's Kenneth Lanning, on this point, has observed that the modern survivor, complete with the usual corpus of satanic motifs, may be something new upon the public stage. He couldn't locate any cult survivors (those telling the Michelle Smith brand of story) who were known before the publication of Smith's book (Advanced ritualistic-crime seminar, September 22, 1988, Richmond, Va.). When I asked Bennett Braun if he knew of any, he admitted that he had not had the time to adequately survey the literature, but pointed out that case histories of *MPD patients* predate Michelle Smith by a couple of centuries—which didn't answer my question.[153]

Of course many accounts exist through the past few centuries of people who have escaped the deadly clutches of the minions of the Antichrist. In colonial America, some women published tales of their abduction into the netherworld of Native Americans; more recently, some women published stories of their escape from Catholics, but the cluster of satanic motifs in a modern survivor's story represents a new version, entertaining us through what anthropologist Mulhern describes as "vicarious heathenism." The new component is not the motifs themselves—the sadistic treatment of children, abductions and murders, orgiastic sexuality to propitiate Satan —but the survivor's impassioned, internalized blend of the images.

The impetus to *believe* such tales has far-reaching consequences, particularly when police and therapists extrapolate on the basis of bogus survivor tales. For example, cult cops push Lauren Stratford's *Satan's Underground* as exemplary of cult survivors' experiences. Gretchen and Bob Passantino and Jon Trott undertook an investigation of Stratford's background for *Cornerstone,* a Christian periodical, and concluded:

> The hard evidence we have uncovered and which we present here speaks for itself. The story of *Satan's Underground* is not true. And the same exploited children it may have been designed to help have been cheated of the truth.[154]

Lauren Stratford is the pseudonym for Laurel Wilson. Wilson, in her book, prevaricates about her background, giving incorrect dates and places of events, offering a chronology for her life's experiences different from her actual history. Like Michelle Smith, she leads the reader to think that she was an only child (she has a sister) and that her mother has died, also not true. Wilson's poor relationship with her mother shows up in the book, where Wilson claims that she was "repeatedly raped and used in child pornography and bestiality" with the connivance of her mother. But *Cornerstone* reveals Wilson's chronic pattern of lying throughout her adolescence and adulthood, her conning of many Christian organizations, counselors, and friends by representing herself as a prostitute, a blind person, and a drug addict. When exposed, Wilson, in most cases, apologized by pointing out that she sought sympathy and attention. She even tried to commit suicide a few times and mutilated herself. She eventually did marry a Frank Austin in 1966. But in *Satan's Underground,* Wilson maintained that she "had been raped and abused since childhood, had been involved in hard-core prostitution for at least five years, and had borne three children" by the time of her marriage; yet Austin points out to *Cornerstone* that Wilson approached the altar as a virgin.[155]

Through a combination of circumstances, Wilson wound up in the Bakersfield, California, area during the early 1980s, coincident with the onset of satanic child-abuse allegations both in Bakersfield and in Manhattan Beach (the McMartin case), both described in Chapter 5. For the first time, she passes herself off as a Satanist. Acquainted with a woman who helped abused children, Wilson confided that the Bakersfield Satanists "were still picking her up late at night and forcing her to watch their rituals, including ritual child abuse."[156] But Wilson is nothing if not melodramatic:

> One of the most macabre stories [Wilson] told [her friend] was that she had a cassette tape of her son Joey's death screams during the satanic ritual in which he was killed, and a black and white photograph of baby Joey that had been taken after his death.[157]

Needless to say, no one has ever heard the tape or seen the photograph. Wilson has never been certain how many children she had or even what fate befell them: she has announced her sterility; she said that her two children were killed during the production of snuff films, and later maintained that she had three children, even stating that for two years she lived in a "breeder warehouse." No evidence has ever turned up that she has had any children at all.

Wilson's satanic allegations caught the attention of authorities and parents of supposedly abused children, but after listening to her, and in fact devoting much time to helping her publicize her claims, parents and law enforcers finally decided she wasn't credible, particularly when she claimed a lesbian relationship with Virginia McMartin of the famous Manhattan Beach case. So how do the *Cornerstone* writers assess not Wilson but the people—including law enforcers—who credit her with absolute veracity?

> However, the most stunning element of the true Laurel Wilson story is that *no one ever checked out the main details* [italics added]. When we contacted Laurel's mother, sister, brother-in-law, cousin, church friends in fact, anyone who would have known Laurel during the book's most crucial years we were shocked to discover that, in nearly every case, we were the first people to have contacted them. . . .
>
> It strains one's credulity to think that no one would notice a teenager who was pregnant three times [to give birth to sacrificed babies], yet never ended up with a baby. Remember, all this supposedly took place in the late 1950s or early 1960s, while she was singing with Pentecostal church groups, attending Christian schools, and living with family members other than her mother. In reality, at least ten people who knew her quite well during that time are emphatic: Laurel was never pregnant during her teens or early twenties.[158]
>
> And what of Wilson's publisher? Did they confirm her story?

> Harvest House [the publisher] had a three-part test: (1) several staff members talked with Laurel at different times and got the same stories from her, and all of the staff members were impressed with her sincerity; (2) they talked with "experts" who confirmed that such things have happened to others; and (3) they gathered character references for her from her supporters.[159]

The publisher's test of veracity comes remarkably close to the reasons why some therapists remain convinced of the literal truth of survivors' claims, and why cult cops such as Jerry Simandl preach a gospel of subversion: the details of the satanic stories seem detailed and consistent; the teller seems sincere and well-meaning; so-called experts proclaim the truth of the tales. But:

> *Satan's Underground* has become the basis, the foundation, for Lauren Stratford's authority as an expert on ritualistic abuse and as a counselor of other victims. Because the story is not true, her foundation is illusory, and her expertise and counseling qualifications are nonexistent.[160]

Police investigators cannot immediately dismiss a survivor's story, but neither should a story command the ongoing commitment of police resources if a few ventures into corroborative territory don't bear fruit. After all, survivors tell stories through their MPD alters that are *fantasies* designed to deflect some kind of trauma, as psychiatrists are the first to admit. Officers must know something of the etiology of dissociative disorders, enough at least to introduce many caveats to processing a survivor's story. For example, an officer who has not been exposed to MPD patients who *don't* tell satanic stories may suggest hypnosis to refresh their memories, not aware of the easy hypnotizability of MPD sufferers and their suggestibility under hypnosis; may not expect a propensity toward self-mutilation; and may misunderstand and misinterpret the physiological changes that accompany various alters. But no justification exists for the police to convert, to become believers, and then cite everything a survivor says as literal truth, thereby alarming the public. Journalist Debbie Nathan provides good advice on this point:

> The next time you hear of one of those conferences where a lady tells everyone how she carved up multiple infant hearts, ask yourself a few questions. Like, how many Satan conferences have the daycare investigators been to? And, how come that confessed baby butcher hasn't been arrested?[161]

If police officers intend to pair with survivors and give seminars, and if the police credit survivors with veracity in their satanic accounts, they must confront one fact: by so doing, police officers ally themselves with self-professed murderers. While MPD patients don't appear as routine and predictable criminals or witnesses to police officers, thus requiring officers to defer to therapists' judgment and guidance in gaining insight into dissociative disorders, neither should therapists try to investigate crimes through clinical work. According to psychiatrist Frank Putnam:

> I do not think that one can be both an investigator and a therapist of the same patient. . . . The message of treatment should be that, taken together, the alters are ultimately one person, and the goal of treatment is a resolution of the perceived differences and the development of internal unity.[162]

In fact, the therapist is in no better position to judge the truth of an MPD patient's story than the police officer is. Two psychologists recently studied whether expert witnesses in psychology and psychiatry can answer forensic questions accurately, and whether such experts can help the court reach more accurate conclusions about people's behavior than would otherwise be possible.[163] The study concluded that professional clinicians can make no more accurate judgments about clinical matters—whether a person tells the truth, for instance—than a lay person. Further, the training and experience of clinicians have no bearing on the accuracy of their judgments in court. "Clinicians miscalibrate confidence and misappraise their own judgmental process and success. Training and experience are unrelated to accuracy."[164] Clinicians should not be faulted for failing to render reliable estimates of truth-telling; rather, the police and the rest of the criminal-justice apparatus should be aware of clinicians' limitations, as well as of their own.

The theoretical foundations of psychology and psychiatry, or for much other social science, for example, rely on the pseudoscientific, that is, the untestable assumption (although some psychiatric problems or propositions are amenable to scientific testing). Psychiatrist Thomas Szasz has written, "I submit that the traditional definition of psychiatry, which is still in vogue, places it alongside such things as alchemy and astrology, and commits it to the category of pseudoscience."[165] One can infer from Szasz's following description of the essence of psychiatric work that therapists engage their patients according to a model of mental illness, a construct that is not real to the patient. What psychiatrists do, says Szasz, "is to communicate with patients by means of language, non-verbal signs, and rules. Further, they analyze, by means of verbal symbols, the communicative interactions which they observe and in which they themselves engage."[166] The complex use of hypnosis to discover and integrate alters, many of whom appear in child personae, is a communicative interaction; therapists must take care not to give shape to their own fears and unknowns through satanic imagery and then suggest them to the patient.

Perhaps part of the difficulty with the psychiatric handling of cult survivors rests with theoretical paradigms in psychiatry. For example, "The core of psychiatric training for practice and research is typically a 3-year residency," and during that time psychiatrists acquire "their knowledge about human behavior and the vast array of theory and data associated with the study of human behavior. . . . There is typically no training in advanced statistics, mathematics, methodology, research design, or related basic issues of scientific work in human behavior."[167] (Kiesler, executive officer of the American Psychological Association, from *American Psychologist,* February 1977).

Therapists who hear spontaneously uttered satanic motifs should examine carefully the therapeutic history of the patient and the theoretical concerns of the past therapists. Remember that Kaye and Klein and Young et al. examined patients who had already been treated by other psychiatrists or clinical social workers. Past therapists' models of satanic cults undoubtedly transfer to the patient. Such is the concern not only of the responsible therapist; even anthropologists must be aware when conducting ethnographies that native informants may invent cultural traits out of whole grass skirts, particularly when informants receive pay for their time. (Much has been written about the pitfalls of dealing with professional informants who sally forth to offer the anthropologist a friendly introduction to the native culture.) But police officers sometimes forget that their investigative models don't necessarily agree with therapists'. Officers generally assume that the people they interview—whether victims or criminals—possess free will and make decisions based on choice. A person entering a police investigation may come from an abusive family or a crime-ridden neighborhood and may display a mental disorder, but a police officer's interview presumes a model, too: through the interview, police will obtain evidence of criminality, either suspecting—or removing from suspicion—a perpetrator, complainant, or witness.

When police officers take their model into the psychiatrist's office, they must realize that therapists seek different ends, that therapists, even by virtue of their training and experience, cannot discern truth-telling except by *feel.* Officers may use that feeling to help make investigative decisions, but not to arrive at conclusions of probable cause. Similarly, they may test that feeling as a working hypothesis. Officers should examine the veracity of a survivor's hypnotically induced story, but if corroboration fails to surface, the officer *must* consider *disbelieving* the survivor's tale *for investigative purposes.*

Chapter Five
"YUKKY SECRETS":
SATANIC ABUSE OF CHILDREN

Be sober, be vigilant; because your adversary the devil, as a roaring lion, walketh about, seeking whom he may devour.

1 Peter 5:8

I beseech you, in the bowels of Christ, think it possible you may be mistaken.

Oliver Cromwell, to the General Assembly
of the Kirk of Scotland, August 3, 1650

In 1983, at the McMartin Pre-School for children in Manhattan Beach, California, police conducted an investigation into the sexual abuse of a three-year-old child. His mother, Judy Johnson, claimed that her son's "bottom" appeared red, perhaps spotted with blood; she suspected that a man named Ray at the day-care center was responsible. This complaint ignited a much-publicized case involving many suspects, a multitude of victims, and legions of accusations of the abuse of children in satanic rituals. An inventory of abusive acts and odd elements in day-care cases nationwide, beginning with and including the McMartin case, reads like the special effects in a collective nightmare: the appearance of strange men and women with only one arm, some limping and some with tattooed bodies; Devil worship; secret subterranean tunnels; burned or cooked and eaten babies; murdered and mutilated babies; ceremonies and other activities held in basements; physical abuse, including beatings, slapping, and assaults, particularly during naptime or in the restroom; mock marriages; nude photography; molesters of different races; Christmas-tree lights; children handcuffed or tied with rope; various objects ranging from screwdrivers to crayons inserted in rectums or vaginas; drowned people or animals; clandestine visits to cemeteries, homes, and mortuaries; oral sex on virtually anyone and even on animals; drug-taking; blood drunk or used in ceremonies; pornographic films; burial of children; transportation out of day-care centers in vans or airplanes to go to secret sites; urination and defecation; strangers appearing to molest children; and so on.[1]

The McMartin case, coupled with a similar one in Jordan, Minnesota, which surfaced almost simultaneously, inaugurated the national suspicion that Satanists have been seeking to run day-care centers in order to exploit juvenile fodder for abusive ceremonies to propitiate the Devil. In fact, the numerous day-care center investigations stimulated by McMartin, plus the influence of *Michelle Remembers,* published in 1980, have both established within criminal justice the indurate opinion that satanic crime exists on a wide scale, permeating all races, professions, and classes.

I have maintained throughout this book that claims of satanically inspired mischief arise from a cultural and historical context. At present, more than a hundred day-care-center investigations similar to McMartin have occurred nationally, and in hundreds, perhaps thousands, of other cases of child sexual abuse, some mention of "ritualistic" activity, whether satanic or not, shows up as a peripheral consideration.

The allegations common to the current seven-year-old wave of satanic fervor present a list of folklore motifs with a long history. The two new manifestations of old motifs are the incorporation of satanic imagery in stories of multiple-personality disorder sufferers and the suspicion that day-care centers front for the satanic megacult. Interestingly, only day-care-center staffs have fallen under suspicion of organized satanic abuse of children; other child-care workers, particularly professional counselors and therapists, have remained generally immune. In Chapter 7, I suggest reasons why day-care centers have emerged as targets of such accusations.

The relentless prosecutions in the day-care cases, occasionally accompanied by persecution of the powerless (middle-class women with insubstantial incomes and little advanced education), have inspired a backlash of public opinion, sometimes organized. In fact, VOCAL (Victims of Child Abuse Laws) arose as a direct consequence of the wide-ranging accusations made in the Jordan and McMartin cases. Nevertheless, the perfervid methods of governmental inquiry into the day-care allegations have netted hundreds of suspects, many of whom have had their children peremptorily removed from their homes for the duration of the investigations. Ironically, the *same* methods that have evolved through professional literature and judicial innovation to afford children legal protection in the face of rising numbers of child physical- and sexual-abuse cases have become the methods used to search for Satan. Or more to the point, the philosophical underpinnings of new methods of detection, investigation, and prosecution of child sexual abuse have been appropriated for the day-care-center cases, which involve scores of purported victims and multiple suspects supposedly committing crimes in concert.

The investigative and judicial innovations have been many—the use of anatomically correct dolls, the appointment of guardians *ad litem* for the child victim, and videotaped depositions and televised testimony. As the day-care-center cases move forward, the investigative, prosecutorial, and judicial innovations undergo tests, not all of them successful. The U.S. Supreme Court, for example, recently found unconstitutional an Iowa law that permitted child victims to testify while shielded from viewing the defendant by a screen. The Supreme Court favored direct face-to-face confrontation in the *Coy* case, yet opined that legislatures and state judiciaries may still find ways to codify exemptions to the Sixth Amendment to accommodate children.[2]

Yet in a more recent case in Maryland, the Supreme Court ruled that a defendant's right to face-to-face confrontation with a victim of child abuse may be denied if the child witness may become traumatized or otherwise suffer extreme emotional distress as a result of testimony in the defendant's presence.[3] These cases illustrate the process of legal innovation; new laws and procedures must always be subjected to constitutional tests. Occasionally, new protections don't last. Justice Antonin Scalia, in the *Coy* case, observed, "It is a truism that Constitutional protections have costs." The court cases also make the point that investigations and prosecutions of child abuse cannot wait for the law to evolve; the cases themselves develop law.

Investigative methods and their rationale, most of them introduced in the past fifteen years as child abuse began to receive public recognition, have been shorn of all caveats when applied to satanic-abuse claims. Some police have therefore taken new methods, infused them with dogmatic assertions about children's truth-telling and the necessity to ferret out *evil,* and made arrests accordingly.

In England, a similar situation has arisen: the notorious Cleveland case had physicians making diagnoses of child sexual abuse in scores of cases based solely on reflex anal dilation and relaxation tests. This caused a public protest followed by a governmental inquiry. As a Scottish chief constable observed of the pressure to investigate child-abuse cases based on research assumptions:

> Whether or not child abuse is on the increase, there is no doubt that there has been a marked growth in the number of cases reported by all organizations; and, with growing professional awareness and training, it is equally true that the more you look for some thing, the more likely you are to find it.[4]

Only recently have medical and social-science professionals and scholars begun to test the new methods to determine whether they really work. Unfortunately, though, the public backlash through VOCAL or through indignation at the conduct of investigators and prosecutors in some instances extends to *all* cases of child sexual abuse. I assert that the hundred-plus cases of day-care-center abuse represent an aberrant phenomenon and have contrived a model of criminality hitherto unheard of and uncharacteristic of what we know of the etiology of child sexual abuse. Further, the pursuit of Satan in day-care-center cases has made the detection and prosecution of actual child-molesting very difficult. In short, the new methods of detection and investigation of child sexual abuse have proven invaluable when *properly* applied by *trained* prosecutors and police officers to "garden variety" abuse cases, that is, within the context of intrafamilial abuse—the most common setting. Public anger over the day-care allegations, then, should not extend to child-abuse prosecutions that do not have a satanic taint.

Since the press has reported extensively on them, I do not intend to simply reiterate the evolution of the various sensational day-care cases; rather, I confine my discussion to law enforcement's participation in them. The law-enforcement role borrows methods implied or suggested by new research. Since that research and the child-abuse ideologies within psychology and psychiatry provide the context within which to judge the justification for and the limitations of police methods, I also offer a lengthy description of current research and examine how law-enforcement officers have subordinated common investigative techniques to the pursuit of Satan, thereby misapplying the new methods and insights. Perhaps the new methods of inquiry into child sexual abuse have in themselves indirectly contributed to the bizarre handling of equally bizarre cases, a conclusion reached by journalists Tom Charlier and Shirley Downing who undertook a comprehensive national look at the day-care center cases and found that

> There is evidence that the child protection system established to investigate abuse reports is seriously flawed and contributed to the spread of unfounded allegations. The system is geared toward finding abuse—but provides no safeguards for those wrongfully accused. There are few checks and balances on investigators.[5]

In their investigative reporting of 36 day-care-center cases, Charlier and Downing found that of 91 persons charged with crimes, 45 eventually had their charges dismissed; 11 were acquitted; 23 were convicted; and 12 had trials pending. Since their report (written in late 1987), the statistics have changed. Two of the convicted, Gayle Dove and Michelle Noble of El Paso, are now free from custody, one having been acquitted on appeal, the other having had her conviction overturned. Others may also have been acquitted; still others may have been convicted. None of the criminal convictions, incidentally, refer to Satanism or satanic motives; all convictions stand on long-established criminal codes. The checks and balances suggested by Charlier and Downing must not only consider the newness of investigative and therapeutic methods in sex-abuse cases but also must recognize that "there are no professional organizations or national standards that license or certify practitioners in [the child-sexual-abuse field]. . . ."[6] In fact, "few, if any, medical schools, clinical psychology programs or social work programs contain a single course in sexual deviance."[7] Charlier and Downing found that in many of the multiple victims/suspects cases they examined, the first person to raise the question of abuse was an untrained, ill-educated, uncertified, or unlicensed worker in a therapeutic role.

Against the background of controversy, reports of child sexual abuse appear to be multiplying. The U.S. Department of Health and Human Services reported that, in 1988, 1.1 boys per thousand and 3.9 girls per thousand were victims of such abuse (a total of 155,300 reported cases that year).[8] In fact, the incidence of child sexual abuse in 1986 was *triple* what it was in 1980. The aggregate numbers do not distinguish the settings or other variants of abuse; day-care statistics mix with those of more "standard" intrafamilial cases. Sociologist David Finkelhor, who has studied child sexual abuse extensively for years, finds the reports of child sexual abuse "epidemic," probably arising from increased public awareness.[9] He continues: "New social problems tend to arise when they are promoted by constituencies that have both political power and public credibility," and in this case two political movements have fused their interests: the child-protection lobby and the women's movement.[10]

Finkelhor may find reporting of sexual abuse epidemic, but national statistics on arrests and prosecutions have not been clear in implying trends. One federal study showed that child abusers may be prosecuted and convicted more frequently than other kinds of abusers but they receive shorter prison sentences. Explaining the meaning of such findings is not easy; perhaps short prison time had to do with the relationship of the child to the offender, but no one can say.

National statistics derive from state figures. Some states, for example, don't consistently report useful background statistics on offenders, such as age or ethnic origin. Other states don't neatly distinguish founded complaints from unfounded ones. In Virginia, for example, the Department of Social Services reported that in 1984, 42,842 cases of child abuse (whether sexual or physical) arose, of which 30,678 were determined to be *unfounded;* in 1985, there were 49,765 cases with 37,449 unfounded; and in 1986, there were 47,888 cases with 35,809 unfounded. Some of the unfounded cases simply lacked sufficient evidence to proceed with an investigation, whereas other complaints were deemed unfounded by virtue of confirming evidence. Of the founded cases, approximately 75 percent were cases of physical and emotional abuse, with approximately 14 percent sexual abuse.

The Genesis of Satanic Allegations: McMartin Pre-School

In November 1989, a jury began to deliberate over "the nation's longest and most expensive criminal case" in United States history: the child-molestation investigation at the McMartin Pre-School.[12] The trial itself, which lasted well over two years, cost more than $13 million. Los Angeles Superior Court Judge William Pounders observed with some annoyance, "This case has poisoned everyone who had contact with it. . . . By that, I mean every witness, every litigant and every judicial officer. It's a very upsetting case."[13] Peggy McMartin Buckey and her son, Ray Buckey, faced conviction on 64 counts of child molestation and one count of conspiracy. The jury found both mother and son not guilty on most of the counts, yet the Los Angeles authorities, in the face of public protest, refiled the remaining charges (over which the jury had been deadlocked) against Raymond Buckey (which also ended in acquittal).

Judy Johnson had taken her young son to the McMartin Pre-School because of its solid reputation; it had been in business since 1958.[14] But even at the outset of the McMartin case, Johnson's behavior since her estrangement from her husband could only be described as extraordinary. She soon became an alcoholic. Told of a yearlong waiting list to enter the day-care center, in May of 1983 Johnson simply dropped off her two-and-a-half-year-old boy at the McMartin front gate and left. The boy carried no note and because of his age, he could tell the day-care staff nothing. But Peggy McMartin Buckey felt sorry for the boy and took him in.

Months later, Johnson took the boy to a doctor because his anus was "itchy" and she thought that he might have become infected as a result of her own vaginal infection. Although the doctor examined and treated Johnson for the infection, he did not examine the boy. Weeks later, Johnson complained to her brother that her son had an inflamed anus.

The boy then returned to the McMartin Pre-School, having now attended the day-care center 14 times. The teacher in charge of the play session that day was Ray Buckey. Buckey ran his own class, but Johnson's boy had never been in it, although he had attended Ray's play session on one other occasion. The day that Johnson's son returned to McMartin, his father found the boy's bottom red and, believing that he had diarrhea, applied an ointment. The father, Bernard Johnson, maintained later that "his son had had a history of hygiene problems."[15] The next day, when the boy was back with his mother, she noticed blood on his bottom and this time contacted a police juvenile officer, Jane Hoag. Johnson reported to Hoag the boy's symptoms "and that he had blurted out something about a man named Ray at his nursery school."[16] Thus the criminal case was inaugurated. Johnson, however, descended into insanity and, eventually, death due to liver complications caused by alcoholism.

Johnson's complaint did not end with her first inchoate allegations. Within weeks, she began to pass on to Hoag other stories, mostly relating to Ray Buckey. For example, she claimed that Buckey had "sodomized the boy while he stuck the boy's head in a toilet." She claimed that Buckey had placed an "air tube in the boy's rectum" and had the boy "ride naked on a horse and then molested him while dressing as a cop, a fireman, a clown, and Santa Claus."[17]

Over many weeks, Johnson continued to feed Hoag and the district attorney stories of abuse of an increasingly bizarre sort: that sodomy was committed by an AWOL marine and by "models" from a health club; that her dog might have been sodomized because it had hair missing; that McMartin Pre-School staff had "jabbed scissors into [the boy's] eyes and staples in his ears, nipples and tongue."[18]; that Peggy McMartin sacrificed a baby and forced her son to drink the blood; that Ray Buckey pricked the boy's finger and then forced it up a goat's anus. On a more mundane level, she accused the boy's father of abuse. Two years later, Judy Johnson underwent psychiatric treatment and received a diagnosis of acute paranoid schizophrenia.

The investigator, Hoag, arranged for a medical examination of the boy. One of the consulting physicians, Dr. Linda Golden, an intern at the time at the University of California at Los Angeles Medical Center, found the boy's anal redness "consistent" with sodomy, but later told a detective from the Los Angeles Police Department that "she didn't know anything about sexual abuse."[19] The other consulting physician, Dr. Jean Simpson-Savary, confirmed the finding but during her testimony she couldn't accurately remember other key details about the boy, maintaining he had been circumcised although his father said that he had not. And *this* medical examination occurred after the first one at another hospital where the physician could not determine the cause of the anal redness.

Hoag apparently developed an idée fixe that Ray Buckey had perpetrated child abuse of the most pernicious sort. According to journalist Mary Fischer, "Based entirely on a telephone call from Johnson [officer Hoag] became obsessed with the alleged guilt of one man."[20] Hoag even tried to interview Johnson's boy, but the boy wouldn't talk to her. Johnson had mentioned to Hoag the names of other abused children whose parents Hoag then called. The result: the parents had noticed nothing unusual.

Nevertheless, Hoag and other police officers scrutinized Ray Buckey and searched the school several times for evidence to corroborate Johnson's stories. "They were looking for a video camera and child-pornography photos but came away empty-handed."[21] But among the items seized by the police were a rubber duck, Peggy McMartin Buckey's graduation gown (later described by prosecutor Lael Rubin as a satanic robe), and Ray Buckey's collection of *Playboy* magazines, also presented in court by the prosecution to corroborate child-molestation charges. With nothing but tentative medical evidence suggesting abuse, among many other possibilities, investigators took their single most controversial step: under the signature of Captain John Wehner of the Manhattan Beach police, a letter circulated among two hundred parents whose children attended McMartin Pre-School. The letter read:

> Our investigation indicates that possible criminal acts include oral sex, fondling of genitals, buttock or chest areas and sodomy, possibly committed under the pretense of "taking the child's temperature." Also, photos may have been taken of the children without their clothing. Any information from your child regarding having ever observed Ray Buckey to leave a classroom alone with a child during any nap period, or if they have ever observed Ray Buckey tie up a child, is important.[22]

The letter ignited a panic among the parents, which set in motion a number of events culminating in the trial. The events merit scrutiny because each cemented a new connection between growing *belief* in the allegations and perceived criminal culpability of the McMartin staff. The entreaties of a psychotic woman to a police officer metamorphosed, through the police letter, into a regional panic. The panic itself constituted a contagious hysteria; the Jordan, Minnesota, day-care case erupted shortly thereafter, the satanic allegations readily transferable from one locality to another through communicating police investigators, therapists, and the press.

The singular phenomenon in the evolution of day-care-center cases of satanic or "ritualistic" abuse is the compulsion of *belief* among people of varying experiences, education, and professions. No one participant, with the possible exception of prosecuting attorneys, could survey the entire landscape of a particular case to view dispassionately the genesis of satanic-abuse claims. Police investigators pursued their own leads; therapists tried to sound out the traumatic experiences hinted at by children's symptoms or affective behavior; parents organized to crusade against the depredations of child abuse in day-care centers, publicly airing investigative information to which they were privy; prosecutors juggled investigative information with the probability of success in court, also taking stock of their position of community leadership in exposing perverse goings-on.

Each line of professional and nonprofessional inquiry strengthened and reinforced the others. Even if at first prosecutors showed skepticism about the evidence in day-care cases, soon the investigative information would congeal to present an impressively detailed account of satanic practices. The universe of detail became self-contained and even self-sufficient. After a time, investigators, concerned parents, and even prosecutors ceased seeking corroborative facts to anchor their scenario in a world of rationality, legally defined criminal culpability, and empirically based notions of criminality. What convinces, what fosters belief, is *detail,* an observation made in Chapter 4 regarding therapists who believe the satanic stories of MPD sufferers. Says the prosecutor in McMartin, Lael Rubin: "I believe strongly in this case. . . . I believe horrible things happened to children at McMartin."[23]

A parent of three boys who attended McMartin between 1972 and 1981 said, "It was fondling, oral sex, rape and sodomy. That was what was going on."[24] The parent, Robert Currie, offered a reward to anyone who could produce pornographic photographs of children taken at McMartin. (None were ever found.) Currie has publicly appeared, even on television, to plead his cause, referring to Satanists meeting in tunnels beneath McMartin Pre-School and the ritual burials of hamsters.

The McMartin story, as carried in the press, explored many nuances to the public appearances of principal actors in the investigation and the local political scene. The key investigative events, however, merit scrutiny since they were the precursors to inquisitional techniques used in other day-care cases.

1. Following the letter from the police to McMartin parents, Hoag continued to receive bizarre allegations from Johnson, continued to focus solely on Ray Buckey as a suspect, and obtained many search warrants for "the school, a supermarket, a photography studio and private homes. Authorities dug up a lot adjacent to the school. They had the floors of the school ripped up, searching for tunnels, or the remains of animals. No evidence was found."[25]

2. After parents complained about the slowness of the investigation, the district attorney's child-abuse unit entered the case. The head of the unit invited a friend, social worker Kee MacFarlane, to interview the children. MacFarlane had no therapeutic credentials or licenses, but did have more than a dozen years in administrative and teaching roles in child-abuse agencies. In Los Angeles, before the McMartin case, she became a staff member of Children's Institute International (CII), an organization that cared for abused children. MacFarlane, CII's medical consultant, Dr. Astrid Heger, and the head of the child-abuse unit then met with parents, still anguished and impatient with the lack of firm leads in the case. The trio invited parents to send their children to CII for MacFarlane to interview them. Although reluctant, the parents agreed, Heger advising them, "You've got to accept it. If your children went to McMartin, they were probably abused."[26] Heger's disposition to believe that widespread abuse occurred led her to diagnose abuse even where her own evidence was lacking, as in her interview of a child who denied abuse. To the child's denials, Heger admonished, "I don't want to hear any more 'No's.' No, no, Detective Dog and we are going to figure this out. Every little boy and girl in the whole school got touched like that . . . and some of them were hurt. And some were afraid to tell."[27]

3. MacFarlane interviewed almost 400 children from 100 families over the next six to eight months. In interviewing the children, she dressed as a clown, offered anatomically correct dolls "in a playtime setting," and recorded her interviews on videotape, telling children that the video camera was "a secret machine" through which kids could purge their "yukky secrets."[28] Of the 400 children she interviewed, MacFarlane found some suspicion of abuse in 369. Interestingly, some of those claiming abuse attended McMartin Pre-School when Ray Buckey was attending high school. Of significant interest in evaluating MacFarlane's approach and technique is the fact that *all* of the children had denied being abused at McMartin Pre-School until MacFarlane and her associates interviewed them. Danny Davis, Ray Buckey's attorney, said, "The case was made at CII, not at the preschool."[29] In fact, MacFarlane's interviewing technique received much probing in court because of her leading and suggestive questions. MacFarlane also rewarded children who gave the "right" answers to questions about increasingly bizarre tales of satanic abuse. Judy Johnson's allegations had been passed on to CII, and the CII staff dutifully incorporated them in their questioning. Johnson still fed odd stories to the police, although her child had never told such stories to the investigators. Johnson herself told the satanic tales to anyone who would listen.

MacFarlane was influenced in her work by Roland Summit, M.D., of the Harbor-UCLA Medical Center, author of a seminal paper in which he described the "child accommodation syndrome." (See pp. 217–222.) Many therapists cite Summit's article as the provenance of the "children do not lie about abuse" ideology. The article offered many ideas about why children might deny abuse, not allowing, as psychiatrist Lee Coleman counters, for the possibility that abuse did not happen.[30] Journalist Mary Fischer recounts one MacFarlane interview with an eight-year-old boy in which he holds an alligator puppet while MacFarlane asks about "Naked Movie Star," a game Ray Buckey supposedly played with children as a pretense for taking pornographic pictures of them.[31]

> Boy: Well, I didn't really hear it [Naked Movie Star] a whole lot. I just heard someone yell it from out in the . . . someone yelled it.
>
> MacFarlane: Maybe, Mr. Alligator, you peeked in the window one day and saw them playing it, and maybe you could remember and help us.
>
> Boy: Well, no, I haven't seen anyone playing Naked Movie Star. I've only heard the song.
>
> MacFarlane: What good are you? You must be dumb.
>
> Boy: Well, I don't really, umm, remember seeing anyone play that 'cause I wasn't there, when I . . . when people are playing it.

> MacFarlane: You weren't? You weren't. That's why we're hoping maybe you saw. . . . See, a lot of these puppets weren't there, but they got to see what happened.
>
> Boy: Well, I saw a lot of fighting . . .

And later:

> MacFarlane: Can I pat you on the head for that . . . look what a big help you can be. You're going to help all these little children because you're so smart. . . . Okay, did they ever pose in funny poses for the pictures?
>
> Boy: Well, it wasn't a real camera. We just played. . . .
>
> MacFarlane: Mr. Alligator, I'm going to . . . going to ask you something here. Now, we already found out from the other kids that it was a real camera, so you don't have to pretend, okay? Is that a deal?
>
> Boy: Well, I haven't seen any real camera.
>
> MacFarlane: How about something that goes flash, remember that? I bet if you're smart, you better put your thinking—
>
> Boy: Yes, it was a play camera that we played with.
>
> MacFarlane: Oh, and it went flash?
>
> Boy: Well, it didn't exactly go flash.
>
> MacFarlane: It didn't exactly go flash. Went click? Did little pictures go zip, come out of it?
>
> Boy: I don't remember that.
>
> MacFarlane: Oh, you don't remember that. Well, you're doing pretty good, Mr. Alligator. I got to shake your hand. You remembered who took the pictures and all that. . . .
>
> Boy: I'm getting tired here.

MacFarlane later admitted that she and other CII staff had assumed unfamiliar roles as go-betweens for the police, that therapists had proceeded in their work even as investigators, despite having no training in evidentiary standards and interviewing techniques. She admitted that all of this gave her "a preconceived bias."[32]

4. After MacFarlane interviewed the children, those she suspected of being abused received medical examinations, usually performed by Heger. Studying 150 children with a colposcope, essentially a magnifier-camera combination, Heger found that 80 percent showed tissue damage "consistent with attempted or complete penile penetration."[33] Although her findings were reviewed by an expert on child abuse—physician David Paul, who concluded that no signs of sexual abuse were present in 9 of 11 children cited by the prosecution as abused—Heger made her diagnosis before

physicians had studied the prevalence of supposed sexual-abuse indicators in *nonabused* children. Later research by John McCann and others (which will be discussed later in this chapter) has questioned the opinions rendered on abuse diagnoses based on genital irritation. Further, Heger received no formal training on colposcopic techniques until a year and a half *after* she used the instrument for her diagnoses.

5. With the CII interviews as the *only* criminal-investigation interviews in the case, a team of three prosecutors, all with extensive trial backgrounds but none with child-molestation training or experience, took on McMartin: Lael Rubin, Christine Johnston, and Glenn Stevens. Rubin, the only one of the three to see the trial through to its end, secured the services of George Freeman, a convicted felon who shared a cell with Ray Buckey and claimed that Buckey had confessed all in jail. The prosecution built its case around child pornography. In court they put the case that the McMartin family and day-care staff had abused the children in order to film their acts (although eventually the prosecution dropped these charges against everyone but Ray Buckey and his mother). To support their case, the prosecution enlisted the help of the FBI and Interpol in the attempt to track down kiddie-porn films starring the McMartin children, fruitlessly searching the preschool itself four times, testing children's clothes and blankets for blood or semen, and hiring an archaeological team to excavate the day-care property for subterranean tunnels. The archaeologists did, in fact, unearth something: turtle and chicken bones, which forensics experts analyzed for evidence of torture.[34]

Glenn Stevens was removed from the case once he turned apostate. He openly doubted the "evidence," eventually believing it all emanated from "a nut case"—Judy Johnson. The letter Johnson wrote to the district attorney accusing men of sodomizing her son and offering stories of a pair of scissors poked into her son's eyes—which was an indication of Johnson's mental condition—was not shared with the defense attorneys upon discovery and did not come to light until almost two years after the trial began. Although Stevens feels that the accumulation of reams of documents simply buried the letter, he found other reasons to doubt the case. He questioned Kee McFarlane's credentials as only academic and administrative, not clinical; although investigators claimed that the children told identical stories of abuse, Stevens found the stories dissimilar; and after watching the CII videotapes of the children's stories, he found their tales influenced by the interview process. If a child denied victimization, Stevens noted, an interviewer would say: "You're not being a very bright boy. Your friends have come in and told us they were touched. Don't you want to be as smart as them? What kind of a way is that to interview children?"[35]

Stevens found other problems; he became suspicious of why the satanic allegations were confined to the South Bay part of Los Angeles County, and also of what followed when parents removed their children from McMartin Pre-School and sent them to other neighborhood day-care centers. Once in other schools, the same satanic stories emerged, causing closure of seven other day-care centers. Some investigators and many parents then claimed that the number of abused children reached 1,200. Stevens reasoned that the fact of the allegations being confined to South Bay corresponded with the area's being the locus of the investigation. All children interviewed by CII came from this area.

Stevens found other bases for doubt: none of the parents had found hints of abuse from their own children, although based on the stories the children should have experienced many signs of trauma, such as bleeding, bruising, pain, bedwetting, and sleeplessness. "None of that ever came up," Stevens later said.[36] If the children learned of some bizarre activities through repeated abuse in day-care, why didn't the children evince revealing behavior once out of the preschool? As Stevens pointed out, one might expect a child, now in kindergarten, to ask an unsuspecting teacher, "When do we play Naked Movie Star?"

Finally, Stevens noted that children did not spontaneously name their tormentors; the names emerged only through interviews at CII. As an example, Stevens found that of the first ten children interviewed at CII, none mentioned Peggy McMartin Buckey as an abuser. The eleventh did, but only after a therapist offered the child an anatomically correct doll and said, "Let's make this the Peggy doll."[37]

6. Further hampering investigative efforts in the case was the instant international attention focused on McMartin following a report by KABC in Los Angeles that aired in February 1984, giving full play to the bizarre stories that emerged through the CII interviews. Controversy exists over how the KABC story came about. While MacFarlane maintains that she gave information to the press only after the KABC story appeared, the FBI has recorded that MacFarlane promised a KABC reporter an exclusive story in February.[38] Further, at some time during the McMartin investigation, the reporter became romantically involved with MacFarlane. The KABC coverage stimulated so much public interest and debate that the investigation stood no chance of reconsidering whether or not a criminal case even existed. The satanic allegations did not surface through police investigation; parent Robert Currie credits himself as the first to introduce the satanic bent. Playing detective, Currie carried on his own investigation, interviewing children, parents, and anyone else who would meet him. But Currie did not keep his thoughts to himself; he appeared on Phil Donahue's television program and later on ABC's *20/20,* and many newspaper and magazine articles soon followed. The news media quickly leaped on each

new story of McMartin, Jordan, and any other case with multiple victims and multiple suspects, constructing satanic links between them. As Charlier and Downing observed in their report, "Each highly publicized case usually produced new allegations."[39]

7. Due to the public scrutiny of the case and investigative myopia in pursuit of Ray Buckey and his mother, evidence that militated against criminal charges was simply ignored. For example, the McMartin school records, coming to light after six years of investigation and trial, present serious obstacles to accepting the veracity of the children's stories. Of the initial 300 children accusing the McMartin staff (through the CII interviews), the prosecution built its case around eleven children. One, David (pseudonym), who was 14 years old in 1989, "claims Buckey molested him over the entire period of his enrollment [at McMartin], yet the records show he left the school a year and a half before Buckey began teaching there."[40] Four other children claimed molestation during the morning classes, although Buckey had not had any of the four in his class. And while the prosecution has contended that Buckey molested kids in the afternoons, "none of the four were at the preschool on the same afternoon as Buckey."[41] When children's accounts are compared with attendance records, the prosecution is left with only two children's stories that match.

The McMartin case adumbrated much of what was to follow in other day-care-center cases: satanic stories that appeared during therapy or through suggestive, leading questioning; heated dispute over medical findings, where physicians insisted that abuse must have occurred because of the presence of symptoms on a checklist of indicators; and massive publicity fueled by parental pressure to obtain convictions. I assert that the inquisitional *attitude* in McMartin and like cases left little room for criticism, for self-doubt by investigators and prosecutors, and for failure to consider circumstances, events, and even evidence that might *not* support a prosecution. For comparative purposes, I outline key investigative milestones in two other similar cases: one alleging abuse by Kelly Michaels in New Jersey, a case that produced a conviction, at this writing under appeal; another alleging abuse by two day-care workers in El Paso, Texas, a case in which charges have been dropped against one defendant and the other was acquitted at a retrial following appeal.

Kelly Michaels

In 1985, a four-year-old boy in New Jersey underwent an examination of a rash, during which the nurse inserted a thermometer in his rectum. While the nurse took his temperature, the boy said, "That's what my teacher does to me at nap time at school."[42] When the nurse asked him to explain what he meant, the boy replied, "Her takes my temperature." This admission sparked an investigation which culminated in the conviction of then-23-year-old Kelly Michaels for 115 counts of sexual abuse against twenty children between ages three and five. The allegations against her included rape and assault with forks, knives, spoons, sticks, and Lego blocks. Some children "described her licking peanut butter off their genitals, forcing them to eat and drink her feces and urine, playing the piano in the nude, making them undress and play sexual games, and terrorizing them into silence."[43]

Journalist Debbie Nathan found in the Michaels case a familiar "preconceived approach" that included "questionable" interviewing techniques and "cross-germination" of stories among children, their parents, therapists, police, and prosecutors. Nathan found as well that Believe the Children, an advocacy organization that promotes satanic conspiracies, had allied itself with parents from the Wee Care center where Michaels had worked, an organization that put out word that Nathan could not be trusted because of her reporting on the El Paso day-care case. And although the judge hearing the case had opened it to the news media, he would not allow Nathan a copy of the trial transcript and prohibited the press from noting that Lou Fonolloras, an investigator with the New Jersey Division of Youth and Family Services, who conducted leading interviews with children, had himself been molested as a child and had mentioned this fact to one of the Wee Care children.[44] Despite Nathan's criticism of the prosecution of the case and her status as persona non grata in the courtroom, two recent books about the case give absolute credence to the prosecutorial claims against Michaels: *Not My Child: A Mother Confronts Her Child's Sexual Abuse,* by Patricia Crowley, mother of a child at the Wee Care preschool (Doubleday, 1990); *Nap Time: The True Story of Sexual Abuse at a Suburban Day Care Center,* by Lisa Manshel (Morrow, 1990).

Public hostility against Michaels during the investigation undoubtedly affected its course. Some of Michaels's colleagues at the day-care center believed she was innocent but feared to say so; when Michaels's family asked for help from the Catholic church to defray hotel expenses in Newark, N.J., where the pretrial hearings took place, the church first assented and provided space in the church rectory. But after the archdiocese received a call from the prosecutor's office, the church withdrew its help. Such was the ambiance of the community in which the investigation took place. The chronology of salient investigative steps includes the following:

1. The four-year-old boy who told the nurse about the thermometer did so days after Michaels quit the employ of Wee Care. The boy's mother then met with the local prosecutor's office but not before she questioned her son at length. While the boy admitted "his own victimization" to in-

vestigators, his tale was ambiguous and indirect. Further, his mother told investigators that her son disliked school naps and *for an entire year* complained of "a sore bum." When prosecutor Sara McArdle talked to the boy and presented him with an anatomically detailed doll, the boy "put his finger into the doll's rectum."[45]

2. The police, McArdle, and parents interviewed other boys, and although three of four denied abuse by Michaels, one admitted it under repeated questioning by his own father. By now, all the boys told bizarre tales of Michaels punching them, fondling their genitals, and threatening to kill their parents if they told anyone. Finally, the police interviewed Michaels, even giving her a polygraph test (which she passed), but one investigator told her, "You are going to have to come up with more evidence. . . . If you don't help us find someone else, that makes you the most suspicious."[46]

3. Later, in the manner of McMartin parents, the Wee Care parents' board sent a letter to parents advising them that an investigation had been conducted of the alleged abuse by a former staff member. By now, Michaels had begun working at another day-care center, but police visited the new school and told the administrator of their suspicions about Michaels, whereupon Michaels was fired. Shortly thereafter, Wee Care held a meeting with parents during which a state social worker told them that Michaels had molested the children and to search for symptoms, including genital soreness, sleep disorders, bedwetting, and temper tantrums.

4. At first, prosecutors reviewed purported evidence and declined to pursue the case. Yet Lou Fonolleras refused to drop the case and pressed on. He did not record his initial interviews with the children. Later interviews with the children were, but they include no narratives of abuse. More often, the tapes contain yes-no answers to leading questions, refusals of the interviewers to accept denials, and the police and social workers suggesting many kinds of abuse and then asking the children whether they participated in or witnessed them. The police even rewarded children with toy badges if they described how Michaels abused them. If children manipulated the genitals on anatomically correct dolls, investigators noted that the children had "victimized" the dolls, thereby symbolically reflecting their own victimization. The investigators carefully recorded children's stories that confirmed their views; but when confronted with fantasy elements (such as a boy claiming that Michaels put a real tree and car on him while she simultaneously molested him), the investigators simply ignored them.
Some of the questioning techniques led children to identify Kelly Michaels as an abuser through a subtle drift from a form of "let's pretend

that Kelly did this" to "how did Kelly do this?" (What follows derives from my examination of tape-recorded interviews with the children.)

In other cases where children did not admit to having witnessed abuse, the interviewer would ask them to *suppose* that abuse had taken place and to demonstrate how it *might* have happened. For example, in one interview of a five-year-old girl, Emily (pseudonym), the investigator provided an anatomically correct doll and told her that many of her friends said they were hurt and that Emily must have known about it. The investigator then asked Emily to demonstrate on the doll good and bad touches, which she did. The investigator repeated that some of the children in day-care "got hurt by a bad touch and that [Emily] might be hurt, too." Presuming that Emily had been hurt, he asked, "Did you get hurt in the music room?" (Michaels allegedly abused children in the music room.) But Emily replied only that she once ran, fell, and got hurt.

Since some of the allegations against Michaels have her using a wooden spoon as an instrument of sexual abuse, the officer hands Nancy (a pseudonym) a wooden spoon and asks, "Can you think of a way that someone might have used the spoon to hurt a child?" Nancy, then, demonstrates *hypothetical* ways to hurt a child with a spoon. The same officer encourages Nancy: "We know how scary it is to tell about it, especially to parents." He then admitted to Nancy having been a victim himself of sexual molestation and pointed out that as a child if he had talked, adults would hurt him, possibly kidnap him, and harm his parents. "So telling about it is important." (The professional literature universally agrees that the formerly abused should not interview children, as a general rule, or might only do so if they have thoroughly reckoned with their own past, a view that holds for anyone interviewing children. "One important factor, often overlooked in evaluating a therapist, is a healthy value system and a personal background devoid of pathology."[47])

The approach of asking a child to give hypothetical examples of abuse and the inferring from the child's answer that such abuse took place has a foundation in the therapeutic literature. Kee MacFarlane has written:[48]

> In cases where children consistently deny abuse but where there are strong reasons to suspect its occurrence, some interviewers have tried to determine whether or not children know any details about abuse by asking them what they *think* an experience would have been like if it *had* happened to them.

Yet on the other hand, MacFarlane advises that interviewers could go too far. She points out that the "let's pretend game" could "only serve to confound any information gathered."[49]

The interviewer resumed the demonstrations with the doll, but with a fork this time. Nancy remained reluctant to identify Michaels as the abusing teacher, but the interviewer repeated his request that Emily hypothetically demonstrate how abuse may have occurred. "You showed how Kelly hit the girls—how else might she have hit the kids?" Such a question blends the hypothetical with a leading suggestion that Michaels was culpable. "How do you think Kelly used this fork to hurt the little girls?" Nancy then proceeded to stick the fork into every conceivable orifice in the doll's body. The child clearly assaulted the doll according to the interviewer's prompting, the interviewer asking her to continue while giving approbation with every jab. The girl gleefully continued the encouraged poking and when she ran out of possibilities, the investigator asked, "Is there any other place you were embarrassed to show where she stuck the fork?" When Nancy stuck the fork in the doll's vagina, the investigator asked, "Did blood come out?"

"Yes," said Nancy.

"Who cleaned it up?"

"My mother."

"Did Kelly clean up the blood?"

"Yes," said Nancy.

"What did she clean it up with?"

"A towel."

The officer had Nancy poke the fork into the doll until she found the vagina, the orifice he sought, to confirm for himself that Nancy must have been thus assaulted, yet Emily clearly remained confused. After the towel answer, the investigator concluded the interview, having obtained what he wanted, telling Nancy that she was "great" and did as well in answering as the other children. "You're being very helpful, terrific. . . . If you show me anything more, you'll be better than Brandi [pseudonym]."

The officer followed the same technique with other children. They did not spontaneously implicate Michaels (or if they did, they said that another child or a parent had said that Michaels was responsible), so the officer presented the children with forks and spoons and asked them to demonstrate how "Kelly" might have abused the children. With another five-year-old girl, the interviewer said, "Some other kids mentioned your name once or twice," and he gave the names.

The child responded, "Why were they saying my name?"

The interviewer mentioned that the *other* kids had been brave and honest in telling what happened. But when the officer displayed a knife, spoon, and fork and asked, "Did you hear of anyone getting hurt with this stuff?" the child answered no. "How do you think little kids could get hurt?" Similar to the interview with Emily, the officer encouraged the girl to jab, poke, stab, and beat the doll until she placed an object in the vagina, whereupon he asked, "Do you bleed when that happens?" The girl said no. Interestingly, the girl tells how her own brother occasionally hurts her, that he even pinches her genitals. But the officer wanted the girl to mention "Kelly" in this context and ignored her brother—who quite possibly could have abused the girl—and asked, "Who else touches you in private places?" The girl responded, "He does!" and pointed to the other investigator.

An interview with Susan [pseudonym] illustrates the persistent use of leading questions to implicate Michaels, a refusal to accept denials of abuse —even when Susan has tired of the interview—and suggests parental involvement in cross-germinating children's stories. The investigator began the interview by referring to Susan's not wanting to talk during the previous interview. When Susan offered nothing new, the investigator asked, "So you don't remember seeing Kelly hurt anyone at all?" The officer then asked if specific children, by name, had been abused; Susan responded that she knew nothing.

"Did Kelly ever take you up to the music room?"

"Yes," Susan said, with other students and another teacher.

"When she was playing the piano, was she wearing clothes?" (The investigator could have offered a less suggestive question by simply asking what Kelly wore. By this point, the allegations have Kelly playing the piano nude.) Susan replied that her mother told her that other kids had worn nothing in the music room, and insisted that she had seen nothing amiss and knew nothing about abuse. To the following questions Susan simply answered no: "Did you see [Kelly] wear robes?" "Did you see other kids cry?" "Did you see kids take their clothes off?" "Did you see Kelly lying on a bench taking a nap?" "Did [Kelly] feed you peanut butter and jelly in the music room?" "Did you see Kelly eating peanut butter and jelly?" (Allegations have Kelly making kids smear peanut butter and jelly on genitals and licking them.)

Finally, Susan became angry and declared the questions "dumb." But the questions continued, again receiving "no" answers: "Did Kelly scare kids?" "Did she play games where she said she could be like Superman?" "Did she say anything bad about policemen?" "Do you like her?"

When the officer asked, "Are you mad at her?" Susan said, "Yes. She did a bad thing."

After Susan failed to describe the "bad thing" or otherwise clarify her remark, the officer asked, "How do you know she did a bad thing?"

"Because my mommy told me."

Her mother, who was present, asked, "What bad thing?"

Susan: "I didn't see it."

The mother presses her to describe the "bad thing," later asking her whether Michaels did "bad things" to other children, asking about each by name. Susan responded negatively to all except for Betsy (pseudonym).

Mother: "How do you know?"

"Mommy told me," said Susan.

5. After Michaels had been arrested, parents began to meet regularly under the guidance of psychologist Susan Esquilin, who was connected with the Division of Youth and Family Services. In fact, long before she had conducted therapy with the children, Esquilin "was one of the principal instigators of the parents' insisting that the investigation go ahead after the prosecutor had closed his file." Some parents still thought that Michaels might be innocent, but Esquilin counseled that they must feel a "tremendous need to deny the possibility of abuse" and should therefore channel their anger into assisting the prosecution. Thereupon a strong affiliation developed between prosecutors and parents. But interviews continued, and when other day-care staff were warned that they, too, could be indicted (because children told investigators that other staff members had known of and ignored Michaels's molestations), they began to remember strange facets of her character: that she once "smelled"; that she might be a lesbian; that she seemed "spacey" and "untidy."[50]

Michaels's own attorneys, incidentally, argued that the abuse allegations simply were not feasible on logistical grounds: Michaels rarely had an opportunity to abuse children because her interactions with them were always either observed or overheard. For example, prosecutors charged that Michaels led groups of children to a choir room, "undressing them, laying on top of them, forcing them to play with her feces, urine, and bloody tampons, and cleaning the mess and re-dressing them, all in less than 45 minutes."[51] Yet none of the obvious corroborative evidence emerged; for example, neither any of the other teachers nor the janitor found blood, urine, or fecal traces anywhere. Further, the prosecution introduced parents' diaries of physical symptoms in their children, such as bruises, sore genitals, and the like. "But no parent reported such symptoms until after the investigators suggested them."[52]

6. Psychiatric examinations (conducted on behalf of the prosecution) of Michaels found nothing significantly amiss aside from a suggestion that she had difficulties with sexual identity. Michaels fit no known profile of a sexual abuser. The lack of a category within which to place Michaels did not stop prosecutor Glenn Goldberg, who told the court "that since Michaels was an actress, she had molested groups of children to fulfill her need to direct 'plays.' "[53]

7. The prosecution introduced evidence against Michaels that emanated from jail guards and an inmate charged with first-degree murder. Even though the inmate wrote a letter of support to Michaels, in court she maintained that in her cell Michaels talked to herself saying, "I didn't mean to harm those kids the way I did."[54] The guards reported on visits from the Michaels family, one guard maintaining that Kelly Michaels's father

"rubbed her breasts" and that Michaels's mother sent her a nude photograph of herself. The press made much of the Michaels family's purported behavior during jail visits, the reporters taking it all at face value. In fact, the prosecution had dropped tidbits to the press periodically; the rumors about the family fondling and the nude photograph came from the prosecutors.

8. In court, children told contradictory stories, and some told tales that not even other children could corroborate, such as one about a boy who claimed that Michaels raped every child in the class with Lego blocks. Another boy said he witnessed Michaels urinating and defecating into a bucket in the gym, whereupon she poured the mess into a toilet. The court heard children's tales in addition to much hearsay, which the judge permitted. Even after two years of interviews, the children's stories remained "erratic" and "self-contradictory." The boy then turned to the prosecutor and asked if the gym had a toilet. Although the children testified on closed-circuit television, the judge also allowed parents to testify about what their children told them, "although such hearsay was subsequently ruled inadmissible by a higher state court in New Jersey."[55]

9. Psychologists testified that the children's behavior was consistent with sexual abuse. Eileen Treacy, the prosecution's "real expert" on the psychology of abuse, who offered such testimony, had exaggerated her experience with child sexual abuse on her curriculum vitae. The judge in an earlier case had found that "she would have been able to elicit the disclosure . . . from many children . . . who had not been sexually abused." Yet in Kelly Michaels's case, Treacy maintained that she provided "psychological services" and proclaimed herself an expert on sex abuse. As attorney Morton Stavis has pointed out, the child-abuse-accommodation syndrome Treacy described to the court was a "therapeutic aid and *not* an investigative device to establish guilt or innocence." Nevertheless, Treacy stated that children's denials of abuse constituted proof of victimization, her basis for saying so deriving from retrospective reports of the children's behavior by their parents. These behavioral changes had gone unnoticed by the parents until they were instructed by the prosecution as to what changes to record. Although Treacy was not a licensed clinician and the syndrome she diagnosed was not recognized by the American Psychiatric Association, the court approved the syndrome nonetheless. One footnote concerning Treacy's testimony perhaps reflects her level of professional acumen. During cross-examination, she was asked, "Why should [a boy supposedly abused]'s mother or father be so concerned with his absence—his lack of desire to eat tuna fish when there's no allegation of any impropriety with tuna fish?" Treacy responded with her interpretation:

I don't know how to say this politely. To some people at certain junctions, the genital smells that emit from a female's vagina, et cetera have been likened to the smell of fish, and it's my interpretation that the reason for the withdrawal from tuna fish in conjunction with the withdrawal of peanut butter had to do with [the boy's association with the smell of tuna fish and the smell of the female vaginal area.[56]

Before discussing problems in investigating such cases, I offer one more: the investigation of Gayle Dove and Michelle "Mickey" Noble of El Paso, Texas.

El Paso

In early 1985, Richard Lescault (pseudonym) called the Department of Human Resources (now the Department of Human Services) in El Paso to report his suspicion that someone was molesting his two-and-a-half-year-old son.[57] The boy had spoken of "someone at the Y" removing his pants, "playing games in the bathroom, playing doggy, licking someone's face and chest, playing doctor, and tickling hineys."[58] Lescault's wife, Ruth (pseudonym), also called in her observations, including her suspicion that her son had referred to workers at the YMCA, mentioning specifically "Ms. Dove" and "Ms. Mickey," among others. Later, Mrs. Lescault would testify from her own notes that her boy *first* mentioned their babysitter, Melanie.

The social worker handling the case, Helga Wright, noted that in her own interview with the boy and his parents, he could not offer any narrative of abuse and could not or would not acknowledge that anyone had touched his "private parts" unless he was asked specific, directed questions, such as, "Did Miss Mickie [*sic*] kiss your boobies?" which the boy would answer affirmatively. Wright wrote of the interview: "I explained my usual method of interviewing alleged victims. My reason for doing so was the parents' frustration and their concern that they would not be believed."[59]

Wright undertook a thorough reconnaissance of the family's situation, noting the mother's concerns that her son's difficulties had been chronic (nightmares, fear of the Big Bad Wolf, some "accidents" with defecation), and observing some stress in the family. The father, employed by the U.S. Border Patrol, had recently moved his family to El Paso from New Mexico and had been working evening hours, "meaning [the son] was seeing much less of his dad than he was used to."[60] Wright even interviewed Melanie, the babysitter, and found her "mentally slow," and therefore was "unable to form an opinion regarding Melanie's care or abuse of [the boy]."[61] When Wright had the family see a psychologist, the therapist also noted that the boy could not respond to open-ended questions, and did observe the boy's lack of anxiety but a great deal of it on the mother's behalf. The psychologist suspected that the boy "might be having flashbacks about an incident of abuse that happened long ago."[62] The other milestones in the case followed a familiar pattern.

1. The parents removed the boy from the YMCA and demanded that the Texas authorities shut down the day-care center. The Department of Human Resources refused to do so, but interviewed the YMCA staff. Wright made unannounced visits to the day-care center, but saw nothing suspicious. Noble told authorities of the boy's problems with bowel movements, that he sometimes refused to go to the bathroom and defecated in his pants.

2. The authorities then interviewed parents of children at the YMCA and had them produce their children for interviews. The social workers described signs of sexual abuse and even had some of the children play with anatomically correct dolls. Wright did ask parents and children some direct questions, such as whether anyone had touched the children's private parts. Records of these initial interviews were not produced at discovery. Based on the social workers' earlier training in *incest,* they offered the parents such signs as bedwetting, nightmares, changes in eating habits, pseudo-adult behavior, unusually aggressive moods, and sudden anger, among other attributes. Journalist Debbie Nathan noted that "these and other sometimes vague and contradictory traits, which probably describe any preschooler's behavior over a few months' time, comprise a checklist used by child protective service workers all over the country as they scout for sexual abuse. The [El Paso] interviews uncovered no evidence of abuse."[63] The local grapevine spread the allegations and details of the investigation among parents. Nevertheless, within months the authorities suspended the investigation as "inconclusive."

3. Later, in the summer of 1985, another Border Patrol agent, Thomas Leppert (pseudonym), approached the El Paso police with an idea that his three-year-old daughter had been molested. He had overheard her say "something that sounded like 'futching,' " and she said that she had heard the word at Miss Mickey's house, a place she had visited three times. But her father related to police other elements of his daughter's stories: that she had had make-up applied; that she saw people wearing monster costumes and "brandishing masks and swords"; that "Miss Mickey 'kissed' and 'tapped' her on her genitals, a black mailman kissed her, and a policeman chopped off a baby's head' "; the girl later telling her mother that "a Daddy monster had showered with her and had shampooed and blow-dried her hair."[64] Further, Leppert said, when a doctor examined the child, she "acted ter-

rified and screamed, 'Please don't hurt me like he did.' "[65] The doctor discovered a ruptured hymen and concluded that something had penetrated the girl's vagina. The same doctor later testified that he was unfamiliar with medical literature suggesting a wide variation in girls' hymens, literature that might suggest that the girl's was normal.

4. The medical examination of the girl and Leppert's statements caused a reopening of the case. Local Texas officials received help and advice from law enforcers and therapists from elsewhere; the case had generated publicity beyond Texas. In fact, the discovery phase of the trial of Noble and Dove produced notes of the Department of Human Resources that showed the cross-fertilization of inquisitional techniques from other day-care cases. According to the notes, Nancy DeWees from the Tarant County Child Protective Services in Texas contributed a list of guidelines for investigating day-care centers; and Faye Greenly from the FBI, based in New York, sent along a list of questions to ask parents and children in such cases, based on another satanic-abuse day-care inquiry. "The FBI's list was big on nightmares, constipation, pencil penetration, pictures being taken, keeping secrets, and playing 'silly games.' "[66] The CPS worker's list included looking "for monsters, masks, dressing up, or going on field trips."[67]

Social worker Marina Gallardo and police detective Sergio Cox then set about visiting parents and children together, alternately asking yes-no questions from the checklists they had obtained. In one instance, they questioned two young boys, cousins, and determined that they probably had been molested. Yet when the boys underwent further interviewing, they did not respond to anatomically correct dolls, and their mother found that the boys evinced none of the behavioral changes attendant upon abuse. But other parents' fears heightened much more easily. As Cox and Gallardo interviewed more children, they eventually found others who would answer "yes" to having nightmares or dreaming about monsters. If children showed shyness in the presence of Cox's police paraphernalia, his badge and gun, Cox told parents that Noble and Dove had used police uniforms to intimidate the children into not talking. After the interviews, some parents began taking notes about their children's behavior and within weeks could describe suspicious goings-on, such as the kids' making adult sexual suggestions. When children denied abuse, Gallardo and Cox construed their answers as "avoidance behavior."

In fact, once Gallardo and Cox had suggested possibilities of abuse at the YMCA and had provided parents with checklists, parents began to notice many anomalies in their children's behavior. One father noted that his son did not seem to "rough-house" with him as much as he used to and that the boy had recently experienced nightmares and bedwetting. Even more unprecedented, the boy had begun to sit quietly and color pictures before dinner. Yet the boy's father had recently been afflicted with bone cancer, and his mother's sister was dying of cancer (a sister had already died), possible explanations for new or unusual behavior. But for the boy's parents, "it all fell into place, every inexplicable or troubling thing Matt did could be chalked up to sexual molestation."[68] And, of course, Gallardo and Cox interviewed everyone except Noble and Dove, who remained quite aware of the investigation, particularly when a local television station aired the story, giving Noble's name and address.

5. Within months, Gallardo and Cox had produced a list of eight children whose parents were willing to have them testify, and the only corroborative evidence thus far was the girl's broken hymen and her fear. The interviews with children had been videotaped, and the videotapes entered the Texas courtroom as permissible evidence. As in other jurisdictions, Texas wished to spare children the further trauma of physical appearances in court, so the videotapes were substituted. Although this judicial procedure in Texas has now been ruled unconstitutional, during the Noble/Dove trial, the tapes appeared on behalf of the prosecution, negating even competency hearings for the children, which are designed to establish whether children can distinguish truth from lies and can promise to tell the truth in court and understand the consequences if they don't. Even when the children appeared incompetent, the prosecution nevertheless showed the tapes. The children appeared pressured to talk, particularly when they could not volunteer details about abuse. Gallardo and Cox refused to accept denials from children,

> as when Cox displayed his gun and handcuffs during the following exchange with one child: "Who went to that party . . . ?" "I don't know. . . . I don't know." "Oh, you do too know." "I do not." "Yeah, you do."[69]

The prosecutor, Debra Kanof, described by associates as quite passionate about and dedicated to her child-molestation prosecutions, was "an avid follower of Kee MacFarlane. . . . She swears by MacFarlane's approach in [the McMartin case] and keeps in touch with her by phone."[70] While Kanof remained unsure about the satanic connection, other child advocates, therapists, and law enforcers had attended MacFarlane's training conference in El Paso the year before and appropriated McMartin investigative techniques.

Kanof interviewed the children herself, and later developed a support group of parents to keep them from "killing" Noble and Dove, but the group also shared ideas and children's stories. That the parents shared stories could be significant because of Texas's hearsay-rule exception that allowed adults to testify about what children might have told them about abuse. In short, the adult could testify on behalf of the child. This "outcry" rule made it possible for the case to proceed without the children. In fact, parents offered testimony based on this principle, offering bizarre stories (syringes stuck up penises, for example) months after the children's initial stories, which did not contain such elements. Even so, many observers were struck by the children's reticence on videotapes when compared with their parents' detailed testimony on their behalf. Kanof explained this difference by alleging that Noble's and Dove's videotaping of their own abuse of the children made them afraid of the prosecutor's video equipment. And parents had colorful stories to tell: "from details about the sucking of breasts to stories about the licking of vaginas to tales of pencils up rectums," much of this supposedly videotaped by Dove and Noble.[71]

6. In their focus on children's testimony, investigators failed to pursue logical leads. For example, they neglected to search Noble's home for evidence of the abuse, particularly photographs or videotapes, fingerprints, associated paraphernalia such as syringes, or even to obtain statements from witnesses who were said to have seen Noble and Dove herd children into their homes for alleged 90-minute abuse sessions. Further, the police never interviewed or checked the background of the babysitter, Melanie. The lack of corroboration led Kanof to introduce theories of Noble's and Dove's criminality just as bizarre as the allegations. Kanof told the press that Noble and Dove had pursued profit in their abuse, that they were linked to a "national porn ring out of Kansas."[72] When the defense described and showed photographs of Noble's breast-reduction surgery to point out that none of the children who claimed to have licked her breasts ever noticed the scars, Kanof "remarked that it would have been just like Miss Mickey to have the surgery during the [Department of Human Resources] first investigation, just to come up with an alibi."[73]

Noble received a sentence of 311 years, and Dove received a new hearing based on a mistrial ruling, but was then convicted. Later, however, years after the local fervor dissipated, both women were released from custody, one acquitted on appeal, the other's conviction overturned. To journalist Nathan, the El Paso case represented a "junior McMartin," an ugly portent of the widely known "California precursor precisely because, unsung and hidden in the suburbs and hinterlands, [these cases] represent something new and epidemic in this country. The child accusers and their parents are almost invariably white and middle class. So are the people they accuse."[74] Nathan found that Noble and Dove were convicted not because Texas "proved their guilt beyond a reasonable doubt, but because the women couldn't prove their innocence."[75]

In a way, these cases—El Paso, Manhattan Beach in California, and New Jersey—illustrate the power of the checklist and the easy reliance on pass-fail tests, cases in which a list of "indicators" of satanic or ritual abuse of children appears as a *vade mecum* under each therapist's or investigator's arm. The indicators, though, should have served as hints, as suggestions, as benchmarks for further inquiries. Instead, taken as a whole, such indicators to many investigators coalesced into a simulacrum of either a satanic ritual or a child-abuse ring. In fact, satanic elements emerged in these specific cases usually as nothing more than an ambiguous motivation to hurt kids since the details of the children's allegations did not compare, except in the broad motifs of coprophilia, forced cunnilingus, and sexual assaults with toys, tools, or kitchenware.

In the Kelly Michaels case, allegations of satanic practice by and large did not appear, while in McMartin they did. Yet even in the Michaels case, some of the satanic elements, such as the wearing of robes, did appear. And the sharing of checklists, followed by the use of leading questions based on them, resulted in investigations turning up the same motifs that appeared wherever the checklists were used. Once the FBI agent passed on such a list to the El Paso investigators, a list that included "references to costumes and video cameras," both elements then showed up in the children's—or parents'—stories.[76]

The checklists of abuse perhaps should not be used as pass-fail criteria, but "they may be of value in determining the relative strength of the accusation."[77] Such checklists normally note that children talk about abuse only with difficulty; that children with sexual vocabularies betraying a sophisticated or "adult" knowledge of the subject may have been abused; that children evince anxieties and depression over disclosing abuse or confronting the abuser. "However, no evidence clearly associates these indicators with true or false accusations, and no evidence suggests the likelihood that a child or parent exhibiting one or more of the indicators is or is not making a true accusation."[78] Psychologists N. Dickon Reppucci and Jeffrey J. Haugaard caution that such lists should suggest hypotheses about abuse, not confirm them. The checklists and the way in which they are used do not allow an investigator or therapist to admit error. Checklists have a way of being transformed into policy, and as social psychologist Frank Osanka observed, "There is 'no room' in the agencies' rules for an honest denial from people accused of abuse."[79]

Checklists may be seductive, particularly to professionals not trained in child sexual abuse or who lack confidence in undertaking such investigations. On the other hand, the prospect of investigating a child-sexual-abuse case appears daunting to even the most experienced detective or therapist. Balancing the vast unknowns of child sexual abuse against its apparent prevalence in United States society, sociologist David Finkelhor observed:

So while there is truth in the idea that our knowledge about sexual victimization of children has been drastically limited because we have studied it through the vehicle of psychotherapy and the criminal justice system, it must be borne in mind that this is not an easy area to study by any method.[80]

But the sharing of checklists, particularly among social workers or police officers untrained or inexperienced in child sexual abuse does not explain the *conviction* with which they pursued cases against persons with no criminal backgrounds. In part, the ideology that investigators and therapists must be allies of or advocates for children derives from the early 1970s with the new-found awareness of rape, its prevalence, the fact of most instances going unreported, and the recognition of severe and lasting trauma for victims. In the late 1970s, shortly after several years of proliferating training programs in rape investigation, in the creation of teams of investigators with physicians, counselors, and the newly invented victim advocate (usually as an extension of a police department or prosecutor's office), the focus shifted to children. Investigators and therapists discovered with child abuse, as they had with rape, that growing awareness of the scope of the problem outpaced supporting literature, research, and the critical give-and-take among professionals. As with rape (the term now replaced by *sexual assault,* which embraces a wider scope of behaviors), training courses and seminars produced checklists and guidelines based on anecdotal evidence, supposition, and assumption. Some of the ideologues who appear as expert witnesses in the day-care-abuse cases, such as Kee MacFarlane, led the way in the late 1970s, borrowing a philosophy of victim advocacy from sexual-assault cases. The contributions of MacFarlane and other early investigators cannot be discounted: while other professionals would not involve themselves in child abuse, MacFarlane and others were determined to introduce a professional awareness of child sexual abuse and offer the first tentative steps toward a multidisciplinary response to the problem.

But since in child-sexual-abuse cases, the victims by definition cannot articulate their experiences as an adult would (and indeed some of the child victims are prearticulate), investigators and therapists have been forced to substitute working assumptions for clinical tests of children's abilities to differentiate truths from fantasy or lies, recall events, and handle trauma. Shorn of all caveats about using untested assumptions or generalizations based on anecdotes, the checklists have taken on a life of their own. I discuss such a checklist later in this chapter. But therapists and investigators in the day-care centers have become adamantine in their child advocacy, perceiving any professional criticism of their methods as a strike against the children themselves.

Some investigative methods may have fostered the satanic horror they try to combat: by planting the fear in parents that their children, in the hands of strangers during the day, have undergone hellish and repeated abuse, investigators have created the very thing they wish to oppose. Children first gave hints of abuse, or at least that something was not right; once parents had been tipped off to the probability of abuse, coupled with their being given checklists of "ritual" abuse signs, the children later began to display the very behaviors that appeared in the lists. The investigations that followed doggedly pursued the motifs in such borrowed checklists to the exclusion of plain and simple empiricism.

The criticism of the Jordan, Minnesota, case by both Minnesota authorities and the FBI concluded that abuse might actually have occurred, yet the flawed investigation that followed, which charged 24 people with abuse, bypassed any real clues of abuse and made several fatal errors:[81] investigators "cross-germinated" stories among the children; the children's stories could not be corroborated by any other evidence; the children themselves retracted their stories upon further inquiry, some saying that they made up the stories under persistent and repeated questioning; that children had been peremptorily removed from their homes for long periods even though they denied abuse. "In the most extreme cases, these children were also told that reunification with their families would be facilitated by 'admissions' of sex abuse by their parents and other adults."

Some of the FBI's conclusions may shock some people who cannot understand how police and child-care professionals could make such mistakes. For example, *suggestibility* can occur during interviews with children quite easily:

> For instance, after a child says that her father touched her in a private place, a suggestive question would be: "Were your pants off when your father touched you between your legs?" In this case, the clinician is assuming that "private place" is the same for the child as her crotch. If this question is asked many times, the child may begin to incorporate into her story the "fact" that her father touched her in the crotch, even if she initially meant something else by her 'private place."[82]

So the only reliable goal of an interview is to ensure somehow that the child's entire experience is revealed. Despite the documented suggestibility of the interviewing process in the day-care-center cases, "the extent to which false information may be inadvertently picked up by the child through questioning is not known."[83] At best, interviewing very young children about abuse is trying, perplexing, and just plain difficult:

> Trying to remember what to ask as well as how to ask it while simultaneously attending to a child's responses, affect, attention span, and anxiety level can cause even seasoned interviewers to omit critical questions, ask questions

that are clumsy or unintentionally leading, or overlook important information provided by the child. It can also be difficult to recall everything later.[84]

FBI's Kenneth Lanning has pointed out several procedural problems
in the handling of "ritual" child-abuse cases.[85] First, although therapists
and police investigators must necessarily collaborate, occasionally their roles
blur. In particular, some law enforcers have used therapeutic interviews
as a source of facts, although the interviews are oriented to the healing
of trauma, not to criminal investigation. In short, officers must investigate;
social workers and psychiatrists must conduct therapy. Second, investigators,
borrowing methods from therapists, govern their work by the immutable
truth that children don't fantasize or lie. As Lanning says, "Children rarely
lie about sexual abuse, but sometimes they say things that are untrue, or
they are confused."[86]

Next, Lanning finds fault with asking children leading and suggestive
questions followed by rewards (e.g., candy, dolls) for providing information. Some interviewers, Lanning finds, have "hidden agendas," and may
themselves be victims of abuse looking to recruit others into "the brother-
hood and sisterhood of the sexually abused."[87] A former victim nevertheless
could conduct a proper interview, but must consider his or her own motivations for doing so. Further, some investigators and therapists have sought
the advice and counsel of experts, people who may have clinical knowledge
in some facet of child abuse—incest, for example—but not in others, particularly cases with allegations that multiple offenders sexually abused multiple victims. Finally, some therapists and investigators, particularly when
armed with checklists of satanic abuse, ascribe narrow meanings to behaviors that could have other explanations, notably nightmares, bedwetting,
and aggression. A proper evaluation of such behaviors must take into account
a wider picture of family behavior and family background.

Given the multiple-victim–multiple-offender cases, of which I have
discussed only a few to establish the pattern of investigation employed in
them, and mindful of Lanning's criticisms of the conduct of such cases,
what constitutes the state of the art? Precisely what do investigators do
in these cases even when trained in child sexual abuse, and what assumptions guide them? And what should be their role as part of a multidisciplinary team of social workers, child experts, and mental-health professionals?

State of the Art

A number of assumptions govern the investigation and prosecution of child
physical or sexual abuse, particularly in respect to the prevalence of false
allegations, the reliability of children's memories, the suggestibility of the

child witness or victim, the harm children may suffer by the investigative and judicial process, the use of anatomically correct dolls, and the type of person who abuses children. This section is a summary of what we know, what we seem reasonably confident in asserting, and what we don't know. Readers may be drawn to the process of questioning children about abuse, that is, the debate about leading or suggestive questions. Readers should remember that the "manner in which interviews are conducted and the information provided by the child will *always* be issues in initiating and trying criminal child-abuse cases."[88] Further, my discussion of the state of the art pertains mainly to investigative and therapeutic procedures, not prosecutorial ones.

1. *Who is the victim? Who is the offender?*

Sociologist Raymond Eve has written of attempts to measure the incidence of child sexual abuse within the United States, quoting estimates ranging from a rate of 336,000 reported and unreported offenses annually, to between 50,000 and one million (against the 155,300 reported incidents in 1988, cited at the beginning of this chapter). "Thus, the unfortunate conclusion seems to be that most empirical estimates of the true dimensions of the problem cannot at present be relied upon with any degree of certainty."[89] Eve concludes by suggesting that child sexual abuse must certainly rank as high on the list as, say, family violence. He questions whether sexual abuse usually accompanies physical abuse. While the physical and sexual abuse of children may not occur simultaneously, various studies estimate that about half of all sex abusers may also inflict physical abuse, although not usually as part of the same act. And sexual acts within child abuse do not necessarily involve intercourse.

Sociologist David Finkelhor points out that most often, sexual abuse takes the form of genital fondling, exhibition, and masturbation.[90] Other acts include sexy talk, voyeurism, oral-genital contact, frottage, interfemoral intercourse, and penetration of a vagina or anus, which could be digital and involve objects as well as genitals.[91] Child pornography and prostitution can play an important role. In fact, Finkelhor eschews the label "child sexual abuse" for the term *sexual victimization,* "which emphasizes that the child is victimized [because of his or her] age, naiveté, and relationship to the older person rather than by the aggressive intent of the abusive behavior."[92] Yet another researcher uses the term *sexual abuse,* which she defines as "any act occurring between people who are at different developmental stages which is for the sexual gratification of the person at the more advanced developmental stage," a definition that doesn't limit the act to that occurring between an adult and a child.[93]

Researchers generally agree about other characteristics of sexual abuse:[94, 95] that relatively few incidents are committed by strangers; that two-thirds of all such incidents occur within the family or among acquaintances and friends; that more than half the victims are girls; that men figure as molesters most of the time; that offenders derive from no particular race, class, or social station; that compared with other interpersonal crimes, child molesters cause a very large number of crimes proportionate to their own numbers (estimated as perhaps "three times the average number of rapes per perpetrator inflicted on adult women"). Although most abusers are men, they certainly don't fit the dirty-old-man stereotype: Finkelhor found that the *largest* group of abusers was teenagers, young adults next, with old men occupying only a tiny percentage.[96] Perhaps related, the National Center for Juvenile Justice attests that from 1976 through 1986 the "arrest rate for 13- and 14-year-olds accused of rape doubled, from 20 arrests per 100,000 children to 40 per l00,000."[97] Further, when confronted with the abuse, the offender "is likely to have strong denial mechanisms at work." Sexual abuse—and physical abuse, for that matter—show a strong intrafamilial and even multigenerational strain. Several studies show an alarming percentage of parents of abused children with histories of child physical- or sexual-abuse trauma. The most vulnerable children, predictably, are preadolescents, not pubertal girls and boys.

Despite what we think we know about the social milieu of child abuse, we are far from having a solid empirical base of observations about abusers and victims. Raymond Eve noted that "those interested in studying child sexual abusers have resorted to the use of small samples, usually made up of atypical cases such as prisoners and persons in psychotherapy. These data are likely to be unreliable because discovery and conviction are likely to be associated with a number of confounding factors, such as social class, race, rural-urban differences, etc."[98] "Determining the validity of an allegation of child sexual abuse is first and foremost a matter of belief. You either believe the child's story or you do not. If you require that there be corroboration of the child's story by physical evidence, witnesses, or a confession by the perpetrator, you will turn many cases into 'noncases.' "[99]

Child sexual abuse remains a newly acknowledged problem and the lack of insightful studies about every facet of it means that research results should not be translated into policy decisions too readily. Nor should preventive literature offer up unsupported statistics designed to make assertions about child abuse. The Virginia chapter of SCAN (Stop Child Abuse Now) circulated a pamphlet a few years ago featuring an intimidating witch with a caption, "To an abused child, fairy tales do come true." Ironically, the pamphlet made no mention of ritualistic abuse claims, but asserted: "Whatever the cause, the effect [of abuse] is monstrous. Both on the family and society. Right here in Virginia, over 80% of the prison population is made up of those who were abused children." The assertion could be true, and the statistic supports the brochure's argument about the prevalence and importance of child abuse, yet the statistic has no foundation, and SCAN could not provide a source for it. Since preventive programs in schools make assumptions based on little or no research (such as the "stranger danger" myth that once occupied a prominent role in such education), we must be very careful about stereotyping the abuser, even though clinical and investigative experience have yielded some insights.

The "stranger danger" myth, which will be discussed later in this chapter, derives from the image of the child molester and abductor as a middle-aged man who lurks furtively around schoolyards. The myth derives from two primary stimuli: our preoccupation with the "other," the stranger or alien who occasionally visits havoc on us; and the lack of data to illustrate the dimensions of the child-disappearance problem. If milk cartons are to be believed, children regularly disappear into a maelstrom at the end of which Grendel's mother munches on their little bones. Because of the lack of data on missing children, the Office of Juvenile Justice and Delinquency Prevention, U.S. Department of Justice, recently undertook to study the issue.[100] The resulting survey, published by a program called the National Studies of the Incidence of Missing Children, noted that most researchers estimate the number of children kidnapped and murdered to be between 52 and 158 annually. "These figures represent, at most, a yearly average of fewer than 2 stranger abduction homicides per one million children under the age of 18."[101] In fact, the new survey constituted "a major contribution to ending the speculation and controversy over the number of these cases— the kind that spark fear in parents whenever their children cannot be found."[102] In fact, very young children did not figure as a particular risk: the highest risk category proved to be adolescent girls, usually between 14 and 17 years old. Interestingly, the abduction/murder rate for blacks was three times that of whites; of Asians, twice that of whites.

For all that we know about abuse, we still don't know what causes adults to victimize children sexually. Research results have been contradictory; the impulses to abuse are dynamic and complex.[103] No clinical method has evolved to identify abusers; "no psychological test or inventory has demonstrated accurate prediction value in determining the propensity toward sexual deviancy. The best single indication of sexual deviancy is history."[104] In general, abusers (who usually admit to beginning a lifetime of abuse while a child or teen) come from dysfunctional families; they have endured harsh childhood experiences; they may indulge in alcohol or drug-taking; and they may have been sexually abused themselves. "While [the perpetrator's] behavior is motivated by multiple factors, the underlying cause is whatever in his personality or functioning compels him to engage in sex with children. The propensity to abuse may be enhanced by cultural supports, environmental factors, maternal dysfunction, marital discord, and sexual dysfunction in marriage."[105]

The FBI's Kenneth Lanning, with support and guidance from psychiatrist Park Eliot Dietz, has written a guide to the behavior of child molesters for investigators that presents a model quite at variance with the new criminal type allegedly emerging in the day-care centers—the middle-class, middle-aged white woman with no criminal background.[106] First of all, Lanning distinguishes the child molester from the pedophile. Child molesters engage in sexual activity with children; they violate laws. Pedophiles, exhibiting a disorder that is defined in the *DSM-IIIR,* achieve sexual excitement through fantasizing about *or* engaging in sexual activity with *prepubertal* children. (*Hebephiles,* an uncommon word these days, refers to such a preoccupation with pubertal ones.) Pedophiles who merely fantasize will not run afoul of the law unless they produce or traffick in child pornography. Importantly, the label of *pedophile* serves diagnostic purposes, not law-enforcement ones. "It is important to realize that to refer to someone as a pedophile is to say only that the individual has a sexual preference for children. It says little or nothing about the other aspects of his character and personality."[107]

Following the work of Dietz, though, Lanning points out that molesters may break the law through either situational or preferential contexts. Preferential molesters simply prefer children sexually, whereas situational ones don't *prefer* children but take advantage of them for varied reasons. Within Lanning's experience, the most prevalent situational molester abuses children because he abuses everyone; the molester is "morally indiscriminate." Preferential molesters, by contrast, display behavior of great interest to investigators; they sometimes go to elaborate lengths to seduce children; others may even marry divorced women to gain access to their children, or get married solely to rear children and abuse them. In fact, Lanning offers four major characteristics of the preferential molester: "(1) long-term and persistent pattern[s] of behavior, (2) children as preferred sexual objects, (3) well-developed techniques in obtaining victims, and (4) sexual fantasies focusing on children."[108] Importantly, Lanning cautions that *"the indicators alone mean little."*[109] For the investigator, preferential molesters leave plenty of evidence of their interests; they are generally young men, unmarried, possibly living at home, with little dating experience (or if married, virtually no sexual relationship), few friends, and a driving interest in children. They may have a large collection of children's photographs, mostly innocuous and nonpornographic, perhaps even a collection of erotica.

> *Collection* is the key word here. It does not mean that pedophiles merely view pornography: They save it. It comes to represent their most cherished sexual fantasies. They typically collect books, magazines, articles, newspapers, photographs, negatives, slides, movies, albums, drawings, audiotapes, video-

tapes and equipment, personal letters, diaries, clothing, sexual aids, souvenirs, toys, games, lists, paintings, ledgers, photographic equipment, etc.—all relating to children in a sexual, scientific, or social way.[110]

Of course, not all pedophiles have such collections. Lanning points out, though, that while more situational molesters probably exist, their victims number fewer than those of the preferential molester.

Even Lanning's work has been criticized for its assumptions about the behavior of those who find erotic satisfaction in children. First, Lanning's typology of molesters rests with his anecdotal experience, not empirical study. Second, Lanning's offender population is just that: offenders. His typology does not reckon with pedophiles or others who do not commit criminal acts, or who refer themselves for treatment (and have been neither arrested nor prosecuted). Lanning of course notes that what defines pornographic or erotic collections of pictographic or written materials about children must be based on context. A single innocuous photograph of a child, for example, doesn't offer criminal associations unless taken in context with much other evidence. Lawrence Stanley, an attorney, feels that Lanning merits some criticism for maintaining that "erotica as generally accepted as *Playboy* or *The Joy of Sex* . . . poses a danger to children because of its potential to lower a child's inhibitions to engage in sexual activity. Lanning has identified as 'child erotica' non-fiction books, articles, and research studies by psychiatrists . . . which suggest that children have sexual feelings and needs, or which discuss pedophilia in less than condemnatory terms."[111] Stanley finds that Lanning's published views, "echoed in professional journals by those researchers and ideologues who share Lanning's perspective, have affected research funding, academic appointments, and publication of articles."[112]

Stanley draws an analogy between public vilification over child pornography and moral panics such as the missing-children campaign. Benjamin Rossen, whose work with a "moral panic" in Holland involving mythical child pornographers is discussed in Chapter 7, takes a similar view, one even more condemnatory of Lanning. Rossen draws a melodramatic comparison between Lanning's *Child Molesters: A Behavioral Analysis* and the medieval *Malleus Maleficarum:*

> The parallels are not accidental. The logic, and sometimes the content, are the same. . . . [The Lanning publication] contains a typology of "offenders" which nearly reaches *Reader's Digest* sophistication and contains the same contradictory racist-like logic to be found in any classical witch-hunting manual. In this, and other similar American "studies," pedophiles are described as socially incompetent, crippled with low self-esteem and unable to relate to their peers. At the same time they are said to have established an international network for the co-operative trade in . . . child pornography. The

FBI handbook, which claims to be a psychological study, has no scientific value.[113]

So back to day-care cases: Where do women offenders fit in? Lanning's guide devotes three paragraphs to them, concluding that he simply knows of too few cases involving women to make generalizations, but "it is thought that the sexual abuse of children by females is far more prevalent than most people believe."[114] For example, while our society abhors the notion of a sexual relationship between a middle-aged man and a twelve-year-old girl, we treat it differently if the adult is a woman, the victim a teenage boy. For the boy, we consider the experience a "rite of passage." But the women who operate day-care centers, the women arrested in the sensationalist cases, don't evince the backgrounds and behavior of preferential *male* molesters, the only model investigators have when building a case. If we consider such women to be morally indiscriminate or satanically manipulated situational molesters, we're left with a similar problem. Lanning's typology even predicts the kinds of evidence we may encounter among amoral, indiscriminate molesters; some are said to have sadomasochistic pornography collections, for example, yet such evidence does not turn up. Even the arrest of Ray Buckey in the McMartin case produced only *Playboy* magazines as anything that approached a pornography collection. To maintain, then, that day-care matrons constitute sexual deviates who prey upon children is to create a new kind of criminal.

2. Do children ever lie about abuse?

Perhaps no topic within the milieu of child abuse/neglect investigation and treatment has aroused so much spirited debate as the extent to which children might not tell the truth about abuse. Parallel with therapists' and investigators' perceptions that they must act as child advocates has been the dogma that children do not lie about abuse. To what extent has research supported or argued against that assumption? For that matter, is the question properly phrased? The phrasing of the question, perhaps, is responsible for the wide differences between estimates of the false reporting of abuse: as little as 2 percent to almost 60 percent, yet "no reliable evidence supports these" estimates.[115] In fact, children may be no more likely now, with their abuse a public issue, to contrive a story than they might have been years ago, but now "the pressures from a parent for a child to construct such a story may be greater."[116]

The ideology that children never lie about abuse, with its corollary that children's denials of abuse must be overcome by persistent and repeated questioning, comes from a paper by Roland C. Summit, M.D. which described the "child abuse accommodation syndrome."[117] Although the "syndrome" has not been recognized by the American Psychiatric Association for inclusion in the *DSM-IIIR*, therapists and law enforcers cite it frequently. Summit argues for his syndrome not on the basis of empirical investigation based on a hypothesis, but rather on his philosophical reflection upon years of working with children's issues. To Summit, both within the context of abuse and the judicial inquiry afterwards, "the identified child victim encounters an adult world which gives grudging acknowledgment to an abstract concept of child sexual abuse but which challenges and represses the child who presents a specific complaint of victimization."[118] Summit asserts that the nature of intrafamilial abuse (which frequently involves no witnesses or physical evidence) coupled with a doubting judiciary must inevitably put the child "on the defensive for attacking the credibility of the trusted adult, and for creating a crisis of loyalty which defies comfortable resolution."[119]

Based on his model of the child's difficulty in trying to violate familial loyalty to voice his or her victimization to a doubting world, Summit believes that therapists must brook no denials in ferreting out admissions of abusive experiences.

> The accommodation process intrinsic to the world of child sexual abuse inspires prejudice and rejection in any adult who chooses to remain aloof from the helplessness and pain of the child's dilemma or who expects that a child should behave in accordance with adult concepts of self-determinism and autonomous, rational choices. Without a clear understanding of the accommodation syndrome, clinical specialists tend to reinforce the comforting belief that children are only rarely legitimate victims of unilateral sexual abuse and that among the few complaints that surface, most can be dismissed as fantasy, confusion, or a displacement of the child's own wish for power and seductive conquest.[120]

Summit posits five categories of the accommodation syndrome: secrecy; helplessness; entrapment and accommodation; delayed, conflicted, and unconvincing disclosure; and retraction. The first category recognizes that victimization happens in secret, when the child and the adult are alone. Helplessness of victims is inevitable, based on the age of the child victim and the age of the adult perpetrator. Young children are helpless in the presence of adults. Because of their helplessness, children respond with self-hate, since, like adult victims of rape, children are expected to resist. So as advocates for children, "both in therapy and in court, it is necessary to recognize that no matter what the circumstances, the child had no choice but to submit quietly and to keep the secret."[121]

Since victimization takes on a repetitive pattern, the child becomes entrapped in a situation he or she cannot control, so the child must then accommodate the abuse but with a psychic price. The pattern takes on "a compulsive, addictive" nature until the abuse is either discovered or exposed, or the child "achieves autonomy."[122] The psychological pressure on the child requires a "splitting of conventional moral values," where the child must lie to "keep the secret" since telling the truth "would be the greatest sin." Therapists must therefore not reinforce a child's sense of guilt or badness and remain alert to a child's self-loathing. In fact, the moral dilemma of entrapment may lead a child to develop multiple personalities. Next, when disclosure of the abuse does surface, Summit says, new problems arise. "The troubled, angry [child] risks not only disbelief, but scapegoating, humiliation and punishment as well."[123] Summit believes that parents and other adults in authority, particularly prosecutors, are unlikely to accord a child's disclosure much credence, either because the story of abuse seems too fantastic or because adults cannot understand why a child would not have reported abuse earlier, or why a child would endure repeated abuse at all.

Next, and most important to therapists' ideology that a child's denial of abuse must be penetrated is the contention that, in the face of pressure from adults' response to a disclosure of victimization, the child may then retract the story. Summit says that "whatever a child says about sexual abuse, she is likely to reverse it."[124] Further, Summit asserts that unless trained professionals can offer the appropriate psychic first aid, *normally* a child *will* recant.

In fact, the expectation that a child will recant a truthful allegation of sexual abuse became an issue in the defense of a man under trial for rape in Alabama, illustrating how pervasive Summit's ideology has become within the courts. The defendant did not want social workers to offer expert testimony that children not only do not fabricate abuse stories but that they even retract truthful stories of abuse. The defendant worried that such testimony might "[bolster] the credibility of the complaining witness" and argued that such knowledge of abuse matters was "within the ken of the average juror" anyway. But the Alabama Supreme Court disagreed.[125]

Finally, though, Summit cautions that however a child sexual-abuse complaint surfaces, we must assume that the child has not lied. "Very few children, no more than two or three per *thousand,* have ever been found to exaggerate or to invent claims of sexual molestation. It has become a maxim among child-sexual-abuse intervention counselors and investigators that children never fabricate the kinds of explicit sexual manipulations they divulge in complaints or interrogations."[126]

Summit's description of a child-sexual-abuse-accommodation syndrome has not met with universal acceptance. Haugaard and Reppucci write that they believe that there is not a sufficient accumulation of evidence to support [the syndrome]. The principal flaw with the notion of a specific syndrome is that no evidence indicates that it can discriminate between sexually abused children and those who have experienced other trauma. Because the task of a court is to make such discriminations, this flaw is fatal.[127]

Checklists do not provide infallible indicators that abuse did or did not take place, and "the lack of infallible indicators means that in each disputed case the clinician's opinion is just that—an opinion."[128]

Summit has also received criticism on other counts. At a sex-abuse conference in California, Deputy Sheriff Brad Darling, who helped investigate the Bakersfield day-care-center case (which will be discussed later in this chapter), championed the view that satanic cults masterminded child abuse in his jurisdiction. As Debbie Nathan reported, Darling told law-enforcement and mental-health professionals

that a large shipment of pesticide-laden watermelons came from the Bakersfield area. And how about the fact that the only African killer bees found in the entire country also were found near Bakersfield? This, Darling implied, proved that Satanist molesters were organized within the "highest elements of society" and will stop at nothing to avenge themselves against child protection advocates . . . . Summit . . . sat in the audience adding supporting comments to Darling's presentation.[129]

In addition to allying himself with the fervent believers in satanic child-abuse rings, Summit advances arguments that, though articulate, do not rely on the studied or the empirical. In his introduction to a book on sexual abuse of children edited by his friend, Kee MacFarlane, Summit wrote:

The nightmare [of society's lack of response to child sexual abuse] is made all the more Kafkaesque by the legions of spectators who serenely pass by as if nothing is happening. But this is no dream that ends with simple awakening. Anyone who is touched by the reality of child sexual abuse moves into a new world from which there is no deliverance.[130]

Summit pleads:

Who will fight for the wretched, soiled, uncertain little kid against all those adult spectators who *know* the child is lying? Child advocacy is not only not reasonable, it is not *professional*. And it's not smart. Those who fight for power are courageous. Those who crusade for the underdog are called hysterical.[131]

But for all his impassioned arguments, as anthropologist Sherrill Mulhern points out, Summit has never treated children in therapy. In fact, "the 'accommodation syndrome' . . . was derived from his work with adult patients who were age regressed and who 'recovered' lost traumatic memories of child abuse."[132]

As a statement of philosophy, Summit's child-sexual-abuse-accommodation syndrome has become entrenched in social-work circles. As a diagnostic tool, the syndrome has been misapplied since it was not intended to aid a clinician in making a diagnosis, and for that matter the syndrome is not a recognized psychiatric disorder. (It does not appear in the *DSM-IIIR.*) But the syndrome nevertheless has entered the courtroom with mixed results. In a California case, a Court of Appeal reversed a defendant's conviction for child sexual abuse because the syndrome, cited at the trial, had not gained scientific acceptance:

> The syndrome is a therapeutic tool that presumes that abuse occurred. . . . As such, it has little utility as a truth-seeking device in the criminal context, in which the presumption is that no abuse has occurred unless proved beyond a reasonable doubt.[133]

Summit, in fact, had testified in the case, explaining a number of myths generally held by society about abuse, myths that are misconceptions (that sex abuse of children is uncommon, for example). The Court of Appeal made a clear distinction frequently lost on some police officers who defer to therapists to conduct investigative interviews:

> Thus there is very substantial conflict between two important goals of society. On the one hand is the need to care and treat an abused child and the need as a treatment device to accept as true his report whether truthful or not; and on the other hand the preservation of the constitutional right to presumption of innocence in a criminal case.[134]

The Court of Appeal listened to Summit at length, and apparently with some impatience. The "criminal court of law should not be the forum for such advocacy [Summit's argument] where due process rights are of a more immediate concern," in the opinion of the judges. One concurring judge observed:

> It is one thing to allow a psychiatrist who has spent hours talking to a child and observing the child's behavior to render an opinion on the narrow issue of whether the child's vaginal injuries resulted from sexual abuse. It is quite another to allow an expert who has never seen the child or the alleged abuser to meander on for some 80 transcript pages about a theory he recently conceived.[135]

The Michigan Supreme Court, on the other hand, viewed the syndrome more leniently. While affirming that the syndrome cannot be used to show that a child testified truthfully about abuse, and that the abuse therefore occurred, the court felt that "evidence of child-abuse accommodation syndrome can be helpful to the jury in explaining certain aspects of child abuse that a lay person would not ordinarily appreciate," a view different from that of the California court. Further, the court found that expert testimony on the syndrome did not have to "meet the evidentiary threshold generally applied to new scientific techniques."[136]

Psychiatrist Lee Coleman criticizes Summit's model by arguing that its fatal flaw "is that [the model] *is based on the classic intrafamilial incest situation*" (italics in original).[137] Coleman similarly criticizes the syndrome not as an insightful observation but as a diagnostic tool: "And while the paper makes no explicit claims that the use of the accommodation syndrome can pick out valid allegations from false allegations, the syndrome is nonetheless being used in precisely this way."[138] A small logical step for some takes the syndrome from a diagnostic model to the notion that children do not fabricate stories of abuse, a notion that "has become an article of faith," and "lack of evidence to support it need not interfere with its fervent dissemination."[139] In fact, Summit has even written that "the more illogical and incredible the initiation scene [the sex abuse] might seem to adults, the more likely it is that the child's plaintive description is valid," evoking the philosophy that our previous skepticism and even disbelief about a child's statements should be supplanted by unrestrained belief.[140]

But does posing the question, "Do children lie about abuse?" involve some misplaced assumptions? Perhaps the question sets up a false opposition that children either lie or tell the truth. The FBI's Lanning has written, "Just because a child is not lying does not necessarily mean the child is telling the truth."[141] The difficulties with glib polarities of "lying" and "truth telling" can be demonstrated in the following extract of testimony by a child (five years old) under questioning from a defense attorney.[142]

Attorney: And then you said you put your mouth on his penis?

Child: No.

Attorney: You didn't say that?

Child: No.

Attorney: Did you ever put your mouth on his penis?

Child: No.

Attorney: Well, why did you tell your mother that your dad put his penis in your mouth?

Child: My brother told me to.

A jury might confidently accept at this point that the child's "abuse" had actually been suggested by his brother. But then the prosecuting attorney takes over:

> Attorney: Jennie, you said that you didn't put your mouth on daddy's penis. Is that right?
>
> Child: Yes.
>
> Attorney: Did daddy put his penis in your mouth?
>
> Child: Yes.
>
> Attorney: Did you tell your mom?
>
> Child: Yes.
>
> Attorney: What made you decide to tell?
>
> Child: My brother and I talked about it, and he said I better tell or dad would just keep doing it.

Clearly, the dialogue illustrates complexities with a child's cognitive abilities, whereas an unsophisticated observer unacquainted with characteristics of child abuse and of child psychology might interpret the dialogue as equivocation.

On the other hand, a recent book by psychologist Paul Ekman[143] finds that children can in fact tell lies, and in the same range and variety as adults: the white lie, for example, or the socially acceptable one; the related social lie, acceptable and usually inoffensive; or the cruel, vindictive, "bad" lie; or the lie to gain advantage or conceal misbehavior. Further, Ekman points out, distinguishing between lying and truth-telling is not always easy. The fib lies somewhere betwixt the two, and young children who tell them do not understand precisely what fibbing is, although they may sense its wrongness.

"Are the children lying?" is too simple and misleading a question. What do children *understand* about sexual behavior, and can a young child separate "bad" (and therefore illegal) behavior from "good" (and therefore legal) behavior? Further complicating the answer, of course, is the notion of good or appropriate sexual behavior; some quite legal adult behavior with children may be construed as improper, for example. Reppucci and Haugaard have recently examined the cognitive abilities of young children regarding sexual abuse as reflected in their responses to abuse prevention and awareness programs. Not unlike the assumptions governing the investigation of child sexual abuse, the "underlying assumptions that power these programs," they argue, "are frequently accepted as fact, even though they are based mainly on clinical anecdote and 'best guess.' "[144] Reppucci and Haugaard suggest that the complexity of sexual abuse and the reporting of such abuse "requires cognitive and emotional maturity and understanding that many young children may not possess."[145]

In contrast to Summit's syndrome, Reppucci and Haugaard delineate the path a child must travel in order to determine the wrongfulness of a sexual or abusive act and then to decide whether to report it, or at least repel the abuser.

> First, the child must recognize that he or she is in an abusive situation. Then the child must believe that he or she can and should take some sort of action. Finally, the child must possess and use specific self-protective skills.[146]

While Reppucci and Haugaard examine this process as reflected in the assumptions made in prevention programs, their suggestions apply to investigative assumptions as well. For example, prevention programs for young children strive to teach the difference between good and bad touching, a difference that investigators explore in their own questioning of victims, "but younger children are very poor at making fine distinctions between abstract entities, for example, between good and confusing touches."[147] Preventive programs do not simply instruct children on the difference between good and bad touching; they also encourage children to refuse the sexual overtures of adults by saying no and running away, and help children to understand that a child's "secrets" of abuse should not be kept, that abuse is never the child's fault, and that children should tell a trusted adult what happened, and continue telling someone until they obtain a response.

Such programs, which have been taught to at least a half-million children nationally and perhaps many more, largely assume that abuse is of the "stranger danger" variety, or that the abuser is a family friend or even a relative. The programs ignore the long-term, intrafamilial, and even multi-generational nature of much sexual abuse, do not address the often violent interactions with abusers or, perhaps most important, the larger context of sexuality. For example, some "bad" touches can be quite pleasant for the child.

To examine the effects of preventive programs on children, Reppucci and Haugaard cite lectures by deputy sheriffs to children (evenly divided between four- and five-year-olds and six- to ten-year-olds) at a day-care center. While subsequent interviews with the children found increased knowledge of the concepts and skills discussed by the officers (that is, of what the officers deemed significant to avoiding or escaping abusive situations), the average number of *correct* responses to questions about the training reached only 50 percent. "Analysis indicated that assault by a stranger was stressed more than had been intended and that several presenters told 'horror stories' to illustrate their points even though these were not included in the training model."[148]

Further, in preventive programs some children may come to view frequent instances of touching in their lives as negative, such as being bathed by a parent or being tickled by a sibling. "It appears that preschoolers were unable to comprehend the concept of a mixed-up or confusing touch" and that "children found it difficult to distinguish how touches can change or how feelings regarding touches can change."[149] Such observations have implications for investigative models of abuse. Preventive programs are based on well-intended guesses, and children undoubtedly pick up *something* from them, but we simply lack definitive answers to the deterrent effect of such programs.

Preventive programs present a model of abuse that contains many untested and unexamined assumptions. We don't know how children assimilate such models into their own experience and understanding, and we lack any evidence of the deterrent effect of such programs. Investigators and therapists undertake their work based on the assumptions of the preventive model. If nothing else, Reppucci's and Haugaard's suggestions simply magnify the complexities of the abuse model and of how children learn about and experience sexuality; such suggestions should cause us to exercise profound caution when investigating criminal cases.

Summit's ideas, however, have translated directly into law-enforcement practice. The *FBI Law Enforcement Bulletin* recently carried an article by Michael Hertica, a police juvenile investigator, that recommended interview techniques in sex-abuse cases based entirely on the attributes of Summit's accommodation syndrome.[150] (In fact, similar to the "tape recorder" theory of memory, which I discussed in relation to cult survivors in Chapter 4, investigator Hertica recommends hypnosis as a way to help abuse victims recall details of their trauma). Another article in a police journal argues that law-enforcement officers must shed certain misconceptions about child-sexual-abuse cases: that a child's sexual experiences with adults must necessarily be unpleasant or hurtful; that children lie about abuse; that a child might have placed an object "into a rectum or vagina in a nonassaultive way"; and that children may contract venereal diseases without sex.[151, 152] The argument that children do not lie about abuse derives from the assumption that children "do not have the experience or knowledge to fabricate a story involving sexual assault."[153] In general, therapists and investigators assume that children have very little knowledge of matters sexual, an assumption that requires testing. Debra Whitcomb of Abt Associates observed, in a government publication:

> For example, when a 7-year-old girl spontaneously asks her father, in child's language, about details of erection and ejaculation, there can be little doubt that this child was sexually abused in some way.[154]

But could the child be precocious? Has the child read one of the many frank explications of puberty and sexuality now available to young children (through their parents) in public libraries? Have the parents never discussed erections and ejaculations within possible earshot of the child? What has the child heard outside the home? Or from an older sibling? A comparatively sophisticated knowledge of sexual matters by children shows up on checklists as a diagnostic index of abuse, but what other explanations exist for the child having such knowledge?

An article by Cecily D. Cagle and Colleen Gallagher, a clinical social worker and a detective, argues that law enforcers have worked with and borrowed methods from therapists and victim advocates and that, therefore, before interviewing a child the officer must have an understanding of the "dynamics of child sexual abuse."[155] A new and influential study of child sexual abuse, written primarily for therapists and social workers by Kathleen C. Faller of the University of Michigan School of Social Work, simply asserts: "First, we believe children rarely make up stories that they have been sexually abused. Young children usually have neither the sexual knowledge to invent such stories nor a reason to do so. Rather, victims have many reasons for not telling when sexual abuse has occurred. . . ."[156]

But before interviewing the child, the investigator must prepare to win the child's trust—for example, by seeking out the child's confidant, if one exists. Cagle and Gallagher assert, "The most important condition to be met before the interview is to make sure the child knows that the investigator believes him."[157] Authorities disagree about how many people should interview the child simultaneously. Most therapists recommend one interviewer, yet others recommend a panel that includes the investigator, the prosecuting attorney, and a social worker.[158] And most authorities proclaim that only *trained* interviewers should talk to the child: ideally, such people have training in all facets of the abuse issue—how abusers behave, how children experience abuse, how children respond—yet considering what we know and what we don't know, we must conclude that investigators and therapists rely on many assumptions. "No profession is automatically best suited to interview children in cases of sexual abuse. . . . It is important to anticipate what the subsequent intervention is likely to be so that appropriate professionals are involved."[159]

Interviews, according to the article, should begin with simple, non-threatening conversation, gradually coming around to the abuse.

> Any investigative interview with a child victim of sexual abuse should have three objectives: to protect the child's emotional and psychological well-being, to ensure that the interview process will not cause further trauma to the child, and to conduct the interview in a manner that will aid in the investigation and successful prosecution of the case.[160]

Interviewers should then ask general questions about the abuse, gradually narrowing to specific circumstances. "If the child responds negatively to the nonspecific suspect questioning, the investigator may consider giving the child the suspect's name and repeating the questions."[161] If the child still refuses, the investigator may mention the name of the person to whom the child first confided the information about abuse. If the child still denies abuse, investigators might try introducing a coloring book designed to focus on the child's fears or feelings. "Finally, consideration must be given to the possibility that the child has not been abused, which would then mandate a close scrutiny of the reporter and any motivation for false representations."[162]

Investigators must assure the child that the abuse was not his or her fault and offer praise for divulging the "secret." Cagle and Gallagher suggest that questioning should proceed by small steps, and should be narrowly focused, *avoiding* open-ended questions, but at the same time *avoiding* leading ones or phrasing questions beginning with, "Let's pretend," or "Tell me a story," ploys that "might engage the child's fantasy world."[163]

Similarly, the National Center for the Prosecution of Child Abuse recommends, "Whatever method you try, *never* ask or tell a child during an interview to 'pretend' or 'imagine' with regard to anything you talk about."[164] (By contrast, Kathleen Faller *recommends* the "let's pretend" approach.) Investigator Hertica, though, cautions that interviewers should not assume they are obtaining all relevant information from a child. He warns that extensive and repeated questioning may be required. Nevertheless, "Don't ask leading questions. This will be hard at times, but let the child tell the story in her own words and then ask clarifying questions. Don't interrupt, but guide the direction of the statement if the child starts wandering."[165]

Kee MacFarlane handles the leading questions issue a bit differently:

> It is one thing to ask a question that is "leading" in the sense that it asks for information about a specific act or person ("Was it Daddy who touched your pee-pee?"); it is another matter to ask questions in such a way that they infer or indicate a desired response ("It was Daddy who touched you there, wasn't it?").[166]

To MacFarlane, the latter question may improperly lead a child's response, while the former "is sometimes necessary." Although the investigation of child sexual abuse must follow rules that dictate avoidance of leading questions, some feel that the same rules don't necessarily apply to courtroom testimony. *Investigation and Prosecution of Child Abuse,* the manual published by the National Center for the Prosecution of Child Abuse, represents the most exhaustive and current compendium of investigative and prosecutorial knowledge. The manual advises that leading questions of small children "is normally allowed and unavoidable in many cases,"[167] at least in the prosecutorial stage. But for the investigation:

> Ask questions that are direct, simple, and as open-ended as possible, depending upon the child's level of comprehension and ability to respond. Avoid leading questions. It is important to be sure that the information given by a child is really coming from her and not provided by the interviewer. Young children will probably be unable to respond to completely open-ended questions such as "What happened?" Instead, give children options and be specific without leading.[168]

Hertica does draw an important distinction, however, between the methods and goals of therapists and police officers when interviewing children in such cases:

> [A therapist's] goal is to provide therapy to help the child. To do so, they must learn the child's "secret," and asking leading questions is often the only way to elicit this information. Police officers also need to know the "secret" to put together a legal case, but they must obtain this information in a manner that will meet legal standards.[169]

And how does one assess the meaning of the interview? Investigators must consider the child's knowledge of sexual matters balanced against what knowledge is appropriate to the child's age and maturity; whether the details of abusive acts match physiological or anatomical fact; whether the circumstances of the child's situation make abuse possible; whether the child has shown behavioral changes consistent with abuse. The behavioral changes are particularly important. For example, sexually abused children may display sexual behavior in other contexts, or they may "have been socialized by the perpetrator to relate to adults on a sexual level and [be] deficient in other ways of relating."[170] (Recall the opinions of Glenn Stevens, the McMartin prosecutor: children in the day-care centers have not evinced such sexual behavior, which is odd when one has heard their stories of repeated, frequent sexual acts.) Physical evidence usually will not turn up, however. And children may later change their stories, which "does not necessarily mean the child has lied. Children rarely lie about abuse."[171] And of course investigators should not limit their interviews to the children themselves: they need to gather statements about abuse that were made to friends, family members, or other adults.

At some point, investigators must decide whether the child has told the truth. Kathleen Faller denotes three "hallmarks" of truth-telling about abuse: first, the child must have the "*ability to describe the context* in which the sexual abuse took place or its surrounding events"; second, the child offers a *description of the sexual behavior* itself," as in, "'He tried to suck pee out of my wiener,'" which relates an identifiable activity within the child's own immature experience; third, the child shows an "*emotional response to the sexual abuse*," such as an affect of fear, anxiety, or anger.[172]

The problem of handling children's denials of abuse shows up repeatedly in the literature on child sexual abuse. Is it correct for investigators or clinicians to continue to question a child after he or she has denied that abuse ever occurred? Haugaard and Reppucci argue that "assessing the accuracy of a retraction may be just as important, and just as difficult, as assessing the initial accusation."[173] On the other hand, Kee MacFarlane contends that child-sexual-abuse cases require new, different rules from those applied to other cases. She asserts that "it is not always in a child's best interests for the interviewer to accept an initial denial at face value."[174] Further, "It is time to recognize that child sexual abuse is not comparable to other types of adult crimes, and should not be investigated as though it were."[175] This view is reminiscent of the opinion of cult officer Sandi Gallant of the San Francisco Police Department, who contends that for occult or cult crimes, traditional investigative methods don't work.[176] To suggest that a *criminal* investigation requires a new fact-finding paradigm has far-reaching consequences for the standards of proof required by the criminal-justice system. The suggestion, in effect, creates a separate, parallel mode of legal inquiry to the rest of the criminal-justice process. Gallant's and MacFarlane's suggestion begs the necessity argument to create a new mode of inquiry.

The necessity argument arises frequently in every facet of the cult-crime model. In Chapter 4 I cited the dishonesty of a therapist who said with some resignation that our work with cult victims can be hampered because of First Amendment restrictions; yet the survivors recount details of kidnapping, human and animal sacrifice, and all manner of sexual and physical abuse, activities hardly shielded by the First Amendment. But the prevailing view among "believer" officers and clinicians is that the First Amendment plays a role in cloaking the satanic conspiracy. In times of stress, people seek to proscribe or criminalize behavior that they imagine threatens the public good; they argue the *necessity* of this based on the inefficacy of "normal" restraints, in this case, our constitutionally derived methods of investigative and judicial inquiry. We must curtail civil liberties for a while, some say, because of an immediate *necessity* to do so. The problem of how to handle children's denials of abuse links to the need, perceived by MacFarlane and others, to conjure up either a new investigative technique or a transformation of a familiar one. Here, repeated, persistent questioning becomes a new method, with few or no records kept of the initial, foundation interviews. There are records, usually video or audio tape-recordings, of later interviews that are conducted after the child has acclimated to the

230 In Pursuit of Satan

pattern of questioning and the interviewer's manner. Such a new method may lead some clinicians, when examining children, to confirm their own suspicions that abuse occurred rather than to try to assess *whether* it happened. As an example of the attempt to confirm suspicions, one physician even accused a child of lying and threatened torment in hell if the lying continued.[177]

Cognizant that interviewing is an inexact art, clinicians and investigators should not make dogmatic assumptions either that children will confabulate when, after repeated interviewing, they begin to describe abuse or that their initial denials betray "what really happened." Some researchers have recommended that "repeated questioning should be done by a clinician who makes a concerted effort to be alert to the possibility that the form of the questions or the manner of the questioning may begin to influence the child's answers inappropriately," and the only way to evaluate what the clinician has done is to videotape all interviews.[178]

3. Is child abuse more prevalent in custody disputes?

Allegations of child abuse may arise in cases of custody disputes, and while the prevailing opinion has it that abuse accusations most likely result from a parent who wishes custody making such charges against the other parent, research has shown that child abuse does occur in many families incident to marriage dissolution.[179] The same study also observed that checklists to ascertain whether or not children are telling the truth about abuse or that list symptoms of abuse should be used very cautiously because reliance on them for quick diagnoses results in many pitfalls.

Another study examined reports of suspected child sexual abuse made to the Denver, Colorado, Department of Social Services (DSS) in 1983.[174] Of 576 reports received, DSS classified 53 percent as founded, 47 percent unfounded. In studying the records, the researchers concluded that about 8 percent were false reports, mostly incidental to custody disputes. Of the remaining unfounded ones, most simply had insufficient information and the rest proved baseless upon further inquiry. The study implied that, at the very least, any clinical findings should be treated cautiously and not assumed to be a priori true or false.

A recent study of abuse allegations in custody disputes funded by the National Center on Child Abuse and Neglect found that *most* such allegations are true, not just ploys by parents.[181] Several recent studies, in fact, suggest that, where allegations have been found to be false, they had at least been made in good faith, and that the notion of large numbers of false reports in custody cases constituting an epidemic is simply a myth. But sometimes the custody cases do occasion children's fabrications. In July 1989, in Pennslvania, Louis Behr abducted his children from his divorced wife who had been awarded legal custody.[182] The ex-wife, Patricia Behr, saw Louis Behr and the children on the *Geraldo* show in October, a program dealing with satanic cults. In fact, the Behr children, four boys ranging in age from two to nine, had told psychiatrists, psychologists, and therapists that they may "have been involved in bizarre sexual games and satanic killings with their mother and her boyfriend." The boys' stories included "ritualistic baby killings and blood drinking." When the FBI arrested Louis Behr and recovered the boys, the truth of the children's allegations emerged. The oldest boy, aged nine, prompted the younger siblings to tell the stories so that he could live with his father. "If I tell the truth, they won't let me live with Daddy," the oldest boy said.

4. Are children's memories of abuse reliable enough for courtroom testimony?

Research to date on the reliability and accuracy of children's memories has been contradictory. Some studies of adults' memories show their vulnerability to suggestion, particularly the tendency to acquire new information, even if untrue, and meld it with memories of events. Psychologist Stephen Ceci chaired a conference at Cornell University in June 1989 that examined the suggestibility of witnesses, showcasing studies that both supported and argued against the accuracy and "truth" of children's accounts of molestation. Psychologist Gail Goodman observed at the conference: "There is much too little research and too much opinion. As things stand now, you either believe abuse charges or you don't."[183]

Many investigators and therapists, though, do not believe that the credibility of children's stories is an all-or-nothing proposition; as suggested earlier, the rigid adherence to checklists by untrained or relatively inexperienced investigators and therapists contributes to this all-or-nothing inflexibility. Those who work with children in a legal context must try different strategies, occasionally circumlocuting to find another avenue of approach, taking hints, suspicions, and hunches to help form new strategies.

Above all, no simple age correlation has emerged in research about the susceptibility of either adults or children to leading *versus* open-ended questioning.[184] Another study, by Karen J. Saywitz, points out that younger children recall fewer details than do older children (but overall they may not differ from adults in errors of recalling chronologies, frequencies of events, or spatial arrangements).[185] Nevertheless, the same study points out that children's recall of complex events, such as an adult's conversation with words the child does not understand, will not prove very accurate, although accuracy improves with the child's age. Yet another study discounts as misconceptions children's inability to separate fantasy from reality and that their memories may prove worse than adults, but does cite courtroom stress and the "fact that the courts liberally permit the use of leading questioning with children [as] aggravat[ing] the problem of suggestibility."[186] Very young children, though, might confuse what they had done with what they had *thought* (although not necessarily fantasized) about doing.

One must remember that most children in abuse cases are quite young: one counseling center found approximately 18 percent of its child victims to be six years old or younger, many so young that they simply did not understand the nature of the investigative and judicial process. "Young children do not possess the cognitive or language skills to be able to fix incidents in chronologial time nor to recount different incidents in detail distinguishing between each in terms of specific events and actions."[187] Irene S. Shigaki and William Wolf agree, and find that when children testify, they are more apt than adults to commit errors of omission and to err in locating events in time.[188]

Another study of eight-, eleven-, and fourteen-year-olds examined their recall of a description of a crime, specifically looking for distortion in memory and the extent to which children introduce extraneous or made-up information to supplement their descriptions.[189] The study found that the *only* difference in recall and distortion between the age groups was that the youngest children studied introduced more extraneous "information" than the older children, implying to the prosecution that younger children may assume that questioners simply want to hear more "facts," not understanding that the information must also be accurate.

Commenting on the Saywitz study, district attorney Peter S. Gilchrist III, of Charlotte, North Carolina, asserts that "if properly questioned by being asked leading questions or being provided cues, [e.g.], 'Can you remember anything about the man's clothes?' young children have the ability to provide additional accurate information."[190] Gilchrist cautions, though, that only a "trained interviewer" should try to extract information from young children by directing their recall of events to points that they would not usually find relevant.

While other studies show that younger children are suggestible when questioned about their recall of events or people, at least one study concludes that the suggestibility is not as severe as we might think. In yet other research, young children were questioned about witnessing a game or receiving an inoculation.[191] Researchers interviewed the children days after the events, and then a year later. Despite interviewers' asking suggestive or leading questions, the children nevertheless resisted the suggestions, so the researchers concluded that even when children are asked leading questions about abuse, their reports can still be relied upon as true. Of course in this study children did not experience the pressure of relating traumatic events or memories of abuse that occurred within their families. Rather, they responded to events in which they had little emotional investment. Nevertheless, based on this study alone, attorney Stephen Goldsmith of Indianapolis, Indiana, opined that "the popular notion that leading interview questions result in false reporting should be rejected."[192]

Related to the issue of the reliability of children's memories is that of witness competency. Each state sets its own criteria for competency: that is, children below a specified age must undergo a competency hearing before they can testify. Children must demonstrate their understanding of the meaning of an oath and generally have to meet four criteria:[193]

> 1. Present understanding of the difference between truth and falsity and an appreciation of the obligation or responsibility to speak the truth;
> 2. Mental capacity at the time of the occurrence in question to observe or receive accurate impressions of the occurrence;
> 3. Memory sufficient to retain an independent recollection of the observations;
> 4. Capacity truly to communicate or translate into words the memory of such observation and the capacity to understand simple questions about the occurrence.

5. What is the role of anatomically correct dolls in interviewing children?

Anatomically correct dolls depict both adults and children with detailed genitals and secondary sex characteristics proportionate to the the age of either the child or adult. Some researchers have preferred to call the dolls "anatomically detailed" because on some dolls not all body parts display proper proportions although the genitals themselves appear accurate. The use of dolls in interviewing children supposedly helps children articulate abuse when their immature vocabularies and shyness or fear may otherwise preclude their doing so. Sometimes the dolls' use occurs in tandem with pseudo-diagnostic techniques, such as art therapy, or having the children draw themselves or their families.

One study has found a significant difference between the handling of the dolls by abused and nonabused children. In observing children's play with the dolls, observers found that abused children generally demonstrated some sexual behavior with dolls, whereas the nonabused children did not.[194] Another study, distinguishing between the behavior of children referred for suspected abuse and those who had not been referred, found similar responses: children suspected of being abused indulged in more sexual behavior with the dolls than those not suspected.[195] The optimum responsiveness to the dolls was found to be in three-year-olds.

Other researchers have tried to examine whether or not the dolls' use actually facilitates children's reporting of abuse. In an experiment, young children played a game and then answered questions about it a week later.

The questions were asked using dolls, one group being given anatomically correct dolls, another identical dolls except that they lacked secondary sex characteristics, and the third group had no dolls at all. In this experiment, five-year-olds proved more responsive than three-year-olds, but the researchers found no correlations at all in the children's responses with or without the dolls, even after the children were asked misleading questions. So in this study the researchers suggested that anatomically correct dolls do not, in themselves, create false reports of abuse.[196]

Nevertheless, the use of the dolls hardly rises to scientific standards. Even Kee MacFarlane has expressed the need for precautions in their use, particularly in determining whether a child's sex play with the dolls derives from abuse or from a response to the sexual nature of the dolls themselves.[197] Other researchers stress the usefulness of the dolls for not only criminal investigations and therapy but in the courtroom. Yet, "anatomical dolls are not a crutch. They cannot be substituted for sound interviewing techniques," say prosecuting attorneys Kenneth R. Freeman and Terry Estrada-Mullaney.[198] They suggest that the dolls' use helps establish rapport with children and reduces stress; helps establish competency of child witnesses in court; helps bridge juries' difficulties in understanding a child's otherwise immature sexual vocabulary; and simply shows what children may find difficult to say.[199] But investigators can't expect children to accept the dolls readily. They must be introduced to them, and through them the investigator must learn what the child knows and doesn't know about sexual behavior and vocabulary. But we simply don't know *why* a child may respond in a particular way to sexually explicit dolls. "The controversy over the use of anatomical dolls also points out the need not to read too much into a child's play alone with them. Children are naturally curious and can be expected to touch, poke, and explore the dolls when first introduced."[200] This same source also cautions the interviewer not to ask children to pretend or imagine when manipulating dolls.

Psychologists Hollida Wakefield and Ralph Underwager, *bêtes noir* to prosecutors of child abuse, argue that incorrect use of anatomically correct dolls can foster false allegations. In fact, they "estimate that for every person correctly identified as a child sexual abuser through such techniques, four to nine are incorrectly identified."[201] They maintain that children who have been interviewed repeatedly before being exposed to the dolls might give contaminated testimony. Similarly, Wakefield and Underwager also criticize the interpretations of drawings made by children, pointing to the lack of research to support such interpretations. On the other hand, Jon Conte, associate professor at the University of Chicago's School of Social Service Administration, criticizes Underwager's and Wakefield's assertions about the prevalence of false allegations by observing the lack of any empirical data to support their claim.

Deputy Sheriff Robert Farley of the Cook County, Illinois, Sheriff's Department has cited the proliferating use of anatomically correct dolls, but notes that the lack of training in their use is widespread among officers. As an alternative, he suggests that officers have children draw their own pictures.[202] The technique, called the "drawing interview," asks that the child draw a picture of his home, his family, and himself; the interviewer then asks the child to identify body parts, and then later has the child draw "what happened." The officer, being careful not to make assumptions, then asks the child to explain the drawing: "Of course, the police officer/interviewer, who is typically untrained in art therapy, must remember not to fall into the trap of playing amateur psychologist and attempt to analyze the drawings himself."[203] In fact, in most of the day-care-center abuse cases, therapists and officers did ask children to draw pictures, although inferences from them played no significant legal role. The pictures may provide advantages over dolls: the child may "express graphically what he may be afraid or unable to express verbally."[204] Curiously, though, while interpretations of drawings can at best be a highly subjective practice, Deputy Sheriff Farley suggests that the pictures can provide "hard evidence" of what actually happened. Others find that the interpretation of drawings should cause concern: "Reliance on them to substantiate abuse is inappropriate at this time" simply because they have not been tested against the responses of abused *and* nonabused children.[205]

6. What is the medical evidence of abuse and how reliable is it?

Suspected child sexual abuse may reveal physical symptoms alone in perhaps 20 to 35 percent of cases.[206] In fact, subjecting a child to a highly intrusive examination risks further trauma. Investigators can only hope to convince the child to cooperate in a timely fashion before evidence of abuse disappears. They must weigh the probability of finding useful evidence against the psychological well-being of the child; by risking upsetting the child further during a physical examination, the investigator may well reduce the number of court appearances the child must make if the case would otherwise depend solely on the child's testimony.

Medical examinations of abused children include complete physicals in addition to tests for venereal disease or pregnancy; the search for hymenal tears and fourchette lacerations in girls; a test of the contraction of the anal sphincter (known as the "anal wink" test) to determine the possibility that the child was sodomized. Further, in suspected incest cases, investigators may wish a child's siblings to undergo medical evaluation. The central problem with a medical examination, however, is that "unequivocal answers about the occurrence of abuse cannot always be obtained," and therefore "the clinician must usually base his or her judgment about the credibility of an accusation on statements, emotions, and behaviors of the child and the child's family."[207]

The medical tests largely derive from clinical suppositions dating to the 1970s, when rape became a matter of more intense public concern. Bruce Woodling, a physician then with the Ventura County Medical Center in California, had developed an interest in sexual-abuse cases and had begun to conduct examinations of women who had been assaulted as adults and molested as children. His interest, plus the local prosecutors' reliance on him, led to Woodling's teaching others how to diagnose child molestation.[208] Physicians focused their diagnoses on what constituted a traumatized hymen, or they at least scrutinzed children's genitals for disease or rape (which might indicate that violence was added to the "stranger danger" image of the molester). By the early 1980s, Woodling had published the results of his clinical work, directing physicians to look for lacerations or scars on the hymen and an enlarged vaginal opening. But Woodling and other physicians arrived at diagnostic criteria by consensus. And as we have seen with psychiatric criteria in child-abuse cases, consensus based on clinical experience yields many assumptions that have not been subject to empirical tests.

> Using "experience" or the consensus approach to define what constitutes medical evidence, however, is not science, because science requires not democracy but controlled studies. To define evidence of sex abuse objectively, for example, a typical "double blind" study would require (a) that there be several examiners, and (b) that there be two groups of kids, the first consisting only of children known to have suffered abuse, the other of kids no one suspects of having been molested. Without knowing who was in which group, each examiner would check each child and document anything that looked abnormal.[209]

Woodling later began to use the colposcope—essentially a camera-microscope combination—and discovered in his examinations that vaginal tissues bore tiny cuts, scars, bumps, pigments, and abrasions; he decided that some of the irregularities were signs of abuse in children. Woodling absorbed ideas suggested by others: that girls' hymenal openings did not exceed four millimeters unless they had been molested; that boys and girls who had been sodomized had stretched anuses that could be detected by spreading and pulling down the buttocks and observing whether or not the anus dilates (the "anal wink"). "This scientifically untested idea dates back to 19th-century England and Europe, when forensic doctors were charged with diagnosing homosexual 'criminality' under Draconian anti-sodomy laws."[210] By the time the McMartin case surfaced, Woodling's views and assumptions had become accepted as "state of the art."

When the Children's Institute International joined in the McMartin investigation, Woodling assisted pediatrician Astrid Heger in examining approximately 150 children. Heger diagnosed abuse based on genital irregularities, scars, tears, and enlarged hymenal openings, even diagnosing abuse in children who lacked even Woodling's standards of evidence, a diagnosis made perhaps in the interest of child advocacy. Woodling himself had advised colleagues, "Never make a diagnosis [of] no evidence of sexual abuse . . . because if you make that conclusion, the case will never go forward."[211] Woodling's views became quite influential by the mid-1980s: he chaired the California State Medical Protocol Committee and participated on various task forces concerned with sexual abuse that were set up by the California Medical Association and the American Medical Association.

By 1989, scientific studies of abuse symptoms in children began to appear. In particular, they compared the genitalia of nonabused children with those of abused ones, finding the natural or normal variability of genitalia so great that prescriptive notions of the size of hymenal openings or the presence of scars can now be doubted. An issue of *Child Abuse and Neglect,* published in the summer of 1989, reported the new scientific studies. In his commentary, Richard D. Krugman, the journal's editor, pointed out:

> The medical diagnosis of sexual abuse usually cannot be made on the basis of medical findings alone. With the exception of acquired gonorrhea or syphilis, or the presence of forensic evidence of sperm or semen, there are no pathognomonic findings for sexual abuse. Critical to this diagnosis is a child's history. A hymenal diameter of [greater than] 4 millimeters alone, reflex anal dilation alone, or a scar at six o'clock alone is not diagnostic of sexual abuse.[212]

But Krugman cautions that the new findings must be sifted because, although many researchers now argue the fact of variation within "normal" children's genitalia, their work is "not comparable since [the researchers] use different populations of children (abused, nonabused), examined by different physicians using different techniques, in different parts of the world."[213]

What are the new findings?

1. Pediatrician Jan E. Paradise of the Boston University School of Medicine examined the contentions of some who insist that hymenal openings of greater than 4 millimeters signify abuse.[214] Paradise, in examining the research of others, questions whether study of the hymenal orifice serves a predictive rather than confirmatory test for sexual abuse, noting that in one study, one-quarter of the girls studied showed abuse yet had hymenal openings *less than* or equal to 4 millimeters. In fact, when used as a predictive test, Paradise suggests that we may end up with a very high percentage of false positives.

238   In Pursuit of Satan

As scientists confronted with poorly defined and sometimes inconsistent information, we should reserve judgment unless this presumably self-evident relationship [that is, that sexual abuse of girls normally involves penetration of the hymen by an object] is convincingly demonstrated to hold true. The costs of overeager acceptance of this hypothesis—to sexually abused children with ostensibly normal hymenal orifice diameters and to nonabused children with supposedly abnormal diameters—are considerable.[215]

2. University of California (San Francisco) Associate Clinical Professor of Pediatrics John McCann and others recently examined the prevalence of scars, abrasions, bumps, growths, enlarged blood vessels, skin folds, and tags in children's genitalia through a study of approximately 250 nonabused children (out of a larger number of children who first had to be screened for possible abuse).[216] Also, McCann and his associates used a colposcope for the survey, which revealed considerable variation and led McCann to caution:

The relatively high incidence of perianal soft tissue changes found in this study does not imply that these findings cannot be caused by sexual abuse. It only means that other etiological factors must be considered before the specter of abuse is raised when unexplained perianal findings are encountered.[217]

Although McCann cautions other physicians about their diagnoses of abuse, the 1985 American Medical Association guidelines "advise doctors that an opening bigger than 4 millimeters could indicate sexual abuse."[218] Another study, by pediatricians Susanne T. White and David L. Ingram, found that, although few "physical objective markers" exist to help diagnose sexual abuse, hymenal openings of greater than 4 millimeters are "highly associated" with it, but such an opening "less than or equal to [4 millimeters] does not negate a history of vaginal fondling or penetration."[219]

3. A study by two English physicians of children in Leeds focused on anal examinations and suggested that a high percentage of abuse involves vaginal and anal penetration, contrary to most prevalent views that abuse usually leaves no physical evidence.[220]

Gross findings (for example, a combination of anal dilatation, multiple fissures, distended veins) may on their own provide sufficient evidence to strongly suspect sexual abuse, although in every case a multidisciplinary investigation and full assessment of child and family are essential to support the diagnosis of abuse.[221]

4. A study of abused girls in Tennessee, balanced against the confessions of their abusers, revealed that even those who suffered vaginal penetration may not evince physical evidence of it a short time later. In fact, "not all children who were sexually abused, if vaginal penetration occurred,

suffered from injuries that can be detected on physical examination."[222] The researcher concluded that "all complaints of sexual abuse must be taken seriously and should be investigated further, even if the physical examination fails to detect any abnormalities."[223]

If the new medical studies suggest the layering of additional but necessary caveats over any diagnosis, physicians must remain sharply attuned to the consequences of diagnoses based on frail or unsupported assertions about indicia of abuse. Journalist Debbie Nathan cites the case of Robin Johnson of Apple Valley, California, who took her four-year-old daughter to the doctor for treatment of a vaginal discharge.[224] The doctor concluded that the girl might have been sexually abused, and notified the San Bernardino Child Protective Services. The physician maintained the diagnosis of abuse (against the girl's denials) because laboratory analysis found that the girl had *Gardnerella vaginalis*, a bacterial infection the doctor said was always sexually transmitted. Child Protective Services then removed the girl into foster care for 11 days, whereupon the CPS physician also examined the girl and found her hymen larger than "normal." But a second laboratory analysis found that the infection was owed *not* to *Gardnerella vaginalis* but to a simple respiratory infection that "could move to the vagina if a child wiped her nose and then her genitals."[225] Also, further studies revealed that *Gardnerella* could be transmitted nonsexually. The Johnson ordeal ended when a judge dismissed the case.

Criticisms Emerge

Some professional literature has begun to appear that takes tentative steps toward discussing the ritual- or satanic-abuse claims against the background of the research and clinical evaluation I have just described. For example, Kathleen C. Faller studied the experiences of 48 children who had been sexually abused in day-care centers or in homes (including some satanic cases).[226] Because the children had all been referred by local child-protective services, investigations had already taken place and suspected perpetrators arrested. Where multiple perpetrators showed up, they were divided evenly between men and women. "In the multiple perpetrator centers, all of the staff at the center were typically involved in sexual abuse, although not necessarily to an equal extent."[227] The child victims were mostly girls, mostly between three and four years old. Faller states: "Children were the primary sources of data about the kinds of sexual abuse they experienced. This information was obtained by asking open-ended questions about their perceptions of the caretaker(s) or the center and by asking what happened at the daycare site or what the caretaker did."[228] Nevertheless, the major weakness of Faller's work in constructing a model of day-care abuse is that the children have already undergone investigations by other police officers, therapists, and social workers. As Charlier and Downing found in their survey, "interviewers, not the children, were usually the first to describe sexual acts, with children required only to answer yes or no or point to the features on a doll or drawing."[229] And Faller does not examine the process by which the children have come to tell their stories.

The sexual activities that Faller found had been indulged in at day-care centers included fondling, oral sex, intercourse, and "other." Perhaps in a reflection of the investigations that preceded Faller's involvement with the children, she describes the category of "other," which

> included such activities as the perpetrator rubbing his penis on the child's belly, the offender kissing the victim's neck, stomach, or chest, and the victim being required to suck the perpetrator's breasts. In addition, such activities as going to the graveyard and engaging in sexual activities, sex with animals, dressing up in costumes and having sex, and apparently satanic practices involving sex were classified as other.[230]

Perhaps not surprisingly, Faller found in the children various responses to the abuse, ranging from stomachaches, depression, anxiety, aggression, and even phobias. About half of the children displayed one or two symptoms, the remainder, three or more. She concluded, "Of pressing urgency is the need to understand the long-term effects of such trauma."[231] But she also turns attention to the offender: "How is it that female perpetrators victimize in day-care?"[232]

Susan J. Kelley, R.N., Ph.D., at the Boston School of Nursing has even elaborated a typology of ritual abuse (building on the work of sociologist David Finkelhor) and discusses satanic philosophy by noting: "[Its] fundamental tenet [is] that followers have a right to abundant and guilt-free sex of every description. Moreover, because Christianity believes that children are special to God, satanism, which negates Christianity, considers the desecration of children to be a way of gaining victory over God."[233] But Kelley's assumption that satanic ideology (which she defines as the "repetitive and systematic sexual, physical, and psychological abuse of children by adults as part of cult or satanic worship") governs the "ritualistic" abuse of children amounts only to dogma of the kind perpetuated and elaborated by cult-awareness seminars. Like other therapists, Kelley imputes the cult presence surrounding child abuse to the usual mind-control methods employed against members, and so on. Articles such as Kelley's don't consider the proposition that some child abusers, who may go to elaborate and imaginative lengths to intimidate children into not revealing abuse, may employ satanic trappings to do just that. Since papers in professional publications, like Kelley's and others, take satanic claims of abuse quite uncritically, the same uncritical treatment is bound to influence other professionals prone to be convinced by tables of data with chi-square tests even though the data themselves have questionable value.

In a more recent study, Kelley examines the stress responses of children who have suffered abuse in day-care centers.[234] As evidence of the satanic problem, she cites recent work by Finkelhor (*Nursery Crimes*), the monograph on cult survivors by Kaye and Klein described in Chapter 4, and work by psychologist Catherine Gould (also to be discussed). Kelley then examines the hypothesis that "children who were sexually abused in day care would demonstrate more behavioral disturbances than a carefully matched group of nonabused children."[235] Kelley's study confirmed her hypothesis. "The extreme forms of physical, sexual, and psychological abuse experienced by the majority of subjects in this study is alarming. The offenders deliberately and systematically terrified their young victims in order to ensure their silence."[236] But what about her data? For this study, Kelley interviewed no children: instead, the information gleaned for her study derived from *parents'* responses to three written surveys. The parents, in turn, had all participated with police and therapists in investigations of day-care centers their children had attended. As with Kelley's other work and Faller's paper, the data were subjected to mathematical tests of frequency of occurrence and significance. But again, the data derive from children who have been subject to unknown therapeutic and investigative probing.

Nursery Crimes, the latest study by Finkelhor and his associates Linda Meyer Williams and Nanci Burns, examined abuse in day-care centers, estimating that abuse occurred at approximately 500 centers over a three-year period, involving 2,500 children, as compared with 229,000 licensed day-care centers in the country, and 120,000 cases of child abuse in *all* settings.[237] Finkelhor whittled his sample down to 270 "substantiated" cases of abuse, of which 17 percent were of the "ritualistic" variety (although accounting for almost two-thirds of *all* child victims). While concluding that, relatively speaking, multiple-suspect/multiple-victim abuse should not receive "disproportionate focus," Finkelhor et al. cut an immense swath through established notions of criminality, of child abusers in particular, by positing a new criminal type: the day-care-center matron-cum-abuser. No one disputes that some day-care employees abuse children in many ways. But in *Nursery Crimes,* the field of data envelopes even the sensationalistic cases, such as El Paso and McMartin, where even if abuse of some sort happened, the satanic sort *probably didn't.* In deciding what cases to study, Finkelhor and his colleagues tried to sift out "substantiated" cases of abuse. Since the authors could not conduct their own independent inquiry, they decided "to base [their] own notion of 'substantiation' on the action of local investigators. *If at least one of the local investigating agencies had decided that abuse had occurred and that it had happened while the child was at a day-care facility or under its care, then we considered the case substantiated"* (italics theirs).[238] By sweeping up all of the much-publicized day-care abuse cases, the study took as a working assumption that the allegations in the satanic ritual-abuse cases were true and then went on to extrapolate theories of criminality consistent with the assumption.

By taking up belief in satanic claims, Finkelhor et al. of course came up with women as common abusers. The study seems determined to hold fast to the new breed of pedophile—women working in day-care settings who have no criminal backgrounds: "Female perpetrators were significantly more likely than were men to have forced children to sexually abuse others and to have participated in ritualistic, mass abuse."[239] *Nursery Crimes* found women as perpetrators in 36 percent of the cases they surveyed. But, as in the Kelly Michaels case, where the allegations did not necessarily take on a satanic dimension (and there were no allegations of placing kids in coffins, sacrificing babies, and so on), Finkelhor and his associates surmise that the day-care women employees simply took advantage of an opportunity to give vent to their "eroticism" concerning children. And Finkelhor points out that the other attributes of molesters that frequently show up in investigations—the ones described in Lanning's typology—don't apply here. For example, no evidence of the production of child pornography has shown up in day-care centers in the satanic cases, a characteristic that seems part and parcel of pedophilia, for instance. Many pedophiles who happen to work in day-care settings *do* keep pornography, however. The authors do take some notice of the fact that the satanic-abuse allegations don't surface immediately, but rather than suggest that allegations could be an artifact of therapeutic intervention, they theorize that the nature of ritualistic abuse is so terrifying anyway that "it is only under conditions of great security and trust, such as after months of therapy concerning the events, that children feel safe enough to remember or reveal these circumstances."[240]

In accepting the satanic-abuse claims, Finkelhor and his colleagues avoid scientific reasoning and avoid reckoning with thoughtful criticism of the handling of day-care cases. For example, the book speaks highly of Believe the Children, an advocacy group notorious for its uncompromising faith in the veracity of the satanic accounts that emerge through therapy. Without naming Debbie Nathan, the book dismisses her criticism of the El Paso case. Finkelhor and his colleages state that Nathan "painted day-care cases in general as simply a modern-day witch-hunt and star-chamber proceedings against innocent people."[241]

In a review of *Nursery Crimes,* Debbie Nathan acknowledges that the book offers sensible observations about "garden variety" child abusers, that is, family members, including male children, and ancillary workers at day-care centers, but errs when mixing the satanic cases into the data (and therefore the conclusions). Nathan has two main criticisms of the study:

> First, *Nursery Crimes* combines data about crimes which, though superficially similar, are so different that to lump them together renders analysis virtually meaningless. Worse, the study uncritically includes many cases whose validity is extremely questionable. From a scientific standpoint, then, most of the authors' conclusions are worthless. . . . But what is disturbing about *Nursery Crimes* is that it seems to have achieved popularity precisely because, rather than in spite of, methodological flaws that contribute more to a climate of hysteria than to constructive thinking about child sexual abuse.[242]

Nathan points out that virtually all women in the study sample were associated with one type of abuse, the ritual variety. Therefore, perhaps some psychiatric speculation is in order. But what history of psychiatric disorders can be applied to the female perpetrators? Nothing unusual or exceptional. They show minimal or nonexistent involvement with drugs, alcohol addiction, abusive histories, or prior arrests. Since Finkelhor and his colleagues did not directly study any offenders, their suggestions about women's motivations to abuse children ritually derive from the suppositions of therapists and investigators in the cases. Nathan criticizes Finkelhor for groping for explanations for the satanic abuse, coming up with the women's "isolation and stress," their need for "power and control" over children, "mortification of a child's sexuality," and "the identification with evil."

Nathan goes on to explore factual errors in Finkelhor's recapitulation of the sensationalist day-care cases, such as describing Michelle ("Mickey") Noble in the El Paso case as having been a battered wife who suffered abuse herself as a child, an assertion with no evidence. In fact, an informant for *Nursery Crimes,* a former prosecutor in the El Paso case, maintained that Noble was guilty of abuse (despite her acquittal) because she fit the female-perpetrator type, the same type her example was used to construct. Nathan similarly disputes the book's characterization of women like Kelly Michaels as being impelled to abuse children because of anger, hostility, and perhaps even multiple-personality disorder, despite the fact that none of these characteristics were demonstrated in her case. In the absence of physical evidence of abuse incident to satanic worship or any hints in the perpetrators' behavior or background, we are left simply with the cult conspiracy theory. Nathan suggests her own explanation of the proliferation of satanic stories:

> [The ad hoc network "of cult conspiracy proponents"] includes prosecutors, police, fundamentalist church activists, social workers, psychologists, psychiatrists, parents, and people claiming to be cult "survivors." This network, which encompasses groups as diverse as Believe the Children (a national par-

ents' group promoting the Satanic conspiracy theory) and prominent hypnotherapists treating patients diagnosed with multiple personality disorders, meets
and share lists of catch words, behavioral symptoms and abuse scenarios said
to evidence a child or adult's previous contact with a cult.[243]

Nathan reiterates the evidence arguing against summary belief in the
satanic or ritualistic claims: investigators' and therapists' a priori assumptions
of the guilt of day-care staff; questionable interviewing techniques; and lack
of material evidence. For this, she feels that Finkelhor should at least have
used "alleged" before "perpetrator," particularly considering that in many
of the cases convictions had not yet been reached. In particular, though,
Nathan criticizes the study for failing to assert what virtually every study
or investigative handbook on child sexual abuse has failed to say: simply,
that children may not have been abused and that satanic ritualism did
not occur. Since the foundation data have questionable validity, Nathan
finds the extrapolated victim and suspect profiles an example of sloppy
work. The profiles of women perpetrators, particularly, come from samples
including

> such data as the marital and educational status of the few hundred people
> who worked at day care centers between 1983 and 1985, and who for one
> reason or another become the subjects of abuse reports. As such, it is impos-
> sible to tell the difference, if any, between these people and the many, many
> more who happened to be working in day care during the same time period
> and who for one reason or another were *not* accused.[244]

Despite the deficiencies Nathan has noted, many have hailed *Nursery
Crimes* as a definitive scientific study. Roland Summit, at the Fifth International Conference on Multiple Personality/Dissociative States in Chicago
in 1988, cited the book as evidence that must be brought to a wider public
to convince people of the existence of satanic cults. The book has been
presented as a definitive work and cited in other contexts as well: in an
appendix to Kenneth Lanning's *Child Sex Rings: A Behavioral Analysis,*
an investigative guide to multiple-suspects/multiple-victims child abuse cases;
in training material used by the National Center for the Prosecution of
Child Abuse; and in a pamphlet entitled, "Just in Case . . . Parental Guidelines in Case You Are Considering Daycare," published by the National
Center for Missing and Exploited Children (also the publishers of Lanning's
two behavioral analyses).

Nursery Crimes represents a way to attempt to put a scientific label
on misleading and unsupportable assumptions, a way to gloss bad data
with sophisticated mathematical analyses. Scientific jargon awes people; data
tables "prove" hypotheses. And *checklists* of behaviors, no matter how ambiguous, evolve into *models* of criminality, and eventually become the *reality.*

How does this happen? Through repetition models gain currency as reality. The most widely disseminated, reprinted, paraphrased, quoted, and used checklist of child sexual abuse originated a few years ago with California-based clinical psychologist Catherine Gould. Similarly, Gould's only published article, which appeared in the professional journal *California Psychologist*, has been repeatedly quoted by therapists and psychiatrists as evidence of the satanic-cult problem. The article, in fact, merely recapitulates presentations made at a cult seminar; yet the opinions expressed within it have evolved into the category of demonstrable proof to those who quote it. For example, Gould quotes Detective Kurt Jackson of the Beaumont (California) Police Department describing the underground megacult, the "black satanic cults" that specialize in child killing and various abusive activities, including production of pornography, animal and human sacrifice, and forcing children to eat human flesh because "they are considered God's favorites, [so] desecrating them is a way to gain a victory over God."[245]

Gould reports her own research based on clinical experience with twenty "ritually abused children," who had undergone torment in child-care settings: "Ritually abused children almost never disclose the abuse to their parents spontaneously because they have received repeated threats that they or their parents will be killed by cult members if they tell."[246] Gould goes on to report familiar dimensions of occult-influenced abuse and how the abuse may be manifested through therapy: a child afraid of shots, for example, borrows his fear from the drug injections he received incident to satanic worship. Gould similarly reports on research with cult survivors, citing her colleague Wolfgang Klebel, a clinical psychologist, who had worked with three "satanically abused boys." "Dr. Klebel emphasized the ways in which highly organized satanic cults systematically brainwash and indoctrinate young children into becoming functioning cult members."[247]

Gould's 1986 checklist, which continues to circulate in unaltered form, consists of 29 "symptoms characterizing satanic ritual abuse not usually seen in sexual abuse cases: preschool children"; 33 "symptoms characterizing satanic ritual abuse and sexual abuse: preschool age children"; 6 "characteristics of schools in which satanic ritual abuse occurs"; 3 notes under "police investigation of complaints of abuse in preschools"; and, finally, unnumbered "common signs of preschool abuse" taken from Gould's own case files. The first list of 29 symptoms includes, for example:

> 1. Preoccupation with urine and feces. Use of words for urine and feces that are not used at home (especially "baby" words like "poopoo").
> 2. Discussion of feces or urine on the face or in the mouth. Constant discussion of urine and feces at the dinnertable. . . .
> 5. Preoccupation with passing gas. Using mouth to make gas sounds repeatedly, attempting to pass gas purposefully, wild laughter when the child

or someone else passes gas. Use of words for passing gas which are not used at home.

6. Aggressive play that has a marked sadistic quality. The child hurts others intentionally, and seems to derive pleasure from doing so. Child destroys toys.

7. Mutilation themes predominate. Child acts out severing, sawing off, twisting or pulling off body parts. Aggressive words include cut, saw, slice, chop. Taking out eyes or removing other parts of the face and head are common themes. . . .

12. Fear of ghosts and monsters. Child's play frequently involves ghosts and monsters.

13. Fear of "bad people" taking the child away, breaking into the house, killing the child or the parents, burning the house down. . . .

16. Preoccupation with the devil, magic, potions, supernatural powers, crucifixions. Questions about these topics in families who do not believe in or discuss them are significant. . . .

23. References to television characters as real people. (This is because perpetrators take on names like "Barney Flintstone" so child's disclosures will be dismissed as television-inspired fantasies). . . .

29. Nightmares or dreams of any of the above.

The second list is less specific on the demonic or satanic elements but emphasizes changes in the child's affect: for example, the list asks that parents observe the child for low self-esteem; fear; anger and aggression; hyperactivity; resistance to authority; overcompliance with authority; rapid mood changes; lethargy or withdrawal from social activities; sleep disorders and nightmares; inability to learn; short attention span; becoming sexually provocative; "detailed and age-inappropriate understanding of sexual behavior"; complaints that adults bother the child; blood or semen on child's underwear; child touches others in a sexual manner; recounts witnessing sex acts or states that someone exposed himself or herself to the child. The list concludes with three medical indicia of abuse:

31. On exam, relaxed sphincter, anal or rectal laceration or scarring, child relaxes rather than tenses rectum when touched.

32. On exam, enlargement of vaginal opening, vaginal laceration or scarring in girls. Sore penis in boys. Blood or trauma around genital area.

33. On exam, venereal disease.

I emphasize that, however Gould intended these checklists to be used, investigators and therapists both promulgate them through cult seminars across the country. Investigator Bill Lightfoot of the Richmond, Virginia, Bureau of Police, for example, includes Gould's lists as part of his "forensic guide" to satanic abuse, which he has distributed to officers throughout Virginia. The entire guide consists of nothing but checklists, in fact, and has also been used as training material by non-law-enforcement instructors who lecture the police—by BADD (Bothered About Dungeons and Dragons) in particular.

Gould's lists present many difficulties. Her symptoms mix observations of children's behavior from bona fide abuse cases of the intrafamilial sort and occasionally include legitimate markers of abuse, such as the important and corroborative blood or semen stains on children's clothing. The problem, of course, is that children become angry, aggressive, depressed, over- or under-compliant with authority, or fearful, have nightmares, experiment sexually, don't learn, exhibit short attention spans, touch genitals, masturbate, and show speech disorders for a variety of reasons. Most of these symptoms are innocuous and attendant upon growing up and experiencing self-discovery, social adjustment, and hormonal surges. Some of Gould's symptoms link to documented and verifiable forms of abuse: indecent exposure, for example, or a child's reference to someone other than a day-care worker who may have displayed unusual interest in, or affection for, the child.

But a "preoccupation with passing gas"? What small child doesn't find flatulence comical and a suitable target for joking and for making fun of other children? Parents—and investigators—don't have to look far for children's interest in monsters, masks, Dracula (who also appears on the checklist), or a preoccupation with "mutilation themes." If a boy mutilates his sister's doll, what should we infer from this behavior? What if the boy collects and dismembers insects and lizards he finds? Parents forget having indulged in such behavior at a young age. Parents and investigators forget children's exposure to other children, and to their fears, anxieties, and fantasies. They forget that unfamiliar children (that is, unfamiliar to parents) commingle with their own children at day-care centers and schools, which results in their own kids' coming up with bizarre or unfamiliar words, habits, and manners. Some of the other children, in fact, may have been abused by their own family members and what such children may not tell adults they may freely tell other kids.

Gould has tried to include in her behavioral checklist elements specific to the day-care-center stories beyond a simple observation of a child's aggression or depression. For example, in her first checklist, she lists:

> 6. Preoccupation with death. Child "practices" being dead, asks if (s)he will die at age 6 (the Satanic number), asks whether we eat dead people. Questions are distinguishable from normal curiosity about death by their bizarre quality.

This symptom requires a parent or an investigator (or therapist, for that matter) to judge a child's interest in death as "bizarre" as distinguished from normal (and therefore not suspicious). What is a child's normal preoccupation with death? If a kid pops the question about eating dead people at the dinner table, how should a parent react? What possible explanations exist for a child's asking such a question? The seduction of the checklist is that each item might be construed as a pass/fail test of abuse, or that an investigator might try to interpret perfectly normal (but unfamiliar) responses, interests, and preoccupations of the child as evidence of satanic abuse. This would be legitimate if the list included symptoms *specific* to satanic abuse in day-care centers. But Gould's lists, even taken as a whole, can reflect a wide range of interpretations that embrace not only normal growing up but also "garden variety" abuse in the familial setting. Most of the behaviors on the list are innocuous and easily explainable; yet the parent, investiator, or therapist must offer a judgment, an opinion of what constitutes cult influence. The only guide adults have is their own judgment of whether the behavior is "bizarre" enough to qualify as satanic.

Gould's listing of "characteristics of schools in which Satanic ritual abuse occurs" is more disturbing. Her list damns anyone even mildly suspected of running a day-care front for Satan. If day-care staff members deny cult involvement, to Gould the denial constitutes an index that satanic abuse probably occurred. For example:

> 1. It is our experience that so-called "open" schools are as prone to Satanic ritual abuse as are closed schools. That is, being able to walk directly into the classroom does not guarantee safety. We believe that a "watch" person alerts perpetrators that a parent is arriving, and the child is quickly produced.
> 2. We have found that several of the offending schools have two-way mirrors in the classrooms. These are almost never "single perpetrator" cases. Rather, from what the children tell us, the whole school seems to be involved. Therefore, the ability to look into the classroom and see what is going on provides no deterrent.
> 3. Personnel at offending schools usually do not seem obviously "strange." After a child discloses abuse at the school, the parent rarely thinks in retrospect that she should have suspected it based on the teachers' behavior. Some personnel at offending schools may even be exceptionally "solicitous" of the child's academic progress. When the child does not progress (because [s]he is being abused) the school may recommend [s]he be retained an extra year.
> 4. The expense, prestige, religious or educational affiliation of a preschool seem to provide no assurance that the school is safe. . . .

In other words, if a parent begins to suspect a day-care staff of satanic abuse, for whatever reason, then the otherwise innocuous and businesslike appearance of the school and behavior of the staff all become evidence, retrospectively viewed, that the school operates as a satanic front. If day-care staff evince concern for the child, proclaim a learning difficulty, and recommend that the child be retained for another year, if the day-care center is widely respected and occupies a prominent position within the community, and if the day-care staff offer their facility quite openly for parents' inspection, then we might have a satanic front. If I extend this logic further, perhaps the safest place to entrust with our children's care is an unlicensed day-care facility operating under a self-proclaimed religious aegis (which in many states may not even fall under licensing requirements), with staff members with no relevant training or experience beyond their professed goodwill toward children, and operating in a run-down building. Gould's checklist of day-care-center concerns represents the worst claims of therapists who contrive checklists: their lists ensure that investigators and therapists will find what they seek. The day-care-center indicia ensure that the mildest, vaguest suspicion of wrongdoing will be confirmed. After all, in the realm of satanic suspicions, innocuous, legal behavior constitutes proof of the malicious workings of satanic cults. In a way, Gould's check-lists parallel the investigative guide compiled by Dale Griffis, examined in Chapter 2.

Psychiatrist and child therapist Lee Coleman has examined the process of interviewing children in prominent day-care centers (and has appeared as an expert witness for the defense in some cases) and finds fault with therapists' interviewing techniques, which are frequently based on checklists.

> In all too many cases, the interviews with the children are horribly biased. The interviewers assume, before talking with the child, that molestation has taken place. The accused persons are assumed to be guilty, and the thinly disguised purpose of the interview is to get something out of the child to confirm these suspicions. It is all too easy, with repeated and leading and suggestive questions, to get a young child so confused that he or she can't tell the difference between fact and fantasy.[248]

Coleman lays blame on therapists who have adopted the ideology that a properly caring and sensitive professional must draw out an abusive story from a child, particularly since children's denials can be explained by Summit's accommodation model. As an example of what he has criticized, Coleman provided the Memphis *Commercial Appeal* with the following interview by a social worker and a four-year-old:[249]

> Interviewer: What's Miss Frances doing while children are in the other room?
>
> Child: I don't know.
>
> Interviewer: Come here. . . . I want to talk to you a second. (Boy's name), you do know. Look at me. Look at me. You know about the secret. But see, it's not a secret anymore, because (another child) told us about it and (another child) told us about it, and your parents want you to tell us. . . . You can be a very good boy and tell us about it . . . .
>
> Child: I don't know.

Interviewer: Yes, you do.

[Later, near the end of the interview, the social worker asks if the same things happened to the boy that were reported by other children.]

Interviewer: She did it to you, too.

Child: No. She didn't do it to me.

Interviewer: It's not your fault, okay?

Child: She didn't do it to me.

Interviewer: Yes, she did; yes, she did (stroking the child's head).

Complicating the interview is the lack of experience coupled with poor training of many social workers who may conduct the first interviews with the children in such cases. Charlier and Downing cite a survey by the National Child Welfare Resources Center, University of Southern Maine, that found 75 percent of abuse cases had been handled by people lacking a college degree in social work. And of those cases handled by college graduates, only a third went to people with graduate degrees in social work.[250]

Philip Jenkins and Daniel Katkin, administration of justice professors at Pennsylvania State University, have placed the recent focus on the putative prevalence of child abuse and sexual abuse within a historic and sociological context. They review the changes in legal procedure that have been suggested to accommodate the many victims of child sexual abuse believed to exist, such as videotaped testimony, other limitations in cross-examined testimony, and perhaps even relaxed standards of proof. "The perception is that we are dealing with a vast social problem; action is urgently needed; and children virtually never make false acusations in molestation cases."[251]

Noting that in the McMartin case the satanic trappings seemed to disappear from the investigators' case two years after it began, Jenkins and Katkin observe that the case emerged during a "moral panic" within an epidemic (or so authorities proclaimed) of child abuse sweeping the country. In fact, during the same year that the McMartin case was investigated, government authorities had pronounced "the remarkable and wholly unsubstantiated claim that 1.5 million Americans under the age of 16 were involved in prostitution or child pornography."[252]

Also in the same year, federal and state law-enforcement officials began a much-publicized campaign to detect and arrest serial killers. The serial-killer model possibly fed the "stranger danger" myth: that is, the lurking stranger who kills and then disappears. Jenkins and Katkin cite Maury Terry's *The Ultimate Evil* as an example of how "the idea that society was under siege by barbaric and alien predators, often with a frightening degree of organization" can seize the public imagination.

Accompanying the serial-killer myth that thousands of homicides annually were committed by such fiends (an issue explored in Chapter 7) was the emerging fear that missing children would become murder victims or targets for pornography. And alongside the thousands of victims of serial killers, the figure of 50,000 abducted (later, *abducted and murdered*) children began to circulate. The then-new National Center for Missing and Exploited Children announced that approximately one million children were declared missing yearly.[253] The public imagination took a small step from stranger dangers, serial killers, and pornography production to find credulity in the underground satanic network of day-care centers.

But as Jenkins and Katkin point out, every modern country has its bogeys but, within this century, "only the United States has so inflated these stereotypes into figures of such awesome power, and so quantified their excesses."[254] And of course such stereotypes have been fanned by the news media, presenting as factual the allegations of day-care abuse (e.g., *Geraldo, 20/20, Inside Edition*). Jenkins and Katkin quite rightly point out that the consequences of our fears, particularly the legal and procedural changes that followed sensational cases, lead to an unknown destination. We don't yet know the consequences of reducing professional confidentiality (e.g., the legislated requirement that therapists and physicians report disclosures of abuse) or of innovations in judicial procedure, such as admitting into evidence some forms of hearsay, and limiting children's exposure in the courtroom. And we can only guess at the long-range consequences of the ideology of therapists and investigators that require as a working hypothesis that allegations of abuse must be a priori true, the McMartin and Jordan cases casting the model. "If children denied victimization, then it was assumed they were concealing the truth, which must be drawn out by some inducement or reinforcement. The therapeutic process thus became an infallible generating mechanism for criminal charges. . . ."[255] At the end of the most expensive trial in United States legal history, the jurors in McMartin agreed: the therapeutic interviews appeared so suggestive that the court could not decide whether a story was a child's own or one developed by a therapist.

Jenkins and Katkin raise an issue with McMartinesque day-care cases that renders the comparison with Salem in 1692 something more than a rhetorical device: the reliance on numbers. With multiple victims and multiple suspects in day-care cases, the legal drive to arrest and convict becomes less focused on probable cause or reasonable doubt that a *particular* suspect or defendant committed crimes, and more focused on a larger group of suspects to be charged or convicted by generalized, less formal evidence. Guilt would be presumed based on an "overwhelming impression." For example, the McMartin case had focused on discrete satanic elements early in the case, such as the network of subterranean tunnels. But prosecutor

Lael Rubin glossed over such details: "A very large number of children were molested at the school. I mean, I don't see that at this point whether one says it was fifty or a hundred or 200 or 300, that really is beside the point. . . . Because what really is the issue is that children were molested at this school—whether there be two or whether it be a hundred."[256] A generalized suspicion was substituted for a particularistic finding of fact.

For historical parallels, Jenkins and Katkin offer examples of notorious cases that eventually showed that witnesses, children or young adults, had lied: the "Mohra" trials in Sweden between 1668 and 1676, which involved the alleged kidnapping and murder of hundreds of children by witches; the case of Mary Glover in Boston in 1688, who was executed for supposedly bewitching children within her charge (the evidence consisted of the affective behavior of the children who became ill in Glover's presence); and finally Salem, which involved seven girls—three under 12 and the remaining under 20.[257] Unlike modern child victims, the Salem girls even became itinerant witch-finders. In fact, the satanic elements in the seventeenth-century stories loom large in those of the late twentieth: Black Masses or other "diabolical sacraments"; a contract or covenant with the Devil achieved through a debasing ritual; and "the stranger," the Man in Black, the Other. Despite the score of executions and some 150 imprisonments, seventeenth-century authorities and their legal processes cannot be dismissed as incomparable to today's methods. Even the Salem prosecutors feared convicting innocent people. Following the unraveling of the Salem case, the jurymen publicly admitted their mistake, but even after the acquittals in the McMartin case in early 1990, no one associated with the prosecution or the investigation admitted the possibility of error or mistaken judgment. Rather, they resolved to take the lessons of the failed case and construct even stronger prosecutions in the future.

Accusations of witchcraft and accusations against child-care workers run parallel. The day-care cases alarm many because communities wonder how such malevolence can happen among friends and acquaintances in their home towns. But witches, or rather the accusations of witchcraft, arose in a social context: first, witches and their accusers were "nearly always people close together, belonging to one neighborhood community or even to one household."[258] Second, accusations in such cases arose out of hostility or antipathy. The McMartin Pre-School had been around for a generation, so wherefore hostility? I suggest that the day-care-center suspicions had coalesced community fears about threatening strangers coupled with ambivalence if not guilt about entrusting one's children to an unknown situation. But when accusations and fears rose to the level of bureaucratic action, the same accusations and fears took on the status of self-evident truths. As historian Norman Cohn observed about witchcraft trials, "[They] illustrate vividly both the power of human imagination to build up a stereotype and its reluctance to question the validity of a stereotype once it is generally accepted."[259] The McMartin case became a juggernaut that propelled a generalized fear in the absence of particularistic, demonstrated proof of *individual* guilt beyond a reasonable doubt.

Jenkins and Katkin suggested a social milieu within the early 1980s that made possible the McMartin and similar cases; certain social dynamics in Salem present a similar and comparable case. Massachusetts in the 1690s had undergone considerable social change within a short period, beginning with a review of established property claims by Charles II in the 1680s, the introduction of the previously forbidden Anglican church, small-scale revolts (such as in Boston in 1689), a weakening of the political structure of the Commonwealth of Massachusetts, and the erosion of a sense of community.[260] "Once man no longer could find the forces of evil (the Devil) working from outside the community, he would be forced to look inward and accuse his fellows."[261]

Future social scientists with some emotional distance from the McMartin and like cases will undoubtedly provide reasoned insights that may elude us at the moment. Nevertheless, in groping for an explanation of how a theory of therapy and that of investigation could fuse, based on certain unassailable assumptions (sometimes based on pseudoscientific or nonfalsifiable hypotheses), scholars will have to consider the larger social environment with its fears and imaginings about what harms children. To set up Roland Summit as the target because of his unproved hypothesis misses the point: Summit is not responsible for the McMartin investigation, and neither is Kee MacFarlane solely responsible. A credulous Greek chorus—the parents and community—drive the cases. Innovations in judicial and prosecutorial procedure reflect community sentiment. Some of these issues will be discussed further in the concluding chapter.

How to Run and Not Run a Day-Care Investigation

Kenneth Lanning's *Child Sex Rings: A Behavioral Analysis,* designed as a guide for criminal-justice practitioners, tries to introduce a reasoned, cautious investigative procedure into the day-care genre of child-abuse cases, placing such cases within the context of other kinds of sex rings (that is, offenders victimizing multiple children). To construct investigative guidelines, Lanning first constructs models of how such rings operate, offering behavioral clues to abusers. Lanning invents new labels for cases that others have described as "satanic" or "ritualistic."[262] But first, Lanning draws a sharp distinction between the roles of law enforcers and therapists in such cases:

Therapists may choose to believe simply because their professional assessment is that their patient believes the victimization and describes it so vividly. The level of proof necessary may be no more than therapeutic evaluation because the consequences are between therapist and patient. No independent corroboration is required.

A social worker must have more real, tangible evidence of abuse in order to take protective action and initiate legal proceedings. The level of proof necessary must be higher because the consequences (denial of visitation, foster care) are greater.

The law-enforcement officer deals with the criminal justice system. The levels of proof necessary are probable cause and beyond a reasonable doubt because the consequences (search and seizure, arrest, incarceration) are so great. . . . The level of proof for accepting allegations of criminal acts must be more than simply that the victim alleged it and it is possible. This in no way, however, denies the validity and importance of the parental, therapeutic, or social welfare perspectives of these allegations.[263]

As many other authors have done, Lanning characterizes people's primary sentiment about child abuse as denial. Perhaps people's denial of the existence, much less the prevalence, of child abuse has led to strident preventive education: Lanning gives the "stranger danger" myth as an example of zealous exaggeration of the facts. He also hints that the "stranger danger" exaggeration might also have assuaged the consciences of people who found it easier to create the evil, lurking molester, who abuses the pristine, good child, than to accept the ambiguous sexuality of children. "Society seems to have a problem dealing with any sexual abuse case in which the offender is not completely 'bad' or the victim is not completely 'good.' "[264] Lanning's guide, however, may be the first to turn urban legend into investigative concern, even branding Satanism as the new version of stranger danger.

Lanning defines his terms, reminding investigators that if they use words like *pedophile* or even *ritualistic,* they should define them. Lanning describes the sexual abuse of children as having three elements: a "significantly older" person who has some "sexual activity" involving a child (by the legal definition). A "significantly older" offender could even be, say, a seven-year-old abusing a three-year-old. Complicating the picture is sex between a 13-year-old girl and a 19-year-old boy, technically child abuse. And while Lanning could not generalize about women offenders in his 1987 guide, here he estimates that female child-molesters comprise between 5 and 15 percent of all molesters. But defining sexual activity presents complications. "Some acts can be sexual acts if you can prove the intent of the individual."[265] If one could prove an intent to obtain sexual gratification, kissing or hugging a child or giving a child an enema could be a sexual act, whereas other actions proved to be for sexual gratification may not be crimes (such as photographing children in a playground). Even the legal definition of a child presents complications, because we do not agree when a child becomes an adult, particularly where the sexual activity involves persons of teen years. Similarly, a photograph of a mature 17-year-old could constitute child pornography.

In considering the sexual exploitation of children, Lanning describes three main activities, child pornography, child prostitution, and child sex rings. Of the latter, he posits two primary groups: the historical type and the multidimensional type, the term he applies to day-care cases in order to achieve analytical and emotional distance from using such terms as *ritualistic* cases. He defines a sex ring "as one or more offenders simultaneously involved sexually with several child victims."[266] As a caution, he also points out that most child-abuse experts have virtually no experience confronting sex-ring cases. In fact, sex rings have characteristics not found in "garden variety" cases of intrafamilial abuse. First, in the latter, typical cases, victims maintain secrecy about the abuse until disclosure to an investigator or other trusted person; yet in sex rings, investigators must examine victims' interactions both before and after disclosure. Second, multiple offenders interact; they do not keep their sexual activity secret. Third, in intrafamilial cases, a parent may be an abuser, the other parent perhaps remaining silent to protect the child; but in sex-ring cases the parents may not have been abusers. "It is a potentially serious mistake, however, to underestimate the importance of [the parents'] role. Their interaction with their victimized child can be crucial to the case. If the parents interrogate their children or conduct their own investigation, the results can be damaging to the proper investigation of the case."[267] The last point is significant: in many of the sensational day-care cases, for example, parents conducted their own investigations, and therapists and investigators could only guess at the extent to which children's stories had been developed through parental questioning.

The historical sex ring, unlike the multidimensional one, can be documented and corroborated. In the historical type, virtually all of the offenders are men, mostly preferential molesters, and two-thirds of their victims are boys, usually between 10 and 16. Such molesters, true pedophiles, almost always collect or produce child erotica or pornography.

> *Child pornography* can be defined as the sexually explicit visual depiction of a minor, including sexually explicit photographs, negatives, slides, magazines, movies, or videotapes. *Child erotica* (pedophile paraphernalia) can be defined as any material, relating to children, that serves a sexual purpose for a given individual.[268]

Characteristically, a child sex ring develops and grows through progressive control over children through seduction. The molester may devote some time to seduction, which involves bestowing attention, affection, and gifts. "The true pedophile or preferential child molester possesses an important talent in the seduction process: his ability to identify with children."[269] Even the pornography collection can become part of the seduction, particularly in arousing adolescent boys with "straight" adult pornography. Molesters exercise control over their child victims in a number of ways, sometimes blackmailing a reluctant victim (with sexually explicit photographs) or organizing a club as a way to "bind" victims together. Clubs could be sports teams, school or church clubs, and more recently, "several offenders have used satanism and the occult as a bonding and controlling mechanism."[270] Interestingly, the progressive and even subtle nature of the seduction and control process may render victims unable to perceive themselves as victims.

By contrast, Lanning posits a model of multidimensional child sex rings, the "ritualistic variety," which have "involved and continue to involve unsubstantiated allegations of bizarre activity that are difficult either to prove or disprove."[271] Characteristics of such cases include multiple young victims, multiple offenders, fear and coercion as the controlling mechanism, and the use of ritualistic or ceremonial activities to further abusive activities. But Lanning cites many difficulties with the word *ritualistic*. In fact, since he cannot come up with a useful definition of "ritualistic abuse of children," he eschews the term. Further, the multidimensional sex ring arises from three sources: the adult-survivor cases, day-care reports, and intrafamilial or isolated neighborhood cases. To Lanning, though, understanding the controlling process offers the main route to explaining multidimensional cases: "It is the author's belief that this fear and the traumatic memory of the events may be the key to understanding many of these cases."[272] Other characteristics of multidimensional cases include extensive involvement by women as perpetrators; molestation as situational rather than preferential; victims as both boys and girls, and quite young; no fixed motivation for abuse, though purportedly to carry out occult ceremonies; alleged production of pornography during abusive sessions (although no such evidence has ever turned up). On the question of the abusers' motivations, Lanning writes "that the motivation may have more to do with anger and hostility carried out against weak and vulnerable victims."[273]

After constructing the model of the multidimensional-abuse case, Lanning confronts the inevitable question of how victims could allege such improbable events. Lanning notes, too, that evidence providing physical corroboration of the odd occurrences has not surfaced despite diligent looking. "Why are victims alleging things that do not *seem* to be true?" Lanning finds, not unexpectedly, no simple answer. "Each case is different, and each case may involve a different combination of answers."[274] He continues, "The first step, however, in finding the answer to this question is to admit the possibility that some of what the victims describe may not have happened. Some child advocates seem unwilling to do this." Lanning comes up with several possible answers: pathological distortion, or tales influenced by mental illness, disorder, or syndrome; traumatic memory (because of fear, young children may distort stories of actual abuse); normal childhood fears and fantasies; misperception, confusion, and trickery; intervenor contagion (by parents, therapists, physicians, law enforcers).

Finally, Lanning offers the explanation of urban legends. He suggests that training conferences may also spread the "contagion," noting how books on the occult sell briskly at professional seminars, observing as well how quickly professionals copy down and then apply as diagnostic criteria Gould's list of 29 symptoms of abuse. "Is a 4-year-old child's 'preoccupation with urine and feces' an indication of satanic ritual abuse or part of normal development? Do intervenors uncover ritualistic abuse because they have learned how to identify it or because it has become a self-fulfilling prophecy?"[275]

By contrasting two types of child sex-abuse rings, Lanning makes an important point: In the historical sex ring, we have a great deal of evidence, both testimonial and physical; we have reliable and predictable behaviors in both the abuser and the child victim; we have a historical record documenting such cases. In the multidimensional case we have what many would dub "bizarre" goings-on yet virtually no physical evidence to corroborate claims; very large groups of people involved as abusers, the abused, and the prejudiced bystanders (parents, therapists, and here I use "prejudiced" in the legal sense). So we are left with children's stories.

Lanning asks the question of whether or not children lie about abuse, pointing out that even if a victim tells a story in which a detail proves untrue, the rest of the story is not necessarily untrue. Children rarely lie about abuse, Lanning says, but they may not tell the truth for various reasons. "[T]hey do fantasize, furnish false information, furnish misleading information, misperceive events, try to please adults, respond to leading questions, and respond to rewards. . . . [Children] should not be automatically believed, nor should they automatically be disbelieved."[276] When children discuss sexual activity, we must consider sources for such knowledge beyond the family: personal knowledge derived from witnessed sex at home, viewing sex-education or even pornographic material, other children, the media (particularly fiction).

Given Lanning's model of the two types of sex rings, how best should an investigator proceed? Many of Lanning's recommendations, and the two investigative guides included as appendices, offer advice that in many ways incorporates the criticisms leveled at the McMartinesque cases. While prosecutors may not have to legally corroborate a child victim's testimony, investigators must still seek corroboration. "It is not the job of law-enforcement officers to believe a child or any other victims or witnesses. It is the job of law enforcement to listen, assess and evaluate, and then attempt to corroborate. Attempts should be made to corroborate any and all aspects of a victim's statement."[277]

In essence, Lanning advises investigators to approach the "big picture" and question one's assumptions continually. Of course the greater the number of victims and the greater the number of suspects, the more corroborative evidence one can obtain. The investigator should carefully document all indicators of abuse; document patterns of offender and victim behavior; identify and interview all possible adult witnesses and suspects; obtain corroborative medical evidence; discover and interview other victims; obtain search warrants as soon as possible; search for other physical evidence (such as clothing, bedding); find corroborative child pornography and erotica; try to obtain a confession for a suspect; conduct surveillance if necessary.

Corroboration through physical evidence does not necessarily mean anything that specifically demonstrates criminality. For example, behavioral evidence can be subtle, and inexperienced or untrained investigators may overlook it entirely. "The fact that a victim does not disclose the abuse for years or recants previous disclosures may be part of a pattern of behavior which in fact corroborates sexual abuse."[278] But where multidimensional rings are concerned, investigators must observe additional guidelines. They should minimize any satanic or occult dimension. "It makes no difference what spiritual belief system was used to enhance and facilitate or rationalize and justify criminal behavior. It serves no purpose to 'prove' someone is a satanist. . . . In one case, a law-enforcement agency executing a search warrant seized only the satanic paraphernalia and left behind the other evidence that would have corroborated victim statements."[279] Further, investigators must separate their religious beliefs from the case. Lanning offers other advice for evaluating the statements of victims, evaluating contagion or cross-germination of stories given by witnesses and victims, and for communicating with—and simultaneously establishing a professional distance from—the parents. "Once the parents begin to interview their own children and conduct their own investigation, the case may be lost."[280]

To further manage an investigation of a multidimensional ring, a protocol from Los Angeles area agencies, included in Lanning's guide, recommends that the law-enforcement agencies in a multidisciplinary task force take charge, and that such control constitutes the single most important aspect of a major case investigation. The investigation should proceed in discrete steps with all agencies following prescribed roles with an equally prescribed protocol for communicating with medical authorities, parents, therapists, and the news media.

It is important that the investigative manager organize teams that interview witnesses and suspects by an almost double-blind method. For example, if one team interviews a child who names other child victims, the case manager assigns another team to interview the other children, a team that doesn't know about the first child's allegations. The double-blind technique helps reduce the possibility of contamination. The protocol, however, does include a letter to parents to inform them of the investigation and to ask their help in affording an interview with their child. Unlike the famous McMartin letter, the phrasing does not mention a suspect, only the preschool or day-care center where the abuse allegedly took place. Neither the Los Angeles protocol nor one from the Tennessee Bureau of Investigation, included in Lanning's guide, warn or caution against multiple interviews with children; both protocols treat multiple interviews as a probable necessity because children may initially deny abuse (the Tennessee document citing Kee MacFarlane on this point), but both still stress the necessity for trained, experienced personnel to conduct the interviews, carefully managing the case—and particularly the parents—to avoid cross-germination of stories. The Tennessee protocol states:

> The mismanagement of the parents may be the single most common mistake in these types of cases and the most damaging to a successful investigation in the long run. . . . The primary damage [a] parent can do to a case is to go to the media and disclose that either (a) the investigation exists, or (b) there are details of the case that investigators are keeping under wraps at this time. They may also turn against the investigators and publicly attack their efforts if they perceive that the investigation is not moving swiftly and the offenders are not in jail.

Both protocols require strictly organized and controlled multidisciplinary investigative teams. Such teams have been used in many sensational cases, however, although their management and direction may have changed almost daily. In Finkelhor's *Nursery Crimes,* he and his associates found poor reports about the worth of such teams. "Investigators in the field, generally, have complained about the problems of teams that waste time, never seem to accomplish anything, spend too much effort fighting turf issues, and allow the bosses to sit around and agree with each other while the staff go out and do the extra work."[281] Perhaps the mismanagement of such teams encouraged parents to strike out on their own and to present their cause to the news media.

Lanning's guide represents the only major attempt by a law-enforcement authority to find a way to "objectively" handle a day-care-center investigation. Despite much sensible advice, the document could present the same problems as does that of *Nursery Crimes:* imposing a logical, ordered, even scientific method atop poor data or faulty assumptions. A danger exists in that investigators, to distance themselves from the publicity difficulties that follow a "ritualistic" case, may borrow Lanning's lexicon, thus declaring that they are pursuing a different kind of case, not a satanic or ritualistic one. Such investigators may use a new terminology to mask the same shoddy techniques or assumptions. So the model *could* confer legitimacy on a bad investigation, thus rationalizing a poor case.

One must be sympathetic to Lanning in trying to devise an investigative path out of a muddle of wild claims, hysteria, and tension, particularly when police have no choice but to examine all claims of child abuse. But by positing a type of case analogous to those involving historically verifiable pedophiles, Lanning runs the risk of legitimizing the very thing he warns against. After all, although he acknowledges the lack of corroborative evidence to support claims of torture and sexual sadism in day-care centers, in positing his multi-suspect, multi-victim mode, he presumes its existence. The model does not cue an investigator to question whether abuse has actually taken place. And the model is not scientific; like his previous behavioral profile of child molesters, his arguments are based on investigative experience, and he extrapolates from past cases to produce tips to follow.

By contrast, psychiatrist Lee Coleman and lawyer Patrick E. Clancy offer their view that what criminal justice needs may not be a new model of criminality within which to reckon abuse in day-care settings but, instead, a rigorous retraining of investigators themselves *away* from pediatric and therapeutic theory:

> In place of the "believe the child" approach, [investigators] must rely on neutral investigation that acknowledges the reality of both true and false accusations of child molestation. . . .
> Investigators who truly understand that finding the truth, and not assuming abuse, is the best way to protect children will be more likely to avoid leading and suggestive interviews. Their retraining must include practice in avoiding such questioning. There is no need for mental health professionals to be involved in such training.[282]

Opposing Lanning's best efforts to find an appropriate investigative protocol, the child-abuse case that developed in Bakersfield, California, in 1984 illustrates what can happen in the absence of investigative expertise and close management. The case resulted in trials and convictions that imposed the longest sentences in California legal history. What happened in Bakersfield represents an object lesson in how to subject children to abusive inquisition, how to destroy reputations of the innocent, and how to subvert the role of law enforcement. The case began with allegations of abuse of three boys in a custody dispute. Almost simultaneously, a few other cases surfaced amid much local publicity about child-pornography rings. Shortly thereafter, Satan entered the fray.

Bakersfield

In 1982, Kern County Sheriff's Department deputies investigated what became known as the "Kniffen-McCuan child molesting ring."[283] Two girls who had been living with their stepgrandmother complained to her of molestation. In the same investigation, deputies arrested two couples in 1984 for molesting their own and each other's children; these arrests produced sentences of up to 268 years. This 1984 case spurred the formation of a multidisciplinary team of deputies, social workers, and members of the attorney general's office to investigate child sexual abuse. In 1984, deputies arrested Jeff Cramer and his wife, Elizabeth Cramer. (Note: The names of witnesses, suspects, and complainants are all pseudonyms.) The arrests were based on reports by Elizabeth's ex-husband's wife that the couple had molested Elizabeth's three sons by her previous marriage. As a result of the boys' statements and Bruce Woodling's physical examination of two of the boys (the two who had denied abuse), deputies moved the three boys into foster care. Eventually, the allegations spread to include a total of eleven children and against seven other adults.[284]

Supposedly, when Elizabeth Cramer's boys spent time with her on alternate weekends, other adults and children would show up and, in a room measuring 10 by 12 feet, the adults photographed the kids with film and video cameras illuminated by three-foot-wide lights (which, oddly, produced no burns despite the heat they generated). In this room the boys (none older than eight) allegedly drank whiskey and beer, inhaled cocaine, were given shots, and were hung on hooks and sodomized. The girls were allegedly assaulted sexually in several ways, and as they screamed, the men ejaculated several times—all of this supposedly recorded photographically (although no incriminating photographs ever surfaced in any of the Kern County cases).[285]

Although the adults continued to insist on their innocence and had passed polygraph tests, they were convicted. Elizabeth Cramer was sentenced to 373 years. But during 1986, the oldest of the child witnesses, Roberta Korin, now a teenager, told her guardian's mother that she contrived her story. Over the following days, Roberta said that "her trial testimony had emerged from hours of interviews with social worker Carol Darling and other investigators."[286] (Darling's husband, Lieutenant Brad Darling of the Kern County Sheriff's Department, lectures church groups on his belief in satanic charges.) In fact, Roberta supposedly had been repeatedly sexually assaulted and sodomized; yet a medical examination revealed no evidence of abuse. Why did she lie? Because Darling told her that "violent friends" of the Cramer family would hurt her and that, if she didn't cooperate, she would find herself in a foster home. But prosecuting attorneys dubbed her confession false. Later, another girl who testified about abuse recanted, saying that repeated questioning by the prosecutors led her to make up a story to avoid further questioning.

At about the same time, two daughters of Bill Grubb were living with his estranged wife. One of the girls told their grandmother, Sally Meyer, that the other sister "was simulating sex with a brother."[287] This caused Meyer to question the children; the older ones, except for one girl, denied any abuse. Meyer conducted her own investigation, interrogating the girls over several weeks and keeping a journal of the conversations. Meyer then reported her suspicions that the children had been molested to a social worker, which prompted the arrest of Bill Grubb and his roommate. But the arrest faltered for lack of evidence.

Meanwhile, Sally Meyer's investigation continued, and she began to allege that Grubb and four men who worked with him produced "snuff" films and by now the children were also talking of cannibalism and the murder of children. In court, the judge dismissed the case, finding that the charges "resulted from 'inhumane interrogation techniques' used by their 'severely mentally ill' grandmother," and the men were released from custody.[288]

Michael Snedeker, an attorney who defended several people in the Kern County investigations, has compared the child-molestation cases with the Salem witch trials, and observed of his own cases that "the possibility of child abuse became the omnipresent inevitability of child abuse."[289] Commenting on the work of the Kern County child-abuse task force, he wrote:

> The enormous momentum of charges against anyone for violating defenseless children was so strong that they obtained early successes even where the evidence was very weak or originated by the investigators themselves. These successes emboldened them to try cases that seemed fantastic, even unbelievable. Their system of witness intimidation and instruction and evidence suppression, together with the aura of fear and titillation that spread through Kern County, allowed them to convict anybody of anything.[290]

Snedeker takes issue particularly with the conduct of Deputy Sheriff Jack Rutledge. Rutledge obtained permission from Cynthia Saunders to interview her son, who might have been molested by a man named Joey, who had been arrested for molesting another boy. Since Saunders knew that her son had been on a camping trip with Joey the previous summer, she requested the interview. Rutledge described sodomy and oral sex to the boy and said that a man named Joey, who had given him rides from school and had taken him on camping trips, had molested another boy. To help him remember, Rutledge "whispered hypnotic, graphic repetitions of sex acts" to the boy. Rutledge wrote in his report that the boy gave him florid details of oral and anal sex with Joey, although what the boy actually offered during interviews "were monosyllabic assents to descriptions of sex acts provided by Rutledge," who took care not to note the boy's denials. The boy was interviewed repeatedly, not only by Rutledge, but also by attorney Colleen Ryan and by Carol Darling. What the boy did say to others did not concern molestation but rather his dislike of his new stepfather, Cynthia Saunders' husband, and his interest in living with his grandparents.

Rutledge continued to interview children, producing reports that they had indulged "in every possible permutation" of sex with named adults, all of which allegedly had been videotaped. Called to the Sheriff's Department on a pretext, Saunders herself was arrested, was not given her *Miranda* warnings, was told that if she didn't confess she would never see her children again, and was threatened with a jail term that would exceed her lifetime. She gave a tentative confession, which she soon repudiated.

Other children complained of Rutledge's techniques, and Carol Darling and Ryan intimidated other children. When one boy wanted to discontinue an interview and Rutledge would not let him, he admitted to being abused. The same boy cried when Darling would not let him leave, and he later told his mother that he had made up a story. A girl said that her denials had no effect on Darling even when she cried, so she finally invented a story of abuse. She and another girl—who had been given anatomically correct dolls and told to pretend they were Saunders and another arrestee and to punch them—told their mothers they had made up stories. The mother called the district attorney to complain, whereupon Rutledge removed the girls from school. When one refused to talk about alleged abuse, saying nothing had happened, Rutledge said, "You know it did," whereupon he slapped her, causing her lip to bleed. The other girl insisted that her grandmother be present for an interview, to which Rutledge agreed. In the grandmother's presence, the girl said she had earlier lied about being molested, to which the deputy responded by twisting her arm and saying, "You're lying!"[291] Rutledge then described, according to the grandmother, "very detailed, filthy" sadosexual acts, forcing the girl, while twisting her arm, to admit abuse.

At about this time, the local paper, the *Bakersfield Californian,* ran a series of reports on "the monstrous unacknowledged phenomenon" of child-porn sex rings. The articles ran opposite reports of the Saunders trial at the same time that the Cramer and Grubb cases surfaced. Snedeker notes that in the Cramer case, the children had been removed from their home and placed in the Jameson Children's Center, where cross-germination of stories undoubtedly occurred because the children attended therapy sessions with other children involved in the investigation.

Eight months after the Cramer children had been removed from their home—eight months during which the children underwent repeated interviewing and therapy—the first satanic elements showed up, ranging from the worship of Satan, the burning of black candles while tossing babies into a fire, and the sacrifice of babies, other children, and various animals. According to the lead therapists at the Jameson Children's Center, most of the babies referred to were "altar babies," or those with unrecorded births who were bred exclusively for sacrifice.

As the investigations—and the interviews—continued, any parent or adult named was scrutinized or even arrested, that is, until April 1985, when the children accused one of the prosecutors, Deputy Sheriff Bill Rutledge, the brother of Jack Rutledge, and a social worker of molestation. But the prosecutor balked at the lack of evidence to bring these accusations to trial. Sheriff's deputies (including the sheriff) then embarked on a public campaign to urge prosecution, mainly speaking to churches to urge people to write letters asking for a prosecution.

The investigators drew heat from the office of the California attorney general, who, despite the earlier convictions in court, conducted an inquiry into the investigations. But the investigators continued their public campaign; Lieutenant Brad Darling even told a church group that Satanists harassed him by leaving dead dogs and cats on his doorstep,[292] a story he later denied.

In 1986, the California attorney general's office issued the *Report on the Kern County Child Abuse Investigation*. It provided a strong indictment of the Kern County investigations, and of the Cramer case specifically. While not discussing the criminal convictions, the investigation focused on the behavior of the Sheriff's Department and its interaction with the prosecuting attorney and the local Child Protective Services. The case examined by the attorney general took on no small proportions: it identified 19 victims, 27 suspects, and a total of 148 interviews.

In general, the Sheriff's Department investigation, according to the report, showed "inexperience and lack of training." In fact, the department had no written policies on standard investigative procedures, particularly on interviewing techniques, or even on more technical matters, such as medical examinations of victims. Further, most deputies did not know what their department procedural manual contained anyway, so that the policies in the manual on supervision and report-writing were not observed. The deputies participating in the Cramer case had little or no training in child sexual abuse, despite the fact that it is a mandatory training requirement in California. The deputies' supervisor blamed the lack of training on "time constraints," yet deputies had found time to attend a satanic-crime seminar in Nevada. Deputies received little beyond casual supervision, the report continued, and perhaps owing to their inexperience they deferred to the prosecutor's office and to the social workers (one in particular) to take the lead in the case. And the principal therapist, despite a degree in social work, had no training in sexual-abuse investigation. In fact, the three main agencies involved in the investigation shared no plan, and their opposing philosophies about the reliability of children's statements hampered their cooperation.

Of the interviews, the report said:

> Deputies allowed overly leading questions, gave the children inappropriate positive reinforcement for many of their statements, and did not question those statements. Only twenty-eight [of 134] interviews were tape recorded. Tapes and reports show that deputies and others told the children what other victims had said. The department also neglected to ask the [Jameson] Center to segregate the victims housed there or to keep them from discussing the case.

Concerning the written reports, fewer than half were initialed by supervisors, and many deputies paraphrased interviews inaccurately and added their own unsupported conclusions.

In all, deputies conducted nine searches that produced virtually no evidence to corroborate either abuse or satanic rituals. In fact, "deputies' efforts to obtain corroborative evidence were limited and poorly documented;" medical tests were not even given to victims who claimed that they had been drugged. But on the satanic allegations, the attorney general's report would not comment, except for the observation that

> the Sheriff's Department uncovered no physical evidence to corroborate the children's stories, and found much to disprove some of their statements. Several alleged victims were found alive, and no reports of missing babies or lost children corresponded with the victims named. No bodies were found in the grave sites described. Deputies searched two lakes where bodies allegedly were deposited, but no remains were found. . . .
>
> The one firm conclusion about the satanic allegations is that they seriously eroded the children's credibility and their ability to testify in court about molestations. The breakdown in the children's credibility as witnesses played a major role in the District Attorney's decision not to file charges against additional suspects without corroborative evidence.

The report did not spare the therapists for Child Protective Services. "A thoroughly experienced therapist and two interns conducted the sessions [at Jameson]. The lead therapist was later dismissed from the center. After her dismissal, she continued to counsel the children on her own." During group therapy, children talked of who had molested them, despite their being told not to do so. But the therapists kept uneven records; the lead one summarized hers "to avoid discovery motions by defense attorneys." The report also noted that when the sheriff's deputies deferred the investigation to a therapist, a central therapeutic assumption tainted the interviews:

The prevailing attitude of the interviewers was that "children do not lie." As a result, interviewers tended to take children's statements at face value and failed to do necessary corroborative investigative work. This attitude seriously impaired the entire interview process and, indeed, the investigation itself.

The following interview took place between a parent suspected of abuse and the social worker:

Social worker: Okay, ah . . . you know when children, when children tell law enforcement or Child Protective Services—

Suspect: Uh huh.

SW: —about somebody, we believe children, okay.

S: Uh huh.

SW: Especially little, ah, would involve children but these are just, you know, four-, five-, and six-year-olds. . . .

S: Uh huh.

SW: Okay, and they don't have, they shouldn't have knowledge of this stuff, they have a lot of knowledge, a lot of explicit details, they say cream was being used—lotion.

S: Have you seen, you know, TV nowadays though, the parents let their kids watch.

SW: Okay, people often do accuse TV, but still children don't fantasize about sexual abuse and they don't implicate their own father.

S: Uh huh.

SW: Okay?

Deputy: Let alone themselves.

SW: Yeah, let alone themselves, especially when they're, when they are feeling so badly about and they know it's wrong.

S: Uh huh.

SW: Okay, it's just they, some you know, if they aren't gonna, if they're mad at their dad and that's when they may say physical abuse.

S: Uh huh.

SW: But, ah, they're not gonna say sexual.

S: Uh huh.

SW: It just doesn't happen.

S: Uh huh.

SW: So we, we do believe the children.

S: Uh huh.

SW: Okay, that you are involved.

S: Then no matter what I, what I say doesn't even matter then?

SW: Well, yeah of course it matters, but, but our stand is that we believe the children.

S: Uh huh.

SW: At all cost, cause that's our job and that's, that's what our belief is.

The report stated of the therapist's lead role,

This dependence upon and deferment to staff of Child Protective Services—who perform functions quite different from police officers in a child abuse investigation—focused the interviews primarily on protecting the child at the expense of investigating and determining the facts in the case. While protecting the child was certainly critical, once that had been assured the criminal investigation should have been the Sheriff's deputies' primary concern.

Deputies' questioning of children violated standards established in 1983 by the California Peace Officer Standards and Training Commission.

Deputies generally did not question the children's statements, and they responded positively to the victims' statements only when the children revealed new allegations or said something to reinforce their previous allegations. They applied pressure on the children to name additional suspects and victims, and questioned them with inappropriate suggestions that produced the answers they were looking for.

In addition to providing reinforcement when they received answers to leading and suggestive questions, in other cases they confused children:

Interviewer: Okay, you said that they touched the privates before they stabbed the baby? Did they take clothes off the baby before they stabbed the baby? Did they take the clothes off the baby when they touched the privates? And then they had you go up and stab the baby? So, did the baby—was the baby's clothes still off after they'd taken them off and you had to stab the baby?

Answer: No.

The deputies fared no better when using anatomically correct dolls, about which most of them had no training. In a flagrant abuse of investigative technique, a deputy had wanted to use a doll in an interview but didn't have one, so he told a child, "I forgot my dolly, then you could point. You want to point on me?"

A year before the attorney general's report appeared, the grand jury that convened to examine the Cramer case concluded that two facets of the investigation ought to be examined: the way in which children are handled by investigators and social workers, and the methods of interviewing the children. The grand jury's letter to the attorney general raised the issue of the "propriety and legality" of the deputies' taking the case to the public.

The report's recommendations mirrored many of those that appear in Kenneth Lanning's guide. The report's summary criticism concluded that the lead therapist's having "clearly exceeded her legally mandated role" and "actually dominating the criminal investigative interviews" led to "the failure of the Sheriff's Department to control and direct the criminal investigation. Sheriff's deputies allowed their role to be usurped by a person with no law-enforcement background and with no responsibility for the successful investigation of an alleged crime, which seriously impaired the investigation."

As a postscript to the Kern County cases, in November 1990 prosecutors dropped charges against four women and three men, including the Cramers and Bill Grubb, each of whom had up to that time served five years in prison. The appeals court overturned the convictions because of prosecutorial misbehavior. The court's opinion reproached the prosecutor, who "in his blind quest to convict, forgot or ignored his constitutional and ethical duties as a representative of the people," noting that he not only pressured jurors to convict but admonished them that Christ "took the side of children over adults in such cases."[293] The prosecutor declared that he would not retry any of the defendants.

Conclusion

Children's claims of abuse in day-care centers incident to satanic ritual, or to sexual sadism, and the tales of cult survivors seem to evoke one of two responses: either people accept the stories at face value or they don't. Those who dismiss the cases out of hand as outlandish or improbable may overlook the strong possibility that some kind of abuse has taken place. Kenneth Lanning says that some middle ground must exist as a foundation for a rational, analytical inquiry into the claims of children and multiple-personality disorder sufferers. Roland Summit finds a "striking similarity" between the confessions of cult survivors and the descriptions of occult activities given by children: "[The children's] descriptions of ritual cult practices come out of nowhere in their backgrounds, and the stories are told to adults—parents or therapists—with no background or knowledge of ritual cults. And they match rather perfectly the descriptions of adults who have survived these things."[294] But as we have seen, such claims don't arise out of thin air: a pervasive and active network of therapists, investigators, and prosecutors continually trade information on "ritualistic" cases. Case strategies are borrowed from other cases: therapists and investigators learn interviewing techniques, for example, from therapists and investigators who have developed the techniques in other cases.

Above all, mistakes arise in complex child-abuse cases when professionals substitute diagnostic checklists for empiricism. I cannot explain why therapists, physicians, and investigators suspend the skepticism produced by their training and experience and adopt fervent and obdurate *beliefs* in murdered babies and daytime airplane trips to cemeteries and, more important, a theory of criminality that envisions women of unblemished backgrounds subjecting children to repeated physical and sexual abuse. In part, this willingness to believe derives from a philosophy of victim and child advocacy. Although the focus of this book examines the police response to satanic claims, I have shown that in many ways police thinking and action about child abuse are inseparable from therapeutic concerns, since the police have relied on checklists derived from research in the psychiatric and psychological fields. If there is one crucial point of this chapter, it is that the conflation of police and therapeutic goals is dangerous.

In 1990, reflecting on six or seven years of law-enforcement concerns with Satanism and cults, I find that the topic is a solid growth industry for many professionals. I can only observe by way of explanation that satanic imagery strikes a particular nerve of fear, partly millenarian, partly apocalyptic. Police officers apprehend the symbols and violence that appear in teenagers' heavy-metal music, their fashions, and their icons. To the officer, the occult-minded teenager represents a being on the precipice: the teenager may have been an abused child, perhaps in a day-care center, and so represents the effect following a cause. The teenager, ambivalent about maturing in a materialistic world, and unaware of the spiritual dangers of "dabbling" in satanic or occult imagery, can easily enter adulthood and acquire multiple-personality disorder as a defense against the satanic violence that he or she unwittingly entered during childhood or adolescence—here the teenager represents the cause preceding an effect that won't fully manifest itself for years.

This long chapter has shown the ambiguities that underlie child-abuse investigations, which translate cautious research into certainties propelling investigations. Much of what appears on checklists as definitive signs of satanic abuse derives from anecdote, someone else's experience, or un-supported supposition, such as that in the early work of Bruce Woodling and others studying the medical evidence of abuse. The day-care-center cases—that is, many of the sensational ones—that include satanic claims fall within a rigidly constructed and tautological universe of investigative and therapeutic ideology where the *possibility* of error is not even recognized; where the rules require a finding of guilt; where even the innocuous or respectable receive suspicion if not condemnation *because* of their innocuousness or respectability. Incredibly, a day-care center that has a reputable, established history with a policy of absolute openness to parents can be rendered suspect *because* of its reputable, established history and its policy of openness.

Police must account for their investigations in a courtroom with scrupulous documentation. But therapeutic interviews with children enjoy confidentiality, which means that therapists conduct their work beyond the public eye. When police give over their investigations to therapists, the process of forming probable cause cannot be analyzed or questioned. We must simply accept therapists' pronouncements.

Kenneth Lanning and other critics consider the rush to find satanic explanations to be a search for simple answers to complex problems. A provocative explanation for the cult-cop view of satanic abuse comes from John Hasek, a retired Canadian military officer and consultant to Canadian police who "views the cult cop reaction as a response to their failures and ambivalences in prosecuting drug and child-abuse cases. If Satanism is a community fear, then the police, he says, 'must be seen to be responding to it, and it's very nice because it's so easy to defeat.' "[295]

The pursuit of Satan in day-care cases presents three tragedies: (1) that real physical or sexual abuse of a child may pass uninvestigated; (2) that children are abused by the criminal justice process itself—children who are victims of nothing except not telling stories that investigators want to hear; and (3) that innocent adults may have their lives ruined. Before her recent acquittal, one young imprisoned mother in one of the Bakersfield cases, whose children had been placed in foster care, looked forward to freedom one day, but she did not want to be united with her kids. She said, "I'm scared of kids. I'm scared to death of kids. . . . I'm glad I can't have any more."[296] Police should follow Lanning's plea to *listen* to children, not simply to *believe* them.

Chapter Six
"WE'RE DEALING WITH EVIL ITSELF"

So whether it be worshiping, whether it be sacrifice, even if it comes to the point where drugs are used, that's Satan. Very definitely it's Satan because it's evil. It's something that can hurt you or harm you. . . . We're dealing with evil itself.

—Detective Gary Sworin (Satanic-crime seminar, Freeland, Pennsylvania, October 4, 1988)

The Devil Owns Our Kids

Because most adults have children, adults have much to say about what's good and what's bad for children. Many adults with offspring think themselves experts on children's behavior. With very young children, we sometimes cultivate the myth of their absolute innocence, their pristine nature, which makes possible our relentless belief in their incorruptibility. With very young children, we describe as "cute" their original utterances about the world.

When children become teens, we react differently to their behavior. Now we begin to perceive them as miniature adults who bring home foreign ideas and notions that may shock parents. These days, such notions include heavy-metal rock music, with lyrics suggesting apocalyptic and violent visions and symbols drawn from the occult. Recall that the lowest level of involvement in cult cops' satanic continuum is the dabbler, the teen who makes use of satanic bits and pieces. Much literature has developed in recent years warning us that such interests have a pernicious effect on teens. Teens who are Scouts, members of churches, or good students a priori cannot do nasty things, that someone or something else *had* to be responsible. Or the literature suggests that teens have so little free will that lurking Satanists will deceive them into attending sex-and-drug parties, swearing them in as card-carrying minions of the Evil One. Or that teens have so little judgment where fantasy is concerned that parents must absolutely control all that they read and hear.

Such literature, written by adults for other hand-wringing adults, relies on supposition, guesses, and speculation, and reacts to music, games, fads, and fashions *meant* to intimidate adults. Very little literature on teens' interests in things satanic involves empirical study. Much of what fuels the literature comes from what cult cops say on the lecture circuit to teachers, counselors and therapists, and parents. I maintain that although satanic or occult symbols seem to be enjoying popularity among teens, their presence does not betoken a kid lost in Satan's thrall. Yet cult cops circulate pages and pages devoted to occult or satanic symbols found on kids' jewelry, schoolbooks, or even in their school essays, implying that teens either have joined cults or otherwise associate with dangerous dark forces. But "[f]or some teenagers, wearing pentagram earrings has all the religious significance of a rosary worn out of admiration for the pop star Madonna, who used to drape herself in the beads."[1] Historian Jeffrey Burton Russell has remarked, "Rooted in adolescent resentment of authority, [kids use] the terms and symbols of the occult to express cultural rebellion rather than personal belief."[2] In particular, I suggest that cult cops, in warning parents about teens' interests, have divorced themselves from law enforcement; what they tell parents consists of their *opinions* of what's harmful, occasionally mixed with specific examples of teens who went astray, implying causal connections not suggested by the evidence.

A brief excursion into the literature and the lecture circuit reveals the guesses, half-truths, and outright concoctions pawned off on gullible audiences by cult cops and their allies. For example, in an article on satanic cults published in *Family Violence Bulletin*,[3] Paula Lundberg-Love, associate director of the Family Violence and Treatment Program at the University of Texas at Tyler, writes of a seminar she attended entitled "Ritualistic Child Abuse and Adolescent Indoctrination" (discussed in Chapter 2). Lundberg-Love writes that "some satanic cults are created for the expressed purposes of child prostitution or the production of child pornography" and that "'religion' has proved to be a good 'front' for organizing child prostitution and pornography rings." Perhaps more damning as a reflection on our collective impotence, she parrots the cult-cop litany, pointing out that "in many states, ritualistic behavior is not against the law." Citing First Amendment protections of "ritualistic behavior," whatever that is, provides the perfect cover for not offering proof of satanic assertions.

The Cult Awareness Council of Houston, which produced the seminar, has concocted a model of cult activities that is specific and detailed. But, of course, we have no evidence of satanic child prostitution, no evidence that women breed babies for sacrifice, and no evidence that snuff films exist. But the lack of evidence has not stopped Lundberg-Love from pandering to cult cops' fantasies. As we have seen, adult professionals who offer such messages about satanic dangers to our children forsake proof of their claims out of what they say is a love of children and desire to protect them from evil.

A survey of adults' claims reveals a widespread belief that not only are an increasing number of teens *worshipping* Satan but also that they join cults to do so. A magazine for teachers begins by asserting that the Missouri death of Steven Newberry "was a sacrifice to Satan," despite the attestations of professionals associated with the case that heavy drug use was the primary cause of the murder.[4] Nevertheless, the magazine quotes unnamed police cult experts as asserting that they "have seen an increase in adolescent obsession with the devil," an obsession that has taken on "all the trappings of an ancient religion." The author cites satanic violence: a teen who committed suicide after she "reportedly" left a note professing devotion to Satan, or the death of a teen at the hands of two others, "allegedly" a sacrifice to Satan. The article advises teachers that dabblers can become "doers," progressing from heavy-metal rock music to attending seances and "ceremonies," finally reaching bloodletting and reading "the satanist bible." And just as psychologists and therapists have provided a checklist of symptoms for satanic abuse of preschoolers, the same article lists symptoms of dabbling (furnished by the National Cult Awareness Network) that include self-mutilation, wearing black clothing and satanic jewelry, sharp changes in behavior (alienation, fatigue, changes in diet, substance abuse), and possession of "a Book of Shadows," a notebook "containing rituals and symbols, and possibly meditations on violent death."

This article, traceable to cult cops, certainly is not alone in its questionable assertions:

—A 1989 editorial in Salt Lake City's *Deseret News* linked teens' interests in Satanism to the Matamoros killings:

> So devil worship is just another silly fad, is it? Though that seems to be the general impression, the sickening reality is that satanism can be extremely violent and dangerous. Just how dangerous should be clear from this week's discovery of at least 12 victims of human sacrifice by a satanic cult of drug smugglers.[5]

—*Denver Magazine* quotes a woman discussing the suicide of her 16-year-old boy:

> From what we can tell, he evidently must have performed some kind of satanic death ritual. He was barefoot and we found symbols drawn on the ground. . . . In his suicide note, he says, "It is time for me to meet my lofty maker. I have now started the lonesome journey to the bowels of the earth; I travel that twisted road that winds its way down to the forsaken pit. My destination will be the foot of the throne where I kneel and greet my father."[6]

The boy had listened to heavy-metal music, had a fascination with knives, played Dungeons & Dragons, and owned a number of occult books, including *The Satanic Bible,* all of which his mother "discovered" upon his death. She reflects, "At first we blamed ourselves. Then we started learning about similar deaths and seeing the pattern. Slowly, we realized we weren't responsible." Importantly, however, the mother reached this realization through counseling by Jim McCarthy, "an expert in paganism and satanism," who also directs Sanctuary, Inc., an organization that offers information and counseling about religious organizations. McCarthy's counseling brought to light the boy's other problems, including intensive use of LSD and hashish. McCarthy believes that "games and fantasy can develop into real and dangerous practices of paganism and satanism," and warns that dabblers experiment with dangerous stuff involving "traditional practices" of the dark arts. The *Denver Magazine* article invokes Patricia Pulling's views on Dungeons & Dragons, maintaining that, at the very least, the game "desensitizes" one to violence. The article also quotes cult cop Bill Wickersham, who discusses the influence of occultanalia in rock music and fantasy games: " 'We are creating an immoral or amoral society by allowing it.' " This last comment, of course, by a police officer, has *nothing* to do with law enforcement.[7]

—Cult cop Greg George of the Bradenton, Florida, Police Department lectures to professionals who work with teens in mental-health and juvenile-justice settings. George's talk presents the usual satanic symbols through slides and videotapes together with the standard assemblage of artifacts: *The Satanic Bible,* pentagrams, and candles. For the titillation of his packed audience, he says, " 'When I travel with my props, the airlines simply won't let me put them on an airplane. They say they simply can't take the chance of having my stuff found at the scene of a crash.' George goes on to say that he has trouble getting airline reservations for himself, even when he's not taking his props with him."[8] Such talk simply magnifies George's daring in taking on the lonely and dangerous pursuit of cultbusting, for which his audiences are undoubtedly awash in gratitude and admiration. Yet airlines don't prohibit other cult experts from flying to seminars with their show-and-tell paraphernalia.

—Dick Burke of the Fellowship of Christian Peace Officers, not one to be left out of the lecture circuit, tells school administrators how to spot Satanism. At the Smoky Hill High School in Aurora, Colorado, Burke offered the standard caveat that First Amendment freedoms must be respected, yet proceeded to link Satanism with criminality. He offered that every teen he had interviewed "and who has told him that they were into the occult or a satanist has had a criminal record. He explained this by saying that occult and satanic activity is oppositional to the Judeo-Christian standards under which our laws are designed."[9] Burke urged parents and teachers to learn all they could about cults: "Find out what your child is being exposed to in the classroom or day care center. Ask what kinds of games, films, programs and classes in which your child is being asked to participate." Other advice includes learning as much as possible about one's child's friends and their families; finding out when, where, and how often adults touch children; and remaining alert to a child being "overly curious" about the supernatural. Clearly, some of this advice derives from sensational day-care claims, yet the advice—from a *police officer*—also implies monitoring teaching, child care, and educational resources for objectionable content.

—A few court cases have seen Dungeons & Dragons introduced either as the focus of evil-doing or as a mitigating circumstance that might excuse a criminal defendant's conduct. In a Delaware case, Jackson Franklin Morgan, known as "Hatchet," was an obese vagrant who charmed children and teens into playing Dungeons & Dragons in the basements of tenements. Although adept at constantly surrounding himself with children, he required girls to engage in sex with him in return for his allowing them to remain in the game.[10] "Hatchet" had set himself up as the dungeon master, the game's master of ceremonies and administrator. In a New York case, a jury convicted Daniel Kasten of murdering his parents "because his grades were poor and he feared that his father would make him get a job."[11] Kasten's attorney argued his innocence by reason of insanity: Kasten, the attorney argued, could not control himself because "his body had been taken over by Mind Flayer, a character in the 'Dungeons & Dragons' game." Unfortunately, Kasten had already confessed to the police that Dungeons & Dragons had nothing whatever to do with his behavior.

—The publicity surrounding some incidents seems to argue that teens sometimes do nasty things because of Satan's influence. Sixteen-year-old Terry Belcher of Georgia testified that after he and another teen strangled a girl, both boys had stood over the corpse "calling upon Satan . . . to be with us, to give him the sacrifice."[12] After he was convicted, Belcher testified at the trial of his accomplice that he had worshipped the Devil but had since renounced the Evil One for fear of going to hell. Although Belcher attested to years of satanic rituals and sacrifices, he said that he planned to kill the girl because she refused to have sex with him; listening to Ozzy Osbourne made him decide to make the killing a "sacrifice." The Cult Awareness Network (CAN) *News* reports on news articles that appear nationally. Noting the increase in telephone calls that CAN receives on Satanism, CAN sounds a warning: "Whether led by adults or other teens, some of these groups emerge into destructive cults implementing behavior-modification techniques (albeit in a hit-or-miss fashion at times) which can reshape the personality of the participants."[13]

The CAN literature stresses behavior modification and mind control by cults. In a seminar to mental-health professionals, the Rev. Mike Rokos, past-president of CAN, relied heavily on Robert Jay Lifton's model of thought reform (see Chapter 2) as applicable to cults in the United States

(October 19, 1989, Richmond, Virginia). As I argued in Chapter 2, the model has questionable applicability to modern cults or small groups of people with nonconformist common interests. In fact, Rokos distributed Catherine Gould's checklist oriented to behavioral symptoms in teens, along with a CAN checklist titled "Warning Signs of Occult Influence," which advises:

> Those who have declared teenage satanism something to be ignored have not made themselves aware, knowledgeable and educated about destructive satanic cults and their persuasive methods of mind-control recruitment. How does a teenager outgrow satanic indoctrination that culminates in child pornography, child prostitution, violence, murder, suicide, drug addiction and a complete loss of free will that leaves the victimized teenager bound in a belief system that they can't get out, even if they want to get out?
>
> *Any* teenager who has not been educated about satanic cult methods and tactics flirts with the occult without realizing it.

The checklist asks parents or teachers to note changes in behavior, such as "increased rebellion"; aggression; depression; change of priorities; interest in occultanalia in books, television, cinema, or magazines; preoccupations with harming people and animals; death; anarchy; secretiveness; an inclination to be "distinterested in church and church teachings of the Holy Bible"; and "involvement in video games that use behavior modification via role playing (Dungeons & Dragons, RuneQuest, Chivalry & Sorcery, Arduin Grimoire, Tunnels & Trolls, etc.)." As with Catherine Gould's checklist, the CAN list has been distributed nationwide.

—A crime-prevention periodical ran an article on Satanism claiming 1.4 million teens and adults "are involved in satanic worship in various ways."[14] The article contains the usual broad generalizations and equally unsupported cause-and-effect relationships. For example, the author links the killer Richard Ramirez "with satan worship and rock music with satanic lyrics"; paints the Matamoros killers as "involved in satanic ritualistic practices"; and claims a "documented" connection between satanic behavior and drugs. The article asks that we remain alert to satanic-cult recruiters, "usually middle-age perverts," who of course lure kids with sex-and-drugs parties. Further, the article suggests that Satanism is a priori criminal: "Followers are predisposed to evil and enticed by their lusts." Finally, the article offers the list of behavioral symptoms, concluding with, "Parents who are suspicious may consider a check of their child's room for bones, whips, small red pillows, swords or knives with symbols, and demon masks and drugs."

—Helping to spread the alarm is Lewis B. Hancock, director of Wasatch Canyon Hospital's Dayspring Program in Utah, a mental-health treatment center. He finds that among teens occult worship has supplanted even drugs:

"It's symbolic of what is happening in our society; we are turning away from traditional Christian values. We are losing our kids out of just about every church on the earth by the droves. Our children are abandoning traditional Christian practices for anti-church and anti-Christian activities and turning to Satanism."[15] Conveying a similar message, but propounding numbers with great authority, pastor David Marchant of Savannah, Georgia, tells the public that "what we're seeing nationwide is a revival of Satanism."[16] In his own tricounty area, Marchant asserts that seven satanic groups exist, and that during the 1970s in Chatham County, a thousand members of the Church of Satan resided (an odd statistic since the Church of Satan has never released such a number).

—All of the preceding claims concerning causal links, the magnitude of the teen satanic problem, and so on appear at law-enforcement cult seminars *parti pris* to the larger context of the myriad ways in which Satan runs amok these days. Detective Gary Sworin of Luzerne County, Pennsylvania, put it all in cult-cop vernacular during a satanic-cults seminar on October 4, 1988, in Freeland, Pennsylvania. He spoke of the influence of rock music:

> There are many more out there who like the music and listen to it. It doesn't prove very definitely that just because you put the headphones on and you're going to listen to Ozzy Osbourne that you're going to go out and start worshiping and start to cut people up and all of this.
>
> But there are some underlying effects that it has, very definitely. You've heard the thing probably in the past couple of years or so that if you play the music backwards, singing chants and worshiping of Satan. Very definitely. I think that stuff is probably done for a reason. They know it; it's been indicated that they've gone and they've played the music back and they've heard certain things. Very definitely.
>
> So someone has the intelligence to think these things up. Someone's putting them there for some reason, and is it just to the point that we're ignorant of the fact, that we don't want to know? Are we afraid? This is probably a big thing. It really definitely means something.

I've presented a pastiche of claims about teens and Satanism, claims that gain currency through repetition. Or they receive reinforcement by such simple means as Sworin's predeliction to punctuate each assertion with "very definitely" as a substitute for analysis of causal connections. Take my word for it, he seems to suggest, I know. I'm a cult cop. Many of the claims resemble facets of satanic child abuse. But many child-abuse court cases were prosecuted on the investigators' *need* to find a criminal conspiracy and on clinical supposition, such as the reduction of physiological symptoms in children to orifice-size tests, or the children-do-not-lie ideology. The suppositions in child-abuse cases came about because the victims were either prearticulate or, owing to immaturity and inexperience, simply cannot articulate sexual abuse as a teen or an adult would. With teens, we have no day-care cases, no forum within which to test the wide-ranging assumptions about the influence of rock music or game-playing or occultanalia on their behavior. Similarly, most of the circulated behavioral checklists evoke the same causal problem exhibited in Catherine Gould's list: teens can be *expected* to become depressed, to change friends, to show aggression, and to become obsessed with new and bizarre things, particularly music, books, or art antithetical to their parents' staid middle-class interests. When cult cops speak of teens as prey for satanic-cult recruiters or for pernicious rock-music producers, they imply that teens, owing to immaturity, have not yet acquired free will or free choice.

Importantly, cult cops tell us that the kids most susceptible to the dark charms of the netherworld happen to be bright overachievers. But bright overachievers sometimes lag behind their peers in developing and sustaining social relationships, they display curiosity about everything, and they may even become secretive about their discovery of sexuality. Kids who are intelligent with poor social skills simply define the process of growing up. By imbuing fantasy games or the reading of occultanalia with some supernatural taint, we deny kids their own intelligence and ability to make choices. When the Pasadena, Texas, school board decided to ban the peace symbol from school property, they did so because a cult seminar advised teachers that the symbol is satanic; that interpretation, in turn, derives from Christian publications that describe the upside-down cross as a mockery of Christianity. How did the kids react to the fuss? One twelve-year-old said, "If they ban peace symbols, they'll have to ban basic geometry because of all its lines and circles."[17] In Maryland, Annapolis Senior High School Principal Kenneth E. Nichols wrote to the parents of his students to alert them to the "eccentric activities" of a small number of students; he took the opportunity to tell parents that "teenagers wearing black clothing, dark makeup and safety-pin jewelry may be perceived as Satanists."[18] But the students have objected to Nichols's warnings about the wearing of black. Some students have launched a petition to demand an apology from the principal, maintaining that the wearing of black betokens more a current and widespread fashion interest than a satanic trapping..

We have other clues about how seriously teens take this talk of the seduction of the occult. In Miami, Florida, in the patois of students one might hear of Cubies, or ideal boyfriends of Cuban descent with strong family values. A pueb or pueba is a boyfriend or girlfriend from Latin America. And "when men on campus whisper sweet nothings in Miami, they tell a woman they are so enchanted by her they suspect she used bruheria on them."[19] In short, the cult-cop warnings of supernatural involvement with *brujeria* appear lost on kids for whom such a word is simply trendy social parlance for a hot date.

Of course, the behaviors listed on checklists might describe a disturbed teen who possesses *The Satanic Bible,* Ozzy Osbourne music, and Dungeons & Dragons, but they also apply to the normally painful process of growing up. Kids change dietary habits, drop and add friends, and undergo phases of resentment, aggression, or depression for many reasons. The teen behavioral checklists match the other checklists I have described in this book: none of them serve as exclusive diagnostic tools, and at best they can only *suggest* that a teen has become mentally unhealthy. The lists cannot serve predictive purposes, either. A clinical assessment of a teen's misbehavior must necessarily reconnoiter the teen's larger familial and social environment, hereditary characteristics, and involvement with substance abuse. Yet this complex milieu is dismissed as of secondary importance if one can come up with *anything* that smacks of the occult, which cult cops assume is so intrinsically evil that kids can easily succumb to its dark lure. Some cult cops attach intrinsic significance to occult symbols and devices but emphasize that a teen's response to them is what counts. Others preach the supernatural influence.

Usually, though, the cult-cop message is ambiguous. If rock-music lyrics can incite suicide, then do we arrest the singer or the composer? If the answer is yes, then cult cops must be prepared to launch a case regarding the First Amendment, which holds, generally, that artists cannot be held responsible for other people's reactions to their work. Are specific lyrics composed in such a way as to numb and seduce young minds into doing evil against their will? If the answer is yes, then cult cops have posited a supernatural explanation for criminal behavior, which certainly hinders the investigation by providing defense attorneys with a splendid opportunity to plead the diminished mental capacity of their clients.

Kids and Crime: What Really Happens?

Cult cops maintain that vandalism represents the primary criminal predilection of the dabbler, who will mark territory with satanic graffiti; the next most frequent crime among dabblers is cruelty to animals (because of their use in rituals or sacrifices). Though most people consider graffiti merely a nuisance, police occasionally report it as a crime. National statistics don't offer much to support cult cops' assertions that dabblers vandalize churches and cemeteries and loot graves. According to the FBI's *Uniform Crime Reports,* 1988 saw 183,117 city arrests nationwide for vandalism of *all* kinds. Of those, 36,928 arrests involved children under 15; 73,679 under 18; and the majority, 109,438 arrests, involved adults over 18. Suburban county arrests totaled 26,177 in 1988, with similar proportions for the three age groups. Finally, rural arrests totaled 16,250, again with the same proportion by age. Such statistics do not report the total damage in monetary terms, the clearance rate for vandalism investigations (that is, the percentage "solved" or otherwise disposed of), or the type or location of property damaged.

But for all the cult cops' admonitions to patrol cemeteries and churches, particularly on satanic holidays, what facts do exist suggest a microscopic problem. Based on statistics obtained from the Virginia Statistical Analysis Center of the Department of Criminal Justice Services, in 1985 the state's courts produced 10,615 "sentencing events" for all types of crimes. (Each time a judge pronounces a sentence, it counts as an "event." If a defendant is convicted for five offenses at one sentencing, it counts as one sentencing event. If a person commits crimes again within a year and is convicted, this constitutes a second sentencing event.) Of these, only three cases suggested "dabbler crimes" pertaining to defiling churches or cemeteries. All three cases concerned trespassing on school or church property at night (trespassing at a school or a church is covered under the same criminal statute). Of the three, two were primary offenses and one was included as part of a burglary charge. In 1986, of 12,370 sentencing events in Virginia, only two involved trespassing; yet neither was a primary offense (one was included with a rape, the other with a larceny). In 1987, of 13,737 events, six cases emerged involving trespassing at churches or schools. Three more involved injury to a cemetery or church property, and one concerned cruelty to animals. In 1988, of 14,966 sentencing events, three cases involved trespassing (two were primary offenses); three involved the related offense of trespassing after having been forbidden, and two involved cruelty to animals.

Finally, the more serious crime (a felony) of violating a tomb or sepulchre saw no sentencing events in 1988, and two in 1989. In the latter year, neither counted as a primary offense, and possibly both sentencing events involved the same criminal.[20] The statistics cannot produce further details: whether or not the very few criminal cases involving churches, cemeteries, and animals had anything to do with Satanism or the occult is questionable. Of course the statistics don't represent the number of cemetery or church vandalisms reported to the police that have produced no arrests, or arrests but no sentencings; such statistics have not been collected in Virginia. Further, all of the sentencing events involve *adult* offenders (18 years of age or older); no similar statistics exist for juveniles. Even if one assumes that the sentencings for church and cemetery crimes plus cruelty to animals represent the criminal results of satanic rituals, they occupy a miniscule percentage of crime that hardly justifies any specialized law-enforcement resources. The sentencing events reflect convictions; the convictions spring from arrests. The number of arrests in Virginia alone, as shown by the preceding statistics, do not attest to cult cops' claims of the prevalence of and dangers presented by putative satanic dabblers.

Teens and young adults do commit murder and suicide, for the same reasons that adults do. Cult cops cite examples in which, they claim, fantasy role-playing games contributed in some ambiguous fashion. Recall the case of Tommy Sullivan of New Jersey, a teen who killed his mother and then committed suicide, a boy who had played Dungeons & Dragons, an association from which cult cops have inferred causality. As a further example of this ambiguous causality, Patricia Pulling of BADD cites the murder trial of Raymond Malin of Salt Lake City, Utah. Malin, 25 years old at his sentencing for raping and murdering a 13-year-old girl, had as a child been physically abused by both his father and stepfather. According to his psychiatrist, Malin grew up quite angry and became abusive to others at a young age. The psychiatrist also maintained that Malin's "extreme involvement" with Dungeons & Dragons and its "[f]antasy violence . . . became an outlet for him. He played close to 30 hours a week. To him, it was like real life."[21] In his game-playing, Malin could make himself dungeon master, thus controlling the game, and he frequently manipulated his characters into sexual violence. Malin's psychiatrist believed that his immersion in the game led to the murder; four consultant psychiatrists, in addition, found that Malin suffered from dissociative disorders, at least in that he could dissociate himself from the persona who committed the murder. Malin's case illustrates the difficulty with D&D causality: Malin could easily have sought any other fantasy, perhaps culminating in a dissociative disorder, as an outlet to his sexual and physical aggression. Dungeons & Dragons did not cause the girl's death. (A newspaper article reported that further complicating the case were possible irregularities in the investigation of Malin; sheriff's deputies may have "improperly obtained a confession from Malin and also obtained permission to search his room through devious tactics.")

Similarly, in the killing of Steven Newberry in Missouri, police officer Larry Jones, editor of *File 18 Newsletter,* quoted local prosecutors, psychiatrists, and investigators who attested that the murder did not represent a satanic sacrifice, as may cult cops believe, but rather involved heavy drug use. Patrick Hayes, an investigator with the Jasper County, Missouri, prosecutor's office, said that the murder "turned up nothing spookier than disturbed kids and heavy-metal songs with nasty imagery."[22] But cult cops continue to cite the case a satanic-crime statistic.

As an example of a teen suicide with some connection to matters occult, two 13-year-old Maryland girls, Marsha Urevich and Nicole Eisel, took their own lives in a suicide pact in 1988. The girls evidently discussed their suicide plans quite openly, even telling friends that "they wanted to meet Satan, that they considered Satan to be their father."[23] The girls' intimidating talk about witches and the supernatural even alarmed two schoolmates into complaining to the school counselor. But the talk of Satanism did not spring forth *sui generis:* educators and investigators commented that both girls "had histories of drug abuse, failing grades and emotional problems." Eisel had repeated the seventh grade. Urevich had been transferred to a school for emotionally disturbed children, whose principal said, "Obviously, the drugs were a negative influence, the peer group probably was. She had serious emotional problems—that may be the underlying reason. The other things [e.g., talk of Satan and the supernatural] I think were just symptoms." Local cult cop Timothy Boyle of the Maryland National Capital Park Police, "an authority on ritualistic crimes," adds that adult satanic worshipers show up throughout the country, but with kids some just "dabble" while others become intensely involved. With the nonspecific satanic gloss, cult cops chalk this murder-suicide to another "occult-linked" crime. Here, satanic and even cinematically satanic imagery (one girl talked of meeting Damian, the devil's son, in hell) occupied a role in the girls' problems, but is of questionable causality; perhaps the satanic talk was intended to alienate and offend others, to create social distance.

I could speculate endlessly, of course, but the important observation is that where satanic motifs or imagery turn up in cases of troubled youth, even a superficial inquiry reveals other misbehavior, destructive preoccupations, even psychiatric disorders. When challenged about causality, cult cops rely on the occult "link" to crime or suicide, an explanation that explains nothing. To posit a "link" serves no other purpose than to assume, imply, or suggest causality. Cult seminars are short on analysis, but long on implication. By offering up ten examples of "links," the cult cop teaching a seminar hopes that the audience will forge from them certainty, if not proof.

Cult cops like Dale Griffis assert that Satanism leads to self-mutilation as well as to murder and suicide in extreme cases. The phenomenon of self-mutilation in a clinical setting has attracted professional psychiatric interest, even to the point of labeling those who do it "carvers." According to *Substance Abuse Report,* clinicians have found that teen girls, "whether out of depression, anger, loneliness, or some other cause, sometimes cut their bodies. They carve boyfriends' initials, satanic symbols, or random slashes."[24] In a clinical setting, girls are particularly likely to "carve" because of the reactions of therapeutic staff. Importantly, the girls don't intend to commit suicide by slashing themselves. In fact, some carving even takes place in settings that some police officers might label as ritualistic; sometimes girls mutilate themselves in order to join a larger social group of girls who do the same, led by a "charismatic carver." Why do the girls carve themselves, if not because they are under the influence of Satan? Most of the girls under treatment come from middle- or upper-class homes, and most have a problem with alcohol or drugs. Richard H. Schwartz, M.D., believes that the kids carve for reasons of resentment and rebellion. And, says Schwartz, carvers can become difficult patients: "Self-carvers are mistresses of manipulation who will ingeniously try to undermine and sabotage management plans and sow seeds of divisiveness between doctors and nurses." But if Schwartz has found self-mutilation among teenage girls who purport to do it in fealty to Satan and for no other reason, he doesn't say.

Whether discussing teen suicide, murder, or self-mutilation, one must remember that, as Mark Twain once observed about science, one gets wholesale returns of conjecture on just a trifling investment of fact. When cult cops posit causal relationships between teen misbehavior—particularly that which seems to adults inexplicably bizarre—and satanic imagery, beliefs, or practices, they either simplify or ignore the circumstances traditionally deemed important by psychiatry, that is, the social and familial environments. Further, cult cops are not qualified to assert clinical opinion about teens' mental health. If one adopts the cult-cop world-view, one seeks the presence of Satan within the antisocial behavior of others, and one will inevitably find it. As I assert throughout this book, cult cops may have invented indicia of satanic influence, but their checklists do not diagnose what they seek; at best, their checklists simply hint at more complex problems beyond which cult cops have no competence to inquire. Yet the cult cops continue to give seminars to other officers and to parents, educators, and therapists, offering their potpourri of nightmares, satanic texts, and rock-music lyrics to prove the existence of a problem.

By similar logic, cult cops make wide-ranging assumptions about abandoned or disused property bearing occult graffiti: that such symbols mark ritually significant sites; that the symbols show dabblers at work; that the symbols mark where crimes have been or will be committed; that the symbols provide instructions or warnings to other cult members. In short, occult or satanic graffiti has something for everyone. In an official satanic-cult presentation by the Virginia State Police, John Polak showed a slide of a bridge in the eastern part of Virginia that was covered with spray-painted slogans and symbols. He pointed to the "significant" graffiti on the bridge, a satanic symbol crowded by much other mindless scribbling. Upon identifying the symbol, Polak mentioned that near the bridge, two years before, police investigated a homicide, thus far unsolved. Though Polak admitted that he couldn't affirm a connection between the death and the painted symbol, it just makes one wonder. Such is the unsophisticated inference drawn by the Virginia State Police: vaguely possible but not probable. So why even mention the symbol and the homicide? Because mention of several such "coincidences" raises suspicions.

The reports of vandalism and satanic graffiti, particularly in "forbidden" places, excite and titillate. The abandoned neighborhood house with its lawn given over to brambles and weeds, its windows smashed, soon takes on mystery. Neighbors see people come and go: who are they and what do they do at night? Any police officer can recount examples of such houses, temporary homes for drifters or meeting places for teens who want to smoke cigarettes, drink liquor, and even take drugs. Abandoned property invites destruction. The mere presence of such places stimulates fear and fascination. For example, residents of Chesterfield County, Virginia, have a run-down abandoned house behind a car dealership that has stimulated neigh-borhood belief that "it is being used by teenagers who indulge in Satan worship or other rituals."[25] The interior of the house is covered with "graffiti that glorifies Satan and sacrificial killing," messages that have convinced many that devil worship attends the place. But even the local investigator has tried to discount such ideas, saying that "we've probably just got a group of teenagers who are fascinated with doing something that is out of the ordinary—something that has shock value to it."[26] Some local ru-mors even place animal sacrifices at the house. But the investigator dis-counts the satanic-cult-meeting-place theory because "the markings are too extreme and prominently displayed to be the work of true devil worshipers. Any of the folks that are truly involved in satanic worship . . . wouldn't be as out in the open. We wouldn't know about that house."

Where police have no suspects, imputing unsolved crimes, particularly distasteful ones, to Satanists makes for easy law-enforcement work. In 1988, someone entered the tomb of a former Virginia governor and one other family, tampering with the governor's casket and removing part of a body from another. A newspaper article reported that "[The] police believe the vandals intended to perform a ritual over the body."[27] At a police-only seminar, Investigator Bill Lightfoot discussed further details of the break-in, showing the damaged coffin and melted candle wax of "ritually significant" colors, an attribute of the crime scene not mentioned in the newspapers (Cult-crime seminar, Petersburg, Virginia, September 8, 1988). To the local police, the matter of the cemetery break-in could no longer be investigated as a vandalism. The newspaper reported that "[Lt. Lawrence Haake] said police believed such incidents in the past were simply the work of vandals. He said that with 'new awareness' police now are investigating such incidents as Satanic or similar rituals."[28]

The police may be treating vandalism with "new awareness," but vandal-ism is a crime that rarely produces suspects, much less physical evidence that would aid an investigation. But when the police actually arrest someone for satanic vandalism, or any vandalism to a church or cemetery, the story proves much different. In Henrico County, Virginia, police arrested six high-school students for digging up graves. Had the police not caught suspects, they would almost certainly have surmised that satanic rituals were taking place; in fact, they originally believed that body parts had been removed from graves, though forensic experts later determined that the bodies had simply disintegrated. So what motivated the boys to disinter the remains? Apparently, they had simply "attended a party and consumed alcoholic beverages. The students told police they were looking for Civil War or Indian artifacts."[29] The family of one of the deceased was relieved to find that "it was nothing satanic in nature."

Similarly, police arrested two boys in Lynchburg, Virginia, for vandalizing a cemetery on Easter Sunday, 1989. They defaced several tombstones, writing "Satan" and "666," plus assorted profanities in spray paint. Why did the boys do it, and on a Christian holy day? Again, the boys, who all attended a local school for the learning disabled, had simply got drunk and gone on a spray-painting spree.[30]

Although satanic fears did not loom large in the Lynchburg case, such fears entered the case of four Florida boys found guilty of "the attempted robbery of a 2-week-old grave" near Myrtle Beach, S.C. According to an article in the *Sun-News,* the boys didn't melt wax over candles or steal skulls; they hurled a tombstone at a small burial vault, making a hole in it but not disturbing any corpses. The local magistrate denied the boys bond because she feared that once released the boys would run amok, worshipping Satan during the upcoming Walpurgisnacht. One of the teens even gave the police some books on Satanism and claimed that "the grave incident was preparation for a Satanic worship ceremony."[31] The remainder of the news article contained quotations from the boys' satanic materials: "On a page with burned edges, a Satanic prayer was written that began, 'Burn the church. Torment the priest. We are the children of the beast.' " In fact, the news article devoted more space to quoting from passages in the satanic books that were irrelevant to the crime than they did to discussing the crime. And the boys' arrest proved so conclusively that Satanism was afoot that a local "expert on Satanic worship from the [South Carolina] Criminal Justice Academy" interviewed the teens.

But despite the teens' admission of their satanic motivation to vandalize the cemetery, what is the meaning of this event? Patricia Pulling, at one of her BADD seminars, circulated the Myrtle Beach article as yet one more proof of the ill effects of satanic worship. The boys indeed "dabbled," but were the judge's fears justified? Did the reporter pander to those fears by giving newspaper space to reporting titillating but irrelevant extracts from pulp writings about satanic worship and other materials available to anyone? Nothing in the case betokens a cult beckoning the boys; since the reporter did not explore other circumstances of the cemetery incident, such as whether the boys had been drinking or had taken drugs, the article leads us to presume that satanic worship provided the sole impetus to the misdeed. Even assuming that it did, how much can we legitimately make of this case? Recall the words of Lieutenant Haake: the police give such cases of cemetery and church vandalism more importance because of their "new awareness" about Satanism. The police cannot view a dabbler incident without placing it high on the threatening satanic continuum. Today's grave disturber could be tomorrow's baby killer:

Very definitely that's what we're talking about here, because of the fact you're starting out—or they're starting out with something that's very, very minimum, very small, which is dabbling, putting markings up and drawings up. And then all of a sudden it starts to progress, and all the contributing factors that we listed all come together and finally something happens where we go from what we know, what we should do, to the other extreme of what they want us to know and they want us to do. And at that point we're lost. And that really is the sad part. (Detective Gary Sworin, Luzerne County, Pennsylvania; Satanic-crime seminar in Freeland, Pennsylvania, October 4, 1988)

Dungeons & Dragons

Detective Gary Sworin, in the cult seminar referred to above, finally gets around to Dungeons & Dragons:

We have Dungeons & Dragons and all these other demons . . . all these games that are out. And luckily within our area, we have had nothing concerning any repercussions from those types of games. . . . It's to the point where—in the game itself, you portray yourself—you take on the characteristic of another person and what you're supposed to do really at that point is make believe that you are this person and you are supposed to rob, to pillage; you're supposed to murder—anything that you can in order to gain [power] in this game.

And [BADD] put together this information and here they find now that because of the fact—what you're doing actually when you play this game is you're playing a role and it's sort of like a role reversal. You're taking on the role of . . . a demon or . . . whatever character you're portraying . . . and as time goes on, the longer . . . that you play it, in your subconscious mind you're storing all of this violence and you're storing all of the things that you're taught by playing this game. . . .

And there [are] people who play [Dungeons & Dragons]. There [are] people out there who play the game, who feel maybe they play it once a week or maybe once a month or something like that and . . . I'm not going to get involved. Well, very definitely you might not, but you've got to realize that depending upon the type of person you are . . . I mean if you're sound as far as mentally and you have yourself set in ways that you're not going to change, all well and good. But what about somebody else? What about the kids that are there?

After Sworin goes on like this for some time, a member of the audience challenges him:

I don't understand where you get the Dungeons & Dragons thing from. I've played the game before and I like it, and I see no satanic anything in it at all. First of all, at the beginning, at the first chapter, it says right off, right away, do not make your characters evil; make sure they're good. They have chaotic and they have . . . good characters, and they say make your characters good; you're fighting evil. You're fighting—you're killing monsters.

Sworin is not used to challenges during his semi-rehearsed talk. His lecture typifies cult-cop presentations: long on hyperbole, short on focus or facts. He faltered during his reply to the Dungeons & Dragons question:

> Sworin: You used the magic word; what did you just say? Killing.
>
> Questioner: But . . . you're good killing evil, and it's not really human. And there's—you know, there's no such thing as monsters so you're only killing imaginary evil.
>
> Sworin: See, that's what the problem is. Again, going back to the research, all right, and if you want, as I said, if you want to give me your name and that, and afterwards I'll send you a copy of this thing that we have for researching [the effects of the game]. But what you're saying, here again, it's not that it's real; they're telling you that, that it's not that it's real, and they're telling you that you're fighting against evil which naturally you're supposed to do. But it's what happens to you and what your perception is as time goes on. While playing this game, you're getting involved in a role reversal, all right, when you're playing it, and it turns to the point where you're going to do anything it takes to rid evil. Am I correct?
>
> Questioner: It warns against that . . .
>
> Sworin: Right. Why does it warn you? If there's a warning on it, there's something wrong with it. You know, I mean I'm not being sarcastic but still, it's to the point where it's determining what good and evil is. And what their research shows here, the sample one, because of the fact that this young boy was playing it, felt that his younger brother did evil to him, he had the right to lash out at him.

The assertions Sworin makes, the research he cites derive from one source: Patricia Pulling and BADD. Pulling's involvement with D&D began with the suicide of her teenage son, Irving "Bink" Pulling, in 1982. Bink Pulling shot himself with his father's pistol in front of his parents' home. Following the suicide, Patricia Pulling began to discover her son's fascination with D&D, an interest, oddly, of which she had previously known nothing. So she began to study the game.

> I continued my Dungeons & Dragons research because some people insisted it was occultic. I read many books on the occult so that I would be prepared to refute or confirm such allegations. The game does, indeed, have a tremendous amount of occult material. Much of what is called "fantasy" in this game is, in reality, drawn from a number of occult philosophies, and it is so specific that it would be ludicrous to suggest that the similarities are mere coincidence.[32]

Pulling maintains that her son took his own life because of a curse placed on him at school by an English teacher, where he played D&D. "The point I am making," Pulling argues, "is that the [dungeon master] has such an omnipotent role in this game, a role I believe can lead to tragedy—as with our own son."[33] Pulling organized BADD to campaign to have the game removed from public schools, where D&D clubs sometimes flourish, and to have a warning label attached to the games in stores to warn consumers of the game's violence. Pulling receives much bolstering by psychiatrist Thomas Radecki of Illinois, chairman of the National Coalition on Television Violence (NCTV), an organization closely allied with BADD. Radecki has proclaimed, "The game is full of human sacrifice, eating babies, drinking blood, rape, murder of every variety, curses of insanity."[34] In 1985 Radecki released a statement that listed D&D-related deaths, citing the book *Mazes and Monsters* by Rona Jaffe, which relates how a fantasy role-playing game took over the lives of college students. But Jaffe's book is a novel, set at an imaginary college in an imaginary town in Pennsylvania. The fact that it is fiction did not stop Radecki from citing it as an "investigative book" for NCTV purposes.[35]

I asserted earlier in this chapter that cult cops like Sworin who deprecate rock music and fantasy role-playing games have abandoned any recognizable law-enforcement role and trifle perilously with First Amendment protections. After all, what business do law-enforcement representatives like Sworin have in warning about evils of game-playing and rock music? The putative harmful effects of both are the province of social scientists and concerned parents, parents who ought to examine what music their kids listen to and what games they play. Patricia Pulling and other parents of children who have committed suicide often claim to have known nothing about D&D before their kids took their own lives, but afterward discovered books, paraphernalia, notes, and letters indicating an advanced interest in the game.

Perhaps the most remarkable phenomenon is Pulling's extraordinary influence on the police, with whom she has an almost symbiotic relationship. Pulling provides the cult cops with misinformation and then makes claims at her seminars based on her access to confidential information provided by cult cops conducting criminal investigations. By citing her information as confidential, she can dangle before her audiences investigative bits and pieces that imply causal connections between game-playing and violence, and make assertions her audience is not likely to question. Her packed audiences have reinforced her new-found identity as private investigator, leading her into odd excursions to Matamoros, for example, or to the prison cell of mass-murderer and inveterate liar Henry Lee Lucas.

The most disturbing fact about Pulling is her assumption of professional roles for which she is unqualified. She has no clinical background, though parents sometimes haul their misbehaving children before her for an analysis of their satanic proclivities. She recently represented herself at a Virginia cult-seminar as being "a private investigator with the state of Virginia," noting that she had received "innumerable degrees and awards." Her "innumerable degrees" consist of a two-year Associate of Arts degree from J. Sargent Reynolds Community College in Richmond, Virginia. The private-investigator business implies some association with state government; in truth, she holds a state private-investigator's license; to obtain this document one need complete only 42 hours of classroom instruction, with an additional six (which Pulling has) if one wants to carry a gun. Then one must pass a one-hour exam and a criminal background check, and pay for the license. In fact, Pulling became a licensed private investigator on October 6, 1987, according to the Virginia Department of Commerce, yet in a radio broadcast on KFYI in Phoenix, Arizona, in October, 1987, she described herself as having been a private investigator for the past six years, a timespan that would have preceded Bink Pulling's death.[36] Huntington House, the publisher of Pulling's book, *The Devil's Web,* refers to her as "a police detective," and attests, "Pat instructs the FBI, local police forces, sheriff associations [sic] and others, and is recognized by these groups as our nation's leading occult authority."[37] Pulling's resume recounts her numerous television appearances (which lends authenticity, because anyone knows that if something appears on TV, it must be true) hosted by such luminaries as Geraldo Rivera and Oprah Winfrey. Even bolder, Pulling lists her expertise as a "jury trainer" and expert witness, though she has ignored my request for an explanation of what constitutes a "jury trainer."

Pulling's work can be summed up in her own definition of Dungeons & Dragons:

A fantasy role-playing game which uses demonology, witchcraft, voodoo, murder, rape, blasphemy, suicide, assassination, insanity, sex perversion, homosexuality, prostitution, satanic type rituals, gambling, barbarism, cannibalism, sadism, desecration, demon summoning, necromantics, divination and many other teachings. There have been a number of deaths nationwide where games like Dungeons & Dragons were either the decisive factor in adolescent suicide and murder, or played a major factor in the violent behavior in such tragedies. Since role-playing is used typically for behavior modification, it has become apparent nationwide (with the increased homicide and suicide rates in adolescents) that there is a great need to investigate every aspect of a youngster's environment, including their method of entertainment, in reaching a responsible conclusion for their violent actions.[38]

And that's just her definition in the glossary to her book. In her seminars, Pulling asserts that 95 to 150 teens have committed suicide related to playing D&D. People at her seminars nod sagely and gasp in astonishment that our government allows such a game to exist. What is her proof of this assertion? In her booklet, *Dungeons and Dragons,* she offers a series of newspaper clippings to prove her point. In one, with no source cited, an Arlington, Texas, boy killed himself with a shotgun in front of his drama class. The first paragraph of the article notes that the boy "was a devotee of the fantasy game Dungeons & Dragons and had a lead role in this weekend's school play," an odd parallel, perhaps. An observation occurs further on in the article that the boy enjoyed the game. But where is the causal relationship? The article quotes the boy's friends commenting on his character, but no one linked the game to his death. Yet this article, for all its superficiality, counts as a statistical fatality in Pulling's reckoning.[39] This and similar assertions are seldom challenged at Pulling's seminars. A journalist offered an observation about Pulling's research in 1985 (when she claimed 51 D&D-linked deaths) that still holds true: "The research is unscientific, consisting mainly of Pulling's interviews with police and parents in cases brought to her attention by newspapers and television. She and her husband want the federal government to investigate the deaths to determine whether Dungeons & Dragons was a cause."[40]

Since Pulling's involvement with D&D came about as a result of her son's tragic death, no one wants to challenge her assertions about him, particularly that he had evinced no other behavioral problems before his death. The picture she paints is one of a happy, well-adjusted boy whose suicide can be explained by only one factor: the dungeon master's curse. One of Pulling's seminar handouts is a newspaper article about her son's death, a piece from the *Weekly World News* (September 20, 1983), with the beguiling title, "Fantasy Game Ruled Honor Student's Life—and Death." The tabloid wastes no time citing Dungeons & Dragons as the cause, citing as a professional authority the Rev. John Torell, "a minister and head of a Sacramento, California, citizens' group that opposes the top-selling game." Torell asserts the familiar explanation that game players no longer can differentiate between reality and fantasy, and expresses shock that educational institutions permit, if not encourage, playing the game. Torell himself is an odd authority for Pulling to have cited in one of her seminars since his main concern seems to be anti-communism and the surrender of the United States to the Soviet Union.[41]

Yet, in a manner similar to the other suicides and murders Pulling cites as statistical evidence, apparently Bink Pulling left several clues to his emotional difficulties. According to cult cop Larry Jones's transcript of a Pulling speech, Bink Pulling had displayed lycanthropic behavior before his death: "He growled, screamed, walked on all fours, and clawed the ground. Nineteen rabbits raised by the Pullings were found torn to pieces in the last three weeks of his life, although stray dogs were never seen. A cat was found disemboweled with a knife."[42] Pulling's inclusion of newspaper articles that note some connection between suicides and the playing of D&D have been dissected, the paragraphs rearranged to present the game in the most damning light. She did this with an August 13, 1983, *Washington Post* article about her son's suicide. The piece originally ran 20 column inches, but was reduced in Pulling's reprint to 14 column inches, leaving out the manufacturer's defense of D&D and, most importantly, critical comments about Bink Pulling by his classmates:

> [Bink Pulling] had trouble "fitting in" and became dejected when he was unable to find a campaign manager when he ran for school office. Shortly before his death, he wrote "Life is a Joke" on the blackboard in one of his classes, a classmate said.
> "He had a lot of problems anyway that weren't associated with the game," said Victoria Rockecharlie, another classmate of Pulling's in the Talented and Gifted program.[43]

As a further example of Patricia Pulling's manipulation of news stories, her statistics include the deaths of two brothers, Daniel and Steve Erwin, 16 and 12 years old. The boys had a "death pact" whereby Steve shot his brother before shooting himself. An article Pulling uses quotes a police officer who claims that "D&D cost them their lives." But Pulling does not cite the comments of the boys' parents:

> Two young brothers carried out a murder-suicide pact last fall because the older boy feared his sentencing in an auto theft case, not because of the Dungeons and Dragons fantasy game, their mother said.[44]

Daniel Erwin had faced a criminal charge for auto theft and, according to his mother, had been "extremely afraid of the criminal justice system":

> The boys' brother, Brian Erwin, 14, said Daniel was upset that a likely condition of probation would be that he return to a school he had dropped out of shortly after his sophomore year began.[45]

Pulling's sloppiness with causality extends to her handling of statistics. Her citation of about 125 to 150 D&D-linked deaths contrasts with the manufacturer's own estimate that 10 million copies of the game circulate worldwide. Game designer Michael Stackpole argues that if Pulling's statistics are correct (she cites a "user base" of 4 million people), then her reasoning "would strongly suggest that involvement in role playing games in fact *reduces* the likelihood of a suicide."[46] Over the first five years of the game's life (between 1975 and 1980), the national suicide rate for people aged 15 to 24 hovered between 11.7 and 12.8 deaths per 100,000. Stackpole points out that "if gamers were killing themselves at the average rate for their age group we would expect between 468 and 512 successful suicides a year among [D&D] enthusiasts. This amounts to about 6,840 successful suicides among the players of role playing games since [D&D] was published, *if role playing games did not incite teens to suicide*" (italics in original).[47]

But although Pulling cites 125 cases as of 1987, she offers newspaper article documentation for only about 65 percent of those, alluding to the many unpublished or unpublicized cases that undoubtedly exist. Yet her "documented" claims still represent only "about 1% of the 6,840 successful suicides expected if [D&D] has no effect at all on the suicide rate of its players!"[48]

Pulling has casually dabbled in estimates of Satanists or occultists. In 1988, she asserted that approximately 8 percent of the Richmond, Virginia, population "is involved with Satanic worship at some level."[49] A reporter examined this statistic later, pointing out that 8 percent equalled 56,000 people, "more than the number of United Methodists in the Richmond area."[50] Pulling responded that her 8 percent figure concerned not just Satanists but also "occultists," including New Agers, witches, and others; she added estimates of 4 percent of Richmond's teens with 4 percent of Richmond's adults. As I recounted in Chapter 3, when shown that 4 percent of adults plus 4 percent of youths doesn't add up to 8 percent of the population, Pulling dismissed her arithmetical sleight-of-hand by saying that 8 percent was probably conservative anyway. Pulling is no statistician, yet virtually no one questions her assertions or her putative facts. Her "8-percent" contention illustrates that one can properly criticize cult cops' numbers.

In September 1988, Pulling quoted "authorities" as estimating 30,000 Satanists nationally,[51] whereas in March 1988, she estimated 300,000 Satanists nationally,[52] along with the unquestioned 8 percent figure for Richmond (implying that one-sixth of all Satanists in the United States reside in Richmond). And whenever she mentions these statistics, she stresses that Satanists can be found in all strata of society, particularly among police officers, doctors, and lawyers. Pulling is equally casual about her knowledge of fantasy role-playing games. In her 1989 book, *The Devil's Web,* she lists thirteen such games allegedly spawned by D&D. But as Michael Stackpole points out, of the thirteen, by 1989 six were out of print; four had seen declining interest, two were not even role-playing games, and one game remained popular but under a different name. Stackpole observes, "Mrs. Pulling's expertise with games apparently ends with 1983 because all of the products she lists in her 1989 book were printed before then, and none that have hit the market since are covered or even mentioned [with one exception]."[53]

Pulling even offers her own checklist for investigators under the title, "Interviewing Techniques for Adolescents," dated September 1988. The guide is designed for investigators who suspect that the D&D player has committed a crime. Similar to other such behavioral checklists, this one posits the kind of young person at risk: "adolescents from all walks of life"; "many from middle to upper middle class families"; "intelligent, over or under achievers, creative/curious, some are rebellious, some have low self-esteem and are loners, some children have been abused (physically or sexually)." In *The Devil's Web,* Pulling states:

... Almost without exception, the teenagers most likely to become involved in satanic activity are white males from middle- and upper-income families. ...

A white male who is intelligent, creative and curious is the most likely to be seduced by the occult. He may be either an underachiever or an overachiever, and he may be going through a stage of rebellion against family, school, church and society in general.[54]

Such behaviors hardly limit for investigative purposes the teens at risk. In a way, her checklist presents both a paradox and an insight. She claims that the students most susceptible to falling onto the spiraling path to hell are bright boys (mainly, although girls are at risk, too) with varied interests who may lack social skills. But the insight in all this focuses on the kids' interests. A recent anthropological study of modern witches and magic in Britain observed that many male adherents of magic groups had computer backgrounds, an observation made by many people about D&D players.[55] The anthropologist T. M. Luhrmann notes that these folks also read science fiction in abundance, an interest shared by D&D gamers. She speculates on why these people gravitate to magic, perhaps offering an insight into people with D&D interests:

[S]everal possible explanations present themselves. Perhaps the most important is that both magic and computer science involve creating a world defined by chosen rules, and playing within their limits. Both in magic and in computer science words and symbols have a power which most secular, modern endeavours deny them. Those drawn to the symbol-rich rule-governed world of computer science may be attracted by magic. . . . One reason that the fantasy games designed for the computer may be so appealing may be because of the complexity of the rules. Another explanation is the sense of mastery and power when the machine obeys your dictates, which may feel like the mastery of magic. . . . The wizard commands the material world, breaking the laws which seem to bind it.[56]

Many D&D players, in fact, link their game-playing to an interest in computers. If one substitutes "fantasy game playing" for "magic," the Luhrmann quotation might apply to D&D gamers.

Pulling includes much technical material about playing D&D in her investigative guide, but it only confuses investigators. For example, a user of the checklist must ask the following three questions, among others:

How long has the individual been playing this role playing game?

How long has he/she been playing the particular character that he is currently playing?

What is his level of his character/characters? Be specific.

In fact, most of Pulling's questions are similar; her guide provides no guidance on how to interpret answers to the questions. An uncritical user of the checklist might interpret any answer to one of the questions as a hint that the player has succumbed to occult influence. Answers to any single question might appear innocuous, but when taken together might lead a satanically oriented investigator to assume the worst. In fact, Pulling follows the Catherine Gould school of checklist design by alerting users to behaviors or responses that supposedly prove involvement in the occult *regardless* of the presence or absence of the behavior or response. For example, Pulling begins her 1988 guide with the statement, "It is very important to understand that not all players of fantasy role playing games over-identify with the game and/or their player/characters." That caveat dispensed with, her very next sentence reads, "However, it appears that a significant amount of youngsters are having difficulty with separating fantasy from reality." Pulling asserts that players may have entered hell without realizing it:

> Or in other instances, their role playing has modified their behavior to the extent that they would react in a gaming situation. This is not always obvious or apparent to the suspect. The personality change is so subtle that in some cases the role-player is unaware of any behavior or personality changes.

This logic has been a prime component of witchfinding techniques since the fifteenth century: that the demonically afflicted person must be examined or tested in a prescribed way because he or she may not realize his or her condition. The Devil's grip is so tenacious that special tests, even tricks and snares, must be applied in order to banish the demon. Of course, another common axiom in such inquisitional techniques is the expectation that those who have compacted with the Devil will lie. For example, Pulling requires investigators to ask the suspect to name the dungeon master, and if the suspect equivocates or states that no one person occupied the role, then the investigator should probe further because, Pulling asserts, only one person occupies the role. But as Stackpole points out, a gamer's answer that several people shared the role may indeed be accurate.[57] Perhaps a better example of a double bind is Pulling's advice that "if an individual is involved in 'satanic activity,' he/she will deny a great deal to protect other members of the group as well as the 'satanic philosophy.' " So denials are to be taken as proof that the player is covering up.

Pulling's main fear about D&D is that the game contains some bona fide occult material, whatever that is. She seems to think that where game designers use demons and monsters from the writings of medieval or nineteenth-century English sources (or from game designers' imaginations), that somehow the game takes on a pernicious magic of its own. In her interview guide she states, "These gods are authentic mythological and authentic occult gods, which some occult religions still actively worship today." Pulling is alarmed at the nature of the demons and monsters invoked by the game, but she seems unwilling to accept that the game creatures bear no evil beyond what people impute to them. She thinks that the game confuses moral sensibilities by reversing polarities of good and evil in young minds, a form of what she calls "behavior modification." Pulling uses "behavior modification" glibly as if the term, scientific-sounding and evocative of clinical psychology, explains itself. For example, Pulling says in her interviewing guide,

> In [players'] minds they are continually gaming whether at the game table or not. Many of them have described things like when they get into situations in real life they think about a solution as to what their character in the game might do. How he/she, the player/character, would handle a situation. There is another problem in that because this game deals with supernatural things and powers like ESP some youngsters think that they gain these powers and that they can do anything, that they are indestructible.

Pulling offers no explication of "behavior modification" but simply asserts its danger. The interviewing guide continues: "Again, remember this is role-playing which is typically used for behavior modification. Players are encouraged to become one with their character or game 'persona.' " She tries to convince us that TSR, the game's manufacturer, has encouraged behavior modification by quoting TSR's publication, *Your Personal Invitation to Adventure*, which states, "Role playing requires that the player become so familiar with their game persona that the player become one with their character in their imagination while playing the game." Pulling hopes that her use of "behavior modification" will imply to her audience connotations of the sinister, the deceitful, an unconscious transformation from Dr. Jekyll to Mr. Hyde.

Behavior modification is a label that applies to a variety of phenomena. Therapeutic techniques involve the modification of behavior; all training experiences involve modifying behavior in some way; mere social performance involves the modification of behavior to suit the context. In fact, the failure to modify behavior according to the dictates of a social context signifies immaturity in the young and possible mental illness in adults. *No one* displays the same persona at all times and under all circumstances to friends, family, lovers. In fact, role-playing has always presented the most challenging type of police training, and the most popular. Through roleplay exercises in police-academy training, novice officers learn how to stop a traffic violator, mediate a family argument, interview a rape victim. Officers are taught how to modify their behavior to best handle a suspect, victim, or witness to gather information. Instructors in police academies quite explicitly tell new officers that they *must* modify behavior in order to defuse a violent situation or intervene in some crisis, whether or not their personal views or attitudes or prejudices oppose the behavior they must exhibit. Would Pulling find such training dangerous? When we read an enthralling book or watch an exciting film, many of us in our imaginations identify with the persona of the hero, the rescuer, the avenger of wrongs; TSR's invitation to Dungeons & Dragons asks us to employ our imaginations to identify with mythological roles, nothing more. Yet few people question Pulling's empty assertions about behavior modification, least of all scores of cult cops who have adopted not only her baseless ideology but also her warnings about rock-music lyrics.

Pulling's undated guide, *Dungeons and Dragons*, tries to argue the occult basis for the game. Rather than make an argument in the booklet, she insinuates the dangerous occult connection with the game by pairing quotations from *Dungeons & Dragons* playing-guides with miscellaneous quotations from sources ranging from *Readers' Digest* to *The Satanic Bible*. Readers of Pulling's guide are supposed to arrive at alarming conclusions abut the occult connection with the game by reading such passages as the following:

ADV. D&D P.H. Page 7 INTRODUCTION

"The game of D & D is a fantasy game of role playing which relies upon the imagination of participants, for it is certainly make believe, yet it is so interesting, so challenging, so MIND-UNLEASHING that it comes near reality."

THE SATANIC BIBLE—by Antone [*sic*] LaVey, Page 125 "Imagery becomes the formula which leads to reality." (p. 14)

.   .   .

ADV. D&D P.H. Page 45-66 (CLERICS SPELL—2nd LEVEL)
NECROMANTIC—SLOW POISON

"The material components of this spell are the Cleric's Holy/Unholy symbol and a bud of garlic which must be crushed and smeared on the victims [*sic*] bare feet."

INTO THE UNKNOWN by Readers Digest—Page 85

"Witches have a most treacherous manner of applying their poison, for having their hands smeared with it, they take hold of a man's garment." (p. 14)

.   .   .

ADV. D&D P.H. Page 70 (MAGIC-USER SPELL (2nd Level)
LEVITATE (Alteration)

"A third level magic-user can levitate up to 300 pounds maximum. If the spell is cast upon the person of the magic-user, he or she can move vertically at a rate of 20' per round."

INTO THE UNKNOWN—Page 62 (ART OF MAGIC)

"Simon Magus was defeated, according to legend, when the Apostle Peter's prayers overwhelmed the evil forces holding him up during a display of levitation. The sorcerer fell to the earth, shattered both his legs and eventually died." (p. 24)

And at the end of her small encyclopedia, Pulling states: "The information contained herein is by no means complete. There is no doubt that the D & D books are in fact an introduction to the occult. In 1801 Francis Barrett published a book called *The Magus,* or *Celestial Intelligencer* which is a complete system of *Occult Philosophy* which can be equated with the *Advanced Dungeon and Dragon* [*sic*] *Books*" (p. 30). So Pulling's argument is no argument at all, merely a recitation of news clippings that sometimes quote earnest police officers attesting to a link between a suicide and D&D playing, plus her inventory of game rules matched with tangentially similar (and in some cases obviously dissimilar) quotations from a myriad of sources on occult matters. But the paired quotations prove nothing; the fact that the game rules advise on how to use levitation magic has no relationship whatever to an anecdote about some ahistorical magician's use of levitation. But the effect of Pulling's guide, when the quotations of game rules are taken out of context and compared with quotations from sources on magic and occult matters, is the communication of something dangerous, something psychologically beguiling and harmful. And cult cops, not ones to dwell on arguments about definitions, logic, or empiricism, go for the effect: Look at Pat Pulling's book, they say. Here's proof of the D&D-occult link. To cult cops—and Pulling—the simple pairing of like with like implies a causal connection.

Pulling has not created the D&D fear alone; she took up the work of others, particularly fundamentalist Christian writers who deprecate the game, but she gained mileage particularly through the story of James Dallas Egbert III. The disappearance of Egbert from Michigan State University, where he was a student, prompted speculation by the local police and others that D&D led to some horrifying end for the young man. Upon Egbert's disappearance, school authorities found that he and his friends had played D&D in the labyrinth of tunnels that serviced the heating and cooling pipes to school buildings. Private investigator William Dear then went after the boy on behalf of his parents. In his 1984 book *The Dungeon Master,* Dear writes of the quest for Egbert in Mickey Spillane style; in the photograph on the book jacket, Dear is accoutered à la Elliot Ness, with a pin-striped suit and broad-brimmed fedora cocked to one side, holding a tommy gun. But Dear found Egbert and learned that D&D had nothing to do with the boy's disappearance. Egbert had been depressed and suicidal; he was a lonely, ignored student; he experimented with drugs;

but above all, his emerging realization of his homosexuality distanced him from his parents, and Egbert told Dear that he disappeared from the university to punish them. (Egbert was reunited with his family but he later took his life.) In conversations with Dear, Egbert talked of D&D and offered a view that has been taken out of context in many cult seminars and offered as proof of the pernicious effect the game has on young minds:

> Playing [D&D]—for real, I mean—was total escape. I mean, I could get into it. Scramble through those tunnels like a monkey. And you can use your brains. There's nothing to constrain you except the limit of your imagination. When I played a character, I was that character. Didn't bring all my personal problems along with me. It's a terrific way to escape.[58]

(Note that D&D is not normally played with elaborate physical props.) One of the earliest denigrations of D&D, from 1980, says this:

> Some endeavors offer a greater temptation for ego to manifest itself in us, however. The next thing to actual defeat of others and self-exaltation as rulers over the vanquished is the voluntary, imaginary role-playing that is offered by such games as *Dungeons & Dragons*. . . . It is not without knowledge that *Dungeons & Dragons* was devised. But it is the knowledge of an evil that mingled the Babylonian mystery religions with a luke-warm "Christianity."[59]

In an unpublished manuscript defending D&D entitled "Local Loonacy," Canadian Pierre Savoie says that the last "line refers to the belief among some Fundamentalist Christians that Catholicism is a mix of true Christianity and pagan Babylonian rites such as pagan forms of communion and the confessional." Albert James Dager's statement quoted above not only condemns D&D but manages to indulge in sect-bashing as well.

The Christian condemnation of role-playing games that present magical, fantastic settings undoubtedly influenced Pulling's views once she began to investigate the game following her son's death. A 1983 tract produced by the Daughters of St. Paul, a Catholic organization headquartered in Boston, states:

> When a student steps into the fantasy quicksands of Dungeons & Dragons, his life can be irreversibly altered—and the lives of his parents and other family members can be deeply affected.[60]

The tract invokes the suicide of Egbert as proof of the game's lure, and describes the process by which an otherwise good Catholic kid "surrenders his self-control and mind to the game":

The graphs and maps he has prepared secretly in his room at night after everyone else has gone to bed become his prized possessions. He is as "hooked" on DUNGEONS & DRAGONS as the addict is tied to his drugs.[61]

The response to Pulling among the lay public generally, and law enforcers particularly, has encouraged her. She has held annual seminars in Richmond, Virginia, for law-enforcement personnel and allied therapists and friends, excluding members of the press unless their coverage has been sympathetic. The seminars even feature doorprizes, sales of "cultbuster" T-shirts and coffee mugs, and evening entertainment. In *The Devil's Web*, Pulling moves way beyond her concern with D&D to highlight her shrewd fieldwork as a private investigator. For example, to embellish her résumé as a consulting detective, she visited the Matamoros ranch two weeks after the murders. In the chapter, "The Devil in Matamoros," she recounts her tale of doing nothing more than visiting the site and becoming nauseated. A photograph shows her pointing to a *nganga* at the site, the text describing the moment:

With cameras in hand, we got out of the car and walked toward the shed. Candles were strewn on the ground, and I saw the *nganga* that I had seen pictures of in the newspaper, and on television the week before. It had been filled with blood, animal and human body parts. Feathers, a horseshoe, gold beads and a pot full of pennies (all items used in Palo Mayombe rituals) also were found at the scene.[62]

Pulling evidently does not find it odd that investigating authorities would leave the *nganga* behind, the incriminating goo within it still evident at the time of her visit. If the police had deemed it evidence, they would not have left it at the site. Further, more than one *nganga* had been found at the ranch, but the other evidence had been removed. The macabre accessories left behind by Mexican authorities were intended to aid in inducing a frisson of terror among tourists.[63]

Pulling also recounts dropping in on murderer Henry Lee Lucas to interview him because of his claims of involvement in satanic sacrifices, and his supposed prediction of the Matamoros murders (an imputation to his prescience widely quoted, but one which I have not been able to verify). Pulling puts stock in his veracity. Although law enforcers have found him willing to discuss new criminal conspiracies and admit to new crimes at the drop of a handcuff key, Pulling writes, "He described rituals and methodology that only could be known by someone who has participated in cult activities."[64] (Or someone who reads popular books or sees film or television depictions of the occult.)

Pulling sidesteps certain controversies, obviously tightening her arguments to respond to criticism. She points out that her concern is with the dabbler, not with conspiracy theories, although she hints that conspiracies exist. Whereas Larry Jones of *File 18 Newsletter* argues that the absence of evidence pointing to a conspiracy simply means that we must adopt a bolder and more disbelief-suspending conspiracy theory, Pulling adopts another approach: "Whether or not a large-scale conspiracy exists, it is apparent that many small conspiracies of deviant criminal adults do exist."[65]

She subscribes to the primary-level-Satanist theory, based on consensus: "Widespread rumors persisted, however, and very recent investigations as well as careful and professional interviewing of victims have led to the general acceptance of this category by the law enforcement and mental health communities."[66] Pulling's assertions rest on sources she cannot identify or quotes out of context; for instance, she uses the Charlier and Downing series on child-abuse cases described in Chapter 5 to support her view that the plight of cult- or occult-influenced kids has been ignored by the government. She then cites secret government reports, sometimes at length, which purport to prove that satanic criminals do indeed lurk out there debauching our children. These reports evidently arrive in her office in plain brown wrappers, sent anonymously. At other times, she cites the popular press, or may even cite academic or scholarly pieces. Pulling even notes the explanation offered by skeptics that some satanic tales are "urban legends," and immediately dismisses the idea because of "overwhelming" evidence; she takes newspaper articles as definitive, forensic evidence. But she dismisses skeptics the same way that cult cops do: "Most of the individuals who minimize the significance of occult crime have never dealt with the documented cases which involve adolescents and children."[67] Similarly, therapists who defend their MPD sufferers' stories as factual rely for evidence of veracity on their patients' trauma, which they alone see. Pulling says that unless one counsels the teens she counsels, one doesn't have a basis for criticism.

Most disturbing of all are Pulling's clinical assessments of wayward youths. Parents take children to Pulling for psychological assessments of satanic or occult influence. One parent brought a girl to Pulling, wanting her to "determine [the girl's] level of occult involvement, whether she was using drugs and whether she needed professional therapy."[68] In the case of a teen named Jill, Pulling learned how the girl had attended parties replete with heavy-metal music, drugs, and alcohol, where she was photographed having sex with adults and the pictures were used for blackmail purposes. Jill later attended a ceremony in which a priest forced her to renounce God and embrace Satan. Pulling concludes that "the specifics regarding the rituals are not known by most persons unless they have a thoroughly grounded occult education. Simply put, Jill could not have made [the story] up. Nothing existed in her background that would have provided her with the kind of information she revealed."[69] However, Jill's errant behavior is not fully described in the book; the reader does not have a complete picture of the girl's family environment and background. Furthermore, even trained therapists, psychiatrists, and psychologists cannot detect truth-telling any better than a lay person can. We are forced to take Pulling at her word, that her clinical analysis explored other possibilities and that she had a good reason for dismissing all but the satanic explanation.

Pulling would represent merely a sideshow of America's current preoccupation with things satanic if she didn't pop up regularly to teach police officers. Ironically, after pursuing satanic stories, counseling teens, and interviewing murderers and pathological liars in prison, Pulling emerges with sensible advice. She urges responsible parenting: parents should learn about what games their children play and what music they listen to. No one denies that teens are capable of criminal, murderous passions; no one denies that some people will intimidate, confuse, seduce, and sexually assault teens and children, perhaps employing D&D or other symbols, imagery, or ideology as lures. But though Pulling's populist proofs, her causal inferences, her all-embracing generalizations have a gut appeal for many plain folks, the explanations she adduces about satanic or occult influences simply don't meet empirical tests, and therefore should not become the basis for public policy. By public policy, I refer to law-enforcement work, the strategies of educational institutions, and the guiding concerns of mental-health practitioners.

Pulling advises parents to suspect the academic or intellectual:

Occasionally, there even can be a problem finding competent outside help since many professionals are not well-informed in the area of teen occult activity, and some refuse to accept that heavy metal/black metal music can present any dangers; they insist that a child's interest in these things (even if it approaches obsession) is a passing one and nothing to worry about. . . .

Remember that a great many professionals themselves subscribe to New Age philosophies of "anything goes," "there is no right and wrong," and "let children do what they will." Unfortunately, many families have had to go through a trial-and-error process to find competent therapy for their children. . . .

Parents should use common sense and the God-given intuition that most parents have. If all the indicators are go, but you get a bad feeling about a situation, trust the bad feeling. "Most of the time, you will not regret it."

Some professionals will say that is hardly a scientific approach. My reply to them is, "It works."

Remember, parents, these are your children. If something happens to them, you will suffer more than you can imagine. Do not be intimidated by well-meaning people who try to give you advice on how to raise your children. This means even those people who have walls filled with degrees and years more education than yourselves. Listen to what they have to say, certainly; then weigh all of the facts carefully, consider what you know about your own child that no one else can possibly know or understand, and trust your instincts.[70]

When Music Is Not Music

Pulling's book leaves fantasy games and launches into musings about rock music, implying more sinister goings-on with heavy-metal music than she is willing to state. In a section in her book running four paragraphs, she dispenses with research under the heading, "Science Probes Psychological Effect of Music." It begins:

> Audio cassettes with subliminal messages deliberately implanted to help the listener break a variety of bad habits . . . and relieve stress and anxiety are widely available. . . . A double-edged philosophy appears to be operating in our society which holds that it is acceptable to use subliminal messages to influence a person's thinking when there is money to be made, but if this issue is raised to hold a company responsible for its actions, we are inhibiting freedom of speech.
>   While the frequency waves of music may sound like mumbo jumbo to the average person, it should be noted that the conscious control and use of sound waves is not new to the United States military.[71]

To prove these assertions, Pulling cites Michael Aquino, head of the Temple of Set, whose Army study on ELF (Extra Low Frequency) radio communications, according to Pulling, showed them to have a "resonant effect," with "infrasound vibration" that can "subliminally influence brain activity to align itself to delta, theta, alpha or beta wave patterns, inclining an audience toward everything from alertness to passivity."[72] Pulling undoubtedly impresses many with her scientific exposition, which includes no citations of such research. But she doesn't need science to make her point:

> What all of this means to us is simply that scientific research now supports the widely held theory that sound waves produced by music can affect the listener both psychologically and physiologically.[70]

Dabbling in terms such as "infrasound" and "delta, theta, alpha or beta wave patterns" no doubt awes some people; after all, assertions cloaked in scientific language appear beyond argument or question to most people. But we should be concerned that in occult-crime seminars, cult cops palaver in pseudoscientific talk about the subliminal effects of rock music, even making sober claims about backmasking, or the implantation of satanic messages on music albums that become clear when the record is played backwards. No cult seminar is complete without a show-and-tell session on rock lyrics. Oddly, cult cops seem to have no reason for discussing lyrics. Do they intend a crime-prevention message, are they saying that rock lyrics incite kids? If so, cult cops have exceeded a crime-prevention interest and infringe on First Amendment considerations. If cult cops perceive rock-music lyrics as pernicious, then why don't they cite Ann Rice's novels as harmful for suggesting that vampirism is an aesthetic experience, for example? Cult cops have freely quoted strident parents' organizations that wish to have rock albums carry warning labels, and they have parroted fundamentalist Christian sources about backmasking messages.

A seminar handout by Sergeant William Valdemar of the Los Angeles County Sheriff's Office identifies a "non-traditional gang group," the Stoners, who have a "criminal potential and propensity for violence" as great as that of any other known criminal gang. "Stoners make up a greater percentage [than what?] of students in Los Angeles schools. They have mass media systems and Heavy Metal fad popularity to spread their sub-cultural philosophy." The handout lists the group's heavy-metal heroes as including music groups such as Black Sabbath, Motley Crue, AC/DC, Slayer, Iron Maiden, and Judas Priest. "Heroes" include Charles Manson, singer Jim Morrison, Hitler, and Aleister Crowley. Stoners evidently commit the following "occult crimes": "animal sacrifice rituals," "recruiting at concerts," "graveyard/church desecrations," and "suicides and murder." But Valdemar's description becomes nebulous: Satanism, he maintains, takes on hundreds of forms, though not all heavy-metal fans are criminals, nor are all people who believe in magic criminals.

Tipper Gore, wife of Senator Albert Gore of Tennessee, heads an organization called Parents Music Resource Center, which "has been working to educate parents about potentially objectionable material in today's music." Copies of Tipper Gore's lecture, "Raising PG Kids in an X-Rated Society," have circulated at cult seminars. In the talk, which cult cops have offered as studied proof of the criminally occult influence of rock music, Gore says:

> Crimes rooted in devil worship are escalating nationwide. Teenagers and adolescents are most often involved and heavy metal music serves as a catalyst for their involvement. Groups whose album covers have graphically portrayed satanic themes include: Mercyful Fate, AC/DC, Black Sabbath, and Celtic Frost. Whether or not these bands are actively involved in Satanism, they are prompting a fascination among teens who—according to law enforcement—are the largest emerging group responsible for cemetery desecrations, animal sacrifices and other occult-related crimes.[74]

Gore goes on to find in rock music themes of sadomasochistic or violent sex and the degradation of women, which she links to violent crime. But the suppositions of cult cops, which Gore has included in her campaign, now emerge as documented proof of causality when presented at a cult seminar. As I pointed out earlier, the prevalence of cemetery desecrations "and other occult-related crimes" has been a matter of anecdote—not statistical record—among cult cops determined to infuse certain crimes with occult overtones. By bemoaning the lack of special statistics-gathering on occult or cult crimes, cult cops can continue to justify the law-enforcement resources invested in "The Problem," which may turn out to be miniscule.

One cult seminar included as justification for an excursion into rock-music lyrics an article by Rob Lamp, a musician and record producer, which discusses the perverse effects of rock music. Lamp offers the example of John McCollum, who killed himself, according to the coroner's report, "while listening to devil music."[75] McCollum's father then sued two record companies, alleging not only that Ozzy Osbourne's "Suicide Solution" prompted the death but also that the record companies involved released the recordings *knowing* that the music could prompt suicide. But the article doesn't reveal the whole picture.

> John McCollum was in many respects like many other 19-year-olds. He was a heavy metal rock addict with earphones and Ozzy Osbourne records to certify it. In addition he was an alcohol abuser and a boy beset by emotional problems of a serious nature well beyond those afflicting other teenagers.[76]

California courts have not been able to support the lawsuit, on the grounds that it violates the First Amendment. The First Amendment, though, doesn't exonerate all forms of speech:

> If, for example, [the speech] is intentionally directed toward the goal of producing imminent and perilous conduct and it is likely to produce such an effect, according to the often cited *Brandenburg* test, protection of the First Amendment will not apply.[77]

The court opined that the Osbourne recording did not meet the test, that the music was a "commentary on this difficult world" and did not urge listeners to react in a specific way. The trial court stated:

> Merely because art may evoke a mood of depression as it figuratively depicts the darker side of human nature does not mean that it constitutes a "direct incitement to violence."[78]

Cult cops carefully point out that they do not wish to enter the controversy about placing warning labels on rock albums, or about censorship generally, yet no other explanation emerges for including in seminars the lyrics of specific songs other than to spur an audience into indignant and self-righteous feelings. Someone ought to be looking into this, cult cops say; the music is dangerous. But to cult cops, heavy-metal lyrics pose only part of the problem; the true dangers of mind control arise from backmasked messages in rock music. Cult-crime seminars normally display tables of recommended books, including Jacob Aranza's *Backward Masking Unmasked* (1983, published by Huntington House, which issued Pulling's book) and Jeff Godwin's *The Devil's Disciples: The Truth About Rock* (1985, Chick Publications). The promoters of these books (which both argue from a fundamentalist Christian viewpoint) "cite studies of subliminal perception and point to advertising conspiracies and to documented forms of brainwashing and mind-control techniques. They also triumphantly reveal the actual hidden messages by listening to rock recordings played backward."[79] Some of the backward messages supposedly contain such apothegms as "Satan, move in our voices"; "Christ, you're the nasty one you're infernal"; "Yes, Satan, he organized his own religion . . . It was delicious . . . He puts it in a vat and fixes it for his son and gives it away."[80]

Cult cops cite backmasking claims as factual, and proven. Interestingly, they never address the crucial questions: How does your average consumer manage to play the messages backwards on a common record player or tape recorder? Assuming the messages are there, what mechanism allows a listener to perceive them, consciously or unconsciously, when the music is played forward at the correct speed? Even assuming that a listener somehow absorbs the messages subliminally, so what? What effects do such messages have? Cult cops never bother to raise such questions, and neither do those who claim to have studied the backmasked comments. "[A]dvocates appear to believe that demonstrating the existence of the messages is not merely necessary to the argument but is sufficient as well."[81] But neither the cult cops nor their fundamentalist Christian sources will ever cite definitive scientific studies that address the crucial questions and demonstrate that such messages, if they do exist, influence people's behavior. Anyone interested in the issue should consult a research report by psychologists John R. Vokey and J. Don Read, University of Lethbridge, Canada, for the definitive treatment of the subject.

> Is there any evidence to warrant assertions that such messages affect our behavior? Across a wide variety of tasks, we were unable to find any evidence to support such a claim. Secondarily, we present evidence to suggest that the apparent presence of backward messages in popular music is a function more of active construction on the part of the perceiver than of the existence of the messages themselves.[82]

As a scientific study, the Vokey and Read report merits close examination, for it did not "investigate satanic messages in rock music per se," nor did it deal with the presence of such messages, only their putative effects on people. Consistent with the theory that "active construction on the part of the perceiver" has much to do with finding satanic lyrics, Stephen B. Thorne and Philip Himelstein of the University of Texas, El Paso, examined specifically the role of suggestion in perceiving satanic messages in rock music. They found:

> There is ample experimental evidence to suggest that, when vague and unfamiliar stimuli are presented, [test subjects] are highly likely to accept suggestions, particularly when the suggestions are presented by someone with prestige and authority.[83]

In a careful examination of what we know and don't know about the effects of heavy-metal music on teens, physicians Elizabeth F. Brown and William R. Hendee, writing in the *Journal of the American Medical Association,* remind us that "total immersion into a rock subculture, such as heavy metal, may be both a portrait of adolescent alienation and an unflattering reflection of an adolescent's perception of the moral and ethical duplicity of adult society."[84] In fact, the authors suggest that physicians should at least examine the role of such music in kids' lives when assessing their emotional and mental health.

Brown and Hendee also remind us that technological refinements have made it possible for teens to immerse themselves in rock music for a total of about 10,500 hours between the seventh and twelfth grades, or "just slightly less than the entire number of hours spent in the classroom from kindergarten through high school," an astounding amount of time made possible by the technology of sound reproduction through cheap, widely available miniature tape- or compact-disc players. Parents quite rightly should perspicaciously consider what their children listen to, how often, and so on, but Brown and Hendee point out that the controversy over the effects of heavy-metal lyrics reflects adults' tastes, perceptions, and interpretations, which may not at all converge with a teen's. "The symbolic meaning of a song, represented more by the rhythm of the music and personalities of the artists, may transcend any explicit appreciation or interpretation of its lyrics and may be the primary attraction for adolescents."[85] The symbolic value of the music should not be underestimated, a view supported by studies that show very few teens "correctly identified sex, drugs, or violence as subjects of their favorite songs," and even when they identified such themes, the few who did so could only come up with "literal and unsophisticated" interpretations. Further, adults should not treat kids' reponses to music and music videos as identical phenomena, for some researchers find that the videos' "surrealistic and abstract qualities" just might "offer a subjective way of addressing these threatening problems in contrast to the depressing and sometimes complacent presention by the news media of the threat of nuclear war."[86] Furthermore, "these young persons may be responding more to the themes of independence and rebellion against parental authority symbolized by rock music than to its actual verbal messages, for music is more than lyrics, rhythm, and melody."[87]

Cult cops take a dangerous route when they present slide shows depicting rock-music albums and lyrics, for they imply causal connections linked to particular and parochial assumptions of what listening to Motley Crue or Ozzy Osbourne does to kids' minds. Cult cops imply a mind-control mechanism or suggest that the music, with its "satanic" lyrics and imagery, is lethal in combination with fantasy role-play games, *ouija* boards, or "dangerous books." Other cult cops don't preach backmasking, but simply assert that listening to the unmasked lyrics repeatedly desensitizes youth to violence. In short, cult cops' use of rock-music lyrics can serve any and every purpose. Brown and Hendee offer, however, that "questions about music preference can be corroborating evidence when other affective behavior of the adolescent suggests potentially destructive alienation."[88] They do not use "corroborating evidence" in the sense of a criminal investigation, though police officers would be remiss in overlooking the music *if* they could demonstrate the corroborative value of such music in a criminal case. But causality is quite elusive where music is concerned. During the Charles Manson murder case much was made of the influence of the Beatles' song "Helter Skelter." Newspapers by and large took the song as a metaphor for Manson's world-view and the ambiance of his small commune, but it hardly took on the form of criminal evidence.

So if cult cops claim that heavy-metal music plays some important role in the life of a suicidal or homicidal kid, what can that role be? A careful investigation of the circumstances should reveal a teen's animosity towards others; difficulties with parents, siblings, friends, or teachers, or social isolation; perhaps problems at school; substance abuse; depression or guilt; perhaps involvement in crime. But the message of alerting other law-enforcement officers to rock-music lyrics may encourage them to seek criminal causality in the music at the expense of exploring solid clues to a teen's behavior. And "solid clues" does not mean documentating one small facet of a kid's interests, that is, the empowerment a teen experiences by having a secret, by indulging occasionally in forbidden (but common and harmless) fantasies and noncriminal activities, by being daring or showing off, by contriving situations in role-playing games, or by dressing oddly or wearing satanic jewelry that sends an unsophisticated, heavy-handed sexual message to other teens. The rock music—that is, the music and not particularly the specific lyrics—a teen listens to helps project an identity of independence, assertiveness, and bravado, not to mention that it fuels adolescent hormones. But cult cops doggedly trumpet the lyrics to their seminar audiences, implying that the words cause problems but simultaneously warning that they intend no transgression of the First Amendment. Stating that one recommends the respect of others' First Amendment rights to believe anything, no matter how bizarre, somehow mollifies not respecting those rights in the next breath.

Conclusion

Earlier in this chapter I mentioned a cult presentation given by Dick Burke, a representative of a Christian police officers association, to the faculty of Smoky Hill High School in Aurora, Colorado. Cult cops give seminars to parents and teachers everywhere, stimulating strong responses whenever a teen mindlessly draws on a washroom wall. The assistant principal at Smoky Hill High attested vigilantly, "We see the graffiti, and we see the artwork. Now we're aware of what we're seeing," thanks to local cult cops.[89] But the school apparently continued to show "a high incidence of occult gatherings." Among the damning—and damned—artifacts police have found nearby were "crude altars," "slain pigs," and "all types of sayings for Satanism, pentagrams and so forth," attests Officer Walt Martin. And what do the newly indoctrinated schoolteachers find as evidence of Satanism at the school? Administrators construed as evidence of the occult a kitten found in a kid's locker with its fur shaved into a mohawk and its ears pierced with "pentagram earrings." But worse, administrators found swastika graffiti. "It wasn't until we met with police that we learned what we were seeing was a satanic symbol, not so much related to anti-Semitism," observed Jill Reed, assistant principal at Smoky Hill High.[90]

Indeed, cult cops have done their jobs well. Frederick County, Maryland, schools canceled Halloween observances in 1989 because 15 to 20 parents had complained about the costumes worn in celebrations. "I personally have trouble defending ghosts and goblins in our instructional curriculum," said John Thompson, one of the Frederick County school superintendents.[91] Some schools didn't stop there: even jack-o'-lanterns and other common Halloween decorations were prohibited. Not surprisingly, a cult cop lurks somewhere behind all this:

> Devil worshipers believe they can make contact with evil spirits on Oct. 31 because it is easier to pass from the living world into the world of the dead on that date, according to Maryland State Police Cpl. L. H. Howland, who investigates satanic-related crimes.[92]

Parents—usually a small number of them—have pressured schools not only to eschew Halloween but also to dump "satanic" books from their libraries. In Billings, Montana, two parents approached the Broadwater Elementary School to request that *The Witches,* a fantasy by Roald Dahl (who wrote *Charlie and the Chocolate Factory*) be banned: "The fact is that there are such things as witches. They are part of the satanic church," said Monte Mutschler, one of the parents.[93]

But not all students have taken school restrictions about witches and Satanism lightly. Two teens have filed federal civil-rights lawsuits against officials of the Sebewaing Township, Michigan, schools, alleging that "their civil rights were violated by school officials who were influenced by a Geraldo Rivera television show on Satanism."[94] The controversy even led the principal of an area middle school to submit his resignation. The principal, Victor Reister, had asked for a state-police investigation into Satanism at his school following the now infamous *Geraldo* television broadcast about the topic that aired just before Halloween in 1988. Although the state police turned up no evidence of satanic practices, Reister, undeterred, conducted searches of school lockers. In one of the plaintiff's lockers Reister found " 'doodles,' poetry, and song lyrics," which he copied. After then conferring with a school counselor, a state-police investigator, and two court officials, Reister told the plaintiffs and two others that they were under "house arrest" during the Halloween weekend, which meant that the kids could not leave their homes or have any contact with each other. Reister justified his activities by saying that students told him of cult goings-on at the school, that the "alleged cult had planned or [that its members] were involved in a possible suicide pact, that animal killings were occurring, and that the cult planned to sacrifice a popular student."[95] The state police officer, Trooper Bernard J. Bator, "did suspect cult activity" and upon interviewing one of the plaintiffs, got her to admit to being involved in satanic worship. But once the school had identified the plaintiffs, two sisters, as Satanists, the school staff placed them under surveillance and even subjected them to some ridicule. When one of the girls requested a pencil in her auto-mechanics class, the teacher "told her in front of the class she could 'just cut your finger off and write it in blood.' "[96] Because of the ostracism, the girls' parents removed them from the school and filed the lawsuit.

Hartgrove Hospital in Chicago has set up a unit of psychiatrists and psychologists to treat satanically infected teens. A bit defensive about the purpose of the unit, psychologist Michael Weiss of Hartgrove says, "The kids who will be admitted will be here primarily because of their behavioral and emotional problems. No one will be hospitalized for strange beliefs or unusual values that we would disagree with."[97] Dale Trahan, staff social worker who has studied Satanism for a few years, organized the unit, the Center for the Treatment of Ritualistic Deviance. According to Weiss, the Hartgrove center has been "staffed by specially trained psychiatrists, psychologists, social workers and nurses. . . . The new program will seek to undermine Satanism's underlying belief system, which hampers conventional treatment." And who has provided the "special training" to Hartgrove staff? Chicago cult cop Jerry Simandl, for one. And what kind of kid does the new center propose to help? Trahan and Weiss describe afflicted teens as bright but socially isolated with poor "problem-solving and coping skills," who join "cults" to gain "membership in a group, power, sex, drugs, freedom from guilt." The therapy consists of breaking down satanic beliefs and replacing them with "a traditional belief system."[98]

The prospectus for the Center for the Treatment of Ritualistic Deviance at Hartgrove posits a need for ministering to satanic kids by asserting that "the phenomenon of ritualistic crime and the destructive practices that are often associated with some occult beliefs and values continues to grow," noting that adolescents are most susceptible to recruitment and to adopting "deviant belief systems." Assuring the public that Hartgrove's staff consists of "professionals with a proven expertise in treating occult connected adolescents," the brochure advises parents what to look for in the susceptible teen, that is, the intelligent, creative, but bored and underachieving young adult. As expected, one finds a checklist that includes:

> Intensified rebellion against society and authority.
> Heavy involvement in fantasy and role play games.
> Heavy interest in heavy- and "black"-metal music.
> Heavy interest in occult.
> Increased use of drugs.
> Use of occult symbols. . . .
> Lack of humor.
> Pleasure at the suffering of others.

To those who inquire about the center's services, Trahan provides two supporting papers. The first is an article from *Social Work* magazine that cites our collective lack of knowledge about counseling teens involved in Satanism and says it needs further research, but suggests that "this relatively new problem" could spring from "psychopathology and sociopathology":

> However, an adolescent's involvement in satanic activities may be symptomatic of a number of disorders, such as psychoactive substance abuse, depression, borderline personality disorders, disruptive behavior, or anti-social personality. Satanic involvement also could be considered as a dissociative disorder or sadistic personality disorder (with or without sexual manifestations).[99]

One cannot read the preceding quotation without musing on what is cause and what is effect, since the authors note that satanic beliefs could simply be symptomatic of other pathologies. To that end they recommend a "comprehensive assessment" of a teen's familial and social milieu. The article also recognizes that a preoccupation with satanic or occult imagery "*does not* necessarily mean satanic involvement," that teens are just as likely to "dabble" to escape boredom. The article's recommended therapeutic intervention includes distancing a client from the satanic subculture, and substituting more "attractive and meaningful" activities that can lead to exhilaration and self-satisfaction.

While the *Social Work* article does not succumb to hysterical rantings about satanic beliefs, it clearly finds such beliefs inseparable from substance abuse and familial or social problems, and the therapeutic interventions appear to correspond to those used for other, more common problems among maladjusted teens. The same cannot be said about the second document used by Trahan, an unpublished 1989 manuscript written by cult cop Donald Story, chief of the Matteson, Illinois, police department, and psychologist Anthony R. Moriarty. The monograph posits a growth in the number of adolescents involved with Satanism and its rituals, and tries to construct a model of the psychological processes at work, called the "web of psychic tension." According to the monograph, "evidence suggests" that increasing numbers of people have become involved with Satanism of late, that Satanism "has leaped from the pages of history to become a perverse reality with potentially disastrous consequences for today's young people." As support for these assertions, the authors cite a cult cop. To support assertions that "ritualistic crimes" have also increased, the authors cite another article by co-author Story that offers no proof of the claim but merely asserts its truth.

The monograph, in establishing the existence of the problem, also asserts, again on no evidence, that "a myriad of cultist beliefs" somehow create "bands of devoted followers who are risking mind and body in the practice of obscure ritualism," failing to point out that most kids simply make up their beliefs. While referring to the lack of benchmark literature, Moriarty and Story borrow from the accounts of cult survivors to justify their views. Moriarty and Story indirectly support their own views by noting the difficulty of obtaining proof from reticient survivors: "Cult members are strongly committed to covert activity and a condition of acceptance into their membership is an oath of silence."

By thus positing the problem, Moriarty and Story point out that therapeutic intervention must be based on the premise that everything in Satanism is a direct inversion of "a tradition of freedom and human dignity as basic values." In fact, the authors cite *The Satanic Bible* as an exposition of this philosophy. They also associate Satanism with other problems such as obsessive-compulsive behavior, poor parenting, and desensitized acceptance of violence (having experienced or witnessed it early in life). But when a teen experiences Satanism, according to Story, he or she finds support for drug abuse and sexual activity (because of the inversion philosophy), activities now "sanctioned and encouraged." And heavy-metal music, while not a "causal factor," is at least encouraging. Though they acknowledge that the music is not that great an influence, Moriarity and Story nevertheless assert that "brought to the fore by constant musical reminders, the adolescent is conditioned by frequent messages that evil is acceptable." Predictably, the authors associate adolescent suicides with Satanism, pointing out that "the ritualistic contract with satan" requires a blood sacrifice. They at least admit, however, that "the relationship between satanism and suicide is symptomatic of pre-existing pathology."

Despite constructing a framework of satanic involvement based not on research and empirical validation but instead on other assertions, suppositions, and generalizations, the authors recommend mostly commonsense solutions; they exhibit a Christian bias, which posits as an alternative to dark practices "the value of good and a concept of God tied to formal religion. Religion serves to give external validity to the pursuit of good in life." This view is "justified culturally and socially, representing a dominant value of our society." Years of "eroding" contact with such good influences will lead the teen, caught in a "web of intrapsychic forces," to "embrace the practice of satanism if exposed to its mystic rituals."

So what must the therapist do? "The use of well-timed open-ended questions conveyed with a sincere interest in the adolescent will encourage free and open dialogue." Oddly, though, Moriarty and Story assert, "Most adolescents who get involved in occult practices fail to recognize that their acceptance of truth and reality are more likely to be subjective conclusions rather than the result of an objective analysis." A rather pompous statement, since *everyone's* world-views, notions of causality, and acceptance of truth and reality derive from both subjective conclusions and "objective analysis," whatever that is. While concluding that satanic teens need "better tools to make decisions about the nature of truth and reality," one can guess *what* reality and truth kids are to learn, particularly when one reads the authors' pious assertion that "the act of locking on to belief through some leap of faith indicates the lack of epistemological tools." Since at this point the authors' self-righteous belief in their own intrapsychic notions has overwhelmed *their* sense of perspective, one might delicately point out that this last assertion also applies to Christians, Moslems, Jews, and just about anyone else who professes spiritual beliefs.

Perhaps we should applaud Hartgrove Hospital's new efforts. Unfortunately, though, the therapeutic assumptions supporting the new center remain untested and unproved; Moriarity and Story have built an edifice on sand. The ideology that cults, that is, organized groups, promote Satanism through deceitful, mind-controlling methods, and that satanic rituals have some inherent magic that particularly attracts bright kids has emerged quite formidably to dominate explorations and explanations of children's behavior. As we have seen, the same ideology exists among therapists who counsel cult survivors, among self-professed police cult experts who teach seminars, and among counselors and educators who supervise adolescents. The ideology bears analogy to religious conversion, as anthropologist Sherrill Mulhern has suggested, in which any dispute about causality disappears and one is left with the given that Satanism not only exists in organized, covert form, but also promotes the mayhem credited to it.

But we *do* have some scientific examinations of kids' behavior. University of Minnesota sociologist Gary Fine, in his 1983 study of fantasy role-playing games, found most players to be well adjusted, well-educated young men for whom the games present no danger but instead a healthy creative exercise in imagination.[100] He observed that game players identify themselves as nonconformists. More recently, a psychologist examined the emotional stability of D&D players and found that "increased exposure to D&D is not positively correlated with emotional instability. Indeed, as a whole group, D&D players obtain a healthy psychological profile."[101] Such references never appear at cult seminars or at Pulling's presentations.

Some newspapers, too, recognize the unscientific nature of claims against Dungeons & Dragons, and have not been so quick to judge the game as teetering on the precipice of evil:

> To single out a game in a world of entertainment involving violent themes seems strange, but the fact that a few suicide victims have left notes mentioning D&D naturally raises questions. In the context of the national epidemic of teen suicides, however, more than a handful of anecdotes is needed to build a convincing argument that D&D is any more dangerous to our mental health than the other intellectual and emotional stimulants in our richly varied society.[102]

The idea of pervasive satanic cults that influence and intimidate adolescents should not supplant a reasonable, cautious inquiry for law enforcers, educators, and therapists. Ironically, despite the cult seminars, which contrive images of the faceless, tenebrous evil that grips us from the bowels of hell, the cult experts who teach seminars often conclude with common-sense advice, as I have noted. One could dispense with the macabre suggestions and innuendo about teens at satanic sex-and-drug parties and get on with simple advice on good parenting that would constitute sound crime prevention. For example, *Woman's Day*'s "Parent's Primer on Satanism" notes that bright, bored, underachieving, talented, and even gifted teens are susceptible to cults.[103] It warned parents to watch for kids exhibiting personality changes or mood swings; kids who drop friends and favorite activities in exchange for other activities and friends; who keep secrets, particularly about new friends; receive erratic grades; misbehave; wear satanic symbols on jewelry, T-shirts, and the like. Now, if one removes the occult from all of this, one is left with teens growing up, dealing with social pressures, handling puberty, running at full tilt on massive doses of pizza and hormones. But what's a parent to do? *Woman's Day* suggests that parents avoid panicking and observe the child; if the teen listens to rock music with offensive lyrics, listen to what the child listens to. "If [the lyrics] disturb you, talk to him or her about it. Ask what the words mean to your child."[104] No matter what ill we believe threatens our children—whether communists, Satanists, the Beatles, or Twisted Sister—the advice is the same: don't panic; observe; listen; talk. Don't ignore satanic symbols or paraphernalia, but don't imbue them with cosmic significance, either. Trust children to behave responsibly *most of the time.* Police officers would perform a valuable public service if they would abandon Patricia Pulling and the cult cops, with their interminable slide shows of satanic graffiti and rock lyrics, and substitute *Woman's Day* as their text for public lectures.

Chapter 7
CONCLUSION:
RUMORS, URBAN LEGENDS,
AND SUBVERSION MYTHS

Thou shalt not suffer a witch to live.

Exodus 22: 18

Necessity hath no law. Feigned necessities, imaginary necessities, are the greatest cozenage men can put upon the Providence of God, and make pretenses to break down rules to live by.

Oliver Cromwell, September 12, 1654

Such mischeefes as are imputed to witches, happen where no witches are; yea and continue when witches are hanged and burnt; whie then should we attribute such effect to that cause, which being taken awaie, happeneth neverthelesse?

Reginald Scot, *The Discoverie of Witches,* 1584

Conversion and Sacred Truths

Since 1980, when the current popular preoccupation with Satanism took root, the focus on training professionals—law enforcers, therapists, psychiatrists, psychologists, educators—has emerged as the salient characteristic of a *movement.* Fundamentalist Christianity has to a considerable extent driven the Satanism movement, despite the fact that many of the movement's representatives are not fundamentalist Christians. But the movement presumes an ideology that, as it spreads, hardens into polarities and absolutes; in addition, it demands that adherents believe the incredible and unprovable. Ironically, in 1990, one must look hard for a professional seminar or conference on child care or adolescent behavior that doesn't have a workshop on cults and satanism, frequently conducted by a cult cop. Professional conferences in psychology and psychiatry include similar workshops and feature believer therapists, social workers, and psychiatrists, and sometimes the cult cops. Even conferences with only a tangential professional interest in Satanism include the topic. For example, crime-prevention conferences, normally taken up with topics from urban planning to forming neighborhood-watch groups, can't resist Satanism and cults, although the crime-prevention value of cult cops' presentations is questionable.

The irony of cult presentations at professional conferences lies in a contrast. On one hand, cult seminars demand that the listener dispel or suspend disbelief and embrace broad assumptions, conclusions, and generalizations about cult-driven criminality and the credibility of "survivors." On the other hand, the same listener attends other professional workshops that presume the longstanding methods of social science: skepticism, empiricism, and debate. The process by which social-science and law-enforcement professionals maintain a largely scientific, or at least empirical, outlook but yet shift easily into cult-seminar beliefs deserves scrutiny by sociologists and anthropologists. That anthropologists and sociologists cannot be found in significant numbers among the believers may indicate the resiliency of theoretical paradigms in those professions and therefore hint at the direction such a study should take.

I assert that the believer movement does create a form of civil blasphemy, to use the term I quoted in Chapter 1. *Civil blasphemy* presumes that we can identify "things so sacred that they must be protected by the arm of the state from irreverence and challenge."[1] Such sacred things include the flag, for example. For my purpose, I assert that what is sacred to cult cops and their allies is the purity and innocence of children. The day-care-center cases certainly attest to the necessity of preserving as sacrosanct children's virtue, to preserve children from adult vice. The stories of cult survivors also reflect the same relationship to the idea of the sacred: after all, the survivors supposedly developed their dissociative disorders consequent to child abuse or trauma of some kind, probably sexual.

But, whether or not some of the putative cult activities in the United States rise to the definition of the criminal, cult cops appear to believe that our behavior and our *thinking* should observe certain moral absolutes. Such absolutes include the notion of evil, a word that has undergone secularization through cult seminars. Cult cops who profess fundamentalist Christianity come with world-views that presume that the antithesis to good is absolute evil. Absolute evil must be fought: as in the fashion of cult cop Larry Jones, the police officer needs spiritual weapons and a special insight to help spot the work of the Evil One. For cult cops who are not fundamentalist Christians, evil does not take on personified form. Instead, it resides in a criminal mind that deliberately inverts anything "good" or anything wholesome and pure. The pursuit of an absolute secular evil has consequences not unlike the pursuit of Christian evil: investigative assumptions that may direct resources away from actual crimes; violations of civil liberties; and an erosion of investigative skepticism and empiricism.

I would like, however, to broaden the definition of civil blasphemy that applies to the believer ideology. Law enforcers and social scientists, whose professional ideologies derive from secular methods but who become satanic-cult believers, experience a religious conversion to a rigid, obdurate new ideology that forbids certain questions and demands absolute acceptance of a corpus of assumptions. A law enforcer or social scientist who fails to convert becomes a blasphemer. A professional who even questions the veracity of children's stories in day-care cases becomes viewed by believers as an enemy, a turncoat of the worst sort: by doubting, one therefore discredits the work of believers and betrays the children. In the case of multiple-personality-disorder (MPD) victims, if one questions or voices suspicion about the literal veracity of their cult claims, one has denied their abuse; and as believer therapists remind us, denial is a product of the prejudices and egocentrism of the investigator. Denial must be breached, disbelief must be suspended, or else one is not among those who stand vigil as protectors of children, guardians of the family. The notion of blasphemy becomes *civil* blasphemy in the sense that the inquisitors, the accusers of nonbelieving professionals are public officials, not ecclesiastical authorities. *Civil* takes on another meaning, that of the public interest, the common good. Skeptics blaspheme against the public interest, offend the common notion of what is right and decent. This common notion presumes to arrogate public power to preserve and protect the family at the expense of the niceties of criminal investigations, which take too long, protect offenders, and insist on observing the obfuscating technicalities of constitutional law.

A police officer who becomes a *believer* has stepped into a worldview with moral absolutes, a realm where traditional investigative methods don't apply, as police officer Sandi Gallant has observed on more than one occasion. The preoccupation with absolute evil justifies the search for the criminal mind and identification of the thought-crimes of death and resurrection, sacrifice, and transcendence of the corporeal that exist in the symbols and rituals of nonconformist believers (i.e., the pagans, witches, Satanists, and practitioners of magic). Such nonconformists are symbol-shifters who appear to either bend the rules or discard them altogether. Larry Jones of the *File 18 Newsletter* cannot cope with nonconformism: he finds that a religious view that doesn't presume *absolute* standards of conduct simply isn't legitimate. So the notion of blasphemy (in Jones's case, not civil but spiritual) leads one to posit absolutes and to derogate beliefs or practices that don't seem to observe the same absolutes.

And as I discussed in Chapter 1, the logic with which the cult cop sallies forth on the quest for blasphemers must necessarily be pseudoscientific. When one searches for moral absolutes, one no longer needs the empirical, the rational, the scientific. In Catherine Gould's checklist of attributes of a satanic day-care center, a preschool's prestigious standing in a neighbor-hood, with decades of history, where the school authorities invite parents to visit the facility at any time, all betoken a satanic cult. Likewise, the same evidence strongly points to *no* involvement with Satanism. Gould creates nonfalsifiable hypotheses. If one finds a satanic cult operating under such circumstances, then the theory (that day-care centers front for satanic cults) has been verified. If one cannot find a satanic cult operating in a day-care center, one can only conclude that the cult's modus operandi has become so sophisticated that the Satanists have eluded identification. But the Satanists are there nonetheless. By such logic, a day-care center that has fallen under suspicion always remains under suspicion: innocence can never be proved. As in the case of other zealots whose failure to adduce proof of their assertions becomes irrelevant in the face of a just cause, Gould's checklist cannot be refuted. The burden of proof falls on the rest of us, then, *to prove that day-care-centers-as-satanic-cult-fronts don't exist.*

Civil blasphemy becomes codified through resolutions adopted by profes-sional societies, by the findings of public commissions, or through new legislation (which I describe later in this chapter). As an example, the final report (January 1986) of the State Task Force on Youth Gang Violence, State of California, convened under the aegis of the California Council on Criminal Justice, cited as a new gang phenomenon "the increasing mem-bership and violence among Punk Rockers, Heavy Metal and Satanic gangs" that involve violence, drug-taking, "anti-establishment orientation," and other attributes. As proof of such activity, the report cites three statements by police: the allegations of satanic practices that emerge through therapeutic sessions with children; the blackmailing of parents by their teen offspring whose satanic practices were discovered and who told their parents that they would commit suicide if anything was done to them; the claim of a parent whose teenage daughter slashed her own arms with a razor blade as part of satanic rituals.

Similarly, the Los Angeles County Commission for Women recently published the *Report of the Ritual Abuse Task Force,* which treats as factual numerous outlandlish, unproved assertions about the cults "out there."[2] Every tale told by a cult survivor or child through intensive therapy appears in the document, served up in checklists of characteristics or attributes. Including checklist upon checklist, the overwhelming impression of the report is one of feculence. One wants to wash up after reading it. All of the symptoms, or *sequela,* to use the psychiatric term, of abusive cult behavior find neat arrangement in categories of use only to an inquisitor, a witch-finder. Under "physical abuse," for example, one learns:

> Ritual abuse victims are physically abused often to the point of torture. Young victims who are being ritually abused without the knowledge of both parents are usually subjected only to physical abuse that is not easily detected.[3]

The report notes "less detectable examples" of physical abuse, which includes "pins or 'shots' inserted into sensitive areas of the body, especially between digits, under fingernails, or in genital areas" and "electric shock to these body areas." More mundane examples listed include sleep and food deprivation, submerging the victim under water to induce fright of drowning, and hanging the victim "by hands or upside-down by feet for extended periods of time. Sometimes hung from crosses in mock crucifixions. Sexual abuse while in such positions."[4]

Anthropologist Sherrill Mulhern has described the process by which professionals become believers as analogous to religious conversion. She observes that the lack of investigative evidence to support the claims of therapists and cult survivors has led both to become more strident in taking the offensive. "Intense networking among 'believers' has been supplemented by a plethora of training seminars organized, ostensibly, to educate the uninformed in the reality and dangers of [ritual abuse]."[5] Mulhern documented the evolution of belief through a two-year study of such cult seminars supplemented by interviews with police, therapists, adult survivors, and parents of victims. Her study found that "proponents of [ritual abuse] have directed most of their educational efforts to 'defining' perpetrators, i.e., describing the organization, motivation, brainwashing techniques, and finality of (satanic) cults—THEM."[6] First, adult survivors parade their claims as corroborative evidence. Cult experts then take the survivors' tales and meld them with disparate bits and pieces from clinical sources, documented cults (of the nonsatanic variety), and actual murder investigations that blend to "complete the tableau." By systematic semantic association, the cult cops (or therapists who present the seminars) link the disparate elements causally.

This technique both masked and justified fundamental semantic deviations such as the systematic substitution of the term victim of *ritual abuse* to signify *any individual who has alleged* [ritual abuse] *victimization.*

In turn, "Victims of [ritual abuse] became the subjects of "scientific" studies of the pathological sequela of [ritual abuse], thus reinforcing the initial semantic deviation. Comparative analysis demonstrated that this process is structurally and functionally identical to proselytizing techniques employed by religious cults to create a "context for belief" which may be acceptable when conversion is the clearly stated goal but which is completely inappropriate when it is presented as education.[7]

Mulhern found that the cult seminars serve to convert "perplexed therapists into 'believers.' " Of course, as Mulhern also found, the faculties slated for cult seminars include "believer" professionals almost exclusively. In fact, Mulhern's two-year study of cult seminars found "a widening gap between clinical data [available through scientific study] and the interpretive grid being proposed."[8]

Does the proliferation of cult seminars (and therefore the believer ideology) show signs of change? What about the future? Within the past six years, police cult seminars have increased in number and still command large audiences, yet their message has not changed. With only occasional slight modifications, the seminars still convey the four-level model, still warn about rock music and fantasy games, still feature pictures of Anton LaVey (in some cases resuscitating twenty-year-old photographs of Church of Satan rituals). The police cult seminars show remarkable indifference to professional thinking in other fields, such as anthropology and sociology, and very, very rarely involve speakers from these two professions. More likely, police officers team up with clergy or believer therapists to instruct seminars. To a degree, professional conferences held by child-care professionals, therapists, and psychiatrists maintain a similar core of immutable propositions, but less so than the police, for the simple reason that, unlike law enforcers, other professionals conduct research and publish papers on their findings, some of which I have described in this book. Law enforcers have neither conducted nor sponsored research. In part, this lack of research has come through the skepticism of law-enforcement administrators, who find other priorities of a more mundane sort, such as paying for additional officers, obtaining new equipment, or providing specialized training in such critical tasks as drug enforcement. Conferences of police executives are notable for the absence of cults/Satanism workshops. Cult cops, by and large, are restricted to the rank and file; the interest largely resides with street cops. Cult-cop ideology spreads also through in-service training, in most states mandated by law. Training officers can ensure interest in in-service programs by offering lectures on satanic-crime instead of on more mundane topics like auto theft.

But within law enforcement one can see signs of some change. Some police officers and officials have learned to advance satanic theories with caution. In a review of unsolved homicides near Williamsburg, Virginia, as with any unsolved major crime, the police inevitably speculate on cult involvement:

> The law officers and families [of the slain] also questioned whether the homicides could be cult-related. Thomas Stanley, head of the Bureau of Criminal Investigation, Virginia State Police, 1st Division, said investigators did discover that the *probable* dates of *some* of the crimes occurred close to an equinox, which is *often* related to satanic activity [italics added]. "But we can't go with the cult theory because usually there's some sort of sacrifice or mutilation," Stanley said. He added: "In this office we've never seen [evidence of cult killing], although we hear that it goes on around us all the time."[9]

In Anchorage, the Alaska Police Standards Council has reviewed, with possible decertification in mind, a cult seminar given to almost 70 corrections officials and police.[10] The attendees thought that the two-day training in

Satanism would give them investigative insight, but instead they found the course "a fundamentalist Christian sermon" taught by Lyle J. Rapacki, who, the Council determined, was unqualified to teach the subject. The Council had initially certified Rapacki to teach in response to application by the Alaska Peace Officers for Christ, who paid Rapacki's expenses. Rapacki had claimed "to be a counselor and former police officer with several advanced degrees,"[11] which proved mostly untrue. In addition, "Lyn Freeman, head of training for corrections, also found that Rapacki had perjured himself in an Oklahoma trial where he served as an expert witness on Satanism, and that he had publicly lied about the death of a teen-age girl. In a televised interview, Rapacki had described her murder at the hands of Satanists. He later admitted that the girl was not dead."[12] With luck, similar councils in other states will scrutinize cult seminars for content and the seminar instructors for their professed expertise.

Other cult-cop debacles have earned appropriate public scorn. In March 1990, in Albuquerque, New Mexico, an environmental scientist studying aerial photographs of the desert discovered an odd configuration of markings near power-transmission lines. Upon visiting the site, the scientist found approximately 400 tires laid out in "a pattern of three hexagons with dots in the middle, connected by jointed lines, and with lines of tires coming in like spokes to the center," and nearby other tires spelled out "TERF" or "TEAF."[13] The scientist claimed, " It looks like nothing on the ground, but in the air it's an incredibly precise pattern. Whoever did this had to have used surveyor's equipment to lay it out so precisely." But what was it? Enter an unnamed senior officer with the Rio Rancho Police Department: "The pattern is identical to a 'seal' used in Egyptian mythology for some type of initiation. It is definitely a ceremonial site used by a cult. A form of church. And it's probably still in use." Referring to the site, Officer Paul Montoya of the Albuquerque Police Department said: "This is definitely witchcraft. . . . And I'd stay away from there if there are any people around. They'll hurt you." Robin Gile, who calls himself "an archetypal symbolist consultant" claimed: "This site was designed to create a focus of will and to draw wisdom in, and it's definitely honoring the female side. There's a magnificent and grand underground of psychic tradition here." Finally, Phillip Wing, "who promotes psychic fairs around the nation" said: "[It's] a very powerful and spiritual symbol."[14]

Almost as soon as the Albuquerque newspapers ran the story, Glenn Shockley emerged to tell of Terf ball, a game he had invented. Photographs of the Terf ball itself and diagrams of the playing field appeared locally. Shockley announced that the mysterious tire patterns—the Terf field—made up goal areas to be attacked and defended. All of this gave the former Albuquerque mayor "the best belly laugh" he had had in years.[15] In the early 1980s, the ex-mayor said, Shockley and his friends "laid out a Terf field . . . and fielded three teams. The mayor's office, the Police Department, and the Fire Department. I was captain of the mayor's office team. It's kind of a crazy game. If I recall correctly, the police won. It was fun."[16] After a trial run in town, Shockley and his friends moved the game to the desert, where they placed the tires to mark the playing field. And the precision of the pattern when viewed aerially? "We laid this out over two weekends in March of '81," said a Terf player, Ron Manyo, "and the only instruments we used were a keg of beer and a cookout."

Local citizens were not entirely amused. One wrote to the newspaper, "It makes you wonder how much any of these 'authorities,' including our police, actually know about Wicca and Satanism."[17] Another wrote, "The media . . . have done their bit to fuel a public hysteria about Satanism and witchcraft by uncritically printing just this sort of absurd speculation, all by self-professed experts, some of whom charge up to $6,000 to lecture to local police departments on the lurking menace of devil worshipers." And, finally, a third citizen hopes that the "Albuquerque Police Department's interpretation of evidence is more rational when it come to real crime."

But these examples of caution are superseded by growing numbers of cult cops who usually surface in newspaper articles, described as the such-and-such police department's satanic-crime experts. Many cult cops pop up like Myrmidons after cult seminars have passed through their neighborhoods dispensing hysteria. The nouveau cult experts then spread the word themselves, creating more proselytes.

Even the tame *Campus Law Enforcement Journal* recently warned university and college police departments that "eight to ten million people have been affected" by cults, as if describing the spread of a disease. Quoting Marcia R. Rudin, Director of the International Cult Education Program, the article reminds campus law-enforcement administrators that they should be able "to recognize the signs of cult recruitment activities—which are often deceptive—and be able to spot warning signs that a student might be getting involved."[18] Of course, the article recommended that eager school officials contact the Cult Awareness Network and the American Family Foundation for help, organizations that promote mind-control models and conspiracy theories. The situation urgently demands police involvement, the article rails, because "satanic-related activity has dramatically increased in the last few years." And another periodical dealing with campus cults parleys the familiar four-level model, citing the particular vulnerability of college youths: "Today's campuses are being called 'spiritual supermarkets' where students are promised unlimited power and guaranteed salvation by an alarming number of satanic or cult groups."[19]

The proselytes of cult seminars also find new ways to cover the faces of their police departments with fresh eggs. As an "example of how offbeat dress and arcane interests are sometimes misconstrued as antisocial or even dangerous," local Massachusetts police raided a bunker at Wompatuck State Park where, they claimed, satanic rites, animal sacrifices, and Dungeons & Dragons playing went on. The local police, through shrewd intelligence work, had found "strange drawings" in the bunker, including an "altar" (a table) and an animal skull and candles. Raiding the site, the police encountered Northeastern University students "in medieval garb" helping a friend with a graphic-arts class project (confirmed by Northeastern University). The students, who had been using the bunker for weeks, decorated the bunker with symbols taken from the alphabets invented by J. R. R. Tolkien for *Lord of the Rings.* None of these findings kept the local press from fanning the satanic fires, which prompted angry parents not only to complain to the police but to try to make public statements to dispel suspicion, although not all local television stations and newspapers that covered the satanic claims were willing to report the follow-up.[20]

> "The police basically misinterpreted everything they saw," said Ted Thibodeau Jr., 21, who hung out in the bunker and whose brother, Chris, was among those caught in the raid. "They were primed for this, and whatever they saw they said, 'Hey, it must be cults.' "[21]

In fact, in the preceding month, Dale Griffis conducted the first conference on Satanism, cults, and associated crime in New England. His teachings in Warwick, Rhode Island, possibly influenced the eager Massachusetts officials. Sergeant Edmund Pierce of the Warwick police described a drawing clutched by a reticent 14-year-old runaway teen that, to him, depicted "a ritualistic human sacrifice occurring in front of a sketch of Satan." "Such an accurate portrayal of a human sacrifice made to the devil would have been impossible if the girl did not have extensive knowledge of Satanism," the good sergeant said.[22]

Even children of little imagination can deduce what might kill a person. Whatever the teen had drawn, the sergeant saw it as a "ritualistic sacrifice" and imputed to it—and the girl—arcane ritual knowledge that one cannot acquire from books, an encyclopedia, or films and television. Only a sergeant who thinks he possesses extensive knowledge of Satanism could find in the sketch an extensive knowledge of Satanism. What, then, might account for not only the prevalence of such beliefs among law enforcers but also their persistence over time?

Folklore

I have suggested repeatedly in the previous pages that *urban legend* plays a role in the creation and diffusion of satanic cult claims. Hitherto, I have circumvented a definition of the term but have used it to represent a larger context of folklore theory, which encompasses rumors, rumor panics, mass hysteria, moral panics, urban legends, myths, and subversion myths. People tell stories; they tell them with different motivations to different audiences with different calculated effects. These relevant folklore terms all have specific meanings and imply specific dynamics at work within populations. The satanic panic that has sucked up police officers has come about through an interplay of all the folkloric story-telling variants. Rumors of kidnapping children for sacrifice and of Satanists worshipping at an altar in the woods lead to police intervention. Children who are influenced to tell stories of day-care-center abuse at the hands of Satanists reflect different dynamics grounded in the same nebulous fears of adults, at least in many cases. Cult survivors and their therapists tell tales that may reflect fears elaborated through clinical therapy, culling from everything and anything: fears of strangers, trauma deriving from earlier abuse of some kind, perhaps even a pathological attraction to symbol-construction that reifies fantasies of sadomasochism, torture, and unconventional sexuality.

The combination of stories deriving from these contexts has coalesced into the four-tiered model of Satanists much trumpeted by cult cops. The theory of criminality that emerges from such tales has been fueled by the sheer force of belief that pervades the training seminars held by cult cops and therapists. The interaction of therapists and the police deserves the scrutiny of folklore research: that interaction produces myths that give the patina of scientific or at least organized thinking. As Sherrill Mulhern has found:

> When one concentrates the research focus on discovering the specific ways in which therapists come to "believe" in the reality of satanic/ritual abuse, one immediately uncovers a remarkable myth-making network of therapists, patients and investigators blending together specific idiosyncratic data into one a-temporal, analytic grid. I say this because, when one examines specific adult survivor stories, it becomes immediately apparent that initially patients were not saying the same things but came to say similar things over time.[23]

As evidence of the analytic grid, Mulhern notes that many therapists—and of course cult cops—have come to hear MPD patients in the same way. She points out that those who work with MPD patients, and who believe in satanic conspiracies, explain at seminars that "it takes an 'educated ear' to understand what patients are really saying."[24] Mulhern's observation underscores the analogy with religious conversion: through participation at seminars, law enforcers and therapists may come to believe, and those who believe adopt the "intimate conviction that they can suddenly see and understand realities which they have never seen before." And with the acceptance of belief comes the dismissal of doubt. "To put it succinctly, the ear educated by belief is also a deaf ear."[25]

History offers many object lessons about not only public panics over Satanism but also reactions to unexplained events that seem to threaten people beyond the principals involved. Recent scholarship recounts the incident of Elizabeth Canning, a teenage scullery maid in mid-eighteenth-century London, who disappeared one day while walking home after visiting relatives.[26] Four weeks later, she turned up exhausted and injured: she claimed that two men abducted her, forced her to stay in a "bawdy house," locked her in a room for a month, and fed her bread and water until she managed to escape. No less an authority than justice of the peace Henry Fielding listened to her story and on meager evidence secured convictions of "an old gypsy" and the owner of the house within which Canning said she had been incarcerated. But enter the Lord Mayor of London with evidence to exonerate the gypsy, whereupon Canning herself underwent trial, was found guilty of perjury, and was sentenced to deportation to the American colonies. But the event had become a media event, attracting even the attention of Voltaire. The media report of the Canning incident, which never produced a satisfactory explanation, coupled with local gossip-mongering, appealed to a public's need for sensation, including ethnic scapegoats, gypsies (considered perverse at best), and important people in high political office. Within this atmosphere, focus on the alleged kidnapping dissipated in favor of speculations about the *victim's* sexuality and innocence.

As I have described, putative cult crimes involve the same public *frisson* with sex, violence, and conspiratorial deceit paired against innocence, truth, and virtue. Occult ingredients feed the public's appetite for sensation; urban legends are thus simply waiting to happen. For example, the Virginia State Lottery once drew a lucky number that "broke the bank"; the number drawn provoked the following comments from a lottery official: "The lucky number was 666. Those who bet on it shared the largest payout in the history of the lottery—245 percent of the total amount wagered. . . . In Revelation 13:18, 666 is described as the number of 'the beast.' Although some people attach a stigma to 666 . . . it doesn't seem to apply to [lottery players]."[27] So folks don't behave too consistently: sporting with the Devil's number can be fun. But in the United Kingdom, the government stopped the number 666 from appearing on license plates "after some motorists complained that the biblical number of the beast had bedeviled their lives, causing everything from fender benders to bad water."[28]

Thus, there are still many who believe that Satan still lurks "out there," awaiting his opportunity to induce discord, suspicion, and deceit, even while he allows us to make light of his symbols and numbers. In northeastern Colorado, for example, 24-year-old Sandra Hilbert believes that witches, Satanists, and occultists lurk about. "I think there's a lot going on out here," she said.[29] Similarly, Norma Rae Bushner, 43, who owns a radio station in rural Yuma, Colorado, asserts, "I really think it could be real. . . . It's happening everywhere in America."[30] As evidence, she offers that someone wrote "REDRUM" (murder spelled backwards) in a substance believed to be blood, on the wall of an abandoned building: as everyone knows, backwards spelling is a dead giveaway for satanic mischief. (REDRUM written in blood also appears in Stanley Kubrick's film *The Shining*.) Interesting enough, in the public library of the small town of Yuma, a book titled *Witchcraft and Magic* has been checked out 22 times since 1980; such a text serves as an obvious source of fear. Virginia State Trooper T. S. Svard, speaking to parents in rural Virginia, instructs on the techniques cults use to conscript teens; his words provide a comparable source of hysteria. Referring to the Jonestown mass suicide and the Matamoros killings, Svard warns parents, "If you think you're safe in Southwest Virginia—you're not."[31] But some authorities—even law enforcers—cite the fears as unfounded and claim that cult rumors are "rooted in anxiety and uncertainty, and, in some cases, anger."[32] All that must happen in order for generalized fears to surface in dangerous ways is one nasty event around which fears crystalize. In southwestern Pennsylvania, for example, after Steven P. Mignogna killed two girls, his attorneys maintained that he " 'exploded' after prolonged exposure to heavy metal music, Satanism and pornography."[33]

Such community fears also produced rumors that led to about half of the Brownsville (Pennsylvania) area's 900 high-school students' staying home because of the story that "a blond, blue-eyed girl would be sacrificed May 5."[34] Stories of the abduction and sacrifice of a blond, blue-eyed child circulate continuously. In 1988, child-abduction and satanic-worship stories "spread like wildfire across a large section of eastern Kentucky."[35] As usual, the stories involved the abduction and sacrifice of blond, blue-eyed children to fill pre-Halloween needs of Satanists. But many law-enforcement agencies in Kentucky investigated the claims. Even the Kentucky State Police found that the satanic stories had reached 25 different counties. For a public willing to believe such a rumor, Captain John Rheel of the Pennsylvania State Police proved to give no support: "We have been unable to substantiate any of the rumors."[36] Such stories, or rumors, involving plots to kidnap children, or nefarious Satanists taking drugs, vivisecting cattle and pets, and writing in strange alphabets on bridges, walls, and roads occur everywhere in the United States. But satanic rumors are hard to play down when people begin to assert that they have suffered at the pitchforks of cultists. Although I do not purport to take an excursion into the psychology of hysteria, folklorists know well the Munchausen effect (named for the famous Baron von M.) whereby people maintain that they have experienced fantastic events, or the Munchausen effect by proxy, by which, say, a parent may claim that his or her own child was menaced by cultists. Nevertheless, a folklore study that found such tales rampant in northeastern Arkansas concluded:

> Considering the extreme opposition between Christianity and Satanism, the Devil Worshipers are blamed for societal ills and criminal acts of a particularly shocking nature. Since there is little chance that anyone would jump to defend a group so diametrically opposed to mainstream values, Devil Worshiping legends provide an outlet for the need to find scapegoats. With ongoing fear of children being kidnapped and the continuing need to assign blame, these legends may endure. Satan remains alive and well in northeast Arkansas.[37]

The Devil is indeed part of our folklore and has been since the country was first settled by Europeans. And the Evil One remains a habitual scapegoat, which can be harmless until we begin to impute satanic powers and rituals to plain folk, such as women who run day-care centers. Or until defendants' attorneys find that "the Devil made him do it" explanations make great arguments in courtrooms to persuade juries that the poor murderers weren't really responsible for their own behavior.

Urban Legends

Stories of child abductions, murders and mutilations at the hands of mysterious foreign-speaking strangers, or ritual abuse (that is, abuse committed incidental to a ritual as a form of propitiation, as cult officers use the term), present nothing new, as folklorist Jan Harold Brunvand has described in his popular books about urban legends, *The Choking Doberman* and *The Mexican Pet*. In fact, stories of abduction, mutilation, and murder of children pervade Euro-American history and mythology. Urban legends about the abduction of children show remarkable variety in their settings and circumstances. Such tales have children disappearing from theaters, shopping malls, stores, restrooms, and amusement parks; such disappearances occur only when the child temporarily leaves the supervision of an adult. And in virtually all cases, someone finds the child before he or she disappears forever. When found, the child may be drugged into a stupor, with his or her hair cut and quickly dyed in order to be removed from a public place without being recognized. Recent scholarship has produced a study of the phenomenon of tales of child abduction and murder in Reformation Germany, stories identical to those of today except that then the scapegoats were Jews, not shadowy Satanists.[38]

According to Brunvand, legends "are prose narratives regarded by their tellers as true. . . . They are generally secular and are set in the less-remote past [than myth] in a conventional earthly locale."[39] Satanic legends enter the fray as migratory tales, i.e., stories "widely known in different places," possibly in cyclical fashion or as several narratives thematically similar.[40] Aside from the stories themselves, their most remarkable characteristic is *movement*. As oral tales, people tell them and tell them often: the stories migrate. Particularly, though, "urban legends . . . often appear to be 'new' when they begin to spread, but even the newest-sounding stories may have gone the rounds before. A 'new urban legend,' then, may be merely a modern story told in a plausible manner by a credible narrator to someone who hasn't heard the story before, at least not recently enough to remember it."[41] Where satanic stories emerge, they place demands on the hearer's credulity because of supernatual if not unnatural elements, and people end up believing them *because* they are incredible:

> Urban legends typically have three good reasons for popularity: a suspenseful story line, an element of actual belief, and a warning or moral that is either stated or implied. Only a few urban legends contain *super*natural motifs, but all of them include at least highly *un*natural details. This fact shakes popular belief in them not a bit, for people in all walks of life credit such stories, and various publications frequently reprint them—or radio commentators report them—as the truth.[42]

Stories of cult activities by Satanists have only recently entered the experience of police officers, and when related by seemingly credible witnesses, some officers suspend empiricism and believe. Brunvand further details the process by noting, "Most urban horror legends, however, combine fully fictional plots with a credible setting and realistic characters to anchor themselves to supposed real-life events."[43] Shorn of modern settings, the urban legends are reducible to motifs that, "in folklorists' jargon, are traditional narrative units—such as characters, objects, or actions—that serve as the building blocks of folk stories."[44] A narrative unit could be an object (such as robes, candles, an altar), a person (a police officer, a priest or minister, a judge, or a child-care worker), an action (eating baby limbs, placing children in coffins with decomposing corpses), or a structural quality (symbols of pentagrams, 666, ritual chants). I have noted throughout this book that although the motifs in the satanic stories of survivors or "victims" from different parts of the country are claimed to be the same, they do not compare in detail. The broad elements, such as the murder of babies, may be the same, but when the stories are forced through the grid of folklore or ethnography, the details don't match. Both folklore studies and ethnography render textual analyses of such stories to examine the manner in which the tale is told (by whom; under what circumstances; with what effect; the "patterns of detail, or clichés of wording," whether told in first-

or third-person, and so on). These considerations do not enter therapeutic concerns but *should* if therapists intend to pass off the stories as truthful and accurate.

In fact, the standard guide to older motifs, Stith Thompson's *Motif-Index of Folk Literature,*[45] catalogs elements of witches' sabbaths, ritual murder and mutilation of children, children abducted by or sold to the Devil, plus a legion of plots involving the Devil. Hundreds of these motifs show up in cult seminars, motifs deriving from Europe, America, and even Africa, the Philippines, and Indonesia. Users of such catalogues must remember that the schemes for listing motifs are an etic, not an emic construction. (See Chapter 4 for definitions of *etic* and *emic.*) Catalogues provide motifs in comparative form to serve scholarly purposes, not necessarily to establish historical or cross-cultural links. Brunvand's books chronicle many motifs that appear in new urban legends, including attempted abduction of children from shopping-mall restrooms; assaults on young boys which result in castration (sometimes performed by black men on white boys), and the kidnapping of girls into prostitution rings.

Some police officers perpetuate new urban legends without taking the time to verify them. For example, a spurious police circular telling of an LSD-impregnated Mickey Mouse decal endangering children found its way through South Carolina.[46] The Pendleton, South Carolina, Police Department even warned the community about the decals, although no one bothered to check the story. Despite the wide circulation of the decals in the early 1980s and despite the widespread news coverage of them, the same story, with the same anonymous police circular, recently traveled throughout New Jersey, alarming citizens and police.[47] The same flyer passed through Richmond, Virginia, in February 1990, ending up in the hands of forensic specialists at the Virginia Division of Consolidated Laboratories. In April 1990, the same flier surfaced in eastern Virginia, leading Corporal G. A. Brown of the Portsmouth Police Department to comment: "No documented cases have been reported to this police department. It raises concern of the parents when there is no valid justification behind it."[48] Chesapeake Police Department Sergeant Richard D. Johnson added, "Every spring this flier goes out, and there is a panic." Rumor, hysteria, and urban legends are easy to produce: simply combine the right ideological leaning with fear and facile explanations for otherwise unpalatable occurrences.

The police have demonstrated susceptibility to cult-seminar hysteria by fomenting rumor and collective hysteria, if not urban legends. The Allenstown, New Hampshire, Police Department received reports during May 1989 that six cats had been found hanging from a tree not far from a decapitated dog, and the sound of drums could be heard in a state park at night. A woman walking her dog came upon what was described as a makeshift altar supporting a carcass of a mutilated beaver. Another skinned beaver turned up, found upright surrounded by stakes. The police decided to turn to a cult officer for help—Sandi Gallant—who, though in San Francisco and unable to inspect the animals—interpreted the findings as indicating satanic rituals. Since the carcasses were found near May 1, the cult officer said that the recent Walpurgisnacht, a putative satanic holiday, probably stimulated the sacrifices. The sergeant in charge of the investigation worried about these events, linking those who sacrificed animals to drug-taking and listening to heavy-metal music, a view confirmed by a local Baptist minister who believed the Devil responsible. The sergeant wanted to find the satanic group behind this. Characteristically, he said, "Their freedom of worship is protected . . . but we want to monitor them."[49] The next day, the Manchester, New Hampshire, *Union Leader* ran an editorial that stated, "We have reached a sorry state of affairs when following the Devil is defined as 'worship.' "[50]

Within a few days, the mystery unraveled. In fact, no dead cats had been found in trees. The beavers were legally trapped in the state park. Other dead animals reported by local residents were those killed on the road and stacked in the forest for later pick-up.[51] But even though the phenomena turned out to be mundane, other officials didn't remember the follow-up news story but only the original news report. After the whole incident passed from the headlines, the mayor of Manchester tried to ban the appearance of a heavy-metal band in town because they would supposedly stimulate more incidents similar to what occurred in Allenstown.[52]

In Chapter 2, I recounted the debacle in Yellowwood Forest, Indiana, involving law enforcers, local residents, a church group, and a neopagan weekend retreat. Readers may recall that a deputy sheriff, who had acquired a cult-cop world-view through attending a cult seminar (conducted by Dale Griffis-trained state troopers), relayed an uncorroborated story of satanic worship that was duly picked up and uncritically published by the local newspaper. Undoubtedly, the news article's circulation prompted, among credulous police through their seminars, at least new rumors—if not urban legends—about satanic rituals. But to cult cops who don't have the opportunity to investigate day-care centers or teen suicides, animal mutilations provide the most readily available fodder for cult speculation. At cult seminars officers exchange photographs of mutilated beasts as children trade football cards. Officers who have no forensic training in the cause of death in livestock or other animals solemnly declare that cultists made gaping holes in cows' necks with "surgical precision." Although occasionally officers find evidence that someone purposefully mutilated an animal, verified explanations of satanic worship very rarely emerge. Even the Church of Satan advises against harming animals. But mutilated animals tell no tales; hence the cult-cop penchant for turning them into urban legends.

In Pontiac, Illinois, in July 1989, Livingston County sheriff's officials pronounced a mutilated goat as the probable victim of Satanism. The goat, when found, had been castrated, had been dead for three or four days, and had its horns removed. Law enforcers pointed out that "small animal sacrifice is common among devil worshipers."[53] This killing, supposed bona fide evidence of cult goings-on, vindicated the work of "a group of ministers, police, school, and social service agency officials" who had been meeting for six months to examine satanic activity in their county. Alas, however, the satanic sacrifice was not to be. After the press picked up the goat story, a man said that the goat was his, that he dumped it after two German shepherds killed it. In fact, the horns had been removed long before the goat's death.[54] The man called the police to dispel the satanic cult stories. Law enforcers accepted the explanation and, apparently, so did the public.

The same cannot be said, however, for the community of Tustin, California. Within three months, 67 cats met with violent ends with "almost surgical precision," some torn in half, others skinned, some disemboweled.[55] A community group formed to investigate the cat murders, convinced that someone, probably Satanists, were doing it. Most of the carcasses turned up on people's suburban lawns, and in some cases just tufts of fur remained. Resident Janet Hampson, who led the campaign to ferret out the truth of the cat murders, even obtained about 60 carcasses from the Orange County Animal Control Center for new necropsies; the carcasses were kept in food freezers. Robert Reinhold, writing in the *New York Times,* explained Hampson's theory that human agents were responsible:

> There is never any blood at the scene, the animals are often dismembered with surgical precision and paws and other body parts are often left on the ground in strikingly similar arrangements. No one ever seems to hear anything . . . nor do dogs bark during the killing. She believes the cats are captured, taken elsewhere, their blood drained and organs removed, then replaced on their owners' lawns.[56]

But local authorities differed with Hampson. Reinhold said that the county veterinarian, Nila A. Kelly, maintained that, "the cats all showed evidence of animal kills. None showed any evidence of satanic cults, human intervention or hacking." The probable culprit: coyotes.

> Typically . . . coyote kills show puncture wounds from the canine teeth, chewing and splintering of bones, signs of which were found in the autopsies. She added that coyotes prefer the internal organs and can cut a cat in half because they instinctively go for the soft middle section where there are few bones. The lack of blood at the scene is not surprising, she said, because coyotes kill quickly and the heart stops beating and pumping blood.[57]

Of course Kelly did not discount human agents, pointing out that Orange County witnesses about ten mutilations annually that can be attributed to people. But the evidence in Tustin points to animals, a theory Hampson doesn't accept: "There is no indication of the shredding, pulling or chewing you'd expect from a coyote."[58] Stories of animal mutilations have circulated for decades, and although explanations for the deaths have evolved from being the handiwork of aliens from other worlds to that of Satanists, the tales still involve a commitment of law-enforcement resources.

Perhaps the definitive—and only—forensic analysis of animal mutilation tales appeared in 1980, authored by retired FBI agent Kenneth M. Rommel, Jr., and Nancy Owen, a University of Arkansas anthropologist. The study, titled *Operation Animal Mutilation,* a "Report of the District Attorney, First Judicial District, State of New Mexico," ran almost 300 pages. The study is set within the wider context of hysteria about livestock killings throughout several western states during the late 1970s, described in *Mute Evidence,* by writers Daniel Kagan and Ian Summers.[59] A rigorous inquiry, Rommel and Owen's study sought to determine the reliability of information on supposed "confirmed" livestock deaths due to UFOs, cults, or secret government programs, to try to determine the actual cause of death of the mutilated animals, to determine if the deaths in fact posed a law-enforcement problem, and, if so, how to best approach the problem. Conversely, if the deaths did not prove a law-enforcement issue, then Rommel was prepared to recommend that no further law-enforcement resources or funding be devoted to the putative mutilations.

In each case of a mutilation where an analysis could be performed, Rommel and his consulting veterinarians demonstrated that the parts of an animal carcass supposedly removed for unknown reasons by aliens or cultists, with surgical precision, are the same parts normally removed by predators and scavengers. Rommel relied on a panoply of experts in conducting necropsies for his arguments. Some birds can "core the anus and remove the eyes and tongue"; larger predators or scavengers attack the soft parts, the genitals, the underbelly, the udders of cows, precisely the parts that cult cops claim that Satanists remove for ceremonies. The "surgical precision" claims proved relatively easy to debunk. Rommel showed that untrained observers (cult cops, nowadays) cannot differentiate between the jagged and uneven cuts made by animals and those made by humans with surgical tools. Rommel found, "It is the rule rather than the exception for these animals [predators and scavengers] to do a neat job and not leave either blood or mess at the site of a carcass."[60] Readers interested in the forensics of mutilations should consult either the Rommel report or *Mute Evidence.*

Rommel's scientific method required a consideration of arguments by "believer" police officers, journalists, and their allies, many of whom held up examples of "definitive" mutilations, that is, mutilations from extraordinary causes, which in the late 1970s were not due to Satanists but to aliens arriving on UFOs (although rumors of Satanism and cult practices surfaced even then). One of the believer law-enforcers, Officer Gabe Valdez from New Mexico, "ruled out Satan-worshippers and predators as the cause of mutilations because of expertise and preciseness, and because of the cost involved in conducting such a sophisticated and secret operation."[61] How times have changed: if Valdez had not been bent on UFOs and associated government conspiratorial coverups, he might not have given Satanists such short shrift. In considering the proofs and the pseudo-authorities cited by the mutilation believers, Kagan and Summers summed up the logic of their approach, an approach that served up nonfalsifiable hypotheses: "The whole thing was part of a closed system, self-referential, solipsistic, which allowed no fresh information to enter unless it was properly polarized to support the prevailing attitude of mystery, conspiracy, weirdness, and/or UFOs and space aliens."[62]

This description of the mutilation-theory mode of thinking applies equally to the current satanic panic. The law enforcers, therapists, psychiatrists, and psychologists who attach literal veracity to cult survivors' stories and the satanic tales day-care kids tell during lengthy interviews construct a reflexive, self-referential model with its own logic. Believers inhabit a bubble within which they convince and reaffirm each other's perception of the satanic conspiracy, refusing to apply scientific tests; instead they apply pseudoscientific methods posing as scientific ones. Mulhern describes how professional conferences with cult seminars never confront whether the phenomena have explanations other than satanic ones, since the seminar speakers always come from the ranks of believers. Scientific approaches to back up satanic assertions, from the studies of ritual-abuse survivors (see Chapter 4) and of ritually abused children (see Chapter 5), upon scrutiny reveal many damning errors of scientific logic and method. But believer arguments and believer studies serve believer ideology, and the more detached from the scientific realm that the bubble becomes, the more farfetched become the claims of the believers.

Rommel found that wherever he had engaged "expert pathologists, veterinarians," and other experts, all agreed that the mutilations were caused by predators. No evidence was ever developed to affirm notions of UFO operations, secret government or business experiments. Again and again, Rommel pointed to the need to employ "qualified investigators" to handle reported mutilations. His description of a qualified investigator bears much relevance to the claims of cult cops, particularly where satanically mutilated cattle are concerned: "A qualified investigator would be someone specifically trained in techniques of criminal investigation, methods of observation of the scene of a crime, and the identification of evidence. Naturally, the more experienced such a person was, the more qualified he would be."[63] So far, so good, but when making claims about cattle mutilation, investigators must additionally have a thorough knowledge of cattle and veterinary medicine. But the mutilation believers—including police officers who propounded conspiracy theories in the 1970s—did not fare well in Rommel's study:

> None of the [mutilation] buffs had access to any experts in veterinary medicine, livestock, or any other fields that bore on the cattle mutilation question, and it was obvious that there was not one seriously qualified investigator in their underground. They were all amateurs, all poorly trained to deal with the subject, and all seemingly uniquely ignorant of research procedures and methods of constructing proven cases, not to mention the subject of animal medicine and livestock raising. Not one of them was a rancher or had even been raised on a ranch.[64]

An unusual claim requires unusual proof, and Rommel quite rightly asserted that "in order to eliminate the verdict of a predator and scavenger damage, one *must show* that the incisions in the carcass have been made by a knife or other sharp instrument."[65] As in the 1970s with claims of UFO-caused mutilations, claims of satanic ones deserve the same tough criticism. And proponents of the Satanism theory, even the investigators who find surgically precise holes in cow bellies, constitute amateurs "poorly trained to deal with the subject."[66]

The Allenstown, New Hampshire, and the Pontiac, Illinois, stories in the forms I have related them may not amount to urban legends, but instead fall into the category of rumor panics or collective hysteria. To become urban legends, the stories need to be retold with a narrative voice that helps shape the audience's response. And while collective hysteria usually produces a generalized response to simply move away from the threatening event, urban legends seem more didactic in asking us to be more vigilant, for the safety of children, for example. Or they function more as cautionary tales to warn us of the consequences of indifference or irresponsibility. But while urban legends may mention specific people, locales, and possibly even dates, "urban legends as a general rule do not identify specific culprits, identify their motives, produce individual victims who testify to the atrocities committed, or advocate specific lines of action for combatting the threat and preventing its recurrence."[67]

Brunvand notes that many urban legends function as cautionary tales in alerting us to typical dangers in the environment, particularly concerning children; the desired effect of such stories is to make us more cautious and responsible. For example, Brunvand cites Commander Joe Mayo of the Youth Division, Chicago Police Department, as telling the *Chicago Tribune* that during a shopping trip in a Chicago department store, a woman suddenly noticed that her daughter was missing. The store security guards conducted an extensive search and found the girl alone in a restroom.

"They cut her long hair and dyed it brown," Mayo said. "Whoever it was changed her clothes. It happens that quickly."[68] And in pure urban-legend form, Deputy Robert Wohler of the Berrien County, Michigan, Sheriff's Department wrote a memorandum dated November 17, 1983 which read:

> Subject: Tips to Make Your Holidays Happy Days
>
> Case #74685-83. Mary Smith had been shopping at the local Jolly Green Giant Supermarket. The time was approximately 7:30 P.M. and the parking lot was lighted only by the overhead lights. Mary had just finished her shopping and was taking her packages to her car. When she arrived at her car she found a woman sitting in her car. The woman gave Mary a sad story and asked for a ride. Mary then placed her packages in the back seat and told the woman she would be right back as she had other packages in the store. Mary then went to the store and got Security. Security accompanied Mary to her car where the woman was removed from the vehicle and found to be a man. What could have been the results? Fiction? No, fact! It did happen. Only the names used are fictional.[69]

Brunvand found, however, that the story *was* fictional; the narrative elements had been popular in the United States since 1983, when the story had migrated from England.

Subversion Myths and Rumors

But urban legends can become more than twice-told tales. Sociologist David Bromley extends the urban legend one step further: he has described a narrative form, the *subversion myth,* which responds "to perceived breakdowns in the social order."[70] Subversion myth reflects social tension. These narratives deal with the tales of cult survivors and others who fear satanic cults, but with a purpose. "They function as cautionary tales which in a metaphorical sense sensitize audiences to the perils of raising children in a world filled with dangerous groups and events,"[71] in a world over which parents have little control. The stories, then, "constitute a significant cultural form through which social disorder is confronted and symbolically contained."[72]

Coupled with a collective readiness to *believe,* the myths present threats that menace not only people but an entire way of life, especially since governmental institutions are not able to help because of constitutional guarantees of religious liberty, which extends even to Satanists. Subversion myths include certain ingredients: description of a danger, identification of a group of conspirators and of their pernicious motives, processes by which conspirators manipulate the unwary to do their bidding, the actual threat to society, and the remedy that citizens must pursue.[73] Subversion myths of the satanic-cult variety reflect deep anxieties about environmental influences over children, particularly when organized groups—the clandestine Satanists—prey upon them. Parents feel powerless to help because the demands of the money-making, home-building world preclude exclusive control over one's offspring. Urban legends might deal with isolated instances that adduce generalized morals; subversion myths presuppose the underground satanic megacult with an ongoing program of kidnaping and murder. By positing "the Other"—"They Who Are Responsible for Villainy"—groups of believers define and then strengthen a collective identity. In describing the ELF incident at Yellowwood Forest, William Guinee hypothesized "that each group theodicy function[ed] to create a sense of group identity in contrast to the other and to self-validate the group. Each ignores certain facts. . . ."[74] The confrontational groups in the Yellowwood incident were law enforcers, a Baptist congregation, and the Wiccans.

But the central themes of subversion myths remain child abduction, physical and sexual abuse, and murder, plus conscription into the cult through mind-control methods. In such tales, the subversive satanic cult emerges as omnipotent, against which conventional *legal* weapons don't work, either because the child victims disappear without a trace, and therefore cannot tell tales of abuse, or because they have been so thoroughly brainwashed that they can't remember what happened to them.

But details of cult life do emerge from the self-professed cult survivors. These days, we have the MPD victims who claim to have experienced upbringing in satanic families. But we have always had the lurid tales of apostates, whether from the Moonies today or, in the previous century, from Catholic schools. And despite the differences in details when comparing the accounts of apostates or refugees, one theme emerges: cults operate to gain and keep power. Many observers of cult claims have noted that the putative cult rituals and paraphernalia seem to evolve in the minds of those who combat the unseen menace. Recall Gordon Melton's observation that conservative Christians have carried on the satanic tradition, if not created it. Bromley notes, on this point, that the persuaded audiences, the believers, cite both the details of satanic cult stories and their sameness from account to account as evidence of their veracity. He also reminds us, however, that "such similarities are primarily a function of the activities of those constructing the subversion scenario rather than the activities of putative subversives."[75] Bromley suggests that, compared with urban legends and collective hysteria, subversion myths seem more plausible to audiences for five reasons: cultural tension conditions audiences to accept the reality of the tales; the target subversive group or individual is identified; self-professed victims or participants arise to offer testimony, thus reducing an audience's distance from the event(s); unlike urban legends, which are spread orally, subversion myths filter through many media, particularly family magazines, and the tales' construction evokes such outrage and indignation that the audience is roused to propose drastic actions.[76]

After urban legends and subversion myths, a third narrative form, *hysterical contagion* or *collective hysteria,* "involve[s] the rapid transmission of the belief that there is an imminent danger in the actor's environment."[77] Bromley cites a 1972 example in which women working at a university computer center complained of illness from exposure to a gas that was never identified. Analyzing such stories means examining their social contexts. At the university center, for example, much tension existed over job insecurity and the resulting job dissatisfaction. But as Bromley notes, analyzing underlying tensions in such stories is difficult because in most cases such incidents pass unnoticed or offer insufficient documentation for study. Collective hysteria stories show less complexity than urban legends (and subversion myths), which also derive from environmental tension but have more specific implications than raising a general public alarm. And unlike urban legends or subversion myths, the narratives of collective hysteria stories "are relatively unstructured and ephemeral."[78] While subversion myths and urban legends might show more developed attributes and complexity of narration, collective hysteria or rumors, I suggest, have the cumulative effect of conditioning a local audience to accept the plausibility of stories properly classified as subversion myths.

Similar to collective hysteria, *rumors* as defined by Brunvand are "unverifiable reports of supposed events" which may "swell to legend proportions as they develop a specific narrative content."[79] This is precisely what I suggest happened to the animal-mutilation story from Allenstown, New Hampshire, or perhaps even the ELF incident in Yellowwood Forest. But rumors, illformed as they are, can powerfully affect an audience unwilling to question their internal inconsistencies or even to question their veracity at all. For example, in February 1989, teenagers in Aliquippa, Pennsylvania, found an old copy of the New Testament near a rock on which someone had written, "And in Arcadia I."[80] The kids told the local police chief that they had found a satanic altar with "a rotting animal hide and a metal box containing small animal bones," which they had thrown away. The animal hide, it seems, was an old wool sweater. But the Bible's owner came forth, explaining that kids had circulated the rumor that he was a Satanist and had been seen reading *The Satanic Bible* in the woods where he had sacrificed a dog. Local people who heard the rumor added that he had been seen wearing a satanic robe in his home. The man explained that he had worn a hooded bathrobe during his bout with the flu. And the phrase about Arcadia was "the translation of a Latin phrase in a seventeenth-century Poussin painting." The poor man, it seemed, liked to take his Bible into the woods to read. But the satanic accusations emerged, and the neighborhood kids even harassed the man's son by "calling him Satan."[81]

Teens, particularly, seem adept at developing and circulating rumors. In Casa Grande, Arizona, public anger had been aroused by rumors that Union High School had allowed a satanic group to rent a classroom where on weekends members conducted worship services.[82] The school's business manager denied that this was so. "That's probably the last group we'd want at the school," said the manager's secretary. In New York, teens have elevated a small, loosely knit gang, the Decepticons, into myth; after a few of the gang were arrested for robbery, high school students began to attribute to them any and all other crimes by local gangs or groups. "So powerful is the [Decepticons'] hold on the imagination of the students that they often use 'Decepts' as a catch-all name for groups of teenagers who commit random violence and vandalism."[83] One boy at West Park High School in Manhattan said, "Everybody's heard of the Decepticons. They're everywhere. No. Don't use my name. They're vicious." In fact, "Most of the same students who swear that the Decepticons are everywhere admit that they have never seen one." Decepticon stories, though, have circulated long enough that they have become urban legend, reifying a specific threat from a generalized fear of school violence. The stories are told as warnings to other kids not to be caught in certain places at certain times. And the Decepticon stories acquire new details in the telling:

> "You know the Decepticons have a secret code," said Claribel Corona, 16, a Park West student. . . .
>   How do you know? she was asked.
>   "My girlfriend told me," she said.
>   How does she know?
>   "Her brother told her," she said. "Do you know how many people would like to know that code? And what they would give to find out? A lot. Nobody wants to get beat up by the Decepticons."[84]

Not only crowded urban settings generate such stories. A similar gang, The Posse, made its presence known in Roanoke, Virginia, in the fall of 1988. In this case, though, Lieutenant J. E. Dean of the Roanoke Police Department said, "We've heard the rumors, but we cannot substantiate that there is a group known as The Posse."[85] School officials speculate that the name of the gang came from a film about gangs and violence. As with the Decepticons, The Posse members do not wear distinctive clothing, so they blend in with other students. Yet the rumors have almost led to violence; in one incident, high-school students showed up at a local bar "armed with baseball bats and riding in a pickup truck," looking for members of The Posse. But Roanoke County Sheriff Mike Kavanaugh understands the rumor process: "All you have to do is get two kids talking at a table in the cafeteria. Two other kids at the next table hear half the conversation, and a rumor is spread."[86]

Sociologist Robert W. Balch and attorney Margaret Gilliam studied the genesis and evolution of satanic rumors in Montana. The study is remarkable for the chronology it provides of the rumors' diffusion over fifteen years. It all began with the murder of Donna Pounds, whose body was found in Missoula, Montana, in 1974. But the nature of her murder ignited public speculation about the crime; she had endured sexual assault, then was "bound, gagged and forced to kneel before being shot five times in the head."[87] Since the homicide did not yield a solution—a murderer—rumors emerged that a Devil-worshipper had sacrificed Pounds, stories that received further elaboration in the telling; her murder occurred as part of an initiation rite that "required three female victims: a Christian woman [Pounds], a virgin and a betrayer." The virgin, rumor had it, was a child who had been kidnapped and killed, but the third victim had not yet been claimed by the Devil; hence the public alarm. Needless to say, the rumors about the initiation rite spread with other attributes that treated Satanism and witchcraft synonymously, offering up elements of animal sacrifices and black masses. "The most persistent story told of a woman who encountered a group of robed figures while driving alone late one night. The figures formed a chain across the road by linking arms, and their faces were concealed by hoods. Terrified, the woman accelerated, hitting one of them before they could scatter into the forest."[88] While the woman claimed to discover blood on her car, the local sheriff's department could not.

Balch and Gilliam found that fifteen years later teenagers in the area who had not yet been born when Pounds died "are steeped in the local folklore about witchcraft and human sacrifice." And yet police finally solved the crime in 1986, and needless to say, Satanism had nothing to do with the murderer's motivation. The researchers' explanation of the rumor process should not surprise readers:

> Rumors are triggered by important or unusual events where factual information is absent, incomplete or disputed. In their quest for explanations, people speculate, exchange ideas and evaluate competing hypotheses in light of pre-existing assumptions about reality. . . . In short, rumor formation is a process of reality construction that can proceed quite readily even when objective support is absent.[89]

Predictably, the rumors included allegations that the police had withheld information from the public, and even that law enforcers had been complicit in a cover-up. Through their survey, the researchers found that of those who had heard that Devil-worshippers had sacrificed Pounds, almost one-third believed the story. Of interest, other competing rumors offered explanations of the killing, but only the satanic rumor gained a firm hold on Missoulans' imaginations. Why? "The satanist rumor had the advantages of completeness and parsimony."[90] Balch and Gilliam found that "three aspects of Missoula's cultural environment contributed to the plausibility of the satanist rumor": widespread local interest in the occult, which emerged through a survey; the influence of rumors of another satanic cult from northern Idaho at the time of Pounds' death, involving the disappearance of two people; and, finally, widespread alarm among fundamentalist Christians about a growing interest in the occult in Missoula.

The fundamentalist Christian beliefs of Missoulans figured significantly in the development and perpetuation of the satanic stories. Fundamentalist ideology about Satanism does not show economy: to such believers, Satanism simply ranks high on a list of undesirable beliefs and practices along with ESP, astrology, and the New Age. During their fieldwork, Balch and Gilliam "found that fundamentalists, especially pentecostals, were rich sources of new rumors and variations on old ones."[91] Apocalyptic notions of the coming confrontation of the forces of good against those of evil ran high in Missoula, stimulated by Hal Lindsey's books and other works much read locally. Add to the books some fundamentalist films, including one titled, "Satan on the Loose," which featured "scenes of devil worshippers dancing hypnotically in a demonic frenzy . . . followed by the stern warning that 'satanic rituals like this one are being conducted in *your* community.' "[92] In fact, the fundamentalists did not take the satanic rumors lightly, and many even refused to talk to the researchers without a nod from their minister, who explained that "many members of his congregation feared that talking to us about Satanism might open themselves to demonic influence."[93]

At one point in their research, Balch and Gilliam found their skepticism endangered by the sheer power of the rumor process. "Although we never found any objective evidence to support the Satanist theory, we had no obvious basis for rejecting it either."[94] Although a quick vacation away from Missoula helped them regain their composure, the researchers hypothesized "that belief in the rumor would be directly related to its currency in one's network of friends and acquaintances." In fact, in their survey, the researchers asked those who indicated a belief in the satanic rumor why they believed it, and respondents most commonly answered, "Everyone was talking about it, so I thought there must have been some truth to the stories."[95] In fact, some of the researchers' professional acquaintances succumbed to belief. A reporter who checked on the Idaho rumors returned only to refuse to discuss the case on the telephone because cult members might be eavesdropping. Although the reporter only learned the same stories that the researchers had already found, "she had been transformed into a believer."

While more than fifteen years had passed since the Pounds murder, local Missoula folklore, particularly among teens, had evolved stories of altars, worshippers who sacrifice animals and drink their blood, naked dancing on satanic occasions, and the like. Balch and Gilliam theorize that two processes have contributed to the spread of new rumors. First, the original rumors accompanying the Pounds murder "provided a novel interpretive framework for making sense of anomalous events."[96] In fact, subsequent deaths of some high-school students, a suicide, and the disappearance of a college student (who had merely taken an impromptu trip), all were ascribed by locals to satanic cults, an explanation that proved untrue in each case. Second, new rumors in Missoula developed through "retrospective reinterpretation," or "the reinterpretation of past events in light of one's current perspective." The second explanation, in fact, coupled with the first, applies to satanic beliefs far beyond those recounted in Missoula. Therapists and police officers who become believers, as I have argued in this book, use their new interpretive framework—the four-level satanic model—as an interpretive grid. And both therapists and police officers who teach cult seminars maintain that their new ideas and findings can now explain past unexplained events. Therapist Kathy Snowden (mentioned in Chapter 4), after working with MPD patients and coming to believe their satanic tales, believes that she was dealing with satanic cult survivors for years and didn't know it.

Despite the prevalence of satanic rumors in Missoula, the local police never gave them credence. In fact, most of the rumors Balch and Gilliam collected seemed rather vague, perhaps mainly due to publicized explanations for some of the anomalous events. In 1986, the Pounds murder was finally solved. The original suspect, Wayne Nance, was killed during the commission of a later crime, and subsequent investigation tied him conclusively to the Pounds murder. Local law enforcers never found any evidence that occult matters or Satanism played any role in her death. While such investigative facts sabotaged the rumors, satanic beliefs persisted even as the rumors waned. Balch and Gilliam attribute the rumors to mass hysteria, or "widespread alarm based on an unfounded belief."[97] They conclude by arguing the necessity for skepticism when hearing satanic claims: "The fact that a story is widely believed or told with deep conviction may be reason to open an investigation, but it is not a good basis for drawing conclusions."[98]

Moral Panics, Rumor Panics

The United States hardly stands alone in witnessing satanic rumors that evolve into panics. Benjamin Rossen, in a doctoral dissertation for the University of Amsterdam, analyzed a case of mass hysteria in Holland, in the town of Oude Pekela.[99] The case arose over two boys' sexual explorations with one another, culminating in allegations of mass child-abuse by subversive cultists. Rossen's study describes the process by which people come to believe in the rumors that sustain a widespread panic or a collective hysteria, providing a fascinating cross-cultural comparison to the day-care-center cases in the United States. He uses the term "moral panic" instead of rumor panic, which he describes as "an often latent fear of an intangible threat against fundamental certainties . . . a time-bomb that needs only a small spark to set it off," a panic resulting from a threat to proper morals.[100] And perhaps Oude Pekela provided such a time-bomb: a small town with high unemployment and widespread feelings of "helplessness and resentment," a town rife with labor protests and heated local political disagreements. The rapid spread of mass child-abuse allegations followed a process understood well by a perspicacious police investigator in the nearby town of Groningen:

> I'll put it in writing for you: If I want to have an Oude Pekela in Groningen tomorrow, it would take me three hours. I would go to a school and tell the teacher, preferably in the kindergarten, that a whole lot of children in her class had been indecently assaulted. I'll bet you that by the end of the day you would have it. That's how it works.[101]

In the United States the imagery that emerges in children's accounts of day-care abuse includes robed adults, nude game-playing, inserting various household implements in body orifices, and even chanting satanic songs, placing children in coffins, and murdering and eating babies. In the Oude Pekela incident, although the social dynamics of the spread of panic, adoption of paranoid beliefs, and so on, are the same as in the United States, the imagery of the children's stories differs: in Holland children reported lion-head motifs, "pubs in deserted places, sex clubs, large expensive cars . . . with smoked-glass windows, men in expensive suits with German accents and cars or busses full of laughing children," but the most prominent symbol was the clown.[102] Clowns, parents believed, enticed children with sweets and, once the children were hooked, clowns and others abducted them. Rossen points out that "stranger danger" admonitions to children backfired with the emergence of a rumor panic about clowns. Parents and some officials warned children to stay away from clowns, but by coincidence, in the nearby town of Winschoter, the local traders' association decided to designate a clowns' month to attract shoppers. They imported well-known clowns to do what clowns do: juggle, ride odd bicycles, hand out balloons, and make up children's faces to look like clowns. The result? A protest condemning the merchants for their insensitivity to the local child-abuse problem. And the Winschoter incident—in July—produced effects the following Christmas when children were warned away from Saint Nicholas because parents did not want their children to receive gifts from "dressed-up people."

Panics and collective hysteria follow definable stages. People's beliefs and their tests for proof of what they believe is happening become narrowly circumscribed within a reflexive microuniverse of rules lacking an outside referent. The cluster of beliefs harbored by people who participate in the panic takes on a life and momentum of its own, eventually playing itself out, either dissipating back into the "rational" universe or transmogrifying into another form. For example, cattle-mutilation stories of the 1970s, which police officers explained as UFO-related or as the product of secret government projects, no longer bear such explanations: satanic-cult causality has fully supplanted any other explanation. As Rossen points out, " 'Moral panic' prevents the people who become caught up in the mass hysteria from appreciating the artificial or inflated nature of their perception of the deviance and the threat they believe it represents, or of the inappropriateness of their behavior."[103]

Rossen defines the cycle of panic as beginning with people's *sensitization* to a form of deviance that becomes the evil Other, the present threat to stability and peace. By now, in many parts of the United States, people have become conditioned to thinking that unexplained nasty events might have been caused by some ill-defined satanic cult. Once they focus on the cult as a threat, people form *symbols* to represent its most significant characteristics, those that highlight the deviance and therefore produce rage and astonishment. As fear permeates a population, people *exaggerate and distort information.* In fact, both informal and authoritative, formal methods of communication become affected, thus engendering a juggernaut of disinformation that, as I noted above, sustains and feeds itself on its own peculiar logic. With a distortion of communication comes an *amplification of roles* in which the "deviants become more deviant, the victims become more victimized, and the heroes more heroic."[104] With polarities of behavior, of good and evil thus established and personified by the major actors in a community—the social workers, police, children, parents—the deviance begins to *diffuse.* At first, the deviant behavior around which people rally to fight might be putative child abuse or the killing of pets and other animals. The deviance may spread to drug abuse, the production of pornography, murder, or theft, all of which people link to the original threat. Next comes *imposition,* or the call to public action. People transfer their anger to governmental institutions, demanding immediate intervention. Finally, the panic reaches *resolution,* either dissipating in the face of hard evidence, evolving into a different form, moving beyond the community afflicted, or continuing in some variant form.

Mass hysteria is the response of people to crises or events that transpire while more generalized fears become entrenched through the model's cycle. The crises or events, of course, are *perceived* crises or events and may not hold any reality for outside observers or bystanding governmental agencies. But Rossen points out that many people may have a misleading idea of what is meant by mass hysteria. "An image of people in a communal frenzy, leaping about, frothing at the mouth and falling to the ground in exhausted faints, may come to mind."[105] Instead:

> Mass hysteria refers to the collective response to an artificial crisis which develops out of shared beliefs and associated fear, but not necessarily out of real threats or real events. Outward behavior may give an impression of rational people at work. They call meetings to discuss the perceived crisis, plans are drawn up and declarations made. As long as the observer believes in the crisis, recognition of mass hysteria remains very difficult. . . . Mass hysteria disasters are characterized by unreal events preceded by plenty of warning and psychological buildup. Over a period the psychological buildup makes increasingly exaggerated behavior acceptable.[106]

But we late-twentieth-century folk don't believe ourselves capable of hysteria. After all, we're too scientific. Kagan and Summers, authors of *Mute Evidence*, point out that our self-perceptions as rational and informed people militates against our taking responsibility for our irrationality.

> Our recent technological and scientific advances and our sophisticated social attitudes probably make us even more susceptible to these delusions because we've allowed ourselves to think we've evolved past the point where we're capable of raw, illogical, irrational belief in implausible events. We figure that if we can be made to believe it, it *must* be scientific.[107]

Relating this to cattle mutilations:

> Once a mass delusion reaches a certain level of momentum, the notion of proof of its central assumptions ceases to play an important part. The extent, the pervasiveness of the delusion, its very existence becomes the proof that it is a legitimate issue.[108]

But Kagan and Summers correctly distinguished the putative cattle mutilations from a cultural phenomenon that employed cattle mutilations as an accessory fact. They experienced a revelation in making the distinction between the fact and the phenomenon:

> The revelation was this: *At bottom, the cattle mutilation pheonomenon had nothing at all to do with dead cows.* The cows were superfluous. The phenomenon was really about the mythologized symbolic *causes* for the dead cows. The dead animals were nothing but a stimulus, an entryway, almost an excuse for people to become involved with the mythologized "others" they believed were causing the deaths: UFOs, conspirators, the government, corporate devils, the military. This was why once the [mutilation] phenomenon appeared in an area, the press, the public, the ranchers, and, most significantly,

the [believers] and [believer] journalists paid almost no attention to the condition of the dead animals and instead became obsessed with the mythic agents they might be able to blame for them. This made perfect sense, since the "others," the *causes,* carry all the symbolic freight that make the myth work.[109]

As we have seen throughout this book, journalists' accounts of despondent teens who commit suicide search for explanations in the occult, in playing Dungeons & Dragons. Investigations of day-care centers have sought Satanists or underground pornographers, and Rossen's study details the public search for international child abductors and pornographers. As a result, professional and public concern shifts to a preoccupation with conspiracies and their *modi operandi.* The four-level satanic model may not amount to a behavioral continuum, but claims about and descriptions of the behavior of people in each level eventually focus on the *phenomenon* of Satanism or cults, metaphors for our own worries and concerns about cultural pluralism, the ascendancy of world powers whose populations don't speak English, fears of losing jobs and of the decreasing value of money and the increasing cost of everything, and, most important, fears of managing our own families.

Ordinary, rational people who succumb to mass hysteria may do extraordinary things, such as search for witches, or at least search for the putative deviants. Rossen recounts a "lynching" that sprang from a developing panic over the Oude Pekela allegations of mass child abuse. In the town of Deventer, a man had been *accused* of engaging in sex with underage boys. The man had not been arrested: the police investigation was under way. The father of one of the victims, with four other men, forced their way into the suspect's residence, abducted him, took him to the home of one of the men, tied him to a chair and beat him, hitting his head and kicking his groin to obtain a confession. After the suspect confessed, the men placed him in a car and drove him around town, threatening to kill him with a knife. They then took him to another home and beat him again before finally driving to the local police station and throwing him out of the car.[110]

If during the process of the panic people meet to demand action, leaders arise who promise to help restore public stability, in the interests of protecting children and family integrity. "The danger that these [community members] represent is considerable. Empowered by the moral panic, their ravings are accredited by experts and ascribed authority by gullible and frightened parents. Appearing as experts, they spread their vision through the media and infect the land with moral panic."[111] Patricia Pulling, as well as cult survivors who claim to have reared and killed their young for Satan, serve as American examples. Recall that sociologist David Bromley found that some women's and family magazines engender subversion myths. A trip to a supermarket checkout line, with its display of such magazines, reveals such tales: pop-psych articles on sexual assault, child abuse, cults, and Satanism, all culled from secondary sources, glibly and superficially written, asserting absolutes, providing warnings and admonitions. But what of the professionals who witness or participate in the hysteria?

Rossen found that professionals proved no less susceptible to mass hysteria than other citizens. In fact, the *repetition* of the incredible, the bizarre, and the (eventually shown to be) fictitious stories seemed to affect many child-care professionals and physicians in Oude Pekela.

> Sustained belief in the unbelievable suggests high levels of credulity and low levels of critical thinking ability. Assertions of certainty represent intellectual risk-taking at the best of times; in the absence of evidence it indicates a form of intellectual pathology.[112]

Rossen points out that "extravagant speculations may also be evidence of credulity," and quotes a physician involved in the incident:

> A child said, for example, that a naked girl was tied to a stake and that the child molesters had thrown knives at her. I didn't believe that until a little chap came and said: It is certainly true because they also hit the girl. I said unbelieving: now, she must have bled. No, answered the little boy, that can't [be] because the knife twisted. Then I knew: naturally they had used a rubber knife for the video they were making.[113]

The result of such thinking, when fed by professionals to parents, parents to children, parents to parents, and parents to professionals is stoked-up paranoia, where the conspiracy model demands that everyone must be suspected. Neighbors begin to suspect neighbors *because* the behavior of friends and acquaintances *seems* normal. So neighbors examine their neighbors more closely, noting any eccentricity or unfamiliar behavior that might offer clues to the workings of the underground child-abuse and pornography industry. People adopt bizarre standards of what constitutes evidence of participation in the subversive megacult; a neighbor may have taken an overnight business trip somewhere on the same day that children at a day-care center were airlifted to a ceremonial site where Satanists sacrificed babies. And everyone knows that the neighbor in his younger days was an Air Force pilot, *ergo,* perhaps the neighbor flew the children to their hellish rendezvous! And wasn't the neighbor's divorce years ago a bit mysterious? Didn't his wife say that her husband didn't want them to have kids of their own? Perhaps he preferred to abuse other families' children? When one willingly sees conspiracies of Satanists or international pornographers, one adopts the pseudoscientific as proof. Notions of perverse criminality come to rely on nonfalsifiable assumptions: "normal" behavior can be taken as evidence of criminality. Unusual or unfamiliar, or "abnormal," behavior can be taken as evidence of criminality. Panics cannot be resolved by a sober presentation of scientific evidence; such evidence cannot transcend the willingness to barricade oneself behind nonfalsifiable speculations.

Rumor panics are alive and well throughout the United States, afflicting rural and urban areas nationwide, as sociologist Jeffrey S. Victor has chronicled. In particular, he recently examined a localized panic that resulted from rumors of satanic-cult activities in parts of Pennsylvania, Ohio, and New York that created what he described as a "collective nightmare."[114]

> The hysterical collective behavior of the rumor-panic was expressed as fearful and angry behavior, in response to a perceived threat in the community. However, the response was far out of proportion to any real threat. There were abundant examples of such behavior on Friday the thirteenth [of May, 1988] in Jamestown [New York]. Many parents, for example, held their children home from school out of fear that they might be kidnapped by "the cult." Absences from elementary schools were three to four times greater than average. Over 100 cars showed up at a rumored ritual site in a wooded area, where they were stopped by police barricades. Some of the cars had weapons in them: clubs, knives and hunting guns. Several teenagers who were falsely rumored to be in "the cult" received telephone death threats from adults. At a warehouse rumored to be another meeting place of "the cult," about $4000 [worth] of damage was done to musical equipment and interior walls. The police, school officials and the youth bureau received hundreds of telephone calls reporting bizarre incidents.[115]

Victor did not find the rumor panic a sudden development. Similar to Bromley's explanation of subversion myths, the New York rumors of cults provided "symbolic meaning, however false, to an evolving collective myth. That myth offered a ready-made explanation for ambiguous, unclear sources of collective anxiety."[116] Victor focused his work with rumor-panics on relatively homogeneous but economically depressed rural areas, but the stories that circulated in such areas resembled stories from other, noncontiguous rural populations: the killing of cats, the abduction and sacrifice of blond, blue-eyed virgin youngsters, and the suicides of satanic teens. All of the stories, Victor suggests, can be interpreted as metaphors for certain anxieties. All of the stories coalesced, over several months, into myths describing the workings of satanic cults, their recruitment techniques, and their effects on the young:

> Myths give meaning to ambiguous, unclear experiences. . . . Powerful, persistent rumors, like myths, cannot be explained adequately as a product of the personal motives of the storytellers. This symbolic interactionist interpretation can help us grasp the reason why so many different individuals, with so many different personal world-views, can come to believe a powerful rumor story and become absorbed by the rumor-making process.[117]

In the case of Jamestown, New York, the rumor-making process began with a punk-rock concert on Halloween, 1987, followed closely by a *Geraldo* program on satanic cults, and publicity surrounding the Sullivan murder-suicide case in New Jersey. Rumors circulated and intensified about the putative Satanism of punk teens, then of many high-school students generally, finally culminating in stories about the ritual killings of cats. The fulminations of a fundamentalist minister about satanic dangers, followed by the importation of church "experts" in Satanism to inspect the community and visit alleged ritual sites, fueled rumors through their pronouncements about community problems. The rumors intensified over the coming months, culminating on May 13, 1988. In the Jamestown case, at least, police acted with circumspection, never supporting the satanic claims and perhaps defusing vigilantes from assaulting nonconformist kids tagged as satanic punkers. No evidence ever emerged to substantiate any of the rumors, including those of cat killings.

The inquiries of Benjamin Rossen and Jeffrey Victor demonstrate the value of social-science methods in showing rumor panics to follow patterns with almost predictable metaphors for the unthinkable, the unconscionable, the dangerous, the subversive, the fearful. Common characteristics of such panics include the gradual intensification of the rumor over time and the highlighting of violent acts and the influencing of unblemished youth by nefarious adults and corrupted teens. The gradual intensification of rumor, plus the emergence of new twists on old rumors that hint at even greater violence, subversion, and nastiness all occur within the bubble of self-contained, solipsistic reasoning with no outside referent. Without an anchor in empiricism, rumor in a community can be transformed into a juggernaut fed by more rumor and stoked by the mass media, outside "experts," and the discounting of the whole business by some public or governmental authorities (denials equal coverup). While Jamestown was lucky in not being subjected to witch-finding visits of cult cops (only cult ministers instead), such experts did visit nearby communities, and the local newspapers dutifully reported their rantings. Victor himself found that *Geraldo* and similar programs were often followed by the visits of witch-finders:

> I found that some people are going around the country making many thousands of dollars from lecture fees, by cultivating fear about satanic cults. Many of these same satan hunters have broadcast their claims to national audiences on the television talk shows of Geraldo, Oprah and Sally Jessy. I am disturbed by their wild, unsubstantiated claims about satanism, which have the effect of inflaming rumor passions. Many innocent people could be victimized by their appeals to the scapegoating hysteria.[118]

When the police succumb to the influence of rumor panics, or when they themselves foment them, their professional thinking has eroded into nonfalsifiable assumptions about cult behavior, and therefore dangerous behavior. Further, the vehemence with which cult cops pursue evil cannot be due to the adoption of nonfalsifiable assumptions alone. I suggest that the four-tiered satanic model, as unsophisticated a construction as it is, gets streamlined in the retelling; the streamlined telling of satanic tales requires a strutting narrator who makes his case without mincing details. Just as cult survivors come to tell their tales without betraying any emotion whatsoever, even as they recount sacrificing their own babies, so do cult cops refine the narrative voice through which they offer up their claims and causal connections, relying more on implication and innuendo than on firm assertion. The apparent unity of their ideology in explaining all that is antisocial and pernicious is *convincing*. Thomas Wedge, for example, has honed his oft-told tales to include dramatic pauses, overstatement, hyperbole, understatement, and any other rhetorical devices he picks up along the way. With his slick packaging, he outshines other cult cops with less histrionic methods, and Wedge remains much in demand as a speaker. His manner, coupled with his all-embracing theory of satanic criminality, converts many into believers.

Different cult cops have different emphases; some evince fundamentalist Christianity, whereas others may not. But all cult cops share the same self-referential thought bubble. The thought-world of cult cops deserves further study. Paul Watzlawick's stimulating *How Real Is Real?* offers some hints on why the satanic model is so compelling. Watzlawick recounts an experiment in which two test subjects, A and B, watch slides of healthy and malignant cells.[119] The test subjects do not communicate with one another. A and B try to decide whether the cell is healthy or sick, so when a slide is flashed, they either press the "healthy" or "sick" button and receive immediate feedback about their decisions. A's light will flash either "right" or "wrong." Theoretically, A and B eventually will become more proficient in making the correct decisions after a number of guesses. But A and B don't receive the same feedback. A receives true feedback, that is, the lights flash according to whether he made the right or wrong choice. But the lights flash for B *according to A's responses.* If A chose the correct answer but B didn't, B's light will flash "right." B does not know this, of course: "He has been led to believe there is an order, that he has to discover this order. . . . There is no way in which he can discover that the answers he gets are noncontingent—that is, have nothing to do with his questions—and that therefore he is not learning anything about his guesses. So he is searching for an order where there is none that *he* could discover."[120]

And the result? At the conclusion of the experiment, A and B explain how to distinguish healthy from malignant cells: A's explanation is simple and economical. B's is complex, convoluted. B's explanation must be necessarily complex because his deductions are based both on correct and incorrect information. How do A and B react to each other's stories? A is impressed with the "brilliance" of B's theory. "A tends to feel inferior and vulnerable because of the pedestrian simplicity of his assumption, and the more complicated B's 'delusions,' the more likely they are to convince A."[121] Watzlawick terms this an example of the "contagiousness of delusions." A and B then take the identical test again, but with different cell slides. When the As and Bs are asked who will fare better on the second round, "all Bs and most As say that B will," and although B performs about the same, A performs more poorly because he has tried to apply B's explanation to distinguishing healthy and sick cells.

Watzlawick's example applies to cult cops. B cop has attended a cult seminar and has begun to reshape his world-view according to the seminar doctrine. He, in turn, teaches A. A becomes impressed with B's model of criminality, which offers a unifying theme to connect quite disparate and apparently unrelated phenomena. A, in adopting B's model, begins to apply it. A becomes a less efficient officer because his newly acquired model of criminality leads him down the wrong path to detecting crime; he spends time pursuing wrong leads, information unrelated to crime, and interviews and maintains records on people with no criminal involvement but with nonconformist beliefs or attitudes. Finally, A becomes less efficient and productive as a law enforcer once he, too, begins to teach cult seminars. Once a police officer has attended cult seminars and has converted to the new world-view with its model of criminality, new information can never violate or correct the seminar model; rather, new information—no matter what it is—will be taken to elaborate or refine the model. So the thought bubble becomes "self-sealing"—"it is a conjecture that cannot be refuted."[122] Through the self-sealing premise, "one arrives at an ultimate certainty of sorts. If the premise is that prayer can heal illness, then a patient's death 'proves' that he lacked faith, which in turn 'proves' the correctness of the premise."[123] Watzlawick cautions about what self-sealing premises can lead to:

> Conjectures of the kind we are considering here are thus pseudoscientific, superstitious, and ultimately, in a very real sense, psychotic. As we look at world history, we find that similarly "irrefutable" conjectures have been responsible for the worst atrocities. The Inquisition, ideas of racial superiority, the claim of totalitarian ideologies to have found the ultimate answer, immediately come to mind. . . .[124]

In constructing a new reality, cult cops rely on superstition to impose meaning on the otherwise explainable. Because the other explanations for inexplicable criminal acts do not invoke a smudgy notion called "evil," fundamentalist Christian cult cops easily substitute their theology in place of empiricism, and nonfundamentalist cult-cops posit a secular evil within the frame of civil blasphemy. And in either case, new facts or suppositions, whether contrary to cult-cop ideology or not, are either denied or incorporated as further proofs of conspiratorial devilry. Proofs and disproofs both vindicate the self-sealing premises of cult-cop theories.

I conclude this section on the application of folklore studies to the proliferation of satanic scares with an examination of an Illinois rumor-panic, one not explicated by sociologists at the time, in which all of the characteristics of such panics—as analyzed by either Watzlawick, Bromley, Victor, or Rossen—appear.

In July 1987, in Ogle County, Illinois, a young adult and a teen committed suicide. Ogle County Sheriff Jerry Brooks posited a connection between the deaths and the occult, which he refused to disclose to the press. Alarmed by the presence of the occult, Brooks invited cult-cop Donald Story, chief of police of the Matteson Police Department (who co-authored a paper on cults and teens that helped justify the Hartgrove Hospital teen treatment center described in the last chapter) to give a seminar. Like many proselytes, Brooks said, after attending Story's seminar, "We may have seen signs of ritualistic cults in the past, but we didn't really know how to recognize them."[125] Story pandered a familiar litany: that Satanists simply reverse the notions of good and bad; that Satanists "worship self-indulgence"; that Satanists occupy tiers of a model, ranging from dabblers to the "very secretive and highly structured" covert, multigenerational Satanists. Of course, youth involvement is on the rise. Story introduced many of the usual, unchallenged assertions: "Go into a bookstore sometime and try to find a book on satanism. Bookstores can't keep them on the shelf, they sell so fast."[126]

(In fact, cult cops frequently offer this statement to prove the popularity of satanic beliefs, usually referring specifically to *The Satanic Bible*. When journalist Ann Rodgers-Melnick heard two "independent charismatic evangelists," John Baker and Larry Mitchell, say this during a tour of churches in which they gave cult presentations, she challenged the assertion. Baker and Mitchell claimed that *The Satanic Bible* was the best-selling book in the Waldenbooks chain, far surpassing sales of the Holy Bible. Yet Dara Tyson, spokesperson for Waldenbooks corporate headquarters in Stamford, Connecticut, told Rodgers-Melnick: "We don't even keep [*The Satanic Bible*] in most of our stores, because there isn't much demand for it." As for how it stacks up to the Christian Bible, Tyson said: "There's no comparison. The Bible is a perennial bestseller."[127] In fact, Rodgers-Melnick found that in the twenty years since its publication, *The Satanic Bible* has sold 618,000 copies, a mere fraction of the two million copies sold of Mike

Warnke's *The Satan Seller,* a Christian polemic against Satanism, which has been in bookstores for only 18 years.)

Story concluded his lecture by asserting the existence of between 5,000 and 7,000 satanic cults operating in the United States, an unfounded figure. He cautioned that Satanists vandalize churches and steal religious artifacts. Ironically, Story hinted at the formation of his own thought bubble. "Previously police officers would see these things, but would assume it was just vandalism," Story said. *"The more we train people to see the signs, the more we're going to see"* (italics added).[128] As for signs in kids, Story said, police should watch for an interest in heavy-metal music, the drawing of satanic graffiti, and obsessions with death.

In August 1987, details began to emerge about the suicide of a 19-year-old pizza delivery boy, Kevin Merfeld. According to friends and acquaintances, just before his death, Kevin attended a séance given by a "high priest of satanic worship."[129] Kevin apparently became quite disturbed about what had happened during the séance. According to his mother, Beverly Merfeld, "He said he didn't believe in what they were doing, and some of the people threatened to lock him in the basement." But the boy later disappeared and eventually turned up dead in the basement of his friend's house. The friend, Chip Oswald, 19, was arrested for the murder of both Kevin and Chip's father, who was also found dead in the home. Friends of Chip said that he "was interested in Satan and that he was kind of weird about it."[130] The séance-leader was not a suspect.

In September 1987, Beverly Merfeld became increasingly convinced that Satanism had played an important role in the deaths and began a public campaign to draw the attention of authorities. She claimed that Chip Oswald had "attended a so-called black mass the night of the slaying."[131] Beverly Merfeld's suspicions bore characteristics of a hysterical response, her evidence part and parcel of the cult-cop thought bubble. "Merfeld has received phone calls that cryptically provide insights into the minds of the numerous young adults apparently involved with a group of so-called satanic worshipers. Callers told her that among worshipers, it is a matter of honor to kill a parent, particularly a father. Only then, say the young people, can they become the 'children of Satan.' "[132] While Paul Logli, the Winnebago County state's attorney, did not deny Chip Oswald's interest in Satanism, he said that the evidence "does not indicate that the occult or his involvement in it was a motivating factor. . . . There's nothing now that draws a direct link between the occult and the murders." But Mrs. Merfeld found such denial "ridiculous" and embarked on a public campaign so that "people [will] know there's a danger out there to their children." What did Beverly Merfeld cite as evidence of the "satanic overtones" in the deaths? First, Kevin had been stabbed to death with a sword, "a weapon which traditionally plays a central role in satanic and black magic rituals" (although in such rituals, the sword's use is only symbolic). Second, a local youth, a self-proclaimed "high priest" of Satanism, held a black mass a week before Kevin died (implying causality). Third, a search of Chip's house revealed drawings of "a goat's head adorned with a religious symbol, and a cross positioned upside down—both classic satanic symbols." Fourth, Chip wrote a term paper on the occult in high school. And, finally, Chip had tried to beat up an acquaintance who told him his Satanism was "garbage." "Now that I know how deeply involved Chip [was] in all this, I can't believe satanism didn't have something to do with" the killings, Beverly Merfeld said.[133]

From September to November 1987, community members responded to the satanic allegations. In a letter to the September 20 *Register Star,* Neva Grady deprecated the public library's having *The Satanic Bible* on its shelves: "Why did the library buy such a book in the first place? The police and some parents are fighting satanism and the good library is putting the satanism bible on the shelves." Following Geraldo Rivera's record-breaking Halloween broadcast on Satanism, in the November 24 issue of the *Register Star,* Kari Martenson wrote to defend the program. "I would like to reach out to everyone out there and tell them that satanism is real and it will not go away without everybody becoming aware of its powers. . . ." Margo Sears wrote, in the same issue, criticizing the U.S. Army for including a section on Satanism in their chaplains' handbook (which she learned from watching the Geraldo Rivera special): "I realize that no one can stop satanism, but as a Christian I believe that it should be somewhere on the record that I object to this material being printed, and that part of my tax dollars are being used to print this garbage."

In December 1987, an assailant clubbed a 17-year-old as he walked home from his job. The *Register Star* headlines announced: "Devil worship suspected in assault on 17-year-old."[134] Why devil worship? The assailant, "with bizarre face makeup," had confronted the boy and asked him for a cigarette. When the boy said that he had none, the man clubbed him, then ran off. According to the victim, the "symbol of devil worship" brandished by the mugger was in the form of an earring depicting an upside-down cross. "Police said that [the earring], and the inverted triangles centered in black paint around the man's eyes, are recognized as symbols of satanism."[135]

In April 1988, a man found "a wooden altar" decorated with a painted pentagram in his barn in the Rockford area. Candles were found on each of the star's points. Local police announced that the pentagram symbolized "the devil and the conjuring of evil spirits, according to Police Department reference materials."[136]

In May 1988, police blamed arson for a fire that destroyed five farm buildings, "and detectives said they are investigating a possible link with occult worship."[137] Again, why the cult connection? Although "no signs of devil worship were found in the burned rubble," Sergeant LaVerne Pickett of the Rockford police said "a detective who specializes in devil-worship cases was assigned to the investigation," although the only satanic evidence was an altar and a pentagram found in a barn the previous month at another site. But detectives cited the arson as falling close to Beltane, a major cult holiday (April 30).

In November 1988, a dead, eviscerated deer turned up in a high-school parking lot surrounded by four purple wax skulls. Lieutenant Joe Walker of the Rockford Police Department said that a pentagram was found nearby. "What we found has definite ritualistic overtones to it," he said, although police did not know how the deer had died.[138] By contrast, the school spokeswoman said that it was probably a prank, with no evidence that schoolchildren were involved. Nevertheless, the school-district directors of elementary and secondary education asked police "to talk about ritualism and the occult." Thus, the local cult cops entered the scene. Detective Larry Anduino said, "Our concern is the criminal violations. These people, from what we've been able to learn, are into the ritualistic abuse of children and the ritualistic sexual abuse of children. This [the deer killing] is highly unusual, one of the first times we've seen it in this area."[139] No one established a relationship between the deer and the pentagram; and because the purple skulls coupled with the deer obviously intimidated school officials, cult cops could now parley their hysteria to the public schools.

In December 1988, vandals attacked a small market repeatedly, stealing money and candles, painting the cash register red, damaging a Christmas display and produce, "meticulously smash[ing] five cases of apples."[140] But while investigating the incident, the nearby Roscoe police found "possible links with satanism and far-right groups." In particular, "The vandals painted deer ornaments, but defaced only the heads and tails of the animals, suggesting members of satanic cults were the culprits. That, combined with the theft of the candles and three red swastikas painted on some ornaments was enough to make Police Chief Richard Lee consider the link."[141] As I suggested in Chapter 2 regarding the satanic musings of cult cop Jerry Simandl of the Chicago Police, where vandalism is concerned (a crime that nets precious few leads or suspects), one can indeed obtain wholesale returns of conjecture based on very little. Most kids who commit vandalism do so pretty mindlessly, spray-painting any intimidating symbols that occur to them. But Chief Lee decided against the Satanism hypothesis. "We think it might have been people trying to make it look like a cult act," he said. Chief Lee summed up the situation by saying, "It looked like they were trying to take out their frustrations." He also discounted the notion that the swastika was in any way related to one painted at the site of a synagogue under construction in Beloit, Wisconsin.

In April 1989, a workshop was held for 11- to 14-year-old students at a local school; it featured Satanism as well as other teen concerns, such as pregnancy, AIDS, and self-esteem. Commented David Dixon, a 13-year-old who recognizes satanic symbols but didn't know their meanings: "We're curious about satanism. Not because I want to get into it, but to make sure friends of my own or people I meet aren't into it."[142] And since the school seminar followed closely the Matamoros murders, kids were a bit frightened. One teen, 13-year-old Eric Bliss, "found deer skeletons in a wooded area near his home. He wonders whether the bones are the result of animal sacrifices to Satan." Illinois State Police "cult expert" Jan Stanton spoke at the seminar, saying, "It [Satanism] may be a fad just like other fads, but it should not be ignored."[143]

Both cult cops and citizens in the Rockford area, for more than a year, seemed willing to leap to satanic explanations for a variety of unsavory goings-on, from murder to vandalism. Once the notion of satanic practices took root, the community mind created an ideological bubble that fed on the absence of immediate explanations by inventing the Other, a demonic mind beyond and separate from the virtues of family and faith. One influential citizen of Rockford, David R. Weissbard, senior minister of the Rockford Unitarian Church, took some time to investigate the area incidents and to interview people; he offered some conclusions in a sermon. He traced the history of Satan in our culture, discussed Satan's relationship to church history, and made observations about the allegations in Rockford, in part based on "an extended conversation with one of the Rockford Police detectives who has been trained in cult activity and specializes in that area." What did the minister conclude?

> There is no evidence that Satan, or his followers, are any more active in Rockford, Illinois in 1989 than in Salem, Massachusetts in 1692.
> It has been said that those who refuse to learn from history are doomed to repeat it. Let us learn, and let us have the courage to speak up in defense of those whose cause may be scorned by others, so that the attention of our community can be focused on the very real problems it faces, and not be distracted by the boogie men who are sacrificing imaginary children at the altar of Satan.[144]

Most disturbing was the world-view of cult cops that the minister encountered through his inquiry.

> The more I have thought about this, the more I have begun to feel that we may be in more danger from professionals whose world view enables them to buy into a belief in Satanic cults operated by community leaders, than we are from such cults. Such people can, no matter how sincere, how well intended they are, serve as the basis of a witch hunt in which real evidence becomes irrelevant.
> The police detective asked me, toward the end of our conversation, how he could be sure that I was not a member of the Satan cult, sent to find

out how much the police knew about it. I acknowledged that he could not know. I thought of that when I read about what happened to the people of Salem who stood up against the witch hunters. Obviously, they were part of the problem, and they were executed.[145]

From the minister's perspective, the police detective, a proselyte in the cause of law-enforcement righteousness, could also have been a satanic plant to mislead the public away from the true proclivities of the Rockford Satanic Lodge. A member of the Unitarian congregation, a counselor who had a client involved in Satanism, maintains that the police gave him names of prestigious community members, "prominent psychologists, ministers, lawyers," believed to be Satanists. And the Rockford police continue their mission; they have made available nationwide a training booklet and investigative guide for law officers entitled, "Ritualistic Crimes." According to Detective L. Slaughter with the Rockford Police Crime Prevention Unit, the guide accompanies an "informational" program "to be given to parents' groups, social workers, teachers, and other interested parties. . . . We feel we have a responsibility to inform these groups of the nature of this type of activity and how it can evolve into outright criminal activity. . . . Our program . . . [focuses] on fantasy games, Heavy Metal music influences, and how these influences can affect some young impressionable minds."[146] Slaughter further explained that a number of officers had received training in how to conduct "ritualistic crime" investigations. But what does the investigative guide contain? Virtually all of the information consists of reprinted seminar handouts showing satanic signs and symbols and providing a glossary of terms along with the inevitable checklists. And most of the information was reprinted from Dale Griffis's materials.

Some skeptical observers point out that the satanic panic may not hurt anyone, since, unlike Jews or blacks or other ethnic minorities, the covert Satanists are fair game for anyone; after all, they don't live in ghettos, worship in recognized public places, or assume a public role in the community. But when police not only suspect but are willing to slander citizens, people do suffer. I have recounted in this book enough examples of damaged reputations, wrongful arrests, and probable cause based on zealotry and nonfacts to argue that people do suffer hurt because of satanic panics. In Chapter 1, I drew the analogy between the cult cops and the witchfinders of a few centuries ago. Do the witch-finding episodes of centuries past provide a comparison with the inquisitional process employed or recommended by cult cops, and do they constitute a precursor of more to come?

Witch-finding

That Satanists are safe scapegoats because they cannot be easily identified for public vilification is, as I noted above, a flawed observation. People suffer *precisely* because evil-doers can be *anyone,* according to the conspiracies put forth by cult cops. That suspicion can fall on anyone has historical precedent:

> Why were witches singled out for a more total and hysterical hatred than any of the other outcasts of Christian society? Perhaps because, unlike Jews, lepers, or out-of-favor politicians, they were *not* physically identifiable, so that the number upon whom guilt and fear could be projected was almost unlimited.[147]

I don't propose a history of witchcraft, so I'll restrict my discussion to that which is relevant to interpreting the behavior of cult cops as witch-finders. Witchcraft as a felonious offense does not, in fact, have a long history. Not until late in the reign of Elizabeth I did witchcraft in England— which supposedly involved the calling up of devils and service in fealty to Satan—stand condemned as a serious crime. The narrative elements of witchcraft accusations—and even some confessions—revealed similar elements: "secret interviews with the Evil One, promises of worldly riches, a contract sealed with blood, little shapes of dogs, cats, and hares, clay pictures that had been dried and had crumpled, threats and consequent 'languishing' and death. . . ."[148] But the crime was heresy. "European witchcraft is best considered a form of heresy, for in order to worship the Christian Devil one must first be a Christian."[149] The powers one acquired as a witch were almost secondary to the pact with Satan, the renunciation of faith, so the heresy of witchcraft was actually a "thought crime."[150] The specific rites and rituals of witchcraft, such as kissing the Devil's arse, *sabbat* ceremonies, the pact with Satan, and the Devil's mark, were all theological inventions that elaborated on the heresy. Historian Jeffrey Burton Russell remarks that the "development of medieval witchcraft is closely bound to that of heresy, the struggle for the expression of religious feeling beyond the limits tolerated by the Church."[151]

Nevertheless, comparisons of cult cops as witch-finders to the witchcraft trials and purges of the mid-sixteenth through the early-eighteenth centuries requires a more exact delineation of the historical context. Modern ethnographies of non-Western cultures that feature witches—such as the Navajo Indian conception of witches and the practice of witchcraft, which I mentioned in Chapter 3—do not bear strict comparison to medieval and Renaissance European witchcraft. Even within Europe, one can distinguish English attitudes toward witches and the legal process of witch-finding from that known on the European continent. Witchcraft prosecutions on the continent multiplied with virtually no legal or institutional restraints.[152] Because of the supernatural nature of witchcraft, standard forms of evidence did not necessarily apply, so shortcuts presented themselves, such as the use of testimony by only one witness (as opposed to two, normally required in criminal cases), supplemented by the regular use of torture. But the standard constraints on testimonial evidence disappeared; disreputable or incompetent witnesses, such as criminals and children, could testify in witchcraft cases, but not in other types. And standards of proof in European trials were opened to the same pseudoscientific reasoning that cult cops evince: if a person accused of witchcraft could summon reputable citizens to testify to the defendant's good character, the court took such testimony as *proof* of witchcraft, since no right-minded responsible citizen could approve of a witch! And if the accused witch offered up her public reputation for piety and service to the church, one again had evidence of devilry; after all, Satan encouraged his witches to appear very forward in a show of religious fervor. Witches in European trials could never demonstrate innocence.

The witch-finding process in England forms a closer analogy to the crusade of cult cops. Witchcraft trials were modernized with a public trial (unlike secret ones on the continent), involved a jury, and separated the processes of prosecution and subsequent judgment. And unlike courts on the continent, English ones at least operated on a presumption of innocence, although their standards of proof of criminal guilt remained rather loose. Torture remained illegal, which meant that witchcraft cases presented difficulties in prosecution; without torture, many accused witches might not confess. And witnesses might not surface to testify to witchcraft. But like the continental inquisition, English courts found that unusual crimes demanded unusual evidence. "Three sources of external evidence became especially significant in English witch trials. These were pricking, swimming, and watching."[153]

Pricking presumed that witches bore the Devil's mark; inquisitors would search a witch's body with a needle, pricking here and there until a spot insensitive to pain could be found. Once found, the Devil's mark would imply guilt. Swimming involved stripping the accused, binding hands to feet (or right thumb to right toe, left thumb to left toe), and tossing the defendant into a stream, pond, or lake. Since air represented the witch's element, a witch would naturally rise to the surface of the water, returning to her element: the defendant, if a witch, should not sink. Of course, if the accused sank and remained under water, she would be vindicated, although also drowned. Finally, watching involved forced, around the-clock surveillance of the witch. The watchers would wait to catch the act of communication between the witch and her familiars. Since inquisitors assumed that the Devil, in fulfillment of the pact with the witch, provided imps or demons to assist her, sooner or later they would return to the witch to be suckled. Woe to the alleged witch if a cockroach should amble into the room. But since witchcraft trials required extraordinary proofs, inquisitors not only invented pricking, swimming, and watching, but conducted trials ad hoc and invented new techniques or methods of ascertaining guilt when necessary. In the Salem trials, for instance, spectral evidence played a key role; that is, in the course of the trial, witnesses (young girls) claimed to see demons flying about; their hysterial reactions to the visions, which none other could see, were taken as evidence of witchcraft. (Here I have repeatedly referred to the accused as "she"; such institutionalized violence against women constitutes another sociological tangent beyond the concern of this book. In this section I am concerned with the process of witch-finding. Today's witch-finding, by contrast, at least recognizes equal opportunity for both sexes.)

Whereas on the European continent the witch-finding bureaucracy became self-sustaining and powerful, in part due to the courts' jurisdiction, which extended even to confiscating witches' property (which ensured that the ranks of the accused included the rich) and forcing the accused to pay the expenses of their own trials, in England no such bureaucracy existed. Because English courts could not confiscate the property of witches, not surprisingly those accused were socially powerless. Ad hoc methods, devised in response to local rumor panics about witchcraft, required a new expertise to conduct prosecutions. Itinerant witch-finders surfaced; for a fee, they guaranteed to find witches. Similarly, subspecialties evolved, such as prickers and watchers. The most notorious English witch-finder of the mid-seventeenth century was Mathew Hopkins, who even hired assistants; he was responsible for the deaths of at least a hundred witches. Witch-finders were self-proclaimed experts in detecting and prosecuting witches and earned generous fees from credulous local authorities. Hopkins, in fact, was an obscure minister's son who worked in maritime law, courted influential friends, and happened to intervene in the right local circumstances at the right time to garner a reputation for finding witches. Although only in his mid-twenties, he became very successful by exploiting the turmoil of the English Civil Wars, although he also stimulated much opposition; in fact, a hostile village crowd supposedly subjected him to a test of swimming, which he failed, coming near the end of his ascendancy. Hopkins was forced, in 1647, to publish a defense of his activities under the title, *The Discovery of Witches*. In defense of his acquired expertise, he wrote:

Querie 3: From whence then proceeded this his skill? Was it from his profound learning, or from much reading of learned Authors concerning that subject?

Answer: From neither of both, but from experience, which though it be meanly esteemed of, yet the surest and safest way to judge by.[154]

In other words, Hopkins read a lot of books and developed expertise as a witch-finder by proclaiming himself a witch-finder. Although Hopkins had no professional credentials in law, he did read much; he studied some law and read voraciously on witchcraft, incorporating many Continental ideas in his work. He learned enough about the law to exploit dormant statutes and obscurities in legal procedure. Theoretically, witches faced capital punishment only if their enchantment caused the death of another (deriving from an Elizabethan statute); so in order to reach the death penalty, Hopkins had to employ extreme methods not only to wring confessions from accused women but also to establish a causal link between the acts of the accused and the misfortune of others. Hopkins engaged in a precarious business, relying on local panic and credulity in order to avoid charges that his own arcane knowledge of witchcraft targeted him for accusation.

As Elliott P. Currie argues, deviant behavior is whatever the authorities say it is. Therefore, authorities identify deviants. If the deviant act doesn't exist, then authorities must necessarily focus on the deviant. Thus, witchcraft became "an *invented* form of deviance, whose definition lack[ed] roots in concrete behavior."[155] By extension, Currie suggests, "There may be a large element of invention in current American definitions of mental illness, and perhaps drug addiction; there is less in the definition of murder or battery."[156] But the United States government—like all governments—invents categories of social deviants to serve political ends; the current demonology about those who buy or sell narcotics and dangerous drugs might serve as an example. Later in this chapter I take up the topic of governmental myth-making about criminality. But government mythmaking and the invention of deviance by government officials begs the question of abuses of power: the persecutions of those who harbor different beliefs or customs from the rest of us. Again, Currie notes:

> The case of witchcraft in England shows that virtually no amount of limitation on the power of a control system can consistently and effectively protect individuals against such abuse once an invented definition of deviance has become officially established. Beyond this, invented deviance undermines the ability of control agencies to maintain procedural integrity.[157]

Jerry D. Rose's study, *Outbreaks,* subtitled "The Sociology of Collective Behavior," chronicles and explicates major persecutory episodes in European history, offering an analysis of why systems of social control reach "the point of an almost obsessive public fear of the dangers emanating from some category of persons," whether witches or otherwise.[158] Whether the purported deviant is a witch, heretic, racial minority, Jew, or unpopular political group, the process of persecution follows a predictable path. First, Rose hypothesizes that a major persecution might occur when a majority population perceives a threat as the consequence "of the willful actions of an identifiable group of sub-human evil-doers"; the persecution takes off when the majority can mobilize officials to take action.[159] In discussing outbreaks of witchcraft persecution, I have not placed sufficient emphasis on the stressful social circumstances that inevitably precede a persecution. Studies of rumor-panics and subversion myths all try to describe precipitating social stresses, anxieties, and apprehensions. Rose, for example, cites the modernization of social life as a persistent stressor; rapid social changes always accompany witch-finding episodes. Insightful studies of the Salem trials offer many examples of such stresses: political and religious disagreements with governing officials, the emergence of capitalism and economic competition. For example, in Salem in 1692, the accusers were "traditional farmers" from the Salem village, whereas the accused persons came from "the industrial-commercial *town* of Salem," a conflict reflecting "sharp ambivalence of Salem villagers toward the modern capitalist world."[160] One particularly prevalent stressor is "intolerance for international ambiguity,"[161] which allies closely with difficulties in adjusting to and accommodating cultural pluralism. For example, parts of the United States have seen large immigrant populations of Asians, Cubans, and other Caribbean populations who celebrate traditions and beliefs that are dubbed satanic at cult seminars.

The threat of harm from putative deviants evolves through exaggeration, distortion, and fantasy, and occasionally certain "vested interests" may even contribute to exaggerations and rumors about the threat, further heightening public fear. But witches, occultists, and Satanists present to modern Americans a *moral* threat to a Christian way of life. Indeed, the historical persecution of witches derives from their moral affront: after all, they were *heretics*. But to carry out retaliation against the perceived social threat, the majority comes to see the minority as the scapegoat for various ills, and the consequent logical step, then, is to dehumanize the scapegoat; Satanists, after all, don't deserve fair play. They forfeit their civil liberties *because* they are Satanists. The dehumanizing process involves the formation of conspiracy theories: "Especially intense fear of a social enemy can be generated if it can be shown that there is a secret and powerful conspiracy among evildoers."[162] To dehumanize supposed Satanists, we accuse them of the ritualized abuse of children, the torture, mutilation, and sacrifice of innocents in fealty to Satan, plus the rest of the grab bag of satanic *maledicta*.

Once the majority has aroused and mobilized itself to persecute an internal enemy, authorities cite civil liberties as impediments to rooting out subversives. Elsewhere in this book I have cited this logic as the necessity argument: the threat looming over us all demands extreme, immediate actions, so we must therefore unfetter ourselves from the Bill of Rights. In a similar tone, cult cops and "believer" therapists and psychiatrists disdainfully observe how subversives receive First Amendment protections as a cloak to their nefarious undertakings. "People may not be deprived of life, liberty, or property without due process of law, and this due process is a thorn in the side of many would-be persecutors who claim that public enemies can use the cloak of civil liberties to avoid their being brought to heel."[163] Once authorities find a way to circumvent civil liberties, a specialized inquisitional process evolves: enter the witch-finder or, for our purposes, the cult cop and his allies—fundamentalist Christians with political clout, believer therapists, and outspoken parents. The advent of the witch-finder represents a "professionalized" finding of enemies, a way of giving an official nod to an irresponsible persecution that transgresses civil liberties and leaves the entrenched authorities with clean hands. But the witch-finder doesn't do his job *in vacuo:* popular support is necessary. Witch-finders court it. After all, cult cops speak to packed houses, usually comprised of non-law-enforcement professionals: parents, educators, and mental-health professionals.

As Benjamin Rossen's study of the Oude-Pekela rumor panic shows, persecutions take place with public support, but precipitating events of real or imagined horror must first occur to trigger an inquisition. News media play an important role, but occasionally, and perhaps curiously, some persecution victims may even participate in exaggerating public fears. Some people do in fact suffer delusions of involvement during a rumor-panic. But during the persecution, the number of suspects multiplies; during the McCarthy hearings of the early 1950s, for example, suspects were encouraged to name communists, a form of public confession that purged them of guilt. When more names surface in such cases, investigation intensifies and commands greater and greater resources. The naming of names daunts skeptics or opponents from surfacing to challenge the inquisition.

Eventually, the persecution winds down. Usually it does so for reasons of costs and benefits; the benefits of trying witches pale compared to the cost of the prosecution. Concerning European witchcraft trials, Currie notes that "the trials terminated not because the judges no longer believed in witchcraft but because they came to doubt their own ability to extirpate witchcraft without destroying the foundations of their communities."[164] But sometimes the persecution wanes because the naming of names extends to "important vested interests that were immune from victimization at the start."[165] In the Salem trials, the furor began to dissipate once the witnesses began to accuse prominent people in power, such as the Massachusetts governor's wife. In Bakersfield, California, the child-abuse allegations eventually singled out the very officials conducting the case. Or the persecution may die because "there are many self-limiting tendencies that [cause a] persecution [to] burn itself out in the absence of external controls."[166]

Based on the foregoing, I posit several analogies between the witch-finding inquisitions of centuries ago in English history and the work of cult cops.

1. *Heresy and civil blasphemy.* The historical distance between modern cult seminars with their recommended police strategies and the heretical basis for witchcraft persecutions creates some problems for comparing the two. Witchcraft trials existed within a medieval thought-world "where the spiritual world was considered as real or even more real than the material, [and] tension and hostility tended to be expressed in spiritual rather than material terms. This explains the wide emotional appeal of heresy. . . . Witchcraft was therefore the strongest possible religious expression of social discontent."[167] Nevertheless, if we accept the term *civil blasphemy* as a contemporary substitute for *heresy,* as a secularization of heresy, then we create a useful analogy. A heretic repudiated not only the established faith but also the entire social order governed by that faith. Similarly, a blasphemer in a civil sense has repudiated social stability and the sacrosanct domain of the pristine child (and therefore the family that rears the child) by *deliberately inverting* common notions of good and evil, right and wrong, legal and illegal, appropriate and inappropriate. Something faintly mythological lurks behind this inversion, with cult cops alleging that Satanists have inverted every moral truth. Further, neither the heretic nor the civil blasphemer can be recognized readily: the nature of the accusation of witch or Satanist can apply to anyone, hence the invention of these two types of deviance and the definition of *sui generis* deviant behavior. Indeed, as Thomas Schoeneman points out, "Witch hunts often create the phenomena to which they are supposedly reacting. Witch-finding techniques operate along the lines of a self-fulfilling prophecy: they are designed to confirm rather than refute the prevalent demonology."[168]

2. *Thought crime.* Because officials with authority invent the categories of deviance and the implied deviant behavior, anyone can be a suspect. Similarly, during the inquisition that accompanies persecution, authorities encourage suspects to name other culprits. The production of lists of names also reifies notions of conspiracies by providing proof to the public of how many people involved themselves in witchcraft then or in Satanism now, clearly illustrating the extent to which deviants have permeated all segments of society. During investigations of purported satanic activities at day-care centers, interviewers pressed children to name other children and culpable adults. Criminal investigations driven more by a search for Satan than a careful consideration of available facts have been concerned with naming suspects and little else. That the modern police pursuit of Satan takes the form of thought crime shows up in the cult seminars; despite admonitions to respect First Amendment rights, cult cops proceed to label books and music as dangerous and to encourage officers to name such materials in search warrants in order to confiscate them. Even worse, some cult cops

have labeled certain people as satanic cult members, and have provided this information to others.

3. *Pseudoscientific logic.* As many skeptics, scholars, and others have pointed out about anything paranormal, occultic, and now satanic, an unusual or extraordinary claim requires similarly extraordinary proof. I have argued that modern satanic panics produce a self-referential, solipsistic thought bubble, a microcosm of causal ideas fed and encouraged by those who have succumbed to the panic. The thought bubble absorbs any new challenge or disagreement in one of two ways: either the disproof becomes proof (easy to do with nonfalsifiable hypotheses; one simply asserts that evidence that appears to negate the hypothesis actually confirms it), or, if the new information challenges the satanic model in a fundamental way, the information gets ignored and declared irrelevant. Sometimes new information must be interpreted in a radical way; the interpretation might strain credulity by posing even a supernatural explanation. In the witchcraft trials, tests evolved out of folk wisdom, rumor, and anachronistic science, or were invented out of sheer desperation for finding methods to prove beyond a reasonable doubt the truth of the accusation. But devising abstract tests of pricking, swimming, and watching does not differ from constructing checklists predicting that children who talk about death, or who fart or show aggressive behavior now and then have been abused by Satanists. Nor do they differ from the psychiatrists who predict that an abused child will usually deny the abuse and not consider the option that the denial means that no abuse occurred. Such pseudoscientific tests suggest self-fulfilling prophecies: one *will* find what one has devised the test or checklist to find.

The tests of deviance must be detached from common notions of proof or, in a legal sense, probable cause or proof beyond a reasonable doubt. To successfully detach from such concepts, the tests necessarily abandon the idea of corroboration except in a very loose sense. To a credulous public, the findings in such tests need corroboration only in a roughshod, nebulous way; better yet, standards of corroboration for witchfinding tests can be simply *invented.*

4. *Mass hysteria derives from social tension.* A vast amount of literature exists that describes the social tensions and stresses that accompanied witchcraft persecutions. The sociological literature on contemporary rumor-panics does the same. Scholars find universal agreement that such stresses precipitate witch-finding. By inventing new categories of deviance and ways to identify deviance, authorities attack those stresses in order to change their own cultures. In fact, a society's focus on the persecution of non-conformists, or of anyone designated a witch becomes a mechanism for cultural change.[169] Our modern preoccupation with day-care cases and other kinds of child abuse has led to judicial innovations regarding the handling

of children's testimony and to a new stature generally for child-abuse cases within criminal justice. The long-term cultural changes that will derive from our satanic panic are difficult to predict at present.

If we accept Benjamin Rossen's definition of mass hysteria and his description of how otherwise sober, discriminating people fall prey to it, then we see immediate parallels between modern community responses to Satanism and the sixteenth- and seventeenth-century English responses to witches. People enter into mass hysteria gradually by digesting progressively subversive stories about the Other, the witch, the Satanist. Once a mind begins to attach veracity to such rumors, or at least becomes quite fearful, then one willingly accepts increasingly more outlandish assumptions, con- clusions, or "facts" about the Other's evil work. One resolves ambiguities into certainties, vague differences into polarities, confusion and uncertainty about how people behave and misbehave into simple tests or checklists. Quite simply, social stress, discord, confusion, and sudden misfortune all must have explanations and causes or life doesn't make sense. When a per- son joins others in a hysterical response, he or she thinks there is a clear vision of what's troubling people. People set up a moral enemy in the Other: defeat of the enemy will bring back goodness and light.

5. *The witch-finder.* Mathew Hopkins emerged from a nondescript background to visit nonurban localities, discover witches, and try them. He had no particular qualifications for this work, but simply proclaimed himself an expert and relied on his résumé of successes in other towns and villages to help prod local credulity in new communities. Hopkins and his assistants earned a living from this work, of course. Deviance became what Hopkins said it was. Rossen's model of a rumor panic can be ap- plied to Hopkins: his work helped exaggerate and distort notions about the evil doings of witches, he amplified the roles of the forces of good (even calling himself the "witch-finder general"), and he brought the machinery of government to bear to prosecute and dispose of witches. To- day's cult cops declare themselves experts in cults and Satanism, no matter how they define the terms, exploit local fears for the safety of children, and preach an ideology of generalized suspicion that heightens rather than allays fears. Their four-tiered model invents a form of deviance, one alleged to be deeply subversive but virtually impossible to detect in its extreme manifestations. Only the cult cop can truly spot the Other. But unlike Hopkins, cult cops cannot have Satanists lynched. Rossen's cycle of a moral or rumor panic predicts that as a subversive model begins to diffuse, governments or authorities may take formal steps to thwart the threat, or at the very least people will demand a formal response from such offi- cials. And cult cops have recently lobbied successfully for legislated ways to attack the Other.

Civil Liberties

During the 1988 presidential campaign, editor Rick O'Connell wrote in an editorial for *Crime Control Digest* that the new president must attend to "major criminal justice problems" in addition to drug trafficking. O'Connell listed three such problems: cults and associated crimes; hate-crime groups; and organized-crime groups, such as the new Asian, South American, and Jamaican gangs.[170]

> Challenges for the new Administration include how to investigate these cults. Where does the First Amendment of the Constitution fit in? And what can be done to stop them?
> Don't forget, these people are masters at the destruction of evidence and horrific subjects are getting into the big-time drug trafficking business.[171]

Law enforcers pose the same demand for official action at their cult seminars. Cult cops issue a call to arms whenever the chance arises. Several years ago, a law-enforcement periodical warned that "the major cult problem facing law-enforcement personnel involves cults which are religiously motivated, groups which hide their misdeeds under the cloak of the First Amendment. Their nefarious activities include: murder, extortion, espionage, drug smuggling, prostitution and child abuse, in addition to such subtle things as mind control and incite [*sic*] to riot."[172]

But cult cops have finally begun to lobby legislators. During legislative sessions in various states during 1989 and 1990, new criminal offenses have been proposed, some passed into law. A sample:

—Impassioned cult cops told the Texas legislature of ritual abuse of children and human sacrifice. Walker Veal of the Killeen Police Academy said that "he had seen a 'satanic calendar' on which some days were marked for human sacrifice, with the sex and age of the desired victim specified. 'Based on their calendars, we have reason to believe they are actually performing human sacrifices,' "[173] Veal told lawmakers. And if state legislators weren't impressed by the calendar, Veal pleaded that Texas must do something, at least, about women he knew who bred babies for sacrifice. At the request of Abilene police officer Lee Reed, state senator Judith Zaffirini introduced Section 49.01 to the Texas penal code, "Diabolic Cult Acts," which criminalizes a number of "ritualistic acts," ranging from consumption of human or animal blood to mutilation and dismemberment, to the more arcane "ritualistic physical abuse of a person" or "ritualistic psychological abuse of a person." The law defines "ritualistic" as "of or pertaining to an act or actions undertaken as part of a ceremony, rite, observance, or procedure intended to glorify." But as Debbie Nathan has pointed out, such law would criminalize the butchery of Thanksgiving turkeys, or even circumcisions.[174]

—The Illinois legislature passed an amendment to state code chapter 38, section 12-31 (under House Bill 1882), which declared the crime of "ritual mutilation," stating that the offense occurs when a person "mutilates, dismembers or tortures another person as part of a ceremony, rite, initiation, observance, performance or practice, and the victim did not consent." At least circumcisions were specifically excluded by addition of a section "c," which says as much. (HB 1882 became law on January 1, 1990.) As a related matter, House Bill 1883 proposed an amendment to the Illinois Juvenile Court Act of 1987, Chapter 37 of the criminal code, adding the offense of "inducement to commit suicide" (section 12-31). "A person commits the offense . . . when he coerces another to commit suicide and the other person commits suicide as a direct result of the coercion, and he exercises substantial control over the other person through" physical control, the "use of psychological pressure," or through the "use of . . . religious, political, social, philosophical or other principles." Clearly, HB 1883 aims to criminalize the behavior of role-playing game leaders if a player commits suicide. The Illinois Code of Corrections Section 5-5-3.2 (13)(B)(6) now states that "misconduct committed as part of a ceremony, rite, initiation, observance, performance, practice or activity of any actual or ostensible religious, fraternal, or social group" can be construed as aggravating circumstances used to lengthen sentences upon conviction.

—House Bill 1693 in the Pennsylvania legislature during the 1989 term prohibited "ritualistic acts," including "the ritualistic physical or psychological abuse of a child when undertaken as a part of a ceremony, rite, initiation, observance," and so on.

—House Bill 928 in Louisiana, 1989 session, proposes to enact a criminal prohibition concerning "the commission of certain deviant ritualistic acts as part of a ceremony, rite, initiation, observance," and so on, in familiar language.

—The Virginia General Assembly, during its 1990 session, passed House Joint Resolution 147, which directed the Virginia Crime Commission to undertake a "study of certain cult practices" in the state (based on testimonials by cult survivors). The bill provides for impossible tasks such as surveying the number of cults in Virginia "that emphasize or promote their members' participation in dangerous, antisocial, or criminal activities," but also proposes to examine law-enforcement problems with cults, "risk factors" governing youth involvement in cults, and the problems cult kids present in schools.

No one can predict the effects of such legislation. Certainly such statutes will not deter anyone from committing crimes; the laws simply provide prosecutorial leverage as well as creating fresh criminal categories for arrests. But when faced with a choice of arresting someone for a "ritualistic" offense or another crime that carries a stiffer penalty, the police will do the latter. Chances are, law enforcers will seek to apply the new statutes to arrest suspects who have transgressed the ambiguities of the new laws, such as causing "psychological abuse."

The Supreme Court has several times affirmed that religious views receive absolute protection, but religious acts receive only *some* protection. The Supreme Court in 1872 established this important and still-cited precedent: "The law knows no heresy, and is committed to the support of no dogma, the establishment of no sect" [*Watson v. Jones,* 13 Wallace 679 (1872)]. In more recent years, the Supreme Court has sought to define tests by which the state should or should not interfere with religious practices. In *Sherbert v. Verner,* the Supreme Court posed three questions:

> 1. Does the issue in question impose a burden on the exercise of religion?
> 2. If yes, does a compelling state interest justify the infringement?
> 3. If yes, the state must show that no alternative forms of regulation suffice to accomplish desired ends. [374 U.S. 398 (1963)]

If the new statutes undergo challenge on First Amendment grounds, the courts shouldn't examine the "truth" of religious claims, although they have sometimes done so, even sometimes examining the *sincerity* of belief.[175] Trying to apply all of this to law-enforcement purposes, FBI agents Orlin C. Luckstead and D. F. Martell, in a series of articles about cults (written before the current preoccupation with Satanism) discuss the constitutionality of intervention in religious practices, even sympathetically describing deprogramming (kidnapping) and its legal problems. Their articles posit a model of cults replete with mind-control methods and absolute loyalty to a charismatic leader, arguing that cults are somehow less "religious" than other beliefs because members give loyalty not to religious principles but rather to the cult leader. So what advice do the FBI agents give law enforcers?

> Congress, the U.S. Department of Justice, and State law enforcement agencies must be responsible enough to avoid interfering with religious belief; but, given this restraint, certain cult behavior (i.e., fraud, violence, deceptive practices) appears to result in substantial harm to society and this outweighs their first amendment protection. Moreover, some cult recruitment methods and behavior-control techniques indicate that decisions to join and remain in the cult often are not freely and voluntarily made.[176]

So what can an officer do? Orlin and Luckstead recommend investigating cults once it is suspected or learned that laws have been broken.

But short of waiting for evidence of criminality to surface, what is a cult cop to do? In the witchcraft cases, judicial methods became streamlined or truncated to make catching deviants easier. Modern cult cops invent other new methods for discovering the identities of true believers in the Evil One in their neighborhoods. Even *Mute Evidence* cites the example of Agent Joe Motsinger of the Iowa State Department of Criminal Investigation, who, in the late 1970s at least, believed in a cult connection between cattle mutilations and cults.[177] Investigators from Motsinger's department decided to visit the Des Moines public library to research the occult.

> When they got there, they found that almost all the books on occult practice and witchcraft, especially those books that had information about animal sacrifice, had been checked out. Thinking this might be an opportunity to make some progress in their investigation, the [criminal investigators] had asked the library to supply them with the names of the people who had taken out the books. The Department wanted to question those people. The Library director refused to give out the information.[178]

Motsinger tried a court order to force the library's hand, which solved nothing but brought lawsuits against his agency. Anyway, Motsinger found out what he wanted to know from other sources.

Motsinger's attempt on the library's patron list has become a de rigeur method among cult cops. Some law enforcers do not stop at book-stomping in their seminars and instead recommend obtaining patrons' lists from libraries. Dale Griffis, in fact, has advised law enforcers to approach local libraries to see who reads about the occult.[179] So has Larry Jones.[180] Similarly, the Rapides Parish Sheriff's Office in Louisiana tried to obtain a list of library patrons who borrowed books on the occult, this time through a subpoena.[181] But the local district attorney intervened and forced the sheriff's office to rescind the request; the chief deputy justified the subpoena by pointing out that "serious followers of satanic cults [connect their beliefs] with narcotics trafficking."[182] In Whitesboro, New York, both police and the local district attorney asked the library to provide names of patrons who borrowed books dealing with Satanism or the occult within the last four years.[183] Not only are law enforcers inspecting our reading habits, but members of the public have also challenged holdings in both public and school libraries on the basis of Satanism. The Missouri Coalition Against Censorship quoted a librarian who observed that "any title with the word *witch* in it," or books on the occult generally, "may be replacing abortion, evolution, and secular humanism as the focal point of conflict."[184] Examining lists of library patrons to see who reads what amounts to a First Amendment threat. Investigators who try this technique simply want to collect names of possible suspects to examine in future reports of occult-connected crimes, or as blind leads in cases with little evidence and no suspects.

New York City Police Department detectives of the "Swami Squad," investigating the multiple murders committed by a man named the "Zodiac killer" because of his post-murder use of zodiac symbols in letters to authorities, found themselves "interviewing psychics, speaking with seers and Satan worshipers and asking astrologers for advice" in an effort to understand their man and predict his next move.[185] Their investigation took them on a hunch to the New York Public Library, which first refused their request to view lists of patrons. Later armed with a subpoena, the officers "reviewed call cards" and ended up interviewing and fingerprinting "a young stockbroker" who had checked out Aleister Crowley's *Book of the Law*.[186] The connection with Crowley? None, apparently, other than the police officers' view that Crowley had inspired contemporary Satanists. The stockbroker didn't remotely match the suspect's description: the stockbroker is white, the murderer, black.

Satanic literature also shows up in prisons, which presents another facet of First Amendment problems. Recently, an Alabama prison denied an inmate *The Satanic Bible* and other related literature because possession of such material constituted a security threat. The inmate sued, alleging a civil-rights violation. The U.S. Circuit Court of Appeals, 11th Circuit, found the inmate was not entitled to such materials at the risk of prison security, but it did not exactly agree with the prison's contention that Satanism did not constitute a religion and therefore did not deserve constitutional protection, and that the inmate wasn't a "sincere believer" anyway. The court found:

> When it is alleged that a prison policy impinges on an inmate's constitutional rights, the policy is valid if it is reasonably related to legitimate penological interests. . . . The court finds that the policy at issue in the present case successfully withstands this scrutiny; it is not an exaggerated response to the situation. [*McCorkle v. Johnson* 881 F.2d 993 (11th Cir. 1989)]

Nevertheless, the court couldn't refrain from drawing a connection between belief in Satanism as defined by Anton LaVey's books and "the violence inherent" in the belief and the "potential disorder" such beliefs would cause in a prison. The prison warden testified that *The Satanic Bible* taught people to "murder, rape, or rob at will without regard for the moral or legal consequences." The court accepted the warden's pronouncements on Satanism without further inquiry or analysis.

Whether prisons will continue to confiscate satanic materials and whether cult cops will use libraries as informants represent a few of the possible First Amendment issues that will continue to surface over occultanalia, because cult cops continue to parrot fundamentalist Christian claims about dangerous books and music. A recent issue of *College Security Report* alerts higher-education professionals to satanic misery on campuses and derives its arguments almost exclusively from fundamentalist Christian sources.[187]

The article on Satanism even encouraged police officers to monitor college courses:

> Many investigators are concerned with the growing number of courses on the occult being taught in many colleges and universities. "It is a very subtle form of introduction to satanism that the college administration should be aware of," says [Lyle] Rapacki. "I just worked with an Arizona college where a group of 35 students invited me down—no faculty or staff were involved. They were concerned about a couple of courses on witchcraft being taught and this was causing problems.[188]

That cult cops seem willing to trifle with civil liberties only reflects the rumor-panics and hysteria (spawned in part by cult cops) that arise within a community. I suggest that civil-liberties difficulties with the campaign against Satanism will continue but will merge with other social movements, such as those connected with abortion, pornography, and child abuse. By and large cult cops will not produce a large impact on civil liberties, nor will the resulting court cases generate wide-ranging decisions and precedents. The threat of cult cops exists on a smaller but more tenacious and sub rosa level: the maintenance and exchange of investigative files and tips between street-level officers, files containing reports on noncriminals named by cult survivors as Satanists, people who sell music, books, occultanalia or New Age materials, and people who play Dungeons & Dragons.

Final Thoughts

A retrospective examination of the cult-cop phenomenon is not yet possible because at this writing it remains in full swing. Nevertheless, I can offer several observations. First, cult-cop ideology is inseparable from a background of widespread belief and credulity about the presence of evil in our communities, an evil with a secular definition, an evil that we suffer from civil blasphemers. Civil blasphemers include purveyors of the New Age, rock musicians, witches and pagans, and, of course, Satanists. Central to the notion of civil blasphemy is the psychology of the Other, the Destroyer, the Subverter, the Devil. For our personification of the Other, we rely on a postulated conspiracy of amoral or immoral enemies of the family. An assault on the family is an assault on stability, purity, and innocence. The new conspiratorial enemy who runs the day-care center substitutes for the fifteenth-century Jew who was erroneously alleged to have abducted and cannibalized children, or the second-century Christian who also evinced a penchant for cooked baby limbs. Norman Cohn describes this Other as a myth that we began to contrive almost two millennia ago, a myth of "another society, small and clandestine, which not only threatened the existence of the great society, but was also addicted to practices which were felt to be . . . anti-human."[189]

The resuscitation of this other society derives largely from two sources: forced cultural pluralism and loss of family control. Shifting populations due to joblessless and poverty coupled with the appearance of large immigrant groups force changes in the North American urban landscape. Old urban neighborhoods once largely white and lower or middle class now feature neon signs in Laotian, Vietnamese, or Spanish. A thoughtful article for urban administrators that anticipated the outcome of the 1990 census observed:

> During the 1980s, the United States has become more deeply multi-ethnic and culturally diverse, as Asians of all nationalities have moved into Fresno and Salt Lake City, Chicago, Los Angeles and Seattle, Honolulu and Providence, while from the south Mexicans, Haitians, Salvadorans and other Central Americans have streamed, legally and illegally, over the border.
>
> That tidal wave of immigrants is only the most dramatic manifestation of how unsettled this country's human landscape is.[190]

A rapidly growing multicultural population produces stress. Working-class white folks now live down the street from new neighbors: Santeria-practicing Cubans. Most white Americans learn about non-Christian or syncretic Christian beliefs through sensational newspaper articles or television news presentations about animal sacrifices, ecstatic religious ceremonies, and worship of deities through trance states. Cult cops have exacerbated public fears by singling out certain beliefs as having a predeliction toward the criminal, the antisocial, the perverse.

Cult cops have tried to shape a world-view that pictures a tangible evil that can be combatted once one equips oneself with a simple ideology, a grab bag of diagnostic checklists, a redefinition of reasonable suspicion oriented to discovering demonic influences. The ideology's evil seems puny when compared with incontrovertible evils that do demonstrably threaten us.

> The Devil no doubt has some interest in cultural despair, Satan chic, and demonic rock groups, but he must be much more enthusiastic about nuclear armament, gulags, and exploitative imperialism, and it is to such problems as these that the serious philosophy and theology of the latter twentieth century has properly been directed. Yet, paradoxically, cynical despair and sharpened determination to confront evil have grown at the same time.[191]

Cult cops would sooner find out who reads books on the Devil, who plays Dungeons & Dragons, and who listens to Slayer or Metallica than confront challenges much less easy to describe, define, and isolate, such as the trafficking in and consumption of dangerous drugs. The popular entertainment media pander images of apocalyptic doom, nightmares, the Other, the mythological, and the occult, against which cult cops purport to crusade as the newest form of crime prevention. Crime prevention used to consist of Neighborhood Watch groups staying alert to suspicious characters, of marking personal property with Social Security numbers, of advising citizens how best to secure their homes and businesses. Now, cult cops make crime prevention a justification for railing against cultural backsliding, against poor taste, against the odious in print, games, or music. The cult cop has taken up the hatchet of Carrie Nation.

Cult cops do have political impact. Several states have legislation pending that serves to confirm cult cops' sputterings about the need for new definitions of criminality, new tools and new laws to attack the menace. The criminal target will be the youngster who heads a fantasy game club, the housewife who works part-time in a day-care center, the immigrant *santero* or *brujo*. Since cult cops maintain a safe distance from analysis and definition, it serves the purposes of rumor-panics and collective hysteria to remain ambiguous: after all, ambiguity permits anyone to become an evildoer. When laws enter the books that aid and abet the rantings of cult cops, such codification should be taken as a clear sign that a government eye has been opened to the threat of Satan. The federal government hitherto has been too busy to notice Satanism because of its preoccuption with myth-making over drug trafficking. Drug traffickers and users represent the public Satanists of the moment, and, in fact, cult cops have frequently linked the putative satanic underground to drug-running and forced drugging of children, abductees, and so on.

The law-enforcement manufacture of a national threat has a recent precedent: serial killers. In a provocative case study of a police-encouraged and government-sponsored subversion myth about serial killers, Philip Jenkins of Pennsylvania State University has written, "If we relied solely on the evidence of the mass media, we might well believe that every few years a particular form of immoral or criminal behavior becomes so dangerous as almost to threaten the foundations of society."[192] Jenkins cites the dope fiend of the early part of the century (now enjoying a renascence) and the sex fiend of the 1930s (and the earlier white-slave traders) as examples, calling them panics that reveal much "about social concerns and prejudices —often based on xenophobia and anti-immigrant prejudice."[193] Jenkins argues that the media defined a serial-murder panic between 1983 and 1985, a panic pursued by law-enforcement authorities who under the circumstances pressed for lessening restraints on their operations and widening their mandate to gather intelligence on citizens. The myth that serial killers were responsible for many unsolved homicides is important because it confirms a traditional notion of an overwhelming threat by lethal predators; and because it distracts attention away from the reality of most homicide—as an act committed between relatives or acquaintances, often in a domestic setting. Crime is thus transformed from the problems of individuals and groups in a particular environment to a war fought by semi-human monsters against society.[194]

Some cult seminars lump Satanists with new threatening criminal types, notably white supremacists, skinheads, and others labeled "hate groups." In fact, the notion of hate crime has gained ascendancy in law-enforcement and legislative circles of late. According to *Justice Research:*

Bias crimes, or incidents of hate violence, are words or actions intended to intimidate or injure an individual because of his or her race, religion, national origin, or sexual preference. Bias crimes range from threatening phone calls to murder. The impact of these types of offenses is far more pervasive than impacts of comparable crimes that do not involve prejudice because the consequences frighten an entire group. The fear that such acts generate . . . can victimize a whole class of people.[195]

Hate crime does not represent a new crime but a new label under which state governments will soon gather statistics. The National Council of Churches has announced that hate or bias crimes have reached "epidemic proportions" in the United States, reporting 121 murders, 302 assaults, and 301 cross-burnings between 1980 and 1986, concluding: "Bigoted violence has become the critical criminal-justice issue of the late 1980s."[196] Similarly, Pat Clark, director of Klanwatch, an organization that monitors white-supremacist activities, finds racist violence growing, although acknowledging that no national clearinghouse on such statistics exists.[197] Klanwatch has also reported that white-supremacist groups have forged alliances with skinhead gangs who have given "new life" to the supremacist movement, "bringing in young recruits and providing a more contemporary image than older organizations."[198]

In fact, at this writing, Congress has supported a bill to "keep statistics on crimes motivated by race, religion, sexual orientation and ethnicity," statistics that will be collected and processed under the Uniform Crime Reporting system.[199] The Justice Department report arguing for national records-keeping upon which congressional action will be based states, "These types of offenses are far more serious than comparable crimes that do not involve prejudice because they are intended to intimidate an entire group."[200] While no new crimes have been defined as byproducts of this new interest, satanic cults will undoubtedly surface through such reporting. After all, many cult cops attribute church and cemetery vandalism to Satanists, but if the interest in bias crime dictates closer law-enforcement attention to such crimes designed to alarm large groups of people, perhaps the documentation will reflect hate groups as culprits and not Satanists.

Constructing a new category of offense—hate or bias crime—means that new definitions may soon follow in criminal law. A murder remains a murder, an assault remains an assault, but if legislatures give play to a wider range of criminal motivations—assaulting a rabbi, for example, to intimidate other Jews—new legislation will take the form of more severe penalties and broadening descriptions of outlawed behavior. If Satanism works its way into bias crime, cult cops will not remain satisfied. After all, they maintain that cult crime requires new law-enforcement tools and strategies. Cult cops may claim that law enforcement has not produced tools adequate to confront Satanism, yet tools for investigating violent crime by repeat offenders do exist. In particular, the FBI has pioneered the technique of psychological profiling of serial criminals. In an unpublished, undated monograph, Special Agent Edward F. Sulzbach of the FBI has written:

> Any officer with a modicum of experience will agree that there is very often at a crime scene evidence that one cannot package, cannot initial, cannot date, cannot send to a laboratory for forensic examination. It is there. You can feel it. You can see it. You cannot package rage. You cannot initial lust. You cannot date ritual. You can't transmit panic to a forensic laboratory.[201]

Sulzbach cautions that psychological profiling, through the FBI model, is only an art, not a science, and should not substitute for proved investigative methods. Still, the FBI continues to modify and develop the model that has been successfully applied to unsolved violent crimes. The model serves to help configure signs, symbols, or evidence of ritual (that is, repeated similar behavior) within the larger context of patterns in the commission of major violent crimes. The technique commands not only the basics of empirical evidence-gathering, but also such disciplines as forensic science and psycholinguistics. Significantly, the model is not guided by ideological considerations, which, by contrast, determine the questions asked in Dale Griffis's cult-investigation manual (cited in Chapter 2). In fact, the FBI's interest in tracking repeat violent offenders led to the creation of the National Center for the Analysis of Violent Crime (NCAVC), a component of the Behavioral Science Services of the FBI Academy in Quantico, Virginia. Its justification:

> Some violent crimes are so unusual, bizarre, and vicious that they are only rarely encountered by local law enforcement agencies. Serial violent crimes often transcend jurisdictional boundaries as the criminal travels from city to city and state to state. The crimes of these highly transient criminals are usually never tied together so that the law enforcement investigators can work in

a coordinated fashion. By functioning as a resource center and a national clearing-house, the NCAVC addresses both of these problems. (From a 1986 FBI brochure on NCAVC)

Law-enforcement literature on applications of psychological and sociological theory to understanding the violent criminal mind has begun to proliferate. Recent journal articles for law enforcers have examined the psychopathy of criminal informants,[202] the schizophrenia of sexual murder,[203] and the psycholinguistics of threats.[204]

I am concerned that the thought-world of cult cops—or, more specifically, the logic by which cult cops make deductions about criminal conspiracies—reflects a wider public and professional shift to pseudoscientific reasoning. Anthropologist Phillips Stevens, Jr., has observed:

> What is significant is that today, in an era of unparalleled scientific discovery, occult interest seems to be moving from the fringe into the mainstream and seems now to be attracting, possibly, a majority of the people. . . .
> But clearly there is growing public confusion and an increased willingness at all levels of society to abandon or sidestep principles of reason and jump to extremely fuzzy supernatural or occult explanations.[205]

Another writer, O. B. Hardison, Jr., of Georgetown University, has recently argued the obsolescence of the scientific notion of an objective reality that we can come to know through the positing of hypotheses and their testing through experiment.[206] Instead, Hardison demonstrates through a survey of modern science, architecture, and even literature that subjectivity, feelings, intuitive understandings, and above all a reality that is egocentric and self-reflexive now run the show. When much of the satanic panic blows over—at least for the time being—I suggest that social scientists ought to reconnoiter paradigms of psychiatry, psychology, and sociology and their application to people's claims of satanic worship, conspiracies, and human sacrifice. Many psychiatrists and psychologists attach literal veracity to the most outlandish and unprovable claims about Satanists; yet sociologists by and large have maintained a skeptical distance. Why? Quite possibly some of the paradigms used in counseling and social work have proved iatrogenic, a possibility therapists *must* at least *consider*. Some of the theoretical models that promote hysteria among professionals might have something to do with the understanding of sexuality. From a dawning awareness of the prevalence of intrafamilial child sexual abuse, we have quickly adopted a defensive posture that presumes that many forms of sexuality, even involving children, are a priori harmful or damaging to emotional maturity. Much of our concern for children's sexuality still resides with supposition, speculation, and hypothesis, not science.

The psychological phenomena bound up in this zeitgeist of satanic-

cult claims include cult cops' world-view, the satanic imagery of cult survivors, the occult tales emerging from day-care centers, the therapists with
obsolete ideas about the functioning of memory, and the usefulness of
hypnosis to obtain push-button playback of traumatic childhood experiences. No one explanation can govern all of the claims, theories, exaggerations, rumors. But cult seminars inevitably miss one central focus: mass
credulity, or collective psychology. Rumors do play a demonstrable role
in stimulating fears of cults and Satanists; yet those with an expertise in
folklore seem to remain in the wings, saying nothing. In part, anthropologist
Stevens observes, to most members of the public, " 'folklore' implies fals-
ity"; yet folklorists should not pass up the opportunity to "provide a much-
needed lesson in critical thinking."

> For example, given the large numbers of unaccounted-for people today, it
> may be *possible* that tens of thousands of ritual murders are going on undetected
> and unreported, or that women are being coerced to conceive, undergo
> pregnancies, and deliver babies for Satanic cults, undetected; but is it *probable?*
> Is it even *likely?* And they might advise their audiences not to fall into the
> trap of twisted reasoning often used in support of occult (or "psychic") claims:
> "You can't prove it *didn't* happen." Of course we can't, nor can science, nor
> should we be expected to. The burden of "proof," as in the courts, is upon
> the claimant; and as magician . . . James ("The Amazing") Randi is fond of
> saying, "extraordinary claims demand extraordinary proofs."[207]

Meanwhile, law enforcers and others could apply a few simple guidelines
to trying to understand and react responsibly to claims about cults and
Satanism. Sociologist Jeffrey Victor has offered simple rules for "dealing
with gossip and rumors about Satanism":

1. Be careful of the labels people put on pre-packaged ideas.
2. Beware of well-meaning gossip-mongers.
3. Remember that when "everyone" gets carried away by fear, "everyone"
can be wrong.
4. Remember "where there is smoke," there is often a lot of hot air.
5. Remember that shared fear makes the "big lie" credible.
6. Contact people whose job it is to know about what is happening in
your community.[208]

Certainly the subject of rumors, rumor-panics, urban legends, and subversion myths require more insightful study to identify the satanic metaphors,
their systematic and sometimes predictable usage, and to explore people's
readiness and willingness to believe. Particularly useful to law enforcement
would be an insight into how collective myths become very personalized
ones, as in the case of cult survivors.
    Law enforcers must not beguile themselves into believing satanic-con-

spiracy theories or conducting surveillance of and record-gathering on people who have shown no criminal involvement. As the FBI's Kenneth Lanning has observed:

> What is the justification for law enforcement officers giving presentations on satanism and the occult . . . ? Is it public relations, a safety program, or crime prevention? If it is crime prevention, how much crime can be linked to satanic or occult activity and what do such presentations do to prevent crime? Law enforcement agencies should carefully consider the legal implications and justification for such presentations. Is the fact that satanism or the occult is or can be a negative influence on some people enough justification for such law enforcement efforts?[209]

Law-enforcement investigators must remove the "cult" from cult crime and do their jobs accordingly, for as Lanning acutely points out, "Bizarre crime and evil can occur without organized satanic activity. The law-enforcement perspective requires that we distinguish between what we know and what we're not sure of."[210]

NOTES

Chapter 1: Talk of the Devil

1. Wallace Notestein, *History of Witchcraft in England from 1558-1718* (New York: Crowell, 1968), pp. 147ff.

2. Ibid., p. 45.

3. Jay Mathews, "In California, a Question of Abuse," *Washington Post,* May 31, 1989.

4. Ibid.

5. Office of the Attorney General, State of California, "Report on the Kern County Child Abuse Investigation," September 1986, p. 4.

6. Ibid., Chap. 4, p. 3.

7. Ibid., Chap. 4, p. 2.

8. Jay Mathews, "In California" (see note 3).

9. Terence Hines, *Pseudoscience and the Paranormal* (Buffalo, N.Y.: Prometheus Books, 1988), p. 1.

10. Ibid., p. 2.

11. Philip Jenkins and Daniel Katkin, "From Salem to Jordan: A Historical Perspective on Child Abuse Cases," *Augustus,* 9, no. 6:15 (1986).

12. Ibid.

13. Ibid., p. 16.

14. Arthur Miller, *The Crucible* (New York: Bantam Books, 1967), p. 108.

15. Jay Matthews, "In California" (see note 3).

16. Arthur Schlesinger, Jr., "The Opening of the American Mind," *New York Times Book Review,* July 23, 1989.

17. Ibid.

18. Arthur Lyons, *Satan Wants You: The Cult of Devil Worship in America* (New York: Mysterious Press, 1988), p. xlii.

19. Raymond A. Eve and Dana Dunn, "High School Biology Teachers and Pseudoscientific Belief: Passing It On," *Skeptical Inquirer,* 13:261 (1989).

20. Clyde Z. Nunn, "The Rising Credibility of the Devil in America," in *Heterodoxy/Mystical Experience: Religious Dissent and the Occult,* ed. Richard Woods (River Forest, Ill.: Listening Press, 1975), p. 85.

21. For example, "Scientific Literacy: New Survey Finds Level Still Low in U.S., U.K.," *Skeptical Inquirer,* 13:343-345 (1989).

22. Ibid.

23. Howard J. Ehrlich and Jack J. Preiss, *An Examination of Role Theory: The Case of the State Police* (Lincoln: University of Nebraska Press, 1966).

24. Chrysti Edge, "Four Satan Worshippers Arrested in Attempt to Rob Conway Grave," *Sun-News* (Myrtle Beach, S.C.), July 28, 1988.

25. Charles McCoy, "Mississippi Town Is All Shook Up Over Voodoo Plot," *Wall Street Journal,* February 24, 1989.

26. Lisa Antonelli Bacon, "Cult Activity in James River Park, *Style Weekly,* 6, no. 42:6 (October 18, 1988).

27. Melissa Berg, "Satanic Crime Increasing? Police, Therapists Alarmed," *Kansas City Times,* March 26, 1988.

28. Ibid.

29. Danielle A. Fouquette, "Detective Delivers Warning on Satanism," *The Beacon* (Virginia Beach, Va.), May 8, 1988.

30. Ed Briggs, "Satanic Cults Said to Entice Teens with Sex, Drugs," *Richmond* (Va.) *Times-Dispatch,* March 5, 1988.

31. Holly D. Remy, "Fears of Crimes Tied to Satanism Rising," *Arizona Republic,* March 20, 1989.

32. Inga Saffron, "In Wake of Deaths, Experts Warn of Satan's Lure," *Philadelphia Inquirer,* January 25, 1988.

33. Rick White, "Ritual Crime Clues Often Ignored, Experts Say," *Temple* (Tex.) *Daily Telegram,* May 12, 1988.

34. Associated Press news release, October 3, 1988.

35. "Satanists Disturb W. Va. Town," *Parkersburg* (W. Va.) *News,* August 18, 1988.

36. Dick Burke, "Satanism in Denver Schools," *The Forum,* May-June 1988.

37. "Self-Professed Mass Killer Says He Belongs to Death Cult," *Crime Control Digest,* 18, no. 19:4-5 (May 14, 1984).

38. "Antiwar or Antichrist?" *Time,* July 3, 1989.

39. Chris Jorgensen, "Expert Tells Utah Conference of Satanism's 'Very Real Evil,' " *Salt Lake City Tribune,* July 31, 1989.

40. Donald W. Story, "Ritualistic Crime: More Awareness Training Needed," *Law and Order,* 37, no. 6:56 (1989).

41. Erling Jorstad, "Satanism: No Figment of the Imagination," *The Lutheran,* June 14, 1989.

42. "Satan Caused Legal Woes, Ex-pastor Says," *Richmond* (Va.) *News Leader,* July 6, 1989.

43. Jacob R. Clark, "The Macabre Faces of Occult-Related Crime," *Law Enforcement News,* 14, nos. 279-280 (October 31, November 15, 1988).

44. G. Olson-Raymer, *Occult Crime: A Law Enforcement Primer,* published as *Research Update,* 1, no. 6:2 (Winter 1989-90) by the California Office of Criminal Justice Planning.

Chapter 2: Believing in Hell

1. Massachusetts State Police, *Roll Call Newsletter,* 88, no. 25 (1988).

2. Ibid.

3. Catherine Crutchfield, "California Police Finding Evidence of Satanic Cults

with Links to Crimes," *Crime Control Digest,* 18, no. 19:5 (May 14, 1984).

4. Fifth International Conference on Multiple Personality/Dissociative States, Chicago, October 1988.

5. Kenneth V. Lanning, "Satanic, Occult, Ritualistic Crime: A Law Enforcement Perspective," *Police Chief,* 46, no. 10:62-83 (1989).

6. Ibid., p, 77.

7. Cult Crime Impact Network, Inc., *File 18 Newsletter,* 4, no. 2:3 (1989).

8. Marjorie Hyer, "Blue Knights and the Black Art," *Washington Post,* April 18, 1989.

9. "Now You Know," *Richmond* (Va.) *News Leader,* August 1, 1989.

10. Jose J. Rodriguez, letter to the editor, *Washington Post,* April 29, 1989.

11. Jacob R. Clark, "The Macabre Faces of Occult-Related Crime," *Law Enforcement News,* 14, nos. 279-280 (October 31, November 15, 1988).

12. *File 18 Newsletter,* 4, no. 1 (1989).

13. Ibid., p. 3.

14. Ibid., 3, no. 3:7 (1988).

15. Arthur Lyons, *Satan Wants You: The Cult of Devil Worship in America* (New York: Mysterious Press, 1988), p. 149.

16. Ibid.

17. Shawn Carlson and Gerald Larue, eds. *Satanism in America* (El Cerrito, Calif.: Gaia Press, 1989), p. 102.

18. *File 18 Newsletter,* 4, no. 4 (1989).

19. Rex Springston, "Experts Say Tales Are Bunk," *Richmond* (Va.) *News Leader,* April 6-7, 1989.

20. Arthur Lyons, *Satan Wants You* (see note 15), p. 20.

21. Marjorie Hyer, "Blue Knights" (see note 8).

22. "America's Best-Kept Secret," *Passport Magazine* (Special Issue), 1987.

23. Inga Saffron, "In Wake of Deaths, Experts Warn of Satan's Lure," *Philadelphia Inquirer,* January 25, 1988.

24. Ibid.

25. Ibid.

26. Kenneth V. Lanning "Ritualistic Crime" (see note 5), p. 80.

27. Wayne King, "A Jersey Enigma: Do Satanists Lurk Among Us?" *New York Times,* March 3, 1989.

28. Ibid.

29. Tony Parker, "Satanic Cults Not Bedeviling Area," *The Pentagraph* (Illinois), August 6, 1989.

30. Ibid.

31. Patricia A. Pulling, *The Devil's Web* (Lafayette, La.: Huntington House, 1989).

32. "Bothered About Dungeons and Dragons," *Dungeons and Dragons* (Richmond, Va., n.d.).

33. Pat Purcell, "Sex, Drug Cult Alleged in Coaldale: Six Nabbed," *Pottsville* (Pa.) *Republican,* April 8, 1988.

34. Karen Blakeman, "Berdella Charged in Murder," *Kansas City Times,* July 23, 1988.

35. "Jurors in Murder Trial Hear 'Satan' Describe Slaying," *Richmond* (Va.) *Times-Dispatch,* November 12, 1988.

36. *Richmond Times-Dispatch* November 20, 1988.

37. "Self-professed Mass Killer Says He Belongs to Death Cult," *Crime Control Digest,* 18, no. 19:4-5 (1984).

38. Ibid.

39. Anton LaVey, *The Satanic Bible* (New York: Avon, 1969), p. 10.

40. Tom Charlier and Shirley Downing, "Justice Abused: A 1980s Witch-Hunt" (6-part series), *Commercial Appeal* (Memphis, Tenn.), January 1988.

41. Anton LaVey, *The Satanic Bible* (see note 39), p. 41.

42. Ibid., p. 69.

43. Ibid., p. 70.

44. Ibid., p. 89.

45. Ibid., p. 116.

46. J. Gordon Melton, *Biographical Dictionary of American Cult and Sect Leaders* (New York: Garland, 1986), p. 59.

47. Aleister Crowley, *The Book of the Law* (York Beach, Me.: Weiser, reprint, 1976), p. 9.

48. Francis King, *The Magical World of Aleister Crowley* (New York: Coward, McCann and Geoghegan, 1978), p. 36.

49. Ibid., p. 37.

50. Ibid., p. 41.

51. Arthur Lyons, *Satan Wants You* (see note 15), p. 111.

52. Ibid., p. 116.

53. Edward J. Moody, "Magical Therapy: An Anthropological Investigation of Contemporary Satanism," in *Religious Movements in Contemporary America,* ed. Irving I. Zaretsky and Mark P. Leone (Princton, N.J.: Princeton University Press, 1974).

54. Robert J. Barry, "Satanism: The Law Enforcement Response," *National Sheriff,* 38, no. 1:38-42 (1987).

55. *The Necronomicon* (New York: Avon Books), p. v.

56. Michael Stackpole, personal communication, 1988.

57. Office of Intellectual Freedom, *American Library Association Memorandum,* January/February 1988, p. 7.

58. Lindsay E. Smith and Bruce A. Walstad, *Sting Shift* (Littleton, Colo.: Street-Smart Communications, 1989), p. 104.

59. Ibid., p. 100.

60. Tom Charlier and Shirley Downing, "Justice Abused" (see note 40).

61. Marjorie Hyer, "Blue Knights" (see note 8).

62. Danielle A. Fouquette, "Detective Delivers Warning on Satanism," *The Beacon* (Virginia Beach, Va.), May 8, 1988.

63. Larry Kahaner, *Cults That Kill* (New York: Warner, 1988), p. 84.

64. Rex Springston, "Experts Say" (see note 19).

65. Ibid.

66. Sonni Efron, "Devilchasers," Associated Press release, May 7, 1989.

67. Melissa Berg, "Satanic Crime Increasing? Police, Therapists Alarmed,"

Kansas City Times, March 26, 1988.

68. Ibid.

69. Larry Kahaner, *Cults That Kill* (see note 63), p. 87.

70. Paula K. Lundberg-Love, "Update on Cults, Part 1: Satanic Cults," *Family Violence Bulletin,* Summer 1989, pp. 9-10.

71. Ibid.

72. "Two Virginia Men Arrested in Attempt to Buy or Kidnap Boy to Make a Porn 'Snuff' Film," *Crime Control Digest,* 23, no. 34:2 (1989).

73. Ed Briggs, "Satanic Cults Said to Entice Teens with Sex, Drugs," *Richmond* (Va.) *Times-Dispatch,* March 5, 1988.

74. Federal Bureau of Invesigation, *Uniform Crime Reports* (Washington, D.C., 1988).

75. Kenneth V. Lanning, "Satanic, Occult, Ritualistic Crime" (see note 5), p. 62.

76. Letter to Debbie Nathan, December 19, 1988.

77. Holly D. Remy, "Fears of Crimes Tied to Satanism Rising," *Arizona Republic,* March 20, 1989.

78. Liz Atwood, "Beware! Cult Symbols Could Be Fatal," *Richmond* (Va.) *News Leader,* March 14, 1987.

79. *State v. Waterhouse,* decided August 15, 1986.

80. Dianne Klein, "Satanic Crime: A New Police Specialty in Demand," *Los Angeles Times,* July 3, 1989.

81. Ibid.

82. Investigator's interview as recounted in: G. Olson-Raymer, *Occult Crime: A Law Enforcement Primer,* published as *Research Update,* 1, no. 6 (Winter 1989-90).

83. Dusty Sklar, *Gods and Beasts: The Nazis and the Occult* (New York: Crowell, 1977).

84. Maury Terry, *The Ultimate Evil: An Investigation into America's Most Dangerous Cult* (New York: Doubleday, 1987).

85. Ibid., p. 162.

86. Ibid.

87. Ibid., p. 166.

88. Ibid., p. 45.

89. Ibid., p. 89.

90. Ibid., p. 170.

91. Ibid., p. 300.

92. Arthur Lyons, *Satan Wants You* (see note 15), p. 93.

93. Shawn Carlson and Gerald A. Larue, eds., *Satanism in America* (see note 17).

94. "UT Student Victim of Cult Sacrifices," *El Paso Herald-Post,* April 12, 1989.

95. Ibid.

96. Ibid.

97. "Cult, Cannibals Blamed in Death." *El Paso Times,* April 12, 1989.

98. Joel Williams, "Twelve Found Dead in Grisly Cult Rituals," *Richmond* (Va.) *News Leader,* April 12, 1989.

99. "Satanic Cult Blamed in 12 Deaths," *Richmond* (Va.) *Times-Dispatch,* April 12, 1989.

100. Peter Applebome, "Drugs, Death and the Occult Meet in Grisly Inquiry at Mexico Border," *New York Times,* April 13, 1989.

101. Ibid.

102. Ibid.

103. "Manhunt Is on for Cult 'Godfather,' " *El Paso Herald-Post,* April 13, 1989.

104. Ibid.

105. Associated Press, "Global Hunt Is on for Voodoo Cult 'Godfather,' " *Richmond* (Va.) *News Leader,* April 13, 1989.

106. Ibid.

107. "Officials Try to Unravel Story of Drugs, Murder and Occult," *Richmond* (Va.) *Times-Dispatch,* April 13, 1989.

108. "En el Rito, se Practicaron Ceremonias Afro-Cubanos," *Diario de Juarez* (Mexico), April 13, 1989.

109. Ibid.

110. Jim Phillips and Morgan Montalvo, "Experts Differ on Voodoo as Motivation for Killings," *Austin* (Tex.) *American Statesman,* April 13, 1989.

111. Ibid.

112. Ibid.

113. Peter Applebome, "Thirteenth Victim Is Found on Ranch Where Drugs and Occult Mixed," *New York Times,* April 14, 1989.

114. Ibid.

115. "Movie Used in Recruiting, Cultists Say," *Richmond* (Va.) *Times-Dispatch,* April 15, 1989, from wire dispatches.

116. Ibid.

117. "Hunt Intensifies for Thirteen Suspects in Ritual Killings," *Richmond* (Va.) *Times-Dispatch,* April 16, 1989, from wire dispatches.

118. Ibid.

119. "Cult Suspects Say Slayings Started After Members Watched Movie" *El Paso Times,* April 16, 1989.

120. "Cult Toll Up to Fifteen," *El Paso Times,* April 17, 1989.

121. Peter Applebome, "On North-South Line, Violence Grows," *New York Times,* April 17, 1989.

122. Ibid.

123. "Police Find Two Bodies Near Cult Site," *Richmond* (Va.) *Times-Dispatch,* April 17,1989.

124. "One Arrested as Probe of Cult Widens," *Richmond* (Va.) *News Leader,* April 18, 1989.

125. "La Direccion Federal de Seguridad Progegia a los Narcos Satanicos," *Diario de Juarez* (Mexico), April 18, 1989.

126. "Drug Cult Victims Largely Ran Drugs, Mexico Says," *El Paso Times,* April 19, 1989.

127. "Cultist Spent Time, Money in Houston," *El Paso Times,* April 20, 1989.

128. "Kidnap Scare Sweeps Matamoros," *El Paso Times,* April, 20, 1989.

129. "Alleged Cult Leader Didn't Use Drugs," *El Paso Times,* April 21, 1989.

130. "El Santero No Acuso a los Narcosatanicos por Temor, *Diario de Juarez* (Mexico), December 24, 1989.

131. "Expert Says Ritual Killings Show Work of Psychopath," *El Paso Herald-Post,* April 25, 1989.

132. "Fear Haunts Cult-Slaying Area Families," *El Paso Times,* April 30, 1989.

133. Joel Williams, "Drug-Cult Killings Cast Pall of Fear Over Matamoros," *Arizona Daily Star,* April 30, 1989.

134. "Cult Leader Ordered Subordinate to Kill Him," *Richmond* (Va.) *News Leader,* May 8, 1989.

135. Ibid.

136. "Cult Leader in Ritualistic Slayings Is Reported Killed by Follower," *New York Times,* May 8, 1989.

137. Ibid.

138. "Killing of Transvestite No Sacrifice, Suspect Says," *El Paso Times,* May 15, 1989.

139. Marjorie Miller and J. Michael Kennedy, "Potent Mix of Ritual and Charisma," *Los Angeles Times,* May 16, 1989.

140. Ibid.

141. Ibid.

142. Ibid.

143. Investiga la Procuraduria las Propriedades de Adolfo Constanzo," *Diario de Juarez* (Mexico), May 18, 1989.

144. Jane Bussey, "Mexican Police Jail Agent Linked to Satanic Drug Cult," *Houston Post,* June 2, 1989.

145. Roy Bragg, "Syndicate's Ties to Cult Probably Only Commercial," Hearst News Service release, July 19, 1989.

146. Gary Cartwright, "The Work of the Devil," *Texas Monthly,* June 1989, p. 82.

147. Ibid., p. 152.

148. Ibid., p. 153.

149. Debbie Nathan, "The Devil and Mr. Mattox," *Texas Observer,* June 2, 1989.

150. Pierre Thomas and Alice Diglio, "Prince William Devil-Buster Aims to Nip Satanism in Bud," *Washington Post,* February 7, 1989.

151. Marjorie Hyer, "Blue Knights" (see note 8).

152. Chris Jorgensen, "Expert Tells Utah Conference of Satanism's 'Very Real Evil,'" *Salt Lake City Tribune,* July 31, 1989.

153. Patricia Pearson, "In Search of Satanists," *The Idler* (Toronto, Canada), no. 25:22 (September/October 1989).

154. Ibid.

155. Ibid.

156. Larry Kahaner, *Cults That Kill* (see note 63), p. 42.

157. Debbie Nathan, "The Devil and Mr. Mattox" (see note 149).

158. W. Stevens Ricks, "Tiffin's One-Man Satan Squad Draws Fire," *Cleveland Plain Dealer,* August 4, 1985.

159. Ibid.

160. Ibid.

161. Patricia Pearson, "In Search of Satanists" (see note 145).

162. Don Baird, "Sympathy for the Devil," *Capitol Magazine* (Denver, Colo.), July 15, 1984.

163. Ibid.

164. Ibid., p. 10.

165. Ibid.

166. "Bill Would Crack Down on 'Diploma Mills,' " *Community Crime Prevention Digest,* May 1989, p. 8.

167. Ibid.

168. David Bromley and Anson D. Shupe, Jr., "The Tnevnoc Cult," *Sociological Analysis,* 40, no. 4:361-366 (1979).

169. Robert J. Lifton, *Mind Control and the Psychology of Totalism* (New York: W. W. Norton, 1961), p. 3.

170. Ibid., p. 4.

171. Ibid., p. 15.

172. Ibid., p. 238.

173. Ibid,, p. 435.

174. William Guinee, "Satanism in Yellowwood Forest: The Interdependence of Antagonistic Worldviews," *Indiana Folklore and Oral History,* 16, no. 1:1-30 (1987).

175. Ibid., p. 1.

176. Ibid., p. 3.

177. Ibid.

178. Ibid., p. 2.

179. Ibid., p. 7.

180. Ibid., p. 8.

181. Ibid., p. 9.

182. Ibid., pp. 9-10.

183. Ibid., p. 11.

184. Ibid.

185. Ibid., p. 19.

Chapter 3: The Other Side of the Case

1. J. Gordon Melton, *Encyclopedic Handbook of Cults in America* (New York: Garland, 1986).

2. Ibid., p. 6.

3. Robert J. Barry, "Satanism: The Law Enforcement Response," *National Sheriff,* 38, no. 1:40 (1987).

4. Dave Jonsson, "Expert Says Some Look to a Cult for Structure in Life," *Salt Lake City Tribune,* April 15, 1989.

5. Dale W. Griffis, "Investigation Manual for Non-Traditional Groups" (Tiffin, Ohio: n.d.), p. 51.

6. Don Baird, "Sympathy for the Devil," *Capitol Magazine* (Denver, Colo.), July 15, 1984, p. 9.

7. Michael Rokos, "Kids, Drugs, Cults: Treating Cult Survivors," cult seminar in Richmond, Va., October 19, 1989.

8. Lisa Antonelli, "Satan's Victim: One Woman's Ordeal," *Style Weekly* (Richmond, Va.), 7, no. 3:38–43 (January 19, 1988).

9. Rex Springston, "Experts Say Tales Are Bunk," *Richmond* (Va.) *News Leader,* April 6–7, 1989.

10. Ibid.

11. Ibid.

12. Charles Austin, Hearst Newspapers release, July 17, 1989.

13. James D. Davis, "The Satanism Scare," *Sun Sentinel* (Fla.), September 16, 1989.

14. Ibid.

15. Allan W. Eister, "Culture Crises and New Religious Movements: A Paradigmatic Statement of a Theory of Cults," in *Religious Movements in Contemporary America*, ed. Irving I. Zaretsky and Mark F. Leone (Princeton, N.J.: Princeton University Press, 1974), p. 613.

16. Ibid., p. 624.

17. Ibid., p. 625.

18. J. Gordon Melton, *An Encyclopedia of American Religions*, 2 vols. (Wilmington, N.C.: McGrath, 1978), p. vii.

19. J. Gordon Melton, *Encyclopedic Handbook of Cults in America* (see note 1), p. 3.

20. Ibid.

21. Ibid.

22. Ibid., p. 5.

23. Ibid.

24. Ibid.

25. Ibid., p. 76.

26. Ibid., p. 243.

27. Ibid., p. 245.

28. Ibid., p. 243.

29. Ibid., p. 241.

30. Ibid., p. 255.

31. Frank MacHovec, *Cults and Personality* (Springfield, Ill.: Charles C. Thomas, 1989), p. 10.

32. Ibid.

33. Ibid., p. 11.

34. Marc Galanter, *Cults: Faith, Healing, and Coercion* (New York: Oxford University Press, 1989).

35. Ibid., p. 5.

36. Ibid., p. 10.

37. Ibid., p. 11.

38. Ibid., p. 35.

39. Ibid., p. 41.

40. Edward J. Moody, "Magical Therapy: An Anthropological Investigation of Contemporary Satanism," in *Religious Movements in Contemporary America* (see note 15).

41. Robert J. Lifton, *Mind Control and the Psychology of Totalism* (New York: W. W. Norton, 1961).

42. Marc Galanter, *Cults, Faith, Healing, and Coercion* (see note 34), p. 64.

43. David G. Bromley and Anson D. Shupe, Jr., "The Tnevnoc Cult," *Sociological Analysis*, 40, no. 4: 361–366 (1979).

44. Ibid., p. 361.

45. Ibid., p. 364.

46. Ibid., p. 365.

47. David G. Bromley and Anson D. Shupe, Jr., *Strange Gods: The Great American Cult Scare* (Boston: Beacon Press, 1981), p. 3.

48. Ibid., p. 4.

49. Ibid., p. 5.

50. Ibid., p. 124.

51. Ibid., p. 21.

52. Ibid., p. 23.

53. This discussion derives from Paul Turner's *Self-Guide for Linguistic Fieldwork* (Tucson, Ariz.: Impresora Sahuaro, 1972).

54. J. Gordon Melton, *Encyclopedic Handbook* (see note 1).

55. Ibid., p. 78.

56. Edward J. Moody, "Magical Therapy" (see note 40).

57. Ibid., p. 357.

58. Ibid., p. 359.

59. Ibid.

60. Ibid.

61. Ibid., p. 362.

62. Ibid., p. 364.

63. Ibid., p. 365.

64. Ibid., p. 368.

65. Ibid., p. 370.

66. Ibid., p. 371.

67. Ibid., p. 372.

68. Ibid., p. 373.

69. Ibid., p. 380.

70. Ibid., p. 381.

71. J. Worthington Montgomery, Letter to the Editor, *Henrico County Line* (Va.), August 3, 1989.

72. Cult Crime Impact Network, *File 18 Newsletter*, 4: 4 (1989).

73. Ed Briggs, "Witches Complain Persecution, Stereotype Still Haunt Them," *Richmond* (Va.) *Times-Dispatch*, March 5, 1988.

74. Ibid.

75. Ibid.

76. "Witchcraft, Satanism and Ritual Crime: Who's Who and What's What?" *Green Egg* (Ukaiah, Calif.), Special Issue, 1989.

77. Ibid.

78. J. Gordon Melton, *Encyclopedic Handbook* (see note 1).

79. Margot Adler, *Drawing Down the Moon: Witches, Druids, Goddess Worshippers and Other Pagans in America Today* (New York: Viking, 1979).

80. T. M. Luhrmann, *Persuasions of the Witch's Craft: Ritual Magic in Contemporary England* (Cambridge, Mass.: Harvard University Press, 1989).

81. J. Gordon Melton, *Encyclopedic Handbook* (see note 1), p. 267.

82. Ibid., pp. 268ff.

83. Ibid.

84. T. M. Luhrmann, *Persuasions* (see note 80), p. 6.

85. Ibid.

86. "Witchcraft, Satanism and Ritual Crime" (see note 76).

87. J. Gordon Melton, *Encyclopedic Handbook* (see note 1), p. 286.

88. Marcello Truzzi, "Towards a Sociology of the Occult: Notes on Modern Witchcraft," in *Religious Movements* (see note 40), p. 628.

89. Ibid., p. 630.

90. Ibid., p. 632.

91. Ibid., p. 637.

92. Ibid., p. 645.

93. T. M. Luhrmann, *Persuasions* (see note 80), p. 7.

94. Ibid., p. 99.

95. Ibid., p. 257.

96. Ibid., p. 258.

97. Margot Adler, *Drawing Down the Moon* (see note 79). Although the author's citations are from the 1979 edition, Beacon Press in 1986 published a version that updated information on contemporary neopagan groups.

98. Ibid., p. iv.

99. Ibid., p. 6.

100. Ibid.

101. Ibid., p. 131.

102. Ibid., p. 389.

103. Max Warwick, ed., *Witchcraft and Sorcery* (New York: Viking/Penguin, 1987).

104. Ibid., p. 17.

105. E. E. Evans-Pritchard, *Witchcraft, Oracles, and Magic Among the Azande* (Oxford: Clarendon Press, 1937).

106. Clyde Kluckhohn, *Navaho Witchcraft* (Boston: Beacon Press, 1962).

107. Ibid., p. 248.

108. Ibid., p. 250.

109. Ibid., p. 255.

110. Phillips Stevens, Jr., "Some Implications of Urban Witchcraft Beliefs," *New York Folklore*, 8, nos. 3–4:29 (1982).

111. Ibid.

112. Blaine Harden, "Liberians Take Introspective Look at Endurance of Witchcraft," *Washington Post*, July 11, 1988.

113. Ibid.

114. Ibid.

115. Ibid.

116. Ibid.

117. Kenneth B. Noble, "Ritual Killings Laid to Liberian Official," *New York Times*, Aug. 8, 1989.

118. Kenneth V. Lanning, "Satanic, Occult, Ritualistic Crime: A Law Enforcement Perspective," *Police Chief* 56, no. 10:64 (1989).

119. Mayra Santos-Febres, et al., Letter to the Editor, *New York Times*, May 15, 1989.

120. Lisa Antonelli Bacon, "Odd Findings in Jackson Ward, Experts Say Ritual," *Style Weekly* (Richmond, Va.), 6, no. 32 (August 9, 1988).

121. Ibid.

122. Judd Golden, "Non-Indian Peyote Worshipers Acquitted on Drug Charges," *Civil Liberties* (American Civil Liberties Union, New York), no. 352 (1985).

123. Ibid.

124. Ibid.

125. Ibid.

126. Alfredo Corchado, "Folk Healers Stay Popular with Poor in Rural Southwest," *Wall Street Journal*, January 4, 1989.

127. Ibid.

128. Ibid.

129. Rex Springston, "Yoruba Followers on Rise in America," *Richmond* (Va.) *News Leader*, August 30, 1988.

130. Ibid.

131. Ibid.

132. Ibid.

133. Charles McCoy, "Mississippi Town Is All Shook Up Over Voodoo Plot," *Wall Street Journal*, February 24, 1989.

134. Ibid.

135. Rex Springston, "Yoruba Followers" (see note 128).

136. G. Olson-Raymer, *Occult Crime: A Law Enforcement Primer*, published as *Research Update*, 1, no. 6:26 (Winter 1989–90), by the California Office of Criminal Justice Planning.

137. Larry Rohter, "In a Most Unsaintly City, a Bandit Wears a Halo," *New York Times*, May 11, 1989.

138. Ibid.

139. Eugene Robinson, "Tour Shows Trafficker Lived in Style," *Washington Post*, August 26, 1989.

140. William Branigan, "Noriega Used 'Evil Magic' Against Enemies, Specialists Say," *Richmond* (Va.) *News Leader*, December 26, 1989.

141. Ibid.

142. William Branigan, "Bewitching the General," *Washington Post*, February 19, 1990.

143. Migene Gonzalez-Wippler: *Santeria: African Magic in Latin America*, 1973; *The Santeria Experience*, 1982; *Rituals and Spells of Santeria*, 1984; *San-*

teria: The Religion, 1989. Joseph Murphy: *Santeria: An African Religion in America*, 1988.

144. George Eaton Simpson, *Black Religions in the New World* (New York: Columbia University Press, 1978).

145. Ibid., pp. 16–17.

146. Ibid., p. 133.

147. Mercedes Sandoval, "Santeria: Afrocuban Concepts of Disease and Its Treatment in Miami," *Journal of Operational Psychiatry*, 8, no. 2:52 (1977).

148. Ibid., p. 53.

149. Ibid., p. 61.

150. Ibid.

151. Ibid.

152. George Eaton Simpson, *Black Religions* (see note 143), p. 299.

153. C. V. Wetli and R. Martinez, "Forensic Sciences Aspects of Santeria, a Religious Cult of African Origin," *Journal of Forensic Sciences*, 26, no. 3:506 514 (1981).

154. Ibid., p. 506.

155. Ibid., p. 507.

156. Ibid., p. 514.

157. C. V. Wetli and R. Martinez, "Brujeria: Manifestations of Palo Mayombe in South Florida," *Journal of the Florida Medical Association*, 70, no. 8:629 (1983).

158. Ibid.

159. Ibid., p. 634.

160. Ibid.

Chapter 4: Cult Survivors

1. Melissa Berg, "Satanic Crime Increasing? Police, Therapists Alarmed," *Kansas City Tribune*, March 26, 1988.

2. Ibid.

3. Ibid.

4. Ibid.

5. Lisa Antonelli, "Satan's Victim: One Woman's Ordeal," *Style Weekly* (Richmond, Va.), 6, no. 3:38 43 (January 19, 1988).

6. Ibid.

7. Ibid.

8. Ibid.

9. Ibid.

10. Melissa Berg, "Satanic Crime Increasing?" (see note 1).

11. Frank W. Putnam, *Diagnosis and Treatment of Multiple Personality Disorder* (New York: Guilford Press, 1989), p. 235.

12. Michelle Smith and Lawrence Pazder, *Michelle Remembers* (New York: Congdon and Lattes, 1980).

13. "Things That Go Bump in Victoria," *Maclean's*, October 27, 1980.

14. Michelle Smith and Lawrence Pazder, *Michelle Remembers* (see note 12).

15. Ibid.

16. Ibid., p. 133.

17. Ibid., p. 134.

18. Ibid., p. 148.

19. Ibid., p. 150.

20. Ibid., p. 184.

21. Ibid., p. 194.

22. Ibid., p. 195.

23. Ibid., p. 207.

24. Ibid., p. 209.

25. Ibid., p. 100.

26. Zeena LaVey, personal communication, 1989.

27. Michelle Smith and Lawrence Pazder, *Michelle Remembers* (see note 12), p. 83.

28. Ibid., pp. 193–194.

29. "Things That Go Bump in Victoria" (see note 13).

30. Ibid.

31. George K. Ganaway, "Historical Versus Narrative Truth: Clarifying the Role of Exogenous Trauma in the Etiology of MPD and Its Variants," *Dissociation*, 2, no. 4, 1989.

32. John C. Nemiah, "Dissociative Disorders (Hysterical Neurosis, Dissociative Type)," in *Comprehensive Textbook of Psychiatry*, 4th ed., ed. Harold I. Kaplan and Benjamin J. Sadock (Baltimore, Md.: Williams and Wilkins, 1985), p. 943.

33. American Psychiatric Association, *Diagnostic and Statistical Manual of Mental Disorders*, 3rd ed., rev. (*DSM-IIIR*), Washington, D.C., 1987.

34. Ibid.

35. Ibid.

36. Bennett G. Braun, ed., *Treatment of Multiple Personality Disorder* (Washington, D.C.: American Psychiatric Press, 1986), p. 3.

37. Richard P. Kluft, *Childhood Antecedents to Multiple Personality* (Washington, D.C.: American Psychiatric Association, 1985), p. 200.

38. John C. Nemiah, "Dissociative Disorders" (see note 32), p. 951.

39. Frank W. Putnam, "The Treatment of Multiple Personality: State of the Art," in *Treatment of Multiple Personality Disorder* (see note 36), p. 183.

40. Ibid., p. 187.

41. Richard P. Kluft, *Childhood Antecedents to Multiple Personality* (see note 37), p. ix.

42. Bennett G. Braun, ed., *Treatment of MPD* (see note 36), p. xvi.

43. Ibid., p. 184.

44. John C. Nemiah, "Dissociative Disorders" (see note 31), p. 947.

45. Bennett G. Braun, ed., *Treatment of MPD* (see note 36), p. 5.

46. Ibid.

47. Frank W. Putnam, *Diagnosis and Treatment of MPD* (New York: Guilford Press, 1989), p. 47.

48. Ibid., p. 24.

49. Bennett G. Braun, *Treatment of MPD* (see note 36), p. 7.

50. Ibid., p. 9.

51. Eugene L. Bliss, *Multiple Personality, Allied Disorders and Hypnosis* (New York: Oxford University Press, 1986), p. 125.

52. Ibid., p. 164.

53. Richard P. Kluft, *Childhood Antecedents* (see note 37), p. x.

54. Ibid., p. 4.

55. Ibid., p. 14.

56. Cornelia B. Wilbur, "Psychoanalysis and Multiple Personality Disorder," in *Treatment of MPD* (see note 36).

57. Eugene L. Bliss, *Multiple Personality* (see note 51), p. 121.

58. John C. Nemiah, "Dissociative Disorders" (see note 31), p. 948.

59. Bennett G. Braun, ed., *Treatment of MPD* (see note 36), p. 4.

60. Ibid., p. 17.

61. Ibid., p. 21.

62. Ibid., p. 4.

63. Eugene L. Bliss, *Multiple Personality* (see note 51), p. 123.

64. Frank W. Putnam, *Diagnosis and Treatment of MPD* (see note 11), p. 85.

65. Cornelia B. Wilbur, "Psychoanalysis and MPD," in *Treatment of MPD* (see note 36), p. 137.

66. Eugene L. Bliss, *Multiple Personality* (see note 51), p. 155.

67. Ibid.

68. Ibid., p. 123.

69. George K. Ganaway, "Historical Versus Narrative Truth" (see note 31), p. 208.

70. Edward J. Frischolz, "The Relationship Among Dissociation, Hypnosis, and Child Abuse in the Development of Multiple Personality Disorder," in *Childhood Antecedents* (see note 37), p. 120.

71. Ian Wilson, *All in the Mind* (New York: Doubleday, 1982), p. 154.

72. George K. Ganaway, "Historical Versus Narrative Truth" (see note 31), pp. 208-209.

73. Bennett G. Braun, ed., *Treatment of MPD* (see note 36), p. 10.

74. Ibid.

75. Frank W. Putnam, "The Treatment of Multiple Personality" (see note 39), p. 188.

76. Ibid.

77. Frank W. Putnam, Juliet J. Guroff, Edward K. Silberman, Lisa Barban, and Robert M. Post, "The Clinical Phenomenology of Multiple Personality Disorder: Review of 100 Recent Cases," *Journal of Clinical Psychiatry*, 47, no. 6:288 (1986).

78. Bennett G. Braun, ed., *Treatment of MPD* (see note 36), p. 14.

79. Daniel Goleman, "Probing the Enigma of Multiple Personality," *New York Times*, June 28, 1988.

80. Ibid.

81. American Psychiatric Association, *DSM-IIIR* (see note 33), p. 271.

82. Frank W. Putnam, *Diagnosis and Treatment of MPD* (see note 11), pp. 55ff.

83. Bennett G. Braun and Roberta G. Sachs, "The Development of Multiple Personality Disorders: Predisposing, Precipitating, and Perpetuating Factors," in *Childhood Antecedents* (see note 37), p. 51.

84. Frank W. Putnam, "Dissociation as a Response to Extreme Trauma," *Childhood Antecedents* (see note 37), p. 81.

85. Frank W. Putnam, *Diagnosis and Treatment of MPD* (see note 11), pp. 61–64.

86. American Psychiatric Association, *DSM-IIIR* (see note 33), p. 271.

87. George K. Ganaway, "Historical Versus Narrative Truth" (see note 31), p. 209.

88. Felicitas D. Goodman, *How About Demons? Possession and Exorcism in the Modern World* (Bloomington: Indiana University Press, 1988), p. 80.

89. Ibid., p. 17.

90. Elizabeth S. Bowman, Philip M. Coons, R. Stanley Jones, and Mark Oldstrom, "Religious Psychodynamics in Multiple Personalities: Suggestions for Treatment," *American Journal of Psychotherapy*, 41, no. 4:543 (1987).

91. Ibid.

92. Frank W. Putnam, *Diagnosis and Treatment of MPD* (see note 11), p. 87.

93. Ibid., p. 112.

94. Ibid., p. 49.

95. Maribeth Kaye and Lawrence Klein, "Clinical Indicators of Satanic Cult Victimization," unpublished paper, 1987.

96. Ibid., p. 1.

97. Ibid., p. 2.

98. Ibid., pp. 3ff.

99. Ibid., p. 6.

100. Ibid.

101. Ibid., p. 7.

102. Walter C. Young, Roberta G. Sachs, Bennett G. Braun, and Ruth T. Watkins, "Patients Reporting Ritual Abuse in Childhood: A Clinical Syndrome," *International Journal of Child Abuse and Neglect,* 1991 (in press).

103. Ibid., p. 19.

104. Ibid., p. 3.

105. Ibid., p. 5.

106. Ibid.

107. Ibid., p. 6.

108. Walter C. Young, Roberta G. Sachs, and Bennett G. Braun, "A New Clinical Syndrome: Patients Reporting Ritual Abuse in Childhood by Satanic Cults," unpublished manuscript, 1988, p. 7.

109. Walter C. Young et al., "Patients Reporting Ritual Abuse" (see note 102), p. 6.

110. Ibid., p. 7.
111. Ibid., p. 9.
112. Ibid., p. 10.
113. Ibid., p. 11.
114. Ibid., p. 12.
115. Ibid.
116. Ibid., p. 13.
117. Ibid., p. 14.
118. Ibid., p. 15.
119. Ibid., p. 16.

120. George K. Ganaway, "Historical Versus Narrative Truth" (see note 31), p. 215.

121. Sally Hill and Jean Goodwin, "Satanism: Similarities Between Patient Accounts and Pre-Inquisition Historical Sources," *Dissociation*, 2, no. 1 (1989).

122. Walter C. Young et al., "Patients Reporting Ritual Abuse in Childhood" (see note 102), p. 19.

123. Sally Hill and Jean Goodwin, "Satanism" (see note 121), p. 39.

124. Ibid.

125. Ibid., p. 43.

126. Richard Noll, Letter to the Editor, *Dissociation*, 2, no. 4:251 (1989).

127. Ibid., p. 253.

128. Frank W. Putnam, *Diagnosis and Treatment of MPD* (see note 11), p. 177.

129. Sherrill Mulhern, notes and taped presentations at the Fifth International Conference on Multiple Personality/Dissociative States, Chicago, Ill., October 8, 1988.

130. Personal correspondence, March 7, 1990.

131. Sherrill Mulhern conference notes (see note 129).

132. Sherrill Mulhern, personal correspondence, March 7, 1990.

133. Ibid.

134. Ibid.

135. Ibid.

136. Ibid.

137. Ibid.

138. Sherrill Mulhern, personal correspondence with Debbie Nathan, 1988–89.

139. Ibid.

140. Ibid.

141. Ann Rodgers-Melnick, "Rumors from Hell" (3-part series on Satanism), *Pittsburgh Press*, Sept. 4–6, 1989.

142. Ibid.

143. Bill Disessa,"Tale of Child's Ritual Slaying Vexes Lawmen," *Houston Chronicle*, March 6, 1989.

144. Ibid.

145. Ibid.

146. Ibid.

147. Debbie Nathan, "The Devil and Mr. Mattox, *Texas Observer*, June 2, 1989.

148. Ibid.

149. Ibid.

150. Ibid.

151. G. Olson-Raymer, *Occult Crime: A Law Enforcement Primer*, published as *Research Update*, 1, no. 6:39 (Winter 1989–90), by California Office of Criminal Justice Planning.

152. "Witchcraft, Satanism, and Ritual Crime: Who's Who and What's What," *Green Egg* (Ukiah, Calif.), 1989, p. 14.

153. Bennett G. Braun, personal communication, May 18, 1989.

154. Gretchen Passantino, Bob Passantino, and John Trott, "The True Lauren Stratford Story," *Cornerstone,* 18, no. 90 (1989): 23–28.

155. Ibid., p. 25.

156. Ibid., p. 26.

157. Ibid.

158. Ibid., p. 28.

159. Ibid.

160. Ibid.

161. Debbie Nathan, "The Devil and Mr. Mattox (see note 147), p. 13.

162. Frank W. Putnam, "Diagnosis and Treatment of MPD" (see note 11), p. 161.

163. David Faust and Jay Ziskin, "The Expert Witness in Psychology and Psychiatry," *Science* 241:31–35 (July 1, 1988).

164. Ibid., p. 34.

165. Thomas Szasz, *The Myth of Mental Illness* (London: Granada Publishing, 1981), p. 17.

166. Ibid., p. 19.

167. Editorial statement by Charles Kiesler, former executive officer, American Psychological Association, in *American Psychologist*, February 1977.

Chapter 5: "Yukky Secrets": Satanic Abuse of Children

1. Tom Charlier and Shirley Downing, "Justice Abused: A 1980s Witch-Hunt" (6-part series), *Memphis Commercial Appeal*, January 1988.

2. *Coy v. Iowa*, 487 U.S. 1012, 43 CrL 3226 (1988).

3. *Maryland v. Craig*, No. 89–478, 6/27/1990.

4. Ian Thomas Oliver, "Child Abuse: Increase or Awareness?" *Police Chief*, 55, no. 9:12–13 (1988).

5. Tom Charlier and Shirley Downing, "Justice Abused" (see note 1).

6. Steven H. Jensen and Coralie A. Jewell, "The Sex Offender Experts," *The Prosecutor*, Fall 1988, pp. 13–20.

7. Ibid.

8. Office of Human Development Services, *Study Findings: Study of National Incidence and Prevalence of Child Abuse and Neglect 1988* (Washington,

D.C.: U.S. Department of Health and Human Services, 1988).

9. David Finkelhor, *Sexually Victimized Children* (New York: Free Press, 1979), p. 131.

10. Ibid., p. 2.

11. Bureau of Justice Statistics, "Tracking Offenders: The Child Victim," *Bureau of Justice Statistics Bulletin* (Washington, D.C.: U.S. Department of Justice), December 1984.

12. Jay Mathews, "Child Molestation Case Goes to Jury in California," *Washington Post*, November 3, 1989.

13. Ibid.

14. Mary A. Fischer, "McMartin: A Case of Dominoes," *Los Angeles*, October 1989.

15. Ibid., p. 128.

16. Ibid.

17. Ibid., p. 129.

18. Ibid.

19. Ibid.

20. Ibid.

21. Ibid., p. 130.

22. Tom Charlier and Shirley Downing, "Justice Abused" (see note 1).

23. Ibid.

24. Ibid.

25. Ibid.

26. Mary A. Fischer, "McMartin" (see note 14), p. 131.

27. Debbie Nathan, "False Evidence: How Bad Science Fueled the Hysteria Over Child Abuse," *L.A. Weekly*. April 8–13, 1989, p. 18.

28. Mary A. Fischer, "McMartin" (see note 14), p. 131.

29. Ibid.

30. Ibid., p. 132.

31. Ibid.

32. Ibid., p. 133.

33. Ibid., p. 132.

34. Ibid., p. 135.

35. Tom Charlier and Shirley Downing, "Justice Abused" (see note 1).

36. Ibid.

37. Ibid.

38. Mary A. Fischer, "McMartin" (see note 14), p. 134.

39. Tom Charlier and Shirley Downing, "Justice Abused" (see note 1).

40. Mary A. Fischer, "McMartin" (see note 14), p. 130

41. Ibid.

42. Debbie Nathan, "Child Molester?" *Village Voice*, August 2, 1988, pp. 31–39.

43. Ibid.

44. Ibid., p. 32.

45. Ibid., p. 34.

46. Ibid.

47. Steven H. Jensen and Coralie A. Jewell, "The Sex Offender Experts" (see note 6), p. 14.

48. Kee MacFarlane and Jill Waterman, *Sexual Abuse of Young Children* (New York: Guilford Press, 1986), p. 81.

49. Ibid.

50. Debbie Nathan, "Child Molester?" (see note 42), p. 35. I am also grateful to Morton Stavis, Esq., for furnishing a copy of the *Brief and Appendix in Support of Renewed Application for Bail Pending Further Proceedings on the Appeal Herein, New Jersey v. Margaret Kelly Michaels*, Superior Court of New Jersey Appellate Division, Docket No. A199088T4, which I quote here (p. 35 in Stavis).

51. Ibid., p. 36.

52. Ibid.

53. Ibid., p. 38.

54. Ibid., p. 37.

55. Ibid., p. 38 and the *Brief* cited in note 50.

56. Ibid., and the *Brief* (see note 50), pp. 35, 50–51.

57. Debbie Nathan, "Are These Women Child Molesters? The Making of a Modern Witch Trial," *Village Voice*, September 29, 1987, pp. 19–32.

58. Ibid., p. 21.

59. Ibid.

60. Ibid.

61. Ibid.

62. Ibid.

63. Ibid., p. 22.

64. Ibid.

65. Ibid.

66. Ibid., p. 27.

67. Ibid.

68. Ibid., p. 28.

69. Ibid.

70. Ibid., p. 29.

71. Ibid.

72. Ibid., p. 31.

73. Ibid.

74. Ibid., p. 20.

75. Ibid., p. 32.

76. Tom Charlier and Shirley Downing, "Justice Abused" (see note 1).

77. J. J. Haugaard and N. D. Reppucci, *The Sexual Abuse of Children* (San Francisco: Jossey-Bass, 1988), p. 174.

78. Ibid.

79. Tom Charlier and Shirley Downing, "Justice Abused" (see note 1).

80. David Finkelhor, *Sexually Victimized Children* (see note 9), p. 35.

81. Tom Charlier and Shirley Downing, "Justice Abused" (see note 1).

82. J. J. Haugaard and N. D. Reppucci, *The Sexual Abuse of Children* (see note 77), p. 171.

83. Ibid.

84. Kee MacFarlane and Jill Waterman, *Sexual Abuse of Young Children* (see note 48), p. 94.

85. Tom Charlier and Shirley Downing, "Justice Abused" (see note 1).

86. Ibid.

87. Ibid.

88. National Center for the Prosecution of Child Abuse, *Manual: Investigation and Prosecution of Child Abuse* (Alexandria, Va.: American Prosecutors Research Institute, 1987), II–2.

89. Raymond A. Eve, "Empirical and Theoretical Findings Concerning Child and Adolescent Sexual Abuse: Implications for the Next Generation of Studies," *Victimology*, 10, nos. 1–4: 98 (1985).

90. David Finkelhor, *Sexually Victimized Children* (see note 9), p. 21.

91. Kathleen C. Faller, *Child Sexual Abuse: An Interdisciplinary Manual for Diagnosis, Case Management, and Treatment* (New York: Columbia University Press, 1988), p. 15.

92. David Finkelhor, *Sexually Victimized Children* (see note 9), p. 17.

93. Kathleen C. Faller, *Child Sexual Abuse* (see note 91), p. 12.

94. Raymond A. Eve, "Empirical and Theoretical Findings" (see note 89), pp. 101ff.

95. David Finkelhor, *Sexually Victimized Children* (see note 9), pp. 73ff.

96. Ibid., p. 74.

97. Felicity Barringer, "Children as Sexual Prey, and Predators," *New York Times*, May 30, 1989.

98. Raymond A. Eve, "Empirical and Theoretical Findings" (see note 89), p. 107.

99. S. M. Sgroi, F. S. Porter, and L. C. Blick, "Validation of Child Sexual Abuse," in S. M. Sgroi, ed., *Handbook of Clinical Intervention in Child Sexual Abuse* (Lexington, Mass.: Lexington Books, 1982), p. 69.

100. Office of Juvenile Justice and Delinquency Prevention, "First Comprehensive Study of Missing Children in Progress," *Juvenile Justice Bulletin* (Washington, D.C.: U.S. Department of Justice), 1988.

101. Office of Juvenile Justice and Delinquency Prevention, "Preliminary Estimates Developed on Stranger Abduction Homicide of Children," *Juvenile Justice Bulletin* (Washington, D.C.: U.S. Department of Justice), 1989.

102. Ibid.

103. Kathleen C. Faller, *Child Sexual Abuse* (see note 91), pp. 99ff.

104. Steven H. Jensen and Coralie A. Jewell, "The Sex Offender Experts" (see note 6), p. 15.

105. Kathleen C. Faller, *Child Sexual Abuse* (see note 91), p. 115.

106. Kenneth V. Lanning, *Child Molesters: A Behavioral Analysis* (Washington, D.C.: National Center for Missing and Exploited Children, 1987).

107. Ibid., p. 2.

108. Ibid., p. 11.

109. Ibid.

110. Ibid., p. 17.

111. Lawrence A. Stanley, "The Child Porn Myth," *Cardozo Arts & Enter-*

tainment Law Journal, 7, no. 2:350 (1989).

112. Ibid., p. 351.

113. Benjamin Rossen, *Zedenangst: Het Yerhaal van Oude Pekela* (Lisse: Swets and Zeitlinger, 1989), p. 8. English translation by the author.

114. Kenneth V. Lanning, *Child Molesters: A Behavioral Analysis* (see note 106), p. 10.

115. J. J. Haugaard and N. D. Reppucci, *The Sexual Abuse of Children* (see note 77), p. 150.

116. Ibid.

117. Roland C. Summit, "The Child Sexual Abuse Accommodation Syndrome," *Child Abuse and Neglect*, 7:177–193 (1983).

118. Ibid., p. 178.

119. Ibid., p. 179.

120. Ibid.

121. Ibid., p. 183.

122. Ibid., p. 184.

123. Ibid., p. 186.

124. Ibid., p. 188.

125. Ex parte Hill, Ala. Sup. Ct., No. 88–684, 9/15/89.

126. Ibid., p. 191.

127. J. J. Haugaard and N. D. Reppucci, *The Sexual Abuse of Children* (see note 77), p. 178.

128. Ibid., p. 180.

129. Debbie Nathan, "Are These Women Child Molesters?" (see note 57), p. 29.

130. Kee MacFarlane and Jill Waterman, *Sexual Abuse of Young Children* (see note 48), p. xi.

131. Ibid., p. xii.

132. Sherrill Mulhern, letter to Debbie Nathan, April 28, 1989.

133. 46 *Criminal Law Reporter* 1140, 11-15-89, citing *People (Calif.) v. Leon*, Calif. Ct. App., 2d Dist., No. B030562, 10-13-89.

134. 46 *Criminal Law Reporter* 1141, 11-15-89.

135. Ibid.

136. 47 *Criminal Law Reporter* 1273, 7-4-90. Case cited is *People* (Mich.) *v. Beckley*, Mich. Sup. Ct., Nos. 81583, etc., 6-5-90.

137. Lee Coleman, "Medical Examination for Child Abuse," unpublished manuscript, n.d., p. 12.

138. Ibid., p. 13.

139. Ibid., p. 15.

140. Ibid.

141. Kenneth V. Lanning, *Child Sex Rings: A Behavioral Analysis* (Washington, D.C.: National Center for Missing and Exploited Children, 1989), p. 23.

142. Debra Whitcomb, Elizabeth R. Shapiro, and Lindsey D. Stellwagen, *When the Victim Is a Child: Issues for Judges and Prosecutors* (Washington, D.C.: U.S. Department of Justice, 1985), p. 14.

143. Paul Ekman, *Why Children Lie* (New York: Charles Scribner's Sons, 1989).

144. N. Dickson Reppucci and Jeffrey J. Haugaard, "Prevention of Child Sexual Abuse," *American Psychologist*, 44, no. 10:1266 (1989).

145. Ibid.

146. Ibid., p. 1267.

147. Ibid.

148. Ibid., p. 1269.

149. Ibid., p. 1270.

150. Michael Hertica, "Police Interviews of Sexually Abused Children," *FBI Law Enforcement Bulletin*, 56, no. 4:12–16 (1987).

151. Cecily Dykema Cagle and Colleen Gallagher, "Bridging the Gap: Techniques for Interviewing Child Victims of Sexual Assault," *Police Chief*, 54, no. 4:24 (1987).

152. Also discussed in Michael Hertica, "Police Interviews" (see note 150).

153. Ibid.

154. Debra Whitcomb, "Prosecution of Child Sexual Abuse: Innovations and Practice," *Research in Brief* (Washington, D.C.: National Institute of Justice), November 1985, p. 3.

155. Cecily Dykema Cagle and Colleen Gallagher, "Bridging the Gap" (see note 151).

156. Kathleen C. Faller, *Child Sexual Abuse* (see note 91), p. 119.

157. Cecily Dykema Cagle and Colleen Gallagher, "Bridging the Gap" (see note 151), p. 25.

158. Jon R. Conte and Lucy Berliner, "Prosecution of the Offender in Cases of Sexual Assault Against Children," *Victimology*, 6(1–4):104 (1981).

159. Kathleen C. Faller, *Child Sexual Abuse* (see note 91), p. 137.

160. Cecily Dykema Cagle and Colleen Gallagher (see note 151), p. 26.

161. Ibid.

162. Ibid.

163. Ibid.

164. National Center for the Prosecution of Child Abuse, *Manual* (see note 88), II–15.

165. Michael Hertica, "Police Interviews" (see note 150), p. 16.

166. Kee MacFarlane and Jill Waterman, *Sexual Abuse of Young Children* (see note 48), p. 93.

167. National Center for the Prosecution of Child Abuse, *Manual* (see note 88), V–23.

168. Ibid., II–9.

169. Michael Hertica, "Police Interviews" (see note 150), p. 16.

170. Kathleen C. Faller, *Child Sexual Abuse* (see note 91), p. 147.

171. Cecily Dykema Cagle and Colleen Gallagher, "Bridging the Gap" (see note 151), p. 29.

172. Kathleen C. Faller, *Child Sexual Abuse* (see note 91), p. 174.

173. J. J. Haugaard and N. D. Reppucci, *The Sexual Abuse of Children* (see note 77), p. 179.

174. Kee MacFarlane and Jill Waterman, *Sexual Abuse of Young Children* (see note 48), p. 82.

175. Ibid., p. 87.

176. G. Olson-Raymer, *Occult Crime: A Law Enforcement Primer*, published as *Research Update*, 1, no. 6:44 (Winter 1989–90), by the California Office of Criminal Justice Planning.

177. J. J. Haugaard and N. D. Reppucci, *The Sexual Abuse of Children* (see note 77), p. 163.

178. Ibid., p. 162.

179. David L. Corwin, Larry Berliner, Gail Goodman, Jan Goodwin, and Sue White, "Child Sexual Abuse and Custody Disputes: No Easy Answers," *Journal of Interpersonal Violence*, 2, no. 1 (1987).

180. David P. H. Jones and J. Melbourne McGraw, "Reliable and Fictitious Accounts of Sexual Abuse to Children," *Journal of Interpersonal Violence*, 2, no. 1 (1987).

181. Diana Jeffrey and Laurie Woods, "Sexual Abuse Allegations in Custody and Visitation Cases," *Youth Law News*, September/October 1989, p. 18.

182. Michael Bamberger, "Some Tell a D.A. That They Lied," *Philadelphia Inquirer*, October 21, 1989.

183. David Gelman, "The Sex-Abuse Puzzle," *Newsweek*, November 13, 1989.

184. Elizabeth F. Loftus and Graham M. Davies, "Distortions in the Memory of Children," *Journal of Social Issues*, 40, no. 2 (1984).

185. Marcia K. Johnson and Mary Ann Foley, "Differentiating Fact from Fantasy: The Reliability of Children's Memory," *Journal of Social Issues*, 40, no. 2 (1984).

186. Irene S. Shigaki and Willavene Wolf, "Courtroom Factors Affecting Jurors' Verdict in a Child Sexual Abuse Trial," *Children's Legal Rights Journal*, 10, no. 3 (1989): 14.

187. Jon R. Conte and Lucy Berliner, "Prosecution of the Offender" (see note 158), p. 104.

188. Irene S. Shigaki and Willavene Wolf, "Courtroom Factors" (see note 186).

189. Karen J. Saywitz, "Children's Testimony: Age-Related Patterns of Memory Errors," in S. J. Ceci, M. P. Toglia, and D. F. Ross, eds., *Children's Eyewitness Testimony* (New York: Springer Verlag, 1987).

190. Quoted in *Prosecutor's Perspective*, 2, no. 1:4 (January 1988).

191. Gail S. Goodman, Jodi Hirschman, and Leslie Rudy, "Children's Testimony: Research and Policy Implications," paper presented at the Society for Research in Child Development, Baltimore, Md., April 1987.

192. Quoted in *Prosecutor's Perspectives*, 2, no. 1:6 (January 1988).

193. Irene S. Shigaki and Willavene Wolf, "Courtroom Factors," (see note 186), p. 14.

194. Lois Jampole and Kathie M. Weber, "An Assessment of the Behavior of Sexually Abused and Nonsexually Abused Children with Anatomically Correct Dolls," *Child Abuse and Neglect*, 11, no. 2 (1987).

195. Sue White, Gerald A. Strom, Gail Santilli, and Bruce M. Halpin, "Interviewing Young Sexual Abuse Victims with Anatomically Correct Dolls," *Child

Abuse and Neglect, 10, no. 4 (1986).

196. Gail S. Goodman and Christine Aman, "Children's Use of Anatomically Correct Dolls to Report an Event," in *Evaluation of Suspected Child Abuse: Developmental, Clinical, and Legal Perspectives on the Use of Anatomically Correct Dolls*, Symposium presented at the Society for Research in Child Development, Baltimore, Md., April 1987.

197. Kee MacFarlane and Jill Waterman, *Sexual Abuse of Young Children* (see note 48).

198. Kenneth R. Freeman and Terry Estrada-Mullaney, "Using Dolls to Interview Child Victims: Legal Concerns and Interview Procedure," *NIJ* (National Institute of Justice) *Research in Action*, (Washington, D.C.: U.S. Department of Justice, 1988).

199. Ibid.

200. National Center for the Prosecution of Child Abuse, *Manual* (see note 88), 11–16.

201. Debra Cassens Moss, " 'Real' Dolls Too Suggestive," *American Bar Association Journal*, December 1, 1988, pp. 24–26.

202. Robert H. Farley, " 'Drawing Interviews': An Alternative Technique," *Police Chief*, 54, no. 4:37–38 (1987).

203. Ibid., p. 38.

204. Ibid.

205. J. J. Haugaard and N. D. Reppucci, *The Sexual Abuse of Children* (see note 77), p. 172.

206. Ibid., p. 151.

207. Ibid., p. 156.

208. Debbie Nathan, "False Evidence" (see note 27).

209. Ibid., p. 15.

210. Ibid., p. 18.

211. Ibid.

212. Richard D. Krugman, "The More We Learn, the Less We Know 'With Reasonable Medical Certainty,' " *Child Abuse and Neglect*, 13:166 (1989).

213. Ibid., p. 165.

214. Jan E. Paradise, "Predictive Accuracy and the Diagnosis of Sexual Abuse: A Big Issue About a Little Tissue," *Child Abuse and Neglect*, 13:169–176 (1989).

215. Ibid., p. 176.

216. John McCann, Joan Voris, Mary Simon, and Robert Wells, "Perianal Findings in Prepubertal Children Selected for Nonabuse: A Descriptive Study," *Child Abuse and Neglect*, 13:179–193 (1989).

217. Ibid., p. 192.

218. Debbie Nathan, "Child Abuse Evidence Debated,' *Ms Magazine*, March 1989, p. 81.

219. Susanne T. White and David L. Ingraham, "Vaginal, Introital Diameter in the Evaluation of Sexual Abuse," *Child Abuse and Neglect*, 13:224 (1989).

220. C. J. Hobbs and J. M. Wynne, "Sexual Abuse of English Boys and Girls: The Importance of Anal Examination," *Child Abuse and Neglect*, 13:207–210 (1989).

221. Ibid., p. 211.

222. David Murham, "Child Sexual Abuse: Relationshp Between Sexual Acts and Genital Findings," *Child Abuse and Neglect*, 13:216 (1989).

223. Ibid.

224. Debbie Nathan, "Child-Abuse Evidenced Debated," (see note 218).

225. Ibid., p. 82.

226. Kathleen C. Faller, *Sexual Child Abuse* (see note 91).

227. Ibid., p. 286.

228. Ibid., p. 289.

229. Tom Charlier and Shirley Downing, "Justice Abused" (see note 1).

230. Ibid., p. 290.

231. Ibid., p. 297.

232. Ibid.

233. Susan J. Kelley, "Ritualistic Abuse of Children: Dynamics and Impact," *Cultic Studies Journal*, 5, no. 2:229 (1988).

234. Susan J. Kelley, "Stress Responses of Children to Sexual Abuse in Day Care Centers," *Journal of Interpersonal Violence*, 4, no. 4:502–513 (1989).

235. Ibid., p. 503.

236. Ibid., p. 511.

237. David Finkelhor, Linda M. Williams, and Nanci Burns, *Nursery Crimes: Sexual Abuse in Day Care* (Beverly Hills, Calif.: Sage, 1988), pp. 11–16.

238. Ibid., p. 13.

239. Ibid., p. 45.

240. Ibid., p. 59.

241. Ibid., p. 246.

242. Debbie Nathan, review of *Nursery Crimes*, unpublished manuscript, 1989.

243. Ibid.

244. Ibid.

245. Catherine Gould, "Satanic Ritual Abuse: Child Victims, Adult Survivors, System Response," *California Psychologist*, 22, no. 3:9 (1987).

246. Ibid.

247. Ibid., p. 14.

248. Lee Coleman, "Therapists Are the Real Culprits in Many Child Sexual Abuse Cases," *Augustus*, 9, no. 6:8 (1986).

249. Tom Charlier and Shirley Downing, "Justice Abused" (see note 1).

250. Ibid.

251. Philip Jenkins and Daniel Katkin, "Protecting Victims of Child Abuse: A Case for Caution," *Prison Journal*, Fall/Winter 1988, p. 25.

252. Philip Jenkins and Daniel Katkin, "From Salem to Jordan: A Historical Perspective of Child Abuse Cases," *Augustus*, 9, no. 6:15 (1986).

253. Philip Jenkins and Daniel Katkin, "Protecting Victims" (see note 251), p. 27.

254. Ibid., p. 28.

255. Ibid., p. 30.

256. Quoted in Jenkins and Katkin (see note 251), p. 32, from a *60 Minutes* broadcast.

257. Philip Jenkins and Daniel Katkin, "From Salem to Jordan" (see note 252).

258. Philip Mayer, "Witches," in *Witchcraft and Sorcery*, ed. Max Warwick (New York: Viking/Penguin, 1987), p. 61.

259. Norman Cohn, *Europe's Inner Demons* (New York: Meridian, 1977), p. 156.

260. Joyce Bednarski, "The Salem Witch Scare Viewed Sociologically," in *Witchcraft and Sorcery* (see note 258).

261. Ibid.

262. Kenneth Lanning, *Child Sex Rings: A Behavioral Analysis* (see note 141).

263. Ibid., p. v.

264. Ibid., p. 1.

265. Ibid., p. 6.

266. Ibid., p. 9.

267. Ibid., p. 10.

268. Ibid., p. 11.

269. Ibid., p. 12.

270. Ibid., p. 13.

271. Ibid., p. 17.

272. Ibid.

273. Ibid., p. 19.

274. Ibid., p. 21.

275. Ibid., p. 22.

276. Ibid., p. 23.

277. Ibid., p. 25.

278. Ibid., p. 26.

279. Ibid., p. 31.

280. Ibid., p. 33.

281. David Finkelhor et al., *Nursery Crimes* (see note 237), p. 175.

282. Lee Coleman and Patrick E. Clancy, "False Allegations of Child Sexual Abuse," *Criminal Justice*, Fall 1990, p. 47.

283. Tom Charlier and Shirley Downing, "Justice Abused" (see note 1).

284. Jay Mathews, "In California, a Question of Abuse," *Washington Post*, May 31, 1989.

285. Michael Snedeker, "Servants of Satan: The Rise and Fall of the Devil in Kern County, California" (2-part series), *California Prisoner*, April, June 1988.

286. Ibid.

287. Tom Charlier and Shirley Downing, "Justice Abused" (see note 1).

288. Ibid.

289. Michael Snedeker, "Servants of Satan" (see note 285).

290. Ibid.

291. Ibid.

292. Ibid.

293. Jay Mathews, "California Drops Abuse Charges," *Washington Post*, November 30, 1990.

294. Debra Cassens Moss, "Are the Children Lying?" *American Bar Association Journal*, May 1, 1987, p. 62.

295. Patricia Pearson, "In Search of the Satanists," *The Idler* (Toronto, Canada), no. 25:25 (Sept./Oct. 1989).

296. Jay Mathews, "In California, a Question of Abuse" (see note 284).

Chapter 6: "We're Dealing with Evil Itself"

1. Ann Rodgers-Melnick, "Rumors from Hell" (3-part series), *Pittsburgh Press*, September 4–6, 1989.

2. Jeffrey Burton Russell, *Mephistopheles: The Devil in the Modern World* (Ithaca, N.Y.: Cornell University Press, 1986), p. 257.

3. Paula K. Lundberg-Love, "Update on Cults Part II: Non-Satanic Cults and Their Consequences," *Family Violence Bulletin* (University of Texas at Tyler), 5, no. 2:9 (1989).

4. Ann Rodgers-Melnick, "Rumors from Hell" (see note 1), September 5, 1989; Jeff Meadow, "Satanism," *Teacher*, September/October 1989, p. 40.

5. "This 'Fad' Is Playing with Fire" (editorial), *Deseret News*, Salt Lake City, April 13, 1989.

6. "Magic: A Deadly Solution" *Denver Magazine*, February 1985, p. 23.

7. Ibid., p. 24.

8. "The High Risk Child: Report on the Tenth Governor's Conference on Juvenile Justice," *Louisiana Youth Care Magazine*, April/May 1989.

9. Dick Burke, "Satanism in Denver Schools," *The Forum*, May/June 1988.

10. Mack Reed, "Dungeons, Dragons and Sex Charges," *Philadelphia Inquirer*, June 9, 1988.

11. " 'Fantasy Game' Plea Rejected, Jury Convicts Man of Murdering Parents," *Star-Ledger* (New York), June 30, 1988.

12. "Teenager Testifies of Satanic Ritual Over Victim's Body," *Florida Times-Union* (Jacksonville), June 10, 1988.

13. *Cult Awareness Network News*, 5, no. 1:8 (1989).

14. Judy Berry, "Satanism: More Than a Childish Fad," *The Sentinel*, August/September 1989, p. 5.

15. Jo Ann Jacobsen-Wells, "Occult Luring More and More Youths, Expert Warns," *Deseret News*, Salt Lake City, July 5, 1989.

16. Tom Butler, "Savannah Pastor to Address Satanism," *Savannah News-Press*, October 21, 1989.

17. "A Chilling Wave of Racism," *Time*, January 25, 1988, p. 23.

18. Lisa Jeff, "Letter on Satanism Angers Annapolis Students," *Washington Post*, December 5, 1989.

19. Jacqueline London, "How to Talk Like a Student," *Richmond* (Va.) *Times Dispatch*, August 20, 1989.

20. I am indebted to Dr. James Creech, Virginia Department of Criminal Justice Services, for the Virginia statistics. No other state has a comparable database on sentencing practices.

21. Mike Carter, "Reality of Life in Prison Awaits a Killer Whose Fantasies Led Him to Murder," *Salt Lake City Tribune*, March 2, 1988.

22. "Networking to Beat the Devil," *Newsweek*, December 5, 1988, p. 29.

23. Amy Goldstein and Paul Duggan, "MD Girls Told Friends of Death Pact," *Washington Post*, November 12, 1988.

24. "Handling Self-Mutilation or 'Carving' in Treatment Centers," *Substance Abuse Report*, December 15, 1989, p. 3.

25. Mark Bowes, " 'Dabblers' Use 'Satanic House,' Police Say," *Richmond* (Va.) *News Leader*, October 28, 1988.

26. Ibid.

27. Gordon Hickey, "Tomb Vandalism Linked to Satan Rite," *Richmond News Leader*, July 9, 1988.

28. Ibid.

29. Mark Bowes, "Charges Pending in Disturbance of Graves," *Richmond News Leader*, December 9, 1989.

30. April Adler, "Cemetery Vandals Draw 17 Days in Jail, Big Fines," *News and Daily Advance* (Lynchburg, Va.), May 13, 1989.

31. Chrysti Edge, "4 Satan Worshippers Arrested in Attempt to Rob Conway Grave," *Sun-News* (Myrtle Beach, S.C.), July 28, 1988.

32. Patricia A. Pulling, *The Devil's Web* (Lafayette, La.: Huntington House, 1989), p. 11.

33. Ibid., p. 10.

34. Billy Bowles, "Group of Worried Parents Links Suicides, Slayings to Fantasy Games," *Charlotte* (N.C.) *Observer*, November 10, 1985.

35. Michael Stackpole, "The Truth About Role-Playing Games," in Shawn Carlson and Gerald Larue, eds., *Satanism in America* (El Cerrito, Calif.: Gaia Press, 1989), p. 255.

36. Ibid., p. 256.

37. According to the publisher's press release, August 1, 1989.

38. Patricia A. Pulling, *The Devil's Web* (see note 32), p. 179.

39. BADD, *Dungeons and Dragons* (Richmond, Va., n.d.).

40. Billy Bowles, "Group of Worried Parents" (see note 34).

41. According to Pierre Savoie, "Local Loonacy: A Catholic (Anti-Catholic) Ban?", unpublished manuscript.

42. "The Emergence of Ritualistic Crime in Today's Society," notes from the seminar given at Ft. Collins, Colorado, September 9–12, 1986, by the North Colorado-South Wyoming Detectives Association.

43. Michael Stackpole, "The Truth About Role-Playing Games" (see note 35), p. 272.

44. Ibid., p. 270.

45. Ibid.

46. Ibid., p. 241.

47. Ibid., p. 242.

48. Ibid.

49. Lisa Antonelli, "Satan's Victim: One Woman's Ordeal," *Style Weekly* (Richmond, Va.), January 19, 1988, pp. 38–43.

50. Rex Springston, "Satanism: Menace or Myth?" *Richmond* (Va.) *News Leader*, April 7, 1989.

51. Gordon Hickey, "Satanic Cults Are Focus of Conference Here," *Richmond News Leader*, September 21, 1988.

52. Ed Briggs, "Satanic Cults Said to Entice Teens with Sex, Drugs," *Richmond Times-Dispatch*, March 5, 1988.

53. Michael Stackpole, "The Truth About Role-Playing Games" (see note 35), p. 245.

54. Patricia A. Pulling, *The Devil's Web* (see note 32), p. 34.

55. T. M. Luhrmann, *Persuasions of the Witch's Craft: Ritual Magic in Contemporary England* (Cambridge, Mass.: Harvard University Press, 1989), p. 106.

56. Ibid., p. 107.

57. Michael Stackpole, "The Truth About Role-Playing Games" (see note 35), p. 248.

58. William Dear, *The Dungeon Master: The Disappearance of James Dallas Egbert III* (Boston: Houghton Mifflin, 1984), p. 268.

59. Albert James Dager, "A Media Spotlight Special Report: Dungeons and Dragons," reprint from *Media Spotlight* (Santa Ana, Calif.), 1980.

60. Louise Shanahan, *Games Unsuspecting People Play: Dungeons & Dragons* (Boston: Daughters of St. Paul, 1983), p. 1.

61. Ibid.

62. Patricia A. Pulling, *The Devil's Web* (see note 32), p. 18.

63. Personal communication with journalist Debbie Nathan, 1989. Nathan regularly reports on cultural and political life on the Texas-Mexico border.

64. Patricia A. Pulling, *The Devil's Web* (see note 32), p. 53.

65. Ibid., p. 30.

66. Ibid., p. 32.

67. Ibid., p. 33.

68. Ibid., p. 21.

69. Ibid., p. 25.

70. Ibid., p. 121.

71. Ibid., p. 68.

72. Ibid.

73. Ibid.

74. Tipper Gore, "Raising PG Kids in an X-Rated Society," *Forum Report* (published by the Council for Children, Inc.), October 5, 1988, p. 4.

75. Rob Lamp, "The World of 'Dark Rock,' " *New American*, February 17, 1986, p. 6.

76. "Suing to Turn the Tables on 'His Master's Voice,' " *Scientific Sleuthing* 13, no. 1:9 (1989).

77. Ibid.

78. Ibid.

79. Tom McIver, "Backward Masking and Other Backward Thoughts About Music," *Skeptical Inquirer*, 13, no. 1:50–63 (Fall 1988).

80. Ibid., p. 53.

81. John R. Vokey and Don J. Read, "Subliminal Messages: Between the Devil and the Media," *American Psychologist*, 40, no. 11: 1232 (1985).

82. Ibid., 1231.

83. Stephen B. Thorne and Philip Himelstein, "The Role of Suggestion in the Perception of Satanic Messages in Rock-and-Roll Recordings," *Journal of Pyschology*, 116: 246 (1984).

84. Elizabeth F. Brown and William R. Hendee, "Adolescents and Their Music: Insights Into the Health of Adolescents," *Journal of the American Medical Association*, 262, no. 12: 1659 (1989).

85. Ibid., 1661.

86. Ibid.

87. Ibid.

88. Ibid., p. 1663.

89. Rebecca Jones, "Smoky Hill High School to Counsel Satanists," *The Forum*, May–June 1988, p. 17.

90. Ibid.

91. "Maryland Town Cancels Halloween This Year," *Jamestown* (N.Y.) *Post-Journal*, October 11, 1989.

92. Ibid.

93. "Parents Who Want to Ban 'Witches' Lack a Sense of Humor, Dahl Says," *Richmond* (Va.) *News Leader*, October 19, 1989.

94. Elizabeth McKenna, "Teen-agers Sue, Claim to Be Victims of 'Witch Hunt,' " *Ann Arbor* (Mich.) *News*, November 1, 1989.

95. Ibid.

96. Ibid.

97. "Psychiatrists to 'Treat' Satanism," *Washington Post*, September 7, 1989.

98. Laurie Goering, "Breaking Satanism's Deadly Grip on Teens," *Buffalo News*, September 11, 1989.

99. Barbara R. Wheeler, Spence Wood, and Richard J. Hatch, "Assessment and Intervention with Adolescents Involved in Satanism," *Social Work*, November/December 1988, p. 547.

100. Gary Fine, *Shared Fantasy: Role-Playing Games* (Chicago: University of Chicago Press, 1983).

101. Armando Simon, "Emotional Stability Pertaining to the Game of Dungeons and Dragons," *Psychology in the Schools*, 24:332 (1987).

102. Editorial, "D&D a Treasure for Many Teens," *Southern Illinoisan*, August 27, 1985.

103. "A Parent's Primer on Satanism," *Woman's Day*, November 22, 1988, p. 150.

104. Ibid.

Chapter 7: Conclusion: Rumors, Urban Legends, and Subversion Myths

1. Arthur Schlesinger, Jr., "The Opening of the American Mind," *New York Times Book Review*, July 23, 1989.

2. Los Angeles County Commission for Women, *Report of the Ritual Abuse Task Force*, September 15, 1989.

3. Ibid., p. 4.

4. Ibid.

5. Sherrill Mulhern, "Ritual Abuse: The Creation of a Context for Belief," paper presented at the National Symposium on Child Victimization, Atlanta, Ga., April 26–28, 1990.

6. Ibid.

7. Ibid.

8. Sherrill Mulhern, "Ritual Abuse: Defining a Syndrome vs. Defending a Belief," paper presented at the International Congress on Child Abuse and Neglect, Hamburg, Germany, September 2–6, 1990.

9. Mel Oberg, "Are Peninsula Slayings Act of Serial Killler?" *Richmond* (Va.) *Times Dispatch*, January 21, 1990.

10. Marilee Enge, "Satanism Class Loses Certification," *Anchorage* (Alaska) *Daily News*, December 14, 1989.

11. Ibid.

12. Ibid.

13. Slim Randles, "The Mystery on the Mesa," *Albuquerque Journal*, March 29, 1990.

14. Ibid.

15. Slim Randles, "Players Claim 'Turf,' " *Albuquerque Journal*, March 30, 1990.

16. Ibid.

17. Letters to the Editor, *Albuquerque Journal*, April 12, 1990.

18. "Cults Still Recruit on Campuses," *Campus Law Enforcement Journal,* 19, no. 4:36 (1989).

19. "Satanic Groups and Cults on Campus, Part 1: Why They Are Proliferating and Who Is Susceptible, *College Security Report*, November 1989, p. 50.

20. Tom Coakley, "Straightening Out Those Tales of South Shore Satanism," *Boston Globe*, May 21, 1988.

21. Aaron Zitner, "Cult Scare Seen as Overrated," *Boston Globe*, May 28, 1989.

22. Diego Ribadeneira, "Police Discuss Violence Linked to Cults, Satanic Worship," *Boston Globe*, April 21, 1988.

23. Sherrill Mulhern, remarks at the National Conference on Child Abuse and Neglect, Salt Lake City, Utah, 1989.

24. Ibid.

25. Ibid.

26. John Treherne, *The Canning Enigma* (London: Jonathan Cape, 1989).

27. "The Lottery Takes a Bath on 666," *Richmond* (Va.) *Times-Dispatch*, August 16, 1989.

28. "Beastly Number Bedevils Motorists," *Richmond Times-Dispatch*, February 4, 1990.

29. Diana Griego, "Believers in Occult Found in Rural Areas," *Denver Post*, August 8, 1988.

30. Ibid.

31. Paul Delinger, "Devil Cults Have Rights, Too, Group Told," *Roanoke* (Va.) *Times & World News*, October 4, 1989.

32. Mark S. Warnick, "Officials Discount Satanism Rumors," *Pittsburgh Press*, May 14, 1989.

33. Ibid.

34. Ibid.

35. "Kentucky Deluged by Rumors of Devil Worship," *Crime Control Digest* 22, no. 38:6 (1988).

36. Mark S. Warnick, "Officials Discount Satanism Rumors" (see note 32).

37. Martha Long, "Is Satan Alive and Well in Northeast Arkansas?" *Mid-American Folkore* 13, no. 2:25 (1985).

38. Po-chia R. Hsia, *The Myth of Ritual Murder: Jews and Magic in Reformation Germany* (New Haven, Conn.: Yale University Press, 1989).

39. Jan Harold Brunvand, *The Study of American Folklore*, 3rd ed. (New York: W. W. Norton, 1986), p. 159.

40. Ibid.

41. Jan Harold Brunvand, *The Choking Doberman and Other Urban Legends* (New York: W. W. Norton, 1984), pp. 405.

42. Jan Harold Brunvand, *American Folklore* (see note 39), p. 165.

43. Jan Harold Brunvand, *The Choking Doberman* (see note 41), p. 73.

44. Ibid., p. 31.

45. Stith Thompson, *Motif Index of Folk Literature* (Bloomington, Ind.: Indiana University Press, 1955).

46. Jan Harold Brunvand, *The Choking Doberman* (see note 41), p. 162.

47. Gina Kolata, "Rumor of LSD-Tainted Tattoos Called Hoax," *New York Times*, December 9, 1988.

48. June Leonard, "Police Downplay Flier on LSD Cartoon Tattoo," *Virginia Pilot*, April 13, 1990.

49. Veronica Noonan, "Satanic Cult Killed Animals in Allentown, Police Say," *Union Leader* (Manchester, N.H.), May 3, 1989.

50. Editorial, *Union Leader*, May 4, 1989.

51. Aaron Zitner, "N.H. Police Chief Discounts Alleged Signs of Cult Activity," *Boston Globe*, May 5, 1989.

52. Aaron Zitner, "Cult Scare" (see note 21).

53. Tony Parker, "Goat Near Pontiac Possibly a Sacrifice," *The Pantagraph* (Illinois), July 28, 1989.

54. Tony Parker, "Goat Killed in Dog Attack," *The Pantagraph* (Illinois), July 29, 1989.

55. Robert Reinhold, "Dozens of Cats Killed, Fears Spread in Suburb," *New York Times*, August 13, 1989.

56. Ibid.

57. Ibid.

58. Ibid.

59. Daniel Kagan and Ian Summers, *Mute Evidence* (New York: Bantam, 1984).

60. Ibid., p. 164.
61. Ibid., p. 171.
62. Ibid., p. 175.
63. Ibid., p. 208.
64. Ibid.
65. Ibid., p. 209.
66. Ibid.
67. David G. Bromley, "Folk Narratives and Deviance Construction: Cautionary Tales as a Response to Structural Tensions in the Social Order," in *Deviance in Popular Culture*, ed. Clinton Sanders (in press), p. 11.
68. Jan Harold Brunvand, *The Mexican Pet* (New York: W. W. Norton, 1986), p. 155.
69. Ibid., p. 203.
70. David G. Bromley, "Folk Narratives" (see note 67), p. 2.
71. Ibid., p. 25.
72. Ibid.
73. Ibid., p. 13.
74. William Guinee, "Satanism in Yellowwood Forest: The Interdependence of Antagonistic Worldviews," *Indiana Folklore and Oral History*, 16, no. 1:20 (1987).
75. David G. Bromley, "Folk Narratives" (see note 67), p. 16.
76. Ibid., p. 17.
77. Ibid., p. 3.
78. Ibid., p. 5.
79. Jan Harold Brunvand, *American Folklore* (see note 39), p. 158.
80. Ann Rodgers-Melnick, "Rumors from Hell" (3-part series), *Pittsburgh Press*, September 4-6, 1989.
81. Ibid.
82. "Satanism Reports Mostly Rumor, Detectives Say," *Tucson* (Ariz.) *Citizen*, December 19, 1988.
83. Dan Terry, "Youth Gang Gives a Name to Students' Fear of Crime," *New York Times*, March 1, 1989.
84. Ibid.
85. Lawrence Hammack, "Fears Grow as Rumors Spread," *Roanoke* (Va.) *Times and World News,* November 25, 1988.
86. Ibid.
87. Robert W. Balch and Margaret Gilliam, "The Social Construction of Satanism: A Case Study of the Rumor Process," unpublished manuscript, 1989.
88. Ibid., p. 2.
89. Ibid., p. 3.
90. Ibid., p. 10.
91. Ibid., p. 14.
92. Ibid.
93. Ibid., p. 16.
94. Ibid., p. 17.
95. Ibid., p. 18.
96. Ibid., p. 20.

97. Ibid., p. 25.

98. Ibid., p. 26.

99. Benjamin Rossen, *Zendenangst: Het verhaal van Oude Pekela* (Lisse: Swets and Zeitlinger, 1989). English translation by author.

100. Ibid., p. 4.

101. Ibid.

102. Ibid., p. 43.

103. Ibid., p. 9.

104. Ibid.

105. Ibid., p. 10.

106. Ibid.

107. Daniel Kagan and Ian Summers, *Mute Evidence* (see note 59), p. 491.

108. Ibid.

109. Ibid., p. 501.

110. Benjamin Rossen, *Zendenangst* (see note 99), p. 151.

111. Ibid., p. 140.

112. Ibid., p. 50.

113. Ibid., p. 51.

114. Jeffrey S. Victor, "A Rumor Panic About a Dangerous Satanic Cult in Western New York, *New York Folklore,* 15, nos. 1–2: 23–49 (1989).

115. Ibid., p. 23.

116. Ibid., p. 35.

117. Ibid.

118. Jeffrey S. Victor, "Jamestown's Satanic Panic: What Really Happened in 1988?" *Jamestown* (N.Y.) *Post-Journal* September 23, 1988.

119. Paul Watzlawick, *How Real Is Real?* (London: Souvenir Press, 1983), pp. 48ff.

120. Ibid., p. 49.

121. Ibid

122. Ibid., p. 50.

123. Ibid

124. Ibid., p. 51.

125. Terry Thomas, "Satanism Specialist Conducts Workshop," *Register Star* (Rockford, Ill.), July 11, 1987.

126. Ibid.

127. Ann Rodgers-Melnick, "Rumors from Hell," (see note 80).

128. Terry Thomas, "Satanism Specialist" (see note 125).

129. Betsy Burkhard, "Satanism Enters Probe," *Register Star* (Rockford, Ill.), August 26, 1987.

130. Ibid.

131. "Beverly Merfield Believes Satanism May Be Linked to Son's Death," *Register Star*, September 6, 1987.

132. Ibid.

133. Ibid.

134. "Devil Worship Suspected in Assault on 17-year-old," *Register Star*, December 7, 1987.

135. Ibid.

136. Janet Kidd, "Occult Worship Suspected in Probe of Farm Arson Fires," *Register Star*, May 3, 1988.

137. Janet Kidd, "More Devil Symbols Discovered in Barn," *Register Star*, April 2, 1988.

138. Ben Rand, "Suspected Ritualistic Activities Investigated," *Register Star*, November 11, 1988.

139. Ibid.

140. Ben Rand, "Satanists or Imitators Suspected in Unusual Break-ins," *Register Star*, December 10, 1988.

141. Ibid.

142. B. G. Gregg, "Curious Kids Want to Learn About Satanism," *Register Star*, April 19, 1989.

143. Ibid.

144. Sermon delivered by David R. Weissbard, Unitarian Church, Rockford, Ill., February 5, 1989.

145. Ibid.

146. L. Slaughter, letter to the Henrico County Municipal Reference Library, Richmond, Va., October 19, 1989.

147. Jeffrey Burton Russell, *Witchcraft in the Middle Ages* (Ithaca, N.Y.: Cornell University Press, 1972), p. 269.

148. Wallace Notestein, *A History of Witchcraft in England from 1558–1718* (New York: Crowell, 1968), p. 125.

149. Jeffrey Burton Russell, *Witchcraft* (see note 147), p. 19.

150. Elliott P. Currie, "Crimes Without Criminals: Witchcraft and Its Control in Renaissance Europe," *Law and Society Review*, 3, no. 1:8 (1968).

151. Jeffrey Burton Russell, *Witchcraft* (see note 147), p. 3.

152. Elliott P. Currie, "Crimes Without Criminals" (see note 150).

153. Ibid., p. 19.

154. Mathew Hopkins, *The Discovery of Witches* (Essex, U.K.: Partizan Press, 1988).

155. Elliott P. Currie, "Crimes Without Criminals" (see note 150), p. 28.

156. Ibid.

157. Ibid., p. 30.

158. Jerry D. Rose, *Outbreaks: The Sociology of Collective Behavior* (New York: Free Press, 1982), p. 137.

159. Ibid., p. 142.

160. Ibid., p. 143.

161. Ibid., p. 145.

162. Ibid., p. 149.

163. Ibid., p. 152.

164. Ibid., p. 167.

165. Ibid., p. 166.

166. Ibid., p. 168.

167. Jeffrey Burton Russell, *Witchcraft* (see note 147), p. 266.

168. Thomas J. Schoeneman, "The Witch-Hunt as a Culture Change Phenomenon," *Ethos* 3, no. 4 (1975).

169. Ibid.

170. Rick O'Connell, "Many Serious Criminal Justice Problems Await U.S. Action," *Crime Control Digest*, 22, no. 46:7–8 (1989).

171. Ibid., p. 8.

172. Kim Remesch-Allnutt, "Cults Organized, Armed & Protected by the First Amendment," *Police Product News*, October 1985, p. 29.

173. Clay Robison, "Children 'Bred' for Sacrifices, Senators Hear," *Houston Chronicle*, May 3, 1989.

174. Debbie Nathan, "The Devil and Mr. Mattox," *Texas Observer*, June 2, 1989.

175. John Richard Burkholder, " 'The Law Knows No Heresy . . .' : Marginal Religious Movements and the Courts," in *Religious Movements in Contemporary America*, ed. Irving I. Zaretsky and Mark P. Leone (Princeton, N.J.: Princeton University Press, 1974).

176. Orlin D. Luckstead and D. F. Martell, "Cults: A Conflict Between Religious Liberty and Involuntary Servitude," *FBI Law Enforcement Bulletin*, 51, no. 5:16–23 (:1982).

177. Daniel Kagan and Ian Summers, *Mute Evidence* (see note 59), p. 442.

178. Ibid., p. 443.

179. American Library Association Office of Intellectual Freedom, *OIFALA Memorandum*, January–February 1988.

180. *File 18 Newsletter*, July 21, 1986, p. 2.

181. "Sheriff's Office Calls Off Witch Hunt," *Richmond News Leader*, March 9, 1988.

182. Ibid.

183. American Library Association Office of Intellectual Freedom, *Newsletter of Intellectual Freedom,* 38, no. 6 (1989).

184. Ibid., 37, no. 6 (1988).

185. Virginia Byrne, " 'Swami Team' Groping for Insight into Mind of Zodiac Gunman," *Buffalo* (N.Y.) *News,* July 22, 1990.

186. Ibid.

187. *College Security Report* (see note 19).

188. Ibid., p. 8.

189. Norman Cohn, *Europe's Inner Demons* (New York: Meridian, 1977), p. xiii.

190. Rob Gurwitt, "How We Spent the 1980s: A Pre-Census Look at a Changing America," *Governing*, 2, no. 1:26 (1989).

191. Jeffrey Burton Russell, *Mephistopheles: The Devil in the Modern World* (Ithaca, N.Y.: Cornell University Press, 1986), p. 257.

192. Philip Jenkins, "Myth and Murder: The Serial Killer Panic of 1983–5," *Criminal Justice Research Bulletin*, 3, no. 11:1 (1988).

193. Ibid.

194. Ibid., p. 5.

195. National Criminal Justice Association, *Justice Research*, November/December 1987, p. 1.

196. "A Chilling Wave of Racism," *Time*, January 25, 1988.

197. "Hate Crime Is Growing, Group Says," *Richmond* (Va.) *News Leader*, January 6, 1989.

198. Peter Applebome, "New Report Warns of Racist Groups, *New York Times*, February 6, 1989.

199. "Senate OKs Counting of Hate Crimes, *Richmond* (Va.) *News Leader*, February 9, 1990. By summer 1990, the U.S. Justice Department had begun to organize to collect bias-crime data. See "Justice Dept. in Early Stages of Action on Hate Crimes Law," *Criminal Justice Newsletter,* 21, no. 13:2–3 (1990).

200. "Hate Crimes," *Richmond News Leader* (see note 199).

201. Edward Sulzbach, "Psychological Profiling Another Weapon in Law Enforcement's Arsenal," Federal Bureau of Investigation, unpublished, undated monograph.

202. James T. Reese, "Motivations of Criminal Informants," *FBI Law Enforcement Bulletin* 49, no. 5:23–27 (1980).

203. Robert K. Ressler and Ann W. Burgess, "The Split Reality of Murder," *FBI Law Enforcement Bulletin,* 54, no. 8:54–58 (1985).

204. Murray S. Miron and John E. Douglas, "Threat Analysis: The Psycholinguistic Approach," *FBI Law Enforcement Bulletin,* September 1979, pp. 5–9.

205. Phillips Stevens, Jr., "The Appeal of the Occult: Some Thoughts on History, Religion, and Science," *Skeptical Inquirer,* 12:379 (1988).

206. O. B. Hardison, *Disappearing Through the Skylight: Culture and Technology in the Twentieth Century* (New York: Viking, 1989).

207. Phillips Stevens, Jr., "Satanism: Where Are the Folklorists?" *New York Folklore,* 15, nos. 1–2:22 (1989).

208. Jeffrey S. Victor, "Victims of the National Satanic Cult Scare," unpublished manuscript, 1989.

209. Kenneth V. Lanning, "Satanic, Occult, Ritualistic Crime: A Law Enforcement Perspective, *Police Chief,* 56, no. 10:77 (1989).

210. Ibid., p. 80.

INDEX